THE KILBURN EPISTLES

James Paul Shaughnessy

Best Wishes: JP Shaughnessy.

1

The Kilburn Epistles

James Paul Shaughnessy

Cover artwork: Shaun Gale

ISBN 9781914615153

A CIP catalogue record for this book
is available from the British Library

Published 2021 Tricorn Books
Aspex Portsmouth
42 The Vulcan Building
Gunwharf Quays
Portsmouth PO1 3BF
Printed & bound in the UK

THE KILBURN EPISTLES

For
Ginny, Lenka and Maria.

With special thanks to my indefatigable literary critic,
nosebag-stuffer and fellow moocher,
Margot North.

Preface

They say that: 'Truth is stranger than fiction' and that, 'euphemism is better than expletive.' What this has to do with the ensuing narrative is beyond me, but my editor suggested that I should start the preface with a statement that would: 'catch the reader's attention' and he thought that this one might be appropriate? If it was left down to me, I would have simply begun with – 'Once upon a time'!

This novel is based on truth, with a little poetic licence thrown in, and where possible I have attempted to keep it within the boundaries of propriety and good taste. It is clear however, that some expletives are far more appropriate and satisfying in describing the moment and feelings experienced, than trying to verbally respond nicely to those veritable *pud-wappers* responsible for rocking our formerly tranquil boats of happiness. However, in a world of cut and thrust selfishness and ignorant manners, my own view is – 'bollocks to euphemisms!' People need to know how we feel.

This narrative opens on 1st January 2012. It follows the life and daily observations of its author: *moi* – a retired single-parent pensioner, in what I like to refer to as *the youth of my dotage.* I am in a relatively good state of mental and physical health, which I attribute to the fact that I never touched a drink (I was teetotal at the time) or associated with members of the opposite sex (apart from nurses) – until I was eight years old.

As a child I had every consideration lavished upon me: breech birth, breastfeeding, circumcision (at birth my foreskin was the length of a reticulated python), tonsillectomy, appendectomy and Buddhism. Apparently, in my cot I looked like a reclining Buddha in repose and apart from the lifelong enduring pot belly, I always had a gummy grin on my face. Later in life, I was to embrace the enlightened doctrines of this beautiful *way of life* and I found its teachings infinitely credible, particularly when confronted with the veritable plethora of confusing, irrational and often contradictory modern-day theological choices.

I have believed in reincarnation ever since I was a young gerbil, and am convinced that my present state and position in life is as a direct result of my actions in previous existences. Since, I am relatively happy, healthy and humble. I must therefore assume that my previous lives could be described as: *mildly irresponsible.* It is clear to me that had I been a complete, *fatherless-person,* that now as a consequence, I could find myself in dreadfully dire circumstances. On the other hand, I could have been an exceptional model of love, goodness and light, and could now be enjoying the fruits of my former exemplary behaviour, and doing nothing more challenging than kicking a football about like Wayne Rooney and others, and earning a veritable fortune for doing it. Clearly, I am somewhere in between the two.

The laws of karma are quite amazing and cunningly precise, and there have been times when I have given the whole philosophy a thorough mental workout.

But during periods of uncertainty and confusion, I would often muse upon those spiritually enlightening words of Chief Geronimo, (1829–1909): "Plenty well, no pray. Big bellyache, heap God!" Everything then becomes clear.

I have been singularly blessed in sharing my living arrangements with two beautiful women: Lenka Brazdova (32) – a Slovakian, working as a croupier in a (respectable) gentlemen's club *somewhere* in central London – and Maria Garcia Hernandez (28) – a Spanish MBA student with an insatiable love for food, life and men. But my greatest companion in life is my seven-year-old Jack Russell terrier called Spike, who has been a veritable blessing from the time that fortune and a rather inebriated Irish traveller (who having sharpened my old carving knife) dumped him on my doorstep as a puppy, and seemingly took the knife in payment.

In describing the lives, loves and occasional – born in the vestry *pud-wapper* of my contemporaries, I have endeavoured to alter their names slightly to avoid embarrassment and to prevent any future possibility of having to attend civil court proceedings in answer to a libellous and/or slanderous action. Knowing my revered and infinitely cunning friends as I do, anything that might: 'bring in a few bob,' friend or not, would be worthy of a little consideration.

As my dear friend, *Ted the Pleb* once reasoned: 'If ever I was to sue a mate for say, defamation of character, or libel and won, why, I'd go half with him on the damages!'

I was employed in the casino industry for many years and as a result am known to my close friends as *Paul Casino,* albeit that my first name is James. On occasion, people do call me James or Jim but I prefer Paul. There are four other Pauls within my immediate circle of friends, namely: *Paul the Dust*, *Paul the Spark*, *Smelly Paul* and *Del the Cab,* (who always wanted to be called Paul) and was afforded the honorary title since at the time of writing, he was going through a deed poll application to change his name to Paul Delusius Finklestein, believing that the name 'Del' sounded too Jewish.

There are so many people that I would like to thank in helping me to produce this novel, but for the life of me, I really can't think of any of them off hand. However, without that august body of men collectively known as 'my friends' (loosely speaking that is), together with the inevitable *pud-wapper* or two (from whom) I have obtained enormous inspiration, this literary masterpiece would never have been completed. Actually, I become quite sentimental and not a little emotional when I consider that to a man, they have always been there when they have needed me.

Being a man of letters (and considerable junk mail) during the latter part of 2011, I began an online literary relationship with an endearing American lady of Italian descent – Virginia Bianchi, a very special talented person who taught me the truth behind the old saying that 'small is beautiful'.

This novel is based upon my daily journal and the emails that I subsequently '*poofed*' to her via email, through that mysterious postman-destroying marvel known as cyberspace.

Finally, special thanks must go out to my former revered schoolteacher: Maynard L Brettle MA BSc BEd for his final written estimation of my future life's potential:

> ***"This young man will never amount to anything!"***

Prophetically he's been spot on!

January 1st 2012

Dear Ginny.

I was watching a mildly pornographic DVD cartoon on the telly as the bells of St Benedict's Church rang out at 23:56 last night. I figured that old Compton (the head campanologist) had got the time wrong again. But then, I understand that the Bulgarian plonk that they use in the Communion Service is pretty potent stuff when ingested in quantity. From what I understand, you need more than one glass to get rid of the taste!

Poor old Father Jessop! I am sure that he gets a little annoyed with arriving into the vestry ever early, due to Compton's erratic twenty-one jewels, gold-plated (fell out of the back window of a local jewellers) retirement watch, which is frankly as predictable and reliable as the eating habits of a vegetarian dyslexic on a diet. Strangely however, his curate, Father Marcus, always arrives punctually, and he, poor man, cannot wear a watch due to some strange or malevolent magnetic power (they either keep stopping or start to run backwards) and as it is, he finds them hard enough to catch when they are running forwards! Father Marcus was never blessed with an 'athletic leaning' although he can sit up straight when sitting down (bless his little white surplice).

But to continue, I offered up a small mental thought of gratitude for making it through yet another year, and thanked providence for the similar safe transit of my remaining family, and remembered that happily (metaphorically speaking that is) I had only witnessed one former friend fall off life's fickle rooftop during the ingloriously ordinary period that was 2011.

Danny *Butter Fingers* Moran was a likeable enough man and I was very sad to hear of his passing. Apparently he broke his neck, nose diving off his toilet seat while trying to wipe his bum with the one hand, and attempting to answer an incoming call on his mobile phone with the other. Sadly, not being *amphibious* as *Alfie the Dip* would say, when trying to describe a person who was ambidextrous, Danny got a little confused, and instead of wiping himself with the paper, and... I am sure that I need not tell you where his Nokia ended up!

In his next life I feel sure that he will become a kangaroo, since he always used to bounce about like one at parties. As a result, he was forever losing what he referred to as his 'hard money' which would be scattered all over the place and, like its final resting place, his mobile phone would also be found in some very unusual locations. As a kangaroo he would now be able to bounce about to his heart's content, and as an added bonus, he'd have somewhere safe to put his personal belongings at least until he'd progressed back to humanity, by which time he would return with a pocket full of very valuable ancient coins and an antique mobile phone in pristine condition.

I have to admit that earlier last night I was tempted to escape for a while, particularly when I anticipated that my evening's peace would be shattered by *Gob Almighty* above, as evidenced by the noise of a lot of people coming and going earlier in the evening. I was quite annoyed with myself that I hadn't even taken notice of the lack of hubbub aloft throughout the entire Christmas period. It's such a nuisance to not be able to acknowledge one's good fortune at the time. However, I was to find out later that she and her entire brood of potential anarchists in training had in fact moved out. It would appear that they have returned to their native country. I am not sure where it is, but am positive that it's a dark and miserable place. I was to meet my new neighbours a little later.

I didn't bother to *go walkabout*, as my red-faced colonial friend *Dunny Greg* would have said, and as I was told later, I hadn't missed out on anything: interesting, life changing, or unusual.

The only noise that came from upstairs was the sound of a child weeping. I thought initially that perhaps my hearing was playing up. However, I was convinced that my one good ear was reliably picking up the sounds of a child's sobs, and I felt that this was simply due to a very tired little soul.

Other than that, my New Year's Eve was peaceful, and joyfully solitary. But then, I have never had any interest in celebrating the arrival of the new year, or *Hogmanay* as the Scots call it, and unlike antisocial individuals like me, they certainly do take it all very seriously indeed. But apart from anything else, I hate crowds, and suffering from claustrophobia, I do not like the kind of close bodily contact which celebrations of this kind naturally occasion. It's bad enough being caught up in a crowd of unwashed Englishmen, quite apart from a newly arrived *abomination of jocks,* straight down from the wild and beautiful glens and mountains of *Inverpimples, McPukeshire*, stinking of booze and bent on altering the facial features of anything in trousers. But then it's nothing personal, they simply enjoy little things like that (bless their little whiskey and urine-stained sporrans).

Having spent out a considerable sum on their rail travel, a little light-hearted New Year's Day *Sassenach-bashing* will almost certainly ensure rent-free accommodation in one of the hastily emptied central-London police cells. Thereafter for the next couple of days, they can sleep off the alcohol, pay their respective fines at the local Magistrate's Court, and stock up on their liquid refreshment needs, in preparation for the trip home, and as fun-loving as ever, the inevitable demolition of their respective train carriages en route.

Clearly, many of my pals on occasion enjoy a few social pints; the Scots however don't ever really need an excuse to get *crapulously compromised,* or *ah wee bit pished!* as our tartan-clad brethren would say. At this time of year in Scotland as a matter of course, all members of the armed forces, emergency services and the judiciary would have been on standby for a full week before and a full week after the 31st December. Historically, the wanton destruction of property and the injuries sustained by drunken revellers has been compared to the mayhem experienced on a Saturday afternoon at the *London Stadium Stratford* (the home of West Ham United) following an all too infrequent home win.

Perhaps the only thing more depressing than staying in is the thought of going out. Although, I suppose it's nice to start another year with a determined resolution, so mine is that from the beginning of March, I will resolve not to procrastinate! Later on in the evening I enjoyed watching *The Great Escape* again for the umpteenth time this century and feel quite confident that I could recite the two-hour script verbatim!

I awoke late this morning, but having soaked the old tonsils in coffee, I dashed over to the gym. The place was virtually empty at 11:00. I thought of all of my friends who would have been out on the sauce last night, ingesting copious quantities of booze, and happily working on their inevitable *Dawn Demolition*. Many of them could literally put away a gallon or two, and some of the more impressionable youngsters, who had hopelessly tried to keep up with them, would reluctantly have had to endure the reappearance of their half-digested evening meals, which *Dunny Greg* colourfully refers to as their '*Technicolor pavement-pizza moments*'. I am sure that a few other unfortunates would have had to suffer the discomfort and indignity of a stomach pump at the local A&E. Sadly, such is the demanding and uncomfortable rocky road towards peer acceptance, and alcohol tolerance.

In the apparatus room, I spoke to one old wag who was busily trying to get into a coordinated rhythmic flow on the cross-trainer. His less than robust frame, baggy shorts and T-shirt reminded me of a demented sock on a washing line being buffeted by a gale-force wind. He enlightened me about his current dietary plans, although God knows what little he has, he should hang on to since I have seen more meat on a butcher's apron.

'Do you know,' he remarked, 'I thought that I'd try something a little different the other day, so I jogged backwards for a mile!'

'What was the point of that?' I asked.

'I put on six pounds!' he replied, and then shaking violently, he broke out into a fit of uncontrollable laughter which didn't do him or the apparatus any favours whatsoever, since it added an unwelcome component in his quest for bodily unity and stability and resulted in him being thrown headlong off the machine. It has since been labelled The Terminator. I gave him what first aid I could, prior to the arrival of the ambulance.

This new year's morning was quite unremarkable apart from a delightful turn in the weather. Formerly, we have had to endure week after week of bruised looking clouds and sun-bereft skies, with bullying gusts of wind that would deter the most optimistic of kilt-wearing jocks from venturing outside (whether pished or not) and copious rain that would have forced ducks to wear their waterproof leggings and sou'wester hats.

But today the darkness and misery reflected in the lugubrious faces of the locals – whom as a collective, could have been compared to the party of confused looking Muslims that had been erroneously dropped off outside St Benedict's Church instead of the Kilburn Islamic Centre by the visually compromised *Paul the Cab* – were suddenly changed to an optimistic hue of happiness and joy. People were smiling again, children were laughing and the streets were full of people in party mood. The marvellously clear blue sky and the bright warming aspect of the watery sun seemed to change the drab monochrome colourless Victorian buildings along the Kilburn High Road reminding me of beautiful pastel-shaded Spanish bodegas. What was formerly cold, sterile and foreboding now appeared tangibly tactile, warm and visually stimulating. Well not quite perhaps, but you can imagine just how inspired and philosophical one can become when nature presents such a beautiful vista.

I was told later that the confusion with regard to *Paul the Cab's* sense of direction this morning was due to his lively alcohol-induced participation in an impromptu *hokey-cokey* last night. Apparently, having been accidentally bashed in the back by an elderly frumpy dumpling, he smashed his only pair of useable spectacles, and without them he was, to quote *Dunny Greg, 'As blind as a welder's dog!'*

But being the remarkably affable and considerate man that he is, and despite the inconvenience of suffering from a real *fatherless-person* of a hangover, he was willing to put his own personal comfort on the back burner as it were, and to make himself available for his ever-nomadic public in holiday mood. He was clearly aware that, what with the very limited bus operation and a reduced service on the underground, people still needed to get around. This kindly altruistic concern for his fellow man was greatly appreciated by all of his passengers and was reflected in the 'good-quality' tips that followed. Visually, apart from being able to identify all current bank notes, whether real or counterfeit, everything else was a little blurred. But being ever adventurous he was willing to take the risk, particularly since legitimately he could charge double fare. At the end of his twelve hours on the road, his takings were the equivalent of a London commodities trader, and from the proceeds he will be purchasing: two pairs of designer spectacles, two airline tickets to his favourite holiday venue (Las Vegas), and since he can no longer safely get into the bath (whether wearing spectacles or not) he will be making a sizeable down-payment on a wet-room installation as well.

While taking Spike out for a late afternoon perambulation across the semi-virgin verdant grasslands of Paddington Recreation Park, even *Ted the Pleb,* who being faced with such inspiring visual stimuli took the time to remain still and take in the beauty of the moment. He was standing outside of Kilburn Park tube station, presumably enjoying the splendour of the heart-warming experience, and as I noted, was being unusually non-responsive to the discordant cacophony of sound associated with passing police vehicle sirens (a noise which through an evolutionary quirk in his genetic physiological make-up would normally have fired up his legs and sent him hurtling away from the area as fast as he could).

I found out later, however, that my romantic notions about Ted's awareness and joy were completely wrong in that the reason for his stationary stance, was not to mentally wax lyrical about the weather, but to consider how he would be able to negotiate the escalators and make the single stop on the tube to Queens Park. Apparently, a little earlier, his underpants had inadvertently been graced with a quantity of semi-liquidised excrement occasioned by a bout of excessive wind, two packets of pork scratchings and the six pints of cheap, out-of-date Guinness that the guvnor at the *Goose and Firkin* had flogged him during happy hour – which normally runs (with no pun intended) between 13:00–23:30 daily. Why on earth he drinks regularly in this veritable den of infamy is beyond my comprehension. My pal *Dave the Voice* Ellis called during the morning to state that he would be gracing The Magpie later in the day. This hallowed watering hole has been in Anglo Saxon hands since before the ink had dried on the Magna Carta. Sadly, through a series of notable calamities, together with the underhanded machinations, avaricious incompetence and inept complacency of a disinterested *Elder's Brewery* (who will remain nameless), the pub fell into the hands of a group of Eastern European refugees who apparently had made a little money from car wash enterprises and organising the catering and entertainment at children's birthday parties and infant corporate events (well that's what they told us). I certainly wouldn't have wanted to meet any of them in a dark alley, least of all a big ugly unsavoury that they called *Uncle Chickle Chuckle*. *Attila the Hun* might be a little more appropriate.

I will join Dave at the pub later, albeit that not a drop of alcohol will touch my lips. I am on the wagon again, at least for the near future, and as you are aware, I have been busier than a one-armed cab driver with pubic lice, what with dodging the potential bodily injuries caused by the women at Sainsbury's (who I am sure all play rugby at the weekends), giving my limpness of musculature a workout or two at the gym, and working on this novel.

I believe that it is time to spread a little happiness and venture out into 'the miscellaneous rabble that extol things vulgar', as Milton would have said when viewing the residents of Susan Atkins Court in general, and The Magpie's locals in particular. But in truth, many of them are dear friends who like that bright morning star, bring such happiness and light to my otherwise very ordinary existence. I can always abstain from alcohol, can happily run the gauntlet at Sainsbury's with wild carefree abandon, and even be relatively civil to *Lenny the Ponce*, but in truth, I could not go without the banter and camaraderie of my close friends. As the old saying has it: 'No man is an island.' But we all need a few pebbles on our particular stretch of the beach!

Happy New Year love! P xx

January 2nd 2012

Good morning, sugarplum.

Now that's what I call a reply. As for expressing the visual joy associated with sunlight, it has always worked that way for me. In the dreadfully dark days of winter, I suppose that I don't really 'see' a great deal other than the perceived darkness and shadow. As you know, I am a bit of an artist and look about me with a searching eye. (Just the one you understand.) In light, the old; *windows to the soul* really do comprehend once again, and for me, the monochrome drabness changes into a veritable kaleidoscope of colour and texture.

In a picture, darkness and shadow are needed of course, but purely to define, augment and give shape and depth to the colour and detail of the main themes. Having stated to *Arnie the Fag* Jones the other evening that 'One day I will donate my art works to a worthy charity', he replied, 'How about the Institute for the Blind!' This reminded me of those wonderful words: 'Happiness is being at peace, being with loved ones, and being comfortable and free from pain. But most of all, being as far away from inept moronic *pud-wappers* as is humanly possible!' I shall be giving Arnold Mountbatten Jones, aka *Arnie the Fag,* a wide berth this year!

And yes, I do remember our time with Helen and Bill this time last year, a wonderful couple indeed. On our first meeting, I just knew that we would become great friends, and while perhaps our emails are a little sparse, I fully appreciate that like me they too have busy lives. I haven't heard from them throughout 2011 actually. I hope it wasn't due to something that I said. Well there was that little incident at that casino, when I told him to be a little prudent with his betting stakes, but he didn't take much notice. You will recall that we drove down there in Bill's $12,000 car and came back in a $130,000 interstate bus. Mind you, I had to admire his philosophical approach to the issue when he stated, 'I just hope that they have more luck with my money than I did!'

I fully agree with you that the end of a year affords us time for inner reflection, but then I tend to do this on a weekly rather than an annual basis. A little like keeping check on the pennies or small things in the hope that the pounds, or the more important issues, will look after themselves. Perhaps not a very good example, but to analyse shorter periods of one's existence can be not only rewarding but infinitely revealing. It will certainly pinpoint or highlight the minor pitfalls and mistakes and thus hopefully will guide one away from any potential major catastrophes. I mean, if one doesn't keep a check on the amount of credit available in one's gas meter for example, one could at some later time be groping about in the dark, and that could result in all manner of potential mischief, particularly if like me you have a half-deaf Jack Russell, who has a little previous for randomly attacking anything that moves during the hours of darkness.

Actually I am quite convinced that Spike was a bat in a previous life since on leaving their caves bats apparently always turn left. Spike does the same thing when he chases the postman. Given the amount of nose bleeds that he's had, you'd think he'd turn right instead, but no, brick wall or not, he is seemingly genetically programmed to turn left! Either that or he is simply as thick as a bag of spanners!

I fully understand your unsettled situation and can also empathise in relation to your views on being alone. While we have so much in common on this issue we are very different. I suppose in many respects I have always been a bit of a loner, and maybe this was in part due to my congenital desire not to hurt or offend anyone. In truth, I feel that my limited talents (such as they are) have been acquired as a direct result of long periods of solitude, self-imposed isolation and experimental bouts of self-help to ascertain and document any changes in my eyesight. Contrary to popular urban myth, it doesn't make you go blind, although my mate *Ginger Tom* was convinced that it gave him toothache. Clearly, earlier experiences have conspired to make me the person that I am today, moulded from a former period in my life when my daily existence was far from being rapturously happy or fulfilled, and my creativity confined to drawing, painting, writing poetry and reading pornographic literature.

But then all of these years later, I meet you and experience at first hand the truth of the old adage that 'wonderful things do come in small packages'. That reminds me love, thank you very much once again for the tortoise, which I have called Eric. Although, shouldn't he be in hibernation at this time of year?

By the way, did I tell you that I am teaching Sebastian my plastic duck to surf? It's all quite simple really. I lay in the bath and gently move my toes back and forth to create small wavelets, which I make bigger and bigger. I then put my little yellow plastic friend on the crest of one such wave, and delight at his swift progress back towards me. Spike nearly had him the first time, but missed, and I do believe that his pride was hurt, since he now watches us with bored indifference. I feel so lucky to have a bath, and I don't mind cleaning up after the dog. I put plastic pads in it at night and place his little stepladder in position. If he wants to go during the night, he runs up it, hops into the bath, does his bit of business and climbs out. It has to be far preferable to clean up a few little doggy droppings and a little pee, than to risk life and limb having to take him down a flight of stairs in the dark. The last time I did that, the little bugger bit me twice!

That's about it for now love. It is 18:00 and time for a little *nosebag* and an early night.

Until tomorrow Gin, adieu.

P xx

January 3rd 2012

Good morning, Ginny.

Do you remember when I commented that I heard what appeared to be a young girl sobbing the other night? Well, having got myself ready for my evening read in bed last night – as you know, I really love to snuggle up with a good book (or to a friend that's read one) – suddenly there was an urgent banging on my front door. It was 23:30. I initially panicked, since I reasoned that at this late hour it could only be either bailiffs or the police. It's quite amazing how quickly the brain works when faced with the fight or flight syndrome, and my ticker-tape thoughts were: It's not the police since these days they don't bother knocking; I am a law-abiding citizen; I don't have any stolen items/goods on premises; I am not into drugs; I am not harbouring any wanted criminals; and the only potential offensive weapon that I have in the flat is Spike.

As for bailiffs, I don't owe anything to anybody. I therefore slowly opened the door, holding Spike in my left arm who, like me, cautiously peered out into the darkness. A disembodied face suddenly appeared in front of us, and I can't say in all honesty who jumped more, me or the dog. This was followed by two smaller faces appearing considerably lower than the first. Opening the door wider to give more light to the area, I found what appeared to be a young Muslim woman aged between twenty and thirty summers, in company with two small children.

How did you know that she was a Muslim, I hear you ask? Well, she was wearing a beautifully embroidered lace hijab, a long dark loose outer garment, affording the requisite modesty expected in Muslim women (so I am informed) and a rather dilapidated pair of Reebok trainers, presumably ruined by rushing through deserts and mountains to get to the mosque on time. I later reasoned that the numerous visible scuffs and stains were probably caused by the normal wear and tear that is to be expected when negotiating the innumerable broken paving slabs, potholes and hip-displacing pavements of Kilburn. But I digress.

The young woman that stood before me didn't appear to have a great deal of bodily coordination, and initially I thought that this was due to the earlier ingestion of either drink or drugs. She pacified my concerned looks and Spike's deep guttural growls (a precursor to attack mode) however, by stating in broken English that she was suffering from 'MS' (multiple sclerosis) and asked if 'I could help her upstairs?' I put Spike out on the balcony, leaving him a few of his favourite biscuits, and gave him strict instructions to leave Eric alone while I was gone. He looked at me as though butter wouldn't melt in his mouth.

I grabbed a torch and, offering her my arm which the young lady grabbed readily, I cautiously helped her up the stairs, the children running up ahead of us. It's a bit of a bugger, Gin, when women no longer look upon you as a potential masculine threat, and treat you like a washed-up old codger. It certainly can be a little deflating to one's ego to realise that one is simply not perceived in the same way that one feels. Women look at me now with all of the comparable enthusiasm of a group of old-age pensioners looking at newly fallen snow.

Having helped her to negotiate the stairs, the children stood holding her front door open and in no time at all, we were all inside what used to be *Gob Almighty's* flat. In the kitchen she stated that there was no heating and the cooker wasn't working. All that I needed to do was to switch on the gas that had been turned off at the mains. I had it all up and running in no time. I then had to explain how to operate her washing machine, and having done so, she loaded it up with children's clothes and was about to squirt washing-up liquid into it to act as a cleansing agent. I managed to change her mind about this, and a little later I ran downstairs and brought her up some washing powder and cooking oil since she wanted to make chips for the children.

'Jasmine' later explained that Elisha was five and her brother Mahmud was six. I offered to cook for them, since the thought of this poor unfortunate girl trying to provide a cooked meal in a small kitchen with two small children running around the place, was a thought that I did not wish to dwell upon. She had some food in the house, but I am to say at the least, very concerned for the welfare and safety of them all.

Sleep tight, Ginny.
P xx

January 4ᵗʰ 2012

Good morning, Ginny.

I got back downstairs at around 02:00 this morning. On opening the balcony door, Spike was looking very guilty. I checked on Eric, who was safely ensconced in his shell, but all of his lettuce, carrots and turnip were missing and his water had a yellowish tinge. It didn't take too long to figure out who the culprit was.

Once inside the flat, my little canine nutcase went into his mad half-hour routine, rushing around the place like a lunatic on mind-altering drugs, and having eventually tired himself out, he picked up his cuddly frog and vanished into Lenka's room. She was out working her normal night shift at her club. Having made quite sure that he was alone, he climbed upon her leather swivel chair and settled down for what was left of the night.

At 04:30 this morning I was awoken by the sound of children screaming outside, and on opening the door found Elisha and Mahmud running up and down the stairs, holding a torch. I put them both back into their flat and really did consider calling the police, since it was my view that all of them were at risk.

It was very clear that Jasmine has no control over these children whatsoever. However, having put them into their beds, they were both fast asleep within five minutes, clearly exhausted.

Back downstairs, Spike slept soundly throughout, and on quietly peering into Lenka's room I found him making little muffled barking sounds, his legs twitching convulsively.

This morning I booked an appointment with the vet to get Spike's hearing checked, and sent an urgent email to our local social services, together with another one to our landlords notifying them of the situation with regard to my poor little lady and her children. I also booked an appointment with Dr Crippen at the dental surgery to get a troublesome back molar pulled.

I have been upstairs with my poor unfortunate neighbour a number of times today and being able to use the good old sign language with facial expressions to suit, Jasmine and I can just about understand one another, although the situation is far from satisfactory. It's a bit like spending an hour or two with James Oscar Fingal O' Finnegan, aka *Whispering Jim,* who has to be the only Irishman I know who his fellow countrymen cannot understand when sober, let alone drunk!

Later in the day I contacted the local social services again, and it seems that they are aware of this young lady and her children. It appears that they are waiting to find her temporary accommodation in a hotel somewhere. I took the name of the person dealing with the case and asked if I could be notified when things were on the move, since I was now, for all intents and purposes, Jasmine's helper, *general factotum* and guardian.

Later, I managed to have a quick 5,000 metres of cardiovascular exercise on the rowing apparatus at the gym and estimated that were I in a boat, I would have covered a distance from Sainsbury's in the High Road to the Marylebone Road flyover. Now there's a thought. Given the dreadful traffic congestion in central London, a narrow ditch, just wide and deep enough to accommodate a thin craft, could be dug. This could be used by 'intelligent' former cyclists who had realised that despite the cycle lanes, they were unwittingly becoming an abundant source of organ donors for the motorists.

Drivers really don't give a *quantity of excrement* about cycle lanes or cyclists for that matter, but they'd certainly keep their beloved mechanised steeds away from ditches. Their use might not get you there in record time, but at least you would arrive in one piece which sadly, is more than can be said for many of the capital's cyclists.

Following my exercise, as usual I finished with a sauna, steam and shower. Will close for now Ginny, and I hope that you have a spiffing day.

My love to you and yours.
P xx

January 5th 2012

Good morning, Ginny.

It would appear that Jasmine has an appointment with her GP at 14:30 on Monday the 9th January, but since previously some of the things she has told me have been *a little confused,* I thought that I'd better check it out. Having spoken to the receptionist, she confirmed that no such appointment had been made, and I therefore arranged another one for the following day at 09:10 in the morning. The receptionist emphasised the point however, that an interpreter should be present since her GP, Dr Hirasoto, 'had enough trouble conversing and understanding English, let alone Arabic!'

I found out later that Jasmine does have a niece living nearby, who it appears is being paid as her official carer. The plot actually thickened when I was told by her social worker, *Mutabeswa Badalatta,* that the lady in question, *Muhulin,* has a car provided by the state to assist in Jasmine's transport needs.

 Following a lot of sign language and facial grimaces by us both, which is about the only way that Jasmine and I can effectively communicate, I got to understand that Muhulin is a late riser and doesn't get up until around 13:00 and hence why I hadn't seen her for three days.

It appears that she was born in the East End of London and had reached the grand old age of twenty-three years. I therefore sent her an email in vernacular language (which I knew she would fully understand) informing her without hesitation, reservation or equivocation of any kind, that unless she got her *tradesman's entrance* down to her aunt Jasmine's flat at her earliest convenience to assist in the urgent provision of toiletry and food requirements, that Norman Stanley Fletcher would have more chance of getting a Barclaycard than she would have in retaining her carer's social allowance and company car! I awaited her anticipated urgent response.

Later that evening, I drew up a small list of Jasmine's more urgent requirements and visited our local halal supermarket run by a very nice group of illegal immigrants from Iraq. When I got back upstairs, I found Jasmine lying in her hallway crying uncontrollably. On picking her up, I carried her into the lounge and sat her down. Both of her children, having been to playschool here in the UK, can communicate reasonably well in English, but it is only Elisha who is familiar with her mother's tongue.

Jasmine's current unhappiness had been caused by Mahmud, who, it seems felt the need to chuck her £400 state-of-the-art mobile phone out of the window. This little child is completely uncontrollable and yet I fully appreciate just how difficult it must be for him and his sister having a severely disabled mother. It was for this reason that I smiled at him benevolently, patting him gently on the head, and I am pleased to say that I resisted the very strong inclination of issuing an appropriate quantity of physical karmic redress. I also quickly forced back several disagreeable impulses of a retributory nature.

On the way down to retrieve the phone – or what was left of it – I collected Spike whom I caught *in flagrante delicto* trying to have his wicked way with Eric and from the look of disappointment and frustration on his face, wasn't having a great deal of luck. In my effort to extricate the little *fudge packer*, he bit me, although I'm pleased to say it was more of a *terrible suck* than a bite since like me, he has more gum than teeth these days.

Having got outside, I hunted around on my hands and knees holding Spike close in my left arm. Needless to say, I couldn't find the phone anywhere, and being suddenly aware of the dog's silent breathing, I turned him into the dim light of the ground-floor passageway to find him staring back at me with a look that expressed the kind of facial emotion usually associated with a psychiatric nurse caring for an elderly Alzheimer's sufferer. There are times when I despair of this dog's lack of the judgement! I managed to find Jasmine's phone, which appeared to be beyond repair, but nevertheless I took it back to her. My heart bleeds for this poor unfortunate woman, which reminds me of Maria's latest upset with her current boyfriend.

She recently got romantically involved with an out-of-work Norwegian actor called 'Bjorn De Bjonk Bjornson,' or some such over-the-top Nordic label. She really has not had a lot of luck in her choice of men friends. She met this one while looking around the junk stalls in Camden market. He was selling brightly coloured plastic butterflies. She was forever loaning him money, and as you know she is far from being financially loaded (bless her little wooden maracas). Anyway, to cut a very long and sad tale short, he dumped her the other day, stating that 'he needed time to get over the loss of his former girlfriend'. It turns out the bloke had been carrying around more baggage that a hygienically-challenged kleptomaniac Sherpa. The disgusting *pud-wapper!*

At 23:50, Muhulin and three young people arrived. Mahmud banged on my door to ask if I would let them into the premises from the outside. All four people were heavily laden with shopping bags, some of which I carried upstairs. Suffice it to say that I returned to my flat very much at peace, my usual congenital belief in the inherent goodness of mankind restored.

Goodnight love.
P xx

January 6th 2012

Good morning, sugarplum.

All was very quiet overhead last night, which frankly had me worried for a while. They say that 'silence is golden!' Well so it might be if one is marooned on an uninhabited desert island, or one had deflected a potential earbashing from *Lenny the Ponce*, by offering him a free massage from the gym's latest masseur (who happened to be a great big hairy former truck driver from Basildon called Dorian). Lenny was totally unaware that he had recently replaced the ever-vivacious Rita.

On the day in question, Lenny arrived back at the pub with a face like a smacked bum and was clearly very agitated indeed. I cannot repeat his exact words, but suffice it to say he wasn't very amused.

But, I digress! Silence under the present circumstances was not so very encouraging given the fact that above my paper-thin ceiling were two uncontrollable children, and a badly disabled, mentally disturbed young woman, who could normally be heard in the *Trossachs Nature Reserve* screaming hysterically at her wayward future anarchists. Formerly the worst disturbances have always occurred at night, seemingly when they are most active and hence my anxiety.

So concerned was I, that I simply couldn't sleep and at 01:20 this morning I got my stepladder out, and putting my stethoscope to the ceiling, listened intently. I heard no sound whatsoever. Even Spike kept looking up at the ceiling and then at me with a rather perplexed concerned expression on his face, one leg cocked expectantly (something that he does during times of stress).

I needed to keep up the tension since to get him to relax would have resulted in my yucca plant becoming liberally doused in urine. I therefore kept a very concerned look on my face as I slowly climbed down the steps, and picking him up, I continued to gaze deeply into his eyes, his leg still cocked akimbo. With the pair of us in this position, perhaps reminiscent of a Torvill and Dean ice skating dance routine, I carried him out onto the balcony.

The look of relief on his face as I gently placed him down was both rewarding and inspiring, although I am sure that Eric wasn't over enamoured at being *urinated* on. Sadly, I didn't have time to scoop him up out of harm's way, and having relieved himself, I do believe that I saw a look of remorse on my dog's face, albeit perhaps fleetingly. It was cunningly short-lived however, since having realised that he wasn't about to receive a summary slap for his unacceptably impolite behaviour, he skipped back into the kitchen with a back leg routine that would have made Rudolf Nureyev rearrange his codpiece.

Getting back to Jasmine's children, Elisha is not a real problem and is so charmingly endearing, but Mahmud, who looks relatively harmless, in truth is an absolute out-of-control *enfant terrible*. But then it seems that their father had left the family home when Jasmine's illness had been diagnosed, the despicable *pud-wapper!*

Sadly, these poor little ones have had little or no parental guidance and have found their own way as it were. But then there is always the hope of a reversal in fortune. All they need is a helping hand and a little disciplined direction. As the great Billy Butlin once said:

'Give me the child from one to seven, and I will give you the camper!'

At 09:20, an earth-shattering scream came from upstairs, and I dashed out of the flat, rushed up the stairs and banged heavily on Jasmine's door. Mahmud opened the door cautiously, and on entering I found Jasmine sitting on the hall carpet in a very distressed condition. It appears that her scream was simply out of frustration. The heating wasn't working again, and I suspected that Mahmud was responsible for turning it off. He really is a very disagreeable child, but then that's nothing new. As one chap noted:

'Children nowadays are tyrants. They contradict their parents, gobble their food, and tyrannise their teachers.' Socrates (370 BC).

The flat was sadly in an understandable mess. Dirty clothes destined for the washing machine had fallen down the back of the gas cooker, and helping her up, I didn't notice that in her left hand she had a large toasting fork which in her uncoordinated condition she inadvertently jabbed into my chest as I lifted her up. Thankfully there was no real force behind it, which is just as well since had there been, this email and indeed my humble offering to the literary world might never have been finished. But mortal flesh does have an annoying tendency to bleed when pricked, and bleed it did.

I cooked Jasmine a couple of boiled eggs with toast soldiers and gave the children a bowl of cereal and chopped banana. One of the quite frustrating aspects of being around very young children is that in no time at all, one begins to talk like them. Anyway, while they were all restoring their bodily tissues, I put a considerable amount of clothes into the washing machine and before I returned to my own flat to start my own morning routine, I took her bag of rubbish, which she now leaves outside her door for me to dispose of at the bins downstairs.

Old 'misery guts' at number 124 complained to me the other day about it: 'Leaving rubbish bags out like that will encourage vermin,' he said authoritatively, until I pointed out that, 'They would have to be something quite special to either break down our front door to the block, or gnaw through solid concrete walls to get to them!'

Later, on the way out of her flat, I responded appropriately to Jasmine's request, loaning her £40 although for the life of me I couldn't fathom out on what she would spend it. The poor young woman is totally immobile.

The rest of the day was pretty uneventful. I fed my beautiful Spanish lodger, who eats as though she'd heard that a tsunami will imminently destroy all of the supermarkets in the Kilburn High Road, and a flood of biblical proportions will cut off our first-floor flat.

Later on, I had a very enlightening chat with Lenka at the Bread Bin pub on the application and therapeutic use of certain sexual toy/apparatus devices. The mind boggled, and so did my Guinness, having spilled it several times! For all of these years, I have clearly been living under a very misguided assumption, erroneously believing that I was a man of the world. Cunningly however, the world that I thought I knew had quietly changed, and had moved on very dramatically without notifying me.

Goodnight love.
P xx

January 7th 2012

Dear Ginny.

I didn't sleep particularly well last night, dreaming that I was sat on a huge Zeppelin drinking Guinness. It was terrifying, the Guinness was going everywhere! I am sure that Freud would have had an enjoyable morning checking out that one from his earlier thoughts and observations as expressed in his books on psychoanalysis. He was a very interesting man no doubt but a complete bore nevertheless. I feel confident that if he were ever to attend a striptease performance, that he'd be the only man in the place watching the audience.

As you know, I am an occasional *mystery shopper*, snooping about for companies that are too tight to employ competent managers, to ensure that employees were doing what was expected of them. It brings in a couple of extra shillings and gives me a bit of an interest outside of the house, the gym, Spike, the pub, and now the welfare of a poor disabled young lady and her unfortunate children.

On getting up at 05:00 this morning, I heard what appeared to be Jasmine putting her children to bed. It is clear that a lot of Middle Eastern people spend much of their waking hours during the night and sleep during the day. This would be sensible when living in their native country with soaring daytime temperatures perhaps, but hardly appropriate in the UK where for most of the year the sun is about as visible as an honest politician.

I arrived in South London's veritable racial melting-pot (Peckham) at 09:00 and entered the *Eyebrows Opticians Shop* at 09:15, to complete my assignment in assisting an examiner from the British Optometrist Society. It involved me acting as a member of the public who had lost his glasses and needed new ones. (Something that *Paul the Cab* will be doing for real soon.) The candidate optician is watched as they go through the motions and on passing they can then become a member of this prestigious professional body. It all went well and I am sure that the young lady passed with flying colours. As it is, I have three pairs of glasses: one for short-sightedness, one for long-sightedness and one to look for the other two. I tried varifocals once and having put them on, I frankly didn't know where to look.

Back home later, Jasmine 'summoned' me up again at the invitation of Mahmud who banged on my door furiously. Upstairs, Jasmine gave me the £40 that I had given her earlier, and a note written in Arabic and asked me to visit our local halal supermarket again and give the note to one of the proprietors. A short time later, I carried a bag full of various items back up to her flat and duly presented them to her. I had to smile when she refused to accept the change, indicating that the change from the money that I had loaned her originally, I could keep as a tip. Still, it's the thought that counts.

It has been a very busy few days and frankly at 14:00 I was feeling very tired indeed and decided to have a very quiet afternoon and evening at home.

Goodnight love.
P xx

January 8th 2012

Good morning, Ginny.

I was rudely awoken at 01:30 this morning. The noise upstairs was absolutely awful. It appears that Muhulin had called, and Mahmud had been summoned from his slumber and ordered down to the outer gate to let her in. Whatever the situation, I think that this is an intolerable way to treat a six-year-old child. I will contact social services later today to see what can be done.

I really didn't sleep very well for the rest of the night, and as I dozed periodically, I was aware of the frustrated screams of Jasmine seemingly trying to chastise her ever-disobedient son. Clearly Mahmud takes no notice of her instructions whatsoever and feels safe in the knowledge that his mother cannot get anywhere near him, so the prospect of being on the receiving end of a little summary justice in the guise of a vernacular clump or two, was totally non-existent. I do not advocate cruelty of any kind, but firmly believe that when all other measures or polite requests have failed, that the moderate physical chastisement of a wayward child may become necessary. The Old Testament is very clear on the issue; *Spare the rod and spoil the child* is very explicit and needs no elaboration.

It seems that they all left with Muhulin at some awful time in the early hours, and I fought back the desire to check my bedside clock, since my eyelids felt like lead curtains.

I eventually got up at 06:00 and having slipped my clothes on, I took Spike out for a quick perambulation around the local park, armed with a couple of those nappy bag thingies which I use to pick up his droppings, and as usual this morning he was very accommodating.

Back home, I left him out on the balcony and picked up my training bag (a term used by gym people to denote a designer bag sporting famous gym brand names, in which are carried: tracksuit, deodorant, shaving tackle and aftershave, talcum powder, toilet paper, and a plentiful supply of moist baby wipes, in case one's enthusiasm at lifting heavy weights becomes a little compromised). But in any event, use of the squats bench is completely banned to anyone who had dined at *The Star of Kerala* Indian restaurant the night before. Reportedly, excessive exercise has resulted in an occasional unexpected anal-relapse and colonic irrigation the morning after, and understandably the gym cleaners have flatly refused to get involved in the considerable clean-up operation.

On my last visit to the gym, I had noticed a rather beautiful thirty-something young lady, with a body far too tantalising to describe in mere words. I have always found a six-pack on a woman exceedingly attractive and strangely erotic. I saw her again this morning wearing a bikini-type training outfit. I sat on the rowing machine and started my 5,000 metres *to nowhere* routine and as she went through the motions on the cross-trainer, she gazed around at me and smiled. I was smitten and went into the quickest ever training routine of my life. What normally took me twenty-six minutes I completed in around half the time.

In the sauna later, I was convinced that had it not been operating, the place would have still steamed up with the heat that was coming from my body! On the way out later, I found the young lady sitting in the lounge wrapped in a big white fluffy bathrobe reading a newspaper, and as I left, she smiled at me again and gave me a little wave.

I don't remember walking home, and only *touched down again* when I opened the door to my balcony to find Spike looking up at me guiltily, a neatly planted cone-shaped pile of poo on the top of Eric's shell. I know for certain that he didn't visit an Indian restaurant last night, and even if he had, there is nothing on the balcony that could have caused him to physically strain himself.

Being a bit of an amateur dog-whisperer, I have come to the conclusion that Spike resents the tortoise and I really don't understand why. I share my love and affection equally between them and do not favour one above the other. Well, maybe I do.

Later, I made my beautiful Maria a breakfast that would have satisfied two Irish navvies during which we had an interesting chat about climate change, the current crisis in Taiwan, the theories on how the AIDS virus originated and whether a dog had ever felt remorse. One could never become bored in the company of Ms Hernandez. Being a typical young person, she is always so interested in giving me the full benefit of her inexperience and is clearly afraid of nothing – well apart from perhaps a stack of dirty dishes that is.

I wasn't in the mood to entertain the three Jehovah's Witnesses who arrived a little later, but gave them a biscuit each and an introductory text to the *Bhagavad Gita* for the walk home. It's nice to be nice.

I contacted Jasmine's case worker (Obijudo Matalebi) and brought him up to date with the latest events. He assured me that everything was going through due process and that 'hopefully' another more suitable living environment for Jasmine and her children would be available shortly. I felt like adding. 'Yeah sure, but I won't hold my breath!'

Lenka surfaced at 15:00 as I was leaving for a few medicinal libations at the pub. I tend to leave her alone first thing, although Spike always makes a fuss of her. He sleeps in her room quite a lot and under similar circumstances, I'd probably make a fuss of her too.

Dave, Jim, Andy and Greg were all in animated conversation when I arrived at the pub discussing the lump that *Ted the Pleb* had found on his big toe. Spike jumped up onto his favourite chair by the window, and a little later he was happily munching crisps from his 'nibbles bowl' (which the lads refill periodically). As usual, he entertained himself watching the homeward-bound passers-by, and like a canine version of *Whispering Jim* in one of his trance-like admonishment sessions, he growled at them contentedly.

Spike is a creature of habit and he is a great people watcher. However, he is not so enthusiastic when it comes to other animals, and frankly I am getting a little concerned at his relationship (if you can call it that) with Eric. I think that I should perhaps move him to a safer environment. *Scotch Andy's* missus is a teacher and she has already suggested taking him for the children's *nature garden* at her primary school. I have given it some thought and feel that he would be far safer and happier there. I would hate to come home one day and find an empty tortoise shell and a guilty looking dog picking his teeth with a can opener. Please don't get me wrong, Ginny, I really do appreciate the very kind gift, but if I have to get rid of one of the animals, it would have to be Eric since Spike was my 'first born' as it were, and over the years he has clearly proved himself to be a prime example of 'man's best friend'. I mean, it might be purely coincidental that he cannot talk, but he has never tried to give me advice, or ask me for money, and best of all, he doesn't have any in-laws.

Goodnight love.
P xx

January 9th 2012

Dear Ginny.

I had to visit Jasmine last night at 23:45 since the noise coming from her flat was totally unacceptable. It now appears that Mahmud has broken her very expensive camera. Being the secretary of our residents committee, I had three phone calls from residents complaining about the hubbub. 'Old misery guts' at 124 threatened to call the police if it continued. I mentioned this to Jasmine and quiet was restored for the rest of the night a little later.

I can positively identify with the subject from my latest bed book: *The Diary of a Nobody* by George Grossmith. Like a latter-day *Charles Pooter,* I suppose that I live well enough and could be referred to as an example of a lower-middle-class impecuniously respectable individual. But then I really cannot complain since I have everything that my credit card can provide. While I appreciate that money cannot buy happiness, it does tend to provide a more pleasant form of misery, and I have found that additional funds lying around, have a tendency to soften my potential for worrying unnecessarily about mundane things, like where my next meal will come from. Actually, by way of an experiment, I would quite happily accept a couple of million pounds simply to prove conclusively that money could most definitely buy me a little happiness. Seriously, I can't complain and I do count my blessings daily.

I visited the gym during the late morning and didn't see the beautiful young lady again today, but my belief in the two forces of yin and yang, the black and white, or ups and downs of daily existence were strengthened in that instead I bumped into *Lenny the Ponce,* that veritable portal of intellectual ineptitude (oh to be able to use the vernacular instead).

As usual, his conversation or perhaps more appropriately his diatribe, reflected on the incompetent and uncaring attitude of the staff at the local DHSS office, notably *a well-nourished, dark-complexioned, fatherless woman,* who has been actively bent on getting him back into work and out of benefits since Moses came down from the Mount Nebo. But then, for as long as I've known him, he has displayed a morbid aversion or disinclination in relation to any form of overt physical or mental activity, whether paid or otherwise.

His only interests in the gym are the sauna and shower, which he states kept his fuel bills low and have prevented him from robbing the gas meter (there being little or no cash in it anyway). Needless to say, he tried to tap me for a few pounds but I declined his request, mentioning that now, being a single-parent pensioner, that I did not have an abundance of spare cash, and what little I had, was destined to provide a few cherished luxuries like dog food and toilet paper.

Later that evening in The Magpie, Lenny was complaining to a few of the lads about 'immigrants taking all of the jobs'. Ted certainly quietened him down.

'Shut up, you slug!' he shouted. 'You are not entitled to an opinion on the subject. If you had kicked those long dangly things out of bed years ago and dare I say, *got a job,* immigrants would have nothing to come to this country for, since all of the available positions would have been filled by the indigenous population.' A short pause followed. 'Your historical contribution, or should I say, lack of contribution to society,' continued Ted, 'has encouraged immigrants to fill the vacant jobs, that lazy good-for-nothing *fatherless people* like you have declined and, I hasten to add that many of them are hard-working people, who are helping to put the *Great* back into Britain!' This was followed by resounding applause from a group of Polish building-site workers who not wishing to associate with the local indigenous rabble, were crammed into the posh bar and had heard every word.

I do not wish to appear unduly unkind, but sadly the general consensus of opinion among my fellow sentient beings is that 'Leonard Maynard Ficks, was put on this earth to teach us that not everything in nature has a purpose!'

I found out later however, that Ted's *very loud* verbal admonishment with Lenny was completely *stage managed,* the scoundrel. He had seen the Polish guys in the other bar earlier in the day, and through a rather shady contact, had ordered a few cases of vodka that had been earlier *relieved* from the back of a local wine store, and following their earlier dramatic exhibition, naturally winning friends with the gullible Poles, he sold them the entire consignment of stolen vodka, making a very sizeable profit in the process.

Back home later, I called in to see if my poor little girl and her children were OK. She stated something about 'someone from her former flat' would be paying her a visit, and 'could I loan her more money?' Sadly I had to refuse, since my funds are a little sparse, but assured her that I would phone her niece, and ask her for a little financial assistance.

You will also remember I'm sure, that I have been on a waiting list to move out of London. I joined this government-sponsored company bent on getting all of the elderly former dazzling urbanites – colourfully referred to as *the old farts* – out of the city, to allow more space for the youngsters, who frankly are the future. I received a phone call from them this afternoon to say that I was fifth in line, and would be getting a possible offer soon. One can but hope.

That's it for now, Ginny.
P xx

January 10ᵗʰ 2012

Good morning, sugarplum.

On my first recollection this morning, I wasn't sure if the screaming and shouting that I heard during the early hours of the morning was real, or was simply a part of a rather disturbed dream. But on waking later in the morning, I felt so frustrated in that all of my best endeavours with regard to Jasmine and her children seemingly are a bit of a waste of time. I found out that having booked an appointment with her physiotherapist which she should have attended today, she attended last Tuesday. The children's social worker arrived during the morning, and he has accepted me as Jasmine's *general factotum* having given him a written letter signed by her, stating that I will be dealing with all issues on her behalf. I just wonder if I am doing the right thing.

It seems that the visitor from her other flat was in fact her former landlord requesting financial reparation for the damage caused during her earlier brief tenancy. It would also appear that she had been unceremoniously evicted and given the second-floor flat above mine as an urgent temporary measure, pending the council placing her and the children in a more permanent residence. Clearly, being so physically disabled, the quicker she is given a ground-floor flat the better, although I really am so concerned about her future, particularly with two young dependent children, one of whom would make Attila the Hun look like Billy Graham at an evangelical concert.

In this modern age, many parents are attempting a gentler approach when it comes to altering the unacceptable behaviour of unruly children. When I was a child (where it was far better to be seen rather than heard), an enlightened kindly approach to unruly behaviour was still decades away, and in the meantime the familiar doctrine of 'when in doubt give 'em a clout' was universally practised. Where were all the social workers then, I have to ask? Strangely, if I misbehaved or was noisy or unruly, I was given a summary clump, and generally put to bed early, but then if I was quiet for any length of time, or behaved myself, I'd be stripped off and every inch of my body scrutinised. I would then have a thermometer shoved up my bum, and as often as not would be wrapped in a blanket like an Egyptian mummy, fed copious quantities of chicken soup and would be allowed to sit up and watch TV all evening, right up to *The Epilogue*?

Then as now, most children think that their parents are a little potty. I heard a tale current at the time which concerned an Irish family who lived at the end of our terraced street. There were twelve children in the family. One day a man came to their door collecting for a local children's home. Shamus tried to give him his five youngest.

Sadly, I can see that inevitably Jasmine's children will have to be put into care, which is dreadfully unfortunate. The only relative that she has in the UK is Muhulin and she has her own children and apparently lives in a very small two-bedroomed council flat in Pimlico. Clearly she would not be able to help even if she wanted to.

I felt rather tired during the late evening, but popped upstairs to wish my little girl and her children a pleasant evening. Returning downstairs, I played with Spike in the lounge for a while and then after a shower and dinner, I had an early night, an event which as a youngster I would have looked upon as a punishment. How one's attitudes change with the passing years.

Until tomorrow, Ginny.
P xx

January 11th 2012

Dear Ginny.

I was at the gym bright and early this morning, and I have often commented that if I were to die tomorrow, I'd be the fittest looking bloke in the morgue, and am a very keen advocate of the observation *use it or lose it,* and over the years I have made a concerted effort to hang on to whatever it is that I have left – and at my age it is precious little.

It's a great pity that I couldn't have done something more positive with my hair which I started to lose in my twenties. But sadly, not much can be done in that particular area of my anatomy, and I'm now as *bald as a badger*, well apart from a stubborn growth of muff on either side of my head which I close crop.

Interestingly, the simile relating to a badger's lack of hair refers to the Victorian custom of catching the poor buggers and shaving them for their very stiff and brittle hair. The actual simile is 'As bald as a badger's bum!' But of course, out of politeness the mention of the animal's derriere was dropped. The hair was used to make men's shaving brushes, and sadly this dreadful trade still goes on in places like China, where badgers are farmed for their hair.

The only positive aspect of being bald it seems is that apparently it signifies that the modern-day *Yul Brynner* lookalikes have more testosterone levels than their gorilla-type counterparts, and therefore are manlier. It is also believed that bald men generally have deeper voices and are more virile with a greater pronounced sex drive, than the hairier variety. Frankly, I think that I could have suffered with having kept my boyish voice level, provided that my testicles had dropped and when walking, I had retained my manly gait and didn't look like a latter-day Mr Humphries mincing around on the set of *Are You Being Served?* I could also live with having a lower sex drive, which together could have potentially given me a luxurious lifelong head of hair, like Chewbacca on *Regaine* in return.

They have a very nice new black receptionist at the gym called Danielle. She has an endearing smile and is such a likeable character. I suppose that I'm still a bit of a flirt, but it's all harmless stuff. When I look at a young woman these days, I remember those very wise words in Ecclesiastes 11:9: *Rejoice, O young man in thy youth, and let thy heart cheer in the days of thy youth.* But it's the old story, Ginny, most youngsters are far too busy to stand still long enough to appreciate just how fortunate they are. In truth, like my peers, I too believed that I'd live forever, had all the time in the world, and was totally indestructible.

While I am not particularly religious as you know, I have always had an abiding interest in theology and studied for the Diploma in Religious Studies over a two-year period from 2007–9 with an illustrious Open University (which will remain nameless) and I enjoyed it immensely.

Actually there was a bit of a scandal at St Phillips last year. It was reported that the bishop had reprimanded the vicar over the less-than-discreet affair that he was having with his Swedish housekeeper. Apparently, the nosey verger had found his vest in her pantry and her pants in his vestry. But then he's only a young man after all and being presumably well versed in biblical dictates is simply living as directed. I congratulate him and offer up a spontaneously verbal ejaculation in crying out 'Halleluiah!' to them both. I hope that the verger will get his well-justified karmic comeuppance in the near future, since any reasonable bloke would have kept his trap shut!

At around 11:15 I met up with Molly (our chair) on the resident's committee, in the Harrow Road surgery of our local MP Adrian Goodfellow, where we discussed several issues of concern brought up by our residents. We met up with our local councillor, Brenda Rothy back at Molly's flat later in the day. I versed Brenda on the dreadful plight of Jasmine and her children and was promised that she would look into this issue when she got to her office the following morning.

Back home, I collected my two animals and having put Eric in a straw-filled shoebox, we went to the pub. Spike trotted along with us happily. As I gave Eric to *Scotch Andy,* I could have sworn that I saw an unmistakable look of a triumph in my dog's eyes. From his vantage place on his favourite chair by the window, he excitedly wagged his little stump of a tail and then proceeded to deliberately fall off the chair on to the carpet, where he went through what looked like a victory roll before bouncing back to his feet and shaking himself with wild abandon.

All was well with Jasmine and the children when we arrived home.

Sleep tight, love.
P xx

January 12th 2012

Good morning, sugarplum.

I had run the gauntlet through the women in rugby training at Sainsbury's in Kilburn High Road before 09:00 this morning, and didn't suffer too many bumps or bruises. But there was a bit of a sale on at the Reject Crock Shop and the queues outside were not only very annoying (since you know how I hate crowds) but I had to risk life and limb by stepping off the pavement into what would normally be a relatively busy road anyway, but on this particular Thursday it had become like a Formula One racetrack, the motorists acting like racing drivers hoping to qualify for the Monaco Grand Prix.

Saturdays are an absolute nightmare. The shops are bulging at the seams with scary looking women, whose lack of war-paint (Kilburnian women don't wear make-up at the weekends) still makes them look like white-faced Apache squaws who are out on their first raiding party of the weekend. Their eyes move at a quite incredible speed searching for their next scalp, or more precisely, that illusive sales item that hadn't been spotted by anyone else. Should you happen to see something that one of them has her eyes on, it is better to admit defeat and simply look away, rather than become embroiled in a potential nasty fracas with a large frumpy dumpling straight off the Kentish Town Reservation, bent on getting (a little something) for her man, *Stinky Tie,* back at the camp.

I've really never understood the mentality of bargain hunters, since many of them buy things that they will never use simply because it is at a price that they cannot resist. It is very clear from watching all of the rugby women in training, that the most dangerous vehicle to avoid has to be the shopping trolley. However, at least you can see them coming, unlike the great lump of a female prop forward in full flight this morning. She had spotted an empty checkout and dashed down the wing unchallenged. Despite the noisy clamour and alarm caused, she was determined to get there before anyone else, even though on the way she dropped two packets of digestive biscuits, four rolls of toilet paper and a large box of soap powder on special. As a spectacle, pretty it wasn't.

Spike was in frivolous mood when I returned home and made it pretty clear that a walk in the park was required. He didn't think much of the squeaky tortoise that I had bought him from the Pound Shop (which was reduced from £3.50 to £1.75) and reluctantly taking it from my hand, he took it out onto the balcony and having determinedly forced it through the railings, dropped it down into the curate's hydrangea plant below. Father Marcus will be pleased.

Maria made a brief appearance and smiled at me good-naturedly on her way to the bathroom, a flimsy towel wrapped teasingly around her perfect cumulative quantity and distribution of muscle and fat that would have inspired the greatest artists and sculptors of the world, searching relentlessly for potential models, and that ever-elusive example of bodily flawlessness and beauty. But I digress.

Following Spike's perambulation, we popped up and visited Jasmine. She seemed to be brighter today and offered to make me coffee (bless her little cotton hijab). However, instead I made her and the children breakfast, and realising that time had flown by and that a hungry Spaniard was waiting downstairs, I hastened back to my flat below to find both Maria and Lenka in animated conversation around the kitchen table.

While I prepared breakfast, I listened to my two girls as they discussed various aspects of feminist liberation. I take it as a compliment that they both feel very free, open and comfortable when discussing personal issues, and often ask my advice on just about everything from the books of Enid Blyton to effective methods of contraception. As mentioned before, Ginny, most young women look upon me as a safe, sexually-challenged pipe and slippers individual, but that is far from the truth. I have never smoked a pipe in my life and I don't wear slippers!

Over breakfast, Lenka wanted to know how she could differentiate between the terms 'erotic' and 'perverted'. I noticed that she had secretly winked at Maria, who looked away and was obviously forcing back laughter.

'Erotic is when you use a feather. Perverted is when you use the whole chicken!' I replied. Lenka stared back at me with a look of amazed disbelief and Maria laughed uncontrollably.

Later in the day, I went through one of my critical awareness episodes which so often results in a modicum of revelatory understanding or acceptance. We had just finished a conversation on the sixties, and it brought back so many vivid memories. It heralded birth control, the Civil Rights Movement, a second wave of feminism following an early era of suffrage and a period where in my view, pop music was at its most influential, and I lived through it! But *time*, that dreadfully illusive commodity, rushed on. When I was young, it was of little importance and while I complacently gorged myself upon it, its passage seemed to drag on like an endless winter. I suppose that I believed that I could turn life's pages at my leisure, slowly one by one like a cherished novel. But suddenly, those pages seemed to have been caught up in a gust of cosmic wind and have fluttered and rushed by uncontrollably ever since. I now realise that my personal library has been all but read, leaving a few old dusty photograph albums and books with missing pages.

It was a very quiet afternoon and evening and I wasn't in any real mood to venture out, and settled on an early night instead.

Goodnight love.
P xx

January 13th 2012

Happy birthday, sugarplum.

I wish I could have been with you today, but surprisingly I have celebrated your birthday vicariously, since coincidentally it also happens to be Lenka's birthday today.

I was up and about pre-dawn to ensure that her special birthday cards and gifts were presented nicely on the kitchen table prior to her getting up. Maria arrived just after 09:00 having spent the night out, presumably living her life to the full, although she insists that her relationship with 'Duncan' is purely platonic, but then she's a very smart young lady and has learnt how to play the piano, tennis and dumb.

Lenka got up at around 10:15 and was a little overcome with emotion when she saw the cards, our gifts and the hastily lit candles on the top of her *Ivor the Engine* birthday cake. A great deal of laughter ensued following Maria's innocent remark of 'Give it a big blow job!' Lenka's breath was quite literally taken away by the remark. It took her quite a time to regain her usual, in-control demeanour, and to stop Spike jumping up and down excitedly, who clearly wanted to join in on the fun. Bless her little wooden maracas, Maria's occasional verbal English mistake is always so charmingly *Manuellian* and in her innocence, it becomes all the more hilarious since she doesn't understand the joke.

Lenka didn't stay for breakfast this morning, wanting to visit an art exhibition in Camden, but as usual I made breakfast for Maria. Having this young lady around in the morning is a veritable joy and cooking for her is usually a very amusing affair. The tremendous sense of fun, love and happiness that gushes from her sets me up for the day and one simply cannot be unhappy or depressed around her. She's also so generous of spirit and is a truly beautiful young lady in every way.

Now, *Ted the Pleb* is a different kettle of fish altogether. Spike and I bumped into him at The Magpie today and contrary to the old saying, it is clear that not every dog can smell a wrong one, since Spike senses nothing sinister about the bloke whatsoever and usually goes into almost rapturous excitement on seeing him. Despite my own personal misgivings about the man therefore, I must surmise that given a dog's intuitive sixth sense as it were, that I have either got Ted totally wrong or that Spike's sense of smell was going the same way as his teeth and hearing.

Ted's latest business enterprise involves organising an *Extravaganza Evening* to be held at the Bread Bin pub later in the month, where light refreshments and a country and western band (*The Blunt Spurs*) would provide a musical interlude. This would be followed by a raffle. Tickets are priced at £20 a head, with free entry into the grand finale competition to identify the name of the *lumpy excrescence* that is currently sprouting on one of his big toes. There are lots of prizes to be won and all proceeds would be apparently donated to an unnamed worthy charity. Hitherto, I have always believed that his personal view on charity (beginning at home) had not changed. Although he is quite an unusual individual, with a very pronounced mercurial personality, so we shall see.

Whatever I might feel about the man, I have to admire his keen entrepreneurial spirit. He has been blessed with what appears to be the congenital ability in relieving others of their meagre financial resources, together with the verbal eloquence to make those thus cunningly deceived, thoroughly appreciate and enjoy the experience. Now this takes incredible talent, but as he explained to me once, 'There is nothing more heart-warming than giving others a good time.' He then went into one of his usual Laurence Olivier inspired, Richard III-type soliloquy verses, which frankly, I always find to be quite impressive and sometimes very moving:

'You may be sorry that you spoke, sorry that you stayed or went,
Sorry that you won or lost, or sorry that far too much was spent.
But as you go through life, I'm sure you'll find – you'll never be
Sorry that you were kind.'

I really never know however, when this man is being serious, or when he's simply engaged in diversionary tactics, bent on cunningly relieving one of excess resources. In his case, I do not ever give him the benefit of the doubt.

My short period of uncertainty and concern in relation to my dog's sense of smell and the truth behind certain canine mythology was relieved as we were leaving. On passing Ted's chair, Spike took a very small perfunctory chunk out of his left ankle.

Goodnight love.
P xx

January 14th 2012

Good morning, sugarplum.

Spike was a little sick on the way home last night and I was very concerned about him. But then it's not every day that a dog can get its teeth into such contaminated flesh! But as unwell as he felt, at home he went into Lenka's room, and snuggled up next to her. Coming back as a little dog is worthy of a little consideration!

I was up at 08:00 and on reaching the kitchen I found her sitting out on the balcony with Spike on her lap. She was dressed warmly but it was still rather cold, so I invited her inside and made her a cup of coffee. Clearly, something was wrong and not wishing to pry, I kept quiet. Within a couple of minutes, she tearfully confided in me that she had received news from home that a beloved friend had passed away. She is a very private person, so I didn't press her further, but I persuaded her to come into the kitchen for warmth.

There is no feeling more dreadful, more distressing or utterly frustrating than having to suffer vicariously. Naturally, this is made infinitely worse when the sufferer concerned happens to be a close friend or loved one. Sympathetic words and encouragement never seem to be quite enough, and one is often left in a state of helpless mental indigence and sometimes considerable self-recrimination, due to the erroneous belief that more support could have been given. However, to laugh during such a period is not only unthinkable, but totally unforgiveable (sometimes).

During my attempt to cheer up my beloved girl, Maria came into the kitchen and in her usual bright and cheerful way smiled at us both good-naturedly, and wishing us both a 'happy good morning', she made coffee, and while stirring the cup wildly she said: 'Mama, she called me yesterday. She is been for the checks on the head. The doctor asked if she'd had ever any illness of the head in the family before. *Oh of course*, she said. *My husband Jose, him is thinking that him is the boss!*'

Both Lenka and I looked at one another in stunned silence. Suddenly, a loaf of bread and a toaster shot down past the kitchen window onto the curate's garden below. A momentary silence followed which was broken by an earth-shattering howl and wild hysterical screams and sobs from our poor Jasmine. It relieved the tension considerably and we both quite literally cried with laughter.

A little later in the day, order was restored. The bread and toaster were returned and Jasmine had somehow managed to shackle Mahmud, who on my arrival was confined to his bedroom. In truth, he is an absolute terror, albeit a fine broth of a lad. The trouble is that some of his noodles are missing. Clearly, he has had no parental guidance whatsoever and thereby hangs the tale. He is totally hyperactive and would appear to be suffering from oppositional defiance disorder. *Alfie the Dip* told me about that one, having been diagnosed with it as a young boy himself.

Back in the halcyon days of the early sixties, when it was believed that to cross a sociologist with a member of the mafia would result in an offer that you couldn't refuse, and during a period when gratuitous violence on the TV was minimal, the daily broadcast of *The Wooden Tops* and more particularly *Noddy and Mr Plod*, was passed by the censors as suitable viewing for young people. Sadly it did nothing to enhance the reputation or credibility of the police.

Having seen big ears doing it to Mr Plod on the television, and also believing that it was the right thing to do, Alfie kicked a police officer up the *jacksie* (bum) one evening, and it resulted in him spending the following four years in a correctional detention facility, where the treatment he received for his oppositional defiance disorder, while apparently being entertaining enough, was about as useful as a third armpit. However, the invaluable tuition that he received from a career thief allowed him to refine and master his earlier leaning as a trainee pick pocket. *Watch with Mother*, has a lot to answer for!

I have already suggested to Jasmine (through her niece) that her wayward son needed to be seen by a behavioural therapist, or at the very least an exorcist.

Later, in an effort to think the matter over, I went to the gym, where I simply sat in the steam room. I find that I can really get my thoughts together in a hot and steamy environment. With my back to the door, I was suddenly aware of a forceful draft of cold air hitting me, and on turning around, through the haze, I saw the outline of a shapely female form.

One does try to act so very nonchalant when one's thoughts are suddenly arrested in such a manner. My earlier mental images were effortlessly wiped away, leaving a residue of helpless confusion and a modicum of imbecilic gestures designed to cover up the embarrassment. You know the kind of thing I mean – sitting in the dentist's chair, for example, with a gum full of novocaine, trying to act all macho and brave in front of the pretty young dental nurse, and dribbling all down your front.

It turned out that the lady in question was the one that I had encountered a few days earlier. Although I couldn't see her clearly (I always leave my glasses outside), I was very impressed with her charming, almost naïve innocence and respectful manner. You could have blown me over with a feather when during our polite conversation; she stated that she was a newly qualified clinical psychologist working at St Mary's Paddington. I am not a religious man as you know, but I was sure that this young lady was heaven sent.

Having explained the issue with regard to Mahmud, she appeared to be very enthusiastic and felt that she could be of help. We met later in the reception area and I gave her my card. She again smiled at me sweetly and reading it said, 'It's been nice talking to you Paul, I will be in touch, and by the way my name is Lisel.'

I floated out of the gym, and while I was negotiating the zebra crossing opposite The Magpie, I almost got run over. But the thought of my life ending on a zebra crossing, opposite my favourite watering hole, having been knocked down by a Robin Reliant, being driven by a very credible Del-boy Trotter lookalike, had me laughing hysterically. As I walked into the Gay Bar I received some very funny looks from the attendant guzzlers, but frankly, I couldn't have cared less. I was on cloud nine and believed that nothing could lower my intense feelings of contentment and happiness, but a little later I was to find out just how fleetingly deceptive such thoughts can be.

When I got back to the flat, Jasmine and the children were sitting outside her front door. It seems that her niece had collected this unfortunate group earlier in the day to take them for an appointment at social services. When they got back home, some moronic *tradesman entrance* had deliberately forced a thin piece of metal into her door lock, making entry into the place impossible.

The poor woman and her children reluctantly left with the niece, to spend what would now be a very uncomfortable night for them all. Yet more problems are on the horizon, it seems.

Later, I went to bed feeling very miserable indeed.

Goodnight love.
P xx

January 15th 2012

Dear Ginny.

There is a saying on this side of the pond that *What goes around comes around!* It's not a new sentiment in the least, and is a simple vernacular version of the biblical exhortation, *As you sow, so you reap!* I really didn't sleep at all well and awoke this morning in a foul mood thinking about the very unhappy treatment that had been dished out to Jasmine and her children, and am convinced that the person responsible lives within the block. I am also pretty certain as to the identity of this *pud-wapper* and am of the opinion that a little karmic redress would be appropriate.

I have been in touch with our landlords with regard to Jasmine, and this morning I had a call from one of the council staff to say that she would be moved into other alternative accommodation tomorrow. I frankly don't know whether this is good news or bad.

Jasmine and her niece plus the children arrived at around 10:00 and a locksmith followed a little later. Access was gained into the flat and the disorganised packing of their humble belongings began with Muhulin taking the reins as it were. I did what I could to be helpful but seemingly just got in the way, so I returned downstairs. I collected Spike and made *for the hills* of the Paddington Recreation Centre where both of us could walk off our individual feelings of helplessness and frustration.

Spike really does pick up on my moods and he knows when I'm down. The last time I was upset he chewed a leg off one of the kitchen chairs, and the time before that, he tried to commit suicide by jumping off the balcony. But then he always was a bit of a drama queen, and there was no chance of him hurting himself anyway, since it was only a three-foot drop into the curate's hydrangea bush. Still, as I reasoned later, it was the thought that counts.

Sitting on our usual park bench surrounded by beech trees, with the muffled drone of vehicular traffic deliriously making its way up and down the Kilburn High Road in the distance, my thoughts were arrested (with no pun intended) by the familiar voice of *Ted the Pleb* who had crept up behind me, and said:

'As you ramble through life, whatever be your goal, keep your eye upon the doughnut, and not upon the hole.'

This rendition was expressed in his usual exaggerated *Laurence Olivier* eloquence and intonation, which again I found quite pleasant and rather amusing, although Spike was not very impressed and his deep guttural sounds kept Ted at a distance. We exchanged pleasantries, and I gave him a complete rundown of my early new year experiences and what had brought me to this new low of abject misery and distress, to which he responded sympathetically. Needless to say, I parted with £40 and was given a couple of tickets to his *Extravaganza Evening* which will be held at the Bread Bin this coming Saturday evening. As he was leaving, Spike was licking his undercarriage with the determined enthusiasm of an itinerant tramp at a soup kitchen, and foolishly Ted remarked:

'I wish I could do that!'

'Well ask him,' I replied. 'He might let you!'

No pleasant euphemism could adequately do justice to his highly colourful reply.

Later, Spike and I took a walk to the infamous Bread Bin Tavern, the scene of Ted's forthcoming extravaganza. If ever there was a person in this world who could cheer a soul up, it is unquestionably the owner of this dump of a watering hole, Rosheen O' Flanagan. I had a bit of a fling with her a few years ago, or should I say got caught up in one as it were, she being busily engaged in throwing out a rather obnoxious individual one evening. I happened to be in the vicinity as the great lump of flaying undignified humanity flew past me and out of the door. He attempted to return, but with my usual snake-like reflexes, I jumped up and closed the ancient portal. I was quite pleased with myself, and Rosheen was very sympathetic and gentle when a little later she pulled me out from under it.

Rosheen is not a lady that one messed around with, either singularly or, worse still, when there was a bunch of them as induced by *Brother Bacchus* and friends, following a night on the booze. She was not like other women and hated the idea of sexual equality, being of the opinion that women who sought equality with men were lacking in class or ambition. She came from a family of six brothers and was taught to box to more or less Olympic standards by the age of eight. But having said all of that, she has an intensely feminine side, and it was only the privileged few that ever saw or experienced it. We became lifelong good friends and trusted confidants.

Back home, I called in to Jasmine's former flat. It was in an almighty mess, although I comforted myself in the belief that things could only get better. They certainly couldn't get any worse!

Goodnight, Ginny.
P xx

January 16th 2012

Dear Ginny.

It was the start of an exhausting day. Jasmine and family were finally moved during the morning and it was a bit of a fiasco. This poor woman has had her fair share of misfortune and I would suggest that enough is enough. Seemingly nothing has gone smoothly for her, and everything that she touches appears to go awry. Her path seems to be festooned with stumbling blocks and even the smallest event lands up becoming a major drama. I think that you get my general drift.

The less than cooperative or friendly council people arrived at 10:15 to collect her belongings. They refused to take the bulk of her goods and chattels, only collecting the barest essentials. She was overcome with frustration and I could have wept for her. Through Muhulin, I told her that I would collect her remaining clothes and would deliver them to her new abode, which I understood was somewhere in the Paddington area. I had a key to her flat and figured that once the dust had quite literally settled, I would start collecting and bagging up items ready for delivery. Muhulin would ring me later to give me details of her new address.

At 11:45 I helped my poor little girl to her niece's car and bade them farewell. She gave me a tearful hug, and I had quite a lump in my throat as the car pulled away. Back upstairs I made a start on packing the veritable mountain of clothes that were strewn all over the place. Later, I had collected four additional carrier bags of personal items and that was the mere tip of the iceberg.

Back inside the relative order of my own humble abode, I hitched Spike to his lead and took him for a walk. It was very chilly and in the park snowflakes started to fall. Within an hour, the area was graced with an icing topping of virgin snow and children were laughing and playing happily. Spike was totally indifferent to the visual changes that had taken place to his former verdant pastures, but remonstrated bodily when he realised that the snow had covered his usual snuffle areas, and there wasn't a decent whiff to be found anywhere.During the week, I had promised Lenka that I'd buy her some oysters. She had never tasted one before and as adventurous as ever, thought that she would like to give them a try. Later in the afternoon, I braved the High Road and visited our local fishmonger. The chap that runs the place is an amiable ruddy-faced cockney who always has a smile on his face, which I find admirable given the smell and below-freezing temperature of the place. He was telling me about a bloke that came into the shop last week, whose son had to write an essay on the intelligence of dolphins. 'Are they really that intelligent?' the man had asked the fishmonger (whom I now know is called Trevor).

Looking at me intently and picking up a limp mackerel which he used to good theatrical effect, it nodding as it were, at the salient points of his narrative, he said:

'Does Dolly Parton sleep on her back?' Before I had time to answer, he said:

'They are highly intelligent mammals, who after a few short weeks in captivity can train a human being to stand on the side of the pool and throw fish at them three times a day. Now that's what I call bleedin intelligent mate!'

He examined his hand-held mackerel critically, and then reverentially placing it back among the ice, he smiled at me good-naturedly, and asked me what I wanted.

'Two dozen oysters,' I replied.

'Best natural aphrodisiac known to man,' he enthused.

'Are they intelligent too?' I asked in jest.

'Absolutely,' he replied. 'I mean, you've never seen one on *University Challenge* have you mate? But then having to look at Bamber Gascoigne for half an hour, you can probably understand why, which proves my point, stupid they are not!'

Needless to say, I bought the two dozen oysters from him, and chuckled to myself just about all the way home.

Muhulin sent me a text at around 16:30 giving me details of Jasmine's new address, and having loaded up the passenger seat, back seat and boot of the car, I delivered her *first consignment* of clothes. She now lives in a small, but comfortable ground-floor flat, which was adequately furnished and warm. But needless to say, the place was in utter chaos. Mahmud was conspicuous by his absence, and

I located him in the toilet busily stuffing underwear down the toilet bowl. Such simple pleasures! While I was there, I received a call from Lisel and brought her up to date with regard to Jasmine's household and she suggested that later in the week, she would visit them with a view to meeting Mahmud. I gave her Jasmine's home address and mobile number and left it at that.

Back at home, Maria and Lenka were in the kitchen discussing urinary tract infections (as one does) and having layered a large platter with crushed ice, I started to open the oysters, which I believe is called *shucking*. I placed them neatly in a circular fashion around its outer rim and worked in a circular fashion towards the centre. Maria's facial expression adequately suggested her thoughts, although she became particularly interested in how one opened them. I demonstrated using my new shucking knife, which I had bought from Trevor at the fishmongers.

'I never did like them things,' she remarked, physically shuddering. 'They look horrible disgusting. How can you put a thing which comes in an ashtray served, and looks like that into your mouth?'

'Oh you should try one Maria, they are really scrummy,' I remarked, passing one to Lenka, who squeezed a little lemon juice over it and unhesitatingly devoured it. Smiling at me she remarked, 'Delicious!'

'They are hypochondriacs as well,' Maria said, poking one with a fork.

'You mean they are aphrodisiacs; hypochondriacs are always sick,' replied Lenka helpfully.

Inspecting one closely, Maria didn't seem to be very convinced, but pointing at another one remarked, 'You could be right, that one doesn't look too well!'

Needless to say, a very amusing fun-filled evening followed, and Maria, true to her word, would have nothing whatsoever to do with them. Later however, she had no reserve or hesitation in demolishing a large offering of steak and kidney pie, mashed potatoes, beans and sprouts, followed by apple crumble and custard.

Goodnight, Ginny.
P xx

January 17th 2012

Dear Ginny.

At 06:10 this morning I received a frantic call from Jasmine's daughter Elisha, asking if I could come because 'Mummy is cold!' Before I could reply she rang off. I was naturally thinking the worst as I trudged across the arctic wastes of the park. I arrived at Jasmine's flat at 06:45 and Elisha opened the front door. The flat was in total darkness and holding the child's hand we made our way slowly along the hall. I really didn't know what to expect, but was quite relieved when I found Jasmine sitting up in bed wrapped in a blanket holding a small torch. The flat was very cold indeed and all of the radiators were off. Mahmud was asleep in his bedroom.

On checking the fuse boxes in the hall, I found that all of the circuit breakers were OK but the mains power terminal had been switched off. Once light and order had been restored, I told Elisha to tell her mother what I had found, and Jasmine simply stared into space. Elisha told me that she thought that Mahmud was responsible and I tended to agree with her. Thankfully, the little devil was out of harm's way and I am so pleased that such was the case, since had he been awake, I feel reasonably confident that my normal restraint could have been severely tested and in all probability ultimately compromised.

I put Elisha back into bed and intimated to Jasmine that she should try and sleep for a while, and ensuring that the heating was back on and all was quiet, I silently left. I sincerely hope that her life will get a little better now, but in truth, I really do not envy the neighbours since they are all in for a very rude awakening indeed. But as it turned out, nothing as comparably offensive as to what the veritable *scrote* at number 124 was to contend with.

More snow was falling as I made my way home, but outside the door to my block, there had been a lot of activity given the amount of footprints. As I opened the outer door, I was almost knocked off my feet by the terrible smell that came from within. Having climbed the stairs, I checked where the smell was coming from, and I found a veritable mountain of raw horse manure almost covering the door of 124. Clearly, this would have to be moved from the outside and in the interim the aforementioned *scrote* would be held captive.

I had to smile to myself when I considered the kind of excuse he would have to make for his non arrival at work, and I felt surprisingly joyful. The commotion and noise that echoed through the stairwell finally abated at 17:15 and the somewhat dishevelled former prisoner made his first appearance of the day a little later.

I was told by one of the other residents, who has a little previous for poking his nose into other people's horse manure, that he had to pay two council labourers £20 each to clear the offensive matter, and he apparently was not overly impressed when the curate asked if he could have a bucketful for his roses.

He was standing at the bottom of the stairs as Spike and I passed on our way out to the pub. I made no comment to him whatsoever and avoided eye contact, but Spike looked up at him intently and on passing, sniffed him accusingly.

I cannot remember a time when the pub was filled with such laughter. The jokes involving horses were never ending. Just as I was leaving, Ted arrived and having bought a large gin and tonic, he took a sip, smiled at me wryly and said. 'What goes around comes around!'

Goodnight, Gin.
P xx

January 18th 2012

Good morning, Ginny.

When Spike and I returned home last night, the overwhelming smell of disinfectant in the stairwell was quite nauseating. Even within my flat, the dreadful odour was overpowering, and my normally inexpressive dog was doing his best to keep a straight face. I for one found it quite difficult to sleep, my mind racing away producing a kaleidoscope of comic images, although as unsympathetic and detached as ever, Spike grabbed his tartan blanket, and confidently trotted off into Lenka's room, where a comfortable good night's repose awaited him.

I awoke at around 07:00 and as usual, Spike jumped up on my bed and greeted me with an enthusiastic exhibition of tongue-licking exuberance of a kind that only a dog can provide. Mind you. in my youth, I met a girl from Aberystwyth once… But I won't go into that.

Dogs are very manipulative and it seems to me that an owner is only considered to be the nominal head of the pack, as it were, when a dog deems that position commensurate with the attention, consideration, food, exercise and comfort-providing qualities of its *partner*. The term *owner* is a little presumptuous when it comes to having a live-in canine for a pet.

I was at the gym quite early today, and as I entered I was greeted enthusiastically by Danielle the receptionist, whom I have mentioned before. She pointed to a newly placed poster advertising an over 50's gym challenge to be held over five days commencing on Monday 30th with wonderful prizes for the winner and runner-up. A young female athlete would be available from the 23rd to guide those interested and to put them through their paces as it were. I've always enjoyed a challenge and I signed up immediately.

At the end of this month, Lenny will be due his annual medical assessment, and normally a few weeks before his interview, he would *throw a wobbly* – usually quite dramatically – which would inevitably land him up in hospital for a spell of observation. Last year, conveniently he was found in an apparent unconscious state behind the nurse's hostel at St Mary's hospital in Paddington.

His medical records are held in a dossier as thick as an unexpurgated copy of Tolstoy's *War and Peace* describing former symptoms as diverse as viral infections to bubonic plague. Very senior and learned physicians have never been able to identify the mysterious phantom medical condition from which he periodically suffers, with any degree of certainty. It had long been suspected that he was nothing more than an unashamed malingerer, simply hoping to keep one step ahead of an ever-vigilant DHSS upon which he relied, to provide substantial financial assistance from the welfare state. However, at a time when litigation against the medical profession for negligence is at an all-time high, he had simply been given the benefit of the doubt and as a consequence, there isn't a doctor in

London who would give Lenny a clean bill of health as a result.

I heard this evening that he had been found by a park keeper unconscious, having apparently collapsed into the rhododendrons by the bowling green. This time however, he got more than he bargained for, since the keeper who found him (Bunny Longhurst) is a little short-sighted, and had used his spike implement to pick up what he thought was an old discarded boot. Apparently, the banshee howl and scream that Lenny made as Bunny enthusiastically sunk it into his boot and foot could be heard all the way to The Magpie, occasioning an all too rare verbal observation from *Whispering Jim*. 'Ah that'll be Lenny then,' he said, having been momentarily distracted from putting on another Jim Reeves record on a jukebox that had become known as *'Whispering Jim's piggy bank'*.

This time Lenny's hospital visit was justified, but as *Ted the Pleb* pointed out, that apart from his mysterious illness, he now had a genuine injury that will be played upon for the rest of his life. Needless to say, it will never get better and will become noticeably worse when the inevitable (compensation) had set in.

Clearly that *well-nourished, dark-complexioned, fatherless woman* at the DHSS will have to get up a little earlier to have one over on Leonard Maynard Ficks, or divert her investigative interests on to a less challenging subject.

I haven't heard from Jasmine today, so I must assume that all is well. I hope that the same applies to you,

Sleep tight, love.
P xx

January 19th 2012

Good morning, Ginny.

I hope you slept well. Mine was a rather disturbed event, due to Spike running around the bedroom seemingly asleep. I really didn't think that dogs could sleepwalk but I might be wrong. It appears that he was looking for something. Perhaps he was missing Jasmine and the kids, or indeed he may have felt a twinge of remorse over the part he played in having Eric evicted.

Lenka didn't come home last night, and maybe he was simply concerned for her welfare. All of these thoughts went through my mind as I attempted to shake off the remnants of a rather disturbing dream, which featured a freezing cold barren landscape and a pair of ghostly wellington boots that were walking towards me in a threatening manner. Freud would have had fun with that one I dare say, perhaps suggesting that I have a latent fear of somebody. But then I do not go out of my way to upset or offend anyone, which logically should provide complete immunity from the hatred or hostility of others. Well there was that little incident where I was selected secretary of our residents association by the majority of the attendant residents last November, taking over from the ousted former incumbent, Nobby Caxton (the caretaker) who took defeat in a gentlemanly manner. Before he returned to clearing the inner courtyard from a heavy layer of snow that had fallen during the night, he shook my hand warmly, pulled on his wellington boots and stated that 'he would always be at my side' which I thought was very kind, until *Tony the Tube* whispered, 'So is appendicitis!'

Too many thoughts so early in the day are not good for the metabolism. It is far better to kind of gently slide into a new morning, and what better way than to see a young beautiful lady dressed in a flimsy toga heading for the bathroom. All negative thoughts are simply blown away like autumnal leaves in a lust of wind, and for breakfast, I quite unconsciously got a pack of sausages out of the fridge, albeit that I had earlier decided on preparing eggs Benedict.

There was a lot of very excited talk at the gym this morning regarding the forthcoming over 50's challenge, and so far fifteen people have signed up. Training will start on Monday and the challenge will consist of an hour's exercise against the clock on Friday. First prize will be an all-expenses paid weekend for two at that scenically beautiful seaside town of Bognor Regis, as described on a poster. The runner-up will receive two tickets to see the award-winning theatre production of *The Wizard of Oz* which is currently running in the West End, and all of the participants will be given free life insurance quotes, compliments of one of the sponsors, and polythene soap bags emblazoned with the gym's logo. I really do so enjoy challenges like this one. Winning or losing isn't really the issue; it's simply a matter of participating that's important.

Some years ago, I took up jogging until I heard of some poor bloke who had been hit on the head by a falling meteorite. Ironically it happened on the top floor of a new Spanish gym, where coincidentally the builders had planned to put the rest of the roof on that very afternoon. Still, I suppose if a meteorite has your name on it, there's not much that can be done, roof or not. But as for coincidences, *Alfie the Dip's* brother Malcolm wanted to visit the States but had a morbid fear of flying, so he worked his passage on a Liberian cargo ship. Halfway across the Atlantic, a 747 fell on it!

I received a rather sweet call from Jasmine's daughter Elisha later in the afternoon, inviting me for dinner with her mother and brother tomorrow evening. When I enquired about her mum, she reported that she was fine and was sleeping. 'What time should I come?' I asked.

'After *The Magic Roundabout*,' she replied. She's such a charming little girl.

At the pub later, the main topic of conversation revolved around Lenny's fortuitous mishap.

Scotch Andy had been in touch with the hospital during the day, and it appears that earlier our poor severely injured friend had undergone surgery, which Ted – who has now taken over as compensation assessor – estimated would put an additional couple of numerals on to his original figure of £18,000, thereby raising his own consultant percentage considerably.

A small deputation on behalf of Lenny's minimal circle of friends, including myself, will visit him tomorrow morning. He may not be one of the most endearing or popular of our associates, but he's one of ours and that makes him important. Ted summed up the situation quite well when he said, 'Lenny is vain, foul-mouthed, selfish and untrustworthy. He can be mean, unforgiving, and most of all childish, but he happens to be my best mate, so none of that really matters!'

Muhulin collected the remaining personal effects from Jasmine's former flat later in the evening.

Goodnight love.

P xx

January 20th 2012

Good morning, Ginny.

Paul the Cab arrived outside of The Magpie at 10:30 as arranged. It was a bitterly cold morning, and prior to his arrival, the four of us – *Ted the Pleb, Tony the Tube, Dave the Voice* and me – huddled together in the doorway of the pub for warmth. In an effort to cheer us all up, Ted said, 'Ah come on boys, it isn't that bad, spare a thought for those poor North Sea fishermen.' In an amazing example of a spontaneous collective of like-minded thought, simultaneously the three of us uttered, *'Shericals!* To the *effing* North Sea fishermen!'

The drive to St Mary's hospital was a miserable affair. Ominously, the inside of Paul's cab was actually colder than the outside temperature.

'I never put the heating on during the winter,' confided a muffled voice that emanated from a full-face woollen balaclava at the front. 'I don't like to put the heating on in case I nod off, besides I never take punters on long trips in case I get lost,' he explained. However, I couldn't help noticing that our driver was wearing a new pair of designer spectacles, and I was relatively confident that unlike those bewildered chaps that were erroneously dropped off at the church instead of the mosque on New Year's Day, that we would (eventually) arrive at the correct destination. But friends or not, *Paul the Cab* Finklestein is a seasoned London black-cab driver, who is genetically programmed to take the longest possible route between two relatively straightforward geographical points. Even when he walks to Sainsbury's in the High Street, he avoids the easy route that would take a maximum of ten minutes to cover, preferring to traipse around the less congested twenty-two-minute alternative.

Having thankfully arrived at St Mary's hospital (in the time that it would have taken us to walk), I was more than simply pleased to get out of the cab, since it negated the very real possibility of developing hypothermia and having to reluctantly cuddle up to Ted for life-saving warmth. A thought that my mind and stomach simply couldn't cope with! Our respective wallets shared the £18 (excursion costs) and I do believe that our driver was a little peeved that we didn't include a small appreciative gesture by way of a gratuity. He got plenty of good old-fashioned verbal instead however!

Lenny's ward was a warm, well-lit depressing place, with a line of beds on either side on which rested various examples of humanity displaying an amazing array of physical conditions. Some evidently suffering from broken limbs were supported by slings and pulleys hanging up at awkward unnatural angles, which looked more like medieval torture apparatus than modern-day medical equipment. Others simply lounged or sat on beds looking like shell-shocked bewildered troops recently back from the front.

Our injured friend was in a bed right at the end of the ward, presumably having been placed there late on Wednesday evening. I was told by a hospital porter years ago, that it was customary in the old Victorian hospitals for late-arriving undiagnosed patients to be placed nearest the door, so that if they died during the night, they could be quietly removed without upsetting the other patients. No such luck here however, since on spotting us making our way towards him, Lenny shouted excitedly and then burst into tears. It took a considerable time to calm him down as he shook our hands, sobbing pitifully. I felt quite sorry for him and did what I could to cheer him up. In fairness, he hasn't had a great deal of luck in his life what with detention at school, borstal, prison and an open psychiatric unit, all of which have weighed heavily upon one of life's misfits, who has simply followed in the fingerprints of his ever-unemployable (never around) father. He was destined to ponce, thieve and con his way through life rather than simply go out and do a day's work. But it really wasn't all due to the influence of his father, albeit that the unfortunate man was reluctantly out of gainful employment for most of his life. In fairness, I could compare his lot to one's religious beliefs since it is evident that it's all about geographical provenance. Born in the west, there's a fair chance that you'd be a Christian, whereas being born in the east in all probability you'd be a Muslim or a Hindu. As far as potential employment opportunities were concerned, had his father been born in Orkney he may have stood a chance, but sadly there were never very many vacancies for lighthouse keepers in Kilburn, or surrounding areas for that matter, irrespective of one's religious affiliations.

Lenny's condition is not too serious and the prognosis is that he will be up and about within a week or so and in the meantime he has to 'take things easy' as the doctor suggested. How ironic is that when you consider that the only two things that *Lenny the Ponce* has ever made are mistakes and fag ash and the only thing that he can do quickly is get tired? His one regret is that he won't be able to attend Ted's charity extravaganza on Saturday and just before we left, he asked him for the return of his £20 ticket money so that he could pay back half of the money he borrowed from *Whispering Jim*. Life in the fast lane can be so complicated.

Back home, I took Spike out for an afternoon stroll in the park, and found that an area around the rhododendrons had been taped off like a crime scene. It appears that the council are taking this matter very seriously, and given the identity of the injured party, I can't say that I blame them. Even Spike, having sniffed the area, cocked his leg and then changed his mind.

Just after the end of *The Magic Roundabout* I crossed over a very cold and frosty park to attend my dinner appointment with Jasmine and her children. Mahmud opened the door, and Elisha came out of the kitchen and taking my hand she led me into the lounge where Jasmine was clearly very surprised to see me. 'It's OK, mummy,' Elisha said, 'Mr Paul has come to take us to McDonald's.'

Goodnight love.
P xx

January 21st 2012

Good morning, Ginny.

Heavy snow fell again during the night and I found it necessary to turn the central heating up a few degrees. There is one thing that I hate more than the snow, and that's the wind. All night it howled relentlessly, shaking the glass in my bedroom windows, and screaming up the stairwell like some demented spectre in a horror film.

Call me an old romantic, but my thoughts suddenly turned to those poor North Sea fisherman risking life and limb out there fighting the elements, braving the storms, and being tossed about on a ramshackle slippery deck and freezing their cods off, just to ensure that there would always be a readily available supply of money in their bank accounts to keep their women and mothers-in-law, as well as the debt recovery people, off their backs. It also ensured a roof over their heads, and enough money to pay a weekly National Insurance Stamp, thus ensuring that after the mandatory accumulated forty years of contributions, that at retirement age (provided that they hadn't been washed over the side in the interim) that they would be eligible to receive a monthly pension payment from that illustrious government body (the Department for Work and Pensions). How about that for romance?

At 07:15, as I kicked my legs out of bed, the smell of freshly made coffee wafted through into my bedroom, followed by the tinkling sound of a teaspoon on a coffee cup.

The smell of morning coffee is so evocative of my childhood. At a period of my life when tea was the normal beverage of the masses, *Pater* being the inveterate snob that he was, gave up drinking it when he discovered that tea had no Latin name. He rode through life like a seal balancing a ball on its nose and chose to spend what little spare cash he earned on things that we didn't really need in order to simply impress the people that he didn't like. Even his old, battered bicycle had aluminium mud guards, a brass horn from a scrapped Austin 7 and a first aid kit.

He gave up drinking the national beverage through inflated feelings of self-importance and reluctantly renounced cycling a little later, following a Communist propaganda scare during the late fifties, which resulted in him developing an irrational aversion to the colour red. It was later to result in his early demise following a serious accident involving him, his bike, a set of traffic lights on red, and a heavily laden Lipton's tea lorry.

His death was covered in *The Bicycle Monthly* and he was buried with full cycling honours. His coffin was wrapped in a large eloquently embroidered red tea cloth, on which was emblazoned the Lipton's coat of arms and a king-size tea leaf. How about that for irony?

Maria is what one might justifiably describe as *domestically challenged,* although in fairness she can make a pretty reasonable cup of coffee. But then putting a spoonful of coffee granules into a cup followed by hot water is hardly difficult. As I entered the kitchen, she was sat at the dining table with Spike sitting on a chair opposite, looking at her intently.

'I'm teaching him to read with the lips,' she confided, continuing to mouth incomprehensible words (that even I couldn't follow) and tapping her lower lip with a wooden chopstick to indicate each syllable. Spike looked at me appealingly.

'Perhaps if you tried it in English rather than Spanish,' I volunteered.

'I am doing it in English!' she replied defensively.

'Ah... but then it must be your accent?' I replied, nodding enthusiastically. Before she had time to answer, Lenka walked in and Spike, seeking sanctuary, leapt up into the warmth and protection of her arms. Needless to say, breakfast was the usual thoroughly joyful and exuberant experience that I always look forward to when my two girls are at home.

I thought I'd give Sainsbury's a miss this morning and go a little *upmarket,* taking my business to Marks and Spencer instead, where one is assured of a better class of fellow aisle walker. No frumpy dumplings in rugby shirts running down the wings in this store. But then, since the cost of a few grocery items here is equivalent to Latvia's GNP, it's hardly surprising. Still, I did find a tin of beans which would normally retail at 45p in Sainsbury's reduced from 70p to 64p so at least I saved a couple of pence at the checkout. The only trouble is they seem to be running out of cashiers, because you have to put each item through a scanner yourself, place them in a bag, press the finish button, put your money in, get your change in 2p and 5p coins and then call for a cashier to sort out the error code, since there was an *unidentified item* on the collection tray (which happened to be my *Sainsbury's Bag for Life*). It all seems so pointless. Besides, I like a little social intercourse when I have to part with money; it makes the separation a little more tolerable.

Later in the evening, Maria and I attended Ted's extravaganza at the Bread Bin, and it was a tremendous success, raising £220 for that undisclosed charity, although no one was able to guess the name of the lump-type excrescence on Ted's toe. The raffle prize of £75 was won by our very own caretaker Nobby Caxton, whose normal lugubrious demeanour suffered a direct hit as it were, and occasioned a fleeting smile, and a clenched fist on the end of a raised right arm. All very militant I thought, and certainly a little unbecoming of a former cub scout. A little later, I found him staring at me good-naturedly.

The Blunt Spurs were a little washed out and frankly not what I'd expected. *Whispering Jim* was well disappointed, particularly since none of them knew any Jim Reeves numbers, which for a country and western band is unforgivable, but then, they probably didn't fully understand what Jim had said to them. He sat by Rosheen's jukebox looking as miserable as a frost-bitten apple, and as usual there was a mini skyscraper of pound coins in front of him which were balancing precariously on a soggy beer mat. He impatiently tapped the tabletop, daring any of them to fall before the band's first break, when he could then stuff a handful into the machine and play some *real music!*

Following their second number, which was called 'I liked you better before I knew you so well' and the unenthusiastic titter and applause that followed had died down, Jim shouted:

'Do you play requests?'

The bass player, a rather portly individual with a somewhat unconvincing American accent of a type used by a Gateshead-Geordie, replied:

'Sure do partner!'

Collecting a few coins from his pile, Jim shouted triumphantly:

'Well in that case, go and play feckin pool!'

The resounding applause that followed, together with the rather unmistakably suggestive glares from one of the bouncers, seemingly out for a night's persecution of itinerant Geordie musicians, convinced the four that an early night would be appropriate. A pro-rata bill for their nine-minute performance would be sent to Ted later, and instead of helping themselves to the prepared sandwiches, vol-au-vents and fairy cakes, they'd collect a Kentucky fried chicken family bucket and French fries on the way back to their digs in Bethnal Green.

Maria enjoyed herself and struck up a friendship with a young bloke that I've seen before walking a poodle in the park. I left just before midnight, leaving her with her new friend and once at home, I didn't want to wake up Lenka or Spike, so I took my shoes off outside of my front door, and did not put the light on in the hall. As I crept into my bedroom on tiptoes, out of my bedroom window I caught sight of a man that looked like Nobby Caxton on the flat roof of our sheds below in the courtyard. I couldn't begin to imagine what a caretaker would be doing in the dead of night on the top of snow-covered sheds, but contented myself with the thought that whatever the reason, it must be a good one. Having safely located the end of my bed, I ran my hand up to the pillow's end to retrieve my pyjamas. Suddenly out of the darkness I heard a deep guttural growl, and before I could take evasive action, Spike attacked and embedded what teeth he had left into my arm.

On switching on my bedside lamp, he blinked, wagged his little tail apologetically, and cautiously crept out of the room.

Goodnight love, sleep tight.

P xx

January 22nd 2012

Good morning, Gin.

I was feeling a little delicate this morning following last night's alcoholic festivities, although in all honesty I didn't really drink that much. (I spill most of it anyway.) I don't care what anyone says about growing old gracefully, I really am beginning to understand how a lifelong fun-loving, charming individual can degenerate into a grumpy, intolerant old bugger in later years.

Time might be a great healer, but it's no expert beautician. My shaving mirror often reflects a face which is slowly becoming annoyingly unfamiliar. I find my bodily readjustments quite frustrating and frankly a little unnecessary. Some changes are acceptable. As mentioned before, my hair started to thin during my early teens for example, but then it was never what you might call fat, besides, baldness is the new chic, and if it's alright with Bruce Willis, Vin Diesel and Clare Balding, it's OK with me,

They say that nature has a purpose, but for the life of me I cannot see the evolutionary logic or the need for a correction to the original working plans purely based on age. What is the point of losing hair from a place where it has always grown in abundance, and replanting it in formerly smooth follicularly challenged areas of one's anatomy like ears and nose, for example? Clearly, the architect has been out for lunch too often and should avoid the judgement-impairing qualities of the 49 claret.

I can accept that, like a car engine, certain components will inevitably wear down needing remedial treatment from time to time, but how would motorists cope with age-related irreversible mechanical changes to their motor vehicles? What if one morning they found that the spare tyre of their old faithful car was now inexplicably situated in a housing on the outside of the driver's door, or the exhaust outlet was now coming out from under the front of the vehicle instead of at the back, or indeed, that their trusty old car horn now played a rendition of *Beethoven's Ninth* instead of an air-horn version of *The Camptown Races*? I would suggest that they'd have the raging hump of a type not too dissimilar to the frustration felt by maturing men when having to have their eyebrows threaded, noses trimmed, and their muff-covered ears waxed on a regular basis!

This morning, as ever receptive to my dark moods, Spike brought me his cuddly frog to play with and finding that this didn't work, he had a dump on the kitchen floor, presumably to brighten up my spirits and to take my mind off my immediate sense of futility. He can be so thoughtful at times.

The girls were not at home this morning so my breakfast was a lonely affair, apart from Spike who as usual sat on his stool opposite, thoughtfully watching every mouthful as I placed it in my mouth. Perhaps he was trying to analyse what my lips were saying as I chewed my food? I shall have to ask Maria how his lip-reading prowess is progressing.

She mentioned the other day that his understanding of Spanish was improving and that he now knew the difference between, *por favor entre,* and *por favor vamoose,* which frankly is more than I do. But then I can change a bicycle tyre!

All was very quiet at The Magpie during the afternoon and I suspect that Ted's extravaganza would have played a large part in the physical absence of many of the lads. *Wino Lucy* was adorning the bar, talking to a bloke that I've never seen before. It wasn't long before she had him captivated enough to part with several pounds in relatively quick succession, buying her large *House White*s which she initially downed with all the grace and finesse of a butterfly gently collecting nectar from a flower. Two financially compromising hours later, the bloke fell out of the place, and she now having to pay for her own drinks, finished off her session on halves of Guinness, which she gulped back lustily like a Doberman lapping up porridge from a bucket. She patted Spike on the head on the way out, waved me farewell and then fell flat on her face.

Uncle Chickle Chuckle graciously volunteered to carry her back to her home nearby. With his wife away, I suspected that his intentions were less than honourable, although I am assured that he will be in for a bit of a shock. When either her honour or money are at risk, this lady sobers up incredibly quickly, and in defence her speed, agility and strength are enough to make Jessica Frettle adjust the elastic on her leotard and the poor deluded, gullible man will quickly learn that she is no wallflower, and that it would have been better to decline the bait, than to struggle later on the hook.

Later in the day, Spike and I visited a charity shop in the High Street to get rid of a quantity of VHS videos that I had piled up in a wardrobe in Maria's room. On the way back, I bumped into Lisel who stated that she had paid a visit to Jasmine's home earlier in the week. She mentioned that the place was in darkness and having been let in by Elisha who was holding a torch, she restored the lighting by switching on the mains in the hall cupboard. Mahmud was initially nowhere to be found, but she located him in the loft a little later, digging out the mortar on an inner wall. She has mentioned to Jasmine that the boy needs a little therapy which frankly is a bit of an understatement, but she will be arranging this through their local GP. I am sure that she knows best, and naturally I wish her the best of luck.

As you are aware, I really love the sound of church bells and I was very content listening to Compton and his fellow campanologist's ringing theirs, which is such a reassuringly evocative sound. It would appear that they must have been sampling the communion wine again however, since it's somewhat unusual to hear church bells ringing at 23:45 on a Sunday evening.

Until tomorrow, Ginny.
P xx

January 23rd 2012

Good morning, Ginny.

I really didn't have a good night's sleep at all last night. The sounds of emergency vehicle sirens kept me awake almost continually throughout the night, and I shall be writing a letter to my local MP and the Commissioner about it. I really cannot understand why police vehicles need to make such an infernal clamorous racket along deserted roads, other than to clearly warn nocturnal drunkards, burglars, rapists and West Ham supporters of their approach, and to do so by inference would suggest that they (the police) *do not want any trouble.* The collective lily-livered *rectal-orifum!* Clearly, those potential or offending miscreants are warned from some considerable distance to *have it away before the plod arrived!* Hence, the consistently empty police cells and the reason why most of the local magistrates are always on holiday.

During the day, I can understand the use of the emergency horns when our intrepid Boys in Blue have to fight their way back to the nick through the normal vehicular gridlock of the Kilburn High Road, particularly if their cocoa is going cold or *The Magic Roundabout* is about to start. But to use them during the early hours of the morning when one could find more life on a tramp's vest, than along an urban thoroughfare that is quieter than nocturnal sin, is in my humble opinion, not only supremely cowardly, but is an unwarranted abuse of their job descriptions.

On a lighter note, I started my week's training in preparation for the over 50's gym challenge which takes place next Monday. The competition is in four parts, each completed against the clock, and the person with the best time will be the winner.

We were told to make our way to the upstairs room which is normally used for yoga classes. (I am pleased to say that our gym has a roof.) The mats were vacuumed to get rid of the small shredded Lycra and knicker-elastic fragments. The contents of the first aid kit were returned to its box, and the heady whiff of fermented body odour and embrocation was covered up by burning a rather nauseatingly sweet-smelling incense stick. I hadn't smelled this sickly stench since the 1969 Isle of Wight Festival, and clearly as one ages, out toleration for such dreadful smells becomes more acute.

My fellow competitors were a mixed bunch of ripening and matured humanity, who like me, were in various stages of physical and mental decomposition. The two other men and six women were all of different shapes and sizes, reflecting a good cross-sectional microcosm of the types of people that one would normally encounter along the Kilburn High Road. It seems now that the powers that be have decided to make this contest a team event, and accordingly we would be split up into groups of three, each team comprising of two women and one man.

The names of the women were written on pieces of paper and placed in a little box, and the two other chaps and I pulled out two names each. My selections were 'Hilda' who works at the drycleaners and 'Myra' who was a retired dentist. Both were quite charming. We were put through our paces by a sprightly little number by the name of Beth, who identified herself as a thirty-one-year-old former track athlete. She was a positively beautiful blonde, blue-eyed Aphrodite with a set of very well-defined abdominal muscles. I have never found the shape of female bodybuilders, or the skin and bone of vegetarian anorexics, attractive, but there is an intangible something about a woman sporting a toned body. (I mustn't keep going on about that.) While I am far from being a chauvinist or inherently sexist in my opinions of the opposing sex, I use the epithet in its fullest sense. I feel quite envious and not a little ashamed that throughout my relatively active life, I have never been able to rid myself of an annoying protective caul of fatty tissue that sits across my abdomen, covering up a magnificently well-defined muscle group comparable with those displayed on Michelangelo's David. But then, every path hath its puddle!

On my last visit to the doctor for my once-in-a-lifetime pneumonia jab, and to complain about the pills that he'd given me which he said 'Would make me stronger!' He clearly hadn't correctly estimated the physical strength and dexterity needed to open the bloody bottle! However, he subsequently gave me more, but this time, he placed them in a user-friendly paper envelope. Before I left, we had a very nice chat about the importance of exercise, and he was very interested in the forthcoming over 50's challenge at the gym. Later in the day, having completed Beth's hour-long preliminary assessment, I had to agree with his sentiments that 'exercise could add years to one's life', since as I hobbled out of the gym, I felt at least ten years' older! However, despite the stiffness and discomfort, I just about managed to take Spike out for a perfunctory loop around the block, have a warm muscle-relaxing soak in the bath, and enjoy a very early alcohol-free night.

Yours in smelly-embrocation.
P xx

24ᵗʰ January 2012

Good morning, Ginny.

I awoke feeling like I'd had a run-in with an unsympathetic steamroller last night, and I quite literally hobbled to the kitchen where Spike was busily engaged with Maria in his lip-reading training. I really do admire her determination and have to take my hat off to my little dog (if I could lift my arms up that far) who patiently endures this nonsense with all of the enthusiasm of a dental patient undergoing root canal treatment, and trying to impress the nurse, sits there motionless like a tailor's dummy, with his hands clamped around the chair arms tighter than an oyster's bum at high tide. But then, he is very devoted to both of my girls.

As I walked past him, Spike's concentration was momentarily broken as he watched me slowly opening the fridge door to grab the milk. For the briefest moment, I could have sworn that he was laughing at me on account of the fact that fleetingly his teeth were visible, and he seemed to shake uncontrollably. Such is paranoia!

I found out from one of my nosey neighbours that a number of sheds had been broken into over the weekend and I hopped, or rather hobbled down the stairs to see if mine had been affected. Ironically, the only two sheds that had been touched were the two either side of mine, which I thought was a little strange and somewhat fortuitous. My shed is just about empty apart from an old tandem bicycle and a brass birdcage. It's quite amazing what old junk one hoards over the years. But both items are of sentimental value. I haven't used the bike since 1998 when my old pal *Tony the Tube* and me visited the glorious Lake District on a cycling holiday.

On one very hot summer's day, as we were negotiating a particularly steep hill near Wordsworth's home, Rydal Mount, it was very hard going indeed. When we thankfully reached the top, Tony said, 'Bloody hell that was some climb!'

panting and perspiring heavily. 'It sure was mate,' I replied. 'It was a good job that I had the brake on all the way up, otherwise we would have gone backwards!' Coincidentally he suffered a hernia on that trip.

As for the birdcage, I lost my canary in 2001 following a rather unfortunate mishap, when at a house party, a somewhat drunken individual of questionable parentage opened *Bubsie's* cage apparently thinking he was a lemon. Fortunately, the canny bird had the presence of mind to slip out of his cage and freedom through the open balcony door, before the veritable *pud-wapper* had attempted to squeeze him into his gin and tonic. He was never to be seen again. We didn't see Bubsie again either!

I really was in no mood, either mentally or physically, for day two at the gym but I didn't want to let Hilda and Myra down. I felt I was part of a team and I take such obligations seriously. Besides, my aches and pains could be relieved by the metaphorical use of a bout of additional *hair of the dog*-type exercise, I thought (well it works with booze). However, I couldn't have been more wrong. Everyone was so sympathetic and supportive as I was helped down from the cross-trainer. I started off alright, but suddenly felt a searing pain in my lower groin, which occasioned a rather uncharacteristically loud guttural howl, stopping everyone dead in their tracks. In the steam room a little later, at the site of the pain, I found a soft spongy lump which, having seen Tony's, convinced me that I too now had a hernia.

My lump was the talk of The Magpie for the rest of the afternoon and Ted sportingly ran a book offering odds at 10/1 that I wouldn't get an operation before the 31st March. Sadly my aspirations of gym immortality, a gratis all-expenses trip away, or free theatre tickets were dashed. However, I was quite moved by the genuine sympathy of my friends and was almost brought to tears when *Lenny the Ponce* stood up unsteadily on his newly acquired crutches (which have added greatly to his now confirmed disabled status) and digging deep into his trouser pocket, he gave me a very dirty crumpled-up fiver which I had apparently loaned him in 2011 during the August bank holiday. 'I only found it this morning,' he confided.

I was in no mood for cooking this evening, so I decided to have a meal at the pub, half of which I took home in a *doggie bag*. Spike didn't get a look in however, since Maria scoffed the lot.

Sleep tight.
P xx

25th January 2012

Good morning, Ginny.

They say that problems usually come in threes, and I had three very noticeable complications banging on my door at 06:05 this morning. Having opened the front door, a police warrant card was shoved in my face by a rather unsavoury looking ruffian who identified himself and his two associates as 'DS Blackstock and DCs Bolton and Little'.

I held Spike close into my body since he was registering body language that suggested imminent attack mode. Before I could utter a word, DS Blackstock produced an official-looking piece of paper which he flashed at me momentarily, barged into the hallway uninvited and stated, 'Mr Shaughnessy, we have reason to believe that you have stolen property in your premises and this is a search warrant. Do you mind if we come in?'

'This has to be some kind of joke!' I protested, holding onto Spike firmly who was now emitting deep growling sounds. I put him out on the balcony as quietly as I could and closed the door.

His anger and frustration that resulted from not being allowed to display what probably would have been for him, his finest hour, in the courageous protection of his beloved partner and a possible nomination for *a Dickin Medal*, sent him into the noisiest frenzy of howls, barks and screams that I had ever heard.

Both Maria and Lenka appeared in the hall, in obvious terror at the commotion. But order was restored when I collected Spike again and gave him to Lenka, who gently carried him back into her room closing the door behind them. Having gone through every conceivable nook and cranny of every room in the flat, they found nothing incriminating. Later, they escorted me downstairs to my shed, which I confidently opened for them, but swayed unsteadily holding on to the door, when inside I saw an array of all kinds of unfamiliar items, none of which were mine. They included a vacuum cleaner, bottles of assorted spirits, a couple of fishing rods, a bag full of pornographic DVDs, a portable television and a set of golf clubs. As each item was pulled out of the shed, I was asked by DS Blackstock if said item belonged to me and each time I replied in the negative. An inquisitive crowd of residents appeared, and there were many standing on their balcony watching the drama.

As DS Blackstock pulled out a large folded tent, I mused on how unfortunate it was that Ted wasn't around, since he would have been in his element, strutting around the yard with the biggest ever audience of his life, witnessing his inimitable rendition of Richard III's famous soliloquy:

'Now is the winter of our discount-tents made glorious summer by this son of York!'

I was later unceremoniously manhandled into the back of a police van and whisked off to the local nick where I was banged up for a while, fingerprinted and later charged with theft. An hour or so later, I was bailed to attend the Westminster Magistrates Court at 10:30 on the morning of Monday 13th February 2012.

On the way out, the duty desk sergeant reluctantly made a theft report relating to the loss of my tandem bicycle and the birdcage, and in a very sarcastic voice remarked, 'You will be hearing from us in due course, sir.' As a consequence, I didn't feel inclined to drop a few shillings into the Police Widows and Orphans charity box that was conspicuously chained to the front desk.

Back home, Maria and Lenka were almost beside themselves with worry and hugged me affectionately. Spike gave me a perfunctory sniff and casually sauntered out onto what he perhaps considered to be the balcony of his betrayal. Whether by accident or design, as he left, his back offside paw caught the door and it slowly closed behind him. He was very reluctant and disinclined to engage with me socially for the rest of the day.

As I walked into the *Gay Bar* (a name that Dave had given to our main watering hole at The Magpie), I was greeted by a chorus of unsympathetic moans and groans from the hastily assembled group of reprobates and itinerant *urine-takers* from many of the local pubs in the area.

News spreads very quickly in Kilburn and I was well aware that I would have to run the gauntlet of merciless mocking and distasteful taunts of the type that normally accompanies any sad soul suffering from misfortune or bad luck, at least until the novelty had worn off or another suitable victim found. I am sure that this kind of thing really does explain the concept of the 'British stiff upper lip', where one displays fortitude in the face of adversity, or exercises tremendous self-restraint in the overt expression of emotion. I figured, therefore, that the quicker I got it under way, the earlier it would cease. An hour, and several well-placed large drinks later, the conversation became a little more refined and serious.

During the morning and following my arrest, Tony and Ted had made a few phone calls, and had seen a number of the local quick-witted and naturally verbose likely lads, whom as a collective, were convinced that I had been 'fitted up', as the colourful local vernacular would describe it. They were confident that with a little collective effort, the scales of justice could be tipped back in my favour, and the despicable *fatherless-people* responsible, (unknown at this present time) brought to book for their loathsome deception. I was all in favour of that.

On the way home later, I was feeling immensely thankful in having such good friends, but once inside the flat, it felt very claustrophobic. The walls appeared to be closing in on me and I felt quite lonely (which for me is a very unusual emotion). The girls were out and Spike was in Lenka's room. But as

I got into bed, I was aware of him jumping onto my duvet. He licked my hand tenderly and then curled up and was soon asleep. It was a wonderfully fitting end to a miserable day.

As I started to drift off to sleep, my thoughts turned to my good and trusted friends, and all earlier thoughts of giving Spike to a family of itinerant gypsies or at the very least having him castrated, were quickly dispelled.

Goodnight love.
P xx

26th January 2012

Good morning, Ginny.

Firstly, let me put your mind at rest. I would never ever do any harm to an animal that over the years I have become more than simply fond of. He is my life's companion for better or worse. Like me, Spike is now getting on in years and we both suffer from those merciless medical conditions associated with longevity. His appears to be more mental than physical.

It really does seem such a short time ago when at school, I remarked about the maturity of one of my fellow pupils, simply because he could tie his own shoelaces and blow his own nose. I feel a little sorry for people like Maria and Lenka, who being four inches along the ruler of life as it were, have all of the questions and are stuck in the middle of confusion. It seems that the answers are only known to the audaciously young or the ridiculously ancient.

Aches, pains and the ever-present 'twinges in the hinges' remind us constantly that we are on the slippery slope heading for oblivion. Clearly, some of us arrive at the bottom fully prepared and ready to start over again (or hoping to do so) and then there are people like me, who accept that my future transition is a bit of a lottery. However, that aside, even if you do not believe in a heavenly Utopia or that your reward for a good and faithful life will be the eternal company and care of a group of nubile celestial virgins, or at the very least, an everlasting first-class box at the annual heavenly Christmas bash, in my experience, a kindly word; or a few shillings to help someone in need, can invoke a very satisfying inner feeling of happiness and joy. Despite one's inherently selfish tendencies or unacceptably destructive ways, one can still manage to live a considerate and peaceful existence. It is a noteworthy aspiration for us all. I've been trying to do it all of my life and have failed miserably (thus far). But then I would have made a useless footballer anyway!

I have read much about religion in its various guises and have to admit that there is a great deal of moral truth and wisdom in the precepts and dictates in many of the religious traditions. I like the idea of clinging on to the bits that appeal, and to discard the rest. Which I hasten to add is what I'd do if ever I was confronted with a group of nubile celestial virgins bent on gratifying and/or satiating my desires whether carnal or not.

The nearest that I have ever got to that was being man-handled, if that's the right term, when I was leapt on by six lady police officers, who arrested me one New Year's Eve in Trafalgar Square, for urinating in one of the fountains. Nubile they were not. It was dreadful.

So there I was, slightly inebriated in the midst of a seething mass of humanity, busting for a pee. As midnight struck, I attempted to make my way to the nearest port-a-loo but the crowd and the sight and sound of all of that cascading water from the fountains, had a quite profound effect on my mental capacity, and more particularly a potentially compromised urinary tract plug, which gushed forth my bladder's contents with remarkable power.

A few weeks later, it was quite an honour to stand in Bow Street Magistrates Court, where a literary favourite of mine (Oscar Wilde) had once stood prior to his committal to the Central Criminal Court at the Old Bailey. I hasten to mention, that our respective reasons for being there were infinitely different. He, poor man, was later sentenced to three years hard labour and I having appeared before Lady Isobel Madeira Jenner, was bound over in the sum of £25 to 'keep the piss for two years!'

Later I hobbled into our local surgery and booked an appointment with the doctor for next week to investigate the lump, but that was perhaps the highlight of my day. Brenda the receptionist was a little too over inquisitive however, and wanted to have a look at it.

I was feeling a little bit down this evening, but following a nice bath, I read a little before retiring and having sipped a sleep-inducing mug of cocoa, laced with a little cognac, I slept peacefully until the early morning arrival of Lenka. A little later, I was fully awoken by Spike's less than ineffectual, exuberantly noisy greeting. I got up for a short time. We had a brief conversation before I showed her my lump (then my suspected hernia) and finally poured myself an additional mug of cognac with another drop of cocoa.

Tomorrow is upon us!
P xx

27th January 2012

Good morning, Ginny.

I really don't know what happened last night. The last thing I remember was Spike barking. I awoke feeling like I had been hit with a sledgehammer. Lenka apparently put me back to bed during the early hours of this morning, or so she tells me. Frankly it has all been a complete hazy blank.

I went over to the gym at 09:15 to hopefully sweat out whatever noxious poison disguised as cognac I'd ingested last night, compliments of *Dunny Greg* who had given me a bottle of what he referred to as *very special cognac* at Christmas. He said that it was imported. However, I really do not want to ponder over its provenance or indeed dwell upon its constituent ingredients.

I was very surprised to find that my normally quiet and dignified gym was heaving with a tumultuous mixture of humanity, most of whom were clothed, or rather not in gym gear. Then I remembered of course that being Friday, this was the day of the over 50's gym challenge. The place was quite literally buzzing with excited expectation. A Jamaican calypso band in the reception area were bashing away on tin kettle drums, creating an exciting carnival atmosphere, and the Lord Mayor, several local dignitaries and members of the press, were sipping sparkling wine, which I found out later was supplied by Ted. Canapés and other appetizers, which together with additional catering and party paraphernalia (including a lunchtime performance by Uncle Chickle Chuckle for the kids), was organised by the proprietors of The Magpie.

I met Beth, our beautiful lady trainer later, who greeted me very affectionately, kissing and hugging me like a long-lost son. She enquired about my health and asked if I would like to present the prizes at the end of the competition, which I thought was a tremendously thoughtful and a very considerate gesture. I readily agreed. I subsequently dashed home and changed into a smart casual outfit, and then hastily returned to the gym.

Later, the competition was won by a team from Queens Park, who dressed like Ragamuffin Street Urchins were collecting for a local orphanage. I heard later that they had raised the very commendable sum of £550. Due to the change in the team structure which instead of single entrants was made up of groups of three, the winners were given six tickets for the all-expenses paid weekend in Bognor Regis, and the runners-up were each given two theatre tickets each, which I thought was tremendously generous of the organisers. I found out later, that a considerable sum had been donated by some of our local businesses, including The Magpie. It was all a resounding success.

Later I met up with my former teammates, Hilda and Myra, who with my replacement (a dustman from Queens Park) came in third place. They all enjoyed the challenge immensely. Myra summed up the collective sentiments of all concerned: 'We may not have won the contest, but have all won a lot of additional friends.' At around 19:30, we all visited a well-attended party at The Magpie.

Lisel came in somewhat unexpectedly to say that Mahmud had been put into care, mainly for his own safety, and that Jasmine and Elisha were being moved to a sheltered warder-assisted flat in Somerset. Both were well it seems and Lisel suggested that it might now be the best time for me to quietly leave the scene, as she reasoned, my presence might upset them. Reluctantly I had to agree. Ted, who had heard our conversation, remarked, 'Remember that, all the world's a stage and all the men and women merely players: they all have their exits and their entrances.' He pushed a large glass into my hand filled with what appeared to be cognac.

'Thanks mate,' I replied, taking a long grateful draught.

'It's not the imported stuff,' he said, as I quickly lowered the glass in alarm. Fortunately, this was the genuine article, unlike *Dunny Greg's* poisonous variety.

I was reliably informed that the moronic cretin had been residing at *Her Majesty's Pleasure* in Brixton Prison since 28th December 2011 on remand, awaiting trial on a charge of 'smuggling illicit cognac' aggravated by the fact that upon scientific analysis, it was found to contain a considerable amount of horse tranquilizer. He wasn't expected to be seen again for the foreseeable future. I'll drink to that!

Sleep well, love.
P xx

28th January 2012

Good morning, Ginny.

My day started off well enough, but like those beautiful winter mornings where for a short time the promise of spring is evident in the clear blue cloudless sky, and one's spirits are lifted immeasurably, temptation arises. The conditions teasingly entice one to foolishly shed the normal heavy layer of outer clothing, in favour of garb more appropriately worn at a July picnic in Henley, rather than a shopping trip along the Kilburn High Road in January. But it's simply all about feelings. Happiness seems to throw caution to the wind, and this often results in a relaxed carefree approach to things which would normally inspire vigilance. Primarily, my feelings of mild elation were due to the wonderful weather conditions, but my emotive temperature was raised even further when for the first time in his seven winters, I was convinced that my dear little canine companion had felt the sting of Cupid's arrow.

He met a rather cute looking Maltese terrier resplendent with a beautiful little pink ribbon and snowy white tresses of downy fur, named 'Binky' in the park, and his very unusual body language and behaviour suggested a rapturous awakening of hitherto dormant emotions. His face nestled into Binky's with a tenderness that was quite touching and most unbecoming in an animal that was normally very antisocial among other dogs, particularly bitches. Binky's lady owner (Celine) was quite enchanting and we chatted together for some time. Both Spike and I had a very pronounced light-hearted spring in our heels as we later walked through the clouds, on our way back home.

A little later, I had a phone call from Tony stating that he had some very important information to impart with regard to my *shed saga* as he put it, and would I meet him and Ted at Brenda's Breakfast Emporium by the bakers at 10:30 sharp. Lenka and Maria were still asleep and Spike was going around in little circles in the hall as I left.

To cut a long story short, Ted explained that he had located my missing tandem bicycle and birdcage. It appears that they had been sold to a scrap metal dealer in

Edgware, who happened to be some distant relative of his. Ted's quite unbelievable vast array of friends and acquaintances never ceases to amaze me. But my joy was almost tangible, although, I fought off the almost overwhelming desire to give him a hug and instead, bought both of my dear friends 'A full English', which for the uninitiated comprises of egg, bacon, beans, tomato, mushrooms and bubble, two teas, four slices and a couple of heartburn and indigestion tablets.

One didn't need to be a budding Sherlock Holmes to realise that whoever was responsible for off-loading these articles, was also clearly answerable for their theft, or at the very least knew the identity of the despicable purloiner involved. I was assured by Ted that the goods would not be sold and that later next week, we could visit the scrapyard.

I later attended the offices of Burt, Lang and Forthright (Solicitors) in Kensal Rise on the recommendation of *Alfie the Dip*, who stated that, 'None of them were very knowledgeable about the law, but they were very down to earth and knew a lot of them people what wear wigs.'

I was seen by Basil Lang who was very interested in my case and was keen to locate the owners of the items that were found in my shed. He stated that he would make an appointment to see DS Blackstock next week (he was busy until Wednesday) but assured me that he would leave no stone unturned in his search for the truth, and that in any event, even if I were found guilty, the most that I could expect would be a £50 fine and a Community Service Order. I hasten to add, this is not a British chivalric award which would entitle a recipient to use the post-nominal designation CSO after their name, or to receive an annual couple of bob from the Privy Purse.

I braved the gym during the evening, but in my somewhat fragile condition found that the cross-trainer was out of the question. I started off alright but like a portable kettle with a faulty cut-out, I soon ran out of steam. Sadly, I also caught a glimpse of myself in the poseur's mirrors by the weights and had to admit for the first time, that in my gym gear I looked like a geriatric poofter in fancy dress, which completely shattered my own long-held personal perception of a latter-day maturing Johnny Weissmuller lookalike. In truth, I suppose if we saw ourselves as others did, we wouldn't want to take a second look.

Finally, to augment my feelings of utter depression and despair, on my evening bus trip to Queens Park with Lenka and Maria where we were to have an evening meal at our favourite Chinese restaurant, a young man had the audacious temerity to offer me his seat, which completely ruined what was left of my already unhappy demeanour and floundering optimism for the rest of the day.

The sun has shone warmly all day, love, but I must protect myself from the inner dark clouds of despond, disappointment and despair. Be assured, that there will be no upper lip quivering for me!

Goodnight, Gin.
P xx

29ᵗʰ January 2012

Dear Ginny.

What on earth must you think of me? I really do apologise for that utterly unacceptable example of self-centred, egocentric bilge that I sent you yesterday. I am not a person that gives in easily, and it takes a lot to get me down. It cannot be denied however, that relatively small problems that mount up while being insignificant individually, as a collective, can wear one down like the proverbial water dripping on a rock, but then I have had a lot on my mind of late.

I am quite worried about this theft charge hanging over my pate, and then there's the medical issue. But while I do wear glasses, for the first time in ages I have begun to see myself in a completely different light. Which reminds me I must get a new bulb for the bathroom. In truth, I really couldn't be more content with my lot, but is that due to intelligence or simple laziness, I wonder? Clearly, it must be very difficult for those poor souls not fortunate enough to have the basics in life to feel content. But then ironically not as difficult as the fortunate few who have everything; for them it seems that contentment is impossible. It's another depressing truism like, half of Kilburn are on full-English and the other half are on bread and jam.

Lenka was out and Maria was still asleep when I got up, and as I walked into the kitchen at 08:10 Spike was lying sprawled out under the table fast asleep, tenaciously gripping in his mouth his Sunday-best lead. How on earth he knew that it was Sunday is quite beyond me. Perhaps this is another example of the kind of endearing quality that our discerning Stone Age forebears found so useful when they decided to domesticate the wild dogs that would sit outside the periphery of their campfires or caves. One thing is for sure, had there been any around at the time, I am convinced that our ancient brethren would never have been late for church, which is far more than can be said for the usual miserably morose and hungover examples of humanity who meander blindly into St Benedict's Church from the time that old Compton had untangled his bell-ringer's ropes, until the doors are gratefully flung open at the end of the service.

Edwina Fewpit's closing rendition of Bach's Toccata and Fugue in D was recently followed by a few discordant muffled shouts, the unmistakable sound of an ancient oak door being kicked open and for those lucky enough to witness the spectacle, the sight of a swiftly decamping hooligan carrying a silver candlestick and the meagre collection plate out into the freedom and secular anonymity of the Kilburn High Road (with half of the able-bodied congregation and choir, close on his heels). With drama like this going on, who needs *Coronation Street*? It has all been very quiet of late, however.

I quietly crept around the kitchen in the hope of not waking Spike up, but he opened one eye and watched my every move critically, while wagging his little tail enthusiastically. This has to be far more preferable to some of my human friends however, since many of them are serial tongue shakers of the worst kind. They do not have a kindly word, let alone a sentence, for anyone or anything.

I put his food down in front of him, which he sniffed perfunctorily and reluctantly fighting gravity, he lifted himself up wearily and slowly walked out onto the balcony where he sat and simply stared into nothingness, gently moaning wistfully. It seems that he is eager to get back to the park. I really feel so very happy for him indeed, I have to admit with a twinge of envy.

Later, in the chilly arctic-type wastes of Kilburn Park, his sense of disappointment was almost tangible. He kept looking up at me appealingly, but all I could do was to shrug my shoulders and try and offer a little verbal condolence of the 'never mind Spike – maybe tomorrow' kind of thing. Sadly, Binky and mum were nowhere to be found. He was inconsolable for the rest of the morning.

Occasionally after lunch on a Sunday, I would take Spike out for a walk along the High Road to visit that other colourful hostelry of note, 'The Goose and Firkin'. Being one of the cheapest watering holes in the area, it attracts all manner of life, mainly from the lower end of the disabled, and hopeful, working-class social strata. Most come from the building industry, and many suffer the consequences of injuries received in an era where health and safety was non-existent, and getting the job done with all of the potential risks involved, was simply a daily reality that nobody ever really questioned. The term 'job and finish', which indicated the possibility of an early day, resulted in risks being taken and corners cut, with the inevitable result of dreadful injury and in some cases loss of life.

With a betting office and mini cab establishment nearby and enormous television screens covering every conceivable sporting event, but concentrating mainly on racing, the place is busier than a cross-eyed rooster on an anthill, making it a very obvious place to meet other interesting like-minded *anal-orifum*. For an impecunious boozer that likes a flutter, cheap intoxicants and the comfort of knowing that the very reasonably priced cab service will get him home (whether inebriated or not), it is a veritable alcoholic Shangri-La amidst a sea of rip-off yuppie-type establishments that had recently appeared in the area.

To be banned from its hallowed portals would mean social ostracism, a loss of self-respect and street credibility, not to mention a reluctantly enforced lower intake of alcohol due to the exorbitant prices elsewhere, together with an unenthusiastic early evening curfew (which naturally would incur additional time spent with the wife, girlfriend or boyfriend, dependent on one's preferences), both domestic and social. As a result, the pub contained the most well-behaved locals in north London. To a man, they were a cautious collective of obsequious toadies, particularly when it came to the landlord, a great mountain of a man by the name of Thomas Patrick O'Mahoney from County Mayo. He doesn't suffer any kind of fool lightly (particularly the educated variety). His hostility to one of the drunken category could never be underestimated, or misinterpreted. His rage is quite tempestuous and the unfortunate felon would be left in no doubt as to his feelings on the matter. Apart from having to suffer a tirade of quite colourful, albeit incoherent, ill-considered observations that even a sober individual would have difficulty in understanding, he would be unceremoniously hoisted out of the place quicker than a plate of grass sandwiches through a goose, never to be seen again.

After lunch, I thought that I'd take a walk up to the Goose, but Spike made it very evident that he was simply not interested. When I went to put his lead on him, he just plonked himself down apologetically and feigned going to sleep, although I knew he was only play-acting because his eyelids were twitching convulsively. Still, I didn't push it. He really wanted to be left alone, and I know that feeling only too well. I therefore put some of his favourite biscuits out on the balcony, and made my way down to the pub.

As I neared the door, the hum of the crowds within and the evocative smell of stale beer and body odour, didn't exactly enhance my earlier need for cultural and/ or social entertainment, in fact, before I'd even pushed open the door, I had the sudden knee-jerk impulse to reverse my steps in favour of attending The Magpie instead. At the very least I could be assured of a better class of cockroach, that didn't have to walk around on stilts, or wear a snorkel and flippers to negotiate the mini urine waves that the locals had to plough through to get to the cascading urinals in the toilets.

In the 'Snug Bar' a delightful name for a former cramped cupboard, I saw my old pal Nobby Caxton, resplendent in his usual company wellies, overalls and woolly hat. He waved at me good- naturedly, hastily drank what was left of his beer, and vanished out of the back door. He was long gone before I had managed to fight my way through the crowd, bent on engaging him on the usual company and tenant gossip.

I may be wrong, but he really does seem to be avoiding me for some reason. However, on later reflection, I recognised that I must stop deluding myself with these ridiculously misguided notions and assumptions when it comes to the actions of others. There's probably a very good reason why he hastened out of the pub, chucking most of his remaining ale down the front of his overalls and scattering his fellow drinkers like scythed hay at harvest time. His bleeper had probably gone off, requesting his urgent attention back at the flats. His unflinching sense of duty has always taken precedence over his need for personal leisure and entertainment. I hold this man in the greatest of respect and have always admired his commitment and integrity.

I didn't remain long in the place, spending the rest of the evening at The Magpie in the convivial company of *Scotch Andy, The Voice, Lenny the Ponce* and the ever-irrepressible *Ted the Pleb,* who as a collective, are as the salt of the earth, giving taste to the watered down tequila of insipid aspiration and flavour to my relatively bland existence. God bless 'em!

Sweet dreams, love.
P xx

January 30th 2012

Good morning, Ginny.

I write you this email with a heavy heart and a sense of abject loss too terrible
to describe. Having left the pub on closing time last night, all was quiet at home.
I figured that both of my girls were in bed and that my little dog was sound asleep
in Lenka's room. Frankly, I did not really consider the matter since this is the
normal course of events when I get back from the pub late. Such is complacency.

I was up at 07:30 and Maria and I had breakfast together a little later. She
left at around 10:15 to join friends at a coffee house in the High Road and Lenka
came into the kitchen at 11:45. Normally Spike would be dancing gaily behind
her, but this morning he didn't appear. I made a bit of a joke of it and stated that
he probably didn't want to leave her bedroom. But her face dropped when she
replied that he wasn't in her room. Frantically, we searched the flat from top to
bottom and he was nowhere to be found. My little companion and friend was
missing!

Initially I panicked and had to be calmed down by my ever-considerate Lenka,
who made me a nice cup of coffee with a cognac chaser. I then mentally went
over my movements of yesterday afternoon and quickly checked the balcony.
The biscuits that I'd left him were still there. His lead was hanging in its usual
place and his water hadn't been touched. I immediately phoned the police, who
advised me to check out various dog welfare clinic establishments, or Battersea
Dogs Home where strays were taken. I spent most of the early afternoon on the
phone, and then with Lenka checked out the pub, the park and our local area, all
to no avail.

Later I told Lenka about Spike's amorous adventure with Binky on Saturday
morning and she suggested that he'd perhaps run away to try and find her, an
idea which had some credibility and eased my sense of gloom and despondency.
Knowing this impulsive animal as I do, I found the idea quite feasible. Clearly,
he could have jumped off the balcony onto the grass below, and made his escape
through the fence in the curate's garden. My worst fear was that he had been
stolen. He would be quite easy to lure away, since a packet of crisps and a saucer
of Guinness and he was anybody's friend. But if he'd gone out on some venture
of his own, he would just as surely return home when the novelty had worn off, or
his bodily tissues needed restoring. He was a creature of habit, and by 17:00 this
afternoon (dinner time) he would not have eaten anything for twenty-four hours
and would have been 'Mad with the hunger', as *Whispering Jim* would have said.

I attended the surgery of Dr Davy Jarvis at 17:00 as arranged, although
frankly I wasn't in the mood to be prodded and poked about with, and I told him
so once I was in the antiseptic confines of his consultation room. He confirmed
that it was a hernia and gave me one of them written hieroglyphics notes which

being translated by Robby Duff (the pharmacist) into pound coins, are to be taken twice per day. I think they call it a 'prescription'.

On leaving, I asked him what were the odds on my having an operation before 31st March. He gave me 14/1.

On the way home, I called into The Magpie for a medicinal livener. I decided not to tell anyone about my missing Spike since like a fart in an echo chamber, I would never have heard the last of it. My little dog was so popular with everyone and the consternation and misery that would have resulted in such intelligence being made public would have been dreadful, so I kept quiet.

As I sat there sipping a large cognac, I suddenly became quite emotional and tears started to stream down my face. To hide my embarrassment, I rushed into the gents, disturbing *Lenny the Ponce,* who being engaged in his late afternoon ablutions, was sucking Brylcreem out from the 50p wall dispenser like a steam pump in a dirty puddle.

Back home, the girls were out, and I sat outside on the balcony in the dark watching the movements of people in their respective flats across the courtyard, simply getting on with their daily lives and evening chores. Nothing really registered however, but I got comfort in the thought that none appeared to be in any distress, happily ignorant to the suffering of others. We should all occasionally pinch ourselves as a personal reminder not to be so complacent in our own contentment, and to remember how those that suffer feel. Amen to that!

Goodnight, Ginny.
P xx

31st January 2012

Dear Ginny.

Needless to say, I didn't sleep a wink last night, but then I was a little concerned that if I fell asleep and my dreams were answered, I might not hear my little itinerant pooch scratching at the door or barking in the curate's garden. But then I reasoned that one must be awake for their dreams to come true, so for most of the night, I paced around my bedroom like a frustrated hamster on a treadmill and drank copious quantities of coffee.

At 07:10 I was sat in the kitchen morosely looking at Spike's Sunday best lead and his two little empty bowls, which normally at this time in the morning he would be sniffing at and looking up at me appealingly.

Lenka arrived home from work a little later and she rushed into the kitchen. Her expectant smile quickly faded as she saw my dejected demeanour. With tearful eyes, she embraced me warmly, gently sobbing on my shoulder. I really cannot cope with a woman crying, particularly one that I love like a daughter and I spent some considerable time consoling her. She was frankly heartbroken. I was trying to act all grown up, macho and brave, but whenever I looked into her beautiful watery eyes, vicarious tears of despair and anguish rolled down my face. To complete this wretched scene, a bleary-eyed Maria came into the kitchen, looked at us both enquiringly and then burst into tears, howling loudly and sobbing uncontrollably. It took us both an hour and more to calm her.

Ironically, grief and laughter are so highly infectious and with both, time spent in recovery is so necessary. However, in my dear Maria's case, the provision of a couple of eggs, sausage, fried bread and beans, together with toast and a cup of steaming coffee, miraculously had an immediate pacifying effect and hastened the process considerably.

Have you ever noticed that it is quite impossible to weep with a mouthful of food? It's a bit like trying to sneeze with your eyes open. Anyway, my point here was that cooking breakfast for my little girl was just the kind of mental distraction that I needed (bless her little wooden maracas).

Sadly, but fortuitously as it later transpired, during the afternoon, another mental diversion arrived in the shape of Father Marcus, the downstairs curate. His bumbling ever-apologetic appearance and never-ending confusing discourse would make the lines from Lewis Carroll's *Jabberwocky* seem intelligible. His appearance in the stairwell has resulted in many a reluctant prisoner being confined to their home until he had left the area, and having been spotted traversing the High Road, he has been known to unwittingly alter the homeward-bound trajectory of a considerable number of my fellow residents, some of whom had reluctantly found themselves in betting shops, pubs and even a mosque in the practice of a phenomenon known locally as 'the curate avoidance technique' or CAT for short. Whoever coined the phrase that 'the art of conversation is dead' had obviously never been *captured* (a word that I use in its fullest sense) by the Reverend (in training), Marcus Byron Tanner in full verbal flow. He has become a veritable expert in rhetorical solemnity and confusion of a kind that could instil dark thoughts in the most optimistic listener, and within ten minutes or so of his non-stop verbal, could convince the happiest and optimistic of men on the merits of voluntary euthanasia.

It is true that most of us at some point or another will talk a little nonsense. For me personally, this rare event has been known to occur when the normal balance in my brain cells and concentration levels are impeded following the ingestion of several large libations. It is also particularly prevalent while in the company of a quota of like-minded individuals involved in what the Irish quaintly refer to as *The Craic,* which in English terms, describes a collective of drunken moronic *pud-wappers* acting like a group of demented children *effin* around and talking absolute *sphericals!*

Following a long meaningless verbal onslaught, two cups of tea and half a dozen custard cream biscuits, he suddenly remembered that he had another appointment. Thankfully, the distinct prospect of being fossilised diminished, as he made his way to the front door. On leaving, he asked if I was now using the services of a dog walker. This brought me down to earth with a bang and awakened me from my former mental lethargy. He stated that he had seen Spike being escorted out of the flats by a tall man wearing a long black coat and a trilby. He had never seen this man before, but did think that it was a little strange because Spike was being led out on a thick piece of rope. Not wishing to have his disappearance known to every person living within a radius of two miles of St Benedict's Church, I did not enlighten Father Marcus any further.

On leaving, he uttered a truly profound statement that had me thinking for the rest of the day. 'Remember Paul,' he said. 'A steam engine approaching a level crossing does not whistle to keep up its courage!' As he left, he gave me a close inquisitive look of the most appealingly kind, presumably waiting for some kind of facial confirmation that I had understood what the hell he was on about. Finding none and smiling wryly, he tapped the side of his nose, as though suggesting that a conspiratorial bond had been made between us, and thereafter he quietly departed.

Like Isaac Newton, I can calculate the motion of *some* heavenly bodies, but I haven't a clue about this one. Fortunately, he very rarely drinks alcohol, which for the rest of secular humanity is a blessing indeed.

By the time that he'd left it was dark, and while initially I felt that I should report this new information to the police immediately, I reasoned that it could wait until tomorrow.

I entered The Magpie with a new sense of purpose. At least I was no longer left in my former dreadful state of uncertainty, albeit that my worst fear had been realised. Although I was far from happy at the heinous kidnapping of my little friend, at least his disappearance could now be explained. The whys and wherefores would hopefully unfold as time progressed, and together with my close friends, we could now make a concerted and determined effort to find him.

The lads cheered me up considerably, and I felt that it was time to let them know what was going on in my life, and to a man, my news about Spike was received with disbelief and rage. Having heard all of the raised voices, Uncle Chickle Chuckle walked into the Gay Bar, obviously inquisitive as to the cause of the rumpus, and bought us all a drink when he was told. I have to say that this generous gesture was greatly appreciated, and I felt that whatever former niggling doubts that there may have been between him and my motley team, that a very positive friendly step towards acceptance and comradeship had been taken. He took me aside just before I left at 22:50 and said, 'Listen my friend, to worry is bad, because is like sitting on a horse of wood made – it gives you things to do, but you nowhere go!'

On my way back home, I was convinced that news of my dear Spike would appear in the not-too-distant future, since apart from myself, I now had the assistance and support of a bunch of loyal friends, who would be relentless in their endeavours in helping to find a little soul who they all loved just as much as me. In times of trouble, true friends always make an appearance.

Back home, the flat was empty. Lenka had gone to work and my Maria was out with friends, presumably enjoying her carefree days to the full (bless her). Lenka had left a note on the kitchen table stating that in my absence she had let in two men from the electric company wishing to read our meter. She assured me that they were wearing the correct ID badges. They apparently took a number of photographs of the inside of the meter cupboard and 'removed something' from it, which they took away with them. Lenka was asked if she had seen it before, and had to sign a receipt which stated that it had been found in my meter cupboard. Lord knows what that is all about. Still, I am sure all will be revealed tomorrow.

Goodnight love.
P xx

1st February 2012

Dear Ginny.

I was awake early this morning and having made myself a cup of coffee, I sat in the kitchen waiting impatiently for Lenka to kick her legs out from under her duvet. She appeared at 13:50. On rising, she is not a morning, or early afternoon person, and does need to be left alone to sort out her own personal demons, so I gave her time to make a cup of coffee and to shake off any remaining mental cobwebs.

Following a bout of self-flagellation with a thing she calls 'a loofer' in the shower (she's a practising catholic), she arrived back in the kitchen, bright-eyed and bushy-tailed a little later, although I'd hate to think what her back looked like. But once my natural curiosity had subsided, I questioned her about the events of yesterday afternoon and specifically the visit by the men from the electric board. She seemed to be as confused about the issue as I have been, stating that, 'They had taken photographs of the inside of the meter cupboard and had produced a small black box, which apparently had *wires* sticking out of it.' They asked her if she'd ever seen this item before, and of course she hadn't. She went on to emphasise the point that: 'She'd never any reason or cause to go into the meter cupboard'. Suffice it to say, this is all very mysterious indeed.

Later during the morning, I again visited our local nick – not wishing to use the personal pronoun *my* – but this time of my own volition, and as luck would have it (metaphorically speaking that is), the same duty desk sergeant was adorning the front office, busily engaged in what looked like the *Beano's* crossword puzzle. On entering, I initially asked him jokingly if he'd been home since the last time I'd seen him? I didn't get any reply whatsoever, he simply turned his back on me and I could hear what sounded like verbal expletives, or the kind of utterances that one would associate with curses that warlocks make at one's local coven. When he approached the front desk again, I noticed that his lugubrious, indifferent facial expression bore a remarkable resemblance to a bull mastiff that had just cleaned its bum. (I didn't feel inclined to share with him my reflections however.)

A faint flicker of recognition momentarily passed across his countenance, which was comforting, either that or he was suffering from trapped wind. Whatever the cause, it was very evident that I was about as welcome as a one-toothed man in a corn-on-the-cob eating contest, and that I should chew, or rather tread lightly. I sensed that he was in no mood for frivolity, and that perhaps he wouldn't appreciate the joke about the ton of human hair that had been stolen from a wig factory in Yeovil. The local police were reportedly 'combing the area.' (I thought it was blinder, it was one of Ted's.) But that aside, I did manage to get the theft of Spike reported.

As I was leaving, I asked him if he would be putting out an APB. He glared at me menacingly. And there's me believing that policemen were employed to help the public. Suffice it to say, that again I wasn't tempted to put a few bob in the Police Widows and Orphans box, nor did I need any reminding about the location of the way out.

On the way home however, I was feeling terribly mean, and not a little guilty at begrudging a poor police widow or indeed an orphan or two of a few bob (for the second time). I even considered returning to the station and surreptitiously dropping a couple of shekels into the aforementioned box, but when I peered into the front office, *Attila* was keeping vigil like a rabid dog, so I gave that idea a miss.

My conscience was appeased a little later however, when as if by divine intervention, I was stopped in the street by a young man selling that free giveaway paper, *The Little Tissue*. He may not have had a pot to *urinate* in or a window to chuck it out of, but at least, instead of sitting on some draughty street corner, wrapped in a sleeping bag, with a hired dog asleep on a blanket beside him begging, he was doing something positive. His clothing did not fall into any recognisable genre, and was perhaps better suited at modern-day fashion shows, attended by the pseudo trendies bent on inspiring a new vogue in bespoke couture, out of clothes that most people would not be seen dead in. The battered balaclava hat was at odds with the harem-type eunuch shirt and baggy long pants pinched in at the ankles, and his feet were covered (loosely speaking) by white moth-eaten plimsolls. This ensemble was completed by a highly decorative African-style blanket which was loosely draped across a pair of very bony shoulders.

It is true that some of us like to dress up, and for many generations, youngsters have done just that. I was no different to my own group of friends in that I too wanted to disassociate myself from the boring respectability of my parents. The first real example of this youth-driven revolutionary mindset began with the arrival of the 'Teddy Boys' back in the fifties. They were into rock and roll, wore clothes modelled on our Edwardian forefathers (hence their nickname), and styled their outrageously well-groomed hairstyles, which were usually plastered in Brylcreem (or lard if they were skint) on the popular singers of the time.

A decade or so later, the youngsters were to emulate the lifestyle and aspirations of their own fashionable music-inspired peer group, and for me it was the 'Mods' and our favourite band, *The Who.* A popular group that we could readily identify with since apart from the clothes, they sang about many of the problems both real and imagined, that the youngsters living through those fun-loving and recklessly hedonistic days (known as the swinging sixties) had to deal with.

The clothes became a readily identifiable source and totem of membership. The more outrageous or brazenly defiant the apparel, the better chance one had of becoming known as *one of the faces,* which was a much sought-after epithet. But then, of the two groups battling for supremacy – and I use the term quite literally – the Mods were clean-cut, suave and sophisticated, whereas the Rockers, were scruffy greaseballs. But employment was the key. It was an expensive game to be a Mod, since fashionable clothes were not cheap, and they were changing all the time. If you were out of work, you could simply buy yourself a load of second-hand clobber (the dirtier the better), a set of assorted *Thunderbirds* cloth badges to sew on the leather-look jacket, and a moped. It really was that easy to change sides as it were.

Latter-day Punks and Goths characterise this need to be identified and in some cases stigmatised, in the same way that the garb of the Teddy Boys was a visible sign of their non-conformist and decadent ways, back in the day. However, *Gabriel's* clothing did not identify him with any rebellious bunch or known social or cultural group. It simply provided substantial evidence of abject poverty of a kind so miserable, that if the wolf were at his front door, I felt confident that it would have brought its own sandwiches and cakes. Clothes aside, while he portrayed a very confident and optimistic individual, his searching and appealing eyes seemed to mirror a suffering soul, projecting the concerned and stressful look of a beekeeper who had forgotten to do up his fly buttons. Nevertheless, I was overwhelmed at his fortitude and not a little impressed at his optimism in trying to sell a paper that I wouldn't even have cut up into little squares for the toilet. However, the front-page leader which read 'Egg laying contest won by local man!' caught my eye, and was enough to kindle my dormant curiosity sufficiently to part with a pound. On leaving, I told him that I would return at around 11:00 daily until the end of the month, with a couple of sandwiches and a thermos of cocoa. Given the problems that I have suffered of late, I felt that my own karmic meter needed a little top-up, and besides, it's nice to be nice!

On bidding him farewell, I gave him an extra 50p and a Sainsbury's coupon for £2.10p off his next shop when he spent £15 or more on toiletries, which was valid until 6th February. I can't quite describe the look that he gave me. Actually, thinking about it later, it wasn't too dissimilar to the one that Father Marcus displayed on leaving me yesterday.

I arrived back home at 12:20. The flat was quiet and there was no little dog to greet me excitedly in the hall. I spent the evening reading, but I simply couldn't concentrate. For some unknown reason, as I sipped my fortified bedtime cocoa, my thoughts turned to those brave North Sea fisherman, which reminded me to add fish fingers to my shopping list for tomorrow.

Goodnight love.

P xx

2nd February 2012

Good morning, Ginny.

During the night, I was vaguely aware of the sounds created by a desktop printer in full work mode. (I must be a little more careful with my English; I'm beginning to sound a bit like Stanley Unwin.)When I got up at 07:10, Maria's bedroom door was wide open. This is a place that I would never enter alone during the hours of darkness, except while carrying a crucifix. As I poked my head around the door, the room looked like a crime scene which involved a group of marauding chimpanzees. A discoloured tangled mess of duvet and bed linen was strewn carelessly on her orthopaedic mattress, part of which was hanging on the floor. Sheets of cut up A4 paper all around the room, suggested the scene and devastating aftermath of a diminutive wallpaper hanger who had finally *lost the plot,* and a great mountain of clothing piled up precariously on a chair was ready to obey the fickle forces of gravity at any moment. The addition of a jam doughnut, with a large bite out of it, carelessly flung onto the windowsill with its jam dribbling down the wall, added a certain concentration-distracting element to a canvas that Salvador Dali would have been raving about.

It looked like she had dressed hastily, and judging by the coffee drips on the carpet, she had tried to dress and drink at the same time. She is not the type of person who can multitask at the best of times, although she once boasted that she was quite good at completing 'one thing simultaneously'.

All was revealed at 09:20 when she arrived at the flat in a very dishevelled condition. Her normally well-groomed hair was a dank tangled unruly mess looking like washed-up seaweed, and her usual pallid sun-bereft complexion took on the florid colouration of a shagged-out long distant runner. Her breathing was fast and erratic and it took a full ten minutes of seated recovery, two almond slices and a large mug of minestrone soup for her to become wholly self-controlled and relaxed again.

It appears that during the early hours she had composed an A5 flyer which bore a picture of Spike, our home telephone number, and the following appeal:

Bisexual Little Dog Lost
Looks up when called: 'Spike or Jose'
Can read the lips, and likes to sleep with
Girls from Spain or Slovakia.
SUBSTANDARD REWARD IF FOUND

She had printed and cut out the flyers from a considerable amount of A4 sheets and had delivered these to every flat (220) of them on the estate, and had also put one on every lamppost and tree along the Kilburn High Road, from The Magpie to the old Bingo Hall (bless her little wooden maracas). I felt so grateful, and indeed not a little humble at the wonderful generosity of spirit and love that my dear Maria gives out so unconditionally.

The fact that I shall have to bear the brunt of a considerable amount of *urine extraction* for the foreseeable future is something that I shall endure with fortitude. Frankly, there's not much else that can be done about the issue, apart from moving that is. A little later I made her a little repast of a breakfast, and while she ate it, I hurriedly prepared a couple of cheese and pickle sandwiches and a flask of cocoa. She was quite interested in my story about Gabriel and asked if she could tag along.

We arrived at the spot where I had bade farewell to him yesterday just before 11:00. He was nowhere to be seen. At 11:30, we had decided to leave, and just as we got to the bus stop, he appeared carrying a rucksack. At a little playground nearby, we found a vacant seat.

Having introduced my very intrigued Maria to my new acquaintance, it was very evident that he was very embarrassed at her presence, but not wishing to stand on ceremony, he got stuck into the sandwiches enthusiastically. As I watched him, I felt certain that he had received a well-to-do upbringing, from the way that he delicately held the sandwiches between index finger and thumb, with his little tell-tale pinkie extended, to the unmistakeably genteel way that he sipped his cocoa without slurping or dribbling. The more I watched and listened to him, the more convinced I became that here was a young man who was more at home with champagne and canapés than milk stout and pork scratchings. His English pronunciation was impeccable and certainly more Etonian than Clapham Commoner. He seemed to be a very gentle, unassuming soul, genuinely appreciative of our small offerings which he accepted with quiet humility and gratitude. Frankly, I was beginning to feel quite protective towards him and for some quite inexplicable reason, a long forgotten but quite distressing scene where *Dumbo,* the baby elephant, realised for the first time that he was alone in the world flashed mercilessly through my mind, resulting in an impromptu testing of the tear-camouflaging capabilities of a recently acquired M&S handkerchief. My puerile distress went unnoticed by Maria and Gabriel however, since both were engaged in animated conversation.

We bade Gabriel farewell at 12:50, and I assured him that I would return at 11:00 as promised each day, at least until the end of the month. I am convinced that providence had brought us together on St Brigit's day for a reason. Since St Brigit was the Irish patron saint of dairymaids, her emblem being a cow, apart from his usual sandwiches and cocoa, tomorrow I shall bring him a pot of strawberry yoghurt as well.

As Maria and Gabriel said farewell to each other, they shook hands cordially, but neither seemed to be in any particular rush in letting one another go. Both were smiling bashfully and speaking softly, and I do believe that there was a look of mutual tenderness in their eyes as they parted. It was all quite sweet. Providence, it seems, is infinitely more cunning than I thought. Suffice it to say that my Maria was uncharacteristically quiet on the way home. Later, having finished off the remainder of her half-eaten doughnut, she confounded me even further by spending the rest of the afternoon cleaning out her room.

I gave both the gym and the pub a miss today, the former from necessity and the latter from a desire to give the booze a little rest, and to avoid (temporarily) the inevitable burlesque, jeer-jeer derision that awaited me in just about every pub in Kilburn.

At 14:00, there were fourteen missed calls on my home phone, which I later unplugged. On reviewing them, one bloke identified himself as 'A little bisexual dog that likes sleeping with Spanish and Slovakian girls' and 'could he come round for a walk?' Another was from a nob who stated that, 'He'd found a little dog, but didn't think it was Spike because it didn't look up when he called it Jose!'

All of us have mobiles, so I think I will get rid of the house phone altogether in the very near future. At the moment, it's about as useful as gossip that isn't worth repeating. Actually my mobile phone has been very quiet today, and on getting into bed later, I found out why. I had inadvertently switched it over to *silent mode* and there were eight missed calls on it.

Until tomorrow, Gin.
P xx

Dear Ginny.

Dave the Voice, Ted the Pleb, Lenka, two calls from Basil Lang, a call from my gym, and two unidentifiable *pud-wappers* made up the sum total of my eight missed calls of yesterday. On phoning them back this morning, Dave wanted to tell me that *Wino Lucy* had been reported missing, having not been seen since last Friday evening.

Ted was eager to arrange a day and time to visit the scrapyard in Edgware as discussed over breakfast last Saturday, and we settled on a meeting next Monday at 10:00.

Lenka (bless her heart) just wanted to know if I was alright, since she couldn't get through to me on my mobile.

Basil Lang wanted to have a meeting as soon as possible, and we agreed on tomorrow morning at 09:00 (which I thought must be important, since solicitors don't normally work on Saturdays). He phoned again later to say that 10:00 would be a better time for him.

Danielle the receptionist at my gym wanted to know if I'd be interested in acting as one of the judges in the forthcoming under-21 ladies gymnastic final, to be held a week on Friday, with the prizes to be awarded by our very own Olympic medal winner, Jessica Frettle. I agreed to do this as a personal favour to Beth, that beautiful young lady who conducted the training at our recent over 50's gym challenge, and finally I chose to erase the unidentifiable callers.

Over breakfast this morning, our collective mood was sombre and the usual high quality of our conversation was nothing short of meaningless drivel. It was clear that my two girls were suffering as much as I was, albeit that I tried to make light of our mutual melancholic state by introducing a little positive action.

'Shall we go for a nice walk in the park this morning?' I suggested, which didn't exactly produce the kind of response that I had expected. Lenka burst into tears and rushed from the room, while Maria began to howl like a demented banshee until the pacifying qualities of a large wad of bread pudding had been placed in front of her. My own feelings of emptiness and loss were suddenly compounded by an intensity of anger so profound, that I was completely beside myself with rage – and what a repulsive couple we made!

A little later, I quietly left the flat and sauntered over to the park where I was hit by an unwelcome kaleidoscope of memories involving my dear little Spike. There was that mental flashback of him chasing Bunny Longhurst through the rhododendrons, and another of the confused look that he gave me the first time that he saw a squirrel, which was followed by that amusing incident at that obedience and socialisation training class, where having had his rear end firmly pushed down on the trainer's command of 'SIT!', he looked up at me appealingly, had a retaliatory dump on the mat and trotted off to the door, picking up his cuddly frog on the way. I found him waiting for me by the Bowling Green,

On my way back to the flat, I remembered that very recent poignant memory where seemingly he had found the love of his life. It was all so bitter-sweet and it brought tears to my eyes. But suddenly, I remembered about Gabriel. It was 10:20 and I would not have the time for sandwich making and to get to our usual meeting place by 11:00. I therefore dashed to the bus stop and bought a couple of sandwiches and a coffee from a local café at the other end. I arrived with two minutes to spare, but when I got there, I found Maria sitting with him on our usual bench evidently in fine spirits. Gabriel was eating sandwiches out of a plastic box, my thermos on the seat next to him. Neither of them seemed to be aware of my presence until I actually sat down next to them.

'I thought that you might have forgotten about Gabby's sandwiches, so I made them for him myself today,' Maria said proudly, smiling at me sweetly. Frankly, thereafter, I couldn't get a word in edgeways, so engrossed were they in each other's company. I decided a little later, that I would make a quiet tactical withdrawal, informing them that I had 'urgent business to attend to'. On leaving, Gabriel stood up and shook my hand warmly. 'I really do appreciate your kindness, and maybe sometime in the future, I will be able to repay you,' he said.

'Well I tell you what,' I replied. 'If you come across a love-sick bilingual Jack Russell that can lip-read and likes to sleep around, having a very definite preference for Spanish or Slovakian girls, give me a call!' This produced a very confused and bewildered look from Gabriel who stared appealingly at Maria. She was giggling nervously and avoided eye contact with me as I left. What a delightful change from the abject misery earlier on in the day.

Back home, all was quiet. Lenka was out, so I spent a couple of hours tidying up the place, washing the bathroom and vacuuming the hall. I phoned the local nick to enquire if there was any news about my Spike, but was told very abruptly that they would be in touch if there were any further developments.

Following a bite to eat, I went out to the pub for an evening libation or two. As I entered the Gay Bar, I initially made a beeline towards the corpulent – or should I say *well-nourished* – frame of my old pal Dave, aka *The Voice*. His nickname is attributable to the somewhat high decibel level of his verbal utterances. Frankly, if he were holding a conversation on Dover beachfront at night, he would be a danger to shipping.

He was sitting on his usual high stool at the bar. I have never known a more quick-witted man in all my life. His anecdotes about his younger days are not only hilarious, but are often brazenly honest to a quite embarrassing degree. He has developed perfect timing when it comes to his usual amusing repartee, and frankly I feel that he would have been a very good stand-up comedian, had he pursued such a career. Many of his off-the-cuff observations are indeed not only hilariously funny, but in many cases are quite profoundly thought-provoking. I call these 'Ellisisms'. Often he seemingly surprises himself following a suitable quip, and laughs with everyone else when he realises just how funny it was. Apart from booze, one of his other favourite pastimes is eating, and I remember one particular memorable utterance, where on this particular occasion we were out dining in a recently opened Italian restaurant, the name of which escapes me. With a mouthful of various culinary delights, he stated, 'Do you know, I wish that food didn't fill you up so much.' 'Why is that?' I enquired. 'Because I love eating!' he replied, with a degree of honesty that wasn't meant to be funny.

On another occasion being engaged in cutting up a steak, the size of which even *Desperate Dan* would have thought twice about getting through in one sitting, he remarked, 'Have you ever got halfway through eating the horse, to find that you wouldn't be chasing the jockey after all?'

Scotch Andy nodded to me as I arrived, and the bar was unusually quiet. Ted was relating a tale about his early years working for a travelling circus and, being a good and interesting raconteur, had most of the lads spellbound. He has had a very colourful and interesting life and had clearly survived through a considerable amount of animal cunning and stealth, rather than hard work or calling. But intrinsically, he is a good man, with a lot of admirable qualities. I found out recently, that the money raised on the night of his *Extravaganza* was donated anonymously to a local orphanage. As I walked quietly towards the loo, I felt obliged to listen to his tale of how he'd lost his job as one of the hands working on the dodgem cars, albeit that I was busting for a pee.

'It was all because of a woman,' he said bitterly. 'I let her have a ride for nothing, but was spotted by the boss and was sacked on the spot.'

The bar went deathly quiet, apart from a sympathetic murmur from *Whispering Jim,* who as usual was in an inebriated twilight zone of his own. Suddenly, Dave's voice boomed, breaking the eerie silence like an inadvertent fart in a country churchyard. 'Don't tell me, Ted,' he called. 'You sued them for Fun Fair dismissal!'

The bar suddenly erupted into a thunderous tsunami of rapturous mirth and I just managed to get into the loo in time to ignominiously urinate down my trouser leg. Needless to say, I didn't remain, and as luck would have it, I was wearing my overcoat so thankfully my indiscretion went unnoticed, as did my silent withdrawal from the pub.

Goodnight love.

P xx

4th February 2012

Good morning, sugarplum.

I was up at around 06:20 this morning and joined Lenka in the kitchen. Over coffee she explained that several things had been bothering her, notably the shed saga, Spike's disappearance and the mysterious affair of the meter cupboard. Her view was that *someone* was deliberately bent on giving me grief, and she suggested that the first thing that should be done was to change the front door lock. Her views had tremendous merit. But while it was highly unlikely that somebody would have a key to the flat, it certainly would make the disappearance of Spike explainable, although I was still at a loss to understand how this could explain about the meter cupboard issue, or the strange behaviour of the Electric Board officials. It certainly wouldn't have anything to do with the shed affair, but as she pointed out, the articles that had been taken from the adjoining sheds that found their way into mine, had obviously been placed there. It stands to reason therefore, that whoever put them there had a key. My own shed hadn't been broken into or tampered with in any way, and the padlock was intact because when I had been instructed to open it by *Inspector Clouseau*, I had used my usual key which I had collected from my cabinet in the kitchen. Her observations certainly gave me food for thought and I hugged her warmly (not that I have ever needed any excuse to do that). It did thankfully remind me to get the breakfast table set, and to prepare the assorted culinary items in readiness for the imminent arrival of a very hungry Spaniard, bent on restoring her bodily tissues. As Lenka left for bed, Maria arrived, wrapped in a blanket. 'You haven't got Gabriel in there with you?' I teased.

'No, but I shall be seeing him later,' she replied, 'so don't bother making him sandwiches today. We are going to McDonald's for lunch, and he's paying.'

I arrived at the offices of Burt, Lang and Forthright in Kensal Rise, at 10:00 as arranged, although the front door was locked. The diminutive figure of Basil Lang appeared from an alley that ran alongside the building a little later. The last time we had met he was wearing a very smart suit, with a shirt and tie that would probably have cost a small fortune. But this morning he was dressed very casually in a woollen jumper, jeans and a heavy duffle coat. At his request, I followed him to the rear of the building and we entered the premises by a back staircase. It was all rather mysterious.

'I didn't want to be seen going in through the front door,' he confided, turning up his coat collar, which didn't exactly clarify the matter.

The office that I followed him into wasn't the same one as last time. One wall was lined with bookcases filled with detective novels, and another decorated with numerous prints and pictures of ancient and modern-day detectives, from Sherlock Holmes to that inimitable inverted detective, Lieutenant Columbo. A deer stalker hat was lying on a large mahogany desk, and there was a violin case on the top of a large grey chest of drawers by the window. Initially, I thought that this was some kind of prank, and fully expected a door or window to suddenly burst open, and a group of moronic cretins to jump out laughing hysterically. But I couldn't have been more wrong. Basil explained that his life's ambition was to become a policeman, but sadly, while Mother Nature had given him the requisite size ten feet, she had not given him the height to go with it. Even when he filled his boots, as it were, he was well below the minimum height required of five feet eight inches, standing a full five feet five inches in his stockinged feet (which, I won't go into). He decided therefore to study the law, and later was to become a partner with Roger Burt and Keith Forthright in the very successful law firm that it is today. Clearly, his height was a deciding factor, and while I have always believed that size is of no importance, in his case, I was of the opinion that a couple more inches could have been potentially disastrous in relation to humanity's loss of his unique investigative ability and formidable prowess in the defence of the innocent.

I really enjoyed his very succinct description of Poirot as expressed by his fictitious friend and mentor, Captain Arthur Hastings, which Basil had clearly memorised:

'He was hardly more than five feet four inches but carried himself with great dignity. His head was exactly the shape of an egg and he always perched it a little on one side.' Smiling at me, Basil remarked,

'So you see *mon ami,* his size was completely irrelevant, *n'est-ce pas?* But as it happens, I am one full inch taller than the great Hercule Poirot, but unlike the blessed man, thankfully, I have a normal-shaped head.'

It appears that this very likeable man actually plays out the professional solicitor formalities when it comes to his weekday office persona. However, at weekends the insignificant diminutive figure of the former office-bound Basil Lang, is let loose into society to mutate into his hitherto unnamed alter ego, bent on saving mankind from oppression and injustice. His interest in the law is specifically confined to criminal jurisprudence, which in his capacity as defending solicitor, allowed him to vent his passion for detective work to the full. His partners gave him the green light to exercise this passion, and in so doing, apparently a fair proportion of his clients were either proven not guilty or had their cases thrown out due to insufficient or questionable evidence, which had a considerable enhancing effect on the credibility and financial side of the business. At the end of this meeting, Basil, in his delightfully articulate legal jargon, stated that following various enquiries conducted by himself and a group that he referred to as his *Kilburn Unreliables* earlier in the week, he was left in no doubt that *Someone,* as yet unknown, was clearly bent on a deceptive course of action, apparently in the hope that such felonious illegality would have a blackening effect on my reputation, and would ultimately compromise my good-standing within the community.'A little later, he went on to explain his theory with regard to the shed theft. He suggested that the culprit had at some time gained entry into my flat, presumably by use of a key, and had then replaced my original shed key with another. This would allow him easy access into my shed, and then once the stolen property had been placed therein, my original lock would have been discarded and another one used to relock the shed. He then pointed out that when I had opened my shed at the request of the police, that I had no way of knowing or suspecting, that the lock and key were replacements.

He further stated that he had visited Nobby Caxton to ascertain the details of the owners of the sheds and remarked that he had found the man somewhat challenging and uncooperative. However, when pressed, he was able to confirm that one of the shed owners had passed away some two years previously, and that there were no known relatives. Apparently, he was very vague and unsure about the identity of the other. Basil confided that one of his *Unreliables* was following up on this, and that he was confident that the owner of the other shed would be identified shortly.

'Why do you call your helpers the Unreliables?' I asked.

'Elementary, my dear Mr Shaughnessy,' he replied. 'Sherlock had his *Baker Street Irregulars*, and I have my *Kilburn Unreliables*, and I can assure you that they are very aptly named.'

As I left, Basil stated that he had a meeting planned with DS Blackstock for Monday to clarify certain issues, and, shaking his hand, I bade him a respectful farewell. I sincerely felt that I had been in the presence of a very special person indeed. Suffice it to say that on my way home to Kilburn, I was feeling considerably more relaxed about this whole issue. It occurred to me later that I had completely forgotten to mention the theft of Spike, but consoled myself in the truth that my mind has been wandering about like a witchetty grub in a Melbourne café attempting to creep out of the back door and go *walkabout*. I have been so wrapped up in my own affairs that I have quite literally had *no time to stand and stare*, as advocated by W. H. Davies in his delightful poem called 'Leisure' which endorses the importance of taking the time to rest and the absolute pleasure in noticing the simple things in life.

As for my own conduct, Ted's somewhat descriptive vernacular of 'Acting like a complete nob!' seemed to sum up my somewhat (out of character behaviour) quite well, and this very succinct observation inspired me to *Get my head out of the clouds, and to step into the transporter!* A little later, I gratefully returned to earth, with a little mental bruising, but none the worse for wear.

As I arrived home later, I found Lenka sitting in the kitchen with a very anxious look on her face. I could hear the sound of male voices coming from the lounge and I looked at her enquiringly. She seemed lost for words and simply stated, 'There are two men here to see you!' stabbing her index finger aggressively towards the lounge.

As I entered, two men who had been resting their bones on my armchair and sofa stood up and introduced themselves. One dressed in police uniform identified himself as PC Hallis from the local police station, and the other introduced himself as Jeremy Pomfret from the Northern Electric Company. Following the usual pleasantries, PC Hallis arrested me on suspicion of *Abstracting Electricity* which he hastened to enlighten me was, 'Contrary to section 13 of the Theft Act 1968 as amended.'

A little later, I was again conveyed to our local nick, but this time, becoming *one of the faces* as it were, I was afforded the relative luxury of a seat in the rear of a panda car, which was far preferable to the cold and uninviting back of a clapped-out police van, with stains and puddles of questionable origin on its filthy floor.

Needless to say, the same confounded desk sergeant was on duty as PC Hallis escorted me into the charge room. I was instructed to empty my pockets, was body searched and then placed in a holding cell until the arrival of DS Blackstock a little later.

As before, I protested my innocence, but my pleas fell on ears as deaf as a tradesman's dummy, and I was subsequently charged by *Atilla* and once again bailed to attend the Westminster Magistrates Court on the morning of Thursday 23rd February 2012 at 10:00. I was released at 19:15 and as I left, I dropped two pound coins into the Police Widows and Orphans Fund on the front desk, and in doing so, was reminded of those wise words by the second century Roman Poet, Martial:

'The only wealth which you will keep forever is the wealth you give away.' Or in other words – it's nice to be nice!

On the way home, I phoned Basil to bring him up to date on recent events, and we arranged another meeting for Tuesday at 10:00. Before he put the phone down, he said to someone who was obviously with him, 'the game's afoot – not a word – into your clothes and come!' Seemingly, I had disturbed him in the middle of a rather delicate situation. Perhaps this is another one of his perks associated with working weekend overtime? Least said, soonest mended!

Back home, I was feeling so utterly miserable. I simply could not believe or understand the dreadful turn of events that had brought me from a state of near bliss a few short weeks ago, to an unprecedented level of sorrow and wretchedness. I realised that my former past life designation of *mildly irresponsible,* needed changing to one of *audaciously reckless,* and in my confusion, I actually considered visiting Father Marcus in the hope that he could provide a little comfort. However, having fortified myself with a couple of large cognacs, I came to the conclusion that he is no more an effective counsellor or spiritual guide, than Sandy Shaw with her top off is to Bruce Lee.

I locked myself away in my room for the rest of the evening, and placed a 'Do Not Disturb' sign on my bedroom door. I was in the mood for a good old-fashioned self-centred sulk.

Night night, Gin. P xx

Good morning, Ginny.

My mobile phone awoke me during the early hours of this morning, buzzing and spinning around on my bedside table like a bluebottle that had been recently zapped with fly killer, and was reluctantly bidding an early farewell to its thirty days of life. I had put it on silent last night, which negates its ringing qualities but switches it to vibration mode.

The last time that it went off unexpectedly in my trouser pocket, it occasioned an involuntary knee-jerk routine, that would have definitely raised a few admiring hairy eyebrows in the front row of the Bolshoi Ballet's Cossack Dancing Team.

It was 04:50 and frankly I was in no mood for social intercourse, or any other kind of verbal engagement for that matter! It was *Alfie the Dip*, who at this time of the morning was either locked in somewhere and trying to get out, or locked out of somewhere and was trying to get back in. And while I have mentioned before that Lenka is no angel of good humour and light first thing in the morning, I too was far from amused, and could have quite happily ripped the *pud-wapper's* head off had he been at arm's length.

Having spoken for a full two minutes without drawing breath, he advised me that he was thinking of moving to Basildon – Jenny his cousin had lost her baby (but found it in the back of her car?) He had his last wisdom tooth taken out (presumably putting the rest of his remaining intellect at risk of imminent collapse) and the name of the owner of the *other shed* is Alexander Barrington Scott at number 96, whom he stated, 'had come clean about his shed and would be at the court hearing on the 13th to explain!' Before I could say a word, he continued, 'Basil sends his regards,' and rang off. This was very good news indeed, and I wondered how on earth this could have happened so quickly. My awe and admiration for my diminutive solicitor is most definitely in the ascendant.

As for Alfie, like Basil he too is quite diminutive in height and as far as his general physical statue is concerned, I have seen more meat on a sparrow's kneecap, but like my dear little Spike, what he lacked in size was more than compensated for in his courageous indomitable spirit. On one occasion in Sainsbury's, I saw this pocket titan challenge a pack of marauding housewives bent on getting to the only available cashier at the checkout before him, and during his attempt at single-handedly holding back this attacking monstrosity, it soon became apparent that he had more testosterone in front of him than an English rugby blindside flanker, taking on the All Blacks at Twickenham. He couldn't walk for weeks and had to reluctantly avoid The Magpie, as he was advised that laughter 'might open up the stitches'.

At around 07:40, I heard the front door opening, and grabbing the pickaxe handle (that happened to be lying by my bed on the carpet), I dashed out into the hall, bent on the physical reformation of any unrecognisable individual I encountered there, but thankfully found my Maria in a somewhat inebriated state leaning up against the kitchen door, smiling at me sweetly. As I helped her towards her bedroom she said, 'What a party we had. The water was flowing like champagne!' She put her arms around me and gave me an ultra-slobbery kiss, which spoke volumes (and I suspected that it wasn't a first edition). I managed to guide her unsteadily to her bed, where she collapsed into an unrefined heap of contented confusion, and taking off her shoes, I gently covered her with her duvet. She was asleep almost immediately.

A little later, I heard old Compton's bells calling the faithful to early morning Mass and for the first time in ages I felt the overwhelming desire to escape for a while, and to sit quietly within the nut-freezing hallowed walls of St Benedict's Church. We all need a change of scenery now and again, free from the inevitable distractions of home and loved ones, and perhaps this is why the pub has always been so popular down the ages.

On entering the impressive Victorian edifice built in the Gothic revival style, with its vaulted stone sculptures and stained-glass windows, I felt very insignificant indeed. Gazing down the long perspective view of the nave, I could just make out the unmistakable figure of Father Marcus through what would have once been the centre arch of the rood screen. (Historically, the inside architectural arrangement of our churches has been changed on numerous occasions to accommodate the current monarch's religious affiliations.) However, it seems that the Victorian church builders retained the screen for aesthetic purposes, and to perhaps suggest that the building was from a far more ancient period. It was in fact built in 1824.

My clerical neighbour, who was silhouetted against the light from the beautifully ornate rose window behind him, was busily placing candles on the altar. He was wearing a white embroidered surplice over a black ankle-length cassock, and I can say in all honesty, that this is the first time that I have ever seen him with his clothes on (ecclesiastical clothes that is). He really made a very impressive sight and later in conversation I found myself behaving like a toadying vassal in the presence of the Lord of the Manor. I felt nervous – out of place – and very confused, particularly with regard to my inexplicable obsequiousness. I suppose it could have been compared with knowing the axe man socially, and then mounting the steps and seeing him for the first time in the garb of his office, wearing his horrid black mask, and tenaciously gripping his chopper. Suffice it to say, that instead of leaving the place spiritually uplifted, I returned home quite morose, with more questions than answers.

As I arrived back at the flat, Lenka was clearing out our window boxes and having spent a little time in conversation with her my spirits lifted, and a feeling of inner contentment was restored. Sensing my mood, she suggested a trip out to Camden Market. Frankly, she could talk me into just about anything. Her endearing smile (that could ripen bananas) belies the immense sadness of a soul that has been through life's wringer a few times, and while she possessed an outward gentle innocence, her inner strength is always politely masked in a veil of good manners and etiquette. Nevertheless, once we were away from the relative safety of the flat, I inexplicably found myself acting like a paranoid mother hen and became embarrassingly overprotective. She smiled at me appreciatively, but suggested that I would be far more comfortable if I relaxed my vice-like grip on her left shoulder and right coat pocket.

Our walk around Camden Lock Market, looking at the vast numbers of stalls selling unusual and original gifts, was a chilly but interesting affair. We bought lunch from a Chinese food vendor, followed by several drinks at a quaint little pub nearby, which was frequented by some very weird and statement-inducing young people. I suppose we were the only couple dressed in what could pass for 'normal attire' in the place. The remainder were clad in a wonderful array of colourful clothes of the degenerate subculture variety, worn by spiky haired punks and spooky, ghoulish fun-loving Goths. If you want to go somewhere to take your mind off a thing, then Camden is the place.

We finished up at The Magpie, and like my dear little dog Spike, Maria and Lenka are very popular with my friends. *Whispering Jim,* was as drunk as a boiled owl, but still managed to make a wobbly beeline for Lenka as we arrived. He hugged her affectionately and murmured something about, 'the day being only fit for a high stool', and unsteadily recovering his balance, he stumbled back to his chair by the jukebox and continued in his former conversation with unseen acquaintances, one or some of whom, were getting a right verbally admonishing. As usual, not a soul in the place was taking a blind bit of notice.

The Voice was in fine spirits relating a tale about a front-page headline he'd seen which said, 'Half of the City Council are Crooks.' 'And so they feckin are!' shouted *Whispering Jim,* momentarily interrupting his private concerns. 'The Council demanded a retraction,' Dave continued. 'And the following day's headlines read: Half of the City Council are Not Crooks,' he said, breaking out into rapturous laughter.

Tony the Tube suddenly arrived, having just completed another eight hours of finance-enhancing labour comparable with that of a successful city trader, and was in desperate need of a lot of light, a few glasses of vision-improving alcohol and a game of darts. *Lenny the Ponce* was distributed between two chairs, sitting on the one with his plastered foot resting on the other, which he proudly displayed with evident affectionate reverence, and Ted was chatting to a seated Nobby Caxton who appeared to be slightly *Brahms and Liszt. Alfie the Dip* winked at me knowingly from behind a magazine that he was reading. Much as I wanted to have a word with him, his body language and facial expressions indicated that this was not the time or place.

It was a typical rough canvas of the Gay Bar on an early Sunday evening.

There were a few notable friends missing, but the main *faces* were in attendance. Strangely, I didn't recall seeing Nobby leave, so must assume that he went out through the posh bar.

Lenka and I stayed for a couple of drinks and on leaving, Ted took me to one side to remind me about our trip to the breakers tomorrow, and 'would I bring a few sandwiches and a flask of coffee – no milk but plenty of sugar'.

We arrived back at the flat at around 21:50. Maria was still in the land of nod, so we didn't disturb her and we crept around as quietly as we could.

Just before bed, I thanked Lenka for her gracious and loving support, which was so welcome and gratefully received today and she hugged me considerately.

I didn't need any rocking and was more than happy to get into bed at 23:15pm.

Until tomorrow, Gin.

P xx

6ᵗʰ February 2012

Good morning, Ginny.

I awoke this morning to the discordant sounds of Maria gargling in the bathroom. I have always associated the sound of jacuzzied-water being violently sloshed around the mouth as a precursor or warm up to her usual culinary decathlon event of food mastication which ordinary mortals refer to as breakfast. Frankly, when hunger sets in, this young lady could eat the horse and chase the jockey. Her grandfather had the farm, her brother had the canning plant and she had the tin opener. But it is one of her endearing qualities, and I really love to cook for her. I am ever amazed at the amount that she can put away in one sitting and would guess that he daily calorific intake would be enough to lighten up a small Yorkshire village. How she manages to keep such a trim figure is beyond me. Clearly she was suffering a little this morning, her usual post-bed shower having no restorative effect on her whatsoever. But at 08:00 most mornings her legs are programmed to carry her into the kitchen, whether her brain wants to go there or not, and in she came at 07:58 looking like a withered tree in a corn field and was evidently not in a particularly sociable mood. She sat down dejectedly and gave me a perfunctory smile. A minute or two later she started making deep, throaty guttural sounds of the type that a dog makes just before it throws up on the carpet, and rushing out of the kitchen, she made it back to the bathroom, where she violently eradicated whatever was left in her stomach.

Given the circumstances and not wishing to exacerbate her delicate condition further, when she returned I avoided mentioning food, but pushed a large glass of water towards her which she accepted gratefully. The pint of water didn't touch the sides as it were, and vanished quickly. The sounds of its passing reminded me to add drain cleaner to my shopping list.

With my back towards her, I made a few cheese and pickle sandwiches, and filled my thermos with hot, sweet, black coffee, as per Ted's instructions. I enquired about food for Gabriel, but she indicated that it wasn't necessary, and that she would explain later. She made her way back to bed.

On the way out of the flats, I passed old misery guts from 124 (he of the horse-manure fame) who nodded at me disinterestedly. Actually, he has been keeping a very low profile of late, and given the merciless verbal drubbing that he has probably had to put up with, it's hardly surprising. If it were me, I think I would have seriously considered emigrating to somewhere safe, like Doncaster. As you know, I am not a vindictive person, but what he did to that poor woman and her children was quite unforgivable. He has lived above me for some thirteen years or more, and I haven't a clue what his name is, and in all that time I haven't said more than two words to him. Actually, at this point in time, I can think of a very appropriate two-word expletive, but sadly there isn't a suitable euphemism that could fully justify the sentiment.

I met Ted outside the revered edifice of The Magpie public house at 09:30 as arranged. We took my car, as his (slippery *fatherless-person* that he is) was conveniently in the garage having its elastic bands changed, and following his less than *National Geographic*-level directional skills, we managed to cover the usual twenty-minute drive to Edgware in a mind-boggling one hour and ten minutes. However, to be fair, we were unlucky enough to catch five sets of traffic lights on red, three on amber and what with assisting a geriatric lollipop lady (who had tripped over her pole) together with the time taken for an over-zealous traffic warden to caution me for driving in a bus lane, as we whizzed the wrong way down a one-way street, it's a wonder that we got to his cousin's scrapyard at all. I could have understood the route taken were he a relative of *Paul the Cab* or if he had secretly been 'doing the knowledge' (a term used by people training to become London cab drivers), since he took me all around the houses to get to what was for all intents and purposes, a simple straightforward road. Suffice it to say, that had he been one of the navigators on the Nuremberg bombing raid, I have no hesitation in saying that 'Southend-on-Sea would have taken one hell of a bashing!'

We arrived at The Buster Lea's Breaker and Scrap Metal Yard at 10:40 precisely, and on opening a very ancient metal gate and walking into the site, we were initially attacked by an animal that was fortunately secured to a concrete block by a length of iron chain. It could be loosely described as belonging to the order *Canis lupus familiaris* (dog), although there was nothing familiar in its bodily form to suggest a relationship with any known species. It was hairier than a werewolf in a mohair jumper and as ugly as a deep-sea racing mullet and frankly, was the most brutal looking beast that I had ever seen. At least I thought it was, until I beheld the less than imposing, but considerably uglier figure of

Buster Lea himself. He was without question a very weird-looking individual indeed. He seemed to be as wide as he was tall with a large misshapen head, a shock of long tangled ginger hair, a profoundly protruding brow under which were hiding in its shadow, two black lifeless eyes that peered around accusingly, and a pair of hands the size of small shovels at the end of two very muscular arms. His legs however were thin and spindly in contrast, as though they had been cut off from his mouth and upper body's food and water supply.

I was under the impression that the Neanderthals had died out some 40,000 years ago. But clearly, this one's prehistoric ancestors had dodged the Stone Age census. Either that or modern-day anthropological scientists had not taken into account his tribe of metal-dealing troglodytes that had settled in the swamps of Stone Age Edgware. Undeniably, this could put the integrity and belief of man's history and evolutionary progress into question, and my belief on the former voyages of the *Star Ship Enterprise* could be forever irrevocably damaged.

After the usual formal introductory pleasantries, I bought back my brass birdcage at the outrageously inflated price of £30, but told him that he could keep the bicycle since I didn't have a readily available supply of negotiable bonds or shares with me, and didn't have any bicycle clips to hand anyway. The description of the bloke that brought my property to him was vague and uninspiring, and frankly he wasn't any help whatsoever. He wasn't much help with regard to a facial description either, being more interested in the physiognomy of HM the Queen and more particularly the watermarks of authenticity on the notes that I'd given him?

On the way home, Ted was relatively quiet for the length of time it took him to eat the sandwiches I had made for him, apart from what could be described as a musical 'verbal slurp duet' which comprised of an interchangeable oral discourse in between a blow, a bite and slurp of coffee.

When the dreadful monotony of this had ceased, and the remaining coffee drunk, he confided that both he and *Alfie the Dip* were on the unofficial payroll of Basil Lang. I found this all quite amusing initially. However, later over a refreshing pint of Guinness, I saw the logic behind using the intellectual resources (such as they are) of two congenital miscreants in the pursuit of other criminals. As they say, 'an old poacher makes the best gamekeeper!'

Back home, I reinstalled my birdcage back into its former place in the shed, and was greeted by Lenka who it seems had been watching for my arrival home. She had called upon the services of a local locksmith who had changed our door lock and for added security had installed an additional mortis lock below it. She can be so thoughtful. Maria was still in bed it seems. At least her bedroom door was closed, and not having a string of garlic available, I thought better of paying her a visit.

I finished off the evening at the Bread Bin, where I met my dear Rosheen and partook of her scrumptious evening fare of slow-cooked bacon and cabbage, which was liberally washed down with a couple of pints of Guinness. The pub was very quiet indeed apart from Bunny Longhurst, the park keeper responsible for injuring Lenny. Rumour has it, that the poor man had suffered terrible remorse over the incident and had used his life savings to pay for laser eye treatment. Initially, I didn't recognise him without his familiar black-rimmed spectacles with their coke-bottle lenses, although he spotted me immediately. Over a pint, he confided that while he still felt terrible regret and sadness over the injuries that he had unwittingly caused, part of him felt that it may have been a bit of a godsend since for the first time in his life, he was able to see the time on his bedside clock without the use of glasses. In an effort to make him feel a little better, I explained that most of us get pretty annoyed about things that we have no real control over. The severity of the itch for example, is always inversely proportional to one's ability to reach it, but as far as this particular injured party was concerned, I explained that his constant inability to reach this metaphorical elusive spot was now over, and in a very positive way his future life would be one of irrepressible joy and contentment. Bunny wasn't too convinced about this, and clearly I couldn't enlighten him any further.

It has now been over a week since my Spike was stolen, and despite the best intentions of my friends, there has been no positive news. As you know, I am not a religious man, but found my knees knocking as I got into bed. I had to answer them and kneeling, I said a quiet few words for the safety of my dear little boy.

Goodnight love.

P xx

7th February 2012

Good morning, sugarplum.

I was at Basil Lang's offices at 10:30 as arranged, bumping into Alfie who was on his way out. He seemed to be in very good spirits and winked at me cheekily. Basil was back to his *other self* this morning, sporting his usual dapper suited and booted weekday attire. He advised me of the following information. Apparently, Ted and I were followed to and from the scrapyard yesterday by an unidentified middle-aged man driving a Morris 1100. The registration number of the vehicle was being checked to reveal the owner, and this should be known later in the day. This intelligence had been gathered by Alfie who had been following the car that was following us. This came as quite a disturbing revelation since Alfie couldn't drive a wet soapy finger up his *anal-orifice* let alone take control of a motor vehicle. Apart from which, he has been banned from driving for years following what he has always described as *that little misunderstanding* that followed his inebriated call to the police informing them that he had just 'crashed into three cars, knocked down two street lights, smashed through a bus shelter and piled through the front of a Burton's shop window'. On being asked where he was, he told the emergency operator to 'go have a burger!' or words to that effect and he was subsequently caught in the toilet of a local Wimpy Bar, with a cheese burger in one hand, and his dick in the other. Another very worrying feature of all of this is that *Alfie the Dip* has never owned a motor vehicle in his life.

Basil was fully aware of Alfie's pedestrian status due to his former claims for foot deodorant, corn plasters and shoe leather and had happily paid him any additional expenses incurred with no questions asked. It graciously included a mileage allowance, irrespective of the mode of transport or vehicle's provenance. This is a very clear working example of my own sentiment – *'it's nice to be nice'* – and Basil's lifelong dictum of *if there is no question, then there's nothing to answer!*

Alfie's capture was due to a very alert individual in a police helicopter on its way back to base to catch the start of *The Magic Roundabout,* They never did recover the vast quantity of missing gents' clothing, which was put down to opportunist thieves. The officer concerned was later awarded the British Empire Medal for his charitable work in the Sudan, having spearheaded the public's awareness to the plight of the country's poor, and the urgent provision of monetary and food assistance for its starving masses. Coincidentally, he later opened what was to become a very successful second-hand clothing outlet in its capital Khartoum. Its shares are currently trading at 105p.

In relation to my forthcoming case before the Westminster Magistrates on Monday, Basil simply stated that there was 'nothing to worry about' and that there was 'no case to answer' and that the case will be 'thrown out of court!' I was very impressed with his confidence and have complete faith in his judgement and resourceful capabilities. He confided that the main reason for allowing it to go to trial was that he wanted to identify the spectators sitting in the public gallery. He was convinced that the person or persons responsible for the planning and commission of the acts or omissions, which were clearly intended to pervert the course of justice, would be in attendance hoping for a conviction. I brought up the subject of my latest charge, to which he simply replied, 'Let's get the first one out of the way before we deal with that issue, but be assured, that tentative enquiries are already under way on that front.'

He then went on to mention that he had become an equal opportunity employer and had recently acquired the services of a female addition to his *Kilburn Unreliables.* As expected, he wouldn't go into detail, other than to confirm that she was a *'pretty-slick-chick-dick'.* While he was on the subject, I took the opportunity of apologising to him for interrupting his 'Saturday afternoon liaison' the other day with my inappropriately timed phone call, to which he replied, 'Oh it was nothing, Ted and I were simply discussing tactics.'

Least said, soonest mended!

I left for home at 11:45 and on the bus back, I received a text from Maria asking if I could meet her and Gabriel at our usual place. I had completely forgotten about the poor boy's sandwiches and flask again, but assumed that Maria would have taken the initiative. I was more than surprised at the reception that awaited me. To cut a very long story short, I was greeted by a crowd of spectators and a film crew. Maria waved at me from the heaving throng and standing next to her was a very smartly dressed Gabriel. It transpires that my dear erstwhile derelict down-and-out was in fact an investigative reporter working for one of the big national newspapers. His task was to spend two weeks on the streets, living like a vagabond, sleeping in hostels and relying for his survival on the generosity of others. The person or group deemed to be the most selfless and generous, would receive an award of £10,000 to be donated to the charity of their choice.

Gabriel put his arms around me warmly and stated that he had chosen me to receive the award. There was a lot of jostling and commotion, cameras flashed, and complete strangers wanted to shake my hand, while others patted me on the back. A number of women hugged me with wild abandon, and an elderly lady dressed in Salvation Army clothes with the rank of a Major General, patted me on the bum with her tambourine and gave me a presentation copy of *The War Cry*. I felt quite overwhelmed with all of the attention and once the commotion had died down, I bade farewell to Gabriel and Maria, who were arm in arm and seriously looking like *an item*, as the modern-day vernacular would describe a couple.

I was still shaking slightly as I walked into the Gay Bar at The Magpie, but a quick couple of cognacs later, I felt revived enough to talk to myself for a while, since the place was quieter than a fly landing on a feather duster. Thankfully, *Tony the Tube* arrived a little later, which started a veritable avalanche of humanity into the place.

My Lenka phoned me at 18:20 and since I wasn't in the mood for cooking, I invited her to join me in an evening meal. We subsequently visited *The Crush* Middle Eastern restaurant run by a very nice group of former Somali pirates. As usual, the food was excellent, and my choice of company could not have been better. Over dinner, I gave her a quick rundown of my day's events and she laughed heartily when I related the Gabriel story. But for better or worse, my Maria it seems has become romantically involved as a result. They do make a nice couple, and I sincerely hope that it will blossom.

Night night, love.
P xx

8th February 2012

Dear Ginny.

I awoke early this morning, and in the darkness I mentally pictured my dear little Spike running around the bedroom, jumping up on the bed and rummaging about in my duvet. I could almost hear his sniffs and grunts as he tried to locate me in the indistinct gloom. Sadly however, it was all wishful thinking and I was quite alone.

I still cannot quite fathom why someone would want to cause me such worry and misery. For the last couple of weeks, I have searched my conscience to ascertain and identify any action, whether deliberate or otherwise, that would cause another to act so despicably. Clearly, when looking after number one, a person must not inadvertently step on number two, and in this case whatever offence, real or imagined, that I have caused to this veritable *pud-wapper,* it will be as nothing when I get my hands upon him, and insert my boot six lace holes deep up his very misguided and soon to be quite excruciatingly painful *tradesman-entrance!*

Before lights out last night as I lay reading in my bed, I received a text from Basil Lang wanting me to meet him this morning near the *Left Foot* shoe repairer and key cutting service shop on the concourse of Euston Station. He suggested 09:30, and if he didn't receive a reply from me, assumed that this would be OK.

Accordingly, I was aboard the 08:15 train bound for Euston this morning. The dark overcast leaden sky reflected my mood precisely. Like a single star noticed on a cloudy night, I was completely insignificant, surrounded by darkness and bunched together with four billion others, or at least that's how it felt, being crammed into a carriage full of fellow travellers, loosely called *morons!*

The train arrived fifteen minutes later, and having been overwhelmed by a monstrous marauding crowd all trying to squeeze through a rather small gap between two doors, I was jostled along the platform, and on the way to the barriers, I had my bum pinched by what could only be described as an unknown opportunist pervert-commuter, who was perfectly camouflaged in a veritable sea of possible suspects. Judging by the swiftness of the action, I was convinced that it had been carried out by a seasoned professional. Having finally made it through the barriers at the end of the platform, I was feeling a little shaken. I reasoned that I could have been bumped off just as easily, and the assailant like my bum pincher, would simply have melted away into the disinterested crowd of somnambulist commuters.

From a very small age, I have suffered from claustrophobia and travel sickness and although it was a relatively short journey, I am sure that I was suffering from a little train-lag. I felt like getting the next train back to the relative safety of my beloved Kilburn, and away from all of this unnecessary battering. However, I really didn't want to let Basil down, but out of curiosity, I checked the display boards anyway and saw that the next Kilburn bound train would leave at 09:10 from platform 6.

Could it be that the discomfort I had felt on my trip down this morning was a vital aspect of fate's plan? A series of events to ensure that I got an earlier train back, instead of the later *doomed train,* that would be derailed on its way back to Kilburn High Road Station, killing everyone on board apart from a trainee chef from Basildon, or was I just being excessively imaginative? As it turned out, I couldn't have been more wrong, since at 11:40 the line was suspended indefinitely due to *a leaf on the track.* But I digress.

I had forgotten what it feels like to have to suffer the indignity and strife of earning a living in a competitive world. The daily tedium and discomfort associated with simply getting to work is something that I now never consider. However, during my years of gainful employment, like many others I suppose, I'd often considered giving up the lousy job, but felt compelled to remain because of the reasonable office surroundings, the comfortable ergonomically designed chairs, a relatively considerate management team, paid sick and holiday leave, retirement fund, and profit-sharing plan, etc. But intrinsically we all resent the idea of having our physical and/or mental energies redirected for the purpose of lining the pockets of others, no matter how comfortable the working environment or the ingratiatingly insincere obsequious tendencies of the bosses.

After all of this time, when my mind wanders back to my working life and I think about those very special colleagues, many of whom I mentally still miss a great deal, an involuntary smile of appreciative respect usually passes across my visage. However, when it comes to my last former boss, an individual who was without doubt the most deceitful, uninspiring, and treacherous, *anal-orifice,* that I have ever had the misfortune to encounter, other feelings and gestures are evoked.

On the very rare occasions when my mind wanders on to disagreeable thoughts in general and nonentities like him in particular, the middle finger of my right hand gets an erection, and like its phallic counterpart, it will not subside until full gratification is achieved. But immediate relief is attained relatively easily, since all that I have to do is present it to the world using a forward and upward movement, which I believe is considerably more offensive than simply sticking one's tongue out and *cocking a snook!* But then, he is worthy of nothing but the best when it comes to discourteous gestures.

On allowing the next cattle truck of marauding wildebeest-like commuters to spew out into the vast and less than endearing chaos of the Euston Road, and having a little time on my hands, I traipsed over to platform 6 anyway. I asked one of those ticket collector chaps standing nearby whether the next train for Kilburn would be stopping at this platform, and my day was completely blessed by his answer. In a soft Irish accent he replied, 'Well if it doesn't now – there'll be a terrible crash!'

I caught sight of Basil a little later, who was dressed in what could loosely be described as 'workman's attire' which consisted of overalls, boots, a rather well-used donkey jacket and a filthy cloth cap. However, the authenticity of his disguise was somewhat compromised by the umbrella and briefcase that he was holding. The general effect was that of a deranged tramp who had just robbed a local Moss Bros store, or a city banker who had forgotten to take off his gardening clothes and to swallow his morning Diazepam.

When I saw him waving at me frantically, which occasioned a fair amount of interest by passing commuters, my immediate reaction was to rush back to platform 6 and to take my chances on the 09:10 back to Kilburn. But of course I didn't, and sauntered over into his general direction avoiding eye contact, and motioning him to follow me to a less conspicuous place where people didn't normally congregate. Finding the gent's toilet closed (due to an unofficial strike), we made our way to an empty *Starbursts* coffee shop nearby. The coffee that they sell here is a special blend of Turkish and Brazilian, as well as yesterday's Turkish and Brazilian.

I was naturally very keen to find out why Basil had adopted the old cloak and dagger routine. Although my estimation of the situation was completely wrong. As far as the workman-type apparel was concerned, apparently he was on his way to paint his mother's lounge, but had to drop off some important (life-changing) papers at the office on the way, and hence the briefcase. The umbrella didn't really need any explanation because the weather forecast this morning predicted 'partly cloudy with sunny intervals' which in meteorological jargon would normally indicate 'torrential rain and gale force winds', and the dirty old cap suggested the possibility that he'd be painting his mum's lounge ceiling as well. Elementary, when you think about it!

This analytical deduction business is really quite simple. I mean, you wouldn't want to get involved in dirty work wearing fine clothes; or indeed would not carry important documents in a rucksack. It follows, therefore, that since most of the commuters I saw getting off trains this morning were carrying haversacks, a number of possible reasons for doing so became evident. Notably, that they were all going to a camping exhibition, or perhaps were carrying overalls in case they were called upon to get involved in a little impromptu industrial painting at the office, or indeed, due to a nationwide malfunction of washing machines caused by the pervasive illegal insertion of fiddling appliances into electric meters, that they were simply going to drop off a load of soiled clothing at a local laundrette, and to collect it again on their way home.

While we were sipping our cups of coffee, Basil enlightened me with regard to the reasons behind this meeting and pointed across the station to a rather dilapidated shop that could have definitely benefited from a coat of paint called *The Left Foot.* It was one of these fancy shoe repair and key cutting establishments that boasted a *while-you-wait* service, which was very useful. Instead of spending their day's pay on an over-indulgent quantity of coffee and/or alcohol at the overly priced station bar while waiting for their usual delayed train, the frustratingly bored and inactive commuters – many of them still on physical comedown following their day's malingering activities – could engage in the constructive pursuits of either getting their shoes repaired (again) or of having (additional) keys duplicated, or both.

In the wink of an eye, a blur passed before me vanishing as quickly as it came. Regaining my composure, I noticed that my unopened packet of custard cream biscuits had gone, and a small square of paper was in its place. Before I had time to speak, Basil opened it and sipping his coffee read the contents. He asked me if the name of Albery Groupenhourst was familiar to me, and I answered in the negative, but added playfully that, 'I did have a sister in the WAAFS', which seemed to fall on very deaf flippancy-deflecting ears. Basil went on to inform me that this was the name of the registered owner of the Morris 1100 that followed Ted and I on our outing to the primordial swamps of Edgware on Monday.

Taking out a small telescope from his pocket, as discreetly as he could, he took a cursory visual survey of the shopfront. Giving it to me, he asked if I could identify the man working at the front desk. I was aghast to recognise the unmistakeable lugubrious features of 'old misery guts' from 124. Pointing a soggy club wafer biscuit in the direction of the shop, Basil announced smugly, 'That, *mon ami,* is Albery Groupenhourst who is not only the registered owner of the vehicle that followed you the other day, but also happens to be a locksmith by trade.'

Having said farewell to Basil a little later, to divert my mind on to more pleasant things, being in town with time on my hands, I thought that I'd visit a few places not so readily available in the wilds of Kilburn. During the early afternoon I visited The National Portrait Gallery, *The Fox and Hounds,* Westminster Abbey and *The Spotted Dog.* On the way home, I had a late lunch at a renowned pie and mash establishment in the Tower Bridge Road, a muff-cut in Camden Passage, a further three pints in *The World's End,* and a cut-price flu jab at an Indian pharmacy that was having a sale. My evening was spent alone in dark reflection with thoughts of revenge too awful to elucidate.

Basil had recommended that I should simply take things easy for a while, and certainly not to challenge Mr Groupenhourst in any way. As he so rightly pointed out, 'There is nothing to confront him with at the moment. Everything gained at this time while being irresistibly compelling, is based on circumstantial evidence and more direct incriminating proof of guilt had to be found.' Basil assured me that, 'If it was out there to be discovered, he will stumble upon it – and if not, there was nothing to be found in the first place!'

Goodnight love.

P xx

9th February 2012

Good morning, Ginny.

I wasn't feeling at all well this morning, suffering from what appeared to be a feverish cold. My arm was also a little sore at the site of my flu jab yesterday. Normally when I catch a cold, I go to bed and take a bottle of whiskey with me. In three or four hours it is gone. I do this for three consecutive days until the cold is also gone.

Both Lenka and Maria nag me rotten about my drinking habits, and I suppose that they are right, but since my life is all about order, balance and symmetry, I do not let it interfere with my innate sense of moderation in all things. It's just that occasionally life throws a wobbly, and I find that a couple of well-placed libations, particularly when taken in company, has a remarkable way of smoothing out the bumps as it were, resulting in the restoration of a little order and balance.

At 08:10 this morning, my Maria was thrown into a state of mental confusion. Initially she had thought that her bedroom clock was faulty. Lately on a normal weekday morning from 07:15 onwards, the tantalising smell of percolating coffee and cooking breakfast fare would waft along the hall into her bedroom, teasingly inviting her to arise and join in the culinary fun.

Following her morning shower, she is programmed to arrive in the kitchen for around 08:00. This morning, however, the unthinkable happened. In her mental befuddlement, she initially checked the kitchen, which she found to be in darkness. Finding my bedroom door closed, which indicated that I was in residence, she suddenly came to a very erroneous conclusion and started to howl mournfully. Falling to her knees on the hall carpet like a dying gazelle, she sobbed uncontrollably. This awoke Lenka who rushed out of her room in panic. Maria was convinced that I had passed away during the night, and pleaded with Lenka to take a look in my room. Lenka cautiously opened my bedroom door and found me sitting up in bed sipping a hot lemon drink and reading a current copy of *The Pigeon Fancier*. Maria was overwhelmed with joy when she realised that I was in fact still breathing, and for the immediate future at least, her normal bodily tissue requirements would be satiated.

She jumped on the bed beside me and seemed rather relieved to be able to touch and converse with living flesh. Needless to say, as selfless as ever, I got up and made my two very special girls' breakfast, and as usual, I couldn't get a word in. The main topic was Gabriel, and it appears that my Maria is in love, bless her heart.

The postman arrived as punctiliously as ever, putting each letter carefully through my letter box. It seems he's a bit of a perfectionist and hates what he calls the shoddiness of public servants. 'A letter should arrive in a clean un-crumpled condition, free from outside contamination,' he maintains. But I've noticed quite a change in the man since Spike has not been around. He appears to be far more confident, self-assured and dynamic, and no longer the nervous spook of a man that would creep up to my door on the one side as Spike crept up on the other, waiting patiently for him to quietly slip the letters through the door. As he timidly did so, Spike would let rip with an almighty banshee howl, and grabbing them violently, would pull them recklessly out of the postman's hand, frightening the life out of the poor bloke, who would rush up the stairs as though the devil himself was after him. That's another thing that I miss about my little lad, he always had the most outrageously funny sense of humour. Although I must say that it is quite a treat to receive my mail in one piece.

Over breakfast, Maria brought us up to date with regard to her blossoming relationship with Gabriel, and her experiences sounded truly charming. Like most of her other bodily attachments, and the functions thereof, my Maria has a mouth which she uses to the full when it comes to eating and speaking. It has never suffered from neglect in either, and over the years she has developed considerable expertise in doing both at the same time. However, in her enthusiasm and excitement this morning, the usual rhythmic flow of the chew, speak and swallow functions became a little uncoordinated and confused, which resulted in small particles of food making their escape – presumably relieved that they would not become part of her digestive tract – to be casually scooped up once more, never to be seen again. Her beautifully expressive eyes reflected the inner truth of her intense feelings. They shone with the light of joyous recollection as she excitedly relived her experiences with us, and both Lenka and I vicariously shared in her intensely satisfying visions of expectation and joy. It was a wonderfully satisfying way to start a new day.

A little later, I opened my mail to find the usual assortment of junk, from advertising crap to final demands. One envelope intrigued me however. It bore half a 2nd class stamp which was stuck on an envelope that had been clearly used before. My name and address had been written on a small square of white paper that had been stuck over the former recipient's details. The envelope was now stuck down with a small length of *sticky-back plastic,* as the presenters of *Blue Peter* would say when referring to S*ellotape.* It all appeared quite strange until I realised that it had come from Scotland and was bearing what looked like an Inverness postmark.

Actually, I really do deplore jokes which suggest that the Scots are miserly skinflints and don't believe for one minute the story that the Grand Canyon was started by an itinerant Glaswegian who had lost a penny in a puddle. I think that the Scottish nation have quite undeservedly borne the brunt of this kind of ridicule for far too long. Apart from *Scotch Andy,* I met another one once, and following the crash didn't suffer from any ill effects whatsoever. It wasn't even his fault since he had the right of way. Unfortunately, the other bloke had the lorry. We sought solace at a local hostelry, and not wishing to appear overly critical, I did notice that he was first out of the cab and the last to the bar. But fair dos though, he did buy a round of pork scratchings. Actually, at the end of the evening I came to the reasoned conclusion that this particular Scot was tighter than a Baptist minister's wife's girdle, at a free all-you-can-eat pancake breakfast!

I examined the envelope critically, and cautiously sniffing it caught the unmistakable aroma of porridge made with skimmed milk, cooked in a brass pot over a peat fire. There was also a subtle hint of woodbines. On opening it, I found the following disturbing message written on what appeared to be an old sweet bag wrapper:

A WEE FEW POONDS WILL BE EXPECTED FER THE RETURN OF YER WEE   DOG DE-TAILS TA FOLLA. NAY COPS OR IT'S A DOOM FA THE POOOCH.

Each letter had been painstakingly cut from what looked like newspapers, and were of various sizes, indicating that the tight-fisted *fatherless-person* responsible had at least bought more than that Scottish newspaper of note: *The Daily Record,* although some of the letters appeared to be rather large for a tabloid. A children's alphabet reader seemed to be more likely. I telephoned Basil immediately with the news. He stated that he'd like to see me this Saturday to run over the theft case in preparation for Monday's appearance at court and that I should bring the letter with me. Although I am not a lover of blackmail, the one positive feature of all of this is that clearly my little Spike is still alive. The despicable *pud-wapper* that has my little boy, would not be trying to extort money from me if this was not the case. Here's hoping.

Later, I received a telephone call from a TV company spokesman asking if arrangements could be made in relation to a convenient date for me to attend the studio for a camera shoot. This is in connection with the prize nonsense, which I had sincerely hoped would simply go away. I am intrinsically a very shy and retiring person and have shunned the limelight all of my life, even refusing a triple gold star for my performance as King Herod in the celebrated play, *A Boy Called Jesus,* performed by the teacher and boys of class 3D Henry Fawcett Junior School in the winter of 1957. But as far as the TV shoot was concerned, I settled for being collected on Monday 20th February at 09:30 sharp. To avoid any unnecessary fuss along the Kilburn High Road, I suggested that the driver of the company limousine should pick me up from within the flats, parking the vehicle outside the estate office (as discreetly as possible). At the studio, a private room was to be provided (preferably with three stars on the door) with suitable mirrors and make-up, together with an en-suite bathroom, a power shower and fresh towels. My additional requirements being a dedicated signed photograph of Radio 2's popular disc jockey Ken Bruce, a full English lunch, three tickets to see the award-winning theatre production of *The Wizard of Oz* and a one-off attendance payment of £150, together with a refund of any out-of-pocket expenses incurred. All was agreed upon.

Later back at The Magpie, Ted was very excited about my forthcoming fifteen minutes of fame, and discussed the possibility of him and me forming an alliance. Dave thought that I should have asked for a great deal more from the television people, like having dinner with Fiona Bruce and a couple of free audience tickets for *The Great British Breakfast Fry off* (tasting section).

Whispering Jim was fighting with his own personal demons at his table by the jukebox, as usual, and I caught what sounded like, 'Dere's none ta keep the puddin warm?' But the good news is that there was nothing sinister about *Wino Lucy's* disappearance. She has now moved to Wales having fallen for a perfume salesman from Pontypridd, who allegedly could sell deodorant to the Venus De Milo. It seems that her days of living the life of a dazzling urbanite are over. Her future life will now be spent in the land of song, castles and very nervous looking sheep, being far happier riding her Honda round the Rhondda, than legging it around the individual tomfoolery and collective arseholery of Kilburn.

Lenny is due to attend another medical interrogation at the DHSS on Tuesday morning next week and has asked me to accompany him to provide a little moral support. Having heard so much about his *well-nourished, dark-complexioned, fatherless female inquisitor* in the past, I felt that it would be very nice to meet her in the flesh as it were. It is not very often that one has the opportunity to meet such a dedicated indefatigable defender of public funds, particularly one that has retained her sanity. She has been Lenny's trainee-nemesis for years, poor thing. I am sure that she can still remember that fateful day back in 2003 when he first darkened her linoleum, and while she has relentlessly tried to eradicate the memory from her mind, she still cannot forget the first time that she laid eyes on him. But like the proverbial dirty puddle, Lenny was always destined to be there to mess up her white plimsolls.

Goodnight, my dear.

P xx

10th February 2012

Good morning, Ginny.

It has been another eventful week, with frustration and anger competing against happiness and peace. My karmic fiddler's elbow has been in limbo and frankly is neither one thing nor the other.

At 07:12 this morning, while I was reading a very interesting article on pigeon husbandry, my bedside lamp blew up, scattering fine shards of glass all over my duvet and carpet. Could it get any worse, I wondered? Frankly, I should never test fate in this way since I firmly believe that to do so, is to invite it to quietly put the hammer in the boxing gloves ready for action.

Following our collective morning meals, Maria appeared to be unwell, since she asked if she could use the hoover to vacuum her room. Initially, I was a little reluctant, since the Anthropology Department at the British Museum had shown considerable interest in carrying out an archaeological excavation of it. Foolishly, I eventually succumbed to her wishes since she can be quite persuasive, but after a few minutes of attempting to suck up several layers of sedimentary detritus, she had to sit down for a spell, and just as quickly, my trusty old Hoover gave up the ghost.

Having switched it on again following her short rest, suddenly, with immense dignity and sadness, its motor burnt out, and to a stuttering smoke-clad climatic whine, it sucked its last, never to suck again. And wouldn't you just believe it, the bloody parts and labour guarantee ran out last Friday.

The morning and early afternoon were very entertaining however, and I was in some wonderful company. I arrived at the gym at 10:00 and was initially greeted by Danielle and Beth. Again, the reception area had a carnival flavour with bunting and streamers hanging all over the place. I had agreed to be one of the judges in the ladies under-21 gymnastic final, and I met the other three judges a little later.

I have always enjoyed physical exercise and was an all-London swimming champion in my youth, winning many cups and prizes. I was in our local swimming baths whenever possible, although such simple pleasures resulted in the spread of athlete's foot, unsightly painful verrucae and later, a subsequent abhorrence of soggy towels and damp socks, as well as communal showers, which I would never use. I would wait until I had returned home, when I would have a wash down at the sink, which wasn't ideal, but at least it prevented the unwelcome attention of predatory eyes, although I still had to protect myself from the inquisitive glances of my infant sisters, who were always vying for a quick flash of my willy. Subsequently I was to develop an allergic skin reaction to carbolic soap, scouring pads and Vim. I sadly had to give up swimming altogether as a result. But I digress!

103

It was a splendid morning, and I was more than simply impressed with the high level of gymnastic achievement displayed by the eighteen contestants. The competition was won by a brilliant young gymnast from Maida Vale, who was awarded a winner's medal by our own Olympic star, Jessica Frettle, who was looking absolutely marvellous following her sex change adjustments. It seems that she wants to be the first person in Olympic history to win a gold medal as both a woman and a man? I have to admire such a dream, but to go through all of that physical pain and suffering, not to mention having your bits messed about with, just so that you can have your name in the *Guinness Book of Records,* tends to induce a comment like *sphericals* to that, for a game of soldiers!

The local press were again in attendance and a number of pictures were taken of the assemblage. Both Ted and Lenny managed to get their faces in on the act, and I had to explain to the organisers that they were simply innocent bystanders. Actually, neither is what you could call photogenic. Prehistoric might be more descriptive!

On one occasion at The Magpie, Ted showed the lads an old black and white photograph of him as a boy. 'This picture,' he commented, 'doesn't really do me justice.' The *Voice* looked at it and said, 'It's not justice you want mate, it is mercy!'

On bidding farewell to Beth, she gave me a wonderful hug and stated that she may have more of these judging jobs available, and would I be interested in joining a select band of like-minded individuals that she laughingly referred to as *The Old Incorruptibles* on a paid basis? Naturally I would be happy to get involved, at least until my hernia had been dealt with and I could once again climb up onto the cross-trainer with confidence. We exchanged phone numbers and email addresses, and she stated that she'd be in touch to arrange a meeting with the two other people involved over the next couple of weeks.

Danielle was her usual exuberantly affectionate self. Her sense of fun is infectious, although she appeared to be a little wary of my two companions, and when they joined us, her quiet composure changed to fully charged street-cred mode. However, in fairness, neither of them would cause her any real trouble, since at heart they are both like an evening draught of milk laced with cognac: quite harmless, particularly when taken in small doses.

A little later, Ted, Lenny and I took a walk down to the Goose for a few well-needed libations with Lenny (using his crutches convincingly). The place was fuller than a seaside public urinal on a Bank Holiday. But then it is Friday, which was always considered the luckiest day of the week to the Norseman when weddings took place. Perhaps getting married in those days was important. It's a wonder that any of them had time to go a-courting let alone getting married, what with all of the raping and pillaging that they were allegedly responsible for.

At the Goose, an unmistakable change takes place in the demeanour of the locals. Gone are the normal lugubrious, mournful features that accompany the visitors to this portal of infamy. In exchange, one can perceive a tangible sense of elation too profound for words, and all because today marks the anniversary of their former paydays.

Most of the regulars in this pub haven't received gainful remuneration since Emmeline Pankhurst was given the vote, and while I really can sympathise with people's terrible pains and troubles, I am dreadfully bored with such ancient delusions whether fuelled by alcohol or not. The simple truth is that for many of us, the regularity of work and Friday paydays are a thing of the past, like the liberty bodice and spam-fritter school dinners. Sadly, we have all had to adjust to the cruelty and unfairness of getting old with all of its inherent problems. I advocate living life to the full in the here and now, since many of us have precious little by way of excitement to look forward to. As one of the lads once commented, 'Just when you're about to score the winning goal, some *fatherless-person* comes along and moves the goal posts!'

Lenny actually bought a round of drinks for the first time this decade which didn't go unnoticed by a group of the lads at the bar, who as a collective, unleashed the genie of incredulity, clapping and whistling loudly, until the mean menacing visage of Thomas Patrick O'Mahoney peered out from around the kitchen door, cleaver in hand. Like a set of collapsing dominoes, a sudden wave of silence swept across the room which stopped at the aurally challenged Buster Crimmond, who was busily chuckling to himself while reading the pub menu. It is quite true that people with impaired hearing do have heightened senses, since I noticed that in the ominous silence that followed, Buster instinctively perceived that *something* was not quite right, and was clearly shaken when he looked up and saw every face in the bar looking at him accusingly. Not wishing to challenge the evident offence that he had caused, he picked up the menu, quietly drank the remainder of his beer, and made his way to the door. On leaving, he nodded politely to the assemblage, replaced the menu on a nearby table and stepped out into the cold and unforgiving anonymity of the Kilburn High Road. Once he had left, the entire inner group became resoundingly animate almost immediately, and the incident completely forgotten within minutes of beer-swilling time.

I really didn't enjoy this blatant example of man's inhumanity to man, and during the build-up of revitalised drunken levity, I slipped out of the back door and caught up with poor old Buster, who was apparently in a bit of a quandary. He had never left a pub earlier than thirty minutes after drinking up time and was clearly a little bewildered. I gave him a fiver and pointed him into the direction of the Bread Bin where I knew he could be assured of another couple of affordable pints with no questions asked.

At The Magpie later, Maria and Gabriel joined us. We spent the remainder of the evening in social conversation. Gabriel gave me a resume of his upbringing and schooling which I found very interesting indeed and my own estimation of his provenance was spot on. I thanked him for nominating me for the prize, but insisted that there had to be other more worthy recipients. But he wouldn't hear of it. He was keen to know where I would donate the prize money, and it seems that the entire Gay Bar had been eavesdropping on our conversation, since the place went deathly quiet waiting for my reply. In the interim, I noticed that Ted had been surreptitiously making his way across the room towards us from Camp Base One (his usual chair by the window) to our vicinity in three nonchalant moves. I told Gabriel that I was thinking about donating the £10,000 to the Police Widows and Orphans Fund and this was met by a discordant foghorn blast of incredulous sighs. Suffice it to say, that within minutes, I was cornered by a group of well-meaning but overwhelming self-opinionated people, all vying for preferment in their suggestions for a suitable charity.

As the evening wore on, I was convinced that my chosen charity was the right one to go for, and this feeling was later supported by the arrival of Father Marcus, who had just escaped from choir practice.

His entrance caused a discreet mass exodus (no biblical pun intended) from the Gay Bar. He had no idea that I was to receive money to be donated elsewhere, but when I told him he quoted scripture, notably 1 Timothy 5:4 which clearly states: '*But if any widow hath children or nephews, let them learn first to shew piety at home.*' This was apparently written by St Paul to a bloke called Timothy, (the Bible doesn't give his full moniker) between the years of AD 62–69. Although it is a little sexist in that the piety mentioned does not seem to include the widow's nieces, it clearly advocates a universal truism that *charity begins at home!* Having made up my mind and being faced with either divine intervention or a collective smack in the gob, I felt like a blindfold camel in a chandelier shop and now simply couldn't back out.

I am pleased to report that I was not physically assaulted in any way, and the rest of the evening was spent in celebration, and in remembrance of those less fortunate.

Goodnight, Ginny.

P xx

11th February 2012

Good morning, Ginny.

As you are perhaps aware, I usually write these emails to you in retrospect, and sometimes very late at night. This one is no exception to that rule, and as is often the case, having had a couple of medicinal libations, I often have to really seriously concentrate to faithfully recollect the day's events. I suppose it's what you might call my daily exercise in short-term memory recall, which can't be a bad thing for a man of my age. The term *senior moment* seems to have initially appeared on your side of the pond in the mid-nineties, but it has now globally fallen into general use to describe any absentminded event irrespective of age.

When I had first left school at the tender age of fifteen, my father would get me up with him for work every morning. His day's labour started at 07:00 whereas mine was an hour later. Nevertheless, we were both up at a time which then, as now, I have always considered to be *the middle of the night.* On one such early morning, I collected an unopened bottle of milk from the fridge for my tea and the old man's coffee. Having shaken it (there was cream at the top of the milk in those days), I proceeded to put the top on the table, and to chuck the milk bottle into the bin. The milk went everywhere, and Pater's responsive expletives were less than charming!

Actually, my old pal *Bucko* related a tale which highlights the bitter-sweet comic aspects of absentmindedness recently, having moved into a two-storey flat off the High Road. On the particular occasion mentioned, having found himself on the landing between floors, he suddenly realised that he couldn't remember how he'd got there and more importantly was unsure whether he was formerly on his way up, or on his way down. Sadly, however, I do believe that his apparent forgetfulness is a little more serious than it seems, bless his little fluffy slippers!

My day started at 06:30 when my bedside table alarm awoke me to find Maria fast asleep in my armchair wrapped in her duvet. I am almost sure that I didn't invite her to do so last night, and I certainly was not aware of her entering my bedroom. In the haze of early morning uncertainty, I tried to piece together my actions upon arriving home from the pub. All seemed to be as per normal as far as my mental recollections was concerned, and I didn't do anything out of the ordinary before bed.

Having silently got up, I donned my silk dressing gown and crept out of the room. I made her a cup of coffee and when I returned, she was awake and apparently quite embarrassed. She was very open about it and stated that when she had things on her mind, she would sometimes sleepwalk. Naturally I made light of the situation and stated that finding her wrapped in a duvet was far preferable than to wake up and find Ted or Lenny playing marbles on my bedroom carpet!

I have to comment that since she has been with Gabriel, I have noticed many changes in her, not least her quiet moods. There have also been times when she has been off her food, which for her hitherto would have been quite unthinkable. But in the quiet of the morning, as we mutually sipped our coffee, the sense of peace and joy that oozed from her every pore infected the very air that I breathed, and the unmistakable feeling of her exultant happiness was almost tangible. Such is love. Needless to say, once she had showered, she didn't need any persuading to partake in a little culinary sustenance and flattened a cooked breakfast of epic proportions. But this morning there was a very evident sense of determination in her demolition of it and, unusually, not a word passed her lips.

On nearing her breakfast completion, she commented, 'Gabriel said that I mustn't talk and eat at the same time,' and having finally finished mopping up the baked bean and tomato juice residue with her remaining soggy slice of bread, she emitted a belch which resounded with forceful vibrations like the inside of a huge defective woofer, and having perfunctorily excused herself with no real apparent remorse or care, stated authoritatively, 'It interrupts with the seminal fluids!'

I was at the office of Basil Lang at 10:10 where I met his *Lady Dick* (which sounds like something that one would find in a Soho sex shop). She assertively introduced herself as Tina Lipseed, who despite her confident manner, was a tiny delicately built young lady in her twenties. She had close-cropped black hair and hawkish features, and was dressed in what looked like a body-hugging all-in-one leotard of the type worn by circus acrobats. There was also a faint aroma of saddle soap and leather about her. She remained quiet and motionless throughout my meeting with Basil, which after the usual pleasantries, moved on to the more serious aspects of our meeting.

His interest and concern in relation to my impending visit to Westminster Magistrates Court on Monday were glossed over in a somewhat cursory way which had it been anybody else may have given me cause for concern, but his confidence has a habit of allaying my fears or anxiety. From the start, he has displayed a convincing ease of manner and charismatic charm, and I am completely assured in relation to his expertise and capabilities.

Enquiries and certain headway have been made in relation to the other forthcoming case, but he didn't want to over tax my mind, believing that one step at a time was important. Once the 'nonsense' of the theft charge had been eradicated, then in due course those other issues could be discussed and likewise eradicated. He would have definitely made the ideal aircraft steward. You know the kind of thing, looking out of the aircraft's window you notice that the wing has just sheared off, there is a pungent smell of oil, and flames are licking up the fuselage. Out of nowhere he appears looking radiant and confident. 'You are perfectly safe,' he asserts. 'Would you like tea, coffee or a cognac?'

Having handed Basil the blackmail letter, he commented that Tina had been on Spike's case and trail since he had been informed of the dog's theft by Alfie, a couple of days after the incident. Her progress was nothing short of miraculous.

It appears that my dear little lad is now being used as a stud in a small dog sanctuary in Sussex. Enquiries had been made at the farm, and it is thought that the owners have hired Spike's services in good faith, believing from counterfeit documentation that he was a direct descendant of the immortal *Trump,* the foundation animal that the Rev Russell (1795–1883) began with, in his quest to breed a strain of dynamic working terrier, which culminated in the breed of the *Jack Russell* that we are all so familiar with today.

A quite clever scam, one would argue. Tina convinced me that he was being looked after very well and seemed to be enjoying his little trip away (and one doesn't need to be told why). It seems that he will be collected within a few weeks by the kidnapper/s and in the meantime that I should not worry about his safety. Basil is in daily contact with his carers at the stud, and while the owners did not wish to carry on with the scam as it were, Basil is of the opinion that at the very least they should make a few pounds selling Spike's pups in the interim. Naturally the person/s involved will be arrested when they come to collect him. He insisted that this information was strictly confidential and that this included *all* friends and relatives.

'But what of this ransom note?' I asked. He picked it up from his desk and took it into his back office and was gone for around fifteen minutes. In the interim, I felt a little embarrassed being left with Tina, who simply looked out of the window with mild indifference. I couldn't help casting furtive glances in her direction, although she acted as if I were simply not there.

Finally she said, 'Please don't feel embarrassed. I am a practising Ninja.'

'Oh I am so sorry to hear that Tina, I hope it isn't too painful.' I replied sympathetically. She smiled at me wryly, but before she could reply Basil returned.

Having examined the letter and contents thoroughly, Basil was of the opinion that this was the work of *an opportunist scallywag* hoping to make a few bob out of the enterprise. He suggested that it could be the work of any one of my own acquaintances since contrary to my own observations, I had missed the obvious. His trained analytical prowess put my own feeble attempts to shame, and I was very disappointed in missing so much. He came to the conclusion that the letter was posted in London and more particularly Ladbroke Grove. Much of the wording had come from a DHSS flyer entitled *Getting back into work,* the rest from a government pamphlet called *Get what you deserve* for people contemplating levels of financial reparation following industrial injury or litigation in actions of negligence. Additionally, the attempts to add a little authentic Scottish fragrance to the envelope and letter were, as he stated, 'a little puerile' and had failed to mask the unmistakable grease and odour of Brylcreem, a small particle from a number 16 bus ticket and what appeared to be part of a toenail clipping, which he intends having forensically tested for DNA.

On my way home to Maida Vale, I decided that I needed a little mental diversion, and fighting off my terrible feelings of claustrophobia, I continued past my stop to Baker Street and changed onto the Jubilee line, catching another train to London Bridge. In former times when I have needed a little peace, I have always found the river walks restorative and wholly therapeutic. I had to smile to myself as I sauntered passed Southwark Cathedral on my way to the South Bank, when I remembered an anecdote of Dave's relating to an earlier visit to his local surgery, when during his medical examination the doctor asked him if he'd every had any trouble passing water. 'Never!' he replied, 'I used to walk over London Bridge every day on my way to work!'

I visited an 'Elder's' pub along the embankment opposite Sir Christopher Wren's monumental masterpiece, St Paul's Cathedral, and enjoyed a pint of their scrummy *Winter Brew,* which tasted like a rich mulled wine. It certainly had a very warming effect.

Looking at Wren's *piece de resistance* a mere stone's throw away across the river, I remembered my two lifelong ambitions: the first, to climb to the very pinnacle of this magnificent structure, and the other, to make wild passionate love to Sophia Loren. It is a wonderful achievement to attain one's ambitions in life, but as I sipped my delicious glass of traditional ale, I reasoned that, one out of two can't be bad, and since I wasn't feeling very energetic anyway, the St Paul's climb would have to wait.

I had a lot to ponder over during the afternoon and the warm and steamy inside environment of the pub was ideal for the purpose. It reminded me of a Georgian opium den. In truth, years ago this part of London was notorious for poverty and licensed brothels called *stews.* The word originally meant a fishpond, then later a public bath house, and eventually a brothel. As I have mentioned before, I seem to think better in steamy environments, and with no saunas nearby, the inside of this alcoholic hostelry provided a superb alternative.

I came to the somewhat obvious conclusion that if one or more of my acquaintances were responsible for the theft of Spike with all of its resultant worry and misery, they could not in my wildest dreams be elevated to the designation of friends, and indeed were clearly mortal enemies.

On the way back to Kilburn, a sudden thought passed through my mind. Why on earth I was thinking about a raspberry I couldn't say, but as I mused upon this friendly little berry, I considered how hard it works during its formative years and once ripe, comes to town, and goes through many adventures just to be able to get a couple of its seeds stuck behind your dentures. Sadly, it would appear that I have one or more such undesirable seed/s close to home and the uncomfortable irritant/s needs to be found and completely prised out of my life.

Goodnight love.
P xx

12th February 2012

Good morning, my dear.

Compton and his group of itinerant ruffians, loosely referred to as *Bell-ringers,* were giving it some hammer at 07:30 this morning, and it is clear that this quite unnecessary presentation is directed predominately at giving the attendees of the 10:30 performance (High Mass) a wake-up-call, allowing them to have a bit of a lie-in. The 08:00 (Low Mass) sitting, is a watered-down version, aimed at the more conservative-minded communicants, who like to experience the puritan austerity of God without the *bells and smells.* However, many of the would-be early morning worshippers had in fact just been released from their all-night pub lock-ins or chucked out of seedy West End clubs.

The quiet, nut-tightening chill and dimly lit smoke-free environment has been found to be an eminently favourable place to assist in the eradication of a hangover, as well as affording a little time for souls in torment (not seeking God's forgiveness for past sins) but to work out a plausible excuse for their non-arrival home after pub chucking-out time, nine hours earlier.

But not wishing to appear hopelessly sceptical, there are those genuinely honest and spiritually devoted people out there, who do not wish to be associated with the poseurs and 'must be seen crowd' acting piously before an audience of peers at the 10:30 matinee. Clearly these simple unassuming individuals prefer to conduct their own Sunday worship in quiet anonymity, unseen by none, apart from the subject of their respect and adoration. I send them all my sincere best wishes.

Having finished my morning ablutions, I noticed that both of my girls were out, since both of their bedroom doors were ajar which meant that they were not in residence.

It was a very cold morning indeed and I found it necessary to turn up the heating. I really wasn't in the mood for eating, but I felt compelled to get out of the flat. Having finished a cup of coffee, I dressed warmly and *made for the hills,* as *Whispering Jim* would have said and to one notable hill in particular.

At 11:15, having caught a bus to Camden, I walked to Primrose Hill, a place where on the evening of Guy Fawkes Night last year, Lenka and I spent a very memorable time. At the top of its 213 feet above sea level mound, panoramic views of London can be seen, and that night I remember we stood in awe watching the numerous displays of spectacular fireworks across the city below us. We finished off in a local pub sipping mulled wine.

This morning the area was relatively quiet, with the usual dog walkers and joggers animating the pastoral scene. I sat on a bench at the top of the hill enjoying the peace and seclusion, when from behind me I heard a faint high-pitched mewing sound. I located the source and found a very young kitten under a nearby bush. I picked it up gently and searched the undergrowth for mum or siblings but there were none to be found. I initially thought of taking it to the local police station, but then pictured the less than pleasing unwelcoming physiognomy of the duty desk sergeant and changed my mind. I tucked him or indeed her (I'm not an expert at sexing kittens) into the top of my duffle coat and decided to take my little orphan home.

On the way back, I called into a pet shop in the Kilburn High Road and bought all manner of feline requisite, from kitten food to a litter tray. It was as much as I could carry at once, and oh how I wished that I had another set of hands. And would you believe it, as if by magic my little female friend suffering from 'Ninja' appeared before me with a large bag of cat litter. 'I think you will need this as well as the tray,' she said authoritatively.

She accompanied me on my walk back to the flat and on the way, light rain began to fall. She was very quiet and even her footfalls were silent. I couldn't resist an occasional furtive glance at this very 'odd' young woman, who even when walking slightly in front of me appeared to sense my every thought.

'It's alright, Paul,' she said reassuringly. 'I understand your reserve and curiosity, it is only to be expected,' she continued, stopping and turning to face me. Her diminutive size suddenly seemed to expand in front of me, her eyes appeared to darken, and her raven black close-cropped hair glistened in the rain like a nose hair after a sneeze. But then, a big black cloud had earlier quite suddenly appeared, and visibility wasn't very good.

Before I had time to answer, she turned and ran off in the direction of the flat at frankly a quite ridiculously fast speed and her feet didn't actually appear to be hitting the paving slabs – I had never seen anything quite like it before. (But then, I do believe that I am in need of new spectacles.)When I arrived home, I realised that I had left my keys at home this morning and rang the outside buzzer to the flat. Fortunately, Maria was at home and let me in. At the top of the stairs, outside of my front door, stood the large packet of cat litter which had obviously been left there by Tina. How on earth she had managed to gain access into the block, however, was a complete mystery.

Maria welcomed me at the door, in her usual inimitable way, kissing me on both cheeks.

'Careful,' I said as I opened the top of my duffle coat, lifting out my little orphan, which I gently placed into her eager hands. She positively screamed with delight when she saw it, and bombarded me with questions which took some considerable time to answer. Lifting it up and examining its undercarriage she said, 'It's a girl!' which she followed up with a ticker-tape narrative of observation and questions of the 'can I look after her – she can sleep in my room – I shall take care of her – we must get her checked with the doctor – she's only about a week or two old – she needs milk' type of thing.

Before the evening was out, our newly christened *'Jimena Isabell, Sophia Hernandez'* had been washed, given a few drops of sweetened sterilised milk, administered through the little finger of one of my new marigold gloves with a hole at the end, and was happily resting in a cardboard shoebox bed prepared by Maria's loving hands, which she had stuffed to the brim with a sizeable quantity of my rolled-up socks. As they say, *necessity is indeed the mother of invention.*

I have to say that I was most impressed with Maria's maternal instincts and considerable knowledge in the needs of cats, although she later confided that her father, having a tomato farm in Spain, had allowed her plenty of time to become familiar with all kinds of animals and had nurtured a considerable number of different types, from chickens to donkeys. It quickly became apparent that she was well versed in the infantile needs and nurture of them all, which was very fortunate indeed since I am to moggies, what Richard Branson is to face cream.

We all spent a quiet evening, and as I curled up under my duvet, I drifted off to the sound of Maria singing what sounded like a Spanish lullaby.

Goodnight, Gin.

P xx

13th February 2012

Good morning, sugarplum.

Maria's howls gave me a very rude awakening at 06:10 this morning, and I jumped out of bed to find out what was wrong, a baseball bat in hand. It appears that during the night our sweet little orphan had left a little offering on the top of Maria's mother of pearl hairbrush. Indecipherable Spanish expletives followed and I am sure that given Spike's knowledge of the language, had he been nearby, he would have run for cover.

After a refreshing shower and a light breakfast, I dressed myself in one of my former work suits and was more than pleased to find that it still fitted me perfectly. I put on a nice blue shirt with a matching tie and even if I do say so myself, I looked pretty dangerous. Before I left home, I asked Maria if she would organise her own breakfast and she was happy to do so. I gave her a cuddle and checked in on our little orphan, who was snuggled up in her little shoebox fast asleep.

Westminster Magistrates Court is located at 70 Horseferry Road, and, what with the usual chaotic Monday morning vehicular and pedestrian mayhem, is about as easy to get to as the *limited free-booze* area at a Jewish bar mitzvah. Having checked on all possible transport routes, I figured that I'd catch a 16 bus to Victoria, make *camp-base one* along Rochester Row and hike the rest of the way across country.

I arrived at this rather unremarkably bland and uninteresting, less than inspiring building, at 09:20. The foyer on the ground floor was busier than an ant at a family reunion party and the discordant noise was not only unsettling, but pre-eminently annoying. As you know, I hate crowds and enclosed places, which despite the counselling sessions even when I think about them now, still brings me out in a profoundly annoying sweating bout. As you are aware, I start to feel giddy and claustrophobic even opening a tin of sardines. But I manfully fought my way through the miscellaneous rabble, searching for a familiar face and eventually located Basil (which was the nearest best thing) sitting on a bench outside of courtroom three.

On the way through, I was like an eavesdropping muppet and caught a snippet of a conversation between a rather official-looking bloke in a uniform, who was busy looking down at a clipboard, and a real tasty looking likely lad.

'What did you say your name was again?' he asked, running a pencil down his list.

'Tommy Shannon from Bow,' he replied, placing a little finger in his right ear, which he proceeded to shake with enough agitated force to loosen the plaster on the walls, let alone any stubborn ear wax.

'Well, are you the victim, witness or defendant?'

'No sorry mate. See, I'm the one what done it. I'm giving me self up, like!'

My normal happy-go-lucky personality was slowly being eradicated as the minutes ticked by. It was a scene of utter chaos which would have made Dante's journey through hell seem like a light-hearted weekend *jolly boys* outing down to Margate.

On our meeting, Basil shook my hand somewhat limply with a right hand which felt like warm laundry and invited me to sit next to him. He seemed very relaxed, composed and confident, which contrasted strongly with my agitated form and restless spirit.

'Don't worry, Paul,' he said reassuringly, 'it will soon be all over.'

'You sound like the executioner, Basil,' I replied absentmindedly.

Following a few meaningless pleasantries, he then went on to explain in detail the court procedure and what I should and shouldn't do. When the charge was read to me, I would be asked if I understood, and that I should reply in the affirmative. When asked how I wished to plead, I was to look at the magistrate and reply firmly, 'Not guilty, your worship!' All further questions put to me were to be answered directly back to the magistrate. Finally, I was advised to 'simply be myself' and in so doing, the unmistakable aura of integrity and respectability would be felt across the entire courtroom. I began to mentally relax thereafter.

Not wishing to bore you with the preliminaries love, having pleaded 'not guilty' as directed, DS Blackstock then took centre stage as it were, and gave his evidence which was subsequently cross-examined by my very eloquent lawyer, who initially threw doubt on the validity of the search of my shed, since the warrant clearly applied to my flat only and not any of my outbuildings. This really flustered the old Blackstock feathers and the magistrate made a written note of Basil's remarks, which I felt was a very positive step in the right direction.

To my amazement, Nobby Caxton was then called in to give evidence, and looking round as he entered the court, I noticed that the public gallery was now filled to overflowing. Just about every face, whether friend or acquaintance from Kilburn and environs, was crowded into a space that looked hopelessly small in accommodating them all. I started to feel uneasy and claustrophobic again.

Nobby walked through the courtroom in a less than confident manner, and appeared to be in a very nervous condition. Having been sworn in, Basil questioned him in relation to the owners of the sheds that had been 'allegedly' broken into, and his testimony was very helpful as far as my corner was concerned. He stated that from his 'limited knowledge' (emphasising the point, that the running of the sheds was dealt with by the landlords) it was believed that the owner of shed number 21 had passed away and as far as he was able to ascertain, there were no known relatives. Basil pointed out the fact that the alleged property that had come from shed 21 was in fact therefore ownerless, an observation that had not gone unnoticed by the magistrate, who scribbled something down on his pad.

Basil then went on to ask Nobby about the owner of shed 23 and, evidently feeling a little more confident, he stated that he believed that this shed was hired to 'Alexander Barrington Scott', who lived in flat number 96. Having no more questions for the witness, he was graciously thanked for his testimony by the magistrate and asked to stand down. Nobby looked quite pleased with himself as he passed me, and finding an empty seat at the back of the room he sat down, emitting what sounded like a very audible sigh of relief.

Alexander Barrington Scott, a middle-aged, very respectable-looking individual, wearing a tweed jacket, grey flannels and an open-necked neatly ironed white shirt and blue cravat, was then called. He had a very authoritative air, and as I was to find out later, was clearly used to public speaking. After the usual preliminaries were concluded, he was addressed by DS Blackstock.

'Mr Scott, can you tell the court where you reside.'

'Yes, your worship,' he replied, nodding respectfully at the magistrate. 'I live at 96 Susan Atkins Court in Maida Vale.'

'Are you the owner of shed number 23 in the inner courtyard of this estate?'

'Well not exactly your worship, we don't actually own the sheds, we simply hire them from our landlords. I pay thirty-one pounds a year rental.'

'Alright, I'll re-phrase that question. Do you hire shed number 23?'

'Yes.'

'A few weeks ago, was this shed broken into and were items of your property removed from it?' asked the detective, seemingly enjoying this part of the proceedings.

'Well in truth, I can say quite categorically that this shed was broken into, but it wasn't actually my property that was taken, your worship.'

'I don't understand,' said the magistrate, holding aloft an official-looking A4 sheet of paper. 'This is the statement you made to the police where you identified items of property that you said were yours which had come from your shed.'

'Well I panicked you see, sir. When DS Blackstock invited me to the station to identify property which was apparently taken out of the two sheds, I simply pointed to a few of the more innocuous-looking items, stating that they were mine.'

'So let me get this straight, Mr Scott,' said the magistrate. 'Are you now saying that no items of your own personal property were taken from shed number 23?'

'That is correct, your worship.'

'You do realise, Mr Scott, that having signed a sworn statement to the police, which you now retract, could put you in a very difficult position? Perjury is a very serious matter.'

'Sir, I am fully aware that I have been very foolish, and I realise now that trying to make money from subletting my shed was a stupid thing to do. I thought the bloke was a reasonable sort, but found out just recently that he is a crook.'

'So where may I ask is the owner of the property that was *resting in your shed*?'

'From what I understand, your worship, he is serving a five-year prison sentence for embezzlement, theft and handling stolen goods.'

An audible murmur of disbelief and frustration echoed around the room, and DS Blackstock cupped his face in his hands, and slowly shook his head from side to side.

The magistrate restored order by banging his gavel on his desk several times, and before anything further took place he declared, 'I have heard enough. Case dismissed!'

A very short period of silence followed, which preceded a veritable cacophony of jubilant joyful screams and shouts, occasioning a very flustered court usher to call for assistance. Shortly after, a number of authorised thugs dressed in security uniforms, physically assisted in the removal of the unruly crowd from the public gallery. Lenny resisted, and having been shaken about like a sprinter's dick, was unceremoniously dumped out into a very startled crowd in the foyer, and needed to sit down for a while to catch his breath. (This was undoubtedly the hardest work that he'd done in years.) A little later he got one of the lads to retrieve his walking stick, which had been recklessly thrown out after him, and found that in the confusion, it had lost its little rubber end piece.

Thereafter, the rest of the afternoon and evening was a booze-fest to end them all. On the way back to Kilburn, we called into numerous pubs and a number of our party, known as mere acquaintances or hangers on, were arrested along the way. Happily, the people that really mattered safely made it back to the hallowed portals of The Magpie unscathed.

In our escape from the courthouse, Basil and I had become separated, and I really had so much to say to him. He has been an absolute star throughout all of this nonsense, and I wanted to thank him, but simple words of appreciation seemed somehow inadequate. At The Magpie, I tried to contact him on his mobile, but it went straight into voicemail. I left him a short message of thanks, nevertheless, and stated that I would contact him at his office anon.

At around 21:35, Nobby Caxton suddenly arrived and smiled at me with a level of facial affection that disturbed me a great deal. He then proceeded to throw his arms around me warmly like a long-lost relative. He has never been what one might call tactile in his life, even to the extent of not ever wanting to put on gloves. I felt somewhat confused to say the least.

'I am so pleased that it has all worked out for you, Paul,' he said, occasioning a very uncomfortable feeling in my bowels which inexplicably suddenly felt as loose as a heron's leggings. He seemed a little unsteady on his feet, and I caught the unmistakable whiff of marijuana from his clothing. This was completely out of character for a man who has led such an upright and respectable life. Forcing back an urgent visit to the loo, I helped him out of the door.

'Leave him, mate,' Ted said. 'I'll take him home. Besides, your two girls are in the other bar waiting for you.'

I thanked him for his kindness and dashed into the loo to relieve myself and a little later entering the posh bar, I found my Lenka and Maria, looking absolutely stunning in what appeared to be wonderful party frocks. They were both looking quite beautiful.

Together with a few other close friends and Uncle Chickle Chuckle (whom I now know is called Vlado), we welcomed in a new day, laughing and crying as the normal inhibitory pathways associated with decorum and restraint were progressively relaxed with each additional libation, and the warmth and friendship of my loved ones, temporarily wiped my unhappy slate clean.

Goodnight, Ginny.

P xx

14th February 2012

Good morning, Ginny.

What a night! I cannot remember a time when I have laughed so much. When I awoke this morning at 06:30, my throat and chest were quite sore. As I lay there in the darkness, I remembered a rather funny incident that happened last night with Dave, who having been challenged by Ted to identify three collective nouns, replied 'fly paper, wastepaper basket, and vacuum cleaner!' It brought about another spell of painful chuckling. Actually, Dave is considerably more intelligent than most people would give him credit, and Ted as a result of his misjudgement, not only had to suffer a bout of derision from the laughing pub attendees, but additionally had to reluctantly part with a fiver as well (which is a very rare occurrence).

Outside in the hall I heard a strange scratching sound and as I slowly opened the door a small black blur shot passed me. I switched on my bedroom light to find Jimena Isabella Sophia Hernandez looking down at me suspiciously from the top of my curtains which in her frenzied excitement, she had scaled faster than lightning through a wet gum tree, as *Dunny Greg* would have said. The trouble now, however, was that having got up there, she was a little reluctant at coming down again. A little later, Maria arrived, uttering indecipherable Spanish expletives, and then proceeded to delicately unpick her little claws from their tenacious grip on the curtains, and displaying considerable patience, she finally prised our little ruffian off.

Later in the morning, I met Lenny outside of The Magpie as arranged to accompany him on his yearly assessment at the local offices of the DHSS. He was looking like a tramp. His clothes were in a disgusting state, his hair unkempt, and his designer stubble looked more like a porcupine's bum, added to which, he was sporting thick-rimmed sunglasses, which, given the dreadful weather conditions, were more suited for the beachfront at St Tropez than the Kilburn High Road.

'I like your optimism, Lenny,' I said, pointing to the glasses.

'No nothing like that,' he replied. 'It's just another one of me medical problems,' he replied, hobbling away and leaning heavily on his newly acquired walking stick.

'Oh indeed! Pray, do enlighten me,' I said.

'Extreme sensitivity to light,' he said proudly.

'You can save all of that old tosh for the establishment, Lenny, you are talking to me now old son, and I have known you for too long to be fooled by you!'

He lowered his glasses and peered at me accusingly. 'What on earth do you mean?' he replied, smiling wryly. 'I am not a well man, Paul, and haven't been for years!'

We arrived at the offices of the DHSS punctually for our 10:30 appointment, and having identified himself to the receptionist at the front desk, we were ushered into a small waiting area.

Shortly after, a small bald-headed man wearing a dark suit and what looked like an M&S cotton tie from their *Man Time* range appeared, holding a great ample file in one hand and a mug of tea in the other. 'I am Malcolm Frobisher, claims manager and I take it, that you are Leonard Maynard Ficks? I have heard a great deal about you, young man!' he said menacingly. Lenny smiled at him, but before he had time to reply, Frobisher said, 'And who is this?' nodding in my direction. Before I could answer, Lenny replied, 'He's my uncle Paul, who insisted on accompanying me here just in case I had a relapse on the way.' 'Oh I see,' replied the less than impressed Malcolm Frobisher. 'Well kindly follow me. Do you think you can make it unaided to the next office? We do have a wheelchair available,' he said, somewhat sarcastically.

Frankly, in the short time that I was in his company, I came to the conclusion that what this jumped-up office boy needed was a good kick in the *sphericals.* I really cannot abide condescending *fatherless-people*, particularly those who believe that their all-powerful superior positions in life gives them the absolute justification and authority to browbeat those that they perceive as lesser mortals. In Frobisher's case, they are folk who sadly have to look to the welfare state for help and succour in times of hardship. From my experience, such *tradesmen-entrances* hide behind the erroneous belief that their unacceptable actions could never result in them being justifiably punished for their less than supportive or disrespectful behaviour to others, which is a common trait of the stereotypical bully.

But then, Mr Frobisher has never met my friend *Ted the Pleb,* and I feel that the man would very definitely benefit from a *charisma-enhancing* meeting with this amazing *life and attitude-altering professional,* and I will be arranging an encounter between them in the very near future.

I am fully aware that Lenny is an absolute scoundrel; but be that as it may, he still has the fundamental human right to be treated with civility and respect, as do the other poor infortunes who sadly have to sit before this excuse for a man, whom I believe would be out of his depth in a car-park puddle.

Frobisher's office was sparsely furnished to say the very least, comprising of a desk, three chairs, a dilapidated filing cabinet and a small seascape print of a young boy trying to eat candy floss in what looked like a hurricane.

'Firstly, I'd like to apologise for the non-appearance of Ms Balalla who sadly has had to deal with a family bereavement,' he said, as we sat in the two vacant chairs available.

'Nothing too serious, I hope,' said Lenny.

Frobisher's eyes suddenly turned quite black, and I sensed that thus far, things were not going too well for my naïve friend. I feel confident however, that being semi-illiterate, Lenny was not being flippant or disrespectful; he simply didn't know what the term *'bereavement'* meant.

Opening the file, Lenny's inquisitor flicked through several pages. It was clear to me that he was obviously aware of every single word of it from beginning to end.

'I don't want to put a too finer point on decorum, Mr Ficks, but firstly may I ask you to remove the sunglasses. Even if we were blessed with a little sunshine outside, in here there isn't very many UV rays being emitted from the fluorescent lighting!'

'I suffer from photo phobia which my doctor tells me is caused by extreme sensitivity to light,' replied Lenny, who took them off anyway, and then proceeded to blink uncontrollably.

Frobisher looked at me appealing. I simply shrugged my shoulders absentmindedly.

Looking through his medical notes and apparently finding no mention of eye problems, Frobisher asked, 'Have your eyes ever been checked, Mr Ficks?' emitting an audible sigh.

'They've never been checked, sir,' replied Lenny, looking at Frobisher appealingly. 'They've always been blue!'

Frobisher slowly repeated, 'They've always been blue!' and put his head down briefly. I thought that I detected a slight tremor of his shoulders.

Returning to Lenny's file, and clearing his throat, Frobisher continued in his inquisition. 'It would appear that over the years you have been subjected to a considerable amount of bad luck, Mr Ficks.'

'Bad luck, Mr Frobisher? I have been a martyr to it. Last year I picked up a four-leaf clover and landed up with poison ivy. You have no idea of the kind of suffering that I've had to contend with. Everything from photo phobia to acute Achilles' heel,' replied Lenny.

'Achilles' Heel is not a medical condition, Mr Ficks; it is a metaphor for a serious weakness, from the myth of Achilles, who was invulnerable everywhere except his heel.'

'Yeah well, I've had that as well,' replied Lenny.'I see that you had an aptitude test last year?'

'Yes, that's right, sir!' Lenny replied excitedly. 'They found that I was best suited for early retirement, and housed, preferably on the ground floor of a warden-assisted establishment.'

'Your medical records make very interesting reading, Mr Ficks. Seemingly your general health is always questionable and the medical profession is completely confounded and not a little confused at your never-ending erratic and confusing symptoms.'

'But then I have hope, Mr Frobisher. Frankly if it was not for hope, my heart would break,' said Lenny, lowering his head slightly and sighing audibly.

'Judging by your previous medical history, you have broken just about everything else Mr Ficks! I have a full medical report regarding your recent accident, and I am very pleased to see that you are walking.'

For some considerable time thereafter, Frobisher scanned page after page of Lenny's file, and a dreadful silence of an ominous kind descended on the proceedings. Finally he looked up and taking a ballpoint pen from his inside pocket, he started to write on the last page of the file. Thereafter he looked up again and with what appeared to be a feigned smile on his face he said, 'After much deliberation on this matter, Mr Ficks, and having taken due consideration of all the facts, I have decided that your benefits are to stop as from Monday the 20th February. My view is as per the old proverb, *A horse that will not carry a saddle must have no oats*!'

Lenny wobbled slightly in his chair. 'But you can't, I mean how will I live?'

Sighing audibly his inquisitor said, 'We have many very severely disabled people in gainful employment, Mr Ficks, many of them being far too proud to claim benefits of any kind. If they can do it, so can you!'

'But I've tried, sir, honestly I have. I've been to loads of interviews, but my previous criminal record, as well as my dreadful medical problems, have always stopped me from being taken on.'

'What I propose is quite simple, Mr Ficks. You are to work here weekly in the DHSS offices for three hours per day. You will report to Ms Balalla who will designate your daily duties. So provided you appear punctually at 09:00 on Monday 20th February and subject to your continued weekday work commitment, your usual benefits will be paid as normal. At least that way you will be contributing to society, albeit in a small way. Now, unless there is anything else, I am a busy man,' he said disinterestedly, and missing his IN and OUT trays, he threw Lenny's file into a third one, which I assumed must be his SHAKE IT ALL ABOUT tray! Lenny attempted to speak, but nothing came out of his mouth.

I assisted my much-shaken friend back out into the usual vehicular and pedestrian chaos of the Kilburn High Road a little later, determined to enlighten Ted on our very unhappy experience.

We slowly walked back towards The Magpie and I tried to make light of the situation by asking him if he'd like to join me in a little breakfast at the café. Having taken off his sunglasses, he silently put them back in their case and on passing a rubbish bin, he discretely dropped them in. Frankly it has been a long time since I have seen *Lenny the Ponce* in such a wretched condition.

As we passed the pub he stopped and looked at its hallowed portal. Tucking his walking stick under his left arm resolutely, he thanked me for my support and encouragement and, hugging me enthusiastically, shook my hand with an amazingly strong grip.

On leaving he remarked, 'You are my hero, see you later mate, I owe you one!' Turning, he marched off like a Guards RSM with a slight limp, whistling the emotive strains of Bette Midler's beautiful song, *Wind beneath my wings*.

I felt quite choked up and not a little emotional, as I walked into an empty Gay Bar taking Vlado completely by surprise. He was engaged in demolishing a rather large steaming bowl of *golabki and rice.*

'You early are my friend?' he said. 'Is there something gone tits up?'

'No, it's just that the papers say that in the UK there are twenty-seven pubs closing every week and I couldn't sleep, I just wanted to make sure that yours was not on the list!' I replied.

A lot of quite unnecessary banter followed, most of it being quite frivolous and amusing which was just what I needed to lighten my load as it were. But even through the laughs, I periodically saw Lenny's formerly ever-optimistic face suffering the realisation of final defeat and my sense of utter futility returned. As Ted succinctly pointed out some time ago, 'He's one of ours, warts and all and personally when one of mine suffers, I suffer too!'

Later in the day, I was to quite literally suffer, as a troublesome back molar that had driven me to extraction, was being tugged and loosened from its fifty-year gummy housing, by that diminutive sadistic former circus star, Derek Lumpington BDS (Calcutta).

The grotesque facial grimaces displayed in his exertion, reminded me of a constipated frog trying to defecate on a water lily. I did not enjoy listening to his taped music of whales calling, and frankly would have preferred the high-pitched sound of a drill engaged in a root canal filling, or someone running a wire brush down a blackboard. His choice of poster wasn't exactly inspiring either. One read 'Be True To Your Teeth or They Will Be False TO YOU!'

After the offending tooth's removal, he asked, 'Do you want to keep it for the tooth fairy, Mr Shaughnessy?' Sadly, I am unable to share with you the choice of my vernacular reply, which clearly suggested a far better place where he could poke it.

Back at home, our newly arrived little feline orphan was running up and down the hall chasing a table tennis ball. Maria was having great fun. She has booked an appointment at a local vet and asked if I could donate £20 to cover costs. She had earlier obtained Lenka's contribution.

During the late evening, as I relaxed in a fragrant bath with Sebastian surfing in the suds, my thoughts turned to my dear old Spike. It suddenly occurred to me that on his return, we might be in for a little trouble when he met Jimena. But she has made herself very much at home, and we all love our little bundle of mischief dearly. We will have to cross that bridge, I suppose, when we come to it.

Having had a nice cognac-laced mug of cocoa before bed, as I was drifting off to sleep, my thoughts turned to my diminutive dentist. He is not really what one could call a midget or a dwarf but he stood a little less than five feet in height. I mused upon the undeniable fact that in the normal course of his transit through this mortal coil that as a matter of expediency, he would likewise seek out friends and acquaintances that were on his own level as it were, and I suspected therefore that his wife or girlfriend would also be of diminutive stature.

I could just imagine a romantic evening in with Derek acting the *Don Juan* attempting to woo his lady. A candlelit dinner for two, gentle romantic strains of Mantovani love songs drifting through the room, and a cool bottle of Sauvignon Blanc resting in an ice-filled bucket.

As the evening nears its close, and following a lustful smooch on the sofa in front of a burning log fire, he looks tenderly into her eyes and, cupping her face in his little hands, gently whispers, 'Darling, shall I run you a nice hot soapy sink?'

Goodnight love.
P xx

15ᵗʰ February 2012

Good morning, Ginny.

I awoke this morning at 06:15 with my pillow covered in dried blood. My mouth, which felt very sore indeed, tasted like I had earlier attended a vampires' convention. My right cheek was rather swollen and looked like it had been slapped with a wet mackerel. My upper lip still felt like it was full of novocaine, and I was dribbling quite a bit. Not a pretty sight! And would you believe it – the tooth fairy hadn't been during the night!

Despite the limited emotional highs and lows of yesterday, I was in a relatively optimistic mood, and pulling my bedroom curtains open, I found that the courtyard below was covered in a white dusting of snow. Maria was absolutely delighted, and like a small child, she ran down the stairs excitedly with the kitten in her arms. Apparently, snow is an infrequent visitor to Maria's part of Spain, and she fully intended making the most of it. She is still so fun-loving and carefree, and there is nothing wrong with that, bless her little wooden maracas.

Needless to say, on their arrival back, my two girls were very cold indeed and in need of warmth and food. I supplied both almost immediately and thereafter they both vanished into Maria's room, where I could hear unfettered laughter (Maria was giggling too!)

Later, my ever-observant Spanish flatmate was the first to notice that there was something wrong. 'Oh dear!' she said, looking at my swollen mouth. 'You poor thing, did you bang your face?' she asked, using her best quivering concerned voice. 'No Maria,' I replied. 'I had a bar of chocolate in my back pocket that I wanted to break up, so on the way back from the pub last night, I chucked myself on to the pavement!' She initially stared at me in utter amazement until she realised that I was teasing her.

'Oh, I now can remember, you went to the dentist yesterday,' she said, putting Jimena down on the kitchen table. 'Do you think she's getting bigger?' she asked.

Jimena tried to escape, and Maria grabbed her tail.

'You should never pull a cat's tail, Maria,' I said.

'I'm only holding it. She's doing the pulling!' she replied. 'What's for breakfast?'

Needless to say that in between gargling with mouthwash (Maria not me – she likes to clear the palate before food) and holding the cat while she got stuck into a sizeable repast (Maria, not me), her eyes glazed over in what I can only describe as a gastronomic haze of ecstasy. I watched in utter amazement at her determination to finish every last morsel. And she always seems to be so genuinely sorry when it is all eaten.

Our newest lodger has settled in very well, although she still hasn't quite found her feet, or more precisely paws. Mind you, she uses her claws like grappling irons as she goes shooting up my curtains whenever the opportunity presents itself. She has not mastered the technique of reversal just yet however, and like the other morning, has to be delicately prised off the curtains like a schoolboy cross-country runner that had inadvertently dashed through a large bramble bush.

I visited the gym at around 14:30. Danielle was her usual radiant self and she smiled at me sweetly as I walked in. Once back into my geriatric poofter get-up, I thought that I'd simply work on my upper body, and completed a few gentle bench-press reps and a number of eyebrow raises, both of which you do lying down. These types of exercises do not involve the stomach in general, thus avoiding any further potential strain on my hernia, and are designed to tighten up the limpness of upper body musculature and my sagging facial hollows.

Later as I walked into the steam room, I found Lenny sitting in the corner who appeared to be a little shrivelled up to say the least. He wasn't looking at his best, although he confided that he could remember having had worse days. But smiling at me happily and having his positive head on he was relatively optimistic. He then went on to inform me about the unfortunate events that culminated in Nobby Caxton's hospital visit, and his later arrest. It appears that after we left the pub on Monday night, Nobby was acting strangely and Ted kindly volunteered to take him home. You will remember that I thought that he wasn't his usual self. I initially guessed that he was drunk, but then there was that unmistakeable smell of marijuana. Inexplicably, at around 02:30 the following morning, Nobby was found by police lying unconscious in the High Road. He was apparently rushed to St Mary's hospital where he spent the night, having suffered the indignity of a stomach pump and a colonic irrigation. After a thorough medical assessment, he was kept in under observation until 16:00 last night. On his release however, he was arrested and later charged with possession of Class A drugs. It would appear that on checking through his belongings, four small packets of what appeared to be marijuana, and six small packets of white powder, which are believed to be cocaine, were found. This is all conjecture, however; since both substances would have to be sent to the police lab for scientific analysis. I asked Lenny where he had got all of this information. 'Ted told me about it this morning in the café,' he replied.

'But where on earth would Ted have got this intelligence?' I enquired. 'Nobby wouldn't have been arrested until last night and presumably released this morning. And there's Ted telling you about it all a few hours later? Knowing Nobby, he would have kept all of this very close to his chest.'

'Dunno,' replied Lenny absentmindedly. 'You know what a nosey *fatherless-person* Ted is, he doesn't miss much!' I didn't like the sound of this at all, and determined to have a word with my nosey friend later.

Back at home, I had a call from Muhulin who asked if she could visit since she had something to discuss with me. I suggested a meeting next week, but she stated that it was rather urgent. If I were free, she could visit today. I therefore arranged a meet-up for a coffee at a small restaurant called *Coffee and Cream*, in the High Road at 16:30.

As reliably punctual as ever, I was dunking custard creams into a cup of cappuccino at 16:20 and Muhulin arrived carrying a large folder a little latter. She gave me an unexpected hug and sat down wearily. Opening the folder, she took out a couple of sheets of A4 paper which she handed to me. The first one was a letter of referral from a Doctor Simpson addressed to what appeared to be a specialist in treating MS sufferers. It recommended a three-week stay at his clinic in Surrey, at a date to be arranged. The second was a booking form.

Muhulin explained that the specialist in question, a Professor O'Donnell, was the best in his field and had achieved quite commendable examples of MS remission in the past. Dr Simpson was of the opinion that a three-week visit to his clinic would be extremely beneficial for Jasmine. I welcomed this news enthusiastically and stated that, if there was anything that I could do to help, I would be only too happy to assist. She then went on to explain that the problem was Jasmine's daughter Elisha and where to put her while Jasmine was away. Apparently, Muhulin had asked Elisha where she would like to go for a holiday, and Elisha had replied, 'I'd like to see Mr Paul.' I was really very surprised and not a little touched.

It then suddenly dawned on me. 'Muhulin, are you asking me to have Elisha for a few weeks, at home, at my place?' I asked incredulously. 'I really would not have asked you but frankly I have no other alternative,' she replied. 'Jasmine has a live-in carer, who has also been acting as an unpaid nanny to Elisha, but as the woman has stated, she is basically employed as an adult carer, not a nanny or childminder. She wasn't qualified enough!'

'As you are aware,' Muhulin continued, 'I am working everyday now, so I really couldn't have her either!'

'But I'm not qualified either, my dear,' I said appealingly.

'I know, but she likes you a great deal, and I know that she'd be safe in your care. Besides, you have two young girls living with you, so you are obviously used to having women about.'

'But they are big girls, love, not infants like Elisha!' I protested.

'All that I'd ask is that you give it some thought, Paul. Frankly, you are our last hope. I do believe that the therapy offered by Professor O'Donnell would greatly improve

Jasmine's quality of life, and I would hate her to miss the chance of attending this treatment.'

I left this 'upmarket rip-off café' at around 5:25pm in a bit of a daze. (I mean, for the price that I paid for two cappuccinos and a small packet of custard creams, I could have bought three pints at The Magpie and would still have had change out of a tenner.) But that aside, on passing Father Marcus on my way home, I saw his smiling face and absentmindedly nodded, but having seen his lips move, I was totally unaware of what he said. I wish that I could switch off as easily during his other, all too frequent visits.

Later that evening, I caught up with Ted in a very busy Gay Bar. He was sipping some kind of cocktail, which in his calloused unrefined hand looked extremely uncomfortable and very out of place, like a dick and a pair of braces on a female statue. (I nearly said 'bollocks' then!)

'What on earth are you drinking?' I enquired, pointing to an ornate glass filled with ice and brown liquid, with a brightly coloured lopsided plastic umbrella hanging precariously on its rim.

'It's what they call a *Grumpy Old Man*,' replied Ted, who stirred the liquid with his left index finger and pointed at Dave who was sat on his usual stool at the bar.

Everyone suddenly stopped what they were doing and looked at Dave enquiringly.

'I dunno why it has such an inappropriate title,' continued Ted. 'I mean, it certainly doesn't make you feel grumpy. In fact, it induces a rather pleasant feeling of well-being and happiness. Perhaps they call it that because it cheers up miserable old *gastric emissions* like him,' nodding in Dave's direction.

'What's your problem, mate?' called Dave. 'Are you looking to be on the receiving end of one of my celebrated *Grumpy Old Man* right-handers?'

'Yeah, and I'd like to see you drink one of them things on a cold Saturday afternoon in the Glasgow Ibrox Stadium next time Rangers play Celtic,' shouted *Scotch Andy*, whose normal soft Dr Finlay-type Scottish accent now took on the unmistakable aggressive verbal intonation of an irate Glaswegian with a grievance. 'You'd be sipping through a straw right enough. Aye, but this time it would be to digest your liquidised food!' Andy certainly does have a way with words and it left Ted speechless. He nevertheless tried to act nonchalant, and bringing the glass to his mouth, he inadvertently poked the umbrella tip up his nose and chucked the rest of his *Grumpy Old Man* down the front of his *Man at C&A* jacket. A great deal of laughter followed, and even Vlado found this rather amusing, particularly since from what we were told, one of his lesser-known pastimes was providing plenty of injured human fodder for the medical profession to hone its repair and recovery skills on.

Once the uproar had died down, and Ted had wiped himself down with a large handkerchief that at some point in its history had been white, *Tony the Tube* said, 'It's a bit bleeding pretentious mate! I know that we jokingly call this the Gay Bar, but leave it out! If this was to become common knowledge, before you know it, we'd be inundated with people from the *Gay Liberation Front*, checking the place out as a potential venue! Not to mention the distinct possibility of the *filth* poking their uninvited beaks in from time to time, hoping to wear in their new Doc Martens, on the innocent buttocks of a few of our fun-loving regulars.'

'I heard a good one the other day,' shouted Dave, distractedly. 'Two deer walked out of a gay bar. One of them turns to the other and says, *I can't believe that I blew forty bucks in there!*'

Looking up from his paper, an unusually lucid *Whispering Jim* warned, 'I'd be very careful if I were you,' he said, tapping what appeared to be an article that he'd been reading. 'It says here that men who use sexist or homophobic jokes, do so to cover up the insecurity they feel about their own masculinities!' The bar suddenly went deathly quiet, and everyone looked at Dave. As if stage-managed, the assembled miscellaneous rabble silently picked up their drinks and to a man, moved their stools away from him towards the front doors. Having seen Dave's bewildered-looking demeanour, the entire group burst into rapturous laughter and applause. One doesn't often get one over on Dave, who likewise saw the funny side of it all and chuckled along with them good-naturedly.

'You bunch of *urine-taking,* misbegotten *fatherless-persons!*' he shouted.

Before I had time to ask Ted about Nobby, *Alfie the Dip* arrived and his body language told me that he wanted to have a chat with me. He's not very subtle, however, since I'm sure that his hand-beckoning gestures were understood by just about everyone else. Once outside the bar, Alfie said:

'Basil will give you a ring in the morning. There have been a few significant developments.' 'What news about Nobby?' I asked. He shook my hand and put his left index finger up to his mouth, followed by a knowing wink. Before I could say anything else he said, 'Basil will bring you up to date tomorrow.'

As Ted was leaving, I caught him at the door. He couldn't offer any further news with regard to Nobby and frankly didn't appear interested in talking about the bloke at all. However, I did manage to convey to him the events surrounding Lenny's recent visit to the DHSS offices, and my utter disgust at the way that he was treated by Mr Malcolm Edward Frobisher. During my unexpurgated version of the events, I could see from his changing facial demeanour that he was not a happy bunny. At the conclusion of my tale, he smiled and said, 'It sounds to me that I should have a quiet word with this person, since it is clear that his very misguided sense of invincibility needs to be thoroughly investigated and challenged.'

Back at home, Maria and Jimena were in playful mode. It seems that Gabriel had visited during the afternoon and had invited Maria for an evening meal at his place tomorrow night. I was therefore roped into looking after our little playful kitten for the evening, not that I minded at all. However, I asked Maria if she could make herself available for a 'team meeting' tomorrow evening at 17:00. She was free and agreeable, but was very inquisitive. I left a note for Lenka on her desk requesting her attendance also. I need to discuss the Jasmine and Elisha issues with them both. I fell into bed at 23:45 quite exhausted.

Goodnight love.

P xx

16th February 2012

Good morning, Ginny.

I received a phone call from Basil at 10:15, and he not wishing to speak over the phone, arranged to meet me at the *Glass House* pub in Cricklewood at 14:30. Basil certainly is a bit of a nomadic type and loves to get out and about a bit. However, as with the *Left Foot* shoe repair and key cutting shop at Euston station, I am sure that there is a very good reason why he has selected this particular venue for our meeting.

Having come in from her work during the early hours of the morning, Lenka had left me a note to say that she was off this evening and would be free to attend our evening meeting. As I left home to meet Basil at 13:55, I reminded Maria about this important meeting.

I gave my London Transport chauffeur an appreciative smile as I placed my freedom pass on his Freedom and Oyster pass authentication slab. It beeped joyfully and only then did the miserable surly *fatherless-person* take his bored indifferent eyes off me, and belching loudly, he accelerated his bone-adjusting conveyance quickly away. I was forced to run down the aisle to keep myself upright, and thankfully landed face first into an empty seat at the back. Still, this time there was nothing broken, and in fairness, I can understand the driver's need for a little bit of light entertainment.

Bus driving in London has to be one of the most thankless and frustratingly stressful of livelihoods known to mankind. Being able to sit day after day in congested traffic, breathing in carbon monoxide fumes and ferrying ungrateful passengers around (many of whom could have taken the tube, or walked) is not for the faint hearted. It requires a certain kind of individual to take on this demanding role and preference is afforded to candidates with substantial life insurance policies, nerves of steel, excellent defensive driving skills, a good working knowledge of the raunchy patois of inner-city kids, and finally a number of vacancies are always available for those less active, or noticeably corpulent (*fatherless-people*) who are unemployable in any other industry (provided they can arrange their excessive body parts into the cab unaided and get there without the use of a hoist).

Being an equal opportunity employer, fast-track management positions are available to candidates educated to GCE O level standard or below, with preference being given to trainees who can demonstrate first-class male *and* female handling skills, provided they can differentiate between the two, and are not on, and have never been on, the sex offenders register.

I arrived at the *Glass House* pub at 14:20. Basil was nowhere to be found so I visited the saloon bar and ordered myself a pint. A little later, a door opened at the far end of the bar and Basil poked his head out. He beckoned me over. I was flabbergasted to find Nobby Caxton sitting behind a desk. He stood up as I entered and shook my hand vigorously.

'It's good to see you, Paul,' he said.

'You too Nobby, I hear that you are in a little trouble?'

'Well, something like that,' he replied. He sat back down heavily like an exhausted marathon runner at the end of a race and stretched his hands out in front of him. He appeared very nervous and timidly kept looking at me furtively, averting his gaze whenever our eyes met. Basil then went on to explain the reason for our meeting.

It appears that my erstwhile friend Nobby, a man whom I have always held in the highest of regard, was responsible for the shed break-ins and also the deception involved in changing the lock to my shed. He'd gained access to my flat some time before with his set of estate master keys. On the day in question, he knew that both Maria and I were out, having kept observation of our block from his office vantage point. Lenka, he assumed being a night worker, would be asleep. Apparently, he had worked on a feasible excuse should he be discovered in the flat and would tell her that he was investigating a gas leak. He was also responsible for planting the electrical device in my meter cupboard. It's a wonder that I didn't spot it when the police raided.

Having gained entry into my flat, he exchanged my existing shed key for one of his own which fitted the new lock that he would later put on my shed. He then planted the electrical device. He later took out my birdcage and bicycle, replacing the items from the other two sheds into mine. Clearly, this was what he was engaged in that night that I saw him on top of the sheds. All that he had to do later was to secure the shed using his replacement lock.

I looked at Nobby while Basil gave me this devastating news. He kept his head down, cupping his hands over his eyes. Naturally, I needed a full explanation. But this would have to wait it seems. At the conclusion of this dreadful news, an awkward silence followed.

Relieving the tension, Basil stood up and, reaching across the table, shook Nobby's hand. 'Thank you very much for your honesty in this issue, Nobby,' Basil said. 'It took considerable courage and strength of character to admit your part in this unfortunate affair.'

'I can't tell you both just how wretched I feel,' Nobby replied, a single tear track making its way down his cheek. He stood and left the room silently. Despite my feelings of bewilderment tinged with anger, I experienced a wave of intense sadness and pity as I watched this dejected and solitary man leave. A friend in need – indeed!

'We will need to discuss certain implications of this at another time, Paul, but I have to rush due to a very urgent appointment in about an hour,' Basil said. He smiled at me reassuringly and patted me on the shoulder. 'Please don't lose any sleep over this, Paul. Believe me, I really understand how you feel, but there are other issues to clear up before we can go any further. Naturally, this is highly confidential and should not be known to anyone. All will be revealed in due course.' Before I could gather my thoughts, he silently left the room, closing the door quietly behind him.

Back out into the main bar, I found that in my absence a lively crowd now occupied what was earlier an empty space. Two barmaids were rushing up and down behind the bar, taking orders as quickly as they could. The sounds of a brass band were thumping out a rendition of *The Floral Dance* and, looking around, I realised that the bar had been designed to resemble a very basic barrack room.

Around the three walls, seats designed to look like beds were positioned, and a large cast-iron woodburning stove was placed in the middle of the room, its large circular metal flue pipe vanishing into the ceiling above. The furnishings bore a military association from the numerous regimental plaques hanging over a considerable area of wall space, to the large prints in frames depicting military battles from Agincourt to Mons which filled any spare gaps. A variety of swords and bayonets were displayed over the optics behind the bar, and regimental flags hung from the ceiling. A large painting of our gracious Queen hung over the main entrance to the bar, with a Union Jack draped across it.

I was to find out a little later that the reason for the crowd was that on a daily basis between the hours of 15:00–16:00, *Happy Hour* takes place. It commences with a taped bugle sounding *Reveille* and ends an hour later with *The Last Post*. Beer, wine and spirits were offered at very low prices indeed during this period. Needless to say, most of the local pubs were just about empty until after 16:00 when their normal trade resumed.

I was in no mood to linger, and having *eventually* been served with a large cognac, I left shortly after. On the way home, I caught another bus and this time my chauffeur was a rather portly black woman. I smiled at her politely as my freedom pass did its thing, although she simply glared at me disinterestedly. But then the bus was very crowded, and it can't be easy to drive one standing up!

I arrived at home at around 16:35pm. All of my girls – feline and human – were in the kitchen. Lenka and Maria were playing with Jimena, who was having great fun chasing a little furry object that Maria was moving about on the table. Having made myself a coffee, I chatted to my two 'big girls' and explained the issue with regards to Jasmine and her daughter Elisha. Both of them were delighted at the prospect of having Elisha stay with us for the three-week period. I have a small portable camp bed in the wardrobe, which she could use, and after a lot of competitive discussion, it was decided that the little one could have it in whatever bedroom and sleep with whomever she chose. I thanked them for their gracious understanding and help. Maria suggested that we start on the week commencing 5th of March, when she would have a week off from college, and Lenka stated that she'd have the following week off on holiday. I would be around throughout anyway. All that needed to be arranged now was to pass on the suggested time frame to Muhulin.

I had a call from Dave a little later inviting me down to The Magpie. I had planned to have a quiet evening at home, but decided that a little distraction was just what I needed. I didn't stay long and was quite happy to return home an hour later.

I managed to have a quick chat with Ted about the Nobby incident, and he made it very plain that he was not interested in the issue at all. I have a feeling that something has happened that he has not been best pleased about. He clearly feels that he doesn't want to elaborate on it, so I shall not bother him again.

Back at home, I phoned Muhulin on my mobile, giving her the news about Elisha's impending visit and having thanked me profusely, she stated that she would pass on the dates suggested and would be back in touch later.

I didn't need any persuading about getting into bed, and my little ball of feline fluff joined me, although she didn't want a bedtime story, and as I read my own bed book – Spike Milligan's final war memoir *(Goodbye Soldier)* – she was soon sound asleep.

Goodnight, Ginny.

P xx

17th February 2012

Dear Ginny.

Just before sleep last night, I had a text from the partner of a dear old friend of mine, asking me to call her this morning. We had lost touch some time ago, and as the old adage confirms, *out of sight, out of mind.* She sent me her home telephone number, which I had either lost or misplaced. Although I do believe that they had moved from their former home in Greenwich some time ago.

Having received her text, my own very unfortunate and sad reflections of the day's events were erased by a veritable kaleidoscope of delightfully happy memories, and last night I drifted off into a deep peaceful sleep, being rocked gently in the warm glow of fond remembrance.

Tommy Grasscon is a scoundrel of the first order, but one of the nicest men I have ever known. He was born in Newcastle during the early forties and in his youth worked in the coal mines, where he was taught how to handle a shovel; at the shipyards, where he was given instruction in the intricacies of steel plate riveting and the medicinal sense in being able to ingest, and retain copious quantities of liquid, notably, Newcastle Brown Ale; and thereafter for a short time, he was employed in a steel factory, shovelling rusty rivets which, as he once stated philosophically, 'is better than shovelling *shite-covered rivets!*'

His main claim to justifiable fame was that for a six-year period he became one of our very own respected and revered North Sea fishermen. This is a quite amazing feat for a man who could quite literally become seasick simply sitting on a pier, let alone being tossed about like *an awakened conscience* aboard an eighty-foot fishing vessel for days at a time. However, it was here that his love for the sea and all things pelagic was to direct a passion that remained with him throughout his life.

It was our mutual fishing interests that brought us together, and for most weekends during the seventies we fished side by side, mainly from beaches or piers, around most of the south coast of England. We would attend various national sea fishing championships and took great delight in wearing suitable high-tech poseur clothing adorned with spurious cloth fishing badges that boasted competitor status at the *Natal Great White Shark Championships* and the *Florida Quays Marlin Open,* among numerous other imposters. One has to remember that it's all very well being on some barren windswept beach fishing, but quite another to look like a complete moronic *pud-wapper* while doing so! However, we did enjoy the attention and apparent high regard which we received from our fellow competitors and had many a laugh over it during our evenings of alcoholic replenishment (another mutual interest of ours).

At the end of a day's *worm drowning*, it is customary for most anglers to carry out an enthusiastically charged period of boasting about *the one that got away* (including fish) and engaging in a considerable amount of boyish camaraderie, fuelled by alcohol in its myriad forms. But it was all a bit of innocent fun. Personally, Tommy and I never actually won anything, but if nothing else, we certainly did look the part.

One of the greatest *Ellisisms* that Tommy ever uttered was on Deal pier. On this particular occasion, he'd crept off with his half-filled can of Coke (which he would cunningly get topped up with whiskey from the end of pier bar). He actually thought that I wasn't aware of what he was doing. On his return, he took a long meaningful gulp, belched resoundingly and then looked wistfully at the tide that was rushing in towards the shore. In his delightful Geordie accent (which I never got tired listening to) he said, 'Ave yer ever wondered how much deeper the sea would be without the trillions of sponges?'

A little later, under the pretence of visiting the loo, which was conveniently located at the end of the pier, I called into the bar. I asked the barmaid if a strange-looking bloke with a funny accent had come in asking her to put whiskey into his Coke can? She nodded enthusiastically, seemingly relieved that she hadn't imagined it. Using my best acting skills (which had been honed during my primary school years) and with a voice faltering periodically for dramatic effect, I stated that, 'I was his hospital carer and that he was a very unstable schizophrenic alcoholic, suffering from advanced cirrhosis of the liver.'

Unhesitatingly, she stated that she would not serve him any further alcoholic drink, and bless her heart, she put her hand on mine, and smiling sweetly, gently squeezed it reassuringly.

I rejoined my unsuspecting friend a little later. He was now staring at the horizon and, to relieve his almost hypnotic trance-like state, I gently trod on the bottom of his rod which made its tip quiver violently. This would normally indicate a bite. He jumped into action, reeling in his rod as fast as he could, to find that he hadn't caught anything. Within twenty minutes or so, he opened his rucksack and turning his back on me, furtively poured Coke from a bottle into his now empty Coke can. As expected, he nonchalantly sauntered off again shortly after, Coke can in hand. Within five minutes or so I saw him standing outside the entrance to the bar, gesticulating wildly. Fortunately, being a little way off, I couldn't quite hear what he was shouting, and perhaps it was just as well. Actually, I did feel a little guilty at the very obvious abuse that the kindly bar lady had to endure as a result of my earlier deceptive prank.

On his way back, his dejected limp frame and bewildered facial expression said it all. Well not quite, since when I got within earshot, I was on the receiving end of what is to this day the most sustained barrage of verbal abuse that I have ever been subjected to. However, Tommy's rage is like a veritable flash of lightning and it is soon over. He simply finds excessive emotion unnecessary and boring. He also has a quite amazing ability when it comes to forgiveness; either that or he has a chronically short memory span. On this occasion, fortunately the tension was hastily relieved when he tipped out the remaining Coke that was left in his can and rummaging in his rucksack took out his bottle of Coke, and with a practised hand, half-filled his can again. The canny bugger then produced a half bottle of whiskey from the inside pocket of his jacket, which he opened and without spilling a drop, refilled and fortified the innocuous space with forty per cent proof whiskey. He stuck a straw into it and gently stirred the contents smiling triumphantly. He then took a long grateful draught and, having belched forcefully, he said, 'I was savin that fer later ya bastad!'

I phoned Clare at 09:00 and she gave me the very sad news that Tommy had been diagnosed with terminal pancreatic cancer some four months earlier and was now in a hospice. He apparently does not have much time left. It seems that he'd asked Clare to contact me, and as luck would have it she'd found my mobile number in one of her old diaries. She emphasised the point that he'd like to see me again, and would I pay him a visit. They live in Sandown on the Isle of Wight, and having nothing planned for the weekend, I stated that I would get a train to Portsmouth Harbour during the early afternoon today.

Having fed Maria, and carrying a hastily filled overnight bag, I left the flat in her capable hands at 11:15. I told her that I would keep her informed, and that should any problems arise she should contact either me or Lenka immediately. I was comforted to learn that Gabriel will be staying with her at the flat. I really do like this boy.

I arrived at Waterloo railway station just after midday and was aboard the 12:45 train to Portsmouth Harbour. It arrived at 15:58. Train lag aside, I have always enjoyed rail journeys, and while I do perhaps feel pity for those thousands of reluctant daily commuters, some of whom travel ridiculously long daily distances, there's something quite nice about starting one's daily employment activities with a rail journey. It affords a soul time to catch up on sleep, consider the day's work schedule, or indeed write another chapter of one's exciting novel. Throughout the journey, I was lost in my own little world, wrapped in a quiet almost meditative indolence, and as the beautiful undulating Hampshire countryside rushed by, I felt very peaceful indeed.

On my arrival at Portsmouth Harbour, I had just missed the Wight Link ferry by a couple of minutes and had another hour to wait until the next one arrived. I bought a sandwich and coffee in the *Terminal Café,* which forcefully reminded me of my reason for being there. It put a dampener on my appetite, so I broke up the sandwich and thought that on the crossing, I'd feed a voracious gull or two. Although I wasn't too sure how a sandwich of tandoori chicken salad would be received. Still, they don't call them *Shite Hawks* for nothing! Ironically, whenever I hear the unmistakably raucous calls of a gull, quite spontaneously, I will always say, 'Howsit Tommy?'

Invariably wherever we were fishing, the only sounds heard were the rushing of the tide, the crashing of the waves, the ear-piercing screams of the gulls, and the unmistakeable sounds of Tommy's bodily gastric emissions, which he intermittently released with evident pride and wild abandon. Strangely, we never really engaged in small talk and indeed hardly spoke a word to one another throughout a day's fishing. But content we were. Normally we would have a daily wager of a pound per fish and a fiver for the biggest on the day, and generally there was never an outright winner. Each fish he caught would be welcomed ashore with the words, 'Come to Dada,' although he was never quite so enthusiastic with mine, and would utter the usual expletive throwing doubt on my parentage each time. But it was all good humoured. We always shared a very special relationship, which was quite unique in many respects.

Having caught the next ferry, I arrived at Ryde Pier some thirty minutes later, and Tommy's partner Clare met me on arrival. Frankly, out in one of our busy streets I would have walked right passed her. She had put on considerable weight since I last saw her, and her former dazzling urbanite chic in dress and deportment, together with the radiant confidence of a no-nonsense feminist go-getter, had been inexplicably exchanged for the unfamiliar disinterested and dishevelled frumpy-dumpling that now stood before me.

We had a fish supper later at a rather uninspiring fish and chip shop, followed by a drink at her local pub during which she gave me a complete rundown of events almost right up until our last meeting, which she assured me, was during the August Bank Holiday of 2003. I have reasoned in the past, that all women have terrible memories, and this clearly proves it. They never forget anything!

We shall be visiting the hospice tomorrow morning at about 11:30. Just before I retired for the night in a spare bedroom which smelt sweetly and had been obviously painstakingly cleaned, with an inquisitive look on her face, Clare poked her head around the door and mentioned that Tommy had asked me to bring him in a 'can of Coke'.

Goodnight love.
P xx

18th February 2012

Dear Ginny.

I really didn't sleep at all well last night, and scientists have discovered a possible reason why it seems. Having read an interesting article in *The Pigeon Fancier* some time ago, it appears that like our feathered friends, humans stay alert for predators when sleeping in new surroundings. However, the only potential threat to my safety and well-being was Clare, whom I heard talking and occasionally shouting in her sleep for most of the night, and during the intermittent breaks in her nocturnal soliloquy, was snoring like a bulldog on Valium. Contrary to the beliefs of the scientific fraternity, in this particular instance, it was clear that the only potential threat that this woman could pose to another would be their loss of sanity following a sustained period of sleep deprivation. As I lay in the pre-dawn gloom, my spirits lifted when I thought of my own dear bed at home, and the satisfaction of knowing that I would not spend another night like this one.

I was wide awake at 05:00 feeling exhausted, irritable and groggy, but thankful that I had not been molested or attacked during the endless incarcerating night. Frankly, I would not have had the strength or resilience to repel a marauding bunch of infant rapists, let alone a frisky frumpy-dumpling like Clare, bent on a little nocturnal gymnastics!

She was bright eyed and in good spirits, when I entered the kitchen, having cautiously groped my way down the stairs in complete darkness. It appears that the landing light was broken. I needed a very strong cup of coffee, not so much to give me a morning buzz, but simply to stop me from falling asleep. It was hard work indeed. We had a light breakfast, and then I asked her where the nearest supermarket was. She was all for driving me, but I insisted that the walk would do me good. God, how I needed a little fresh air!

I arrived at the local supermarket fifteen invigorating minutes later. The wind was very bracing, and a light sea mist was falling, providing a refreshing facial spray which was just the ticket. I bought a litre bottle of Coke and two half bottles of whiskey (which I hid in the pockets of my duffle coat), together with an assortment of chocolate bars and crisps. I took my time returning, and at 10:40 we left for the twenty-minute drive to the *St Mollimus Hospice* on the outskirts of Bembridge.

The hospice stood in a large area of woodland. The drive which meandered around a circuitous path, finally arrived at a modern brick-built building comprising of a number of floors, each containing private rooms. Tommy was in room 24 on the second floor. I was quite shocked to see his emaciated body lying in the bed. He was propped up by a number of pillows and he was hooked up (if that's the right word) to an intravenous drip and a plastic pipe up his nostrils which were presumably administering oxygen. He smiled at me as I entered the room and made an attempt to shake my hand. Sadly, he couldn't hold out his frail bony arm for long and before I had time to grasp his hand, it sank down onto the bed beside him. I sat down on a chair next to the bed and simply patted it. We chatted for some considerable time.

It was all really distressing for me, but I'd hoped that he wouldn't see my intense concern and sadness. With considerable forced bravado, I did my utmost best to hide it in a load of waffle, and jokes of a type that were once our usual familiar banter. Twenty minutes or so later, Clare stated that she would go to the visitors' café and left us alone. As soon as she was gone, Tommy became very animated and considerably more alert. From under the bed linen, he lifted out a brown envelope which he gave me quickly. He made it evident that he didn't want Clare to know about it, and explained that the contents were between 'him and I'.

I put the Coke bottle and the goodies on his bedside table, and he looked at me enquiringly. I returned his gaze, intimating that I didn't understand his confusion. However, I couldn't keep up the pretence for long. I put the two half bottles of whiskey under his bed clothes.

'Bastard!' he said, smiling appreciatively. 'I thought for one horrible moment that you might not have understood my coded message,' he said, looking very serious indeed.

'Are you kidding?' I replied. 'I understood fully!' However, he told me to put the bottles under the towels in his cabinet. It seems that he has made a friend of one of the orderlies and later when all was quiet, 'Tim' would be able to pour him out a libation or two.

Clare and I left at 13:50 and I briefly collecting my bag from her home. She kindly drove me back to Ryde Pier where I later caught the ferry back to Portsmouth Harbour. After a pretty uneventful journey, I was sitting in the Gay Bar at 18:35pm. It was completely empty, and I wondered if some major catastrophe had taken place in my absence.

In the solitude of the empty space, I amused myself thinking about a few of the quite ridiculous events that could have taken place in my absence. Maybe the entire motley Gay Bar crowd were outside the local nick demonstrating at Lenny's arrest for leaving the scene of an accident, having been knocked thirty feet along the road by a speeding hit and run driver. Or being the unlucky *fatherless-person* that he is, *Alfie the Dip*, had inadvertently run into an accident that started out happening to someone else, and the Gay Bar crowd were at the scene gloating.

Suddenly, my mental reverie was interrupted by a loud steady stream of locals entering the bar. They were all in a very inebriated state, and I found out later that Ted's luck on the horses had changed, and instead of having to thumb a lift back from his bookmakers in Cricklewood (which was a usual event on a Saturday afternoon), this time he travelled back to the pub in a cab, and invited the entire motley group of bar attendees on a gratis pub crawl (much to the disapproval of Vlado). It started with *Happy Hour* at the *Glass House,* followed by a visit to the five pubs on the main road, from Cricklewood to Kilburn. They were not a pretty sight! Mind you, none of them are exactly attractive or physically alluring examples of humanity sober! As a collective, they'd make a freight train take a dirt road, and Dickie Mumford was looking out of a bus window last Thursday and got arrested for *Mooning.* Pretty he isn't!

I got home at 22:25. The flat was empty, apart from Jimena who hurtled herself down the hall carpet towards me, which was a comical sight. She still hasn't quite mastered the dexterity needed to keep her on a straight course, and she bounced from one wall to the other on the way down. She is obviously a very sociable little thing and enjoys company. My thoughts again turned to Spike. It can't be long now for his return and the robber's justifiable fate. I shall phone Basil tomorrow.

Maria had left a note on the kitchen table to say that Nobby Caxton had left a letter for me, which frankly I wasn't in any mood to read. It could wait until tomorrow, I thought.

Following a refreshing shower and shave, and feeling thoroughly exhausted both physically and mentally, I thankfully got into bed, and even forgot to make myself cocoa. Frankly, I didn't feel the need of anything to help me sleep, or at least, I'd hoped so. Jimena curled up on the pillow beside me and was soon asleep purring contentedly.

Goodnight, Ginny.
P xx

19th February 2012

Good morning, my dear.

I had a marvellous night, and having regained consciousness at 07:40, felt very refreshed indeed. The delightful smell of freshly made coffee permeated the air. I heard the sound of a M&S silver-plated teaspoon hitting the sides of a plastic mug and called out, 'Is that you, my little Spanish sugarplum?'

'Near enough, Paul,' called Gabriel chuckling. 'Would you like a cup of coffee?'

'Oh go on then, Gabriel, just to please you!' I called. A long pause followed. 'You are so kind, Paul,' he replied finally.

Kicking my legs out of bed and peering into the kitchen I said, 'Milk and two sugars, if you please.'

Later, my dear little Spanish sugarplum arrived in the kitchen looking more radiant and happy than I have ever seen her. I made them both breakfast, and shortly after Lenka came home. She looked quite exhausted poor thing, but joined us at the kitchen table. Quite out of character she asked me if she could have a cognac, and of course I duly obliged. She confided to me later that she was having a little bit of a problem with one of the new managers at work, who was giving her a little too much unwanted attention, which she thought was bordering on sexual harassment.

I reasoned that should the issue continue, I would ensure that the matter was dealt with expeditiously and the veritable *pud-wapper* warned off. She made the point that she wouldn't want me to get involved. If that was the case, she should have kept it to herself, and normally that is what she has done in the past. She has always been a very private person. I was convinced that this was serious however, since she felt that she needed to tell someone else about it and needed to let off a bit of steam, as it were. I stated that I wouldn't get involved if she felt that she could deal with it alone, but I'd be there if needed. Just before she left for bed, she hugged me and, kissing me on my cheek, whispered, 'Thank you my dear, but don't worry, I'm a big girl now!'

'That's what I'm afraid of,' I replied.

Later I opened and read Nobby Caxton's letter which gave me great cause for concern. In it he expressed his profound sadness and intense regret over his actions. He offered me his heartfelt apologies and expressed his relief that the shed issue had been satisfactorily dealt with, but warned that the electric meter issue might not be quite so easily resolved. He stated that his actions were directed by another, and implied that he had been blackmailed, although he didn't point a finger at anyone in particular. I could believe that, since hitherto Nobby had always acted in a decent and respectful way to everyone no matter how grand or lowly. His integrity was consistently beyond reproach, and I always considered him to be one of life's true gentlemen, which made his involvement in this dreadful matter all the more poignant. He signed the note, respectfully yours *Nobby Caxton.*

During the late morning, I visited the gym for nothing more strenuous than a revitalising visit to the steam room. While sitting there poking fluff out of my navel, Alexander Barrington Scott, my saviour in relation to the shed saga, entered. He sat down next to me and shook my hand vigorously. We had a very nice chat, and I instantly liked the man. He is a professional toastmaster, and it is a wonderful choice of employment since he has a very interestingly rich sonorous voice. He enjoys his work it seems but confessed that he would have preferred to be a judge. His reasoning being that toastmasters who are no longer fit for the job, are gently pensioned off, which is quite the opposite when it comes to judges. The more incompetent and bumbling they become it seems, the longer their stipend lasts. I found this a quite amusing revelation and had to agree that there was an element of truth in what he was saying. I have never seen a young or immature looking judge. But then, I do not make a habit of checking out the ages of our current serving judiciary.

Apparently, his case comes up next week, and he philosophically declared that he would completely accept the findings of the court, since, as he so succinctly put it, he had been 'caught bang to rights!' Although not exactly, since he had put the record straight as it were, and had freely admitted his part in the unfortunate affair. I pointed out that it took a great deal of grit and character to own up as he did, since he could have just played it all along, and no one would have been any the wiser. Had he done so, it is my belief that despite Basil's best efforts, the axe would have fallen, and I would have had to suffer the disgrace and indignity of having a criminal conviction added to my relatively clean former police record. We arranged to have a meeting one evening next week for a drink, and I felt it incumbent upon me to take him out for a meal. It's nice to be nice.

On leaving the steam room before me, he stated, 'Crime really doesn't pay, does it?' I nodded enthusiastically. 'Perhaps one way of ensuring that crime would never pay,' he continued, 'would be to let a bloody government department run it!'

I phoned Basil later in the day, and he was in a very quiet indolent mood, which for him is a little unusual. He stated that Tina had been keeping an eye on the dog breeder's place in Sussex and reported that Spike was 'enjoying his holiday'. She is in liaison with the local police and the owners of the puppy farm and between them, a date would be set for the miscreants to collect Spike as planned. Naturally, he or they would be justifiably welcomed into the cold blue gabardine arms of *The Wallopers,* (as *Dunny Greg* would have put it). I would be notified in good time and will be kept informed with regards to developments. As far as the additional case which will be heard next Thursday, he had 'high hopes of a breakthrough' which frankly wasn't very encouraging.

As I sat in The Magpie sipping a large cognac, my thoughts turned to dear old Tommy and I suddenly remembered the envelope that he had given me. I located it in my inside pocket. On opening it, I found a small key and a short hand written note on which he had outlined his request. I was to take the second letter, which had been formerly typed and signed by him (and witnessed by the manager of the hospice) to the Canterbury branch of the Listowel Bank and to seek out its manager, a bloke called Robert Levington. I was to give him the typed letter, which he would be expecting, and on the production of some form of positive ID, I was to be given access to the safe deposit box area. I was to open box 44 and collect its contents, which were now mine. His hastily written note further stated that the box contained £18,750 in £50 notes. He asked that I seek out his only living next of kin, a daughter, 'Siobhan' (which came as a complete surprise to me). She was last heard of living in Kinsale, Southern Ireland. I was to keep £3,750 to cover expenses and to have a drink or two, and if she was located, to give her the remaining £15,000. If she could not be found following 'an honest and diligent search', then I could dispose of the remaining cash in any manner that I saw fit. It was signed, *your good friend Tommy*. I was absolutely flabbergasted.

Both of my girls were out when I returned home. I had a light supper in The Magpie, since I really wasn't in the mood for cooking, particularly since it would have been for me alone. Jimena was pleased at my arrival, and we spent a meaningful hour together. I was trying to teach her to chase and retrieve a little round ball of wool. It wasn't very successful however, since having chased and caught it; she simply wouldn't chuck it back!

Goodnight, Ginny.

P xx

20th February 2012

Good morning, Ginny.

I was up bright and early this morning and, having hastily showered and shaved, had a light breakfast. Jimena had spent another night curled up next to me and was no trouble whatsoever. Maria had spent the night out, presumably with Gabriel, and Lenka was out at work. The peace was quite wonderful.

Jasmine's former flat above has not been occupied since she left, and I feel blessed indeed that it has remained empty ever since.

At 09:00 a chauffeur was waiting for me, and as I left the inner courtyard of the flats, a large group of residents were waiting outside. As I came out, the ecstatic applause was quite deafening. I felt very humble and not a little embarrassed as I made my way to the Daimler. As we journeyed to Maida Vale studios, I mused upon the spontaneous goodwill that I had received from my fellow residents.

When one lives in such a communal housing environment, it is quite difficult to know every neighbour. In fact, it would be quite impossible. Out of the considerable number of people that reside in Susan Atkins Court, I am friendly with a handful of them. But when one of our members, no matter how anonymous or unfamiliar, has a bit of good luck or achieves something notable or special, then the entire community vicariously shares in the recognition and sense of achievement.

I was to finally get my fifteen minutes of fame, which, not wishing to bore you with the details, was all over in ten minutes. In front of the cameras I was given a large facsimile cardboard cheque for £10,000 from Gabriel which, with much pomp and ceremony, I presented to Deputy Assistant Commissioner Sir Cecil Frank Bancroft KB QPM, which at my behest he confirmed would be deposited into the Metropolitan Police Widows and Orphans Fund the following morning, and thanked me cordially. I later had a cold coffee and a slab of tasteless bread pudding in the studio canteen, met various celebrities, (none of whom I recognised), was given a signed photograph of Ken Bruce and an M&S voucher for £50. The cheap skates! They didn't even give me a lift back home, and to add insult to injury, I had to pay £3.50 for the tube fare back, since I didn't think that I would need my freedom pass today.

I was glad that all of this nonsense was over relatively quickly, and that I was in time to meet the lads outside the DHSS offices at 11:55, when five minutes later an event of epic historical importance was to take place. I had cajoled a local reporter from *The Kilburn Times* to attend, stating that it was a story that would be of immense public interest, and particularly for all those on benefits. A former claimant (I nearly said sponger then) had courageously kicked his legs out of bed two hours earlier than normal, and for the first time in his thirty-two years of inactivity would emerge from a virgin office at midday following his *first ever* three hours spent in gainful employment.

At fifteen minutes past the hour, the unmistakable, dejected and wretched figure of *Lenny the Ponce* emerged to a rousing vocal chorus of 'For he's a jolly good fellow' which resounded above the vehicular cacophony of the Kilburn High Road. Cameras flashed and passing pedestrians stopped to ascertain the cause of the rumpus, thinking perhaps that they'd see someone famous and milled away disappointed when they saw Lenny's less than inspiring shape and wan-looking physiognomy being hoisted on to the shoulders of an excited miscellaneous rabble. I heard one woman say, 'I thought it might be one of them Rolling Stones. But he doesn't look anything like Keith Jagger!'

Being close to the Goose and Firkin, we crashed en masse through the doors a little later. News spreads fast in Kilburn, and just about everyone in the place applauded Lenny, who looked so very bewildered and needed to sit down. He was the first to put his hand in his pocket and, as usual, he left it there, since he didn't have the proverbial pot to pee in. But I reasoned that it was the thought that counted and believed that one day he would find a note of the realm, albeit perhaps one that could no longer be used as legal tender, since paper currency had been discontinued some considerable time before.

I was very surprised a little later when Basil arrived. Again, he could not give me any real comforting news other than to inform me that arrangements had been made for Spike to be collected at around 10:30 on the morning of Friday 2nd March. The police would be nearby ready to apprehend the despicable *fatherless-people* involved. However, I did manage to tell him about Tommy's request and he suggested that I have a word with Tina, whom he stated, 'had proved herself more than worthy when it came to tracing people.' With a little help from Ted and Alfie, she had been the one to locate Spike's whereabouts, which frankly given the lack of positive leads was no mean feat. On leaving the pub, he stated that he would ask her to give me a ring.

Later in the Gay Bar, Lenny was to give a blow-by-blow account of his first three hours spent at work to a crowd that listened in hushed reverence as though he was relating a heroic epic about how he'd crossed the snow-covered Pyrenees on his belly. In all fairness, nobody would have believed that this momentous event could ever have happened, but happen it did and while he related his incredible story, with the reporter scribbling away furiously, he looked about as happy as a penguin in a microwave, and his attentive audience could justifiably be described as an incredulous open-mouthed collective abomination. Vlado was lost for meaningful words and Dave, who normally has plenty to say, was dumbstruck. *Whispering Jim* completely ignored Lenny's verbal *codswallop* and was busily playing cards alone, and judging by his colourful expletives, he was clearly losing.

A little later, I met up with my girls at home, and together with Jimena, I really felt so very joyful that I had such a wonderful family around me. We spent an hour or so chatting and laughing. It has been a very interesting day, and I was more than happy to jump into bed relatively early.

Goodnight, Ginny.
P xx

21st February 2012

Good morning, Ginny.

I spent a most comfortable night getting up at 06:30. More snow had fallen during the night, and on spotting it Maria couldn't wait to be jumping around downstairs. But at 07:00 it was still dark outside and (reluctantly) she scoffed a light breakfast of waffles covered in maple syrup instead.

Lenka is off work for a couple of nights now and I suggested to Maria that a trip out somewhere during the day might be fun. She was all for it, and once

Lenka had shaken off her morning demons, and had completed her morning devotions with her loofah in the shower, so was she. All that we had to decide upon was a potential destination and suitable itinerary.

Maria couldn't take her eyes off the newly fallen snow in the courtyard, and without conviction absentmindedly stated that 'Jimena, couldn't be left alone for too long'. Lenka pointed out that this would limit our choices but then had a brainwave. 'Maria would like to play in the snow, so let's go up to Primrose Hill, I could teach her to snowboard,' she said excitedly and vanishing into the kitchen came back with our extra-large metal tea tray.

We got the bus to St Johns Wood and walked from there to Primrose Hill. This is a very affluent area and it would appear that the nobs in general and the local residents in particular enjoy a little time spent on the piste. (They like skiing too!) I understand that this particular sport is a very expensive one, and frankly I have never seen the point of spending a couple of thousand pounds on equipment and clothing just to get *Brahms and Liszt* in some obscure Alpine bar.

Needless to say, *The Hill* was inundated with poseurs on snowboards and skis, but I cannot remember a time when I have laughed so much watching Maria hurtling down the slopes sitting on a tea tray. It was absolutely hilarious. She enjoyed it all very much however, and we all had a marvellous time.

Before we returned to Kilburn, we had a very nice lunch in a rather expensive bistro in the High Street. Maria studied the bill of fare like a duchess to the menu born, and ordered an all-day breakfast, Lenka had a sandwich and a selection of assorted petit fours and I had the bill.

Later in the afternoon, I had a call from *Ted the Pleb* to say that Nobby Caxton had been reported missing. His son Lionel had told him that his father had failed to return home last night. I didn't like the sound of this at all and I seriously hoped that he would not do anything silly. Clearly he is suffering, and being a man of principle, the balance of his mind might be considerably disturbed.

Lenny's mind was *very* seriously disturbed following his three hours of work yesterday and last night he had to have a sauna, a deep tissue rubdown, and a session of Thai foot massage. Instead of his usual uninspiring evening meal, he settled for a large glass of soluble aspirin, a handful of vitamin pills and two strawberry-and-banana-flavoured protein drinks. He was sitting in the Gay Bar when we got back to Kilburn, chatting to *Scotch Andy* who was wearing a new pair of designer spectacles, which Alfie thought made him look *quite extinguished*!

Looking up from his paper, an unusually lucid *Whispering Jim* said, 'They can make a person look quite intelligent.' Walking over to Andy, Jim asked him if he could take a look at them. Andy reluctantly gave them to him, which he then put on Lenny. Studying Lenny's bewildered-looking face critically, Jim scratched his *scrotum* and said, 'Oh I dunno though?'

Alfie who was sitting in the corner of the bar trying to look a little intellectual, had his head buried in *The Observer*, or at least was studying the pictures. Looking up, he said, 'Glasses can actually alter your appearance and personality quite considerably.'

'Yeah! If you empty them regularly enough you mean,' called Dave, as he left the toilet and was having a bit of trouble doing up his fly.

'Having a little difficulty there, Dave?' shouted Ted.'Nothing that I can't handle,' replied Dave. 'But then being as well-endowed as me, one has to be a little careful.'

'Why, in case you can't find it?' replied Ted mockingly.

'You wouldn't want it on the end of your nose as a wart, mate,' replied Dave.

Sadly, nobody could give me any real comforting news about Nobby, and frankly none of the buggers seemed in the least bit interested when I brought up the subject. I took my drink and walked outside, sitting down at a damp uninviting table. The shock of the chill wind and a wet seat enlivened me sufficiently enough to hasten back into the bar, but before I could get to the door, I was stopped by Tina who appeared out of the shadows, frightening the living daylights out of me. I cowered before her like a vanquished foe, with a heart that was banging away like a headboard in a brothel. 'Good gracious me!' I said (or words of near similar import). 'Why on earth must you always make such a dramatic entrance? It seems to me that you have a very pronounced over-inflated sense of entitlement in frightening the hell out of people!'

'Oh sorry Paul,' she said. 'It's a force of habit.' After, a few minutes, my heart rate had slowed sufficiently and I became more self-composed. I took her into the posh bar and initially necked a large cognac, after which I bought her a large vodka tonic and a vegan green goddess pizza topped with extra mozzarella and cashew nuts, which she devoured with amazing finesse.

A little later, we got on to the subject of tracing Tommy's daughter. I gave her all of the information that I had, and that was precious little. I told her that her name is believed to be Siobhan, although it wasn't clear what surname she would now be using. Her father was Thomas Lucknow Grasscon, although the name of her mother was unknown. I had nothing further to add apart from the belief that she was last heard of in Kinsale, County Cork, but even with this snippet of semi-reliable information, I couldn't provide an exact date, apart from confidently stating that it would have been sometime after 'the turn of the twentieth century!'

Tina had been making notes throughout and didn't seem to be in the least bit perturbed at the very sketchy information that I had provided. I asked her if she was free to take on this assignment, and she stated that things were pretty quiet at the solicitor's office and she would be more than happy to take on a challenge like this one.

We agreed to meet at my flat in the morning, where I would give her £200 which should cover her immediate expenses, and would pay her £40 a day labour. Should she locate Tommy's daughter I would give her an additional bonus of £25. All was agreed upon, and on leaving she shook my hand and then gave me a very surprising kiss on the cheek.

Goodnight love.
P xx

22nd February 2012

Good morning, Ginny.

I tried to phone Basil first thing this morning, but he was apparently not in the office today. I am very anxious about my court case tomorrow and perhaps more so in that Basil has been very uncommunicative over this last week or so. But then I haven't given up hope in this quite remarkable man. I am sure that he has everything under control.

Maria hadn't come home last night and it seems that Jimena had curried a little favour with Lenka and had spent the night with her. They both arrived in the kitchen just after 08:00.

Tina arrived at 09:20. I introduced her to Lenka and something quite extraordinary happened. They shook hands warmly and I sensed an indescribable mutual bond had taken place between them. Perhaps it was some kind of sixth sense, but I knew that they were destined to become very good friends indeed. They are very similar in many ways and are both very strong-minded individuals.

I gave Tina the £200 for expenses as promised, and she gave me her bank details so that I could put the promised daily bank transfer of £40 into her account. The exchange rate on the euro is quite good at the moment, so she will not be short of cash in Ireland.

I will be contacting the Listowel bank in the not-too-distant future, which hopefully will enable me to top up the short fall in my personal finances. My bank, which hitherto has always been quite full, is getting lighter and it is not quite as noisy when I shake it now!

Lenka was fascinated at Tina's latest assignment and was quite impressed given the limited amount of information that her new friend had to work on. 'I would love to go on an adventure like that one,' she said.

On leaving, Tina shook her hand again and smiling sweetly replied, 'Maybe next time Lenka.'

A little later I went up to see Lionel Caxton to ask if there was any further news with regard to his father. He was in a very distraught condition. Nobby's wife Gretchen had left the family home in 2009 and being the devoted dutiful son, Lionel had remained at home. I comforted him as best as I could and reassured him that his father perhaps needed to spend a little time alone, and was convinced that when he had sorted himself out, he would return home safe and sound. Perhaps I was simply trying to convince myself that such would be the case. Frankly, I am very worried about Nobby's state of mind and his safety. However, Lionel did tell me that he and his mother were in regular contact (which was news to me) and that periodically they would meet up. It seems that Nobby wasn't aware of this.

I received a letter from St Mary's hospital in Paddington this morning to say that an appointment had been made for me to have my hernia reversal procedure on Monday 2nd April. Oh *sphericals!* I thought. I'd had a tenner bet with Ted that I would have the operation before the 31st March. Normally I do not gamble and believe that a man shouldn't gamble when he can't afford it and perhaps more importantly, when he has an excess of available funds. However, I foolishly took the wager and will therefore pay what's due, but not until well after the 2nd April.

I had a very quiet evening.

Goodnight, Ginny.
P xx

23rd February 2012

Good morning, my dear.

Once again I had to make the laborious trek across London to the infamous Westminster Magistrates Court, which frankly is a veritable nightmare. I was in no mood for being polite and snarled at the bus driver on my first leg of the journey. This was completely out of character, and on leaving I made a point of apologising to my Sikh chauffeur. He smiled at me good-naturedly and replied, 'If you never make a mistake, you may live and die without anyone ever noticing you.' Actually, this changed my entire thought process and I seriously considered becoming an *utter rotter* for the rest of the day.

I arrived at Horseferry Road Magistrates Court at 09:30, thoroughly exhausted and genuinely annoyed that yet again I had to defend myself in a court of law and had to answer spurious charges (of which I am totally innocent). Having played Abraham Lincoln in a school play years ago, as I walked through its less than inspiring front doors again, I remembered my best ever soliloquy:

'I do the best that I know how, the very best that I can; and I mean to keep on doing it to the end. If the end brings me out all right, what is said against me will not amount to anything. If the end brings me out wrong, ten angels swearing I was right would make no difference.'

Sadly, I hadn't realised at the time that I was actually verbalising this recollection, which resulted in a large swathe of the *miscellaneous rabble* parting and allowing me to walk through them, like a leper at a royal garden party.

A copper with a clipboard raised a very hairy pair of eyebrows and was scratching his bum with wild abandon, and a young child in one of those frontal hammock thingies was vomiting copiously down the neck of a rather baggy blouse that its mother was wearing. Not a pretty sight for one having a somewhat weak constitution, which had earlier ingested a bowl of porridge. Still, at least it looked as though the child was enjoying itself.

I found Basil sitting outside courtroom two, where a little later my case would be heard. 'So how's it all looking Basil?' I asked. 'Without Nobby Caxton's evidence, not good at all, in fact, quite impossible,' he replied.

'I wondered why you hadn't been your normal regular self. I thought that you might have left the country,' I said flippantly.

'I shall be seeking an adjournment,' he replied. 'This case cannot go on without Nobby!'

A little later, my name echoed through that dark satanic hall of infamy and once inside courtroom two, Basil went straight on to the offensive. He succinctly stated his observation that without the testimony of a crucial witness, 'a very serious miscarriage of justice was likely to take place and as a result an innocent man condemned!' This produced a collective incredulous gasp and a murmur of disbelief from the public gallery, which prompted the magistrate to give his gavel its first perfunctory wallop of the day. Without uttering a word, his well-practised condemnatory glares towards the offending rabble had an immediate effect and an ominous silence ensued.

As usual, I thought that Basil's rhetorical eloquence was marvellous, although perhaps the word *condemned* could have been omitted and another more suitable term or euphemism used instead. It conjured up a less than desirable verdict which resulted in my being roughly slapped in irons, thrown onto the back of a cart and transported for life to darkest Bradford, with no chance of a reprieve, or ever setting foot in my beloved Kilburn again. However, his statement and the following theatricals thus produced, certainly aroused me from my earlier mental wool-gathering.

The magistrate (who appeared to be in his nineties) having looked up from his notes, granted 'a stay of execution' as it were, and stated that 'the case will be adjourned, *'sine die!'* which frankly, I didn't initially understand, but having seen the look of relief and joy on my solicitor's face, who whispered, 'It will be adjourned until we are ready to proceed,' I too breathed a sigh of relief. Those few words were as delightful to my troubled mind as an ice-cold lager is to thirsty lips. My spirits lifted immediately and despondency slipped from my drooping shoulders like a large soggy cloak.

On our way out, I was quite surprised that on this occasion, the public gallery was not packed to capacity like the last time. It consisted of a few reporters scribbling away in their notebooks, a limited quota of the local *miscellaneous rabble*, none of whom I recognised, and a great lump of a security bloke, who simply stared into space. Actually, he reminded me of one of those street entertainers that mimic statues and will only move when a coin is placed in their box. On our way out, I chucked a 5p coin at him just in case, but it had no effect whatsoever. Someone had either forgotten to top up his meter or had blown out his pilot light. A possible job for Lenny, I thought.

Outside in the courtroom corridor, I again passed the young child in the hammock thingy, who was having a marvellous time bashing its mother's vomit-filled blouse and laughing deliriously.

Basil appeared to be quite relieved that for the time being at least, the case was on hold. He shook my hand, and stated that he'd be in touch, and that maybe we could have a meet up for lunch at the *Glass House*, next week.

'I never did understand why you had chosen this pub for our former meeting with Nobby,' I said.

'It's all rather simple,' he replied, closing his briefcase, and straightening his tie. 'It happens to be Albery Groupenhourst's favourite watering hole, and as the very wise proverb states, *keep your friends close, but your enemies closer*!' Tapping the side of his nose with his right index finger, he silently left.

This got me thinking. So far I have been a very passive transient being, allowing personal events to take place and offering no resistance whatsoever. Those wonderful lines from Hamlet suddenly came to mind and inspired me to take a more active interest in my condition and fate.

'To be, or not to be, that is the question;
Whether 'tis nobler in the mind to suffer the
slings and arrows of outrageous fortune, or to
take arms against a sea of troubles and by opposing end them.'

I therefore decided that since I was already in town, that instead of heading straight back to Kilburn, that I'd call into Mr Groupenhourst's place of business intrinsically for him and I to become a little better acquainted. Besides, I am just about ready to play him at his own little game and to become more than simply friendly with this *fatherless-person*. Of course, I really do not enjoy the thought of behaving in a less than straight forward manner, but it sometimes becomes necessary to forget one's principles and to not be afraid to wear trousers with rubber-lined pockets at the soup kitchen (metaphorically speaking of course).

To set my plans in motion, and to provide a legitimate reason for my visit, I would ask him to make a couple of new door keys, copies of which I felt sure he would retain for his own future use. But first, I would pay a visit to a very old former police pal of mine who has an office nearby.

It is always so nice to meet up with trusted friends again and with Bill Robinson it was indeed a great pleasure. We were at school together, and I was the best man at his wedding. Later I was to become a godfather to each of his three daughters. He chose the police service and I selected a career in the gaming industry. On retirement in 2007, he opened a small home security business, selling burglar alarms and providing advice on surveillance and home security matters. This became very successful, and now he is one of the leading lights in the security industry, particularly in matters of covert home and industrial surveillance.

We spent a very enjoyable two hours together and having brought him up to date with regard to my own unfortunate issues – which he listened to with considerable interest and sympathy – he gave me a great deal of very useful advice. He will pay a visit to the flat on Saturday, and was confident that he could help. On his advice, our meeting and any subsequent conversations were to remain completely confidential, and this was to include (everyone) within my immediate circle of friends and applied to relatives as well. However, I will need someone to confide in, and I hope my dear Ginny that you will step into this uncertain and lonely breach and become my confidante and guide over the dark and uncertain days that lie ahead. You have always proved to be a loyal and loving friend, and frankly you are the only person that I can truly trust at this time.

I stepped into the lair of the villain at 15:20, my entrance being made known by a buzzer that sounded as I opened the door. He was involved in key cutting and had his back to me. Above the noise of the cutting device, and without turning around, he shouted, 'I'll be with you in a minute or two!'

Having finished, he turned around, and wearing what could be described as a somewhat grotesque mask of geniality, he joined me at the counter. Suddenly, his facial expression changed to one of abject horror as the coin of recognition dropped, and the false smile started to twitch and curl up at the edges. Clearly he was having tremendous difficulty fighting back the snarl that was doing its best to achieve full expression. I acted just as surprised, but offered my hand anyway, which he reluctantly took. I won't bore you with the less than sincere verbal *sphericals* that passed between us, other than to say that I asked him to make a copy of my two front door keys, which I left with him. I told him that I had to dash due to an urgent appointment, and that perhaps if it would not be too inconvenient, we could have a meet up with one another tomorrow evening at a pub of his choice. I even intimated that it would be nice to have a pint or two with him, which seemingly put him at a loss for words, although he appeared to relax a bit more thereafter. I shook hands with him again on leaving.

Later back in the Gay Bar, I mentally considered my first ever acting role in a real-life scenario, and although I was quite saddened that I have had to take this course of action, I was quite pleased with my initial steps into the deceitful world of skulduggery.

Following a call from him later, he suggested a meet up at the *Glass House* pub on Saturday evening at 19:30.

Goodnight, Ginny. P xx

Good morning, Ginny.

Despite having a very disturbed night's sleep, dreaming quite vividly about a cold, damp, dungeon, I awoke at 06:10 sweating profusely, with Jimena trying to attack my feet under the duvet. I do believe that she would be excellent at catching mice, but in the interim is content to practise on toes.

Maria wasn't home when I got up, and I am beginning to feel a little superfluous to requirements. Like her, my almost robotic early morning activity revolves around breakfast. For me it involves preparing same, while for her it is a simple matter of getting rid of it. I am a creature of habit from my early morning culinary extravaganza to my late evening ingestion of medicinal quantities of cocoa and cognac, and I become quite disorientated when my normal routine is disturbed. However, following her morning shower, Lenka joined me, and having explained to her my sense of unhappiness and futility, was delighted to know that she was 'a little hungry' and liked my suggestion of banana pancakes liberally coated in maple syrup. Thanks to her, my morning needs and expectations were satisfied, and thereafter all was right with the world, at least for the time being.

At 10:00 I phoned the Canterbury branch of the Listowel bank where I spoke to its manager, Robert Levington, who, by his friendly and amusing repartee, gave me the impression that he had been expecting my call. Having nothing planned, I enquired if it would be convenient to call upon him later in the day.

I left home at 10:30 and got the tube to Victoria and was aboard the train bound for Canterbury East at 11:20. The one hour thirty-minute journey was memorable in that it passed agonisingly slow. There was a bloke sitting opposite me that looked like he'd just escaped from a lunatic asylum (perhaps the pyjamas and teddy bear gave him away). But seriously, there are many times (like on rail journeys) where I simply want to be left alone. I won't even make eye contact with the ticket inspector, as he struts through the carriages like a frustrated Gestapo agent on community service, hoping to catch a fare-dodger.

When out in the bigger world, I have developed considerable cunning in personal self-restraint, particularly where an innocent single word or gesture on my part might encourage the unwanted attentions of a potential pest, no matter how innocent looking, and there are plenty of them out there.

Ten minutes into the journey, while reading my paper, I realised that the bloke opposite kept looking at me furtively, and when I looked out of the window I saw his reflection gazing back at me, which I chose to ignore. He was an unmistakable serial verbaliser looking for his next victim. However a little later, an elderly woman pulling a trolley came struggling along the aisle and wearily plonked herself down next to me, puffing loudly. She kept looking up at the luggage rack and was clearly too weak to lift her case. As gentlemanly as ever, I stood and hoisted it up for her, and having regained my seat smiled at her absentmindedly. It was then that I realised to my horror that this single humanitarian gesture would be perceived as a green light and would be rewarded with a veritable earhole bashing for the remainder of my journey. I had unwittingly fallen into her trap; an innocent miserable captive, and thereafter I was to experience the truth behind the old saying that 'no good deed goes unpunished' since now that the ice had been broken as it were, 'himself' of the cuckoo's nest was inspired to join in. I could tell that he had a lot of very uninspiringly dreary and mundane things to get off his chest and wouldn't rest until a considerable quantity of over-flowing verbal irrelevance had been eradicated from his being and systematically stuffed down my *external acoustic meatus* (earhole). And stuffed down it was! Still, as I thankfully hastened off the train at Canterbury East, I felt confident that my karmic balance had received a few extra nectar points, in that I had helped two needful transient beings to let off a bit of steam, albeit stale and monotonously tedious. But then, it's nice to be nice.

As I legged it out of the station, I offered up a silent prayer of thanks to the karmic assessor in that I had been able to patiently overcome an unpleasant experience, and hoped that if ever I was to meet up with either of my fellow travellers again, it would simply be on passing and hopefully on different trains. Mine going to Waterloo and theirs on a night-sleeper to Inverness.

Thankfully my cab driver was far less talkative, mainly because, as I was to find out later, that he couldn't speak a word of English, although he seemed very proficient when it came to abstract expressions like, 'It will be ten pounds fifty sir!'

It was a pleasant journey to the Listowel Bank which was near the city centre, and I was sitting in the office of its manager, Robert Levington, at 13:55. He made me feel very much at home, and after a very welcome cup of coffee and the usual pleasantries were concluded, we got down to business. I gave him Tommy's formal letter and as requested, produced two forms of positive ID, my passport and driving licence, both of which he photocopied. A little later he took me down to the safe deposit box area, and on opening box 44 I found the money. I took it back to Bob's office where he passed it through a note counter and it totalled £18,750, just as Tommy had stated. I certainly didn't want to be walking about with this amount of cash on me, so Bob very kindly opened up an account in my name, and I deposited it all therein. My account details, plus cash card and cheque book would be sent to my home address in about four working days.

Following a very quiet and peaceful journey home (I had found a straw bale to sit on in the mail car), Sebastian and I were romping in the surf suds at 20:55pm.

Goodnight, Ginny.
P xx

25th February 2012

Good morning, Ginny.

At 07:50 I was awoken by a scratching sound outside of my bedroom door, and on getting up to investigate, I found Maria sitting on the hall carpet holding a fork in one hand with Jimena balancing precariously on her right shoulder. She was smiling at me sweetly and giggling wildly.

'I bet you thought that it was Jimena scratching on your door,' she said, getting up off the floor with considerable effort and displaying an appreciable amount of bodily instability and confusion like a drunk holding a kitten in one hand and a fork in the other, that had just tripped over a dustbin. 'We've missed you,' she said, kissing me on the cheek. 'What's for breakfast?'

At around 09:45 having showered and cleared away an assortment of kitchen utensils, washed Maria's breakfast plate (which had been licked clean of every suggestion that it had once been used as a receptacle on which food had been placed) and secured the padlock on the fridge, I thought that a revitalising trip to the gym would be in order.

There was a new male receptionist at the desk when I arrived who introduced himself as Simon. He was immaculately turned out in a blue silk shirt, matching cravat and a pair of grey chinos. His unmistakable accent suggested an Australian provenance and sure enough he told me later that he hailed from Earls Court. He was actually born in Balham but had lived and worked in a place that had become known as *Little Australia* for years, and being constantly surrounded by Aussie colonials, had become infected with the unmistakable twang of the outback and that quite annoying habit of theirs in using rising intonation when making a statement. I'm no language prude but have a fundamental belief in the English language as amended, which having been forged over centuries from utter gobbledegook to its present definitive expressive form, is as good as it can get. Quite simply, a statement should not sound like a question!

Having given my limpness of musculature a wake-up call, I found Lenny sitting in the steam room. I really wasn't in the mood to listen to his monotonously whining drivel and was about to turn tail when he asked me to stay. Normally I would avoid friends in need (unless there was no clear route of escape) but since I had patiently sat through a considerable time listening to the dull observations and reminiscences of two complete strangers yesterday, how could I turn my back on one of my own?

I sat down heavily and sighed, awaiting the depressing verbal onslaught, but I couldn't have been more wrong. The former *well-nourished, dark-complexioned, fatherless woman* at the DHSS was now referred to initially as Ms Balalla and as his five-day recollections unfolded, a more familiar term of Eugenia was used. She had apparently taken him under her maternal wing and, despite the years of frustrating torment that Lenny must have given her, she had gently guided him through his very first work experience. And I got the impression that he had enjoyed the journey.

On leaving, he casually stood up and the towel that was wrapped loosely around his waist slipped down to the floor revealing a distressed-looking dick that had been suddenly exposed to the hot stream and was twitching like an agitated meerkat on guard duty. He casually picked it up again and absentmindedly holding it in front of his genitals said, 'I am not a failure because I didn't succeed, but simply because I haven't tried. But all of that is now in the past.' He left shortly afterwards, letting in a very unwelcome gust of cold air, which didn't exactly have a positive effect on my bodily extremities either.

On the way home I bumped into 'Alex' Barrington Scott and invited him to join me and Albery at the Glass House pub later in the evening. I thought that he would be a welcome addition and a distraction as it were, while Albery and I got to know one another. He will join us at around 20:00 this evening.

Back home, Jock Robinson arrived at 13:15 and completed an internal survey of my flat, concentrating on the hall, my bedroom and the kitchen. He will be putting in pinhole cameras linked to a time-lapse VCR, which will only record movement. Maria was very inquisitive throughout his stay and questioned me ceaselessly when he had left. However, this was all completely confidential. I eventually had to give her a feasible reason for his visit and told her that he would be doing a little painting and decorating. At some later date, Jock will install the system, which will have to take place when both of my girls were out. This necessary subterfuge will hopefully achieve the desired result – to catch a horribly unscrupulous *anal-orifice.*

Later, for the first time in many months I felt that I needed to have a quick afternoon nap, however, I didn't sleep. I never do if I have a lot on my mind, and in this case it was Jimena trying to curl up on my face. In fact she was a real pest. I turned over and she climbed up onto my hip, sat down, stretched luxuriously and then started to purr contentedly. Initially it was a quite comforting sound, until she started to suck on my belt noisily and then began kneading my jeans, which ended any further hope of sleep.

Actually I have always been a light sleeper, and would often be disturbed by snoring. My former canary *Bubsie* was dreadful. Sadly on one fateful night, its long-term cage-partner, *Lucky,* had simply had enough and tragically he chucked himself into their water trough.

My initial social meeting with Albery was far from memorable. Having been given my newly cut keys which I received with the usual thanks and pleasantries, it soon became painfully obvious that we were about as compatible as a doughnut and a dumper truck. Frankly, when there was nothing more to be said, he kept on saying it. However, on the arrival of Alex, my fear of dying of boredom ceased. Happily, his ready wit and interesting subject matter enlivened the proceedings immensely, and following Albery's ingestion of five large gin and tonics, the evening started to brighten up. A little later, my former verbally reticent neighbour was giving us a complete unabridged account of his life, aspirations and disappointments. (He would obviously be one to avoid on a train journey.)

An hour and a half later, I was convinced that after a few more libations he would have happily given me the keys to his flat, the names and addresses of his henchmen, and the details of his offshore bank accounts.

During the build-up in relation to his later years, he stated that he was, 'A former regimental sergeant major in the *Kings Own Royal Brunswick Grenadiers'* and perhaps this would explain his evident love for military paraphernalia in general, and his utter hatred for anything on two legs in particular. He is clearly a very bitter man, and in conversation his statements were delivered like threats that no one dared to question. Apparently, he fought with Mountbatten in Burma, had a row with Alexander in Tunis, and couldn't get on with Montgomery at Alamein. If all of this was true, he certainly wouldn't have been nominated as a possible candidate for the prestigious 'NCO OF THE YEAR AWARD' run by the NAAFI, or nearer to home 'THE GOOD NEIGHBOUR CUP' (which I understand is currently under review by our landlords, due to the evident lack of interest on the part of the estate office personnel, the temporary caretakers, and the residents).

As the evening progressed, it became clearly evident that Albery was immensely proud of his disagreeable nature and seemingly enjoyed the notoriety of being considered a complete *fatherless-person* by anyone who had the misfortune of coming into contact with him. I am sure you will agree that this is very unusual behaviour indeed.

My own personal description of him would use the following terms, although not necessarily in this order: disagreeable, egotistical, self-opinionated and charmless. Perhaps more revealingly, he could be described as one bearing the characteristic traits and intellectual capabilities of a three-toed Malaysian sloth. He is also an unashamedly prodigious lying *fatherless-person* who tells *porkies* with unbelievable enthusiasm, particular those that relate to his non-existent military career.

Having checked later on *Google, Yahoo* and *The Encyclopaedia of British & European Regiments,* it quickly became evident, that he had been talking complete *sphericals,* since 'The Kings Own Royal Brunswick Grenadiers' is as fictitious as that celebrated Highland Regiment, *The 3rd Battalion Foot And Mouth* which featured in that marvellous sixties film *Carry on up the Khyber.* Additionally, for him to have engaged in active service during the last conflict, and assuming that he would have been around eighteen at the time, this would mean that his current age would now be around ninety-three. At a rough guess, I would estimate that he is in his late fifties or early sixties. Either that or he had secretly discovered the fabled *Elixir of Youth,* which the Greek Gods called

Ambrosia. Personally, I'm not too keen on it, although their creamed custard is rather scrummy on apple pie.

As the evening progressed and Albery's timidity subsided, reluctantly I have to admit that he began to slowly grow on me, but for all of the wrong reasons. In truth, I really couldn't believe that a man like him could exist in our modern age. He is undoubtedly the worst example of humanity that I had ever met, and as a result my fascination intensified. However, the story of his parent's escape from Nazi Germany during the last war, and their heroic tale of survival living rough in the forests of Bavaria during the dreadful winter of 1941 (if it could be believed) would have made Scott's expedition to the North Pole seem like a summer picnic at Henley and would probably have been nominated for a *Booker Prize* had it been made into a novel. However, if the tale was true and Albery had inherited his parent's survival capabilities, then clearly this man was very dangerous indeed, since he would stop at nothing to ensure his own personal safety and survival.

Before Alex and I left at 01:35, he invited us both to a (men-only) regimental reunion luncheon on the afternoon of Saturday the 3rd March, to be held where we were now sitting. He told us that the food and speeches part of the proceedings would be over relatively quickly, and thereafter a free bar and *suitable* entertainment would be provided. His lascivious grin and the way that he rubbed his hands together, clearly suggested an evening of alcohol-fuelled debauchery.

On our way home later, Alex made the comment, that he'd never met anyone quite like him. And I had to agree with him, but added that, 'Let's hope he was the last of his kind!'

As I lay in bed a little later contemplating sleep, I commended myself in that I had achieved stage two of my master plan, although I considered that I would have to tread very warily, since Albery was a cunning old *fatherless-person* and like a close relative of his, the fox may change his fur, but not his habits!

Goodnight, Ginny.
P xx

26th February 2012

Good morning, Ginny.

I had a phone call from Tina this morning. She has been in Ireland since last Thursday and is staying at a 'very nice guest house' just off the High Street in Kinsale. Mrs Murphy's Irish stew is 'to die for' and the Guinness at the *Nutty Monk* is 'the best she has ever tasted'. So far 'it has rained every day non-stop', she has had 'two proposals of marriage', has bought a bottle of 'Bushmills Blue' fifteen-year-old malt for Basil, 'who loves a drop of the Irish', and 'has two possible leads with regard to the whereabouts of Siobhan Grasscon'. (I knew that she would get around to it eventually.) Before she rang off she asked how Lenka was, and that I should pass on her regards.

You may remember that my ancestral family came from County Mayo. They escaped that terrible time of famine back in the 1840s, and with their meagre belongings apparently trekked right across Ireland to the east coast, and sailed over the Irish Sea, landing up in Glasgow. They quickly realised that a Scot is a man that keeps the Sabbath (and anything else that came to hand) so what little possessions they had they guarded jealously. It was here that they learned their own personal art of survival, and after many adventures, they finally settled in Dumbarton.

A few generations later, my great,-great-great-grandfather *Hamish* opened up a fish and chip takeaway called *Avast – Chips – Ahoy*. He always had a good sense of humour. He was a tough old bird and a notorious scrapper in his day that never backed down when it came to a little row-induced fisticuffs. Early in the last conflict, he was one of the first to volunteer for active service. However, he was never destined to prove his patriotic mettle and was reluctantly prevented from winning his Victoria Cross since he was severely wounded during his medical examination. Thereafter, he flatly refused to mention the war.

It was a very quiet and uninteresting morning, and frankly I felt a little isolated in the flat. Both of my girls were out, and while Jimena is an amusing and lively companion, I felt that I needed a little human companionship and stimulating conversation. I settled on a visit to the Gay Bar instead, which would have been the next best thing. Besides, I reasoned that it would be inexcusably self-centred of me to remain lonesome, companionless and solitary, particularly when I could experience the same thing among friends.

When I arrived at the pub, the usual motley crew were in attendance. Ted was having a pretty heated conversation with Vlado on the merits of placing little snacks on the bar like cheese, baked potatoes and various nibbles which used to be customary on Sunday visits to British pubs during the 'good-old-days, pre-dinner imbibing session'.

'We are a pub, not kitchen for soup,' pointed out Vlado. 'Tell you what though,' he continued. 'If you want foods, buy a Martini, and I'll stuff olives in it with sticks!'

Whispering Jim looked up from his game of scrabble and shouted, 'I hate them feckin things! I got one of them caught in me throat once, and a bloke attacked me from behind, and held me in one of them bear-hug grips and violently lifted me off the ground with his fists in me stomach. He had me loose change rattling in me pockets, which sounded like a major pay out on the fruit machine, and I was bouncing up and down like a puppet on a string!'

'That'll be the *Heimlich Manoeuvre* Jim,' said Tony helpfully. 'At least he got rid of the lump blocking your airway.'

'I was more concerned with the lump that was sticking in me back!' shouted Jim indignantly, banging his fist on his table, which catapulted his packet of fags and lighter into Ted's lap, who appreciating the windfall, helped himself to a cigarette, stuck it behind his right ear and said, 'Thanks Jim, I don't mind if I do, I'll save it for later.'

'So did you die then, Jim?' asked Dave, evidently in *urine-extraction mood*.

'No, course I didn't, but a couple of them paraplegic blokes had to regurgitate him!'

'Why did someone want to eat with him was?' asked the wide-eyed, open-mouthed Vlado.

'Not at all,' replied Jim absentmindedly. 'But the judge did ask why I had beaten him. I told him that it was probably due to me weight advantage, longer reach and superior footwork. But one thing is for sure, he won't be so keen on carrying out any more of them personal-space invading *How's-yer-fathers* on innocent people again. I've never felt so humiliated in all me life!'

'It's what you might call a life-enhancing experience Jim,' said Dave chuckling. 'Without that dreadful humiliation, perhaps you wouldn't have been able to lighten our day by telling us about it!'

Jim looked at me appealingly. 'I wish he wouldn't talk such complete *sphericals,'* he said, and looking down, continued in his one-man game of scrabble. Two gulps of lager, and a bag of pork scratchings later, the whole incident was forgotten.

Suddenly the front door burst open and an unknown distressed-looking face appeared which simply shouted 'CAT!' and there followed a very undisciplined hasty retreat, as though a grenade had been rolled into the place. Some sought sanctuary in the crowded gents, with the overflow cramming into the ladies, and others having made it into the posh bar. The Gay Bar was cleared in an amazing 35.5 seconds. You will recall that this acronym means, '**C**urate **A**voidance **T**echnique' and is used as a verbal warning of the approach of Father Marcus.

On this occasion it was a false alarm, since he simply passed by without venturing in, presumably on his way home from church. However, one can never be too complacent and these drills are a vitally important part of our daily lives in Kilburn, and aimed more particularly at the locals whose pastoral care is provided by Curate/Reverend in training, Marcus Byron Tanner.

Don't get me wrong, Ginny, I am quite fond of him, but as far as spiritual guidance and pastoral care, he is about as useful as a banjo player in Beethoven's Fifth. However, I bet that he would be absolutely devastated if he knew the lengths that some of his parishioners go to in avoiding him. Actually, having returned to the bar, I felt a little remorseful since I know that he is a good man, trying his best to come up to the expectations of his senior clergy and in his own very unusual way, is sincerely trying to do the right thing for those in his pastoral care. I decided then and there that I would be more available and visible to Father Marcus. He's not perfect, but then neither am I. He accepts me with all of my faults which are of a deliberate nature, whereas his are innocent and are unsympathetically ill-perceived by us all. Tomorrow is a new day, and I believe that a little change in direction is called for.

On the way back into the Gay Bar, I caught sight of *Scotch Andy* sitting on his own in the posh bar. This is most unusual, since he is normally such a fun-loving gregarious person. I simply had to join him. It appears that through the unexpected arrival of a relative of his mother's from the Ukraine, he had been told that he was in fact Jewish. While he is not a practising Christian, at the insistence of his wife (who is a devout Catholic), he has attended Mass every week since they married in 1987. I personally didn't see any real conflict of interest in this. In fact, I felt that it could be positively advantageous. 'There can't be many Jewish-Catholics about for a start!' I pointed out, although this didn't really lighten his mood. Standing up, he dusted himself down and said, 'Paul, I know that you are only trying to be helpful mate, but I need a little time alone. I'll catch up with you later.' He drank the last dregs of his beer, smiled at me in a rather embarrassed way and left the bar.

Late into the evening, I simply couldn't get his self-conscious smile out of my head. Clearly he had taken the news pretty badly, although for the life of me I couldn't understand why. As I lay soaking in the bath with Sebastian surfing in the suds, I considered the two religions. Both are monotheistic, with one basing its beliefs in the Old Testament and the Talmud and the other on the New Testament. Out of the two, the Old Testament is clearly older, but some would say that the later New Testament is simply a re-worked, revised and edited version of the first. However, I have never felt inclined to criticise religion in general or religious scripture in particular. It would be more than simply absurd and highly presumptuous of me to do so. Whatever their provenance or intrinsic accuracy or truth, they have been guiding mankind in their respective beliefs and religious customs since time immemorial.

Still, as I read another chapter of my latest bed book from the philosophical pen of *The Marquis De Sade,* I mused upon just how wonderfully romantic it would have been being in that beautiful garden, with the world's first woman.

Clearly on the plus side there would be no mother-in-law, no kids running around the place or drunken yobbos messing up the daffodils. It must have been quite something to be romping around together naked, without shame, guilt or belly buttons. A beautiful story that like all tragic dramas would be perhaps a little repetitive and boring for some latter-day party-poopers, at least until the villainous snake turns up and puts a right old spanner in the works.

A beautiful picnic can be ruined by a few drops of rain, a beautiful painting destroyed by a slash of a knife, and a beautiful heart broken by a few deceitful words.

I never did like snakes, particularly the talking kind. One only has to remember Disney's dreadful depiction of *Kaa* the python in *The Jungle Book*. He has been described as an hypnotic, conniving, seductive and thoroughly crafty predator, and while it is clear that Adam and Eve did rather mess things up for the rest of us, and it's easy to sit in judgement of them, I wonder just how many of us would have been *led up the garden* in the same deceitful manner. But at a time when the Guinness Book of Records had not been invented, they certainly would have scored a double first in modern times. They were the first people to walk the earth and the first pair to eat an apple!

Goodnight, Ginny.
P xx

27th February 2012

Good morning, Ginny.

Father Marcus caught me a little off guard this morning. Having knocked at 09:45 I opened the door excitedly since I thought that it was the postman. (Not that I get turned on by people in uniform, you understand, or get over-stimulated at the thought of seeing Norman Frederick Chisholm, a man whom I know in a purely business capacity, but because I was expecting a new toaster. Maria likes a few slices of *cooked bread* with her breakfast and this one does six slices at a time.)

Having got himself seated in his favourite position at the breakfast table (fortunately Maria wasn't in, since at this time in the morning, the kitchen table would have been *a no-go zone* being piled up with her usual post breakfast assortment of crockery and plates), but before he had uttered any meaningful words (which are few and far between anyway) he had devoured a strawberry yogurt, a bowl of crunchy nut cornflakes and eight custard creams. It seems that it had taken a lot of willpower, but he had finally managed to give up dieting.

Having allowed the unexpected repast to be masticated and drunk a large milky coffee to wash it all down, he finally clarified the reason for his visit. He explained that following a survey that he had conducted with residents –those that he could capture that is (about three I would imagine) – he found that there was 'quite a lot of interest' in holding a weekly bingo afternoon in the resident's hall (presumably to be attended by the three aforementioned captured residents). He asked if I would be available to assist him. It would be held for two hours on a Thursday lunchtime, and I would be responsible for selling the bingo ticket books and giving out the prize money. I told him that I would give it my due consideration and would get back to him later on in the week. However, as I mentioned to you yesterday, I am going to be more helpful to Father Marcus, and tomorrow I will let him know that I would be happy to assist him on his weekly bingo spectacular. I really didn't want to initially appear too enthusiastic. Besides, how difficult could it be to sell three bingo ticket books?

On leaving, he stopped by the door. 'It's a shame that I can't call out the bingo numbers in Latin,' he said, chortling happily.

'But wouldn't that confuse them?' I replied.

'No, my beloved churchgoers would be fine, but it would certainly bugger up the atheists,' he said, nearly choking with laughter as he made his way down the stairs. There is hope for this boy yet!

Danielle was on duty at the gym this morning, and her radiant, welcoming smile really sent a warm glow of happiness through my being. I asked her how she was getting on with Simon, but people started to arrive behind me and before she had time to answer, all she could say was, 'He's a triple N!' Which had me completely baffled.

The reception area was empty on my way out, and as I left, Danielle said, 'He's a nasty, narcissistic narshole!' Well that certainly cleared up that little mystery.

Later in the morning, I visited a small local nursery called *Paint Pots & Crayons* in readiness for Elisha's arrival next Monday. I spoke to one of the owners, a delightful young lady called Poppy, who very obligingly took me around the place, giving me a complete rundown on the children's daily activities. The weekly fees are very reasonable and I thought that Elisha would enjoy the daily four hours of stimulating activity that the nursery provided.

As you are aware, I have two grown-up sons and a daughter, but naturally they no longer live at home now. Strangely, a few years ago I would have quite enjoyed listening to the pitter-patter of little feet again. Fortunately at the time, I was awoken from my whimsy when my beloved Spike was dumped on my doorstep, and he has proved considerably cheaper and has more feet.

I haven't seen my two girls for a while, but have been constantly followed by my other little girl Jimena, who is an absolute delight to have around. However, Maria and Gabriel arrived at 16:00 and my little ball of fluff rushed excitedly down the hall to greet them.

Imitating her usual curtain-scaling routine, she shot up Gabriel's outer clothing faster than a crocodile out of a handbag factory, and once aloft she sat contentedly purring on his shoulder. Maria made a great fuss of her, and I got a nice cuddle too, but would have preferred it to have been from Maria. However, she did give me a perfunctory kiss on the cheek, followed by a meaningful passionate hug when I suggested making sandwiches and coffee.

Maria's relationship with Gabriel has truly blossomed, and they seem like a perfect couple. He is articulate, gentle, attentive and considerate, and she is more than simply fond of him. She is a beautiful, intellectually compromised, submissive young lady who suffers from the occasional mood swing and pre-menstrual tantrum, who displays a very obvious reluctance to engage in matters of a domestic nature in general and has a distinct abhorrence to washing-up liquid in particular. But she responds well to gentle words, a good old-fashioned cuddle and a couple of her favourite toffee-coated doughnuts, and he loves her to bits. He has obviously seen through the common, everyday facade that she has chosen to present to the world, and has discovered the wonderful hidden beauty of spirit that lies beneath. What a delightfully perfect couple they make.

Later in the day, I received a call from Basil asking if I would be free for a 'catch-up type meeting' tomorrow at 10:30, and he jokingly asked when he could have his *slick-dick-chick* back. He was obviously referring to Tina. 'It shouldn't be too long, Basil,' I replied. 'She's in the haystack as we speak.'

'Well, I sincerely hope that she doesn't prick herself,' he ventured. I felt it wise at this point to change the subject.

At the Gay Bar later, the boys were in animated conversation.

'In my world, before wedded, a woman never sees her husband,' said Vlado, pouring a large tomato juice for *Scotch Andy,* to which he added a considerably larger measure of neat vodka.

'Yeah well in this part of the world she doesn't see very much of him afterwards,' replied Dave. 'That's why publicans like you do so well. I bet you have never had a set of bicycle clips in your life, have you?' Before Vlado had time to answer, Lenny chucked in a few words.

'I should be so lucky,' he said dejectedly. 'Actually, I wouldn't mind being married.'

'You're not intelligent enough,' interrupted Ted, putting down a rather crumpled-up copy of *Woman's Weekly* (he gets it for the recipes).

'That's not very fair, mate,' replied Lenny. 'Eugenia thinks that I've got a lot of potential and believes that I would make a very good husband and father. Besides, just be careful, you're talking about a person that I am very fond of,' stabbing a finger into his chest. 'I am a changed man stepping up the newly discovered ladder of life,' he continued. 'So when would I be intelligent enough?'

'When you start thinking that marriage is completely out of the question,' replied Ted, disinterestedly thumbing through a copy of Kate Garraway's book The Joy of Big Knickers, which was one of the course books that *Alfie the Dip* had to read during his recent part-time evening GCE O'Level English Literature

161

studies at the Kilburn Institute of Further Education. Sadly, his normal education had been severely disrupted by his various and sporadic terms of incarceration in various government-sponsored institutions. Apparently, when he had asked *Miss Hodges* where she thought he would come in the class, he was absolutely delighted when she confidently replied that 'he would certainly come with the first twelve'. The fact that there was only twelve in the class was neither here nor there! He was later to receive a grade C minus. But then God loves a tryer!

Interrupting his scrabble game, *Whispering Jim,* suddenly said, 'Yeah well I was well annoyed! My best made suddenly upped and had it away to Australia, and the *fatherless-person* didn't even have the decency to take the missus with him! How do you spell insipidasious?'

One could never be bored at The Magpie, Ginny, and frankly no matter how far I was to travel in this vast and beautiful world, I would always gravitate back to this unassuming hostelry of delight.

There has still been no news regarding dear old Nobby, and as the days pass my concern deepens. But at least I got to talk with Andy again. He has come to terms with his mid-life crisis change in religion. 'I think that the next time that I go to confession, I'll take a lawyer with me,' he said, laughing hysterically.

I have always felt very close to Andy. Unlike most of the others, he brings an intelligent meaningful element into an otherwise chaotic scenario of an existence. He has always been a pretty unassuming character, last in judgement but always first in advice and succour to those of our collective motley crew that need it. He's one of life's unsung heroes.

On my way out of the pub, Ted gave me a copy of *The Kilburn Times* with its front-page leader which read, *'DHSS MANAGER ARRESTED'*. I read the first couple of paragraphs which stated: 'A senior manager with the Department of Health and Social Security has been arrested for handling stolen goods. His home was raided by police on Friday the 24th February, following an anonymous tip-off. Several boxes of what appeared to be stolen watches and jewellery were located in his garage. His personal computer and mobile phone were seized by the police, and he has been bailed to attend the Westminster Magistrates Court on Tuesday 10th April at 10:00. The Management at the Kilburn offices where he works were not available for comment, although it is understood that he has been suspended from work pending the outcome of the case.'

I was absolutely gobsmacked, and frankly very upset indeed. I really couldn't believe that Ted could come up with such a dreadful form of retribution. But then, do any of us really know our friends and acquaintances that well? While I am aware that he is a quite remarkable and generous man when it comes to helping people in need, he is also utterly ruthless in the pursuit and punishment of anyone who needlessly inflicts pain or suffering on those who are unable to fend for themselves, particularly the weak and vulnerable. It is clear that occasionally his sense of propriety and judgement may become a little distorted and his retaliatory methods a little excessive, albeit that as a modern-day karmic assessor, I believe that his simple philosophical approach of 'what goes around comes around' is spot on. All he needs to learn now is that the punishment must fit the crime!

Goodnight, Ginny.

P xx

28th February 2012

Good morning, Ginny.

I didn't sleep at all well last night and awoke with a sense of regret too dreadful to explain. How I wished that I hadn't mentioned Lenny's visit to the DHSS offices to my self-appointed, *righter of wrongs*. But I cannot turn back the clock. What's done is done, and I must live with the guilt, and frankly, I was far from happy with myself this morning. I believed that accordingly, I too should be in line for a little karmic redress, which as it turned out was to arrive a little sooner than expected.

On a lighter note, our new toaster arrived this morning, and in a very uncharacteristic display of domesticity, Maria was the first to try it out. She got through the best part of a full loaf of bread experimenting with the timer mechanism, and finally found the correct setting that toasted the bread to her preferred colour and texture. A little later she had the usual substantial cooked breakfast but didn't fancy *cooked bread* this morning.

I was at the offices of Burt, Lang and Forthright at 10:29 sharp and was greeted by a very sombre-looking Basil. He invited me into his inner sanctum and sat down heavily in his large leather swivel chair. He told me that he had a call from the Sussex police earlier to say that Spike had again been abducted. It appears that he was taken from his cage sometime during the night and boltcutters were used. I was absolutely devastated. The only possible lead that they have is that during the early evening, a tall man wearing a trilby was seen standing near a telephone box outside the breeder's property. Basil's theory is that the people responsible must have been informed about the police operation. Spike was due to be collected at around 10:30 this Friday morning. Clearly, these *fatherless-people* are giving us all a right royal run around. He did mention that 'if Tina had not been engaged elsewhere, it might not have happened'. Which frankly I thought was an observation too far!

'And perhaps if you had obtained a written confession from Nobby when you had the chance,' I said, 'I wouldn't now be in judicial limbo.' However, I accepted his explanation, which he expressed convincingly. He had hoped to arrive at a way of dropping Nobby from the equation completely. He believed his story that he was blackmailed into it, and so do I. Unfortunately, before a plan could be formulated Nobby went missing.

A little later, our brief differences of opinion over, in his usual charming way, he invited me out for lunch at a local Indian restaurant. But since it was a little early he took me to a local pub, where we had a couple of aperitifs. Well he did, I had a couple of pints of Guinness instead. I really didn't need anything to stimulate my appetite, since I was feeling very hungry and could have eaten the horse and chased the jockey. We had a pleasant couple of hours together. Strangely, he didn't mention Albery once. However, he did his very best to reassure me about the safe return of Spike. Nearer to home, I think I am more concerned about Nobby.

Later, as I walked through the doors of The Magpie, Ted was in conversation with *Whispering Jim*.

'I'm going to give you a nice bottle of Irish whiskey for your birthday tomorrow, Jim,' Ted said.

'That's very kind of you mate, but please don't. My doctor has told me to lay off the strong drink,' Jim replied.

'OK I'll give you something even better then, which I think you'll appreciate.'

'What's that?'

'The name of a new doctor,' replied Ted.

Following the usual pleasantries with the attendant team, I made a move on Alfie whom I found sitting at a table outside cutting his toenails. And they say that romance is dead. He was so engrossed in what he was doing, that he didn't hear or see me sitting down. When he had finished, he casually looked up and nearly jumped out of his skin when he saw me. 'Do you have to come creeping up on people like that?' he said.

'Sorry Alfie, next time I see you sitting out here cutting your toenails, I'll blow a horn to announce my arrival,' I replied. Before he had time to answer, I asked him, if he'd like a drink.'Well it is a little early in the day,' he replied.

'What, for a drink?'

'No, for stupid questions,' he replied. 'I'll have a pint of lager.'

Having brought him his drink, he looked at me suspiciously and asked what it was that I wanted. It took me quite a time to convince him that this was a spontaneous gesture, free from any form of skulduggery, and having drunk two thirds of it, he began to relax. Six hastily refilled pints later, he was ready to sell his grandmother's Victorian chamber pot to the highest bidder.

As an initial step, I asked him how his new-found employment with Basil was going, and he was very enthusiastic. He clearly enjoys the work and gets on with both Basil and Ted wonderfully. Ted was a good laugh, but Basil was a bit of a tyrant, who reminded him a lot of his father. He explained that although Basil was a bit of a bully, he'd never actually thumped him, unlike his dad who apparently only ever hit him once. However, it had left quite an impression. He suffered three broken ribs, a dislocated shoulder and his new Levis were ruined. Apparently, his father had driven into him in his milk float. To this day, the mere thought of yoghurt and semi-skimmed milk has him running for cover.

On leaving a little wide-eyed and legless, Alfie mentioned the regimental reunion dinner. My mind went into overdrive. On pressing him further, he stated that Basil had been invited by a masonic friend of his, a bloke called Albery, who happened to be the current master of his lodge. I was very surprised indeed, and not a little confused.

A little later, I had a word with Ted regarding the Frobisher issue, and made it more than simply plain that I didn't agree with the way that he had dealt with the issue. I had reasoned that the level of punishment didn't fit the crime as it were. In my view, a good kick up the *anal-orifice*, particularly if witnessed by his office juniors and subordinates, would have been sufficient chastisement. But I was nevertheless intrigued at how he'd managed to pull off such an incredible deception. He stated that 'it all fell into place' as a consequence of an insurance fraud. An old friend of his, who had a jewellery shop in Lisbon, had 'an unfortunate fire' at his premises which was apparently caused by an electrical fault. Reportedly, much of the stock was destroyed, although a large quantity of the cheaper goods were later to find their way into Frobisher's garage. The good-quality merchandise had been removed from the premises a few hours before the night-time conflagration, and an inflated insurance claim was submitted. On its anticipated pay-out, Ted would be handsomely rewarded for his assistance.

The considerable amount of cheap watches and jewellery found by the police were smuggled into the country by a likely lad from Wigan, who, with others, regularly worked for Ted on his illicit bi-monthly trip to Calais on what he referred to as 'his booze and cigarette run'. The smuggled goods were dropped off at Ted's lock-up in Maida Vale, two days before the police received their anonymous tip-off about Frobisher. In the meantime, a friend of Ted's planted the boxes of watches and jewellery in the unsuspecting Frobisher's garage four hours before the call to police and their arrival a little later. Being a professional, he left no outward signs or evidence that the garage had been tampered with in any way. Uniformed Plod was waiting for Frobisher when he arrived home from work that evening.

The clever part of this whole issue was that the merchandise would never be identified, particularly since it had come from abroad, and in any event, it had apparently been incinerated in a shop fire and therefore for all intents and purposes no longer existed.

Clearly, Frobisher's solicitor would have one hell of a job in providing a feasible explanation for the presence of the 'alleged stolen goods' that were found in his client's garage, and frankly a bloke with wooden legs would have had more chance of surviving a forest fire than he would have in being able to produce a modicum of convincing doubt in relation to his client's innocence.

Goodnight, Ginny.

P xx

29th February 2012

Good morning, Ginny.

I am sure that I have had worse nights, but for the life of me I couldn't remember when. I was tossing about like a peanut lost at sea just about all night long, and it was a very tiring experience. When I finally got up at 07:05, I frightened the life out of myself by looking in my shaving mirror. It wasn't a pretty sight.

All three of my girls were up and about when I poked my head around the kitchen door at 07:45. They immediately knew that something was wrong, since great streaming tears were inadvertently running down my face. It's very difficult to hold a satisfactory conversation under such circumstances, particularly since a short time later both Lenka and Maria were howling pitifully. I simply couldn't explain my intense feelings of utter despair, mainly due to my throat tightening up in an effort to stop myself from howling with them. I told them about Spike's further disappearance, and this simply added fuel to the fire of our intense misery. After we had all settled down, the phone rang. It was Tommy's wife Clare, informing me that my dear friend had passed away peacefully during the night. It seems that he wanted to be buried at sea, which frankly would be a very appropriate place for his interment.

Having put the phone down, I punched my bedroom door with such force that I broke my wrist. I landed up in St Mary's hospital, being ferried there in an ambulance. Having been through surgery, I awoke some time later in a ward with my forearm in plaster. However, the experience had allowed me to catch up on a little meaningful sleep, and I had a bit of colour in my cheeks once again.

There's nothing like a little karmic redress to lighten up one's mood. My girls visited me later, followed by a motley crew of very lovable friends. When Lenny arrived, he took one look at me and burst into tears.

I was cared for by a number of very charming nurses. Later I was given a sleeping sedative, but a nice cocoa and cognac would have been just as good. However, I would have had more chance of throwing off my earthly shackles, sprouting feathers and flying off into the sunset, than getting one.

Goodnight, Ginny.
P xx

1st March 2012

Good morning, Ginny.

I remained in the hospital overnight and the medical care and attention that I received was first class. I slept very soundly indeed.

At 11:30 I was collected by Tony and Ted, and I really appreciated their concern. They talked me into buying them a couple of large full-English *nosebags* at Brenda's Breakfast Emporium on the way home. Ted is wonderfully adept at receiving his karmic credit in advance, or as soon after his altruistic action as possible, and isn't slow in coming forward when it comes to negotiating suitable reparation.

Tony, on the other hand, is naturally generous of mind and spirit, being blessed with a very relaxed and gentle outlook on life, which is a common feature of most long-term tube drivers.

Unlike their long-suffering bus driving counterparts, a normal twenty-four hours of a tube driver's day (whether spent hurtling through underground tunnels or rummaging around under duvet covers trying to find their partners) is spent in many hours of complete darkness. This has had a quite profound effect on their lives and aspirations. As a consequence, it has produced a body of gentle, stress-free, tolerant, and extremely wealthy people, who are fluent in German (making communication with their Swiss banking staff easier), have children in prestigious public schools, together with holiday homes in desirable European countries. Having plenty of free time has allowed Tony to attend charitable functions hosted by international celebrities. He has been to loads of them, and his greatest claim to fame is that at a very posh evening dinner, Arthur Scargill asked him if he could borrow his cummerbund, since he had dropped a bowl of porridge on his. But then Tony does have a bit of a wild imagination, since in his celebrated book, *Once More Unto the Face*, Scargill stated that, 'He was a lifelong supporter of Weetabix, and wouldn't be seen dead eating porridge!'

In the animal kingdom, bodily organs that are rarely used will become weak, and inevitably through *natural selection* could be lost completely. However, animals that spend their lives in complete darkness depend on other sensory modalities. Some mammals that are completely blind, like the star-nosed mole for example, can detect, grab and eat food faster than the human eye can see. (This would be slightly quicker than my Maria.)

In human blindness, it is a well-known fact that the condition produces heightened sensory perceptions and awareness, resulting in an acute sensitivity in relation to touch, and a considerably enhanced hearing capability.

In the case of tube drivers, long periods of darkness have resulted in a heightened sensory ability when it comes to touch and smell, particularly in relation to British bank notes. They can identify a note's denomination simply by touch and can smell *a wrong one* from some distance away. It is also documented that, on average, a tube driver has a smaller penis than say a man that works in an office. This is due to an erratic shift work pattern and a lack of regular sexual stimulation and/or use. While many can locate their partners through touch or smell, their quarry's physical presence had often left the marital bed. Which is hardly surprising since the thought of being groped by a pair of freezing cold hands, or a (lukewarm dead-man's handle) in the middle of the night, together with the less than romantic attempts of a bloke sniffing about in the dark like a Bullmastiff suffering from chronic sinusitis, is hardly a sexually arousing experience. The prospect of a nice cup of tea and a chocolate digestive is often an infinitely more exciting alternative, and often results in yet another barren night of frustration and loneliness, suffered by our ever-hopeful tube driver and his ever-diminishing dick.

Both Tony and Ted were devastated when I told them about Spike's additional abduction, and were very specifically vocal in their utter disgust and condemnation of those responsible, so much so, that Brenda had to leave her culinary activities in the back and, hastening across the counter, performed a marvellously executed scissor-jump, the speed of which made Tony twitch convulsively, occasioning a neatly packed forkful of sausage, bacon and beans to be catapulted across the table hitting a very surprised Ted in the left ear. She gave them both a very clear warning that 'such language and noise would not be tolerated in her establishment!'

The old adage about 'not biting the hand that feeds one' came to mind, although I feel confident that the large toasting fork that she was waving about menacingly had a lot to do with their almost immediate compliance. I couldn't help laughing though, since they looked like two naughty schoolboys, being admonished for not doing their homework.

Back at home later, Lenka gave me a very welcoming cuddle, and Jimena came hurtling along the hall excitedly, and, clearly liking a more lofty position, ran up my outer body clothing and perched herself on my shoulder as she had done with Gabriel recently. Maria was apparently at the library, so I decided that a little walk would do me good, and I went down to meet her.

The Manning Thorpe Library is just off the High Street in a dilapidated condition. It was built during Queen Victoria's reign, got bombed during the last war, and fell down in 1959, evidently quite exhausted. It was restored to its former ramshackle state by unemployed builders who were looking for a second chance (and seemingly were never offered one). Loving they were not!

Inside the main entrance, hung a rather suspect looking fire extinguisher below a large printed sign which read: **IN CASE OF FIRE – SSSHHHH!**

I found Maria in the cookery section looking – or rather *drooling* – over an illustrated book on French cuisine.

She saw me approaching and rushed into my arm (the one still able to cuddle) and gave me a large smacker on the cheek, much to the very evident annoyance of the reception librarian (an elderly spinster type). Having selected a book on *animal husbandry* which she apparently thought would give her some good social advice on her boyfriend, and not wanting to disillusion her at this stage, we ventured up to the reception desk to complete the final act in the borrowing process.

The book was duly stamped by the elderly lady, who carried it out silently and efficiently. On leaving, she gave Maria a rather endearing smile and a little wave. I got a somewhat disinterested perfunctory nod and a rather loud sniff, which didn't go unnoticed by Bunny Longhurst, who having spotted us leaving, took out one of his hearing aids, blew on it resoundingly and then waved his newspaper as us. This silent gesture, were it clearly audible, would have said, 'Hiya folks, haven't seen you for a while! How's the lump?' In reply, I pointed at Maria, shrugged my shoulders and gave him a large over exaggerated smile and thumbs-up. His loud raucous laughter echoed through the formerly soundless hall, as we hastened out into the comforting freedom and unrestricted chaos of the Kilburn High Road, giggling like a couple of desert cobras who had inadvertently wandered into the middle of a mongoose convention and had seen the funny side.

Later at the pub, I related the anecdote about our earlier visit to the library, and the grumpy overly officious elderly spinster type who had made our visit less than pleasant.

Ted said, 'Oh that'll be Arnold Entwhistle, or should I say, Louisa, Rebecca, Dutoit from Wigan. He was a long-distance lorry driver with a penchant for dressing up in women's clothing, but a few years ago, having had hormone therapy, he finally decided to shed his former transvestite image, and to fulfil his lifelong quest in becoming a real female. He therefore underwent the necessary transitional surgery that was required, and having changed his name by deed poll, has now the legal status of a woman.'

'How come you know so much about all of this?' enquired Dave. The Gay Bar suddenly went deathly quiet, and even Vlado forsook another mouthful of his favourite golabki and rice, the spoon hovering a couple of inches from his mouth.

'Oh I know about a lot of things that have taken place in this fair parish,' replied Ted rhetorically. 'Indeed, I can tell you about things that have yet to take place,' he continued, swallowing a large quaff of rum and cranberry juice.

Vlado sighed with disappointment and shovelled the expectant spoonful of food into his mouth quicker than one of those star-nosed moles.

Having clearly downed sufficient *sphericals-inducing* alcohol, Ted slowly sauntered into the centre of the room and cleared his throat. I had the distinct feeling that my feet should be directed back to my humble abode, since he was obviously in the mood for talking. His face took on the appearance of a hungry robber's dog, and he paced the room excitedly, seemingly searching for inspiration.

For those of us that recognise these tell-tale body language signs like me and the inimitable Dave, a discreet withdrawal from the area often becomes necessary. Dave refers to this as 'making like a hockey game and getting the puck outa there!'

Needless to say, we both 'made like a hockey game', Dave leaving through the back door and I crept out through the posh bar.

Goodnight, Ginny.

P xx

2nd **March 2012**

Good morning, Ginny.

Today was meant to be one of joyous celebration since my dear Spike was scheduled to be collected and returned home. Sadly, that was not to be the case following his additional abduction recently. How on earth this was allowed to happen given the undercover police operation is beyond me. I was certainly not in a very happy mood as I slouched into the kitchen.

Both Maria and Lenka were sat around the table. I really had to laugh when I saw my Maria holding a knife and fork and looking expectantly at the cooker, panting with her tongue hanging out. 'I think she's hungry,' Lenka said, laughing hysterically which set Maria off as well. This was just what I needed to shake me out of my ridiculous self-centred lethargy and misery.

A very amusing time was had with my two girls doing their very utmost to gently sooth away my unhappiness, and our mirth made the time hasten by undetected. It is a truism that those who are happy become blind to the passage of time. For those in abject misery, however, it hangs on in there relentlessly, and this can be seen in a lot of recently retired pensioners who, sadly, simply do not know what to do with themselves and they no longer wish to play. Ironically when a man retires and time is no longer a matter of urgency, he is usually given a watch or a clock (which for many elderly people seems to go backwards). But for the elderly newly-retired people, it is worth remembering that 'we don't stop playing because we're old – we get old simply because we stop playing!'

At around 10:30, Clare texted me to say that she had checked out the burial-at-sea issue that Tommy had wished for and was of the opinion that it would be too much to arrange. The red tape is quite demanding and very exacting. The Marine Management Organisation (MMO) is the regulating body and before a decision is made, Tommy's body would have to be medically examined and be certified free from fever or infectious diseases. He must not have undergone embalming and the permission of a coroner had to be obtained for his body to be removed out of the country. The coffin had to be of a certain type with a considerable number of honeycomb-type holes drilled into it and his body had to be dressed in biodegradable material. Apparently, this was the mere tip of the regulatory iceberg. It is certainly a long way from the Georgian Navy's custom of wrapping the body in its hammock, weighting it down with a cannon ball and chucking it over the side. There was also the cost of a licence fee and the funeral itself, which was far from cheap. However, given the considerable time, effort, and money involved, she decided to have him cremated instead and have his ashes buried at sea. She asked me what I thought, and clearly was looking for a bit of encouragement and support. I reminded her that Tommy was a very pragmatic man, who frankly didn't like a lot of fuss, and had he been faced with this decision would have wholeheartedly agreed with her conclusion. I also reaffirmed that I wasn't a million miles away and should she need my assistance I would be only too happy to help. I also stated that I will attend the funeral provided that I am given a little notice.

A little later I had a call from Muhulin checking on the arrangements for Elisha's drop-off on Monday. Fortunately, Maria will be available and she will be taking over the reins, as it were, for the first week, Lenka for the second, and me for the final week. But this will be a shared venture. I shall be available for most of the time anyway and will muck in as appropriate, as will Lenka. This is going to be a very new and quite challenging experience for us all, and to be honest I think we are all looking forward to it. We shall all experience the patter of tiny feet again, apart from Jimena's.

At midday, both Lenka and Maria went out as arranged to meet Gabriel. During the early afternoon, Jock Robinson called and installed my pinhole cameras. They will be electronically linked to a small monitor in my room and will only record movement.

Over at the gym later, I met up with Alex again and we had a natter for quite a while. He stated that he had been looking forward to the regimental dinner which takes place tomorrow. I felt that it would be wise not to attend, particularly given the recent revelation about Basil's masonic relationship with Albery. While this all came as a bit of a shock, I feel that there is a simple explanation for it all, and indeed that Basil has some plan in mind. If I were to show up, I might blow his cover as it were. I made my apologies to Alex, stating that I would be away visiting a sick aunt but would be very interested in knowing how it all went at a later date. I really do hate telling lies, Ginny, although clearly a little honest imprecision will sometimes prevent a ton of dishonest waffle and bare-faced *porkies* later.

Lenka phoned a little later to ask if I'd like to join the three of them for a late lunch in Camden, which I declined. Apparently later on in the afternoon, she would be joining in on some march or other that was taking place in central London. She can be a bit of a militant type, particularly when it comes to those who are disadvantaged, dispossessed or skint. As Dickens once said, 'No man is useless in this life that lightens the burden of someone else.' Apparently, the people that she will be marching with are supporters of the LGBT movement, which I think is something to do with the railways.

Our enlightened modern railways are equal opportunity employers, and while this type of work has long been considered the realm of the male, I have a friend in Cardiff whose sister is an engine driver, as well as a housewife and mother. She gets the kids off to school at 09:00, drives the 09:55 train from Cardiff to Swansea, has a bit of lunch in the staff canteen, and brings the 13:06 train back to Cardiff, collecting the kids at 16:30. They all sit down to a home-cooked dinner at 18:00, and her husband does the washing-up. His colliery closed back in the late nineties and from the time that his wife (Bronwyn) had found one in the glove compartment of his car, he has worked in a local corset factory ever since. What a wonderful carefree life they must all lead.

I haven't heard of any disputes in the transport sector recently, so I really can't imagine what they are all protesting about. Still, I'm sure that all will be revealed anon.

At around 16:00 I ventured off to the *Mother's World* shop in Cricklewood, mainly to buy kiddies cartoons and colouring books which I hoped might appeal to Elisha, whom I believe is now six years old. I bought her a *Cut & Create Station Set,* which will be a wonderful way of making necklaces, bracelets and all manner of interesting things, together with a *Unicorn Colouring Set* and *crayons.* I also bought her an assortment of *Disney DVDs,* excluding Dumbo, since emotionally I don't think I could watch it again without blubbing, and various little storybooks and a little girl doll, completely made of cloth, which I have called Jessie. Finally, I couldn't resist buying the *Little Princess* jigsaw puzzle. I'm sure that Maria will have a great deal of fun playing with this lot. However, I was quite shocked when I presented these things for payment. I could have eaten very well for two weeks on what I was to spend and there's me, a single-parent pensioner. I asked the cashier if she'd take anything off for cash. 'Not bloody likely!' she snapped 'This is a shop, not a bleedin strip joint!'

It had been a nice enjoyable day until that happened, and I really did get some very dirty looks from my fellow shoppers, and one old battleaxe with a face like a bucket full of busted crabs, went out of her way to remark critically at the top of her voice. 'You ought to be ashamed of yourself, a man of your age!'

Unfortunately, I am not one to turn the other cheek without considerable justification and will not be made to look like a fool (unless it is completed warranted), which is fortunately a very rare occurrence. Borrowing the very appropriate motto of the Black Watch which states *Nemo me impune facessit* – which loosely translated into Scottish means, 'See you Jimmy! None shall take the *pish* outa me without me putting tha boot in!!' – I felt therefore that a little appropriate verbal retaliation was necessary.

On leaving the shop I simply called out as loudly as I could, 'You'll have to excuse her; she's going through a bit of a nonentity crisis!'

My evening was spent at home alone apart from Jimena whose hilariously funny antics cheered me up a great deal. I watched *Snow White and The Seven Dwarfs* on DVD and before bed I had finished the *Little Princess* jigsaw puzzle; all seventy-five pieces of it!

Goodnight, Ginny.

P xx

3rd March 2012

Good morning, Ginny.

I had a great night's sleep, and when I awoke at 07:20 Jimena was curled up on my duvet purring contentedly. I initially checked out my camera recordings and found that Lenka had come in just after midnight, and Maria and Gabriel followed a little later. I was pleased that my covert camera situation is working well and that the girls are none the wiser.

I could hear voices in the kitchen, and on getting up found Gabriel, Maria and Lenka in fine spirits, sipping coffee around the table. Jimena, who had condescended to join me for the night, on hearing the commotion went rushing into the kitchen like her little bum was on fire. Her arrival was greeted with a lot of laughter.

A little later, Gabriel suggested that he would like to prepare breakfast this morning, and opening the fridge brought out a large bag of kippers. Maria wasn't at all impressed, but Lenka couldn't wait to sample a food that she had heard so much about. 'Are they Arbroath smokies?' Lenka asked. 'I've heard so much about them!'

Gabriel seemed a little lost for words. 'I don't know, Lenka,' he replied nervously. 'When I asked the bloke for kippers, he told me a story about how intelligent they were.'

Lenka and I smiled at one another. 'Oh, so you've met Trevor our local fishmonger,' I said.

'Indeed, although I didn't believe what he said about Bamber Gascoigne,' he replied.

I had previously arranged to meet Ted, Dave and Tony at Brenda's Breakfast

Emporium, and following a shave and a quick shower, I donned my best *Man at C&A* – jeans, sweater and cord jacket. I saw this outfit on a window-dressed model. It was smart and yet casual, I hate to be overdressed, and yet like to look the part, no matter what the occasion. My motley friends, however, were all in *urine-extraction* mode.

Having entered the busy steam-filled café, I found the three of them sitting at a table by the till. As I pulled the remaining chair out from under the table, they all stood up quickly, as though I was some visiting dignitary. Their action caused a ripple of stifled mumbles, and a loud metallic crash of cutlery confusion. Playing along with them, I remarked, 'Thank you gentlemen, please be seated.'

Apart from the ominous hiss of steam from the coffee machine, the room fell uncomfortably quiet, and Brenda stared at us as if she had spent the night in the stable and had eaten her bedding.

'Don't take any notice of them morons!' she shouted to the assembled miscellaneous rabble, many of whom were left in a state of helpless confusion and indecision, not knowing whether to eat their sausages and bacon, or to save them for later when the intensity of the moment had passed.

We ordered our quadruple full English breakfasts – or should that be more accurately expressed in plural as *breakii* or *breakinum*? The English language can be somewhat confusing, although I believe that it has reached the pinnacle of perfection. Englishmen are renowned the world over for their expertise in the art of complaining for example, and the language allows them to practise this innate quality with considerable aplomb and eloquence.

Needless to say, as expected, I had to bear the inevitable gauntlet of unrestrained *urine- extraction* with regard to my attire, they as a collective looking like they had just treated themselves to a complete change of clothing from the local charity shop.

'No don't be unkind Ted,' said Tony. 'They do say that cord jackets will come back into fashion, although it might not be this century!'

'Yeah, but come on lads!' remarked Ted. 'Just look at the creases in them jeans!'

'That's why he uses the tube,' said Tony. 'It's the best way to get your clothes creased.'

'They say that you should not judge a man by the clothes that he weareth,' Dave remarked.

'He doesn't have enough evidence,' said Ted, which confused the lot of us.

'What about the company that a man keepeth then?' I asked, leaning back casually with my hands folded behind my head.

The subject changed very quickly thereafter and to cut to the chase, in-between mouthfuls of Brenda's artery hardening fare, we discussed Spike, Nobby, my impending court case, and various snippets of gossip, mainly of an unsavoury nature.

But then I suppose that man is by nature a nosey bugger, ever on the lookout for any juicy piece of tittle-tattle, naturally aimed at the people that he does not like. Ironically, the term 'gossip' changes to 'slander' or 'defamation' when aimed at those that we have time for, or who are one's relatives. Needless to say, it is therefore very important to have vetted one's listening public prior to engaging in gossip generally and thereby avoiding a probable nasty fracas or a potential smack in the gob from a listening associate, friend or relative of the person being slagged off.

On our second cup of liquid (loosely referred to as tea), I brought up the subject of Basil's recreational event at the regimental bash this evening, and initially Ted seemed somewhat reticent in enlightening me further.

Tony cleared his throat, excused himself and escaped into the toilet. I regarded Ted thoughtfully, and he was clearly ill at ease. I added to the tension by not questioning him further, but simply stared at him. He really does hate this kind of thing and I knew that were I simply to continue in what I like to call the old *fish-eye* treatment, that he would inevitably break under the pressure. Actually, he has the breaking strain of a soggy sausage roll, and I can always tell when he is lying, because his body language becomes about as subtle as a skeleton masturbating in a biscuit tin.

After sufficient eye treatment, I said, 'Right then Ted, enough of the old *sphericals*, clearly you are aware that Basil will be in Albery Groupenhourst's company this evening, and I would like to know why it is such a big secret. I am paying the bloke to look after my interests, and therefore I should be kept informed of developments.'

He looked up at me sheepishly and was about to reply when Tony rejoined us. He sat down heavily in his chair, and realising that there was a bit of tension between Ted and I, commented, 'I tell you what boys, I needed that! I can say in all honesty that my best dump of the week is always after one of Brenda's breakfasts, they go through me quicker than a two-man bobsleigh.'

'Yes, thanks very much for that mate, we really wanted to know about that, you uncouth moronic *pud-wapper,*' said Dave, belching resoundingly.

Ignoring Dave's remark and evidence of his own disgusting table manners, Ted said, 'Both Alfie and I have been sworn to secrecy, mate.'

'Oh, you mean that same Alfie who like you is a member of that illustrious crime-fighting trio appropriately called The Kilburn Unreliables? A man of unblemished reputation, a bastion of discretion, honour and sobriety, who following the hedonistic pleasures of a tongue-loosening few pints of lager, and a packet of pork scratchings, told me all about it a few days ago,' I said.

Ted sighed and gazed at me with a look of exasperation and hopelessness. 'Well, as they say, loose lips sink ships,' he replied. 'God be praised that he wasn't even a Guinness on the bar during the last war. With him about, Hitler would have been playing marbles in Whitehall as early as 1940.'

'Boules!' Dave shouted, which caused an additional moment of uncertainty among the assembled diners, many of whom had remained vigilant following the earlier little misunderstanding.

'What on earth are you on about?' I asked.

'Germans don't play marbles; they are more likely to play boules,' said Dave authoritatively.

Taking no notice of Dave's inconsequential, albeit interesting snippet of trivia, Ted said,

'Basil has a plan, which I hasten to add, we have not been informed about. He has been acting very strange lately though and keeps himself to himself. He's normally such a gregarious, happy-go-lucky sort of a bloke. But the last time I saw him, he was looking as though he'd just come from a funeral.'

'Or a masonic meeting perhaps?' I suggested.

Back at home later, I had a nice relaxing evening, and was in bed quite early.

Goodnight, Ginny.

P xx

4th March 2012

Good morning, Ginny.

I was wide awake at 04:30 which is the consequence of going to bed early. Actually, if practised regularly, it can then develop into a bit of a vicious circle, since the earlier one gets up the earlier one tires and naturally is ready for bed earlier than normal. And so the cycle of consciousness and sleep revolves continually, each state totally dependent on the other. This is why you will often encounter elderly people walking their dogs at around 04:00 each morning, carrying torches and wearing brightly coloured high-viz jackets and luminous wellies. It's all a simple matter of lifestyle.

My little curled-up ball of fluff looked up enquiringly as I switched on my bedside lamp. The vacant stare suggested annoyance and when I squeezed her squeaky cloth mouse, she yawned, rolled over disinterestedly and was soon fast asleep again. I checked my camera recorder and saw my girls coming in at various times during the early morning. Actually, I feel a little guilty about spying on them since they are not what I am interested in; what I mean is, they are not the ones that I should be looking at. I think you know what I mean.

The flat was very quiet, and rather chilly. Both of my girls' bedroom doors were closed and unlike me they were probably both sleeping contentedly. Jimena had no desire in joining me in the kitchen. I made myself a cup of tea and instead of putting the central heating on I got back into bed and read a couple of chapters of my latest bed book called *Animal Husbandry*, which Maria couldn't understand. Much of it is a little beyond me as well, but I found the section on pig breeding fascinating, which reminded me to get a packet of sausages out of the freezer,

Later, following a quick shower and shave, I felt like a trip out somewhere, although I wasn't sure in which direction my wanderlust would lead me. I really do enjoy spontaneity, it makes life so interesting, and I often can't wait to find out where I shall go next.

I left my flat and my slumbering girls at 07:15 and made my way to Maida

Vale tube station, still unsure of my intended destination. However, once at the station I realised that it being Sunday, the gates would not open until 09:00. I therefore caught a number of buses, taking the overland route instead.

Being the Sabbath, my thoughts were channelled along a church discovery theme and having found myself at Waterloo railway station, decided that I would visit Winchester Cathedral. I'd heard that amusing song by the sixties band, *Scaffold*, and felt that I'd like to see the place. I caught the 08:30 Portsmouth Harbour train and although I would miss the 08:00 Holy Communion, and probably the 09:45 choral matins, there was every chance of my attending the 11:30 Sung Eucharist. I always did enjoy a good old sing-song.

The train journey was a happy solitary affair in an air-conditioned moderately inhabited carriage of slumbering passengers. They were a mixed bunch of miserable *fatherless-people,* who clearly, like me, simply wanted to be left alone. I had deliberately sought out the *quiet carriage* and there wasn't a mobile phone to be seen or heard anywhere. However, after the first stop, an audible rumble of discontent was heard coming from my reclusive fellow travellers, which followed the arrival of a young woman and a somewhat unruly child, who crashed through the carriage looking for a likely place to park. But following the less than welcoming glares by those that were awake, she hastened further along the train. As they passed one old bloke who had been rudely awoken from his slumber, his less than charming verbal expletives had a dominoes effect on others in the vicinity, and the noise and rumpus that followed was quite deafening.

Once the furore had died down, order and peace was restored, and I am pleased to say that for the remainder of the journey there was not a single murmur or titter to be heard anywhere. Most of the grumpy old *fatherless-people* had fallen asleep again anyway, which I was pleased about since it limited the possibility of being confronted with an eye-contact hopeful. As a result, I arrived at Winchester fully refreshed and completely willing to rejoin humanity again.

The road from the station was a steep downhill affair and I arrived at the Cathedral at 10:55 just in time for sung Eucharist. It was a quite beautiful ceremony and begun with the arrival of the choir and clergy in full regalia. It was carried out with great solemnity, and the choir sang texts to music, some of it having a distinctly medieval flavour.

Later there was a sermon preached about the importance of Christian fellowship and, given my sincere lack of any kind of fellowship on the train down, I was feeling a little guilty. But then I suppose that's what religion is all about, and as I sat there listening to the inspiring words of tolerance, forgiveness and brotherly love, I determined that on the train journey home, I would be the same reclusive, intolerant, pain in the *anal-orifice* that I was on the journey down. It is very easy to nurture warm and compassionate feelings towards others, particularly having been subjected to the hypnotic rhetoric of a clergyman, the heavenly sounds of the choir and beautiful music in an awe-inspiring medieval church, but it is quite another in the secular anonymity of a South Western train carriage on its way back to Waterloo.

Following the service, I had a very quick bite to eat in a local café, and was safely ensconced on the 12:30 train back to London. I arrived back in Cricklewood at 14:40 and called into *The Lord Falcon* for a quick libation. I like visiting unfamiliar pubs, it's like looking up old lost friends – they are all so different and yet familiar. I thought about last night's reunion, and I can't wait to have a few words with Basil, whom I believe owes me an explanation.

On the way home I thought I'd call into the *Glass House* pub, but before I arrived, Alex phoned to say that his night at the *Regimental Reunion Dinner* started off pretty civilised but following the speeches, it degenerated into a repulsive show of debauchery, with the strippers mixing with the crowd, and performing all manner of degenerate and disgusting acts upon what he called 'a collective of revolting drunken louts!' He apparently left early.

As I walked into the pub, a taped rendition of *Reveille* was being played on a bugle and checking my watch I found that it was the start of *Happy Hour*.

The place was busier than a beachfront urinal on a bank holiday, and the smell was reminiscent of a fertiliser factory in a heatwave. I only just managed to squeeze in through the front doors. I hate crowds as you know and as I turned attempting to make a hasty retreat, I just managed to get outside, when suddenly out of the crowd a large disembodied hand grabbed me, which was followed by an arm, and squeezing out from under a man's armpit, I saw the bewildered face of Lenny, who smiled up at me apologetically.

'Sorry Paul, I just needed a bit of a helping hand to get out of here,' he said.

'You're a little far away from home,' I replied, pulling the rest of him out of the scrum.

'It was Eugenia's suggestion. Fifteen minutes ago the place was just about empty and then – Suddenly – all hell broke loose! I've never seen anything like it.'

As we walked along Cricklewood Broadway, Lenny hanging on to my one good arm tenaciously, he skipped into step with me like an out-of-step squaddie on a parade ground.

'She thought that I'd like to witness one of the natural wonders of the world and said that I should get in at around 14:45.'

'Well it's certainly a memorable sight,' I replied. 'It could be likened to a shark feeding frenzy; the only difference is that sharks have better table manners.'

A little later we landed up in an almost empty pub called the *Hippo* and having bought a couple of beers from the bar, we found a table by the door.

Lenny took a swig and, wiping the froth from his mouth with the back of his hand, smiled at me pleasantly and sighed. I felt that he wanted to offload, and I gently initiated an opening.

'So how's the job going, Lenny?' I asked, taking a sip of my beer, which tasted suspiciously like froth-flavoured water, and as I did so, quite unintentionally I looked up and saw the barmaid regarding me critically. Our eyes met briefly and she quickly looked away, knocking over a tray full of glasses from the counter.

'If I'd known it would be like this, I'd have joined up sooner,' he replied. 'And all of those horrible things that I had called Eugenia were simply unfounded.' He stopped and suddenly looked quite embarrassed. 'Frankly,' he said, clearing his throat, 'she's been like a mother to me, well I suppose more like a sister really, at least I think so, not having ever had either.'

'I'm glad to hear it, Lenny,' I said, being ever more distracted by the barmaid's behaviour which was becoming more bizarre as the minutes passed. She clearly had something to hide and evidently was trying her utmost to cover it up.

'I never thought that I'd ever live to see the day that you were gainfully employed, well albeit on a part-time basis that is,' I said.

'Yeah well, I am seriously thinking about going the whole hog,' he said with evident pride in his voice.

'You mean – full-time employment?' I gasped.

'Well, I dunno, maybe something part time, or job sharing to start off with.'

'Doing what?' I asked.

'Something sitting down,' he replied. 'People what work sitting down earn loads more as them that works standing up,' he asserted, looking at me for encouragement or approval. 'There's one bloke at the office that never seems to leave his seat at his desk. He's obviously being paid and his desk is always piled high with papers, but I'm not sure if he's busy or simply confused. I could do that!'

'Do what?' I asked.

'Sit at a desk all day looking confused and getting a lot more money than the poor old security bloke at the door, wearing his smart uniform with the medal ribbons he won during the war, who has to stand there all day looking efficient, wearing out his shoe leather and earning a pittance for doing it. See what I mean about earning more by sitting on your bum?'

'Well it's not quite like that, Lenny, people who sit down at work have to do so in order to carry out their job functions. How could an accountant examine a person's tax returns, or a typist make out a written report standing up? Why, it would be as daft as a window cleaner trying to clean windows, or a labourer on a building site trying to dig a trench sitting down.' Lenny's mobile phone suddenly rang and having answered it, he walked outside.

On his return he looked decidedly embarrassed. 'What's wrong?' I said. 'You are flip flopping about like a dying fish, is it bad news?' I asked.

He sat down heavily and momentarily starting to shake. I became quite concerned and wondered if I should call an ambulance. I have never seen him in such a state. 'What on earth's wrong, Lenny?' I asked, grabbing hold of his hands. 'You are shaking like a leaf!'

'How do you want me to shake?' he asked absentmindedly.

A short pause followed, during which Lenny's eyes suddenly glazed over, and beads of sweat appeared on his forehead as though he had just taken a large mouthful of the *extra special chicken vindaloo* as served up by *Rudra Khatri* and his fellow culinary sadists at the *Star in Kerala* Indian restaurant. (It's certainly not for the faint hearted or indeed those who do not enjoy exhaling like a fire-breathing dragon.)'It's Eugenia,' he replied incredulously. 'She's invited me for dinner this evening. AT HER PLACE!' he shouted.

'You mean that you'll be actually sitting at the same table and being fed by that formerly *well-nourished, dark-complexioned, fatherless, DHSS lady*?' I said teasingly. 'But do sit down boy, you're beginning to give off steam!'

'Actually, we have become quite close,' he replied, clearing his throat and taking another large gulp of his watered-down lager. 'She's quite sweet when you get to know her.'

Before I had time to answer, he finished the dregs in his glass, belched resoundingly and made a hasty retreat towards the door.

'Sorry Paul, must dash, I need a scrub and a shave, and will have to dig out some decent clothes, which I don't have an abundance of. Still, I'll find something.' Standing up, his flushed cheeks having returned to their usual sun-bereft hue, he said, 'will catch up with you later.'

He dashed out of the pub, bouncing into a wall on the way, like a novice drinker learning the curate avoidance technique, and suddenly he was gone.

I felt very happy for him. Not only has he got over his innate abhorrence to work, he has found a woman who, it seems, is genuinely concerned about his well-being and happiness. Apart from Ms Balalla, the last woman that he had been involved with was his unfortunate mother who sadly died giving birth to him. He was brought up by a very strict and seemingly resentful father. He told me once that at school, kids used to come up to him and say, 'My dad can easily beat up your dad!' He would reply, 'That's great, when?'

Before I left the pub, I simply had to find out what was going on with the barmaid. I therefore casually sauntered over to the bar and asked for a large cognac. Putting our empty glasses on the bar, and trying to strike up a little conversation I said, 'not very busy in here, is it?'

'Well I can only work twenty hours a week,' she replied.

'Really, that's unfortunate, since I am sure that that wouldn't bring in much income.'

'It's enough, what with my benefits,' she replied. 'I know who you are, so let's stop the pretence. Why are you spying on me?'

I was quite flabbergasted. 'I really don't know what you mean, young lady,' I replied.

'Don't give me that!' she replied. 'You and your mate are DHSS snoops, I saw you both there the other week, you were with that bloke Frobisher, who has already lowered my benefits because he reckoned I was working full time.'

Needless to say, after much debate and paternal encouragement, I finally convinced her that I was not working for the government, or indeed, for any other organisation. Thereafter, I reminded her of my earlier request for a large cognac.

She leant across the bar and whispered, 'I wouldn't if I were you,' nervously looking towards the kitchen door. Pointing to a large array of optic bottles she said, 'There's more genuine cognac on me pinny than in that bottle!' The thought of *Dunny Greg's* horse tranquiliser-laced poison almost make me retch and I made a very hasty retreat.

I wasn't in the mood to engage with my London Transport chauffeur on my way back to Kilburn so I simply walked. It was quite chilly but the thought of a nice couple of warming cognacs at the Gay Bar gave me a quite pronounced determined bounce to my step. On the way I had a call from Basil, who asked if we could meet up tomorrow. However, Elisha is being dropped off in the morning and I want to be around all day to make sure that she settles in well. We arranged to meet at Brenda's Breakfast Emporium at around 10:30 on Tuesday instead.

Both Lenka and Maria were in the Gay Bar as I arrived, and were in animated conversation with *Whispering Jim* and Dave. The atmosphere was lively and convivial and both of my girls were in fine spirits laughing uncontrollably. But then both Dave and Jim are great to have around if you need a good laugh.

Ted and Alfie were sitting in a dark corner, seemingly trying to act secretive and were chatting conspiratorially. I really do have to admire their enthusiasm but as would-be detectives, neither of them could track a three-legged elephant with a nosebleed in the snow.

Back home later, Jimena did her usual bit rushing down the hall and running up my outer clothing. She seems a lot more coordinated now though, and can at least run in a straight line, bless her. I reminded Lenka and Maria about Elisha's arrival in the morning, and both were very obviously excited at the prospect.

Goodnight, Ginny.
P xx

5th March 2012

Good morning, Ginny.

Muhulin and Elisha arrived at 11:00 and within ten minutes the flat looked like a mini tornado had been through the place. When she saw me, Elisha rushed into my arm and hugged me. She squealed with delight when she saw Jimena, who coming out into the hall to investigate, took one look at this diminutive titan and ran for cover. It was then that Elisha noticed the cast on my forearm and wasted no time in producing her colouring pencils ready to draw a picture on it.

Muhulin dropped off several bags of clothes and a few toys and stated that she'd 'keep in touch'. But as far as we were concerned, Jasmine's treatment would last around three weeks and that Elisha would be collected sometime during the week commencing 26th March. This would all be confirmed later.

Having settled in and the excitement had lessened, Elisha made friends with Jimena, who despite her initial shock and timidity, slowly allowed Elisha to stroke her and was on purring terms with her within half an hour or so.

Maria decided that since it was her turn to act as *mama temporal* for the first week that she would care for Elisha fully and therefore that she should sleep in her room. I was more than happy with this arrangement as was Elisha who walked around with Maria hand in hand. I was told in no uncertain terms that Lenka and Maria would be taking the little one out to our local McDonald's for dinner, and that if I didn't wish to join them I was 'to make my own evening meal arrangements'. I am not too sure if I am over enamoured at the bullying, although I figured that I will have to watch my step, since there's four of them now!

I phoned the local nursery to confirm that Elisha would be arriving tomorrow at 09:00 and asked if Maria could stay with her for her first morning. Poppy was OK with this and I was happier knowing that for her first real sojourn into nursery school that our little girl would be with someone that she knew. Although I feel confident that she will make little friends quickly.

At 13:00, Maria had made an assortment of sandwiches cut up into little triangles, and had taken Elisha to our local Middle Eastern establishment and on the child's recommendations had bought various sweet cakes and juices (none of which we had tasted before). We all had a wonderful lunch. Elisha didn't stop chatting and had clearly made herself very much at home. Sure to form, following lunch, Lenka went out for a walk, Maria, Elisha and Jimena vanished into Maria's room, and I was left with the washing-up. Still, I felt relatively safe since historically no woman has ever injured a bloke while he's doing the housework.

At around 14:30 I received a text from Tina to say that she was following up on two promising leads and hoped to have something more positive in a few days. She was now in a place called *Skibbereen* which she tells me means 'little boat harbour' which is apparently on the southwest coast. It appears that she's learnt a lot about Irish social etiquette and is getting plenty of the *craic* and yesterday, following a seafood supper and a little *soakage,* she went to bed *banjaxed!* I do hope that it is not contagious.

But I do love her indomitable spirit and lust for life. She's a bit of an enigma really. I found out what a ninja was the other day. But what I find really strange is why this little lady needs to hide behind such a ridiculous persona. I have seen the tenderness in her nature, like the day that she met Lenka. The façade dropped for a short time and briefly she was herself. This reminds me, I must ask Lenka how her railway demonstration went the other day.

In the Gay Bar at 18:30, *Whispering Jim w*as in fine voice. His rendition of the 'Camptown Races,' had them rocking in the aisles, although Vlado was not very amused. Jim's version is a little left of politically correct and not for the easily offended ears of someone brought up in a communist regime. He shouted at Jim to quieten it down, and Jim took umbrage. Jim, in an agitated state, is not one to be messed about with, and in a sudden blaze of fury, he picked up his chair and threw it at our unfortunate pub landlord. Happily it missed, but it completely obliterated an optic display of some nine bottles, which all smashed to the floor. A few of us managed to get him outside, before a fracas of enormous proportions could take place.

'You is barred!' screamed Vlado as we led Jim away.

'It's about time we took a stand against this *anal-orifice!'* Jim stated, or rather screamed, as we sat him down on a low wall next to the pub. We all did our very best to calm his rage. His fists were tightly clenched, his eyes were bloodshot and he was shaking violently. One couldn't be uncertain in relation to his general mood or feelings.

'Good God Jim!' I said. 'What's wrong with you? Why did you throw the chair at him?'

'Cos the feckin table was too heavy, that's why!' he replied aggressively.

A little later, Dave led him away and order was restored.

When I went back into the bar, a number of the lads were sweeping up glass and doing what they could to help Vlado who was clearly very angry indeed. In fairness, he had a perfect right to feel annoyed since it's hardly the kind of thing that one would expect in polite society. But then this is Kilburn on a cold damp Monday evening in March, and not a warm Ladies Day at Ascot in June.

Jim has never been what one could call passive either verbally or physically, and sadly when it comes to personal restraint, particularly during times of provocation, he has all the finesse of a lobster on heat.

On behalf of my poor undisciplined friend, I made profuse apologies to Vlado who nodded understandingly. I have come to respect this man a great deal, and he is very popular with all of the lads. Later, when the mess had been cleared away, he passed me a large cognac and there was a great deal of sadness in his eyes as he said, 'There's none else to do. His many lifes are used up!' I understood what he meant but appreciated his genuine regret at having to ban a true local character.

Jim has been using the pub since the late sixties. His personal use of the jukebox was legendary, and rumour has it that from the profits obtained, the landlords of the pub had raised enough cash to completely redecorate the posh bar, provide the new oak tables and chairs for the front, and leave enough over to pay for Vlado's annual return air fare to Kosovo every year. Needless to say, Jim liked the odd *gargle* or two, which kept Vlado pretty fit having to change Guinness barrels in the basement on a regular basis.

As I lay in bed later, contemplating the evening's events, I realised that of all the natural disasters of this world – earthquakes, tsunamis, hurricanes or sudden audits – for a man to lose one of his dearest friends from his local watering hole, is a quite profound and disturbing event of unparalleled proportions.

Whispering Jim is a part of the very fabric of The Magpie public house in general and the Gay Bar in particular, and without him the place would simply not be the same. Yes, he can be a cantankerous old bugger, occasionally full of mischief and sauce, and yet in many respects his faults pale into insignificance when one considers his kindly attributes and general goodwill to others. He was always the first to welcome strangers into the pub, albeit that most of the time the said strangers didn't understand a word that he was saying. He had a very quick wit, although sadly when provoked an even quicker temper. But I had to chuckle to myself when I remembered one of his funniest and most original excuses for arriving home late. On the occasion in question, he was in a pub in Dublin and, as one does, he got caught up with a few of the lads having the craic. As mentioned before, time passes so quickly when you are having a good laugh.

His late wife was sadly no stranger to loneliness, since he would be out most evenings at the pub. But he was always home for around 21:00. But on this occasion, having forgotten about time due to the good company and the better Guinness, he suddenly realised that it was three in the morning.

He phoned his wife a little later and putting on his best out-of-breath voice he said, 'Don't pay the ransom Clodagh, I've managed to escape!'

Goodnight, Ginny.
P xx

6th March 2012

Good morning, Ginny.

My household all slept peacefully last night, and as I entered the kitchen at 06:30 all was quiet. Jimena followed me out and looked up at me enquiringly. She is getting as manipulative as Spike in that she makes it quite evident when she's hungry. Likewise, she's also beginning to exhibit some of Maria's eating habits in that once food is placed in front of her, it is determinedly devoured with gusto, although in Jimena's case it is carried out with gentle feline grace.

Both Maria and Elisha took control of the bathroom at 07:15 and their laughter echoed along the passage. They evacuated the area at 07:40 cleansed and ready to wreak havoc on an unsuspecting world, but were happy to initially hone their skills on me and Jimena in the kitchen.

I bade them both a very good morning as they entered, and Elisha hugged my leg. Maria didn't appear to be interested in such intimate physical contact so early in the day and simply settled on planting a slobbery kiss on my cheek. As she did so she uttered a rather loud 'MWAH' which had Elisha giggling delightfully. There's nothing quite like the pleasure-giving sound of a child's laughter, it is so very infectious.

Maria had her usual substantial cooked breakfast washed down with a copious quantity of coffee, while our little guest had a bowl of crispy pops and a banana, and clearly enjoyed a glass of the passion fruit juice that she had suggested. I suspect that having this beautiful little girl with us is going to be more than a simple learning process.

With an hour or so before they would have to leave for Elisha's playschool, they vanished into Maria's room to watch a DVD which as it turned out was *Beauty and the Beast*, which reminded me of my intended meeting with Basil at the café at 10:30, so I hastened into the bathroom for a refreshing shower and shave.

Maria and Elisha left home at 08:50 and I got to Brenda's Breakfast Emporium at 10:05 in readiness for my appointment with Basil a little later. In the meantime, I bought a couple of rounds of toast and a mug of coffee. Apart from a few reckless diners bent on testing their bodily resilience to Brenda's life-shortening fare, the place was quieter than one of her sneaky kitchen mice, creeping around and trying not to disturb the cockroaches that were enjoying a sauna under the cooker.

At 10:30 precisely, the doors of our nearby local dosshouse were flung open, spewing out an assorted array of unfortunate men. Heavy rain had coincidentally started to fall, and a little later a considerable number of very damp itinerants entered the café filling the place with steam and condensation. Within minutes, visibility was down to around eighteen inches, and the smell was a tad less than antiseptic.

Basil arrived a little later. He poked his head around the door, took one sniff, pulled a rather comical face and mistakenly beckoned to what he thought was me. However, I was more than a little affronted when the bloke that he had invited to join him outside was a rather portly young black skinhead with pink spiky dreadlocks and a club foot. I simply sat sipping the dregs of my cold coffee and awaited results. A few minutes had passed without anything happening, so I ventured outside to find that the young man had hoisted Basil up a brick wall, his shoes a good two feet from the ground, with his somewhat large claw-like fingers locked tightly around his neck.

I quickly took a tenner from my wallet (something which I do not engage in normally) and having flashed it in front of the assailant's face, my unfortunate red-faced solicitor was dropped quicker than a leper's lunchbox, and the note snatched violently from my hand. The young man looked into my eyes menacingly and, smiling briefly, presented a set of misshapen discoloured teeth, together with brown swollen gums that had clearly never felt the sting of a novocaine prick or a tap from a palaeontologist's rock hammer for that matter (which in his case would have been more appropriate). Folding the note carefully, he placed it into his jeans pocket and hobbled away, emitting loud maniacal laughter of the type used by the stereotypical villain in a Hammer House horror film.

I am not one to laugh at the genuine misfortunes of others, but as I helped Basil to his feet, I was fighting back and attempting to mute the sounds of a restrained giggle that was simply bursting for freedom. I had to let it go since trying to withhold it was beginning to feel quite painful. However, in my usual respectful manner I had time to squeeze out the words, 'I'm sorry Basil', before I let rip with a veritable tsunami of raucous laughter.

'I'm glad that you find it so amusing,' Basil said, dusting himself down.

'When the world laughs at you, Basil, laugh back, it's just as funny as you are,' I replied.

He quickly walked off in a very determined fashion and I had to run to catch him up. He had parked his car nearby and we were soon speeding north along the Kilburn High Road.

On the way to his office, I broached the subject of the regimental reunion and asked him how it went. He completely ignored me and only became mentally responsive again once we had entered his place of business and two cups of tea had been made.

'It went better than expected! Although, I left after the dinner was over. I knew what was to follow and it isn't very pleasant!' he remarked, slumping heavily into his leather swivel chair and changing the date on his wooden perpetual calendar.

We spent some considerable time in conversation, Ginny, which frankly I don't want to bore you with, but when I broached the subject of Albery Groupenhourst, the light went out of his eyes and he morphed into a quite different man from the one I knew.

'I have to admit that I have been suffering from a distinct conflict of interest,' he began. 'I was more than flabbergasted when I discovered that Albery is, to say the least, a very devious and most disreputable individual. From my investigations, I have uncovered his involvement in a considerable amount of criminal activity.' He sighed heavily. 'Just about everything, including blackmail, extortion, drug dealing and vice. It would appear that he uses his shoe repair/key cutting shop as a front for his money-laundering activities. Together with DS Blackstock, we are building up a case against him, and when it all comes to trial, I believe that he won't see the light of day for some considerable time.'

Taking a long satisfying swig of his tea he said, 'Although, if he were to come clean, as it were, and provide useful testimony, particularly with regard to his associates, the court might be lenient. I heard recently that a 225-year sentence imposed by a Bangkok court on a sixty-five-year-old man charged with extortion had been cut to 180 years because his testimony had proved useful.'

'Yes and I am also aware that he happens to be the current master of your masonic lodge,' I said which seemed to take him completely by surprise.

'Quite so,' he replied, looking rather embarrassed. 'You will remember when we visited his shop the other week?' I nodded assent, and strangely felt a little upset that I had put him into a bit of a tight spot. 'You could have knocked me down with an extra light feather when I realised that it was him,' he said.

He walked into an adjoining room and returned carrying a packet of chocolate digestive biscuits which he placed reverentially on his desk. Eyeing them critically, he suddenly slammed his clenched fist into them; the unexpected noise thus created, made me jump, and caused my ears to ring for a short time. The blow scattered particles of different sized biscuit all over the desk.

'I felt like that the other day Basil, but smashed my fist into something a little firmer,' I said, sifting through the wreckage and selecting a number of intact bite-sized morsels, which I moved to one side. 'So where do we go from here?' I asked, tucking a couple of chocolate biscuit pieces into my mouth.

'I think that I owe you an explanation, Paul. Firstly, I did not wish to keep you in the dark about Albery and intended to come clean, as it were. This morning seemed to be the right time.'

'Well if it's any consolation to you, Basil, I can assure you that I am completely trustworthy and anything that you tell me will be held in the strictest confidence.'

'Thank you,' he said, opening his desk drawer and placing a packet of ginger nuts on the table which he opened with finesse. He took a bite out of one and smiled. 'I can't stand chocolate digestives!'

I felt that I should tell him about my own little bit of skulduggery as far as Albery was concerned, and the trap that I hoped he would fall into.

I explained that, having convinced Albery that I had a ready stash of cash in my flat, and he having recently obtained a newly cut copy of my front door keys (which would give him clear unrestricted access into my flat), I felt that he would be presented with an opportunity far too difficult for him to resist. Clearly it wasn't a case of whether he would rise to the bait, but simply a matter of when. As Oscar Wilde once said, 'The one thing that I cannot resist is temptation.'

'I admire your independent resourcefulness,' said Basil. 'But Albery's no fool, and one that was not likely to stick his neck out needlessly. He would need considerable persuasion that the rewards involved justified the risks taken. What on earth did you tell him?'

'I simply asked him where I could buy a small safe to install at home, to house a considerable sum of cash that I was trying to hide from the avaricious and prying eyes of the Inland Revenue and other sundry sticky-fingered blood-suckers.'

'Has he any idea of just how much in ready cash this entails?'

'No, but to give the story a little more credibility, I emphasised my lack of trust in financial institutions in general and my bank in particular.' I explained that it had been my experience in life that people naturally feel comfortable and often unwittingly gravitate towards others that can make them laugh. Clearly this is something that politicians haven't yet realised. I therefore tried to give my feelings on the banking industry a little flippant humour in stating that 'I had never been very impressed in getting my bank statements handwritten on cocktail napkins, and was very disappointed a few years ago when I was turned down for a bank loan, explaining that perhaps I'd been a little foolish in mentioning that all I needed was enough to pay for a one-way flight ticket to Argentina.' He did actually find this quite amusing.

'Well, I wish you luck Paul, but please be very careful, Albery has some very nasty people on his payroll, many of whom are seasoned criminals.'

Thereafter, the conversation turned to more worrying matters. 'So is there any further news about the fate of poor old Nobby?' I asked.'That is another subject altogether,' he said, and he seemed to suddenly become very ill at ease. 'For the time being, Paul, I can assure you that he is fine, albeit a little depressed. The main thing is he is being well looked after, and I can state quite categorically that in due course, you will be fully enlightened as to the very valid reasons for his apparent disappearance.'

I trust this man implicitly and, not wishing to cause him any further unnecessary worry, I didn't press the matter further.

Later in the evening I called into The Magpie and caught up with a few of the regulars. Poor old *Whispering Jim* was conspicuous by his absence. His usual well-worn chair by the jukebox was empty, and someone had put a small sign on his desk which read *Gone but not forgotten*.

Dave was in conversation with Vlado and clearly the assembled motley group of potential inebriates (it was early evening) had forsaken another viewing of *The Magic Roundabout* in favour of a little live entertainment at the pub.

'Yeah well when I was married, I used to have coffee every morning with two lumps – my wife and her mother,' said Dave, which occasioned a titter of mirth from the audience.

Looking closely at Vlado's luxuriant *walrus moustache,* its thick, bushy whiskers drooping over his mouth which was just about invisible, he continued. 'But judging by the state of that lot mate, all you'd need to do is sprinkle coffee grounds over it and drink a cup of hot water.' Dave was obviously on good form.

I had one single very large cognac and then had another quiet word with Ted regarding the Frobisher issue. It seems that he had purloined several of the more desirable jewellery items (to cover costs) and the rest was planted in Frobisher's garage. Taking out a folded handkerchief from his pocket, he dangled a rather nice-looking watch in front of my eyes. 'It's a replica, but you'd need to be an expert to tell the difference,' he said. 'If you ever need a bit of *Tom,* just let me know mate.'

This is an example of cockney slang, Ginny, which apparently originated in London during the 1840s, and was originally used by market traders and costermongers (who sold their fruit and vegetables from handcarts). It was probably used to disguise what was being said. The reason why has never been fully explained.

When used in rhyming slang, a *Ruby Murray,* for example, could in all probability be worked out to mean a curry. However, to make the issue more confusing, it is only the first part of the term that is used. An example would be the word *bread* which means money. It comes from the rhyming slang for, *bread and honey.* As for the word *Tom,* this comes from the term *Tomfoolery* which rhymes with jewellery. Other examples would be the word *Apples* which means stairs, and comes from the slang *apples and pears.'* Likewise, the word *Barnet* means hair, and comes from the term *Barnet Fair.* It's all quite simple really.

But getting back to Frobisher, I still believe that Ted's sanction was, to say the very least, a bit severe, and I reminded him again of my feelings on the issue. He simply shrugged his shoulders and replied, 'What goes around comes around, me old China!' *China plate* = mate.

** INTERLUDE **

7th March 2012

Good morning, Ginny.

I am very sorry that I didn't send you yesterday's email last night, but I was otherwise indisposed. I will send it later today before this one.

On my way home from the pub last night at around 22:10, as I got to the outer door of the flats, I noticed a tall bloke wearing a trilby in the phone box opposite. He looked in my direction and quickly turned his head. Suddenly, I completely lost all of my teetering good humour and patience and I dashed across the road and was narrowly missed by a speeding police vehicle.

I pulled the door open and grabbed the *fatherless-person* by the throat, dragged him out of the phone box, I kneed him violently in the groin, and lashing out, planted a swinging right hook which connected forcefully with the side of his face. He fell to the ground uttering obscenities.

I was suddenly grabbed from behind and forced facedown onto the pavement with my right arm held painfully high on my back and a knee forcefully keeping my left arm pinned to the ground. I was panting like a rabid dog, and my right fist was agonisingly painful. I heard the person holding me say to another, 'Call for an ambulance and the van, Pete!'

The ambulance was the first to arrive at the scene, and a little later my groaning potential nemesis was stretchered into it and whisked away, to the very unnecessary sound of its emergency vehicle siren. The vehicular *Rush Hour* and more particularly, *The Magic Roundabout,* were over hours ago!

A little later, I was quite violently manhandled by two ruffian police officers and quite literally thrown into the back of a police van. As he closed the back door to the van, a police officer whom I later found out was PC Andrew Cunningham said, 'Sorry about the state of the place, but my cleaner didn't show up this morning. And by the way, you're nicked for assault!'

The combined smell of stale urine and vomit was quite nauseating, and on the way to the police station I was tossed about like a plebe in a blanket (as you people in the States would say). However, I was very pleased to find that my short journey was siren-free, and as I was man-handled out of the van a little later and frogmarched into the charge room, I gave the driver an appreciative nod of thanks.

Once inside, the usual standard police procedures took place, which included the emptying of my pockets. I was searched from head to toe (with inquisitive fingers rummaging around in some pretty delicate areas). My fingerprints were taken (again) and finally I was interviewed by a young detective constable apparently on some kind of mind-altering substance, either that or he had overdosed on the canteen tea.

Thereafter, I had to suffer an unwelcome six-hour reflection period in an airless and miserably cold and dark cell that had an aroma subtly suggestive of urine and excrement which was in odoriferous competition with a squirt or two of disinfectant. A small, almost overflowing urinal, complete with its less than resplendent former occupant's turd (the size of a bacon baguette) floating on its top, added to my general feelings of apprehension and dismay. I sat on the cold plastic mattress, which made dreadful farting sounds every time that I moved. Initially, it brought a smile to my face, in that it reminded me of my fishing days spent with Tommy Grasscon (who could fart like a Brewery dray horse). But it soon became dreadfully irritating, and I found myself standing in a corner (reading the varied and colourfully offensive wall inscriptions) for most of my incarceration, while consciously praying for the night to end and my freedom regained. But in any event, on my release I shall be putting in a formal complaint to the European Court of Human Rights, the Police Complaints Commission and my local MP since the disgusting conditions in which I was confined were utterly unacceptable. Actually, as an interim measure I might have a (quiet) word with *Ted the Pleb*, who I'm sure could suggest and implement an appropriate retaliatory gesture or two!

Unfortunately, I wasn't allowed a phone call during the night, because apparently their telephone line was down, which was dreadfully frustrating since I wouldn't be able to phone the girls to allay their fears with regards to my inexplicable disappearance and safety. Although a couple of hours into my stay, I was informed that 'Lenka had phoned' and she had been informed about my situation. Presumably on my non-arrival home, she would have initially checked the local hospital and police station (bless her).

Later, I was offered a cup of tea from a very elderly special constable, whose florid well lived-in face suggested an active outdoor lifestyle like gardening, and more particularly, stepping on rakes.

Finally, I was escorted back into the *Walloping Room* as *Dunny Greg* would have said, my property was restored, and I was charged with causing Actual Bodily Harm (ABH) which the charming young lady police sergeant graciously informed me was contrary to Section 47 of the Offences against the Person 1861. I was given a copy of the charge sheet and bailed to appear before the Westminster Magistrates Court (again) at 10:00 on the morning of Monday 26th March 2012. With the number of times that I will have visited this venue, I am seriously considering renting a room nearby. It would certainly save on all of the unnecessary travelling.

I was released at 08:25 this morning, feeling pretty sorry for myself, particularly since I didn't have my freedom pass with me so I had to walk home in a fine drizzle, which unlike torrential rain drenches you to the bone. When I got home at 09:05, the flat was empty apart from Jimena, who did her usual streak along the hall towards me, running up my clothing and skidding off the top of my soggy jacket shoulder. I had a much-needed shower, drank three large cognacs and went to bed, leaving a note on my bedroom door to say that I was OK and was sleeping. I would enlighten my girls as to my nocturnal adventures later in the day.

I awoke at 16:15 and was greeted by a very concerned Lenka and Maria. Elisha hugged my leg and then gave me a very comprehensive tick-a-tape account of her time spent with the girls, concluding her narrative with her clearly enjoyable adventures at her playschool. She has obviously settled in well. I then gave my two beloved big girls a summary of my own less than happy experiences over the last twenty-four hours.

I phoned Basil a little later and brought him up to date with the events of last night and he suggested an urgent meeting on Friday at 10:00 in Brenda's Café.

I needed to get out for a while and felt like a little change of scenery in the search of a mentally and spiritually uplifting experience, and apart from anything else, I was as hungry as a diamond without a carat.

I landed up in a newly opened fish restaurant in Queens Park. It is at times like this when my mind is in turmoil that I simply jump on a bus or a tube and get off when the mood or inclination moves me. This evening, Queens Park was my potential Utopia.

I had a most enjoyable fish supper and was served by a very nice attendant waitress. Her name was Susan, and she worked some evenings as a part-time waitress in the restaurant, but was a philosophy student at the Willesden College during the day. In between courses, we had a very interesting exchange of philosophical ideas, at the end of which I gave her one of my cards, which all sounds very posh, but it simply has my name, email address and phone number on it. I left her a two-pound tip on leaving, and she shook my hand warmly as I made my exit. I certainly needed this very welcome distraction.

I called into the Gay Bar at 21:15 to have a quick couple of sleep-inducing night caps. On entering, I caught the tail end of a discussion between *The Voice* and Vlado. The usual 'entertainment seeking groupies' were in attendance, sipping their respective poisons and listening intently to the verbal discourse.

'I can't be doing with those nonsense appetiser how's-your-fathers mate.' said Dave. 'I don't need gastronomic foreplay, Vlado, I like the real thing!'

'In best events, hors-d'oeuvres are given before a food. With served an aperitif, which is like a glass of wine David,' replied Vlado.

'I've seen those things at posh dinner parties, not for real like, but on the box. I wouldn't be very impressed if I was offered one from a large plate. At the end of the day, they are only a ham sandwich cut into twenty triangular pieces.'

'I've got to that way in life when food, it takes the place of sex,' said Vlado.

'Well I haven't got to that stage yet mate, besides, it would be a little bit awkward to fit a large mirror on the ceiling over my cooker since I don't have a large stepladder,' replied Dave.

The assembled group collapsed into almost uncontrollable mirth, and frankly what made it all the funnier, was that Vlado in his innocence, didn't have a clue what Dave was on about, or why it was so funny.

I felt it wise to keep my additional brush with the law quiet, since I was in no mood to put up with the inevitable *urine-extraction* that would follow. Thankfully, I was in my own bed at 23:30.

Before I shut my bedroom door, and while Maria had left her room to visit the bathroom, Jimena seizing her opportunity to escape, dashed into mine. She clearly likes a bit of variety in her life.

Goodnight, Ginny.

P xx

8ᵗʰ March 2012

Good morning, my dear.

Both Jimena and I slept very well last night. She is a very easy-going bed companion.

First thing this morning, I penned an email to the secretary of the European Court of Human Rights in Strasbourg, complaining bitterly at the less than humane treatment that I (a subject of the British Commonwealth) was subjected to recently in the care of a government-sponsored institution. I copied in our own police commissioner, Sir Bernard Hogan-Howe, and our local MP Glenda Jackson, who apparently took a hiatus from acting to pursue a political career. I hope that the waiting list for her reversal procedure is not as long as mine. Later on this evening, I shall be having exploratory talks with Eduardo F. Cordona, aka *Ted the Pleb* on matters involving karmic-redress and sundry matters.

Elisha and Maria had taken over the bathroom at 07:05, which was ten minutes after I had made my way there in the hope of urgently relieving a very full bladder. I knocked on the door gently and Maria opened it cautiously.

'Any chance of a quick pee, love?' I pleaded. 'I really do need to go quite urgently.' She left the door open, and got back into the shower with Elisha, pulling the shower screen behind her. I gratefully entered. The noise of the cascading shower water veiled the sound of my own little water fountain and having washed my hands at the sink, I hastened back into my bedroom. Lenka's bedroom door was closed, so I assumed that she was in bed sleeping.

When I entered the kitchen, Jimena was sat by her food bowl looking up at me expectantly. Nothing much changes in this household until I have fed the masses! I fed her accordingly.

I made breakfast for my two other girls at 08:00 and thereafter they dashed into Maria's room to watch a cartoon DVD until it was time for Maria to drop

193

Elisha off at the playschool.

Having spoken to Father Marcus about it recently, and it being Thursday, I had forgotten all about the lunchtime bingo session that our new gaming entrepreneur had arranged. He phoned me at 09:15 to ask if I was 'still up for it'. I replied in the affirmative and we arranged to meet in the estate community hall at 11:30.

Following my shower and a bite to eat, Maria returned from dropping off Elisha at her playschool and asked me what plans I had for the day. I told her about the bingo extravaganza, which surprisingly she seemed quite excited about. She said that she'd like to tag along. Accordingly, at 11:25 Maria and I were waiting outside of the community hall as arranged.

Father Marcus arrived ten minutes later in what could be described as *very plain* clothes. Actually, it's the first time that I have seen him in a pair of denims and a rollneck sweater. When he opened up the community hall, tables and chairs had been earlier laid out in a circular fashion. In the middle of which was another chair and desk, on which stood a large wooden bingo roller, if that's the right expression.

I was given a large stack of bingo books and I had to admire the curate's optimism. There would be three games in total, the first game was for a top line, the second for a bottom line and the last and star prize, would be won by the player with a full house. Each strip was £1.50 and red pens, which I was told later are called *dibbers,* were 50 pence each.

The afternoon's bingo session would start at 13:00 and I stood by the door, welcoming in the participants and selling the bingo books. At 12:05 the first couple arrived who purchased two books each, but didn't need dibbers as they had brought their own. As time passed, more and more people arrived, and I was quite flabbergasted to find that at 12:50 there were fifty-five attendees. Just before the first game was about to start, another nine people hastened into the hall. Shortly afterwards, Maria left to do a little personal shopping and then to collect Elisha from her nearby playschool.

Prior to the start of the session, Father Marcus announced that 115 tickets in total had been sold, which together with twenty-seven dibbers amounted to the very creditable sum of £186. Using a calculator, he stated that the first game winner would receive £25, the second game winner would receive £61 and the full house winner would receive £100.

Maria and Elisha arrived later and quietly tiptoed into the community hall, taking a couple of seats at the back. Elisha waved at me enthusiastically from her seat, smiling sweetly.

The afternoon was a resounding success. It was clear that Father Marcus enjoyed his role as the bingo caller and his choice of words to identify the numbers were hilarious. *Winnie the Pooh* for forty-two, *The Lord is my Shepherd* for number twenty-three and *Grandma's getting frisky* for number sixty, to name but a few. It certainly added a new glossy touch and amused many of the more seasoned bingo enthusiasts. There was much fun and laughter, and later as they were leaving, just about all of those in attendance thanked us for our participation and hoped that this would be a regular feature in the social life of our ailing community hall.

Father Marcus had clearly enjoyed himself as had Maria and I, and on leaving he thanked us for our help and gave us both a big hug. Elisha's usual hug of my leg came in a close second. I picked her up and cuddled her adoringly, and she placed a kiss on my cheek accompanied with a long loud verbal 'MWAH!' which had the three of us laughing like loons. I am extremely fond of this beautiful little child, who in the short time that she has been with us has enriched our lives tremendously.

We called into the Gay Bar for a short time and Vlado was very obliging in allowing our little guest to join us. I do believe that this is the very first time that she had ever been into a pub.

We were in time to hear what also happened to be another first. It's the first time that I had ever heard Vlado say something amusing. But then he's not the most talkative person at the best of times. However, in fairness I feel that much of this is due to his somewhat sketchy grasp of the English language, and rather than make himself look foolish, he simply keeps quiet.

Ted was at the bar deliberating on what to have. Looking at Vlado he said, 'I'm really not in the mood for a lager, since it's too bleedin fizzy! Your selection of house wines are dreadful, and since *Whispering Jim* has been stripped of his watering-hole status (which brought about a genuine collective sigh and murmur from the bar attendees) your Guinness has the consistency of warm paint stripper!' Looking around for inspiration and picking up one of the pub menus he said, 'I tell you what Vlado, I'll have something tall, cold and full of gin.'

Vlado walked to the end of the bar and cautiously peered into the posh bar next door. On his return, he leant across the bar and in a relatively quiet voice he said,

'Sorry Ted, my wife, she has just left for the meets with her hair-messer!'

The bar erupted into a loud appreciative bout of laughter, and some of the lads were applauding enthusiastically until Vlado's inquisitive wife called Zora-Aleena (who sadly it seems, has suffered a severe charisma-bypass) *materialised* from the ladies' loo passageway, eyeing us all accusingly. Suffice it to say, she is a very scary looking woman indeed. She has to be a good 6ft 4inches in height (which is about seven inches taller than Vlado). Her powdery facial skin is almost the colour of white marble without the warmth, and her black accusing eyes augment perfectly her non-existent passionless personality.

Vlado became as a wilting lily at her appearance and nervously sauntered off upstairs into his own safer private domain. I thought that he was made of stronger stuff. But then, every path has its puddle! Sadly, I am sure that his daily walks with her are very muddy affairs indeed!

It is at times like these that I thank providence for decreeing that I should remain single in my later life. Almost on a daily basis, I count my blessings and often remember my dear old mum's words when she reminded me that 'I am a thing of beauty and like Peter Pan, will be a boy for ever!'

The truth of this became clearly evident following the divorce of my second and final wife during my fifty-second year.

Back at home, I made Elisha and Maria dinner. Lenka had left a note stating that she was out visiting friends for the evening.

At 20:10 there was an urgent knocking at out front door reminiscent of Elisha's brother's less than sedate attempts to be heard, a few weeks previously. I cautiously opened the door to find Father Marcus. He appeared to be in a very agitated state. I invited him in which he declined.

'Sadly, we shall have to put the bingo sessions on hold for the foreseeable future,' he said.

'I thought that it was all a tremendous success, Father Marcus,' I replied.

'And so it was, Paul. However, the three winners were all systematically mugged on their way back to their homes and had their winnings stolen. Fortunately, none of them were hurt.'

It was a miserable end to a very happy day.

Goodnight, Ginny.
P xx

9th March 2012

Good morning, Ginny.

I didn't sleep at all well last night, thinking about the despicable people responsible for mugging those poor people yesterday. Frankly, with all of the nonsense and worry that I have had to put up with lately, I am getting a little paranoid myself and as far as becoming as aggressive as I was the other day, I cannot rationalise my behaviour at all. I am still very unhappy about it. But then as you know, I've had a lot on my mind lately, and it seems that the only days on which I do not worry are yesterday and tomorrow.

I met up with Basil at 10:00, joining him for a light breakfast of eggs Benedict and coffee. He made it very evident that like me, he wasn't impressed with my behaviour on Wednesday evening.

I really did feel quite embarrassed and tried to present a rational explanation for my actions, but in truth, no real appropriate justification could be given for what I did. To quote Lenny, I had simply 'lost the plot!'

He made it clear that I would have to plead guilty at the court appearance and would have to face up to the consequences. He smiled when he pointed out that as far as the prosecution was concerned, I couldn't have picked two better witnesses.

He felt that next time I was in the mood for a little aggressive behaviour towards innocent pedestrians that I should get 'a Supreme Court Judge to witness it. It would save the police a hell of a lot of paperwork!' I do so hate sarcasm!

I took Basil's expected and well-deserved admonishment with quiet humility, and simply sat there, eating my breakfast and nodding in agreement at his remarks.

He suddenly changed the subject. 'However, it's not all bad news, Paul,' he said. 'There have been further developments as far as Nobby is concerned. He is willing to totally exonerate you from the extraction of electricity issue, but sadly in doing so, he will be condemning himself.'

'As noble as that is, Basil, I cannot allow that to happen,' I said.

'I firmly believe that he was being blackmailed, Paul, but for some reason he cannot or will not give me any information on the issue. However, I suspect that all will be revealed in due course. But seriously, are you willing to put your hands up for an offence that you simply did not commit, and to risk your good name, not to mention your potential loss of liberty for someone else?'

'Basil, I have always had the greatest of respect for Nobby Caxton, and I refuse to believe that his actions were self-motivated. Clearly, it would be the only honourable thing to do.'

'Well you had better seriously think about what you are doing here. Your case in relation to the assault charge comes up on the 26th March; you have no option but to plead guilty. I believe that given your clean previous record, the worst scenario would be a suspended prison sentence, a community service order and a fine. However, I know that I could provide considerable mitigating circumstances due to the very unfortunate state of affairs in your private life, and would confirm that you are very remorseful over the incident, and that your actions on the evening in question were completely out of character. I could provide many statements from friends to that effect.'

'I will accept whatever sanction that the court deems appropriate, Basil,' I said. 'Clearly I am in the wrong here and deserve to be punished accordingly.'

'It's a good job that all of my other clients are not so chivalrous, since I would be out of a job in no time if they were,' Basil replied. 'But in fairness, I take my hat off to you, dear boy.'

'I just want this issue over and done with, Basil,' I said, beginning to lose my temper. 'This nonsense has been going on for far too long. I want to go to bed at night with a clear conscience, and not to have to worry about bloody court cases! You are my solicitor, acting on my behalf, are you not?'

'Yes, of course I am, but...'

'Right then, I would like you to reinstate the outstanding case, if that's the right term. The one in relation to the abstracting of electricity *sphericals,* as early as you can. Under the circumstances, I have no intention of letting Nobby suffer. The *fatherless-person* responsible for coercing this virtuous and trustworthy man is the *anal-orifice* that should be standing in the dock!'

'You have obviously made up your mind, Paul, but you have a way out of this charge if you are willing to let Nobby tell his story. Needless to say, if you allow this case to go ahead before the assault case, and you plead guilty, you will have a criminal record and on the assault case would therefore be likely to serve any earlier suspended sentence, together with any additional time added for this later offence. At that rate you'll be knitting mittens and crocheting toilet-roll holders for some considerable time. Is that really what you want?'

Before I had time to answer, laughing hysterically, he said, 'Still there's one consolation Paul, you would be relatively safe from the *Shower Bandit Queens*, apart from the ones with bad eyesight that is!'

I wasn't amused. 'Just do as I ask, please Basil, and get that electrical court case on the go as soon as possible. After all, that's what I am paying you for!'

He clearly didn't like that. He stood up suddenly, paid the bill at the counter, and as he passed me on the way out he said, 'Good morning Mr Shaughnessy, my secretary will be in touch!'

As he reached the door I called, 'When is she starting, Basil?' which he obviously heard but chose to ignore. He left, slamming the door behind him. I had never seen this side of a man that I thought I knew well and was left quite speechless at his childish behaviour. I understand fully that he is simply trying to protect me, although I was not best pleased at his earlier insinuation that I am an ugly *fatherless-person* and an out-of-condition old reprobate.

Later in the day I received a text from Clare to say that Tommy's funeral would take place at midday on Friday 23rd March. I sent her a reply to say that I would travel down to the Isle of Wight on the Thursday.

Later in the Gay Bay, Ted gave me £166.'What's this for?' I asked.

'Well, *a little birdie* told me that three of our more senior residents were robbed by a group of *scrotes* from the Hinkler Estate yesterday so I had a nose around. I met up with one of the lads involved and had *a friendly chat* with him so to speak, and surprise, surprise! He told me all about it and gave me the name and address of *the boss*, who turned out to be sixteen-year-old yob who professes to be a trainee money-launderer. He is currently working in a dry-cleaning establishment in Camden.'

'That's absolutely marvellous, Ted,' I said, patting him on the back.

'Think nothing of it, Paul. As the old saying goes *crime doesn't pay* – unless of course you can do it exceedingly well! The novices involved in this litter caper were a little green.'

'Young, you mean?'

'No it was the colour that they went as we dangled them over the roof of Tumbleton Tower, in pursuance of the truth and the money stolen. It's quite amazing how people can be so very cooperative under such circumstances.'

'Yes, I suppose that your methods can be quite convincing, Ted,' I said, shuddering at the thought. 'Not for the faint hearted, kind of thing!'

I bought him a drink and counted out the cash. 'There's £20 missing, Ted,' I said.

'All's fair in love and war, son,' he replied. 'Call it my ten per cent handling fee.'

Thereafter, I gave him a complete rundown relating to the less than pleasant experience I had endured recently, compliments of our local nick's disgusting accommodation and en-suite facilities. He listened attentively. 'Leave it to me!' he said reassuringly.

On my way home, I called in to see our revered pastoral guide, but he was out, so I visited Father Marcus instead. Sorry Ginny, a little bit of inappropriate humour always seems to cheer me up in times of uncertainty or stress.

Father Marcus was in his dressing gown when I knocked. He invited me in and asked if I'd like to share a glass of sherry with him.

'I haven't got any straws with me, Father,' I replied. As expected, he really didn't understand what I was saying (bless him).

Having filled two small crystal glasses with amber liquid from a rather suspect ancient-looking bottle, that looked like it had been buried for a very long time in some dark cavernous hollow, he invited me to take a seat.

Holding his glass to the light, he stated, 'This is very special stuff, Paul.'

Before I dared to put the glass anywhere near my lips, I said, 'You didn't happen to buy this from a bloke called Greg did you, Father? He's a big ginger-haired ugly looking Australian bloke.'

'No Paul, this came from the wine cellars of an ancient French monastery.'

'Thank the good Lord,' I said, with genuine sincerity. Before I had time to continue, Father Marcus sighed and said, 'On top of the muggings, the community centre was broken into last night and the audio equipment, which I had borrowed from the Scout's Hall, was also stolen. I shall have to personally buy them new equipment.'

'I am very sorry to hear about that, Father, but at least I have a little bit of glad tidings which I hope will give you a little comfort.' Having added Ted's 'handling fee' from my own wallet, I gave him the stolen £186.

He was absolutely delighted, so much so that he threw back the remaining sherry in his glass (it made such a mess on his carpet). Sorry love, I couldn't resist that! He refilled both of our glasses with additional sherry and with a smile on my face, I stood up and raised my glass to this kindly well-intentioned man, and recited the following toast:

'May the wind be always at your back, and the sun upon your face, and may the wings of destiny carry you aloft to dance with the stars.'

For the first time since I have known Father Marcus, he seemed to be utterly lost for words and not a little embarrassed. 'I do so love those Irish toasts,' he said.

'It may have been inspired by the Irish, Father, but it came from the pen of a bloke called George Jung,' I said.

'A relation of Carl's, no doubt,' said Father Marcus confidently.

'Near enough, Father,' I replied. 'He was a drug dealer who was the first person to introduce Columbian cocaine into America.'

Later, my own flat was in darkness with both of my girls' doors closed. There was no sign of Jimena, and as I got into bed I smiled to myself at the thought of my four precious girls slumbering peacefully, and a fifth probably preparing supper in Florida, five hours behind.

Goodnight, Ginny, enjoy your meal.

P xx

10th March 2012

Good morning, Ginny.

I was awoken from my slumber at 06:15 this morning by a loud knocking on my front door. My first thought was that Father Marcus had suddenly understood my joke about the straws last night, and simply wanted to get it off his chest. On cautiously opening the front door, I was confronted with a very tired looking Tina Lipseed holding a rucksack.

'I am so sorry for my early arrival, Paul,' she said, 'but I have other things that I must do before midday today.'

My first question to her was, 'How on earth did you get into the block?'

'Oh it's all very simple Paul, it's called a key!' I hadn't even considered that possibility.

I invited her in and made her a cup of coffee. 'So how did it all go?' I asked.

'Well I found Siobhan,' she said. 'Sadly she's lying in a grave in the St Magnus churchyard, in a small village called Inneshbell in County Cork. I have a photo on my phone of her headstone.'

'I'm so sorry to hear that, Tina,' I said, as Lenka walked into the kitchen looking very bleary eyed. She smiled at us both good-naturedly and made herself a coffee.

'What did you find out about her?' I said, smiling at her expectantly.

'She died in 2006 of complications following a heart operation. I have a copy of her death certificate,' which she handed to me from the front pocket of her rucksack. 'She was a nun and lived and worked in the St Joseph's convent, just outside the village of Inneshbell. I understand from the Mother Superior and other sisters that Sister Angelica, as she was called, was a beloved member of the convent and highly thought of by the residents of the village. Her death came as a great shock to the community. She used to run a pre-school class for young children.'

Lenka excused herself a little later, but before she left for her morning appointment with her loofah, Tina shook her hand and they exchanged mobile numbers.

As Maria, Elisha and Jimena came into the kitchen a little later, Tina made her exit. But before she left, I asked her if Siobhan had any other living relatives in Ireland, and she replied that from her investigations it appeared that she had entered the convent in 1968 at the age of sixteen, and apparently had never had a relationship with a boy. She spent thirty-eight years at the convent and died on the 31st March 2006 aged fifty-four. She was an illegitimate child and spent her early years in the care of the Magdalene asylum or laundries as they became known, ostensibly to accommodate fallen women, or in Siobhan's mother's case, to house young women who became pregnant outside of marriage, which I suppose was the same thing. Not much is known about her young mother who appears to have vanished from the scene when Siobhan was a child. Sadly, she was never to know the identities of her parents, or any other relative.

'Her father Tommy told me that her last known whereabouts was in Kinsale,' I said.

'That's where the Magdalene asylum where Siobhan spent her childhood was situated,' replied Tina.

'So if Siobhan was born in 1952, Tommy died just recently at the age of seventy-four.' Getting my electronic abacus from my bedroom, I did a little calculation. 'So, that means that at the time of her birth, he would have been...'

'Fourteen,' said Tina.

'Yes, and what a dreadful tragedy it was for all involved,' I said.

'As far as the residents of Innishbell are concerned, her presence among them was a blessing, and she has been greatly missed by the sisters at St Joseph's, so it's not all bad Paul.'

I really appreciated all of her hard work and effort and gave her £250 since she had located the whereabouts of the unfortunate Siobhan. She was quite embarrassed and gave me a very nice hug in return.

'I can't thank you enough, Tina,' I said, as I walked her to the front door. 'I dare say that we shall meet up again soon.'

'You can count on it,' she replied. 'I will dash home for a shower, and then at around lunchtime, I have a meeting arranged with a man to discuss the finer points of a bottle of twelve-year-old Bushmills Blue Label.'

Smiling, I replied, 'No names, no pack drill, but I have a feeling that he has an office in Kensal Rise and a penchant for reading detective novels.'

Before she could give me a reply, she was down the stairs and out into the courtyard very quickly indeed, and in truth, had she tripped on the way down, in all probability she would have been wearing her knickers on her head as she left the flats. Why on earth she hides behind her ridiculous alter ego is beyond me.

I made my girls a substantial breakfast and as usual it was a very entertaining affair. Elisha gave us all another tick-a-tape narrative of her first week at playschool, which she had clearly enjoyed. Maria, in between mouthfuls of tissue-restoring egg and bacon, gave us a similar edited version of her experiences with Gabriel, and I asked Lenka about the railway demonstration that took place the other day.

'What railway demonstration?' she said.

'That LBGT demo thing that you went on.'

Both Lenka and Maria went into almost uncontrollable fits of laughter, which amused Elisha enough for her to join in as well.

'What's so funny?' I asked.

'LBGT are the initials that relate to the lesbian, gay, bisexual and transgender movement. Originally it was simply called the LGB back in the nineties but was enlarged to include the transgender group as well. Paul, you really should get out more!'

'Well, perhaps under the circumstances, I'm glad that I have stayed in. But what were they demonstrating about?'

'They were not demonstrating about anything. They were simply publicly celebrating their non-heterosexual allegiance, in whatever form that may take. Have you never seen the six-band rainbow flag which represents the LGBT movement?'

'No.' I replied. 'But I did have a sister in the WAAFs that went AWOL once.' She totally ignored my attempt at a little flippant humour.

'For far too long, the gay community has been the subject of ridicule, scorn and discrimination,' she continued. 'The movement promotes toleration and acceptance in our clearly prejudiced society. My own view is that people should be allowed to live their lives free from bigotry, intolerance and prejudice, and to be accepted for who and what they are, instead of being judged by their sexual preferences, religious leanings, colour of their skins or social habits. I have always been a champion for the underlings and the downtrodden in society.'

Before I could reply, Gabriel knocked on the door, apparently to take Elisha and Maria out for a pre-arranged visit to London Zoo for the day. On stepping inside, he was positively mobbed by adoring females. Jimena ran up his outer clothing and perched herself on his shoulder, Elisha hugged his legs and Maria cuddled him from behind, kissing his neck passionately, which was accompanied by the inevitably loud verbal 'MWAH!' This set Elisha giggling uncontrollably again.

A little later, they left for their visit to the zoo.

At 11:10 my mobile phone rang, and I was asked by Ted if I could attend The Magpie. He was rather evasive when I questioned him further and he hung up, which added to the mystery.

When I told Lenka, she was intrigued enough to want to join me.

A little later we arrived outside The Magpie, and the scene that greeted us was one of utter chaos. There were some fifteen or more men standing outside the pub carrying what appeared to be hastily constructed placards. One of which read

Reinstate Whispering Jim and another read *Free The Six* on one side, which clearly related to the false convictions of a group who became known as the *Birmingham Six* back in the mid seventies, and on the other was written *Whispering Jim is not just for Christmas – HE'S FOR LIFE!* in red paint, that clearly had not been allowed to dry, since each letter bore the tracks of running paint.

I met up with Ted who was trying to keep the ever-excitable mob under control. Looking around at the familiar faces, it became clearly evident that the demonstrators were the regulars of the Gay Bay in its former entirety.

Vlado joined us and was clearly very ill at ease. But then he had a pretty hostile crowd in front of him and worst still, his wife Zora-Aleena was standing at the entrance to the Gay Bar behind him, uttering indecipherable oaths which, to an untrained secular ear, could be confused with the satanic verses used during the *Virgin Disembowelling Ceremony*. Given the choice, I think I would have been happier taking my chances with the hostile crowd.

'What's on for this, Ted?' Vlado nervously enquired.

'It looks like you have a bit of a problem, my friend. You will, I am sure, have no difficulty in recognising all of those that are gathered here?'

Vlado looked around solemnly, and slowly nodded. 'But what is they after Ted?'

'I seem to get the feeling that they are not happy with your decision to ban *Whispering Jim* from his usual watering hole,' said Ted. 'He has been using this place longer than *The Shawshank Redemption* with commercials! In fact, he has been a regular feature of this pub since the early seventies. What you see here is simply a spontaneous example of English loyalty, and apart from death, when it comes to the disappearance of a friend from one's favourite watering hole, it is the kind of loss that cannot be fully rationalised to anyone, particularly unsociable people who don't drink, or who prefer to drink alone.'

'But he had to be gone. Unhappy, very much was I,' Vlado said.

Looking around, Ted counted the assembled crowd. 'Well sadly Vlado you are being given an ultimatum. The seventeen men that you see before you will boycott your pub until the full and unreserved reinstatement of James Oscar Fingal O'Finnegan, also known as *Whispering Jim,* has taken place.'

'But if I allow him again, I will become as a laughing thing, drinkers will think, that as you say I am a soft tickle and I cannot like that. Jim was to go!'

'Not wishing to add insult to injury, Vlado,' said Ted. 'But to mirror your own views, it could be that should you persist in this understandable decision of yours, and I do sympathise with you, that in the near future you and your wife may also *have to go!* It might be a little difficult to explain, when you are asked to account for the sudden substantial loss in your public bar takings, to an unsympathetic area manager. And then of course that's without mentioning the empty jukebox tin, or should I say, *The Whispering's piggy bank*, which for years he has enthusiastically patronised and is normally overflowing with pound coins.'

Walking up to Ted, Vlado said, 'Please Ted, I must be seen to be in violence, you understand?'

Ted lowered his head and quietly replied, 'Do what you have to do, Vlado.'

Checking that Zora-Aleena's gaze hadn't softened – the look that she gave him could have turned hot magma into ice – Vlado's feigned anger looked convincing, and suddenly he pushed Ted back violently.

Bringing his former skills as a trainee stuntman to the fore, Ted made a big over-exaggerated scene of crashing back into the crowd, and falling at their feet, moaning loudly. This took the boys totally by surprise, and many of them started to back off. But for the very first time, I saw Zora-Aleena smile.

Vlado turned and walked defiantly back to his wife, who held his hand as his opened the door to the Gay Bar to allow her to enter, but before she did so, he faced the now very quiet crowd and shouted, 'Vlado and my woman, Zora-Aleena, will not become disgraced or intimated in masturbate crowds!' He and his wife then quickly turned and vanished into the pub.

Getting to his feet and dusting himself down, smiling wryly, Ted said, 'What more can one say?'

A little later, Lenka and I joined the former regulars of the Gay Bar who en masse invaded the public bar of the Goose and Firkin, taking the landlord and his usual group of morning regulars, collectively known as: *The Mess,* completely by surprise.

Lenka, Ted and I sat apart from the others and we enjoyed a relatively quiet drink, until the sun went in on the arrival of the landlord Thomas Patrick O'Mahoney, who appeared from out of the men's toilets, mop and bucket in hand. Looking at Ted enquiringly he said, 'And to what do we owe the pleasure of your visit, Ted?' Before Ted could reply, he added sarcastically, 'And before you answer, just remember that your tongue is a very wet place and slips can easily happen.'

'Now is that any way to welcome a fellow countryman, Tom?' said Ted, putting his drink down and slowly standing. An awkward silence followed, apart from the sound of the aurally challenged Buster Crimmond who like the last time, was looking at the pub menu and chuckling to himself happily. He suddenly stopped and, looking up, found everyone in the place glaring at him accusingly. He sighed audibly and said, 'Oh fa feck sake, not again!' He stood up timidly and placing the menu down reverentially, he cautiously made his way to the door.

'No!' I shouted, and rushing over to him, I escorted him back to his seat. He smiled at me awkwardly and sat down again.

The landlord slowly made his way towards Ted, their eyes were fixed upon each other, and it was a rather worrying moment. As they stood face to face, the tension was quite dreadful. Suddenly Ted said, 'Well are you goin to buy me a feckin pint, ya big bollix?'

The landlord burst into raucous laughter and they hugged warmly. An audible murmur of ecstatic relief floated heavenwards, and the decibel level of the place quickly got back to its normal ear-shattering level.

Later in the afternoon, Lenka, Ted and I visited *The Peony Chinese Buffet Restaurant* (a pay-an-entrance-fee-and-scoff-as-much-as-you-like kind of thing). Having loaded our plates with all manner of exotic culinary dishes, we found an empty seat by the window.

The main topic of conversation of course was the Vlado–Zora-Aleena issue, and Lenka took the chair, as it were. Her view was that given the quite unacceptable behaviour of *Whispering Jim,* a suitable punishment had to be administered. Clearly Vlado wasn't happy about it, but he is the publican, and as hard as it must have been for him, he really had no alternative.

'I agree that Jim had to be punished Lenka, but to ban him completely is in my view a little severe,' said Ted, popping a rather large forkful of miscellaneous vegetable matter into his mouth.

'That's the answer Ted,' I said. 'We agree that he had to be chastised, it's just the severity of the sentence that seems to be a little harsh. All that needs to be done is to soften Vlado up sufficiently, by indicating to him that we all agreed to Jim being punished, but to alleviate any potential future problems, why not give him a month's *cooling off* period. This could become part of his new disciplinary procedure. It would indicate to his regulars that unacceptable behaviour would not be tolerated and would result in an initial one-month ban. Thereafter, any further serious transgression would end in lifetime banishment from the pub, with no chance of a reprieve. Apart from any other consideration, it would indicate to the pub regulars that although he was a strict disciplinarian, Vlado was a fair-minded man, willing to give a person a second chance.'

'Absolutely!' said Lenka. 'But from what I saw, Vlado, is a pussycat, however his wife is a veritable tigress. She's the one that needs to be severely softened. Getting through to her will provide an easy way out for him, a way of winning without losing face. Although there's no question in my mind as to who wears the trousers in that household.'

Ted and I resolved later in the evening that 'the softening up processes' of our incumbent tigress currently caged at The Magpie would begin on the morrow, and in the interim we agreed with the former regulars that our temporary replacement watering hole would be the Bread Bin.

Goodnight, Ginny.
P xx

11th March 2012

Good morning, Ginny.

The sound of Compton's bells at 07:30 awoke me this morning, and I was thinking of Vlado. Not erotically, you understand. (Perish the thought.)

As Lenka made clear, she thought that *Whispering Jim's* problem could be settled through Vlado's wife and last night, Ted, Lenka and I resolved to formulate a plan aimed at toning down a very strong-willed woman, and in so doing, hopefully, we might also be able to bring two people, who clearly loved one another (at some stage) back into some semblance of a meaningful relationship.

Lenka noticed yesterday that Zora-Aleena seemed to soften towards Vlado following his staged assault on Ted, which suggested that while she might be a very confident and assertive lady, she clearly needed a dominant alpha-male in her life, to presumably take control in any unpleasant social or professional event in their lives. She had become quite submissive following Vlado's performance, holding his hand tenderly as they went back into the pub. I had not really considered this show of affection, but Lenka doesn't miss much and can be quite analytical when it comes to overt physical actions. Clearly her deductions were correct.

Lenka was working today and was out first thing, so we decided that the three of us would meet in the Bread Bin at 19:00 this evening to discuss tactics.

Breakfast this morning was its usual period of fun and laughter, with Elisha and Maria in verbal competition to give me a complete account of yesterday's visit to the zoo, evening meal at McDonald's, critical appraisal of the *Jungle Book* cartoon, and a very descriptive account of the pre-bed hilarious antics of Jimena, who apparently had them both in fits of laughter chasing a table tennis ball along the hall.

Being Sunday, another day of carefree relaxation was in store for Maria and Elisha. Gabriel picked them up at 10:00 to begin another adventure, this time heading for the south and the seaside resort of Brighton. I am very grateful to both Maria and Gabriel for the unconditional love and care that they have given to our little girl. She loves them both dearly, and one day they will both make superb parents. I hope to be still around when that happens. The trouble with dying is that it always seems to happen at the most inconvenient time.

Lenka is holidaying all of next week and had planned on having Elisha over this period, but Maria wouldn't hear of it. She made it very evident that she will have her for the duration of her stay, and in the meantime her MBA studies will be, as she put it, 'thrown into the freezer!' I am sure that what she meant to say was 'put on ice'!

During the afternoon, I ventured through the park to the Bread Bin. Rosheen was clearly very pleased to see me and after her less than unenthusiastic cuddle,

I hobbled to a vacant seat. I didn't think that anything was broken, and reasoned that a nice long soak in the bath and the bruised area massaged with ibuprofen gel later, would prevent an evening visit to our local A&E. It wasn't really painful unless I coughed or laughed. I therefore did neither for the rest of the afternoon.

The public bar was sparsely patronised, with three paying customers, one of whom was Bunny Longhurst who gave me a double-handed thumbs up as I arrived, which wasn't half as painful as Rosheen's earlier physical show of affection.

Having regained my composure, as I slowly walked up to the bar Bunny said, 'Why are you limping, Paul, are you still having problems with the lump?'

'No.' I replied. 'Maria is fine, Bunny. She's going down to the seaside today.'

He nearly choked with laughter, which seemed to annoy the two other very well-dressed bar attendees, one of whom glared at him disdainfully.

Having collected a pint of Guinness, I sat down at Bunny's table and whispered, 'What's wrong with him, Bunny?' casually nodding in the direction of the bloke giving him the fish-eye treatment.

'Oh don't mind them two,' he said. 'You only ever see them at lunchtimes. They are usually out bright and early every Sunday morning, asking people why they are not at church.'

'Jehovah Witnesses?'

'No, I think that they might be out-of-work burglars, checking for unattended houses!'

Rosheen gave me a very large cognac on the house, and as I sipped my aromatic 'water of life' she sat down with us and gave me a full verbal rundown of the more notable occurrences in and around the pub since our last meeting. She is the living embodiment of the truth behind the belief that 'talking is a woman's sport'. For a full thirty-four minutes she held me captive, as I listened to the unexpurgated version of the events that had touched her life and business both socially and privately over the last eight weeks. In future I shall not leave such a big gap in between visits, but then until *Whispering Jim's* saga is over, me and the other former members of the Gay Bar will be gracing her pub on a temporarily daily basis anyway, provided of course that Vlado doesn't throw in the towel earlier than expected.

When Rosheen took over the pub many years ago, she wanted to turn back the clock and to try and reawaken what she believed is the normal innate social nature of her customers (like in the friendly pubs back in the forties). People in those days, she maintained, used to sit chatting to one another about their families, friends, work and politics, and not glued to television screens watching football matches, or screaming at losing horses. But then, in those days, television sets were very rarely seen in people's homes, let alone in pubs. But I have to admire her vision and determination. She was always totally against televisions or fruit machines in the place, and accordingly she attracted a particular type of customer who preferred a quiet pint or two in convivial company. The pub was never really what one might call busy, but it attracted a nicer type of clientele.

Bunny left at 15:10, followed by our two suspect burglars. I was concerned that the *fatherless-people* were following him, so I went to the door just to check what was happening. My fears were quickly allayed however, since Bunny went one way, and they went in the opposite direction.

A little later, Lenka and Ted joined me and we spent an hour or two discussing the Zora-Aleena issue.

Just before closing time, Lenka and I poked our heads into the Gay Bar which normally on a late Sunday evening would be a veritable hive of beer-swilling regulars. It normally closes at around midnight on a Sunday, an hour and a half after permitted licensing hours.

Vlado looked up expectantly and smiled at me appealingly. I pointed to the Posh Bar and walked outside and into an area which I would only formerly use in emergencies like a police raid – when *Ted the Pleb* was in verbal diarrhoea mode – or when I was warned of the impending arrival of Father Marcus.

Holding an empty pint glass expectantly, he said, 'Will you have drinks, Paul?'

'Vlado, please don't get me wrong, but at the moment, me and the other regulars of your public bar are sadly in dispute with you. Frankly, I feel so dreadfully sorry that it has come to this, and I do hope that in the very near future our grievances will be resolved to the mutual satisfaction of all concerned'

'I hoping so too, my friend,' he replied, putting the empty glass on the counter. 'But, words that are said are of easier than actions done.'

'We fully appreciate the dilemma that you are in, Vlado,' I said, 'but if it's any consolation to you, we believe that there may be a possible solution.'

'The biggest problem that I have to smile with is, when you people are away! Our first shout with anger, was at the wedding when I say, *I do!* She says, *oh, no you don't!*'

'Absolutely! And it is that kind of issue that we would like to discuss with you, Vlado. Could you meet us tomorrow lunchtime, somewhere on neutral ground?' I said.

'Like where?' he asked, gazing around nervously.

'Well how about the Peony Chinese Buffet Restaurant at noon?'

'I'll be there!' he said, smiling in anticipation like a hungry fox in an overcrowded hen house.

Goodnight, Ginny.

P xx

12th March 2012

Dear Ginny.

Our home was in complete darkness as Lenka and I crept into the flat at 00:25 this morning. On bidding her a fond goodnight, I hugged her affectionately, and told her not to get up too early. I set my alarm for 07:30 so that I could be up and about for my other three girls.

I was in the shower at 06:20 this morning however, and frankly I really do wonder why I ever set my alarm clock, since when I know that I have to be up at a certain time, my biological timepiece never fails me. It always wakes me in good time, usually an hour and a half or so before the alarm rings.

The breakfast table was set at 07:20, with Elisha's bowl of Choc O Pops and chopped banana together with a glass of passion fruit, while Maria's uncooked bacon, sausage and black pudding rested on a metal tray, which would be grilled and presented to her breakfast plate at 07:58, two minutes before her usual limp body and its emaciated tissues (needing urgent restoration) entered the kitchen at 08:00. Two cracked eggs rested in saucers awaiting their watery fate.

As I sat waiting at the kitchen table sipping a rejuvenating cup of coffee, my reverie was disturbed by the sounds of laughter coming from the bathroom. A little later, Jimena trotted into the kitchen and jumped up onto my lap, her head meeting my hand as I stroked her. Following this charming feline gesture, she started to purr gently, and despite my own comfort, her actions cunningly persuaded me to avert my attention to more pressing issues. I therefore robotically opened a small tin of salmon and mackerel cat food, which unlike Maria's impending grub-fest (reminiscent of a holiday camp custard-pie eating contest), she devoured with unhurried finesse and charming feline grace.

I put the sausage, bacon and black pudding under the grill at 07:46 and having added a couple of drops of vinegar into a pan of simmering hot water, which I stirred gently to create a whirlpool effect, I slipped the eggs into the pan at 07:56 and allowed them to cook for the requisite three minutes to ensure that the yokes remained soft and the whites delicately firm. Maria is very particular when it comes to her poached eggs, although she is not quite so fastidious in relation to the more common varieties like scrambled, boiled, fried, shredded or mashed.

At 08:00 precisely, Maria and Elisha entered the kitchen hand in hand, both giving me a hug and emitting a giggle before they arrived at their respective chairs around the table.

Later, having dropped Elisha at her playschool and clearly bored, Maria asked me what my plans were for the day. I told her about our arranged meeting with Vlado at midday, which she didn't initially seem to be particularly interested in, although once I mentioned where it was to be held, her former negativity suddenly changed and she asked if she could tag along until it was time to collect Elisha again. Without wishing to sound sceptical, I liked to believe that the glint that I saw in her beautiful blue eyes simply portrayed a longing to be with us and had nothing to do with the fact that she loves Chinese food nearly as much as English, Indian, Spanish, Italian, Turkish, French, Bulgarian, Australian and Aboriginal. She had a particular fondness for *bush tucker* in general and *witchetty grubs* in particular, the taste of which she stated, when raw, was similar to almonds, and once cooked, the skin became crisp like roast chicken with a yellow egg-like inside. And there she was a couple of weeks ago, turning her nose up at the sight of a bowl full of delicious oysters! However, she conceded that she 'might' be tempted into joining us in a few morsels, 'just to be sociable'.

Lenka surfaced at 10:35 and, following her shower and breakfast, she was eager to 'get out there amongst it!' A saying that she always uses when having to deal with matters of a contentious or disputatious nature, or when she was simply in the mood for getting completely *plastered*, irrespective of the time, the place or the company.

She has always been a very spontaneous and strong-willed woman, who has never been ashamed of saying what she thought, and has been ever ready to lay down her own personal comfort and reputation for an honourable cause.

At midday, having paid our entrance fee at the door, Lenka, Maria and I joined Ted and Vlado at their table in the Chinese buffet. Vlado seemed a little ill at ease, particularly when he saw the two girls. However, Lenka smiled at him encouragingly, but Maria (her mind on matters gastronomic) simply winked at the waiter seductively and feeling that five people sitting around a table intended for four might be a little crowded, selected an empty table some distance away from us which was conveniently placed behind a pillar, making her just about invisible.

Thinking about it later, it became very evident that her sacrifice wasn't entirely based on humanitarian or practical issues, but rather her wish to be away from the censorial eyes and incredulous comments of her fellow diners when it came to witnessing the vast amount of food that this voracious Spanish *monster-muncher* could put away. A once-in-a-lifetime spectacle, made all the more incredible when at the conclusion of her mammoth overindulgence, she would be able to stand unaided, without having to engage the services of a forklift truck to get her out of the place.

Having selected our various assorted meals from a mind-boggling array of unidentifiable dishes, we regained our seats. After the usual pleasantries had taken place, Vlado was the first to speak. 'I would like to thank you Ted, for the helping you granted for me on the other day.'

'Think nothing of it, my friend. I have been in worse situations, believe me!'

'I am hoping that I didn't hurt anything of you.'

'He's made of unbreakable parts, Vlado,' I said.

Matters then took on a more serious note and Ted instigated the proceedings.

'As you saw on Saturday, Vlado, the boys are most unhappy with the fact that you have banned Jim. This whole issue is about him, although there is another element to the subject that perhaps we could help you with.'

'I was too also was unhappy, but I must persist in my future, and be happy for myself and Zora-Aleena.'

'Certainly, Vlado,' Ted replied. 'We fully understand how difficult it was to have to ban Jim, and we all truly sympathise. But that doesn't alter the fact that as a result, you have a big problem. What I would like to suggest is that you ban Jim for a month, rather than for life.'

To cut a very long story short, we convinced him that by doing so, he will be seen as a no-nonsense publican, with a zero-tolerance policy when it came to abusive and/or aggressive or disputations customers. Without exception, this policy would apply to all, and instances of bad behaviour would initially be dealt with by a verbal warning. A second or subsequent antisocial violation would result in an immediate one month's banning from the premises. Thereafter, upon reinstatement, any further infraction of this house policy would result in life banishment from the pub, with no possibility of clemency or an appeal.

At this stage, Lenka turned the conversation on to more personal matters. 'I couldn't help noticing, Vlado, that your wife seemed to enjoy your forceful stance against Ted yesterday,' she said.

'My Zora-Aleena, is really of nature gentle. But she comes from very tough family. Her daddy, Dimitri, he was killed in fight with cousin, who called his Svetlana, name of pig. *Big Juri* (her brother) cut him up with meat chopper, and dish him up for food to his own Svetlanas. Sorry!' he said apologetically, 'I mean his own pigs.'

But nevertheless, it seemed to us that Zora-Aleena, enjoyed the way that you protected her,' Ted said.

Smiling, Vlado blushed and said, 'She likes me when I play like soldier on white horse. But if I treat her bad, her brother, Big Juri, give warnings of my legs cut off!'

'All women like to feel protected by their man, Vlado,' Lenka said. 'It is all part of the classic love story. If a man makes his women feel, safe, valued, cherished and loved, she will create a home fit for a king and around it, she will build him an empire.'

'In evening when I pushed Ted, she was loving for long time, which is nice, but all of the time makes head pain. We even in bed together were!' said Vlado.

Throughout all of this, Maria was seen only fleetingly when she returned to the ever-diminishing dishes of Chinese food. I noticed that the waiter watched her intently as she rebounded back to her seat numerous times, and the look on his face suggested utter disbelief.

A little later, she left to pick up Elisha. Bidding us farewell, she declined our invitation to join us with Elisha at the Bread Bin later, stating that she would have a bit of a lie down, which was hardly surprising, since the amount of food that she had probably demolished would have hospitalised a cart horse.

I do believe that the proprietors were more than simply relieved when she left, since their profits for the day must have taken a bit of a nosedive. I am sure that the floor staff would be given her picture produced from the CCTV cameras, to be carried on their person during their hours of duty, and having been identified on her next visit, she would not be allowed normal cutlery and would be given a single chopstick instead. Her visits to the food counters would be restricted and monitored under full camera surveillance, and on leaving her coat and bag would be searched and any request for a doggy bag would be politely declined.

We left Vlado at 14:45 and ventured off to the Bread Bin. During the early evening, the usual Gay Bar regulars started to drift in, and Rosheen was rushing around like a mad thing trying to serve them all. Ted intimated to them that progress had been made with regard to *Whispering Jim's* potential reinstatement.

As an initial step at placating Zora-Aleena, Ted felt that a good quality gift from Jim, together with a suitably worded card expressing sincere regret at the distress that he had caused, would pave the way for a little additional softening up later, and hopefully, like water dripping on a rock, Zora-Aleena's former hard and unforgiving stance would be systematically worn away. At least, that was the theory.

Whispering Jim would not be told about the goodwill and effort made on his behalf by the Gay Bar regulars, or the gifts given to Zora-Aleena which had been generosity scraped up from cash that was formerly destined to whet a few lips, and to provide a few hours of alcohol-fuelled joviality. This amounted to the very creditable sum of £35. Ted suggested that initially a beautiful floral bouquet should be sent to her, together with an appropriate card. This would leave enough for a large box of Swiss chocolates to be sent the following day.

Back at home, Lenka and I agreed that it had been a very successful day. Vlado was of the opinion that he could convince Zora-Aleena to accept the new pub disciplinary code. His excuse for being away from the pub today was that he and other pub managers had been asked to attend the Brewery's Head Office in Kennington, to receive instructions on a new procedure for dealing with unruly or disputations customers.

It is very fortuitous that Vlado's wife doesn't speak or understand one word of English, and therefore, when involved in a little innocent subterfuge, or indeed for that matter was blatantly subjected to a modicum of open-handed deceit, he could be able to cover up his tracks with relative ease. However, Vlado is an honest man, and only tells *porkies* when the truth is unavailable or inappropriate, which I suppose are the only valid reasons for telling lies anyway.

Goodnight love.
P xx

13th March 2012

Dear Ginny.

Alfie the Dip awoke me at 05:10 this morning, or rather his mobile phone did. His early morning calls are becoming both annoying and disruptive, although in fairness, I shouldn't be too hard on him since he doesn't know his own mind and sadly he hasn't missed much.

Forcing back unprintable but expressively colourful language, and trying to be as polite as I could, I said, 'Don't you ever sleep, you moronic, limp-dicked cretin!'

'Sorry,' he said, 'did I wake you?'

'No not at all Alfie, I was outside on the balcony, feeding the Fringillas.'

'Oh I'm sorry,' he said. 'I hope that they all got plenty!'

Before he had time to go into a lot of inconsequential verbal nonsense, I said, 'What do you want, Alfie?'

'Tina wanted you to phone Basil.'

'What, at five in the morning?'

'No, any time after ten. Ideally at eleven when he's having his coffee break and a couple of slices of tiffin.'

'What the *flip* is tiffin?'

'It's a cake made from crushed biscuits and...'

'Never mind, Alfie!' I said, quietly uttering unrepeatable blasphemies. 'So couldn't you have phoned me just before ten?'

'No I had to phone you as soon as possible in case I forgot.'

'So what time did Tina ask you to phone me?'

'Around lunchtime... yesterday.'

I quietly turned my phone off and tried to catch up on a little more sleep, but try as I might, there wasn't another wink to be caught anywhere.

A little later, I visited the gym for nothing more strenuous than a session in the steam room, followed by a refreshing shower and a shave. I bumped into Albery as I entered the estate, who has been keeping a bit of a low profile lately.

He was presumably on his way to his place of business and was making for Kilburn railway station. We exchanged pleasantries on passing and he stated, 'By the way, I may have a small safe for you. I'll give you a call later.' I was back indoors at 07:30.

There was a note on the kitchen table, which Maria must have put there last night on which she had written, 'Don't bother doing me any breakfast in the morning. I think I have a buggy tum!'

Having showered with Elisha, they came into the kitchen at 07:50 with Jimena following behind. Cuddles and kisses followed, although Maria was not herself. She was very pale and asked me if I would take Elisha to her playschool. Naturally I agreed and nodding at me she went back to bed.

I gave my little girl her normal cereal and chopped banana and fed my little purring ball of black and white feline fluff, which is now beginning to fill out bodily. Her confidence, like her ability to jump and reach impossibly high objects, gets better by leaps and bounds daily, and she is a very considerate and companionable little ruler in our household.

At 08:55 I dropped Elisha at her nursery and called into our local newsagent to buy a paper. I have always had a good relationship with the proprietor; Gupta Sarkar from Bangladesh, although I haven't seen him in the shop for a long time. Initially, I thought that he was a very dedicated and hard-working individual.

His newsagent shop is open from 05:00–23:00 daily and he was never late opening (but then he probably got his early morning call from *Alfie the Dip*). The first time that I met him, I was enthusing on the respect that I had for Indian businessmen in general, stating that many of them could teach our own company directors a thing or two when it came to running and building up a business.

Coming from a third world country, and diligently working and saving enough to come to the United Kingdom and start a business could not have been easy. However, my view changed slightly when he told me about his particular story.

'My formula for a good thriving business was initially based on many years of self-denial, for myself, and considerable deprivation for my wife and family, in raising the money necessary to get here,' Gupta said. 'But as my dear old revered father told me, *Success is guaranteed by getting up early every day, and working long into the night.* However, after winning £750,000 on the National Lottery in 2010, my revered father's opinion then changed to *Why work hard when you don't have to?* So now I get up at 08:00 and my cousin Ranbir opens the shop and works until 12:40. I then keep an eye on the place until 13:20 when my half-brother Reyanash takes over until close. It's a pretty hectic day, particularly when weather permitting, I try to fit in a game of golf between 14:00–17:30 which is then followed by a late afternoon nap and dinner. To round off my day, I enjoy a social evening playing bridge at my local club, from 20:30–22:45. Thereafter, I count and put the day's takings into my safe and am usually in bed by midnight.'

My view on immigrant shopkeepers has since changed quite dramatically, and following my chat with Gupta, I have tried to abstain from stereotyping anyone, particularly those indefatigable owners of corner shops which are open all hours, to provide us with our daily provisions and are coincidentally all owned exclusively by people from poverty stricken former British protectorates. I should be so lucky – perhaps in another existence!

Lenka was in the shower when I arrived home. After breakfast, she said that she would be out for the day visiting friends who had recently arrived on a holiday from Slovakia. She wanted to take them on a London sightseeing trip.

I phoned Basil a little later, who despite our rather disagreeable last meeting asked me to come in and see him. I had a couple of hours free before it would be time to pick up Elisha again, so I got the bus to Kensal Rise.

Basil greeted me enthusiastically when I arrived and offered me a cup of his coffee, which I declined. I am a real coffee lover, but sadly Basil's variety – which he told me 'was imported' – is quite disgusting. After sampling one cup recently, I had to unceremoniously dash to his toilet. I didn't know which end of my person to point at the loo bowl first. I settled on the top bit and having *barfed* with unrestrained abandon, managed to get the other end pointing into the right general direction with seconds to spare. Pretty it wasn't.

'I've received more positive information in relation to the whereabouts of Spike,' Basil said, biting into a rather large slab of an unidentifiable confection, which I assumed was tiffin.'Well that's marvellous, Basil,' I said excitedly.

'My Kilburn Unreliables have been on the case since his last abduction and were beginning to make a little progress, but since the return of my super slick-chick-dick, Spike's whereabouts has been determined. In fact, Tina met him and an elderly lady that he is currently staying with yesterday.'

'She really is quite marvellous, Basil,' I said, with genuine admiration for this amazing young lady. 'So where is he Basil, and is he OK after his stud-farm experience?'

'Tina said that he's fine. He has been staying with a Mrs Beryl Young since shortly after his last unfortunate abduction from the stud farm.'

'I am so happy Basil, and I will be more than simply happy to give Tina a sizeable gratuity for her diligence and hard work.'

'That's fine, Paul,' Basil said. 'She would like to join you when you collect Spike and will give you a call when an appointment to visit Mrs Young has been made.'

'Marvellous, Basil,' I said. 'Where does she live?'

'In a small village on the outskirts of Southampton,' Basil replied. 'Oh, and not wishing to put you under any undue pressure Paul, I thought that I would take this opportunity to bring you up to date as far as your bill is concerned.'

Opening his desk draw he took out a file which he opened and, looking at its contents, said, 'For my previous and recent services, your account stands at £720, which I would ask you to settle up as soon as possible or at least before the end of our fiscal year, which would be March 31st at the latest.'

'Good gracious!' I said, in mock surprise. 'Is another fiscal year nearly over?'

He was about to answer, when he realised by the smirk on my face that I was taking the *urine*. I subsequently paid him my outstanding bill, using my new Listowel Bank VISA debit card and it didn't hurt a bit. We bade a fond farewell a little later.

On my way to collect Elisha from her playschool, I realised that I am in a bit of a quandary in relation to what I should do with Tommy's surplus money. Following the sad news about his daughter's death and remembering the contents of my friend's letter, effectively I was now at liberty to use or dispose of the funds in any way that I saw fit. The logical recipient should be his wife Clare, but then surely if Tommy had wanted her to receive it, or part of it, he would have said so in his letter. Clearly this money was kept from her in life, and should I therefore go against his very clear wishes now that he was gone?

On our way home from her playschool, Elisha said, 'Can we go to McDonald's tonight?'

'Well that depends.' I said. 'Maria has been at home, and she may have made us all a scrummy dinner.' I was just teasing her of course, since the chances of my Maria making an evening meal was about as likely as her buying a pair of marigold gloves and volunteering to do the washing-up for a week.

When we arrived home, the flat was empty, the breakfast dishes were still in the sink, but happily it seems that my Spanish monster-muncher had managed to put a little sustenance into a stomach that probably thought that her throat had been cut. A slice of discarded toast and a globule of peanut butter lay ominously by the drainer, and the remains of a half-eaten chocolate digestive biscuit was on the top of the tea caddy.

Jimena was clearly pleased to see us both and for the first time that I can recall, she dashed down the hall in a straight line to greet us.

Elisha and I had a couple of hours playing with her puzzles and we watched the Disney classic, *Sleeping Beauty* on DVD which we both enjoyed.

Later I took her to McDonald's, a place where my little house guest feels totally at home. She knows the names and prices of every different meal and is a very enthusiastic critic of the various dishes. She is clearly to the menu born.

Maria phoned me at around 18:10 and she joined us a little later. I was quite happy to leave my two girls at 19:20 and made my way down to the

Bread Bin where I met up with the boys. Ted and Dave were in animated conversation as I entered.

'No, I've always liked her free spirit,' said Dave authoritatively, biting into one of Rosheen's less than inadequately filled cheese and pickle rolls.

'C'mon man, that's not being very kind, she's just a little slow,' said Ted.

'Well that's one way of putting it, she's about as quick as a geriatric slug on tranquilisers,' said Dave, taking a sizeable swig of his pint of lager. 'Actually, she can be talked into just about anything. The only difference between her and a supermarket trolley is that the trolley has a mind of its own. Mind you, there's a lot to be said for being associated with adventurous easily led nubile females, particularly those with the breaking strain of KitKat.'

I never did find out who they were talking about since like the usual topics of conversation in the Gay Bar, the subject matter changed very swiftly from one thing to another. It's so annoying!

Ted was usually the main culprit, bouncing from one subject onto another before a satisfactory point or conclusion had been reached, just like many of the pointless televised debates in the *House of Commoners*, who unlike Ted, actually get paid for talking absolute *sphericals*.

Rosheen was her usual affectionate self, but fortunately her strength had been earlier sapped in giving her new regulars gratuitous hugs as they entered. In comparison to the inevitable enthusiastic rib-bruising crushes given to the early arrivals, my hug was a quite pleasant affair.

It is also clear that Lenny's former trainee nemesis at the DHSS has certainly had a quite profound influence on him. Not so long ago, his idea of roughing it would have been for him to turn his electric blanket down to medium, and now for want of a more objective description, he is a hard-working, confident yuppie in training. But then, there's much to be said for the love and guidance of a good *well-nourished, dark-complexioned, fatherless woman*. Bless her little cattleprod!

All was quiet at home when I arrived just after midnight. Before bed, I checked on my covert camera recordings and found nothing untoward. Long may it last, although I will have a chat to Albery about the small safe that he has available. My intended trap is still ongoing.

I can just picture his cunning plan. I buy his small safe, to which I'm sure he would have a key, and then how easy would it be for him, or one of his henchmen, to walk in at their leisure and empty it of its contents? I'm sure that he has another key to the flat following my visit to his work premises recently.

Goodnight, Ginny.
P xx

14th March 2012

Dear Ginny.

Maria and Elisha were awake earlier than normal this morning. I heard the sounds of laughter coming from their bedroom at 05:15 together with what sounded like furniture being moved around.

All was revealed at breakfast time when Elisha explained that they were playing 'mothers and fathers'. I didn't quite follow the rules and wasn't too sure about why the furniture had to be rearranged until Elisha enlightened me. 'Well you see, daddy goes to work and mummy stays at home,' she said authoritatively.

'Oh I see,' I replied. 'And are you the mummy or the daddy?'

'I am the mummy,' she replied indignantly.

'And Maria then is the daddy?' I said. She looked at me in surprise. 'Well she couldn't be the mummy as well, because I am the mummy, silly.'

'Of course you are Elisha, but eat up your wheatie pops darling, because you won't grow up to be a big girl if you don't,' I said.

'I'm already a big girl,' she replied, and having popped a spoonful of her cereal into her mouth, she appeared to be lost in thought. Suddenly, she said triumphantly, 'All mummies are big girls!'

'But why were you moving the furniture around?' I said.

'Because I'm going to have a baby, and before we collect her from the baby shop, daddy must make her a bed and put it by the window.'

How cute was that? Throughout this chat, Elisha was deadly serious and while Maria covered the smirk on her mouth with her napkin, I had to excuse myself and dashed into my bedroom, pretending to make a call on my mobile.

On my return, Jimena welcomed me back, brushing her side along my leg. Thereafter she simply switched off and while our indecipherable utterances droned on around her, she remained passively disinterested throughout. Like most, if not all cats, she is the epitome of cleanliness, and started to clean herself in that inimitable feline way, running her abrasive tongue seductively along her legs and paws. Periodically she would stop and look up at us enquiringly. Thereafter she would start to purr again before returning to her morning grooming session.

Like my dear little Elisha, she has won my heart, although I really do feel quite guilty, since her presence has taken my mind off the dreadful sense of loss that I have felt. She has become Spike's replacement, albeit on a temporary basis. However, had he found out about it, I am sure that he would have happily left, taking his squeaky frog, his Sunday best lead and a mouthful of dog biscuits with him. But then he always was a bit of a drama queen.

Ted phoned during the morning to say that a beautiful bouquet of flowers and a card purporting to have been written by *Whispering Jim* had been delivered to The Magpie, and it seems that Zora-Aleena was quite touched.

During the phone call that Vlado had made to Ted, he stated that she was so overcome with emotion that she started to weep. Apparently, when Vlado tried to comfort her, she confided in him quite forcefully.

It appears that her tears were not shed in gratitude at Jim's show of remorse, but it simply reminded her that her own husband had never bought her flowers, and as a result he landed up wearing his lunchtime plateful of minced meat dumplings, complete with rice in a yoghurt and garlic sauce.

Notwithstanding this unfortunate *little domestic*, Ted was very optimistic and, now that the softening-up process was underway, he felt very positive. A follow-up would take place tomorrow with the arrival of another conciliatory card and a large box of Swiss chocolates.

In an effort to prevent any further wastage of food, or another potential 'domestic,' I did mention to Ted that this follow-up delivery should take place between Vlado's normal daily eating hours, since I was convinced that he had never bought his wife chocolates either.

Having dropped Elisha at her playschool, Maria was again at a bit of a loose end this morning and asked me what plans I had for the day. Jokingly I told her that I might have lunch at the Chinese buffet, which prompted her ultra-hasty retreat to the bathroom.

Lenka got up quite late this morning and when she came into the kitchen she wasn't looking at her best to say the very least. However, a lightning shower and a bite to eat changed all of that.

'Let's all go out for a walk,' she suggested.

Looking out into the courtyard and then up at the cloudless sky, Maria said, 'Well I'm game!'

'How about a mooch around Hyde Park?' suggested Lenka.

Shortly afterwards we were all on a southbound bus into town.

We had an enjoyable time together, wandering around one of the larger of the Royal Parks, which covers 350 acres, simply feeding the ducks and people watching, which Maria revels in. We walked around aimlessly, confident in the belief that one could never become lost in such a place, since provided one had a reasonable knowledge of London, at every point on the horizon, familiar landmarks pointed out one's geographical position and therefore the correct direction home.

We were back in Kilburn for 12:45. Maria left us to collect Elisha and Lenka and I visited the Bread Bin. It was pretty quiet, with the bulk of the lads still at work. But the two people that really mattered were in attendance. As we entered, Dave was in conversation with Ted, and as I went to the bar to order a couple of warming libations, I caught a snippet of their conversation.

Dave was in fine voice and said, 'The difference between a drinker and an alcoholic, Ted, is that like me, the drinker doesn't have to go to them AA meetings.'

'Whether you like it or not, Dave,' Ted replied, 'it is a recognised fact that people who drink daily are alcohol dependent, which in effect means that they are alcoholics. The only reason you do not drink every day is because there are not nine days in a week. However, you do drink daily during the remaining seven.'

'I suppose that there must be some kind of logic in that statement,' Dave said, puffing out a loud lungful of frustrated air. 'But for the life of me, I can't quite make my way through the mental antifogmatic of what you are saying.'

'What I am saying, my friend, is that whether you like it or not, you are just like me.'

'And what's that then?' asked Dave.

'The unadulterated, walking personification of an alcoholic in denial!'

A little later, Dave was asking everyone what the word unadulterated meant.

Lenka and I were home at around 17:20 and I had to rustle up an evening meal for us all pretty quickly, since Maria was looking quite faint through lack of nourishment. However, a large plateful of spaghetti bolognaise followed by apple pie and cream and she was back to her old robust, indefatigable self again.

Having finished, she smiled at me contentedly and said, 'I think, that later on tonight, just for the fun of it, I'm going out to get...' A long pause ensued. She put her head down and was seemingly trying to get her thoughts together. Suddenly, with a smile on her face, she looked up and said triumphantly, 'I'm going out to get *mouse-bummed*!' and holding Elisha's hand, vanished into the lounge with Jimena following them closely.

As she left the kitchen on the way to her room, Lenka smiled and said, 'I think she means *rat arsed!*'

We all had a quiet evening in our respective bedrooms and Maria didn't leave the house.

Goodnight, Ginny.
P xx

15th March 2012

Good morning, Ginny.

Not wishing to be repetitive, our usual morning activities took place with no mishaps or notable episodes.

I received a phone call from Basil at 08:00 this morning, which is considerably earlier than normal. He doesn't usually get to his office before 09:30. He requested that as a matter of urgency I should attend his office. His abrupt and forceful request had me leaving home half an hour later, and I arrived at his office at 09:20.

On my arrival, I found a rather dishevelled looking Nobby Caxton, biting hungrily into a rather large slice of tiffin. He stood up as I entered and tried to say something, but his mouth was fuller than a centipede's sock drawer. He mumbled a few indecipherable grunts and sat down in frustration. I patiently waited until his current mouthful had been masticated and he had got his breath back before I shook his hand and bade him a very pleasant good morning.

After the usual pleasantries with Basil were concluded and I had declined his offer of coffee, he took over the proceedings in his usual competent way. He explained that during his recent trial on a charge of possessing a quantity of class A drugs, Nobby had been found guilty and was given an eighteen-month prison sentence, suspended for two years. He was also ordered to pay a fine of £250 with an additional £50 costs.

I did my best to offer him my sincere commiseration and sorrow regarding the dreadful downward spiral of his life, although he fervently denied that the drugs were his, and stated that while on occasions he enjoyed a *spliff,* this was not a regular occurrence. He clearly believed that he had been framed. I had no hesitation in believing him and told him that he had my full and unconditional support. He became quite emotional.

After a short recess (I'm beginning to sound like a member of the legal profession), Basil went on to invite Nobby to tell his story.

Nobby explained that Albery Groupenhourst was his father-in-law. His estranged wife, Gretchen, was Albery's only daughter. They had lived together in Susan Atkins Court with their son Lionel, a twenty-eight-year-old paramedic for some fifteen years. But as a direct result of Albery's constant interference and influence in their relationship, a serious rift developed between them. She subsequently left the family home some seven years ago and is believed to be living in Huddersfield.

To date, she has not filed for divorce and it was this issue that kept him under Albery's direct malevolent influence, since he made it plain to Nobby that provided he was willing to 'assist him' from time to time, there would be no divorce and a very good chance that Gretchen would return to him.

Sadly, it seems that Nobby fell into Groupenhourst's trap, where he has been ever since. It started off slowly, with him giving Albery a master key to the estate flats, which over time was then systematically used by his henchmen to gain access to selected homes.

Nobby was used as Albery's eyes and ears, and carried out surveillance at the flat that was to be targeted, and passing on such intelligence as to the potential wealth and lifestyle of the occupants and their daily routines. This home would be subsequently ransacked and anything of value removed. Cunningly, these burglaries were carried out with a considerable gap in between each other, to hopefully indicate that they were simply random occurrences with no regular pattern. This gave the *Plod* the impression that they were not inside jobs. It appears that Albery has *caretaker helpers* in other housing estates scattered around London.

In the first two years of this skulduggery, out of the 220 homes on the estate, a mere five burglaries were conducted, but given the substantial wealth of their occupants, the money and goods stolen were considerable. The investigating CID detectives clearly did not grasp the fact that those targeted were occupied by some of the wealthiest occupants living on the estate.

After his first step into the dark world of organised crime, Nobby was trapped and Albery put further pressure on him by threatening to *temporarily suspend* his beloved son Lionel's walking capabilities, should he fail to carry out any further instructions given to him. The subject of this threat also happened to be Albery's own flesh and blood grandson, the despicable *anal-orifice*!

Later I was frankly astounded to be told that two flats within the estate were used as brothels. I don't walk about with my eyes shut, although I certainly didn't put two and two together when occasionally I wondered at the amount of men milling about during the evenings, particularly after dark. Needless to say, Albery's criminal activities included local drug dealing, and as Basil pointed out, his shoe repair and key cutting business was simply a front through which he laundered his ill-gotten gains.

DS Blackstock and the Serious Crime Squad were investigating Albery's activities and are convinced that with the additional evidence against him (which Nobby could provide) he wouldn't be seeing the blessed light of day for some considerable time. However, for this to be achieved, Nobby would also have to come clean about his own involvement, and in testifying against Albery, his own freedom could also be put in jeopardy.

After a brief tea break, Basil stated very convincingly that he could prove beyond all reasonable doubt that Nobby's actions were based on underhanded coercion and prompted by the very real threats made by Albery towards his son, and were not of his own volition. In his defence, this would provide pretty strong mitigating circumstances.

On leaving later, I shook Nobby's hand and wished him every success, and reminded him that I was completely on his side and was only a phone call away should he need anything.

Basil's parting words were decisively positive, and he reminded me that our meeting was completely confidential. He assured me that it was only a matter of time before Albery was arrested, and in the meantime, I was to continue in my normal daily activities. As I left, Basil stated that under no circumstances would Albery be granted bail and would therefore remain incarcerated until the date of his trial, which could literally be months away!

On the bus back to Kilburn, it suddenly dawned on me that a man that I always referred to as 'old misery guts at number 124' was probably the cretin responsible for the theft of Spike, and he had obviously made a few measly pounds on the deal, the despicable *pud-wapper!*

On leaving the bus in Kilburn High Road, I received a phone call from a woman purporting to be 'Basil's secretary'. I thought that it was Tina, who had tried to disguise her voice. She notified me that a new date for my pending court case in relation to the abstracting of electricity charge would be heard at 14:00 on the 21st March at Westminster Magistrates Court. When she had finished, I said, 'Thanks Tina!' I found out later that it was Alfie.

This reminded me of my other pending case for ABH which was due to be heard a mere five days later, when for the third time I would have to stand in the witness box at Westminster Magistrates Court and try and give a rational explanation as to why I assaulted a complete stranger causing him actual bodily harm. This really is like some dreadful nightmare!

They say that 'a problem shared is a problem halved', but I am of the opinion that it's better to keep your troubles to yourself, since experience has taught me that by repeating them over and over to one's various acquaintances, that intangible entity known as fate could think that you like them and could then proceed to give you more.

Later, I visited the Bread Bin where I met up with Ted who was in good spirits. He stated that Zora-Aleena was very pleased at the additional card and chocolates that she had received this morning. Vlado had also stated that his wife was warming to the idea of a formal disciplinary policy, and he had mentioned the possibility of Jim's reinstatement after his four-week banishment from the pub.

This period would effectively elapse on Sunday 1st April. A more appropriate day could not be found, since April Fool's Day would be one that all concerned would remember, quite apart from it being hilariously ironic that is.

Later, as I relaxed in a warm fragrant bath, with Sebastian surfing in the little wavelets that I made for him, I cannot quite express the intense feelings of elation I felt. In a short while I shall hopefully be picking up my little boy Spike who has been away from me for a full forty-six days. I can't wait to see him again, bless his little heart.

God bless my dear, sleep well.
P xx

16th March 2012

Good morning, Ginny.

Having had a refreshing sleep, on waking this morning, to quote one of my Lenka's favourite sayings, I wanted to 'get out there amongst it!' I was feeling particularly joyful and frisky, if that's the right word, enjoying a sense of happiness of a kind that I hadn't experienced in a very long time. The thought of seeing my beloved little dog again made me realise just how much I have missed him.

I gave both Maria and Elisha an affectionate cuddle as they came into the kitchen at 07:59 this morning, and both were in mischievous mood.

Elisha proudly presented me with a delightful crayon drawing of myself, which was amazingly accurate in its delightful childlike crudity and honesty.

Children do not pull any punches when it comes to drawing reality as they see it. However, I was a little displeased with Maria when in a very concerned voice Elisha asked, 'Is your *Ernie* better now, Paul?' Maria gave me a very embarrassed smile and looked away.

Fortunately a child's train of thought can be easily distracted, and smiling at her, I simply replied. 'He's much better thank you, darling. Where's Jimena?' I asked which provided enough of a diversion to deflect her attentions elsewhere.

Later in the morning, I phoned Tina to ask if she was free to have a chat. She replied in the affirmative and she duly arrived at midday with a large smile, and an even larger bag of assorted doughnuts.

She was her usual bubbly energetic self, and following a brief summary of her life since our last meeting, she asked if I would be free on Monday to visit Spike. I reminded her that it would be to 'collect' rather than to visit him. She smiled at me ruefully, which I didn't quite understand, but before I could question her further, she asked what I wanted to see her about. I asked her if she would be free to take on another little assignment, and then went on to explain the situation with regard to Nobby's wife Gretchen, and asked her if she would be available to track her down and to get her side of the Albery story. I was convinced that he had a hand in her sudden departure from the family home.

I provided her with all the relevant information about Gretchen's last known whereabouts and gave her £50 to cover her initial travel expenses, and a further £100 by way of a token of my thanks and gratitude for her invaluable help in locating Spike's whereabouts. She stated that she would start her investigation regarding Gretchen's whereabouts on the day following our journey down to Spike, and we then arranged a time for us to leave on Monday morning. I will be driving us down to a village called North End in Southampton to collect my beloved little boy, and my sense of excitement is almost overwhelming at the thought.

On leaving, once again she gave me a very warm affectionate hug together with a much unexpected kiss on the cheek. Lenka didn't come home last night since her bedroom door was left ajar, which as I've mentioned before, indicates that its occupant is not at home. But I am not worried since she is very streetwise. However, just to be on the safe side, and to stop any later niggling doubts concerning her safety intruding into my present euphoric state, I phoned her on her mobile, which went straight to voicemail. This didn't exactly put my mind at rest. However, I left her a short message asking her to give me a ring.

I was in need of a little time alone during the afternoon and felt in the mood for engaging in an interesting mental distraction, so later I visited the Imperial War Museum in Lambeth, South London, which now stands on a site within the Mary Harmsworth Park, to give you its correct name. I later learned that it is housed in a building that was on the site of a former lunatic asylum, the best part of which had been demolished.

The locals call the area *Bedlam Park*, and the name *Bedlam* became a word synonymous with lunatic asylums or an environment of insanity generally. It is also used to describe a state of uproar and confusion and conjures up the dreadful conditions of the early mental institutions. (Something like the recently televised reading of *The Palace Bar Bill* in The House of Commoners which advocated the introduction of a thirty per cent levy on all alcoholic drinks served within the confines of The Palace of Westminster after 18:00 hours.) This bill was introduced by a 'temporary' Green Party backbencher from Cheam, who I'm sure will be getting her P45 in the not-too-distant future.

On the various tube trains across London, I enjoyed honing my furtive people-watching skills on an unsuspecting public, and one can never be bored trying to guess what people do for a living for example. It's not a good idea to stare at anyone however, since this could result in two possible outcomes. Firstly, by doing so one may inadvertently become a perceived threat to another, and may land up being summarily bashed up by an insecure, paranoid individual, simply because he doesn't like the look of you, or he had forgotten to take his morning pills. Or worse still, one may fall prey to a predatory gasbag, suffering from verbal diarrhoea, who erroneously looked upon you as an interesting potential passive listener, and then proceeded to narrate an unexpurgated version of their life, from the nappy to their retirement watch, with the only possible escape being an impromptu hara-kiri using a discarded wooden Starbucks hot chocolate stirrer, or to jump out of the carriage at the next stop, even though it is light years away from your intended final destination.

I arrived outside of the quite imposing front façade of the building at around 14:20 and I enjoyed my visit immensely. I was particularly impressed with the First World War exhibition of the front-line English trenches, complete with the authentic sounds of the small-calibre high-velocity shells, called in slang terms *whizz-bangs* by the British troops, who often used humorous language to describe the awful conditions and dreadful events of their miserable lives. The dark environment and the rotting musty smells really brought home just how awful their lives in the trenches must have been. I was also particularly moved by the Holocaust Exhibition. It was a very powerful and emotional reminder of the atrocities that took place in the German concentration camps in Poland during the Second World War, and I had to turn away in horror at some of the video clips.

As far as the abhorrent treatment of the Jews by their German captives, I couldn't help but remember a saying by the late great Samuel Johnson who observed, *'He who makes a beast of himself gets rid of the pain of being a man.'* This could be used in describing the inhumanity and hatred that a very small, misguided section of the German nation in general, and their nemesis, Adolf Hitler in particular, advocated and ruthlessly practised.

Outside of the building later, I took a large lungful of semi-fresh air and mentally thanked providence for having been born after the last war. From the top steps of the entrance, I looked across Bedlam Park at the traffic chaos outside and imagined that if Johnson could now stand next to me and look out at his present-day beloved city, would he now rephrase his earlier sentiment of 'When a man is tired of London, he is tired of life; for there is in London all that life could afford' to a more realistic observation like, 'When a man can no longer afford to live in London, and is tired of trying to make a living. He should bugger off to the country!' Which I hope to do in the not-too-distant future.

With one thing and another, the cost of living in modern-day London is, for many, a simple mathematic equation: earnings plus ten per cent.

My final ambition in life is to move away to some sleepy little village, where the only yellow lines to be found are on the hats of school-crossing patrol ladies, and a traffic jam relates to having a bit of breakfast in the car outside of a rural cake shop.

In the country, one has time to stand and stare, as advocated by William Henry Davies in his delightful poem. Sadly, you couldn't do it in places like the London Underground as mentioned earlier. But I do seriously like the idea of getting up very early each day, simply because there is so much to do, what with standing and staring at the beautiful countryside and following rural pursuits. I also like the idea of going to bed earlier, due to one's mind and body having been satiated to excess with joyful thoughts and activities (which I believe can only be found close to nature). I go to bed early these days simply out of boredom!

Being gently lulled to sleep by the evocative calls of a tawny owl has to be far preferable to being thrown out of bed in the middle of the night by the sound of a passing emergency vehicle's siren, and then on the cold floor with one's heart banging away like a headboard in a brothel, to have to check one's pyjamas for any evidence of an involuntary bowel evacuation.

On the way back to Lambeth North tube station, my Lenka phoned and invited me to join her in an Indian meal at a newly discovered Punjabi restaurant at Marble Arch. Before I replied, I phoned Maria just to make sure that all was well at home. I heard Elisha's beautiful laughter in the background and knew that my other girls were fine. Maria had brought them both fish and chips for dinner, and then they were getting stuck into some 'scrummy doughnuts' that they had found on the kitchen table. I phoned Lenka back thereafter and told her that hopefully I would be with her within the hour.

Having fought my way through the evening rush hour, I met her outside of the *Guryev Punjabi Restaurant* at 18:44. I was both surprised and delighted to find that she was in the company of our little ninja lady friend, Tina.

We all had a lovely time and at 20:45 I left them and caught a bus back to Kilburn. I couldn't resist a quick visit to The Magpie and walked into the posh bar a little later.

Vlado was very pleased to see me and gave me an enormously large cognac on the house, and Zora-Aleena actually smiled at me. I had a peek in the Gay Bar and it was depressingly deserted.

Out of earshot of his wife, Vlado stated that the new pub disciplinary policy was now in place, and two copies of it were placed in suitable frames and screwed on a wall in both bars. He also commented that both he and Zora-Aleena would welcome *Whispering Jim* back into the pub on the 1st April. I was delighted and shook his hand warmly. As I left him I said, 'Thank you Vlado, your former Gay Bar regulars can't wait to get back!' He smiled at me joyously, and I am sure that his eyes glazed over as he said, 'Thank you, my friend.'

Later at home, the door to Maria's room was shut and there was no sound whatsoever coming from inside. It was the end of a very interesting and pleasant day.

Goodnight, Ginny.
P xx

17th March 2012

Good morning, Ginny.

My day started off relatively well. It being Saturday again, there was no immediate necessity to cook breakfast early, since Elisha would be at home today. Accordingly, all of my three girls sleeping in *The Shambles* (a very appropriately named description for Maria's bedroom) were all still down to it at 08:45. At least, there were no usual tell-tale noises or disturbances coming from the room, which would indicate that an impending human and feline tsunami was gathering momentum, and that a sudden unstoppable noisy rush along the hall, and an excited eight-limbed tidal-wave crash through my kitchen door was to be expected.

The first signs of life coming from the room coincided with the aromatic fumes emitted from my coffee percolator's flue, which for ten minutes or so before had wafted its unmistakable enticing fragrance along the hall, and had cunningly made a vaporous assault on Maria's keyhole (which isn't a euphemism). Being blown by the ever-constant draft from under the front door, its alluring aroma had filled her room, and by a simple process of mental imagery associated with food, it had offered her a seductive invitation to start a new day. This request was acted upon shortly afterwards.

As mentioned before, Maria's room is a place that I would not normally enter during daylight hours, and at night, without a string of garlic bulbs around my neck and a crucifix in my hand, it is a complete no-go area. However, hearing an unfamiliar sound, I knocked on her door and cautiously peered in. I was suddenly struck on the head by two pillows which had been thrown by Maria and Elisha, which made me jump. Following the little noise that they had made earlier, they had waited patiently to ambush me as soon as I opened the door. It resulted in rapturous laughter by us all.

Needless to say, our morning breakfast period was a memorably happy and jovial time. Both Maria and Elisha were laughing throughout the time we spent together, comparing their own experiences and observations on yet another week that had quite literally flown by.

Lenka hadn't come home again last night, but this time I wasn't unduly concerned since she was in the company of our diminutive tiger Tina. Under her protection, I am sure that no harm would have befallen her, or anyone else for that matter.

Ted phoned at 09:15, enthusing about the news of *Whispering Jim's* impending reinstatement at the pub, and we arranged to have a meet-up later in the day and to pay him a home visit. I couldn't believe that I had not seen or heard from him for the past thirteen days, and frankly I wasn't best pleased with myself or Ted for that matter, since neither of us had bothered to contact him throughout this time. In our defence however, he's not the easiest of men to get in touch with, since he has no home or mobile phone. Secondly, I never had any reason to visit him at his home, since as friends we simply shared the same watering hole. A place which I believed was more of a real home to him than his warden-assisted flat in Notting Hill could ever be. Fortunately, as I was to find out later, Ted knew exactly where he lived.

Just as I was leaving home at 11:50 to meet up with him, Gabriel arrived to take the girls out to the Longleat Safari Park drive-through, something which I'm sure they will all enjoy He is such a wonderful lad, and all of my girls are very fond of him.

I met Ted outside of Maida Vale tube station at midday and we travelled on the underground to Ladbroke Grove station, which Ted informed me was about five minutes' walk away from Jim's home, just off the Portobello Road. On the tube, I had fought against my feelings of claustrophobia very convincingly.

Later we mooched along through the very busy and well-attended market, which Ted informed me dated back over 150 years, and looking at the articles for sale, it appeared to me that during this time, the type of items for sale hadn't changed that much, since they consisted mainly of second-hand clothes and all manner of antiques and miscellaneous junk-type objects and ornaments, quaintly referred to as *bric-a-brac*. However, I enjoyed the atmospheric buzz of the place a great deal.

We arrived at Jim's warden-assisted accommodation at around 12:30 and following Ted's use of the outside buzzer system, we got no reply from Jim's internal intercom. Ted checked his notebook to confirm that flat ten was the correct one. He pushed the buzzer again and likewise we didn't receive any response. Looking through the glass on the front door, I could see into the warden's office and noticed a large man reading what appeared to be a newspaper. I pointed this bloke out to Ted and looking at the information on the wall nearby, found that the warden's office was listed as buzzer number one. Ted duly gave it a buzz, which enlivened the warden sufficiently to open the door for us and to enquire what our business was.

Whispering Jim had apparently left the premises at 10:50 sharp, a habit that he engaged in daily, apart from on a Sunday when he left an hour later. His morning departure was the first of his twice daily expeditions to his local pub. Daniel (the warden) laughingly explained that Jim had told him that these visits were *fact finding missions* to ensure that firstly, *The Pig & Whistle* remained open and that it had not become one of the casualties of the current economic climate. Secondly, being a lifelong philanthropist who liked to give to worthy causes, he believed that in his own small way, his daily twelve pints of Guinness, together with the endless pound coins that he stuffed into the pub's jukebox, quite apart from the sandwiches, crisps and pork scratchings that he consumed daily, would help to ensure that the landlord, his wife and their two charming young daughters would keep a roof over their heads, and that *Viljoen*, their very vocally friendly Indian mynah bird, would always have a plentiful supply of fruit, seeds, mealworms and Guinness.

As Ted and I walked into the pub at 13:15, the unmistakable voice of Jim Reeves singing *Distant Drums* was playing on the jukebox, which convinced me that *Whispering Jim* was not too far away and sure enough, sitting at a table in the alcove of the front bay windows, with a pile of lop-sided one-pound coins, looking like the leaning tower of Pisa in front of him, was our dear old friend Jim. As we neared the bar, Viljoen screeched 'SHOP!' which alerted the bar staff of our arrival and awoke Jim from his normal daydream stupor. He recognised us immediately and rushed to the bar to greet us, mumbling short sentences, all of which sounded pleasant enough, albeit totally indecipherable. Having bought us a pint, we followed him back to what had clearly become *Jim's seat* in the house.

Following a few catch-up words, designed to enlighten him on the events both social and domestic that had occurred in his absence, we informed him about all of the efforts made by the Gay Bar regulars on his behalf, and he seemed both grateful and very touched. However, he then went on to completely ruin our day by stating that in his couple of weeks away from The Magpie, he had done a lot of thinking and had come to the conclusion that, like the lyrics of the famous song 'Wherever I lay my hat, that's my home', that now *The Pig* was his new watering hole!'

He stated that he had moved on from the initial sadness and frustration associated with being banned from his favourite boozer, but he had found a pleasing alternative. The pub had a lot of added benefits in that it was a mere walk away from his home, and that unlike his former pub, he wouldn't have to pay a fortune in weekly cab fares getting there and back. The locals were all very friendly and the South African landlord and family were all very kind and considerate.

I was totally flabbergasted. But then, we were all to blame. While our motives were a little selfish in that we simply wanted him back in our pub, we had clearly acted under the very misguided belief that he wouldn't survive the disruption and terrible sense of loss that he would feel out there on his own, as it were. It was clearly impertinent of us to believe that he was not resourceful enough to sort out his life accordingly, and to witness at first hand the incredible strength of character and obvious capabilities of the man, was both a pleasing and humbling experience for us both.

During our stay, we could see why he was so enamoured of the place. Many of the locals greeted him warmly as they entered the pub, and the bar staff were all so very pleasant. The landlord shared a few jokes with him, and his daughters teased him delightfully, and even Viljoen kept repeating *'Mine's a large one, Jim'* which we found absolutely hilarious. In truth, I was feeling a modicum of envy. Before we left, I asked him if he would make an appearance in the Gay Bar on Sunday 1st April, since all of the lads would love to see him again, even if it was for the last time. This seemingly struck a bit of a sentimental note and with tear-glazed eyes, which he tried to hide, he readily agreed.

Both Ted and I were uncharacteristically quiet on our trip back to Kilburn. Later, I wasn't in the mood for any further social activities and was home and in bed sulking at 21:55. Feeling the way that I was, had I been on a bus, I would have most definitely laid down in the aisle and stamped my feet in annoyance and frustration.

Goodnight, Ginny.

P xx

18th March 2012

Good morning, my dear.

As I lay in bed gathering my thoughts at 04:45 this morning, I realised that both Ted and I had been completely mistaken and not a little presumptuous in believing that *Whispering Jim's* social life would have been thrown into utter chaos following his banning from The Magpie. But I comforted myself when I thought about Oscar Wilde's observation on the making of gaffes: 'Whenever a man does a thoroughly stupid thing, it is always from the noblest of motives.' With those words resonating in my mind, I slept on again, until the peace and quiet had been thoroughly compromised by Compton's itinerant yobbos, who seemingly had been at the Communion wine again, given the over-enthusiastic hammering that they were giving their bells at 07:30 this morning.

I heard the front door close, just after Compton's lunatics had started, and leaping out of my bed, I checked my video recorder and saw Gabriel, Maria and Elisha creeping softly along the hall and leaving the flat, clearly off out for another day's adventure. After the front door had quietly closed behind them, Jimena initially looked a little bewildered, but a little later she curled up on the hall carpet and was fast asleep in no time.

I eventually got up at 08:15 and Lenka arrived home a little later looking thoroughly exhausted, and I assumed that she had just finished another night shift at her club. She smiled at me on arrival and gave me a quick hug (which is better than no hug), and then headed for her bedroom.

A little later, I was sitting in the kitchen. Jimena jumped upon my lap and started kneading my knee, which Maria informed me she does 'when she's happy, and it is a reminder of the former comforts she received while being nursed by her mother'. Apparently, it could also be a signal that she was hungry. I duly obliged a little later, and having been fed, she no longer needed my attention and rushed into Maria's room, the hussy!

Having had a light breakfast of porridge with chopped banana, I had a shower and a shave and was ready to 'get out there amongst it' and happily surmount any difficulty that life could throw at me. Curved balls, however, are a little more difficult to handle and at 10:25 a rather large one was cast in my general direction.

Lenny phoned to invite me for lunch with him and 'his friend' Eugenia at a pub off the Cricklewood Broadway. I was quite surprised to say the very least. Initially, I wondered if this was a coded cry for help in disguise. However, he appeared to be very self-assured and confident. A table for three had been booked at the *Horse & Plough* in Burrow Street for 14:30 aperitifs and the lunch would follow at 15:00.

As a matter of urgency, I dashed over to the gym, and did nothing more strenuous than to sit in the steam room. However, I was pleased to meet up with Alex Scott, who informed me that following his recent court appearance, given his former clear record and the fact that he had stepped forward to quite literally save an innocent man (me), he was given a conditional discharge, but ordered to pay £250 towards costs. I was very pleased for him and once again thanked him for his wonderful humanitarian gesture, which took a tremendous amount of courage. It's not very often that one has the chance to meet a real-life hero in the flesh.

Later back at home, I phoned Ted to discuss my lunchtime appointment with Lenny. Initially he thought that I was joking, but when his laughter had finally died down, he asked me to ensure that for posterity, I would take sufficient photos to celebrate what he called 'The boy's coming out'. It was clear to me that the photos would later be used as *urine-extracting* material, which I pretended to go along with. However, under no circumstances would I allow that to happen and my simple excuse would be that I had forgotten to take my mobile phone.

I had never heard of the Horse and Plough pub, and indeed didn't have a clue where Burrow Street was situated. However, I checked out the place on Google and read the gushing reviews. The restaurant part of the pub was completely separate from the three bars and looked quite posh. The extensive culinary dishes on offer were very impressive, and having attained a two-star Michelin rating, the prices were correspondingly expensive. I mean £14.50 for a small dessert crème brûlée, consisting of an egg and a couple of spoonfuls of demerara sugar, certainly isn't cheap, in fact I think that it is nothing short of taking the *gastronomic urine!*

I couldn't help wondering where on earth Lenny would have got the money to be able to fund a three-person sojourn into such an expensive restaurant, and paying what I would conservatively estimate to be the equivalent of a week's wages for the skipper of a North Sea fishing trawler.

The dress code of *smart casual* had me thinking, since the last time that I had seen him, he was wearing clothes that he said were new. Well new to him maybe, but I suspected that they had been previously worn by others before they had been finally dropped off at a Kilburn charity shop.

I thought that I'd wear my latest Man at C&A creation consisting of a white open necked faux-silk shirt, with a contrasting grey cravat, grey chinos and a grey blazer. A fashionable clothing ensemble, that was smart and yet infinitely casual.

Instead of using my London Transport chauffeur, I booked a cab that arrived promptly at 14:10 and subsequently conveyed me to the pub. Thankfully, it was an uneventful experience but only just. Driving along the Cricklewood Broadway at any time of day or night is not for the faint hearted. I gave the driver a two-pound tip on our safe arrival by way of thanks, and gave him directions for his relatively safe return to his base in St Johns Wood, using what the locals refer to as *A safer rat-run.*

As I walked into the pub, I found Lenny sitting at the bar with what looked like a cocktail in front of him. He gave me a warm handshake and cuddles on arrival, and asked me what I wanted to drink. Not wishing to appear pretentious, I acted unsure and doubtful. 'Well how does a beer sound?' he said. 'I dunno Lenny,' I replied. 'I usually finish them before they can get a word in!'

Before he could reply, I saw a quite beautiful young woman walking towards us. Looking at me she smiled and said, 'I take it that you are Paul?' and offered me her hand.

Jumping off his stool Lenny said, 'Oh I'm sorry Paul, this is Eugenia.'

To say that I was surprised is a bit of an understatement. She was absolutely gorgeous and nothing like what I had imagined. She was clearly of mixed race, with a beautiful light coffee colouration. She was around five feet six inches in height and her emerald-green eyes, like her smile, were radiant. Beautiful long tresses of raven-black plaited hair fell softly down her back and a tight-fitting dress and pink cotton top accentuated her slim hourglass figure. She was delightfully soft spoken and had clearly been very well educated. I would estimate that she was in her early thirties, and clearly there were not too many years between them both.

To cut a very long-winded story short, Lenny stated that he had been contacted by solicitors who were looking for the relatives of the late Rebecca Anne Ficks. She was Lenny's father's older sister, who, apparently had never married. It was established that Lenny was her only known living relative and therefore he had become her sole heir and beneficiary. His inheritance included her former detached house in Chertsey, a small farmhouse on the outskirts of Cannes, a shares portfolio relating to various concerns, the current value of which was around £260,000, as well as loose change to the value of around £10,000 which was resting in two banks. I was absolutely delighted for him.

But during the dessert, he dropped a bombshell stating that he and Eugenia were engaged and would I be his best man at their forthcoming wedding. Frankly, I nearly choked on my croquembouche and clotted cream (which I find easier to write down than pronounce). I really wasn't prepared for all of this exotic food and mental excitement in one day, but I was so very happy for him.

Later, having been notified by one of the waiters that my cab had arrived, I offered them both my sincere congratulations and, giving them a hug, I made my way deliriously to the door. Lenny came with me, holding my hand. Just before I left, I made the comment that now being part of the jet-set, he would have to learn a little French.

'I know a few words already,' he said proudly.

'Like what?' I said.

He thought for a minute, and with a passable French accent said, *'Bonjour monsieur, vous avez, pas des deux.'*

'Which means?'

'Well, the *Bonjour monsieur, vous avez,*bit means, hello mate, have you...'

'Very good Lenny,' I said. 'And, what about the *pas de deux?'*

Opening the door for me, he replied, 'Oh that's simple, it means father of twins!'

During the cab journey home (via a rat-run) I considered just how quickly a man's life can be changed by a few shillings and the love of a good woman. There he was a few short months ago contentedly *messing* his way through life, and suddenly, instead of walking away from responsibility, he will now be running down the aisle, without anyone chasing him either!

I am quite convinced that he will make a wonderful husband, and with Eugenia still being a mere *slip of a girl* as it were, is well capable of having children, and I know for sure that Lenny will make a wonderful father.

Ironically, while his interpretation of *pas de deux* was charmingly amusing, and of course was completely wrong, ironically it is very appropriate in that it quite literally means 'a dance, or an intricate relationship or activity for two'. Having hopelessly stumbled around the ballroom of life, I sincerely hope that together with Eugenia, Lenny's future dance routines will be long, fruitful and ecstatically happy.

As I got out of the cab, and walked through the inner courtyard of the estate, I suddenly had a quite profound thought. Success is relative, the more success, the more the relatives, and when it comes to people like *Ted the Pleb*, who looks upon Lenny as his surrogate son (in training), a close watch on Lenny's acquired assets, whether liquid, fixed, tangible or intangible would be advisable, particularly when the interested party in question, could charm the drawers of an Armenian nun.

My sweet home was very quiet on my arrival, both of my girls' doors were closed, and before I walked into my own bedroom, I blew a kiss at them both.

Goodnight, Ginny.

P xx

19th March 2012

Good morning, my dear.

I was 'ready to get out there amongst it' at 06:15 this morning. I have been without my beloved Spike for long enough, and the kind of immense excitement that I felt at the thought of seeing him again today had no precedent. But sadly, it was all to end so bitter-sweet.

Maria was aware that I would be out early this morning and had agreed to prepare breakfast for Elisha. In a show of what could be described as 'the eccentric divergence of my normal rational behaviour', I removed the fridge door padlock first thing this morning and left her a note stating that she could 'help herself', which I was sure would be acted upon with considerable enthusiasm.

The fridge contained an ample supply of cheese and ham to make toasted sandwiches, five small pots of strawberry yogurt, four cream doughnuts and seven chocolate club wafers, although I was quietly confident that on my return she would have kindly 'created a considerable space' ready for a provisions reload, and that my fridge would be as empty as a cobbler's curse.

But during those ecstatic moments of joy, where one's normal sense of propriety and judgement are abandoned – or simply forgotten – irrational or unaccustomed behaviour is likely to occur. A good example of this is when the West Ham United football team actually succeed in winning a game. The usual gentlemanly, good-natured behaviour of the club's supporters is lost in an *uncharacteristic* show of post-match elation.

The injured are ferried to the local hospitals in a never-ending stream of ambulances and public vehicles, reminiscent of the tiny boats that went to the rescue of our troops at Dunkirk, and the inevitable destruction and carnage to local property and shops that follows has been compared with the allied bombing of Dresden. The volunteer St John's Ambulance Brigade teams who had strategically placed themselves at the exits, had hastily decamped from the area just as the final whistle blew, and subsequently all leave for the local constabulary and judiciary was cancelled, since for the near future both the police and local geriatric judges would be busier than a group of randy roosters in a hen house.

I met Tina outside the estate at 06:30 as arranged. She wasn't as talkative this morning, and quite surprisingly, she held my hand as we crossed the road to my car. She was dressed in very smart clothing and for the first time, instead of smelling like saddle soap, the gust of fragrant air that waffled towards me as she sat down in the passenger seat of the car had the unmistakeable aroma of *Chanel number 5*. As I turned on my ever-ready torch to program my satnav (which I had bought from Ted) I noticed that she was also wearing make-up.

Driving across London at this time in the morning is a nightmare. The Edgware Road was busier than a cross-eyed air traffic controller who had lost one of his contact lenses, and there had been a serious accident around Hyde Park Corner. The Brompton Road was at a complete standstill, and in the time that we sat there, I could have changed a flat tyre without losing my place in the queue before the traffic had started to flow again. But such is the misery of driving in the Met-trollops.

An hour and twenty minutes later, we were thankfully heading south on a very busy M3. We had a break at the Winchester Services at 10:25, and the food and coffee wasn't bad. Tina had a cheese salad and I had a *semi full-English* breakfast which consisted of a fried bantam egg, an anaemic-looking rasher of bacon, a small quantity of button mushrooms that needed to be chased around the plate, and half of a fried tomato, which looked like a large red boil just waiting to burst. However, my spirits lifted as we left. Needing to empty a rather full bladder, as I stood at one of the numerous urinals, one of their former visitors had written on the wall *'Kindly refrain from dropping toothpicks into the urinal. Pubic lice can pole vault!'* I was giggling like a schoolgirl as I rejoined Tina at the car.

Later we were driving south along the M27, and my satnav ordered me to 'KEEP LEFT!' 'TAKE THE NEXT EXIT!' 'KEEP LEFT!' 'TAKE THE NEXT EXIT!' I kept left and took the next exit, and then following its precise directions. 'IN TWO HUNDRED AND TWENTY YARDS YOU HAVE REACHED YOUR DESTINATION!' In precisely 220 yards I was told again 'YOU HAVE REACHED YOUR DESTINATION!' I found myself parked in a lay-by on a lonely featureless road, with a field full of cows on the one side, and a lake on the other. I apologised to Tina, who was looking a little flustered. She opened her bag, and taking out a compact mirror, quietly checked her make-up. I believed firmly that she had things on her mind, but I simply kept quiet.

After a couple more wrong turns and another annoying adventure involving a muck spreader, a turnip field and a no-left-turn sign, we finally drove into North End village at 12:50, and more by luck than judgement, we eventually found the bungalow of Mrs Beryl Young a little later. It was situated in a very pleasant rural setting, with undulating woods and pastures front and back.

My heart was thumping away wildly as I rang the bell. Initially all was silent and then I heard the unmistakeable sound of my dear little Spike barking and snuffling behind the front door. A little later I heard a woman's voice which shouted, 'No Buster, down boy!' The door opened slowly and cautiously an elderly woman peered out at us. She clearly recognised Tina and her face lit up.

As she opened the door fully, Spike came charging out barking at us furiously. Suddenly he stopped and, cautiously sniffing at my hand, his tail started to wag furiously and his excitement was almost as overwhelming as mine.

As she invited us in, Tina introduced me. Mrs Young said, 'He's certainly taken a shine to you, young man!' and after the usual pleasantries had taken place, we were led to her sofa in the lounge, Tina sat on a rocking chair opposite and in true *Worzel Gummidge* fashion we were offered tea and a slice of cake, made all the more charming by our host and her delightful Hampshire accent.

Mrs Young was a very small elderly woman whom I would estimate to be in her eighties. Her hearing was clearly bad since she wore hearing aids in both ears, and she needed the help of a stick when walking. She wore a chequered blue dress over which was an apron which had probably started off the day black (it was now covered in flour).

Before I could get a word in edgeways, Tina and Beryl were engaged in what for me was an example of inconsequential discussion of a type not unfamiliar to the female tongue, and after ten minutes or so of *feminine craic-type blathering*, I looked at Tina appealingly. 'Beryl,' she said. 'Why don't you tell Paul about how you came to get Buster?'

Sitting next to me on her sofa, with Spike sitting in between us looking up expectantly, she said, 'My husband Albert passed away five months ago.' Tears started to well up in her eyes and she quietly excused herself and left the room. Spike followed her out. They returned shortly after, with Beryl holding a tissue and Spike had a large Bonio-type biscuit in his mouth. Beryl regained her seat next to me and Spike slumped down by my feet, and as well-mannered as ever, quietly sucked his treat.

'I'm so sorry,' she said, wiping tears from her eyes with the tissue.

'That's quite alright, Beryl,' I replied. 'Please go on with your story.'

'Albert and I were childhood sweethearts,' she continued. 'We were together for sixty-two memorable years and we were never apart. Well there was the war, when he was away for five years, but that couldn't be helped. When he passed away, I was heartbroken. I have never been on my own you see, and I simply couldn't cope. Our children live in America, and apart from a younger brother who lives in Aberdeen, I have nobody. Well, I do have a good neighbour next door, but that's not quite the same, is it? But then, as if by heaven sent, I found Buster in my back garden one morning. He was very emaciated and was terribly cold. I let him in and he curled up in front of my fire and was soon fast asleep. I truly believe that my Albert had sent him to keep me company. He is such a good boy and he has given me a new lust for life. I love him dearly.' Smiling at him tenderly, she said, 'He follows me everywhere, bless his heart, and I don't ever feel lonely anymore.'

I suddenly became aware of Spike looking at me intently. I looked at Tina, whose eyes had glazed over with tears. She smiled at me apologetically and slowly looked away.

Later, Beryl got out her prized photograph album and I patiently sat and looked at each picture and listened to the stories that they evoked, many of them being genuinely interesting. My little lad sat patiently at my feet throughout and I wondered if he remembered Lenka and Maria. At around 15:30, I suggested to Tina that we should be thinking of heading home. Beryl thanked us for our visit, and on opening the front door, Spike sat next to her as we left. I turned and, stroking his head gently for the last time, I tearfully rejoined Tina. A little later, we were on our way back to the smoke.

We had a very quiet and uneventful journey back, and I dropped my little ninja off at Marble Arch. She gave me a lovely hug and kissed me sweetly. On parting, she simply smiled at me and said, 'Thank you, Paul.'

Goodnight, Ginny.
P xx

20th March 2012

Good morning, Ginny.

I was awake at 06:10 this morning, and as I gathered my thoughts, I came to the conclusion that during the last two days I had been through an unprecedented journey of emotional highs and lows.

The intense joy that I had experienced following Lenny's fateful nudge into the real world, where he had found the love of his life and had inherited a sizeable financial windfall, which would ensure a stress-free existence for them both for the rest of their lives, filled me with intense joy, and I couldn't have been happier for them both.

A mere day later, and my own sense of personal light-heartedness was overshadowed by a dreadful state of abject sadness and despair. Having seen my beloved Spike again, I was later to realise that it would be for the last time. Fate had decreed that I would have to leave without him, since in all conscience given the circumstances, I simply couldn't do otherwise. At least I was convinced that, like Lenny, he would spend the rest of his life in a loving relationship with his new partner, and while neither of them is in what could be described as the *flush of youth,* I was convinced that their remaining years together would be spent in love, happiness and peace. I had to smile to myself at the thought, that one of us was destined to spend his remaining years out in the country after all. Amen to that!

Perhaps that's what karma is all about? Hypothetically in Lenny's case, his first thirty-one years of life and the misery that went with it, could be due to his previous lives misbehaviour, but once the sentence had been completed, as it were, his remaining transit through this mortal coil could then continue with all of the uncertainties and temptations that modern life cunningly provides. But for the time being at least, his karmic slate had been wiped clean, and hopefully he would keep it that way.

Thinking about the Frobisher affair, which I am clearly responsible for, if the sad loss of my beloved Spike is connected to this issue, then my subsequent karmic scourging had been dealt with very swiftly indeed. But then, given the world's population, which is estimated to be at around, 7,800,000,000, maybe a *pay-as-you-go* type of operation was now in place. This would be a logical step, since I am sure that keeping tabs on everyone, not to mention the mind-boggling time spent in penalty assessment as well as the considerable administrative processes involved, has to be a logistical nightmare!

Clearly, there is a lot of truth in the biblical observation of 'as you sow, so you reap', or its modern-day equivalent of 'what goes around, comes around' and I firmly believe that people who ignore such warnings, do so at their peril.

Such heavy philosophical thought, so early in the morning, particularly when one's system had not been suitably enlivened by caffeine, is a mentally draining affair. But a few cups of coffee later, I was alert enough to read the note that Lenka had left for me on the kitchen table. Bless her heart, she had bought food for Spike's return, which she had left out on the balcony. I couldn't thank her personally since her bedroom door was ajar, and she was clearly out there amongst it!

Maria's door was shut and therefore just before 08:00 I could expect the arrival of my remaining three girls into their dining area. I quickly prepared breakfast for them. I hadn't figured out just what I would say to Maria in relation to Spike's non arrival, but not having had the time to work out a feasible excuse, I thought that I would state that it was all a simple case of mistaken identity, and that the dog that we visited yesterday, although being very similar in looks, wasn't Spike.

On their way to the bathroom at 07:15, Elisha and Maria were in fine voice and laughing hysterically. Jimena peered into the kitchen and on spotting me she jumped up on to my lap. Needless to say, her breakfast was provided a little later.

On their arrival into the kitchen, I was mobbed by my two remaining girls and I hugged them both adoringly. They did not need any persuading in relation to demolishing their respective breakfasts. After which, Maria suddenly said, 'Where's Spike?' Clearly, before her morning bodily tissues had been restored, Maria's normal brain function was in neutral as it were, but enlivened by a considerable amount of nourishment, it quietly slipped easily into first gear, and after a couple of slugs of coffee it was in overdrive.

Crossing my fingers, I explained my earlier hastily concocted story about it being a simple case of mistaken identity. I really do hate telling porkies, but I would have never lived it down if I had tried to tell her the truth. Like us all, she adored Spike, and if I had told her that I had left him with another, she would have been heartbroken, irrespective of the motives involved. However, clearly being upset, with tears in her eyes, she accepted my explanation and as caring as ever, she gave me a supportive hug and said, 'I can't even ask for doggy bags anymore,' and howling pitifully, she dashed down to her bedroom with Elisha and Jimena in close pursuit.

A little later, all hell broke loose in the stairwell. The sound of a considerable amount of heavy footfalls on the stairs was almost deafening. This was followed by loud banging upstairs. Peering outside of my front door, I was greeted by a uniformed police officer who simply said, 'There's nothing to worry about sir, could I please ask you to go back inside?' I duly obliged.

Looking out into our courtyard, I saw a considerable number of police officers and two police vans. It was 08:45 and I felt it best for Maria and Elisha to stay at home. I phoned Elisha's playschool to inform the staff that she would not be attending today.

At just after 09:00 I saw police officers carrying boxes and a computer which they put into one of the vans. It would appear that Albery's flat had been searched and any incriminating evidence found retained by the police. At this time of the morning, he would have been at his place of business, but I found out later that the raids on both his home and business were conducted simultaneously. Apparently, his shop was just about ransacked.

I phoned Basil a little later, who stated that Albery had been arrested and was currently being interviewed by detectives from the Serious Crime Squad. He would be held overnight and would appear at Westminster Magistrates Court first thing in the morning on a charge of drug dealing, which Basil informed me was the mere tip of his criminal iceberg, and that a substantial amount of other serious charges would be added later. Due to the very complicated nature of the investigation and the very real possibility that if released, Albery would flee the country, any application for bail would be strongly opposed by the Director of Public Prosecutions himself.

I have never enjoyed witnessing the downfall of others, believing wholeheartedly that people who make mistakes in life can change. But when I considered Albery Groupenhourst's crimes and his innate merciless nature, I really couldn't find it in my heart to offer him the slightest modicum of sympathy. As Robert Louis Stevenson once said, 'Sooner or later, everyone sits down to a banquet of consequences,' and the inconvenience of his pre-trial remand experience, will be a mere *hors d'oeuvre* prior to him getting stuck into the serious business of his criminal main course and pudding.

The entire meal would be supplied free of charge, as would his future dining and sleeping arrangements, and his removal and subsequent incarceration away from society would be greatly appreciated by the public in general and our Gracious Queen in particular. Being a bit of a patriot, I am sure that Albery would be tickled pink when he found out that his imprisonment would be at:

Her Majesty's Pleasure.

At the pub later, I had a phone call from Tina who was with Basil at his office. Given the news about Albery's arrest, she was curious to know if I still wanted her to seek out the whereabouts of Nobby's wife Gretchen.

With all of the excitement of the last couple of days, I had completely forgotten about my earlier request, but nevertheless, I felt that she should continue on this assignment, since I am passionate in my desire to see Nobby and his estranged wife back together again.

Tina stated that she would start first thing in the morning and asked that if and when found, was she to give Gretchen any message? 'Yes,' I replied. 'Simply tell her that it is now safe for her to return home to her husband and son.'

Before she rang off, she said, 'Basil sends his regards, and will see you tomorrow afternoon at the court. Oh and don't be late!'

How ironic I thought, as I sipped my cognac, Albery will be appearing in the morning performance and I would arrive at a follow-up matinee later in the afternoon. However, I decided that I'd make a bit of a day of it, and for the first time (providing that there was enough room, that is) I would sit and watch the court proceedings from the spectator's gallery, at least until after lunch when it would then be my turn to face the music, as it were. Not that I would ever want to make the sitting in courtrooms an essential part of my social calendar, you understand!

Strangely, as my mind went through a veritable kaleidoscope of poignant scenes from my earlier court appearances, the song *Jailhouse Rock* suddenly came to mind. It went again, considerably faster!

Before I left for home, I was intrigued to find out the outcome of a story about a young lady that Alfie was positively gushing about. 'I met her in the launderette,' he said, 'and I asked her if she would like a squirt of me fabric softener.'

'And they say that romance is dead?' quipped Dave, who was clearly in *urine-extraction* mode and was smiling mischievously like Adam when he told Eve that he preferred pears.

The Gay Bar suddenly became as quiet as dreaming trees, and all eyes and ears were upon Alfie, who sadly is to public oratory what Richard Branson is to face cream.

'She smiled at me sweetly and blushed,' he said, taking a long satisfying swig of his gin and grapefruit. 'I think she must have been foreign, because she didn't answer me. She just sat down and started to read a book. I have never seen a woman with such beauty! I was smitten!'

'That sounds like a classic case of love at first sight, Alfie,' said Ted authoritatively.

'No, I mean I was walloped! Some old battleaxe with a face like a broken mangle, that I was sitting next to, gave me a hefty swinging clump with her bottle of *Lenor,* and whispered, *she can't hear you, she's deaf!'*

'So what did you do?' asked Dave. The assembled open-mouthed bar attendees held in acute suspense.

'The only thing that I could do!' he said, rolling up a fag. 'I sauntered over to the woman in charge and asked her if she had witnessed me being assaulted and would she sign a statement.'

Since Alfie is a well-practised grand master of the anti-climax, I had a distinct feeling that his anecdote, like many of his others, would lead his audience into what could be described as a verbally induced state of colic, resulting in his listeners becoming hard to control, difficult to soothe, and displaying a tendency to burst into tears for no apparent reason. I therefore made a strategic withdrawal, being certain that at some later date, the complete pointlessness of his epic narrative would have become abundantly clear, and that my earlier decision to retire prior to the tale's conclusion was justified.

On my way out, I bumped into Lenka who was looking very concerned indeed. I had to go through the same deceptive porkies that I had given Maria earlier, and frankly I'll be glad when this matter can be finally put to rest. Apart from anything else, I am hoping that time's healing process will get a bit of a move on and give me some peace. But while people keep reminding me of it, the scab keeps getting picked as it were, and then I'm back to square one, with all of the intense sadness and despair that this inevitable brings.

Lenka was very supportive and as we walked back towards home, she held my hand, like Tina had done yesterday and said, 'C'mon, the night is yet young. Let's go down to the Bread Bin for a night cap!' I didn't need asking twice and having blindly groped our way through an ominous freezing fog, a little later we were thankfully sitting in the warmth of Rosheen's hostelry.

Later, Lenka brought up the subject of Spike again, but I cunningly steered the conversation on to other considerations, notably my visit to the court tomorrow, followed by the trip down to the Isle of Wight on Thursday, in readiness for my dear late friend's funeral at midday on Friday.

She asked me if she could join me on my travels, since she was off work for a few days. I was more than pleased to accept her request. My only reservation was whether Maria would be able to cope with Elisha single-handedly. I phoned her from the pub and she was more than happy, and I believe that in a small way, she felt quite pleased that I would trust her with such a responsible undertaking. But then Lenka and I would only be away on the Thursday and we would be back on Friday evening.

Maria is a big girl now, and while I tease you about her, she really is a very capable young lady. So what could possible go wrong? What am I saying? I shouldn't tempt fate in this way.

When we returned home, all was quiet. I gave Lenka a hug and blew a kiss at Maria's door. I was more than happy to close my eyes – *to sleep; perchance to dream.*

Goodnight, Ginny.
P xx

21st March 2012

Good morning, Ginny.

Kicking my legs out from under my duvet gave me my first real challenge of the day. Not that my reluctance in getting out of bed was due to laziness, you understand, since I had slept very well indeed, and I was simply itching to 'get out there amongst it!' But my central heating is timed to come on at 06:00 each morning, and since the heating had gone off at 23:00 last night, my bedroom was now colder than a well-digger's testicle, the thought of which was all the justification that I needed to remain where I was, at least until my programmed heating device had moved on to a more agreeable time and had prompted my boiler into action.

In the interim, I dug out the remaining fluff from my belly button and having a little time on my hands as it were, I considered the issue relating to the 'well-digger's testicle'. I tried to imagine the dreadful work conditions that this would entail, and I mentally envisaged the poor bloke digging away in the semi-darkness, looking forward to his tea break up above in the blessed heat and light of the sun. A welcome thought made all the more appealing at the suggestion of being able to warm his vulnerable extremities, or in his case (extremity), at least until the foreman's disagreeable glances prompted his hasty return back down the ladder.

It is clear that the singular reference to a part of the poor man's *family jewels* must indicate that on some earlier occasion, during the cold and heavy work involved, he had tragically lost one of its precious stones, as it were. Clearly this event must have taken place during those halcyonic carefree days before the overly pedantic, dole-inducing *Health & Safety Brigade* had put all well-diggers (with or without testicles) and their ancillary workers out of gainful employment.

But when one considers some of the more unpleasant conditions for a man to find himself in (apart from losing a testicle that is), being cold is one of the most unpleasant. However, in my honest opinion, being wet as well as cold is the worst of possible combinations.

As I lay there in the warmth and comfort of my bed, I remembered some of those classic war films that I had watched on TV – where our gallant American GIs, having jumped (or were chucked) out of landing crafts into waist-deep freezing cold water, are seen courageously rushing up the beach head, like the first few *jolly boys* dashing off the charabanc at Margate, searching for the nearest pub.

With their cold soaking wet socks, underpants and trousers that had been earlier drenched in the icy water, and with the very real prospect of having a high-velocity *whizz-bang* up their *tradesman's entrance,* they are then seen hastily digging in and preparing for a long damp engagement. Their formidable enemy (all as dry as negative farts) are comfortably ensconced in their warm trenches, and after putting away their buckets and spades and (reluctantly) breaking up their sandcastles, are now also ready for the impending encounter.

Clearly under such circumstances with bullets whizzing past you, and bits and pieces of former friends' bodily parts being blown all over the place, the last thing that you'd be thinking about would be the condition of your clothing, whether sodden or not. But during all of the time that the troops are pinned down, I cannot believe that they simply ignore the discomfort caused by their icy cold, soggy knickers and socks, which throughout the conflict never get any warmer than a penguin's briefcase. Clearly during the ensuring hostilities, they will not have had a chance to dry out, or indeed, had not been changed from the time that they had hit the beach, and unbelievably, nobody complains in the slightest.

In these action-packed American war films, one never sees a laundry truck, or clothes drying on lines in the trenches, which doesn't exactly inspire confidence in the film makers sense of realism.

In the later shots of the field hospitals where you see the gallant injured, with parts of their anatomy hanging off, you will never hear any of them discussing their creeping hypothermia, trench-foot symptoms, or the cold-induced haemorrhoids, let alone being given any advice on what they should do about their creased and shrivelled up nobs and testosticles!

But then the American GI is made of pretty robust stuff and is clearly willing to undergo all manner of unpleasant physical discomfort and suffering for his *Uncle Sam*, or any other relative for that matter, provided that the cause is just, or Cecil B. DeMille is watching. One only has to consider the military history and acting career of Audie Murphy to see the connection between the two.

During the last war, he was one of America's most decorated combat soldiers. He received every US military award for valour, as well as French and Belgian awards for heroism. After the war, he then went on to a very successful acting career.

He was a relatively small man in stature (which could possibly account for his being able to creep up to enemy lines, bash em all up, and return unscathed and undetected in time for his cocoa and cookie before lights out). He also had a rather high-pitched voice, which one biographer attributed to his military service, or more particularly, the considerable amount of times that he'd engaged in combat with damp and freezing cold trousers, knickers and socks, as a result of having been chucked into the sea from landing craft. It beggars the question, why on earth weren't those who were destined to be dunked into water, not issued with fleece-lined all-in one romper suits, or at the very least given waterproof wellies and breathable waterproof leggings? One possible reason could be that a formidable enemy wouldn't be able to take it all seriously if they saw an attacking force of American GIs fighting in *Yves Saint Laurent* designer wet-gear or bright yellow mankinis.

But getting back to our diminutive all-American hero. He initially starred in the autobiographical war film *To Hell and Back* but most of his roles were in cowboy films. Later he was asked by a reporter why he had chosen westerns instead of war films. He unhesitatingly replied, "Have you ever seen a cowboy being chucked out of a landing craft?"

The sound of my trusty old boiler kicking into life again curtailed my mental wool-gathering and inspired me to hasten to the bathroom. Following a refreshing shower and shave, I was ready to start another day and to deal with an impending tsunami of hungry females, which crashed into my kitchen door at 07:50.

Lenka and I were on the first leg of our journey to Westminster Magistrates Court at 08:25, and having arrived forty minutes later, we called into a local café for a quick coffee, before we joined a small group of people queuing to get into the spectator's gallery.

At 09:45, when the security blokes had put their slobbering guard dogs into their respective cages and (with no euphemism intended) had tucked their truncheons down their trousers, they opened the large bomb-proof outer doors to the Court. This protective measure was deemed necessary following the actions of some *very unhappy* relatives in the past, who were not overly enamoured at the substantial prison sentences imposed on their loved ones, and were anxious to exhibit their displeasure in a more positively expressive way. This often resulted in mindless destruction to courtroom fixtures and fittings and on one occasion the complete demolition of the lead-reinforced front doors by a *very-very unhappy* axe-wielding frumpy-dumpling octogenarian from Wigan.

Ten minutes before the court was due to sit, Lenka and I had secured front row seats to watch the morning melodrama. She had never seen the inside of a British court before, and prior to the start of this year, I too was happily ignorant of the inner workings of a court, well, apart from that brief occasion when I had to reluctantly visit one, following that *little misunderstanding* involving that impenetrable crowd, a cascading water fountain, an overfilled bladder and three very dedicated watchful lady police officers, who in just about complete darkness had clearly spotted a very small white dick, in among a heaving mass of dark humanity. An optical feat that is still spoken about in the respected academic halls of *The Royal College of Ophthalmologists.'* But, as the man said, *'It is illegal to make liquor in private or water in public!'*

The theatricals began at 10:00 precisely, with the court usher's polite verbal request of 'All rise!' The entire assemblage shuffled to their feet, and once the magistrate had taken his place in front of his chair (which looked more like a regal throne), he nodded politely and then sat down, This was the cue for the audience to regain their seats, and after a short pause to allow for any further noise to die down, the magistrate gave the wooden reinforced pad on his desk a perfunctory wallop with his gavel and thereafter complete silence was achieved (apart from one bloke who kept coughing, much to the annoyance of the clerk of the court, who producing a small bag from his desk, instructed the usher to give him a *Fisherman's Friend* to suck and this isn't a euphemism either!).

The clerk of the court, who was sitting in front of and below the lofty seat of the magistrate, gave Sir Gerald his morning list, and throughout the following scenes was clearly the director of the performance. The magistrate gave it a cursory glance, since he had obviously studied it earlier in his chambers while biting into his morning tiffin and sipping his coffee. (But then, one must be seen to go through the standard motions relating to our ancient court rituals.)Looking at the clerk, Sir Gerald said, 'Call Albery Groupenhorst!' The clerk then addressed the court usher, and in a louder voice said, 'Call Albery Groupenhourst!' The usher left the court via a side door, and shortly after Albery was led into the court, being supported on either side by two burly security guards who placed him in the dock. Gone was the former cocky swagger and belligerent confidence of untouchability and instead an unfamiliar grovelling wimp that exhibited a pathetic figure of dejection and despair stood before us. He looked about him in bewilderment and confusion, with his dark eyes expressing trepidation and hands that were visibly shaking. For one brief moment, I couldn't help feeling an immense sadness for a man that had brought me, and a considerable number of others, such dreadful heartache and misery, and I really wasn't enjoying the spectacle.

The charge of the importation of controlled drugs which was contrary to section 3 of the 1971 Misuse of Drugs Act, was read to Albery and he was asked to plead. He responded immediately stating, 'I am not guilty of the charge, your highness.' A very cunning ploy, I thought, trying to indicate to the court that his incorrect address to the magistrate suggested a naïve innocence and unfamiliarity with courtroom etiquette or procedure. But then the magistrate looked like a wily old *fatherless-person*, who had heard it all before, and one that certainly knew the difference between a mayonnaise salad and a plate of chicken *excrement*.

Albery's defence lawyer on the other hand, was a middle-aged scrawny looking individual, with a clipped Oxbridge accent, who was wearing what looked like a black double-worsted suit from the *Man at C&A* range, together with a white shirt and grey bow tie. He stood up and formerly introduced himself, but sadly his presence went just about unnoticed, apart from the clearly indifferent magistrate, who out of politeness gave him a perfunctory nod of recognition.

After a thirty-minute display of his less than convincing rhetorical ability, he didn't come across as being half as smart as he looked, and unlike the magistrate, I was of the opinion that his identification of certain food items would always be questionable, and that in any event he should avoid future dinner parties. As for his client being granted bail, I was convinced that despite all of his very best monotonous articulate waffle, that we had more chance of watching Lord Lucan riding into the courtroom on Shergar.

To cut a few sorry scenes from the drama, which could be described as 'a well overdue day of reckoning', as expected, Albery was denied bail and remanded in custody on committal proceedings to stand trial at the next available sitting of the Crown Court, which like an appointment for having a hernia reversal operation, could be months away.

Outside in the court lobby, I simply had to phone Basil, who was just as pleased as I that the 'fiend of Susan Atkins Court' was finally on his way towards his well overdue karmic retribution.

Lenka was absolutely fascinated listening to the legal cut and thrust of dialogue between the parties, and seemingly enjoyed it all immensely.

The court recessed for lunch at 12:30 and back out into the fresh air, we called into a nearby pub for a bite to eat and a libation. Fortunately, I had readily negotiable bonds with me to pay for it. Central London pubs are a complete rip-off!

During our chat about the court system in general and Albery's case in particular, it became clearly evident that Lenka hadn't realised that my Abstracting Electricity case was to be heard following our lunch. It seems she was under the misapprehension that my only motive for visiting the court was to witness Albery's case. She wanted to know where we would be going after lunch, and crossing my fingers, I simply replied that there would be a very interesting case at the court which was scheduled to be heard at 14:00. My refusal to enlighten her further was enough to fire up her naturally inquisitive nature.

Having finished our watercress rolls and halves of bitter, we arrived back in the court lobby at 13:40.

Basil was sitting outside of courtroom two, and for Lenka's benefit, I acted surprised to see him. I introduced him to her as 'an old friend of mine'. Basil's face was a picture of anxious concern, but winking at him, I told Lenka to go back into the public gallery and that I would rejoin her a little later.

As the court opened for business, Basil and I entered, taking our seats at a desk in front of the clerk of the court. I looked round at Lenka, who was looking at me in disbelief with her hands held out in front of her in a gesture of abject uncertainty and supplication. I smiled at her reassuringly and blew her a kiss. A rather large scruffy individual who was sat next to her, seemingly had got his wires crossed, since he smiled at me coyly and gave me a little wave. A little later, having been invited into the dock, the charge was read to me and I was asked how I wished to plead. Looking at the magistrate, I replied, 'Guilty your worship!'

Before anything else could take place, the outer door of the courtroom was flung open and Nobby Caxton came rushing into the room. He ran unchallenged along the entire length of the court and stood looking up at the magistrate, who demanded an explanation. Two uniformed security thugs appeared out of nowhere and grabbing him forcibly then proceeded to grapple him down to the ground.

The noise in the room and the spectator's gallery was quite explosive, but the magistrate's pounding gavel restored order quickly.

Having been allowed back to his feet, Nobby shouted, 'This man is innocent! I am responsible, you mustn't believe him – I did it!'

The magistrate temporarily adjourned the case and asked for the legal teams, together with both Nobby and myself, to attend his chambers. In the interim, the court and spectator's gallery was cleared.

Without wishing to bore you with what followed, after Nobby and I had finally convinced the magistrate of the real truth of the issue, the police were called and Nobby was arrested, and the case against me was dropped. However, on passing, the magistrate stated that there could be no justification for lying to a court under oath, no matter how noble the motive. But in my case, due to the rumpus that had followed, the clerk of the court hadn't had time to record my plea, and therefore no evidence of perjury, or conduct likely to pervert the course of justice, would be appropriate. I was therefore free to leave. Both Basil and I therefore made a very hasty retreat.

Thankfully, the bloke who had waved at me from the spectator's gallery was nowhere to be seen, as Basil and I met Lenka in the lobby. Bidding Basil a fond farewell, a little later Lenka and I were on our way home. Having received a matronly-type earbashing from my very patient Lenka on the way back, which I fully accepted, we collected Maria and Elisha from home and took them out for a veritable banquet at our local McDonald's. Thereafter, Lenka and I had a few very large night caps in the Gay Bar, but Maria was happy to take Elisha home.

We didn't stay long and we were home at 20:15. Jimena was very pleased to see us and after her usual affectionate greeting, was more than happy to rejoin Maria and Elisha in their bedroom.

Before bed, I phoned Basil and thanked him for his help today, and when I enquired about Nobby, he stated that he had been released on bail and would be back at home during the evening. I was so very pleased to hear it. It was a fitting end to a relatively perfect day.

Goodnight, Ginny.

P xx

22nd March 2012

Good morning, Ginny.

Following the usual feeding frenzy around my kitchen table at 08:00 this morning, and having written out a comprehensive list relating to the evening meal preparations for her and Elisha later in the day, I reminded Maria to phone me if there were any problems. I was more than pleased to learn that Gabriel would be calling during the evening and in all probability would be staying overnight.

Lenka and I finally bade them both a fond farewell at 08:20 and on the way to the station Lenka reassured me that the girls would be OK in our absence, but being the worry-guts that I am, she had obviously picked up my signs of anxiety.

However, she was not aware that I suffer from acute claustrophobia and as we waited on the platform at Maida Vale station, I started to become breathless and a little uneasy, which she thought was due to my concern for our girls left behind at the homestead. Normally I would always prefer to travel by bus but if and when I had reluctantly taken a tube, I always ensured that it was outside of the rush-hour periods. The thought of squeezing into a veritable sardine can of a tube carriage was very disconcerting indeed, although over the years, I have been able to control many of the unpleasant physical manifestations of this potentially debilitating condition, following psychotherapy and counselling sessions. But without doubt I have found that the best treatment currently available relates to simply using *That big six-wheeler, scarlet-painted London Transport, diesel-engined, ninety-seven horsepower omnibus* instead!

As our train arrived however, my first hurdle was to push myself into the confined space of a very crowded carriage and, holding tightly onto Lenka's hand, we forced our way inside. I was sweating and breathing heavily. But as if by heaven sent, being at the end of a line of seats, a very pleasant young lady asked me if I would like to sit down. This was all the distraction that I needed, and as I thankfully sat down on her lap, she initially appeared to be very startled, but when she realised that I was completely harmless, she smiled at Lenka good-naturedly, and then simply carried on as if nothing out of the ordinary had happened.

Lenka was profusely embarrassed and apologetic, but the young lady ignored both of us and continued reading her novel, perhaps aware that her actions may have been wrongly interpreted as 'a green light' for a couple of serial ear-bashers, bent on engaging her in monotonous meaningless drivel, that would bore the living *excrement* out of her all the way to Waterloo.

But nevertheless, our farce-like arrival into the carriage brought a few smiles onto some formerly very severe laughter-inhibited faces. But sadly, many of these poor buggers had taken this same monotonous morning journey for years, and frankly that was nothing to laugh about! I therefore felt obliged to cut them a little slack as it were, and to accept that their unapproachability and aloof detachment could be understood and therefore forgiven. Like my own personal space-repelling techniques, I recognised the usual signals that they simply wanted to be left alone. But then most of these people are professionals who had honed their people-avoidance techniques to a very high level of expertise, and no issue whatsoever would persuade them to utter a single syllable during their twice-daily underground incarceration.

Ironically, once back into the safe world of their familiar work environments, happily their former introverted travel masks are lifted, and miraculously they are transformed into their usual corporate personas which for many of their long-suffering work colleagues, is about as stimulating as reading the back of a hair conditioner bottle when taking a morning dump.

Thinking about it later, Lenka and I could have been mistaken for a mental patient and carer out for the day and it is certainly something to bear in mind for future underground journeys. But happily, the thoughts induced during our temporary imprisonment completely took my mind off my unfortunate condition, although on leaving the carriage at Waterloo, I thanked the young lady for her gracious unflappability and patience, and leaving her one of my cards, I breathed an audible sigh of relief.

Apart from having to bear a relatively sustained verbal barrage of abuse, albeit interspersed with unfettered laughter from Lenka, our rail journey to Portsmouth Harbour was very pleasant and uneventful. We enjoyed our ham and cheese sandwiches and coffee that I had prepared during the girls' breakfasts earlier, and our topics of conversation were varied and interesting. Needless to say, that on our arrival at Portsmouth, we had just missed our connecting Wightlink ferry to Ryde Pier Head by a couple of minutes.

I am beginning to get the feeling that as the trains from Waterloo arrive at Portsmouth Harbour, someone from the ferry waves a flag at the skipper, who then hastens his ferry away from the quayside. Later in the *Terminal Café* while eating their tandoori chicken-salad sandwiches, the crew can then have a good old laugh watching their CCTV footage of the disappointed faces of the arriving rail-passengers, as they gape in horror watching (their ferry) sailing away to Ryde without them. Clearly, it's not only London bus drivers that need a little light-hearted, daily entertainment to brighten up the gut-wrenching tedium of their daily lives.

I phoned Clare to notify her that we would be on the next ferry, which was expected to arrive at Ryde for around 13:20. Lenka enjoyed the Solent crossing immensely, although due to a rather choppy sea she was beginning to feel a little delicate. However, she made it across without any need to visit the loo.

We met Clare on our arrival, who drove us back to her home in Sandown. The two girls got on famously, and my sense of worth and usefulness diminished with each passing mile. By the time that we had reached Clare's home, I was clearly superfluous to requirements, and having dropped our overnight bags in her hall, 'I made for the hills' and walked to the local pub.

Frankly, once inside I got the impression that the pub's regulars had either been abducted by marauding aliens, or were all visiting their relatives at HMP Parkhurst. Apart from one old boy and a scruffy looking border collie, the place was as empty as a eunuch's Y-fronts. However, the landlord was a very jovial character and was clearly in the mood to entertain his two customers. But then having drunk a pint of his local ale (and had managed to keep it down), I felt that I was entitled to a little compensation of some kind. His rendition of the old Al Jolson's song of 'My Yiddishe Mama' wasn't bad, but I could have sworn that it was Tom Jones that had sung it, or was it Englebert Humperdinck?

A little later, I took a stroll down to the beachfront, which reminded me of the very many happy days that Tommy and I had spent together, fishing off the end of piers. Actually, we would fish off the end of anything, provided there was water in front of us and a bar behind us. But nostalgia isn't what it used to be; and with a fading memory it can be a little confusing and infinitely uncertain.

It only seems a short time ago when Tommy was teaching me how to cast and I was instructing him in how to use an ATM, but that was over forty years ago! Strangely, he never really got the hang of getting money out of a hole-in-the-wall machine as they become known, particularly when it related to money that he owed me. Apart from our one pound per fish bet, I often had the biggest one of the day as well (and fish). Sorry Ginny, I couldn't resist that one!

I think that the most that I ever won on any single day was nine pounds. However, winning it was all very well, but then receiving the money, particularly from a man who was suffering from what he called *dyslexic fingers*, apparently made all the more severe by his being left-handed, was another matter altogether. He positively refused to allow me to operate the machine for him and stated that with patience and practice he would eventually master it, and in the meantime, I was simply to run up a tab, which was subsequently adjusted on each trip, with his fish being subtracted from the outstanding amount owed. At the last count he owed me fifty-seven pounds, but thereafter following his move, we sadly lost touch, and my fifty-seven pounds went poof!

But then as I sat in the amusement arcade looking out to sea, the very gentle inner voice of my conscience was suddenly aroused, and my thoughts turned to Clare. As mentioned to you before, Tommy had made no mention of giving her any part of his hidden wealth, and as per his instructions, 'that following a diligent search' if his daughter couldn't be found then 'I was at liberty to dispose of the remaining cash in any way that I saw fit'.

My thoughts were suddenly arrested by a phone call from Lenka stating that a table had been booked at a local restaurant for eight, and as time was pressing, could I please return home to 'sort myself out!' One woman can be a little bossy, two women together morph into oppressive dictators.

On my way back, I phoned Maria, who stated that all was well. Gabriel would be collecting them both shortly to take them out for an evening meal, and that 'I must not worry!'

Back at Clare's, the girls were engaged in animated conversation, and after I'd unpacked my dark suit, shirt and tie from my overnight bag, I asked Clare if I could have a quick shower.

Following my scrub, and a change of knickers and socks (which were all bone-dry and had been neatly ironed), I joined them downstairs in the lounge. They were engrossed in looking at photographs in a large album, and Lenka was positively gushing at infantile pictures of Clare's children from a previous marriage and her subsequent grandchildren. I was aware that Tommy and Clare had never actually tied the knot as it were, albeit that they had been partners for many years. Tommy had always boasted that he would be a single man all of his life and often joked that as a bachelor, he had 'never made the same mistake once!'

Thinking about him, I suddenly felt quite emotional and I truly hoped that his next transmigration would be a happy one, and that being the relatively good man that he was, that the karmic assessor would look upon him favourably and would deal with him kindly.

I asked him once if he could come back as an animal, which one would he choose. He sat and thought for a moment and replied, 'Oh I think being a hippo would be rather nice.' Naturally, I wanted to know why.

'Well they like water, and so do I,' he said confidently. 'And although they do live in croc-infested rivers, due to their size and aggressive leanings, they are very rarely preyed upon. Like most human bullies, crocodiles and lions would only have a go at the little ones. They are herbivores and as you know, I do like the occasional spliff, but eating like a vegetarian would suit me just fine, since I've never really been a meat eater, apart from which, my dentures have trouble dealing with a bacon sandwich, let alone chomping through an eight-ounce steak with all of the succulent consistency of a dried up wellington boot!'

'Anything else?' I asked.

'Yeah, it must be quite nice to soak and play around in water all day, what with them little birds eating them annoying little ticks and lice from yer back. But best of all, they don't have any mother-in-laws or money worries.'

'Animals don't have any use for money, Tommy,' I replied, jokingly.

'And that's just as well,' he replied. 'I mean, if you thought that I had trouble, what with me dyslexic fingers and all, just imagine the *effin* trouble that a hippo would have in getting its money out of one of them cashpoint how's-yer-fathers!'

After our evening meal at a small Italian restaurant followed by a few libations at Clare's local pub, we headed back to her home.

Lenka was given the spare room and I was pointed into the general direction of Clare's sofa on which a duvet had been neatly folded. If it had been down to Tommy, in all probability I would have been offered the floor and a blanket, but then had I been with my old friend, I would have probably been slightly *Brahms and Liszt* anyway, so such inconsequential considerations as a comfortable night's sleep would not be of any real importance. Not until the following morning that is, when you awaken as stiff as a board, with a tongue like an emery board, a head like a train crash, a mouth like a gorilla's armpit and a bowel as loose as a pair of flamingo's leggings.

Those first few tentative steps can also be so rewarding, since on waking, the extremities (including testosticles) are often completely numb and lifeless, and the thought of being wheelchair bound for the rest of one's life becomes a very real possibility. But having bashed a little bit of life back into them, and finding that they were able to take a few cautious steps without collapsing, a potential career with West Ham United is once again on the table.

Tommy and I slept under Brighton Pier one night, and when I awoke and had finally got to my feet, I was walking around like John Wayne with a pebble clenched between the cheeks of his bum for days. Tommy spent three hours in the local A&E with follow-up physiotherapy on a collapsed kneecap, and treatment for a case of acute groin eruption (which he didn't want to talk about), other than to say that, it only hurt when he laughed. Naturally this presented a challenge that I simply couldn't resist, and later in the day, he was in a lot of laughter-induced pain.

As I lay on Clare's sofa contemplating our day, I realised just how strange it was to walk into a place and not to have an animal come charging down the hall to greet you. It's amazing the things that one takes for granted in life, and such simple pleasures are so very important. But then being Spanish, my Maria is so naturally excitable and is always so happy to see us when we return home, bless her little wooden maracas.

Goodnight, Ginny.
P xx

23rd March 2012

Good morning, Ginny.

We were all up early, and ready to get out there amongst it at 07:30. It was to be a day of ultimate drama, with Tommy's funeral taking centre stage, as it were.

We were all dressed soberly. I wore my dark suit, a white shirt and black tie, and the girls were in similarly respectful attire. Clare wore a black dress and top, finished off with a pillbox hat and a dark silk chiffon veil, which added mystique and a certain unapproachable aloofness to her ensemble. Lenka wore a dark grey trouser suit and black rollneck silk blouse which together looked both elegant and pre-eminently suitable for a lady who would be getting in and out of a hearse, and at the wake later, as fun-loving as ever, would be joining in on the alcohol-fuelled hokey-cokey albeit briefly, since we had a ferry, a train and a tube to catch.

Before we left Clare's home, I phoned Maria. All was well and she stated that both she, Elisha and Jimena were looking forward to our return home. I told her that we should be back home by 21:00 at the latest, but if we encountered any problems on our journey home, I would phone her.

The two hearses arrived punctually at 11:00 and Clare, Lenka and I got into the one behind Tommy's. The drive to the crematorium was as expected, a sombre affair, but then none of us were in a talkative mood, and for the first time since I had heard of his death, I suddenly became aware of the finality of it all, and that I would never see my dear old beloved friend again. I firmly believed that our immediate world would be a far lonelier place without him, and that he would be genuinely missed.

Having arrived at the crematorium, a small crowd of around ten people were standing outside of the chapel, none of whom I recognised. Clare, Lenka and I were invited into the chapel first, and having gained our seats, the others followed.

As Tommy's pallbearers brought him in on his last mortal journey, Eva Cassidy's beautiful rendition of 'Over the Rainbow' started, and the truly lovely sentiments of the lyrics hastened many an emotional tear from the mourners, including me and my beautiful Lenka. However, Clare seemed to be completely detached from the proceedings and simply stared at the coffin.

Since Tommy was a lifelong unapologetic atheist, the service was conducted by a very capable and eloquently charming humanist celebrant. I was very surprised indeed when he introduced me to Tommy's brother Larry (whom I never knew existed) who was later to deliver a very commendable eulogy, which was a delightful celebration about a simple man, who had lived an interesting and varied life. A life mixed with poignancy and joy, chastised with an ever-present element of laughter and happiness, which was one of Tommy's innate characteristics.

He finished with Robert Lee Sharpe's beautiful poem, 'A Bag of Tools'.

*

'Isn't it strange how princes and kings,
And clowns that caper in sawdust rings,
And Common people like you and me.
Are builders of eternity?'

*

'Each is given a bag of tools,
A shapeless mass and a book of rules;
And each must make ere life be flown
A stumbling block; or a stepping-stone.'

And finally, to Frank Sinatra's beautiful ballad, 'My Way', Tommy's coffin slowly passed along a moving conveyer and out of our sight behind a red curtain, to start his uncertain transmigration into the karmic unknown, which I hoped would be some faraway croc-infested river, where my dear old friend could wallow away happily to his heart's content. Amen to that!

Lenka and I did not stay for the wake, and we got a cab back to Ryde, where a little later we were on the ferry chugging its way back to Portsmouth Harbour.

Before I left, I gave Clare two envelopes, which I said Tommy had wanted me to give to her. Each contained a cheque for £3,000, one for her, and the other for Tommy's brother Larry. I included a simple note to both, which read:

'Gone Fishing!' – Love Tommy xx

After a very uneventful journey, Lenka and I arrived home at 19:50 and we were welcomed by my three other adorable girls, who all came rushing down the hall to greet us on our arrival. Frankly, both Lenka and I were exhausted, and really didn't need convincing that a relatively early night was in order.

Goodnight, Ginny.
P xx

24th March 2012

Good morning, Ginny.

I was awake at 06:15 this morning. My trusty boiler's intervention a little earlier, and the lukewarm temperature of my bedroom having been heated up sufficiently, I was prompted to kick my legs out of bed fifteen minutes later (which basically meant that I was up at 06:30). Robotically, I made for the bathroom to complete my usual morning ritual which consists of a pee and a periodic shave. As considerate as ever, and not wishing to monopolise an area potential needed by three others, I then hastened back into my bedroom.

I prefer to have a shower when the flat is empty, which reduces the possibility of any of my three girls having a quick flash of my willy. When I had finished, I would cautiously open the bathroom door and listen for any signs of movement in the hall. If all was quiet, I would quickly streak the fifteen feet or so into my bedroom (which is not a pretty sight), where a fluffy radiator-warmed towel awaited.

Normally I have my daily dump following my initial ingestion of food and drink (which must initiate the bowel evacuation process). Life can sometimes become quite tedious, particularly when it comes to a daily routine of a repetitive nature. Having got a little bored with constantly reading the same old conditioner bottle, I found an old tube of sun lotion in the bathroom cabinet recently, and the back of it looks like an interesting and informative alternative. I shall give it a perusal later,

Being Saturday, the normal weekday morning feed-fest can be relaxed once again, and a gentler approach to another day can be considered. Well at least that is the theory.

The first real sign of additional life in my humble abode was the unmistakeable sound of Elisha's laughter. However, Jimena having spear-headed the attack as it were, arrived in the kitchen first. She jumped onto my lap with all the confidence and familiarity-bred audacity of a fat kid getting seconds at school dinners. Before she had got herself comfortable, she stroked her head on my hand and then proceeded to knead my leg with all the enthusiasm of a baker who had overslept and had a lot of catching up to do. I am no cat behaviourist, but was satisfied that her body language, and the intense eyeball treatment that she was giving me, suggested one simple unequivocal command:

'FEED ME!'

As mentioned before, I am convinced that the relationship between a man and his dog isn't one of master and servant but is based on egalitarian principles, whereas with a cat, it is completely different. Our little Jimena doesn't have any masters, but she certainly has plenty of servants.

Two other girls (whom she is currently training) arrived in the kitchen a little later. Maria gave me a warm hug followed by a slobbery kiss on the cheek and said, 'It's good to have you home Paul, and we've missed you! What's for breakfast?' Elisha simply hugged my leg.

Gabriel arrived at 09:30 and was welcomed by a group of adoring females all vying to get at him first. Needless to say, Jimena was standing on his shoulder before Maria or Elisha had even left their starting blocks. He is taking them both out again today, although he wouldn't tell them where they were going. 'It's a magical mystery tour,' is all that he would tell them.

Later in the morning, I had a call from Muhulin who apologised for not contacting me sooner and asked how Elisha was. I gave her a quick update on our little girl and stated that she was very well and appeared to be enjoying her holiday with us. She then went on to ask if I could keep her for a little longer, but seemed to be very vague about the time frame. Apparently, Jasmine had responded well to the treatment that she had been receiving at Dr O'Donnell's clinic, and the team felt that a couple of extra weeks would prove very beneficial.

Naturally, I agreed to keep our little girl with us for as long as Jasmine's treatment was destined to last. Later in the Gay Bar, however, I realised just how important Elisha was to us all, and the thought of not having this delightful child in our lives anymore brought a lump to my throat.

I will have to have a chat with Maria and Lenka about this, since apart from any other consideration, I cannot expect Maria to put her studies on hold indefinitely. She really should be encouraged to return to her college.

Later in the day, Ted's less than quiet entry into the Gay Bar awoke me from my reveries. He appeared to be slightly intoxicated, and at 13:30 on a Saturday afternoon, it was completely out of character.

I guided him to his usual chair and sat him down. 'What on earth's wrong, Ted?' I asked.'Lenny's getting married!' he said finally. 'He told me about it last night, and I haven't been able to sleep a wink thinking about it!'

'I don't understand Ted, so what's the problem?' I asked, ordering him a large rum and grapefruit.

'He's only gone and asked me to do the *effing* catering, and that presents a considerable problem, particularly since I have only just started up in my catering business. It's only a small concern at the moment, but with a little effort, I think that such an enterprise could be very successful, particularly in the age of the liberated woman!'

Having caught the tail end of Ted's remark as he entered the bar, Dave said, 'Oh no, not another one of your get-rich-quick schemes? So what is the latest earth-shattering corporate venture all about this time?'

'Food mate. Fast food – only faster food! A bit like an up-market version of meals on wheels,' he said, ordering a drink for Dave, who held up a pint glass expectantly. 'It's all about doughnuts! A fast home-delivery service, free from overheads or running costs. My delivery agents would be on roller skates!'

'It all sounds a bit too good to be true!' said Dave. 'A bit like that bicycle breakdown insurance cover that you tried to get off the ground last year. That all went as flat as a witch's tit after your first week of trading!'

'Well punctures are few and far between, what with the reinforced modern-day bicycle tyre being what it is. But at least I am willing to get out there and try, which is more than can be said for you moronic bunch of *anal-orifum*. Frankly, I've seen more get up and go in a ward full of geriatrics suffering from terminal constipation!'

'But why would you need to get involved in all of these money-making projects, Ted?' I said. 'You clearly make a considerable amount from your various ongoing projects, I mean come on mate, how many of us can afford gold-plated bicycle clips!'

Suddenly his facial expression changed from its normal miserable lugubrious look into an aspect of bewildered confusion. 'It's just that over these last few days, I have done a little soul-searching and have come to the conclusion that I should change my ways.'

Being relatively early in the day, the bar was very quiet and Ted's only audience was Dave, Vlado and me, which perhaps under the circumstances of this profound revelation was just as well. Was it to become common knowledge, it could inspire a few young pretenders to seek a place on the top table as it were, and to ultimately attempt to knock the overlord out of his seat.

Initially, I thought that this veritable maestro of satire and intrigue was having us all on, but I was very surprised when he suddenly hugged me and said, 'I know that you have had your fair share of problems over the last few weeks, and frankly I haven't helped. In fact, I have a bit of a confession to make.' Suddenly he seemed to be lost in thought, and appeared to be very ill at ease and not his usual self. He started to pace the room, like an agitated caged tiger and then looking at me he said:

'He didn't wear his scarlet coat, for blood and wine are red, and blood and wine were on his hands when they found him... found him... It was only meant as a bit of a laugh mate, and I really didn't mean you any harm. I had a bet with Lenny that I could prise a few bob out of you using underhanded methods. When I told him about my plan, he wasn't at all amused. However, since there was fifty pounds riding on it, Lenny went along with it, and even helped in cutting up various books and magazines to provide the necessary lettering. It was me who sent you that blackmail letter, which I made out had come from Scotland. But, I hasten to add, that had you fallen for it and paid any subsequent cash demand, I would have naturally come clean about the whole issue and would have returned any money involved.

I was absolutely devastated, and really couldn't come to terms with the notion that a friend could do such a thing to me, particularly when it involved my beloved Spike. Vlado turned and walked away into the posh bar, and Dave simply sat there in stunned silence.

My initial thought was to leave, but as I stood up, Ted held my arm and said, 'Yet each man kills the thing he loves by each let this be heard... Paul I am so very sorry mate, it was all just a bit of a laugh, and I would ask you to forgive me.'

Dave looked at me expectantly, and tried to change the frown on his face to one suggesting a little forbearance and forgiveness, which I chose to ignore.

I walked to the door but before I opened it, I turned and said, 'Did you give Lenny his money?'

'No, not yet mate,' he replied timidly, with all of his usual confident panache absent.

'Well I'll tell you what, Ted, there are two things that you can do for me,' I said defiantly.

'Anything mate, just name them!' he replied, his voice sounding relieved and a little hopeful.

'Firstly, you will pay Lenny the fifty pounds that you owe him, since he clearly had won the bet.'

'No problem mate!' he said confidently. 'I'll give him the money tonight. What's the other thing?'

I walked back to the bar and ordered a large cognac from Vlado, who had been waiting in the wings and appeared just as I arrived at the bar. I sat down at Ted's table and he looked at me appealingly.

'And then, you can sort out the Frobisher mess!' I said. 'I really didn't think that you would go to such lengths and I haven't had a good night's sleep since. What you have done to that man is completely unforgiveable, although I am just about as much to blame, but if it's any consolation, I have already had my fair share of personal misery and fully expect to be on the receiving end of a little more suffering of the outrageous fortune kind, in the very near future!'

Standing, he held his hands out appealingly. 'That might be a little difficult mate, why didn't you choose something a little less demanding like asking me to get you a front row seat at an Elvis concert for example?'

'He's dead!' Dave said helpfully.

'Exactly!' replied Ted.

'I don't care how you do it, Ted, but the punishment doesn't fit the crime. Admittedly, his behaviour towards Lenny could have been considerably improved upon, but it doesn't warrant the potential life-changing consequences that a criminal record for handling stolen goods could bring!'

Banging his fist on the table in front of him, his voice slowly rising in volume reaching its crescendo on the last two words, he said, 'I may not agree with what you say, Paul, but I'll defend to the death your right to change the *effing* subject!' He was clearly getting out of his pram, and I felt that I should stop rocking it for a while and give him his dummy back.

But fortunately, Vlado came to my aid and in an effort to relieve the tension he started to hastily remove bottles of spirit from their optic devices. He played the part of a very apprehensive publican expecting trouble wonderfully, and his facial grimaces and nervous looks were very convincing indeed. It was certainly enough to divert Ted's attention long enough for me to hasten to the gents. I remained there until I estimated that the immediate danger had been averted.

On my return, Ted, Vlado and Dave were laughing loudly and clearly the mood had changed.

'That was very good, Vlado,' said Ted, giggling to himself. 'You could have won an Oscar for that performance!'

'I am not like to see the hate of friends,' said Vlado. 'It was like Paul was in fright like a seed of melon couldn't be pushed up his bum with hammer? Friends must not war!'

I had to admit that Vlado's acting skills were very good indeed, and I was very thankful for his quick thinking. He averted a potential nasty fracas, since like Mount Vesuvius, Ted's temper can be quite unpredictable and once aroused can be very destructive indeed. However, unlike the semi-dormant volcano that hadn't erupted for over sixty years, Ted's temper is a little more volatile. It reared its ugly head again last week Thursday, when apparently due to a little misunderstanding between him, a rag and bone man and a flatulent cart horse, he couldn't wear his new designer patent leather shoes to the traveller's ball after all, and the rag and bone man missed his night out at the disco to raise funds for the tree society. But as they say, *excrement* happens!'

As the unfortunate bloke was transported away to St Mary's Paddington, he is reported to have said, 'The axe forgets, but the tree always remembers!' A veiled threat, if ever I've heard one!

On leaving the pub later, Ted put his right index finger to the side of his nose and said, 'I'll see what I can do about Mr Frobisher!' I found out the other day that this physical gesture means, 'We are sharing a secret.' Actually, his speech is often accompanied by appropriate statement-enhancing physical gestures of one kind or another, in fact were he to lose his hands, he would be just about speechless – a condition, that would be met with considerable approval by many of his long-suffering contemporaries I dare say. However, Ted has always been a very resourceful man, and if ever that were to happen, I am sure that he would use some other bodily appendage. Perish the thought!

As he opened the door to the bar, he turned and said, 'Some do it with a bitter look, some with a flattering word; the coward does it with a kiss, the brave man with a sword!' The door slammed shut behind him, leaving an uncomfortable silence and three very bewildered faces.

A little later, Alfie arrived, who, like sunshine following rain, brightened up our spirits and his beautifully inept observations had us all laughing in no time. However, he did pick up the tension between us. 'Gawd! What's a matter with you lot?' he said. 'I've seen happier looking people queuing up for their annual colonic irritation procedures.'

'Irrigation!' said Dave.

'What?' said Alfie.

'It's colonic irrigation, not irritation!' replied Dave, who started to chuckle.

'Have you ever had one, clever dick?' Alfie asked.

'Well no I haven't, but that doesn't alter the fact that the correct term is…'

'Irritation!' shouted Alfie. 'I've had one and take it from me, I know what the *effin ell* I'm talking about mate! I can't think of anything more irrigating!'

'What's wrong with you, Alfie? The word is irritating!'

Looking at me helplessly and smiling mischievously he said, 'Isn't that what I've just been saying?'

Hearing raised voices, and seemingly appearing out of thin air, Zora-Aleena suddenly materialised. Vlado smiled at her timidly and holding her hand reassuringly, he mumbled something to her in a strange tongue. But then, I've told him on more than one occasion to get some new dentures fitted! She nodded and, looking at us all accusingly for what seemed like an eternity, she smiled at Vlado wryly and evaporated off into the posh bar like an ethereal mist out of a stagnant cesspool. Vlado returned her smile, but I sensed that in his case it was simply an instinctive spontaneous response to her departure from his immediate area. As the sound of her footsteps vanished away, his smile together with ours widened considerably.

'Phew! That was close,' whispered Alfie, theatrically fanning his face with a beer mat. 'I don't scare very easily, but that woman frightens the living daylights out of me. One thing is for sure, I wouldn't want to wake up one morning and find her lying next to me!'

Vlado beckoned us to the bar, and putting his face close to Alfie's he quietly whispered, 'Neither I would!'

A lot of unfettered laughter followed, until Zora-Aleena returned to the Gay Bar again, this time with an enquiring look on her face.

A little later I left and made a beeline for *Whispering Jim's* watering hole in Notting Hill. They say that a change is as good as a rest, and I was certainly in need of a little respite from Kilburn for a while. I was on the tube to Ladbroke Grove at 12:50, and am pleased to say that once again I had controlled the usual physical manifestations associated with my claustrophobia. An elderly lady with a beautiful little shih-tzu sitting on her lap provided me with all of the mental distraction that I needed for the first leg of the journey. A little later, I caught a bus from Paddington and arrived at the Pig and Whistle at 13:45.

I met up with Jim, who was seated at the same chair as last time, and indeed he could have been there from our last meeting two weeks ago. He greeted me warmly as did the licensee, a well-nourished amiable man called Danie Goosen, which I found out later is pronounced Darney Ghoosen. He was born in Johannesburg and came from an Afrikaner lineage, and was clearly very proud of an ancestry that could be traced back to the early Dutch-settlers in southern Africa. He was fiercely patriotic and apparently, in common with most Afrikaners, was a devoted rugby fan. Springbok regalia and paraphernalia were displayed all around the bar.

A picture of a younger looking Danie in military uniform hung in a silver frame behind the bar, and a large, framed photograph of Francois Pienaar accepting the Rugby World Cup from Nelson Mandela in 1995, hung proudly over the ornate brick fireplace. A wonderfully well-stocked blaze of logs and coal crackled away enticingly in its hearth and my mood was light and cheerful.

As I walked up to the bar, Viljoen screamed *'SHOP!'* which again alerted the bar staff to my arrival and had me giggling helplessly. I bought Jim and me a drink, and smiling at my dear old friend, who was straightening up a lop-sided stack of pound coins, I asked Danie if he had driven them all mad yet.

He smiled good-naturedly, and in that beautiful clipped South African accent replied, 'Och man, he's a real character! He generally keeps himself to himself, but is usually well attended by his unseen friends, who are seemingly ever present when he's around. He's certainly never without company. But having heard some of his less than polite admonishments, I wouldn't want to offend him!'

'Yes, like a drunken Glaswegian with a grievance, one can never be uncertain as to his mood, I said. 'In the past I have sometimes wondered if he has simply been able to latch onto a different reality; a different plane so to speak. He seems to go into a form of transcendental meditation, and he came up with a quite profound observation the other day,' Danie said, placing a pint of Guinness and a large cognac in front of me on the bar. Nodding towards Jim he said, 'He told me that if Darwin's theory of evolution is correct, we should be seeing a lot more indestructible pedestrians soon! Which is a pretty intelligent statement and is not as daft as it sounds.'

As I brought our drinks back to Jim's table, he jokingly said, 'He's a nice enough bloke, but don't mention the Boer War,' and then taking off the voice of Lance Corporal Jones from the comedy sitcom *Dad's Army*, he said, 'They don't like it up em Mr Mainwaring! They don't like it up em!' and then proceeded to burst out into hysterical laughter, which wasn't heard by anyone who was more than a foot away from him, since even when laughing, Jim does it quietly.

We spent a very enjoyable few of hours together, and I can say quite honestly that if I were to attend a quiz show on Jim Reeves, I feel relatively confident that I could name just about every one of his songs, and if I was ever to appear on *Mastermind*, I'd certainly have it as my specialised subject.

Before leaving, I reminded him of his return visit to The Magpie on the 1st April, and we agreed on a meet up outside of Brenda's Breakfast Emporium at midday.

As I left, I decided to walk the couple of miles back to Kilburn instead of taking the tube, since I felt that I needed to get a bit of exercise and the chances of my meeting up with another dog owner willing to have their animal commence lip-reading training, would perhaps be a little remote anyway.

Just like our walk around Hyde Park recently, familiar landmarks pointed me in the right direction for home and it was an enjoyable stroll. However, it reminded me of the fact that I no longer had an animal that needed daily exercise, and as a result I had gotten out of the habit of walking. A thought, that I quickly erased from my mind. Nevertheless, I blew my Spike an affectionate kiss, which didn't go unnoticed by an elderly traffic warden, who hastily wrote out her next victim's parking ticket and then disappeared quicker than a fart in a fan factory.

I eventually arrived home at 18:10 and was greeted by a houseful of people. All of my girls were in attendance, including our delightful little Jimena. Gabriel was his usual charming self and has now proved beyond question that he is more than worthy of the title, 'one of the team'. We are all very fond of him.

It was clearly evident that both Maria and Elisha had enjoyed a wonderful time with him exploring Chislehurst Caves in Kent. Apparently, these were man-made tunnels that had been manually dug out over hundreds of years, to extract chalk which was used in lime burning and brick making. It seems that much of ancient London was built from the chalk of Chislehurst.

Having verbally exhausted her Chislehurst experiences, Elisha then went on to describe her subsequent grub-fest at McDonald's which was clearly the highlight of her day. She went into great detail with regard to the quality and quantity of the food and drink consumed. Her descriptive eloquence was positively astounding for a six-year-old, particularly when it came to her appraisal of their newly introduced *Beef and belly pork burger with skinny chips and cheesy mayonnaise dip.*

Just before bed, I winked at Lenka and Maria and asked her if she would like to stay with us for a bit longer. She hurtled herself into my arms and replied, 'I want to stay here for ever and ever!'

Just before bed, I put the clocks forward an hour, and was more than simply happy to welcome back the start of our lighter evenings. Roll on summer!

Goodnight, Ginny. P xx

25th March 2012

Good morning, Ginny.

On waking at 06:20 this morning, I had *Whispering Jim* on my mind. He drinks on average twelve pints of Guinness every day, or eighty-four pints every week. There are 2.3 units of alcohol in each pint. This means that he is knocking back on average 193.2 units of alcohol per week.

I do not wish to appear flippant about this serious issue or those well-meaning medical people who have our best interests at heart, since I am sure that following their intensive research into the harmful effects of alcohol abuse that their findings are to be taken seriously. At present, they state that a safe level of daily alcohol consumption is between three and four units. In Jim's case, this would equate to around two pints per day. At his present level, he is therefore drinking around 23.6 units over this recommended intake daily.

Frankly, every time that I have seen him, he appears to be fitter than a butcher's dog, and from my limited knowledge of his medical history, he hasn't ailed much throughout his entire sixty-two years of life. So either the medical profession have got it all hopelessly wrong, or taking his own thought processes on Darwinian theory a step further, Jim could have evolved into one of the first (as yet undiscovered) new species of mankind that had developed a complete immunity to the harmful effects of alcohol. Since I am presumably the first person to identify this new species, in true Linnaeus fashion, I would like to formerly name it as *Homo sapiens whisparensis*.

Following such intriguing intellectual considerations so early in the day, our morning breakfast was a pretty mundane affair. I discussed Elisha's prolonged stay with us and both Lenka and Maria were all for it. Elisha had made her own sentiments on the issue very evident last night, bless her!

I was feeling a little superfluous to requirements again a little later, when after a discussion between them, they decided that they would all go out on 'a girls' shopping day'. Lenka was of the opinion that Elisha needed new clothes. The small suitcase that came with her only consisted of a few basic items of clothing, and clearly her wardrobe needed restocking. The girls generously chipped in £65 between them, and I donated a further £50 to the venture, and a little later they were all on their way to that overrated and over-priced shopping Mecca called Oxford Street.

After I had cleared away the breakfast debris and put the cutlery and crockery onto the draining board, I suddenly remembered my covert camera arrangement. I hadn't looked at the recordings for some time, so while I drank my coffee, I checked them out. I found nothing untoward whatsoever, and I gave serious consideration to getting rid of it completely, particularly now since our former neighbour was no longer a serious threat to health.

Tina phoned a little later to say that she had located Gretchen, who apparently was more than simply happy at the unexpected turn of events relating to her father. She has been in touch with Nobby and once she has cleared up her personal affairs, she will be making her way back to London. I was so very happy about that and I arranged to meet Nobby at The Magpie later in the evening, but first of all I felt I needed a change of scenery and an invigorating mooch and settled on another meander along the South Bank. This time, however, I would fully utilise the services of my London Transport chauffeurs, who as a collective didn't disappoint me. They were all a bunch of despondent, melancholic and thoroughly depressing *fatherless-people.*

At 12:39 after an uneventful journey, I was again sitting in the Swan public house with its beautiful views of St Paul's Cathedral, a stone's throw across the river. I was pretty exhausted from my mental activity en route, with my mind considering the following truths as I saw them.

In this part of London there are a considerable number of pubs, and on this Sunday morning most of them were bursting at the seams with insatiable alcoholics. How on earth they all survive, being in such close proximity to one another is a mystery indeed, and the same goes for the pubs! (Sorry Ginny, but I couldn't resist that.) Earlier, as I passed one after the other on my way to the South Bank, I considered the reasons why a particular pub was preferred above all others. I came to the conclusion that firstly, a man is by nature a relatively social being, particularly when it comes to his favoured watering hole, and like his innate love for watching spectator sports, he prefers to do it in company.

Clearly, it follows then that a man will gravitate to the places where his friends are to be located. But other factors are just as important. For example, the quality, price and consistency of the beverages, together with a friendly, capable and obsequiously disposed bar team.

As for the types of individuals that one is likely to encounter, two types are worthy of mention. The first relates to that ever-green, randy old *fatherless-person,* who when it comes to being served, arrives at the bar a nanosecond before his preferred cheeky, voluptuous barmaid, who loves to tantalise and tease the oldies. He is usually very particular about his preferences in this regard, and if the barmaid is late for work for example, he would prefer to die of thirst, rather than be served by a bloke. Apart from his incredibly swift arrival at the bar, he is normally quite easy to spot. He favours dark distant corners away from the bar, and can be seen sipping his ale and innocently perving at the girls. He normally has a small pile of tissues in front of him and sits quietly away from the limelight, presumably reminiscing on those former excruciatingly bad *good old days,* reliving his heroic activities on the beaches of Dunkirk, his little skirmish with Rommel in North Africa, or nearer to home, trying to remember when he could last look at a beautiful young woman without having to wipe his misted up spectacles, or discretely clean up the evidence of his involuntary drooling. Sadly, there are not many of them left.

The other type of individual that one is likely to encounter is that ever-miserable *pud-wapper* whom as a collective are referred to colloquially as complete *anal orifum*. The type of person belonging to this sub-group is ever on the lookout for something, or someone, to complain about. He never has a positive or a good word to say for anything or anyone, and understandably he is always alone. He is to be avoided at all costs, since like a virulent infection, he can spread his toxic influences without physical contact. He is the type that could cause discord at a church outing picnic, and is capable of having an argument in an empty phone box. Sadly, there are far too many of them wandering abroad unchallenged, and due to the understanding and forgiving natures of most UK inebriates, they are unfortunately tolerated in many of our beloved watering holes.

Comfort always plays a very important part in one's choice of venue, particularly where the quality of the alcoholic beverages or the friendliness of the bar staff are questionable. In such cases, on entering, one is likely to find an extremely friendly licensee with a wonderful sense of humour, together with a flirtatious wife, who together tend to level out the playing field as it were, making the possibility of having to sit on a hard seat or to stand throughout 'the session' tolerable.

Personally, I prefer to avoid pubs with outside gardens bedecked with tables and umbrellas, particularly those that have a play area for the kids. I'm no prude, but believe that public houses are meant for adults, and equally I avoid school playgrounds, particularly those that sell alcoholic beverages.

Pubs with outside recreational facilities tend to indicate that the inside décor and/or comfort of the seating, together with the quality of the beverages and/ or food, are questionable. It may also indicate a general inadequacy in the non-existent personalities of the landlord, his wife and the bar staff, and that disappointment should be expected. But on the positive side, at least the brewery, having recognised the considerable shortcomings of the enterprise, had provided a viable alternative, albeit that during the winter months, the kids' swings become a no-go area anyway. But the ever-tolerant British boozer simply throws caution and his solidified beer to the wind, and with testosticals colder than that poor well-digger, he sucks his solid pork scratchings enthusiastically.

The hostile weather conditions often reminds him of our brave North Sea fishermen, and the sub-zero temperatures afford the more imaginative to consider the discomfort felt by that heroic Sherpa Tenzing Norgay who on the final assent of Everest, gave Edmund Hillary his last cup of hot cocoa, and settled on a frozen strawberry mivvy ice cream and chocolate flake instead. They don't make them like that anymore!

The Magpie is a relatively nice watering hole, being run exclusively by the management team. Initially, however, we were not too sure about the guvnor whom we were told was called 'Uncle Chickle Chuckle'. At first, we believed that he was involved in children's entertainment as a sideline. However, that was all nonsense as we were later to discover. His outward aggressive persona was all a big act as well, since he has proved himself to be a very gentle and considerate man.

The beer is always good and the décor and general comfort of the place is more than simply pleasant, and of course my favoured friends meet there. So for me, it has all the requirements necessary to be called 'my favourite watering hole'.

Had Zora-Aleena been running the pub alone, however, she would have undoubtedly caused a bit of a problem, but with Vlado's calming and encouraging influence and support, she has clearly proved herself manageable. Although he always has his pair of kid gloves available, should he need to assert his manly authority.

I really do count my blessings in that I have escaped the kind of daily misery that my poor purveyor of alcoholic refreshment has to contend with. I simply cannot imagine what dreadful circumstances in her life have been responsible for producing such a disagreeable individual, or indeed, what unimaginable behaviour in a previous existence could have warranted the very evident unhappiness of her present condition. However, I personally feel that she really does deserve our support and sympathy since I have never seen another soul in such a sad and wretched condition. I believe that one person capable of addressing the evident problems she has is my beloved Lenka, and I shall have a chat with her about it when I catch up with her again.

Back on home turf later, I met up with Nobby Caxton at the Bread Bin.

He was looking a little tired but managed to force down a few pints in a relatively short space of time, and thereafter all was right with his world, at least until the deceptive effects of the alcohol had worn off.

As expected, his less than honest relationship with the former occupant of 124 Susan Atkins Court had become common knowledge with his employers, and he has been subsequently fired from his caretaker duties. His flat within the complex came with the job, and he has been given a month's notice to vacate the premises.

Fortunately, Gretchen will be retaining her two-bedroomed flat in West Yorkshire, and as far as Nobby is concerned, a complete break from his present surroundings and a new start somewhere else would clearly be the best option. Although it seems that his son Lionel will be staying in London.

At 18:45, Ted phoned and asked me to join him in the Gay Bay, and bidding a fond farewell to Nobby, I joined him a little later. On my walk in between, I phoned the girls. Lenka had prepared their evening meals and they were now watching *The Jungle Book* movie on DVD. Elisha's laughter in the background was all the confirmation that I needed, and clearly all was well at the homestead.

Dave and Ted were in conversation when I arrived. As I walked up to the bar, they nodded at me perfunctorily

'But she's such a nice little thing,' said Dave, having put his Sunday paper down. 'She's always getting involved in raising money for charity and puts her heart and soul into caring for the elderly.'

'Admirable!' said Ted, 'particularly in a seventeen-year-old!'

'In October last year she raised £5,000 having completed the London marathon.'

'That's very impressive!' said Ted.

'Well it is when you consider that she wouldn't have normally walked to the bus stop if she could have got a cab instead!' said Dave. 'Her determination to finish the 26.2 miles was absolutely astounding for one so young.'

'How long did it take her?'

'Eleven hours and sixteen minutes!' said Dave.

'Hang on a minute!' said Ted. 'Some of these distance runners have completed the course in a few hours?'

'Yeah well, she didn't exactly run. The reporter from *The Kilburn Times* described it as *A cross between an energetic mooch and a very slow jog.* But then she had a few tea breaks on the way as well. Her time wasn't important; it was all about finishing!'

'Now you're talking,' said Ted, licking his lips lasciviously.

'And then in January, following her sponsored parachute jump aimed at raising funds for *Help the Senile,* she later collected a further £2,750,' said Dave enthusiastically.

'That takes a lot of bottle, that does! I have trouble stepping off the pavement, let alone intentionally chucking meself out a plane!' said Ted, shuddering noticeably.

'You don't do it alone mate, you're strapped to an instructor,' said Alfie helpfully, who had suddenly appeared from the direction of an area that he always referred to as his *Water-Loo*. 'I could be strapped to Gina Lollobrigida! You still wouldn't get me involved in all of that nonsense. I hate flying too, what with being thrown about all over the place and that dreadful flatulence!'

'I think that you mean turbulence,' said Dave helpfully.

'I know exactly what I mean, mate!'

Having drunk the last few dregs of beer, and bidding us a collective farewell, Alfie walked to the door. 'Who was it that you were chatting about?' he asked,

'That lovely young lady, who has been so actively involved in raising funds for elderly people,' said Dave. 'She's a real one-off! This country could do with more young people who give so much care and attention to the elderly!'

'Hang on!' said Alfie. 'You don't mean Libby Plummer? She's a very athletic little number, who is always getting involved in fundraising activities?'

'Yes, that's her,' replied Dave excitedly. 'We need more of her kind!'

'Well the magistrate wasn't of the same opinion. There is now a court order prohibiting her from entering or being near any place that is set up exclusively for the care or housing of the elderly. It seems that she has considerable previous for getting physically *playful* with elderly males.'

'You're having a laugh!' said Ted.

'Apparently over a six-month period, she systematically went through just about all of the able-bodied male residents at the *Bide Awhile* senior citizen's rest home last year. Suspicions were raised following a number of inexplicable sudden deaths, made all the more strange in that the three men concerned all apparently died with smiles on their faces.'

Opening the door to leave, Alfie said, 'Mind you I believe that she was providing a very important social service, and in her case, I think that she should have received recognition of some sort, well apart from the one about her *having been cocked, more times than Davy Crockett's musket* that is!'

As the door to the bar closed, an uncomfortable ominous silence fell upon us like a large black cloak. It's very rare for either *The Voice* or for Ted to be completely lost for words, although both made an attempt to string an appropriate word or two together. As for me, I would have gladly swapped places with that testicularly compromised well-digger, rather than explain my own feelings on the issue. We were all clearly left in a state of helpless facial indigence, and probably looked like three open-mouthed cod fish on a fishmonger's slab. This didn't go unnoticed by the ever-alert Zora-Aleena who has that uncanny ability to instinctively sense when something is wrong and to mysteriously materialise accordingly.

We became considerably more animated following her critical visual appraisal of the Gay Bar in general, and a close-up inspection of our faces in particular. The welcoming sight of Lenka entering the bar however allowed us all to relax a little, and for our former eternity of silence to thankfully cease.

A little later, Ted invited me to join him and a friend of his at the Bread Bin at around 17:00 tomorrow evening. He intimated that this had to do with the 'Frobisher issue'.

Lenka and I returned home at 21:50, and had to run the gauntlet along our hallway, being chased by our other girls who were clearly very pleased to see us.

We all had an enjoyable evening together.

Goodnight, Ginny.P xx

26th March 2012

Good morning, Ginny.

Elisha's playschool is shut for a week, to coincide with the normal school half term, presumably allowing a little more flexibility for parents who have children in pre-school nurseries and junior schools. I do believe that Elisha was a little disappointed that she wouldn't be attending for a while.

Maria has decided to have what she calls *a gap year* from her MBA studies. She really has put her heart and soul into her mothering duties, and Elisha is clearly enjoying the ride.

She insisted on making breakfast this morning, however it was of the non-cooked variety and consisted of cereals and fruit juice, which is certainly a positive step forward. She asked me the other evening if I'd give her a little training in cooking generally, and I have agreed to assist her in this later next week. For the time being, I have other pressing matters that needed my attention.

I won't bore you with the details of my trek across London again, other than to say, it was a very depressing affair. Hundreds of miserable faces everywhere, and not a single smile to be seen from Maida Vale to Horseferry Road.

I arrived at the court at 09:10 and was very surprised to find Basil and Tina sitting outside of the clerk's office in the foyer. I understood that since I was clearly guilty of this assault charge, Basil could not be reasonably expected to come up with anything more than mitigating factors. But there was nothing discussed along these lines, and I certainly didn't expect to see him.

I sat down next to them dejectedly. 'This is all becoming rather tiresome, Basil!' I said.

'Yes, I know Paul,' he said.

Tina gave me an embarrassed smile and lowered her head.

'Does the name Mullins ring any bells?' said Basil.

'No, why, should it?'

'Stephen Mullins is the name of the man that you assaulted, and he happens to be sitting outside of courtroom two,' he said, surreptitiously nodding in his direction.

I glanced in that area, and saw a man of around forty years of age staring at me malevolently.

Being a veritable expert when it comes to the old eyeball treatment, I returned his glare. For a good few seconds or more we were locked in ocular combat, which finally ended in my antagonist's ignominious defeat, which he tried to cover up under the guise of blowing his nose.

Frankly, even when shaving, I avoid looking into my own eyes directly for any length of time since I really do hate confrontations, and having to explain to others the cause of the early morning disturbance in the bathroom while being alone, can also prove a little difficult.

Just before 09:30, Mr Mullins collected his trilby from the seat next to him. Our eyes met again, and briefly I picked up a fleeting sense of recognition, which I simply couldn't explain.

My case was called at 09:50. Before the proceedings started, Basil identified himself to the magistrate. She was a no-nonsense robust-looking woman of around *ninety-five*, who thanked him for his polite introduction and gave him a perfunctory nod.

I went through all of the usual pre-trial requirements and a little later was asked how I would like to plead.

Looking at her worship, I stated that I fully understood the charge and that I wished to plead guilty.

The police officer who arrested me then went into the witness box and gave the brief circumstances and facts of the case. The injuries described in relation to the complainant were detailed, although in all honesty they were hardly life-threatening and consisted of a little bit of superficial bruising, that's all.

I periodically checked out the spectator's gallery and try as I might to engage Mullins in another little eyeball joust, he simply turned his head every time that I looked in his direction. Tina, however, kept smiling at me from her position a few feet away from him.

Basil gave one of the best performances of his life when it came to giving mitigating circumstances on my behalf, and if I were the magistrate, I would have been lenient given my relatively clean police record. However, she deemed my actions serious enough to warrant a three-month prison sentence suspended for two years, and a fine of £250.

On checking the spectator's gallery, both Mullins and Tina were missing.

Outside in the court foyer, I saw him leaving. He turned put on his trilby and shouted, 'This is not over!'

I rushed to the door and grabbed him. 'What's not over?' I asked in my best menacing voice. He broke free and quickly left the premises.

Two security thugs were making their way towards us, and Basil pushed me out of the door and said, 'Time to leave, Paul!'

Once outside, Basil and I walked away quickly. The security blokes were stood in the entrance to the court looking like two tethered shih-tzus just dying to escape and to go walkies. There was no sign of Mullins or Tina.

Basil explained that he wanted Tina to follow our injured party, and to have a bit of a snoop to hopefully find out a little more about him. He was of the opinion that this was the man responsible for the abduction of Spike, and had the feeling that he and Albery were not connected in any way.

This was an interesting theory and one that gave me a considerable amount of mental comfort. If this was true, then the bloke that I had bashed clearly deserved every little bruise and cut that I had administered. His discomfort and pain was a simple example of poetic justice in action.

Having had to change a number of times on my way home, my last bus from Marble Arch to Kilburn was driven by one huge lump of a driver. As I got on, he smiled at me radiantly. It really cheered me up until I realised that his facial grimaces simply indicated trapped wind, as evidenced by the considerable disagreeable noises he made before he drove the bus away. Melodic it wasn't!

I called into the old homestead at 16:00 and wasn't ready for the sight that greeted me. Maria was preparing an evening meal. That simple sentence should be enough to conjure up the scene.

Lenka and Elisha were sat on one side of the kitchen table, the other half of which was being used as Maria's food preparation area. Maria was wearing a brightly coloured pinafore and one of those mob caps of the type that the girls on the deli counter wear. I really had to stop myself from laughing, but I forced it all back when I saw that this issue was being taken very seriously by the girls.

Having carefully unwrapped the two Neapolitan pizzas, which she placed reverentially on our large baking tray (the same one that she used as a ski-board recently) she carefully loaded it onto the middle shelf of the preheated oven, and quietly closed the oven door. A short pause followed. After a second or two, Elisha squealed with delight, hugging Maria tightly, and Lenka smiled at her encouragingly.

I looked at Lenka enquiringly, but before I could make any comment she said, 'Rome, like their pizza Napolitano, didn't happen overnight!'

Clearly, Maria was pleased with her first tentative steps into the world of domestic science, and I gave her a congratulatory hug. It was only a little later that I realised just what a momentous step my dear Maria had taken. It was such a simple series of actions that she went through, but in levels of pure achievement, she had become the *nouveau riche* of attainment. An appropriate analogy could be to compare her initial actions to those of a young novice learning how to drive a motor vehicle. Clearly the first step in the driving process relates to getting in and out of the car safely.

Before we had time to consider the matter further, Maria invited us to vacate the kitchen, to enable her to set the table. We duly complied.

A little later, the tantalising smell of burning pizza wafted along the hall, and shortly after I heard what sounded like a few choice Spanish expletives, followed by a general racket reminiscent of a large bass drum and a couple of cymbals being thrown down a flight of concrete stairs.

Lenka felt that we should remain completely detached, since to disturb her would be to interrupt a very important part in her learning process. In this case, however, I suspect that a cursory glance at the recommended heating time would have been a step in the right direction. She will never forget this simple but important lesson. Bless her little cotton fire blanket!

Likewise, the loss of his driving instructor's offside front door is also a very important lesson that our dispirited learner driver will never consign to oblivion. As for the heart-broken instructor, he too would learn an important lesson when it came to giving his pupils clear unambiguous instructions, particularly when teaching people with hearing loss or who had forgotten their hearing aids. But then in both cases simple mistakes were made, and as they say, 'nothing is insurmountable'. I mean, new cookers are relatively cheap these days, and a second-hand car door from a local scrapyard could be easily obtained. But more importantly, the person who never makes a mistake must lead a pretty solitary and lonely life, and I am pleased to report that there are no social hermits or *foul-ups* as your charming American euphemism would say, when it comes to my immediate and far-flung friends.

At around 17:15, following our cheeses and pickle dinners, I meandered up to the Bread Bin where I met up with Ted and a distant cousin of his called Dickie (Tesco) O'Toole, who was an amiable, sixty-five-year-old dapper looking individual. On being introduced to me, he hastily put his pint of Guinness down, stood up smartly and shook my hand. His vice-like grip took me completely by surprise, since he was pretty small and frail looking.

But to cut a very long story short, Dickie had spent most of his life in prison and was basically a harmless petty criminal who simply couldn't cope on the outside. Over the years he had become completely institutionalised and was more than happy with prison life. He was apparently always on the lookout for any unlawful opportunity that would ultimately result in his return to his beloved confined environment.

Due to the pettiness of his former crimes, his sentences seemingly were getting shorter, and without physically hurting anyone, he was in need of getting involved in a more serious unlawful act which would ultimately lead to a longer prison term, the longer the better. Enter Eduardo Filepe Cordona, aka *Ted the Pleb,* looking for a person who would be happy to act as a scapegoat for another, in return for a sizeable custodial sentence and a small monthly allowance paid into his prison account, the details of which would follow.

I am sure that you can see where this is heading? Frobisher's case comes up on the 9th April, but somewhere in between, Ted will put his master plan into operation. He started to explain the finer details, but frankly I really didn't want to know, so he quickly changed the subject, and in no time at all we were discussing the FTSE and the reasons behind the fall in shares in relation to *Colonial Cocoa,* and sundry issues. I jest of course!

Dickie's tales about his life were both innocently charming and dreadfully disturbing. As a young boy of ten, he was sold to a childless farming couple in Ireland. Like Tommy's daughter Siobhan, he never knew his parents and was initially brought up in what became known as the *Magdalene Laundries,* which as mentioned before, was an organisation that was run by Catholic nuns, which in effect was nothing more than workhouses for *fallen women.* This dreadful derogatory term was used by the very influential clergy of the time, to describe young unmarried girls with children. In reality, however, it was a very profitable church-sponsored business which exploited the vulnerability of the ostracised girls, many of whom were still children themselves. Most of the poor souls had been abandoned by their own families and quite literally, had nowhere else to go.

He escaped from his home and tyrannical bullying guardians when he was twelve, and like Paddington Bear, after many adventures he arrived in London. It was downhill all the way thereafter. He lived rough for the first couple of months and was constantly being arrested on petty theft charges, most of which related to the pilfering of food items from supermarkets, and hence his less than inspiring criminal nickname. Over the years he found that prison life suited him and following release from his latest prison sentence, within a week or so he would ensure that he was back within the confines of the only real home that he had ever known. What a heartbreaking story.

In relation to the Frobisher issue, his story to the police would relate to his sudden conversion to Christianity. Apparently, after planting the illicit jewellery in Frobisher's garage, he had suddenly *found Jesus,* and thereafter he simply couldn't live with the guilt associated with condemning an innocent man (like a latter-day Judas Iscariot) to a life of pain and hardship.

Ted was of the opinion that the police would not be very interested in his motives, and even if pressed, he would simply state that he had been paid to plant the goods, but under the obligations of the criminal fraternity and its (honour among thieves) type of constraint, he would never reveal the culprit's name.

Given the poor man's lifelong criminal convictions, he would surely be imprisoned for a minimal term of five to ten years, and his eyes lit up with excitement at the prospect.

On leaving, he thanked me with a kind of genuine solemnity that I have never witnessed before. He was positively relieved that hopefully in the very near future that (God willing) he would once again be able to renew his membership of a very exclusive club, and to be among the only true friends that he had ever known. Apart from the rent-free accommodation, regular meals and his daily gym workouts, through his occupational therapy classes he had learnt so many new skills. He had taken up art classes some years ago and had become a bit of a minor celebrity at his last open prison, where many of his paintings are displayed in the public areas and the prison library.

On my way home later, I realised that in some cases the line between right and wrong occasionally overlaps. Clearly, Ted's disgraceful behaviour towards Frobisher was completely wrong and unjustifiable. But is Dickie's implication in a crime that he simply didn't commit any less wrong? In both cases, wrongful and/or illegal acts have been, or will be committed.

If the wrongful acts in question both result in satisfactory outcomes, however, then surely the original wrongdoings are simply a means to an end and thus must be justified? The obvious conclusion therefore seems relatively straightforward. They are simple examples of a kind of rightful dishonesty or virtuous wrong in action, and I think that the term 'Duggskulery' could be used to describe any future applications of this nature.

It has been a very exhausting day and I am very happy that it's time for bed.

Goodnight, Ginny.

P xx

27th March 2012

Good morning, Ginny.

I didn't sleep very well last night and was awoken at 07:05 by a very gentle tapping on my bedroom door. On opening it I found Elisha, who in her usual inimitable way, rushed into my bedroom and bounced on my bed. Maria was still asleep it seems.

After I had sat her in my armchair, I asked her how her evening went last night.

She was positively gushing with enthusiasm and gave me a complete rundown of her experiences from the time that I had left last night until her bedtime story, which apparently was read by Lenka.

A little later, a very bleary-eyed Maria arrived followed by a very excitable Jimena, who was dashing around the bedroom like her tail was on fire, which resulted in rapturous laughter from Elisha, and even my sleepy Maria had to have a quiet chuckle.

I had a call from Father Marcus during the morning who had only recently heard about Nobby's troubles. Clearly the CAT scheme was still alive and kicking, and this would perhaps account for the delay in his knowledge of current events. He was very sad to hear that Nobby and his family would be leaving the estate, and asked my advice on whether he should attempt to raise enough money from the residents to buy him a farewell present? I thought that it was a very good idea and told him that to get the ball rolling as it were, that I would donate £10 to his collection.

Needless to say, his regular Thursday bingo sessions have been shelved following the very unfortunate events that had befallen a few of our winning residents on their way home on his inaugural session, although he will be reintroducing it following the Easter celebrations, during the week commencing 9th April, and had secured the services of a tenant to act as his full-time helper.

Muhulin phoned a little later to ask me if I'd be available to attend a meeting with Jasmine's case worker and herself to be held at the social services offices on the morning of 30th March at around 10:00. Naturally, I wanted to know the purpose of this meeting, but she seemed to be a little evasive, and stated that 'being a rather delicate issue' she'd prefer to discuss it all fully on the appointment date, but assured me that it was nothing to worry about. I trust her sufficiently to take her at her word and stated that I would attend the meeting as arranged. However, I was more than a little intrigued when she stated that I should bring Elisha with me.

Maria prepared breakfast for herself and Elisha which consisted of cereals and fruit juice, which frankly would have been a mere hors d'oeuvre for a young lady who could normally eat two more potatoes than a pregnant pig together with a sizeable pudding to follow. Having finished her meagre meal, it became clearly evident that she was still as hungry as a church mouse on a diet, and I simply couldn't see her suffer in this way.

I suggested giving her 'a lesson in the art of grilling bacon' and her face lit up with excitement. She had six rashers of thick-cut back bacon resting on a metal tray in the blink of an eye. With feigned interest, she watched me closely as I placed it under our eye-level grill. She had four slices of bread in the toaster before I had turned the now sizzling bacon on its tray, and within minutes the pleasant evocative smell which reminded her of her last toasted bacon sandwich, filled the kitchen. For a brief moment she appeared to salivate, which she hastily disguised with a tissue that she removed from its box with amazing dexterity.

The two-bacon filled toasted sandwiches were consumed with evident satisfaction and were soon consigned to culinary history. In a show of evident appreciation, she excused herself from the room and returned wearing a colourful pinafore, but if that was not enough to warm the cockles of my heart, on her upturned hands (looking like a surgeon entering an operating theatre) she wore a pair of blue marigold gloves. A sight that I thought I would never live to see.

Both Elisha and I watched her with concerned interest, and Jimena, who presumably sensed that a seismic change in direction was about to take place, tiptoed out of the kitchen, dragging her little comfort blanket behind her.

Elisha and I sat at the kitchen table spellbound. My Maria washed and dried up all of the breakfast crockery and cutlery with commendable aplomb, and when the last items had been cleared away into their respective resting places, we nearly raised the roof with our enthusiastic applause and praise. She actually appeared quite moved at our response.

Naturally, this momentous event could not go by unrecognised or unrewarded, so later in the day I took them both to a newly opened pie and mash shop along the Edgware Road.

Neither of them had tasted this traditional cockney dish before, and while Elisha didn't really like the mashed potato, she loved the pie and liquor. Maria however, downed a 'double, double' doused in chilli vinegar with all the enthusiastic gusto of a Bermondsey stevedore.

On our way home, we bumped into Father Marcus who looked like a man with a lot on his mind. I noticed from some distance that he seemed to be talking to himself.

His exuberant greeting was tinged with the suggestion of relief, which I can only surmise indicated that our dreadfully cruel avoidance issue was taking its toll on a man, who simply wanted to communicate with others. Actually, I really felt quite sorry for him, and not a little guilty.

Within ten minutes of our meeting, he had verbally covered his Easter preparations, the hard work and effort experienced by two itinerant piano tuners, who had 'given his organ a good going over', the current funds relating to Compton's bell ropes, and the cost of two new church cleaners, the last pair having apparently moved on to 'pastors anew'!

He doesn't very often come out with funny quips like this, but when he does, he goes into fits of hysterical laughter, which for those who may be in the vicinity, is often more amusing that the joke itself. He has a very high-pitched laugh which initially vibrates at a low frequency, and powers its way up the scale. Clearly, this mirthful expression is not one of his most endearing features, indeed it is simply added to a considerable list of additional peculiarities, which sets him apart from humanity.

However, I sometimes wonder whether it is us that have it all wrong, and that he is the prototype of the perfect man of the future. He is infinitely kind and gentle, pre-eminently sincere in his love for others, and has a bloody awful sense of humour! But that aside, as Ted would say, 'he's one of ours, and that will always make him special.'

Listening to his very amusing laughter started off Elisha, which in turn had Maria and I giggling like a couple of loons. As we walked along the High Road laughing wildly, we cleared a great swathe of homecoming pedestrians, who had earlier been regurgitated out of Kilburn Park Tube station, some of whom risking life and limb had foolishly stepped into the road to avoid us. As we neared The Magpie, and being in mischievous mood, I convinced Father Marcus to join us for a drink.

Being relatively early in the evening, most of the usual Gay Bar crowd were either still *en route* from their daily commercial incarcerations, or were just getting up, following the preliminary twenty-four hours at the wake of one Michael Murphy, a long-time regular of The Goose.

An Irish wake is a very serious business, and one held at Thomas Patrick O'Mahoney's pub is not for the faint-hearted, the weak-willed or anyone hoping to have an early night. The last one was to continue for a full four days and nights, and punters were attending in twelve-hour shifts, with meal breaks every six hours.

Ted provided the bacon and cabbage followed by poteen-flavoured doughnuts, at discounted rates for the deceased's relatives, or anyone suffering from a terminal illness. It was a tremendous success, so much so, that Thomas was able to offer discounted rates for future bookings, as well as pre-paid discounts to 'protect against the ever-rising cost of wake arrangements'.

As we entered the Gay Bar, I noticed two *decampees* making a hasty retreat towards the gents. Dave and Alfie were caught like two rabbits in a car's headlights, and simply stood riveted to the spot. Dave good-naturedly accepted his capture and chuckled to himself, whereas Alfie smiled at us with that stupid kind of embarrassed facial expression of a bloke who had walked into a lamp post, and then as he hobbles away, tries to make out that he wasn't hurt.

Once inside, I looked at Vlado and pointed to Elisha, and he nodded his approval. We all sat at what was once *Whispering Jim's* table by the jukebox, and then I ordered our round of drinks.

I tried to talk Father Marcus in to sampling a pint of the brewery's finest bitter, and he immediately declined having physically shuddered. He preferred his usual sherry instead. Maria had a Malibu and pineapple and Elisha had a mango juice, and I had my customary large cognac.

Suddenly from out of the darkness along the loo passageway, Zora-Aleena wafted into the bar like the proverbial ethereal mist, and she made a point of greeting Father Marcus warmly. As gentlemanly as ever, he stood up on her arrival and gently took her welcoming hand. This was a side of this enigmatic lady that I had not witnessed before, and I didn't find the experience disagreeable.

She morphed into an amiable example of a very elegant and confident young lady, and I do believe that Father Marcus was a little embarrassed with the attention that he was being given. Her use of the English language was very basic, but she somehow managed to convey her happy thoughts marvellously, and she even gave me a very warm smile.

Elisha appeared to be a little uncomfortable initially as she then became the centre of attention. However, Zora-Aleena's very obvious maternal instincts were accepted with good grace, from a child who recognised the very evident protective and loving gestures that she was being given.

None of us understood a word of what Zora-Aleena was saying to Elisha, but the softness of her voice, together with her smile and gentle eyes, projected an abundance of warmth and love of a kind that almost left me breathless. Frankly I was captivated.

Before she left, Zora-Aleena kissed our little girl on the forehead, and walking behind the bar she joined Vlado, who appeared to be a little ill at ease. Finally, she waved at Elisha tenderly and then disappeared once again into the darkness of the loo passageway.

During all of this time, the two *decampees* who had made their escape on seeing Father Marcus enter the place had been hiding in the gents' toilet, so I thought that I'd pay them a visit.

As I entered, I heard the two cubicle doors bang shut. I told Vlado about the chaps in the loo and being in a bit of a mischievous mood himself, he quietly locked the outside door and switched off the light inside the loo, telling those remaining in the two bars that he was going to test the fire alarm.

The noise of the alarm caused Zora-Aleena to suddenly reappear with a very concerned look on her face. Vlado whispered something to her, and she was clearly amused at the prank that was about to take place.

Vlado banged noisily on the outer lavatory door and shouted 'FIRE!'

The noise associated with sheer panic that came from inside the loo was very funny indeed, and our poor captive's shouts and screams were competing admirably with the almost deafening sound of the alarm, together with the good Father's less than inaudible nervous howls of delight.

Elisha giggled along happily, although she was clearly confused about what was taking place, and I am quite sure that this was the first time that she had ever witnessed grown-ups behaving like playschool children in their sand pit.

Before Vlado had switched off the alarm, and had given light back to his captives, he had motioned to the ten or so people in the posh bar to come into the Gay Bar to witness the release of two very frightened individuals.

Vlado very quietly unlocked the door and then hastened back into the bar. Having switched off the alarm, the pub fell into a short period of unprecedented silence like a comedian who was about to insult a heckler with an appropriate reply.

Two much-shaken individuals suddenly appeared in the bar to a tumultuous cheer from the crowd, who were clearly enjoying the joke and the resultant spectacle.

Without saying a word to anyone, they hastily left the pub. I feel sure that should they ever feel inclined to engage in curate diversionary tactics again, that their sanctuary would never be sought within the confines of a public convenience in general or a pub bog in particular.

After our adventure-filled day, our evening was joyfully peaceful and quiet.

Goodnight, Ginny.
P xx

28ᵗʰ March 2012

Good morning, Ginny.

Alfie is evidently suffering from acute insomnia. Either that, or like some precocious attention-seeking child who during the hours of darkness solicits outside reassurance that the world as we know it had not ceased to exist, and that he was not the only living mortal left on the planet.

This is not the first time that this moronic *pud-wapper* has woken me up during those precious hours where my mind and body are in the process of rebooting, and I am giving my pillow some *head*. Previous experience has taught me that his calls generally are about as pointless as trying to put toothpaste back into its tube.

However, when one's phone rings at 01:53, an initial sense of panic ensues. On a scale from one to ten, with one being not important and ten being very important, to be called at this time in the morning, one must be looking at a score of nine in relation to the caller's apparent urgent need to impart the unexpected dreadful information, that simply couldn't wait until later in the day. But then, this would generally relate to those gifted with a modicum of that often-illusive commodity, 'common sense', which in *Alfie the Dip*'s case, is about as common as a person like *Alfie the Dip* having a modicum of common sense.

Fortunately, mobile phones allow one to see who is calling and I declined the call, switched off my phone, went to the loo for a quick pit stop, and then returning to my bed, I snuggled back under the comfortable warmth of my duvet. But try as I might, I simply couldn't go back to sleep. I tossed and turned for around thirty minutes, trying to get Alfie and his call out of my mind.

I tried reading for a time, but that didn't help, so I got up and made myself a nice milky cup of Horlicks, into which I slipped a couple of measures of *eau die vie*. As I sat on my bed sipping its malty intoxicating goodness, my thoughts turned to that fateful day when our paths first crossed. I really cannot forget the first time that I saw him, although for the intervening ten years or more, I have been trying my very best to do so! But then, all of my friends are unique quirky individuals, which is possibly one of the main reasons why I am so very fond of them. Boring, they are not.

My impromptu nightcap had the desired effect, since a little later I was once again in the care of *Brother Morpheus* and slept on until 07:10 when the infectious laughter of Elisha in the kitchen awoke me from my very peaceful slumber.

Maria prepared their cereal breakfast, which I later followed up with an action replay on yesterday's bacon grilling lesson, which she again enjoyed. She suggested that tomorrow she would try her hand at cooking boiled eggs, with toast soldiers. However, following her morning breakfast she again washed up and left the kitchen clean and tidy. From tiny acorns mighty oaks do grow!

Gabriel arrived at around 10:00 to take them both out for the day, although like last time, the destination was to remain a secret.

I visited the gym at around 10:30 and received a very warm welcome from Danielle, who stated that she had missed me. I had given the gym a wide berth recently since I really didn't want to strain myself in any way, and to give my *Ernie* a bit of a rest.

I simply had a poach in the steam room followed by a shave and a refreshing shower, but I came out feeling on top of the world. All of that was to change pretty quickly a little later.

At home, my Jimena welcomed me back with a little more enthusiasm than I had received earlier from Danielle; but then I wouldn't have fancied Danielle on my shoulder anyway.

As I made myself a cup of coffee, my nocturnal nemesis phoned again.

'Good morning, Alfie,' I said. 'I'm dreadfully sorry that I couldn't take your call earlier on, but I was skydiving!' 'No problem, mate,' he replied. 'I just thought that you should know that Nobby Caxton was involved in a hit and run accident last night. He is in a critical condition but is staple.'

'The word is stable Alfie...! Where is he?'

'He's in St Mary's Paddington. His wife and son are with him. I thought a stable is where you kept a horse!'

'No Alfie, that's a staple!'

A little later, one of my London Transport chauffeur chappies collected me from my bus stop opposite the estate, and within the hour I was in the intensive care unit of St Mary's hospital.

I am pleased to report that Nobby's injuries are not life-threatening, and to cut a very long story short, it seems that on his way home from the Michael Murphy's protracted wake last night, apparently a blue Morris 1100 mounted the kerb, ran into him, and was last seen heading north along the Kilburn High Road. Coincidentally Albery's blue Morris 1100 has not been seen for some time.

Lenka phoned at around 12:50 asking me if I'd be free to meet her and Tina for lunch at The Carpenter's Arms in the Edgware Road. It seems that Tina had news for me with regard to Mr Mullins.

I met up with them a little later. Tina seemed to be a little on edge when we met, but both girls hugged me warmly. We had a very nice lunch together with a few notable libations.

Following our meal, Tina asked me if I had ever lived in Yorkshire, and more particularly in the village of South Oaksall.

I explained that when I was around sixteen, my parents moved up to South Oaksall, which would have been around 1971. They had bought a bungalow on the outskirts of the village, on a new building estate. Our time there was brief, because neither of my parents could find gainful employment locally, and there wasn't much work in Doncaster (our nearest town) either. So after a memorable year or so spent in a quite beautiful area, reluctantly, we had to return to London.

Tina's next question took me completely my surprise. 'Am I right to say, Paul, that it was in this idyllic setting where you had your first meaningful relationship with a girl?'

I really felt quite embarrassed and believe me that doesn't happen very often.

'Well there was a young lady that I became quite fond of, but for the life of me, I cannot remember her name.' I said. 'She was so very pretty and had a great sense of humour. Yes I liked her a lot.'

'Would her name be Anna?' Tina asked.

'Yes!' I said excitedly. My mind was suddenly filled with a cornucopia of wonderful memories. 'But how on earth did you find out about her?'

'It wasn't too difficult, Paul. After your court appearance I followed Stephen. He lives in Hackney. He visited his local pub on his way home, and he appeared to be in the mood for downing a few drinks. He clearly didn't recognise me and we got talking.'

I had a feeling that Tina had offloaded her discovery to Lenka prior to my arrival, since periodically our eyes met, and she smiled at me sweetly.

'Can you remember when exactly you left Yorkshire?' Tina asked.

I didn't like the way this was going. I felt that instead of the friendly chat that I had expected, I was being interrogated.

'We left for London during early April 1972.'

'Are you completely sure about that?'

'Absolutely,' I replied. 'I started work as a trainee photographic printer in Victoria at the end of April 1972. It was my first real job!'

Smiling at me, she raised her glass of gin and tonic as though she was about to deliver a toast. 'Well that certainly puts you in the clear, since Stephen was born on the 3rd March 1973,' she said.

'Whatever you are on, Tina,' I said, 'please get me a couple of boxes, since then I might be able to understand what the hell you are talking about!'

Putting her glass down, she tenderly put her hand over mine. 'Well apparently, the first real love of your life sadly passed away during June of last year. Stephen is her son, and clearly having been given false information was told that you were his father, and that you had abandoned his mother when you had discovered that she was pregnant. I have a feeling that whoever smelt it dealt it!'

'Stephen had sought you out after his mother's death, and was clearly bent on retribution, and seemingly he still is!'

'You need to get a paternity test,' said Lenka helpfully. 'That would clear up the matter beyond all reasonable doubt.'

'Yes indeed!' I replied. 'However, in his rather depressed and misguided condition, I would have more chance of surviving a forest fire wearing petrol knickers, than being able to arrange a simple meeting with him, let alone to get him to agree to a paternity test!'

'Leave that to me,' said Tina. 'I have his telephone number and shall give him a call. I have always found that by not feeding a grievance for a while, it will slowly die of starvation. What he needs is a little mental diversion.' Her complacent smile suggested a modicum of feminine wile, and I was left in no doubt with regard to her persuasive capabilities, or her indomitable spirit when tested.

Following my lunch and subsequent grilling by Tina, I was in the mood for a good stretch of the old legs and decided to walk back to Kilburn. On my way home, I considered the general cleanliness of the area. Road sweepers are relatively frequent visitors, and occasionally a motorised sweeper can be seen laboriously brushing along the kerb sides, with the driver absentmindedly flicking his fag ash all over the place.

I suppose the cleanest place north of the Marylebone flyover has to be my gym. The spooky looking cleaners patrol the premises like prison warders searching for contraband. Being armed with environmentally friendly cleansing aerosols in one hand and a cloth in the other, they attack any recently used item of equipment, washing away all traces of embrocation, shredded Lycra, body fluids, or organ parts, prior to the apparatus being used again.

Clearly one could not expect such a stringent cleaning regime along our streets, but as a matter of course, I do believe that pedestrians, who reside in any of our busy inner cities, should be given masks to filter out the life-shortening carbon monoxide fumes. This is an ever-present problem in and around our busy vehicular thoroughfares.

Edgware Road during the morning and evening rush hours for example, is a veritable no-go area in relation to air pollution. A little further up the road, the last time that a nightingale was heard singing in Berkeley Square it was so hoarse that it was mistaken for an Atlantic Puffin suffering from laryngitis, which had been blown off course during its southerly migration.

In places like Kilburn, during the winter the sound of the *dawn chorus* simply reminds the populace to restock up on cold and flu remedies, and to book their respective influenza vaccinations.

Out in the country, listening to the exquisitely beautiful calls of the tits and warblers welcoming in a new day in some idyllic leafy glade, is far more preferable than having to endure the asthmatic chokes and rasping sounds of Kilburn wood pigeons, suffering from smoker's coughs first thing in a morning, all fighting for space in trees which are about as plentiful as ice cream vans in the Arctic.

I arrived at the Bread Bin at around 17:25 and was greeted by my ever-vivacious bone-crusher Rosheen, who welcomed me with all the enthusiasm of a mother who had just found her long-lost son. However, her hug was relatively restrained, and in any event, I had a very bulky jacket on which provided a very effective buffer.

I was very surprised to see Basil and two of his KUs (Alfie and Ted) sitting at the bar, who seemed to be just as surprised at seeing me. They certainly weren't astounded enough to buy me a drink however!

It soon became evident that Basil's visit wasn't purely social. It appears that they were discussing Nobby Caxton's run-in with the Morris 1100, and it became clear from the vehicle's identification as supplied by a relatively sober witness, that the car used was indeed Albery's missing vehicle. The assumption is therefore that the incident was no accident, and that Nobby had been deliberately targeted by one of Albery's henchmen.

Basil went on to explain that Nobby's testimony with regard to his own involvement in the burglaries on the estate, was vital. He is the main witness in the case. There is no doubt that Albery was the man behind all of the illegal issues, and clearly if Nobby was no longer around, this part of the case would possibly collapse. However, there were plenty of other issues pending, and that in the opinion of DS Blackstock, the charges relating to the offences committed in Susan Atkin's Court, were the mere start of a considerable avalanche of additional criminal charges which inevitably would be brought to bear. Nobby's evidence was of the utmost importance, and keeping him safe, therefore, was vitally important.

Basil had passed the information with regard to Albery's vehicle to DS Blackstock, who not wishing to take any further chances, had provided a 'safe house' for Nobby and his family, and in the meantime they would all receive police protection. He left shortly after.

While Alfie was in the loo, Ted quietly mentioned to me that Basil was acting for Frobisher.

I was quite flabbergasted at this unfortunate turn of events and felt very uneasy about it. I know that there is a perceived honour among thieves, but apart from any other consideration, Basil is a friend of mine, and I really can't imagine what he would think of me if he knew the duggskulery that Ted and I were involved in. Things are really getting a little out of hand!

Back at the homestead, I was invited to join my three girls in an evening meal of corned beef, chips and peas, which I was pleased to accept. Apparently, it was a bit of a team effort. Maria opened the two tins of corned beef, Lenka had prepared and cooked the chips and peas, and Elisha had set the table. She also ensured that the tomato ketchup was placed in a prominent, easily reached position. Paper napkins and small tumblers of mango juice had been invitingly placed next to each diner's knife, which Elisha confirmed would 'whet our whiskers'. I think she meant whistles, bless her heart.

Over dinner, Elisha gave Lenka and I an unbiased appraisal of the Legoland Windsor Resort. She had enjoyed the visit immensely, and Gabriel had bought her a doll that had to be constructed out of those little Lego bricks, which she had hoped to make a start on after dinner. However, that would be after watching their latest cartoon DVD which happened to be Walt Disney's *Dumbo*.

In the rather fragile mood that I was in, watching this film with its heart-rending story would have completely finished me off, and any semblance of good humour and happiness that I had retained would have been irrevocably lost. I know that it all worked out well in the end, but that's not the point. To put a single-parent pensioner through all of that dreadful emotional trauma, would be totally unforgiveable. Even when I think about it now, I get a lump in my throat.

After a quick shower, I thanked the girls for our evening meal, and in bed I started to read a new book called *Marley & Me* by John Grogan, which I thought might provide a mental escape from my considerable fears and concerns and would ultimately put a smile back on my face.

Goodnight, Ginny.

P xx

Good morning, Ginny.

I really had a very peaceful night and having read the first two chapters of Grogan's charming book, my depressed state eased and my spirits lifted considerably. It brought back so many wonderful memories of my dear little Spike. He always was my beloved little boy. I really do miss him a great deal, but console myself in the sincere belief that he has a wonderful life with his new partner, whom I suspect he can twist around his little dew-claw. Beryl is understandably besotted with him, but then he always did tend to like the females.

Actually, the latest research on our ancient forefathers suggests that it was the women who domesticated the wild dogs, who were ever present outside the camps and caves of ancient man. How on earth they have come up with this quite revelatory information is beyond me. Maybe ancient women simply didn't get on with the blokes; obtaining more sincere love and loyalty from a dog, which seems to be completely feasible.

Apart from any other consideration, all of the artistic depictions of typical troglodytes that I have ever seen, are hardly what one might call inspiring when it comes to attracting the opposite sex. As a collective they are depicted as great big ugly hairy brutes. The blokes aren't much better either!

Maria and Elisha were their usual bubbly selves over breakfast, and Maria made a very commendable offering of boiled eggs and toast soldiers. Needless to say, in Maria's case this was a mere starter and a sizeable helping of bacon sandwiches was to follow.

Later, over her own breakfast of muesli and fruit, Lenka stated that she had arranged a meeting with Zora-Aleena, since as I have mentioned before, she is of the opinion that the poor woman needs help. It's typical of my Lenka to actively consider the sufferings of others, and to spend some of her own free time in helping those that she comes into contact with. I believe that she would make an excellent counsellor because she's a very good listener, and I am sure that under her gentle persuasive guidance, Zora-Aleena will be able to escape from the socially inhibiting shell in which she has apparently been hiding.

Back in Slovakia, Lenka was an English teacher and her first step towards Zora-Aleena's social conversion will be to give her a good working knowledge of the language, and I couldn't agree more.

My guilty feelings with regard to Basil are ever present, and I really feel as though I have betrayed the trust of this kindly man. Fortunately it is only Ted and I that are involved in the Frobisher duggskulery, and I will be so pleased when the whole distasteful episode is over.

Muhulin phoned during the morning just to confirm our earlier arranged meeting at the social services office tomorrow at 10:00, and once again she reminded me that I should bring Elisha with me. For the life of me, I cannot fathom what this is all about.

Over at the gym later, to my astonishment I found Lenny lying under the bench press apparatus. He was just lying there you understand and had no intention of attempting to push the 110 kgs that was loaded on its bar. Still, as they say, it is the thought that counts.

All is still go as far as his forthcoming wedding is concerned, and the first reading of the banns, making public his intended marriage, was read for the first time by Father Marcus at the church service last Sunday morning. A definite date has not been decided upon, but he is hoping for the wedding ceremony to take place before the end of April.

Despite his financial windfall he is still actively seeking work, although he is very unsure as to the type of employment that he should seek. He likes animals, so he thought that he might try his hand at becoming a trainee ostrich babysitter, or being a very friendly person, he'd even consider a position as a professional cuddler. Sadly, at present, there are not too many openings for either. Still, he is diligently searching the adverts placed in our two local veterinary surgeries, and has placed his own ads offering his cuddling services in a few well-known girlie magazines, although, I have a feeling that Eugenia might change his mind on that issue.

At 13:45, the Gay Bar was completely empty apart from Vlado, who told me that he had spent the morning 'cleaning out his pipes' which I thought was a little too much information! He stated that Lenka and Zora-Aleena had just left the pub and were going to have lunch together. Once my Lenka is 'out there amongst it', she certainly doesn't waste any time. I can't wait to find out from her later how it all went.

I had one quick pint with Vlado and then thought I'd pay a visit to The Goose. The place was in a disgusting state. Apparently, the last few *wake* attendees had staggered from the place at around 05:20 this morning, and Thomas Patrick O'Mahoney was squeezing out his mop and dropping it back into a bucket of dirty water as I arrived. He was like his urinals (in a quite disgusting state of repair). The smell of the bar hastened me out of the place considerably quicker that I had entered, and I thought better of engaging him in conversation, since this big lump of a man is not universally known for his bonhomie or abundant sense of humour. Besides, I like my facial features just as they are.

Since I was on a bit of a pub crawl, I finished up at the Bread Bin, which apart from Rosheen was as empty as a bird's nest in December. But then, as far as our feathered friends are concerned, it won't be long before they will be putting away their thermals and wellie boots for another year. A little later, on the arrival of the spring flowers, they will be donning their party plumage and checking out the local birds in the hope of a quick 'hop on' (which is the avian equivalent of a leg over), followed by a whirlwind romance, a little nest building, and a spell at fatherhood, prior to taking their well-earned autumnal breaks down south in Littlehampton.

This beautiful little seaside town in West Sussex is a stopping-off point for many of our migratory birds, and a regular destination for pigeon's *down from the smoke*, where they can enjoy a little sea air, a better class of lodgings and if a more exotic one on its migration route cannot be found, they'd happily settle on a quick *hop on* with one of the local birds. An important feature of these trips away from Kilburn is that whatever happens in Littlehampton, stays in Littlehampton.

Bunny Longhurst arrived at 17:30 having completed his park-keeper duties in the Paddington Recreation Centre, and was clearly ready for a pint or two. I have always enjoyed this man's jovial nature and fun-loving attitude to life. Coincidentally, he is a lifelong *Twitcher* (a bird watcher who is ever on the lookout for rare species). He has been known to take unpaid leave, simply to go dashing off to some remote and often inaccessible location, following reports that an infrequent avian visitor had been spotted.

He has had a lifelong love for ornithology and is a very active member of the Royal Society for the Protection of Birds, and on leaving school he longed for an outdoor work life, and settled on a job as a park keeper. Like me, his schooling wasn't geared up to produce prospective university students, and was aimed at providing industry with yet another generation of machine-minder fodder of the labouring class, to be poorly paid and exploited for the rest of their working lives. We were chucked out into society in the mid-sixties, with a certain amount of optimism, ever cheeky smiles and thankfully, the ability to read and write. *Tony the Tube* quite succinctly summed up our future life prospects, having once stated, 'The world was our lobster!'

Bunny's choice of job allowed him to follow his abiding interest in birdwatching and kept him relatively close to nature.

We got chatting about a number of the more interesting items of local gossip for a while, and when that had dried up, the subject matter naturally changed to ornithology.

Following a very interesting discussion on the merits of bird ringing or banding, as it is sometimes called, we got on to seabirds. I've always enjoyed interesting conversations and Bunny's very descriptive information about the common shag was fascinating. I was frankly amazed when he told me that this particular seabird didn't have waterproof feathers.

'Who would believe that an aquatic seabird could evolve without the requisite waterproofing,' I said.

Bunny smiled at me complacently. 'Perhaps you are of the opinion that this is what one might call an evolutionary cock-up,' he said.

'Well, it does seem to be a little daft,' I said, taking a swig of my beer. 'I suppose it could be compared with finding a flat-footed arboreal kangaroo?'

'When it comes to evolutionary change, animals must adapt to their environments or face extinction. I can give you many extraordinary examples of almost unthinkable changes in animal species that have taken place due to evolutionary processes. Mankind is a typical example of this.'

I smiled to myself, when I thought about *Alfie the Dip's* innate mental inability when it came to processing outside information correctly or efficiently. 'Mankind's evolutionary progress is clearly not foolproof, Bunny. Some of our species are still in the process of evolving,' I said.

He looked at me enquiringly.

Changing the subject, I said, 'So like the American GIs that had been earlier chucked out of a landing craft into waist-deep water, this water bird also has to suffer the discomfort of sodden clothing, or in their case, feathers,' I said.

'So it would seem,' he replied.

'Well, at least they do have an opportunity to dry out, which is more than can be said for our heroic soggy-bottom boys.'

Taking a sip of his beer, Bunny chuckled and said, 'But there is a very good reason why this particular seabird doesn't have waterproof feathers.'

Before he could continue, *Alfie the Dip* suddenly arrived, seemingly in a bit of a panic.

'Sorry boys, but I need to get to the Water-Loo,' he said, dashing through the bar and vanishing behind the toilet door.

On his return, he sauntered up to the bar, bought a sandwich, and seemingly not intending to stay, walked to the door and opening it said, 'I hope I didn't disturb your conversation. I tend to do that quite a lot these days,' with a suggestion of genuine regret in his voice.

'Not at all Alfie,' I replied. 'I was just asking Bunny here why aquatic birds like shags, do not have waterproof feathers.'

'Well I think that's pretty obvious,' he said. Closing the bar door, he slowly walked back toward us. Bunny was clearly interested in what he had to say.

'I would really be obliged if you could enlighten us on this particular subject, professor,' I said unfairly, and I regretted my words as soon as I had said them.

'No need for the soccasim, mate,' he said, biting into his sandwich ravenously. 'It's so... so... not nice!' He walked back to the bar, ordered a small whiskey, with a small whiskey chaser, and returned shortly afterwards, smiling at us mischievously. Placing the two glasses on the table, he sat down.

'Why don't you just order a large whiskey?' I said. 'It would certainly save on the washin-up.'

'Well I'm trying to cut down you see, and two small ones are better than one large one.'

An ominous silence followed. 'Well?' I said finally. 'So... what about the shag then?'

Rosheen suddenly stopped wiping the bar counter and looked at us enquiringly.

Alfie, raised a glass, examined the contents against the light, and then knocking back the whiskey in one go, like a cowboy in a western film, he said, 'Shags are quite cute, they even have a little tuft or muff of feathers on the top of their heads, and that's where they get their name from,' he said authoritatively. 'I was watching a very interesting documentary on the box the other night, presented by that bloke David Atten – Atten – something or other.' 'Borough,' I said.

'Yeah, that's him, David Borough!'

I looked at Bunny in exasperation, who shrugged his shoulders and chuckled to himself.

'But how…?'

'It's a seabird what relies on seafood for its survival, although them *shite-hawks* are rather fond of fish and chips, which they swoop down and nick from unsuspecting holiday makers, but I'm told that they don't like wally gherkins.'

'Yeah, but how?'

'Some of the more flashy bigger birds dive in the sea from high up, but the shag is a little more refined in its habits and dives from the surface.' Smiling, he took another swig of his remaining whiskey and said, 'In scientific terms, this action is called *a muff dive!'*

Bunny stared at me in disbelief, took a large swig of his beer and then started to laugh uncontrollably.

'Alright Alfie,' I said, 'you've had your little bit of fun.'

'No, let him finish,' Bunny said, trying to regain his composure. 'I'm enjoying this.'

'Well as I was saying, shags are quite fond of sand eels, what coincidentally happen to live on the bottom of the sea.' He looked at me with an intense expression of seriousness of a kind that I have never seen on his face before. 'Now that I have given you all of this information, why on earth do you think that the bird doesn't have waterproof feathers? It's all very logical when you think about it.'

I looked at Bunny appealingly, who was about to say something when Alfie said, 'No Bunny, let Paul answer.'

I felt that I should play along with all of this. 'I give up Alfie,' I replied.

Standing, he picked up his remaining glass of whiskey which he initially sipped, and then having licked his lips, he threw back the remaining dregs and putting his empty glass down on the table he made for the door. Smiling he said, 'During its little muff dive, water soaks its feathers, so out of water it has to dry them. It lays prostate on a rock.'

The word is prostrate, Alfie!'

'Yeah, it stretches out its wings like one of them show-off pheasants.'

'Peacocks, Alfie!'

'Yeah well anyway, while he's stretching out his wings, and looking all macho like, with his feathers drying in the sun, like that Vosene bird on the telly, the females get all horny and before you know it, Bob's yer sister's brother, and a few months later, another little shaglet is born.'

'I like your theory, Alfie,' said Bunny enthusiastically, 'but it has one major flaw.'

'Wass 'at then?'

'Shags are monogamous.'

'Wass' at then?'

Rosheen, who had been listening to our discourse throughout, seized the opportunity to put in her very well-timed observation. 'It means, Alfie, that they don't shag around!'

'Well I suppose that might be another reason why they lay about on rocks trying to attract passing talent. I mean, Robert Redford look-a-likes they are not. But even so, they've got to find the right one, and that's why they have to try out a few first before settling down, so to speak. As the old saying goes, 'any old bike is good enough to practise on, but you need a good one for keeps!'

As he left, he smiled at me and said, 'I really thought that you would have figured that one out though, mate.' With a very smug look on his face, he said, 'It's all simply about compilation!'

Before I could answer, he was out of the door and gone.

In an effort to answer the very confused look on Bunny's face, I said, 'I think he meant copulation.'

Shortly after, both Bunny and Rosheen were howling with laughter.

When quiet had been restored, I simply had to find out the reason for the shag's lack of waterproofing.

'Mother Nature doesn't make mistakes,' Bunny said. 'Like the cormorant, shags feed on seafood. However, their methods are slightly different. Cormorants, like gannets plunge into the sea from above, whereas the shag dives from the surface. They are much smaller and lighter that their seabird cousins. Their feathers become waterlogged, making them heavier, which enables them to reach their staple diet of sand eels which live on the seabed. It's as simple as that!'

Goodnight, Ginny.

P xx

30th March 2012

Good morning, Ginny.

Today our collective rituals of bathing, dressing and bodily tissue restoration were completed by 09:00 (separately that is!) Elisha asked me if Maria could come with us on our visit to the social services office, and I was more than happy to allow a lady, who has acted like a surrogate mother to our little girl, to accompany us. My Maria has been absolutely marvellous in every way.

We arrived at the offices at 09:50 and met Muhulin who was waiting in the foyer.

A little later, Elisha and I were invited into an office. We were greeted by a man who introduced himself as Simon Stockton. He then introduced me to Emily Brand, a middle-aged frumpy dumpling of around fifty-five summers. Both appeared to be very pleasant types.

After the usual pleasantries had taken place, Simon informed me that he was the head of the fostering section, and that Emily was his assistant. I was dumbstruck for a short while.

To cut a very long-winded story down to a manageable comprehendible précis of the meeting, I was told that I had been nominated to act as Elisha's foster guardian, at least for the foreseeable near future. It appears that her mother Jasmine would be hospitalised for the remainder of her life, and Elisha would therefore have to be put into care as an interim measure.

If I was willing to take on this responsibility, I would initially be given practical training, and as a foster parent would be paid for my services. I would be under the supervision of Stockton and Brand and could 'contact them at any time!' My thoughts suddenly turned to Alfie's penchant for making nocturnal phone calls and I couldn't help smiling to myself.

Elisha was asked if she would like to remain with me, and her response didn't leave any room for doubt. She was absolutely delighted, and jumping into my lap, giving my *Ernie* a bit of a jolt, she very nearly choked me to death, as she enthusiastically hugged my neck.

On our way out, Elisha hugged Maria, who couldn't get a word in edgeways. However, she soon got the general drift as to the purpose and the result of our meeting.

Muhulin quietly wept when she heard that I had accepted the request to act as Elisha's *tempus a patre,* and she nearly squeezed the life out of me as well.

Following a brief lull in our verbal narrative and overt gesticulations, like the unmistakable calm before the storm, my sweet Maria suddenly became overcome with *emulsion* (as Alfie would have said) and started to howl uncontrollably. The horrendous noise thus produced, resulted in the very swift attendance of two rather fearful looking unsavoury individuals in security uniforms.

To control Maria's pitiful sobbing on our way home, I dashed into a nearby newsagent and bought her a Mars bar to suck for the remainder of our ten-minute walk home. It quietened her down considerably, but on our arrival at Susan Atkin's Court, her visage took on the appearance of a well- digger's face, which had been subjected to a session of productive lamentation on its way home from work. Pretty it wasn't!

Our little Elisha skipped, danced and giggled delightfully all the way back to our humble abode. Being off playschool for the day, she asked if she could go to the swings in our local park. She was clearly in wanderlust mood.

Having washed away her former tear and chocolate-mascara marinade, which had hardened to a crust-like facial coating, Maria reapplied her cosmetic mask, and shortly after was happy to venture out once again. A little later, my two girls were both hand in hand on their way to the park.

Lenka was at home and intimated to me that her progress with Zora-Aleena was 'very productive and promising'. She would like to bring her home periodically for English lessons, and naturally I agreed.

A little later Ted phoned to say that Dickie O'Toole, aka *The Tesco Kid*, had given himself up to the local constabulary and was being held for questioning. He asked if I'd like to join him for a few libations at The Glass House pub at around 15:30.

Being halfway through Happy Hour, the place was fuller than a centipede's sock drawer, and it took me a considerable amount of time to get to the bar. On the way, I had my bum pinched, but search as I might, I couldn't find my illusive little ninja, who was clearly responsible for my bodily assault and was hiding somewhere in the pub.

I eventually found Ted sitting on a stool at the bar. I wasn't in the mood for a drink initially, and would have rather settled on a couple of good lungful's of oxygen, although the chances of finding a paramedic wheeling an oxygen cylinder in this den of iniquity was about as likely as ingesting a *lentil vindaloo* from *The Star of Kerala* Indian Restaurant and to not suffer a rectal prolapse the morning after. It's certainly not for the gastronomic lightweight or the involuntary colonic irrigation sufferer.

Apparently, Ted had not heard anything more from Dickie following his recent surrender to our boys in blue.

I reiterated the fact that for Basil's sake alone, I wasn't happy with this dreadful example of underhanded subterfuge and was suffering pretty badly with guilt.

Having taken a rather large swig of his lager, he commented, 'The world is full of quite indescribable pain and suffering mate.'

'I simply feel that we have betrayed Basil's trust,' I said.

He smiled at me ruefully. 'Frankly, if you can't remember what you were worrying about last week, your troubles are as a dandelion floret blown on the wind.'

'I sometimes tire of all of your Shakespearian clever-dickery,' I said, looking around furtively, hoping to spot my little ninja buttock-molester.

'While my depiction of a troubled conscience may be a little poetic, it is not from the pen of the bard.' Taking a large swig from his glass of lager, and looking around for a bit of an audience, in a voice decibel level which promised the immediate and unequivocal attention of those poor unfortunates nearby, he shouted, 'Conscience is but a word that cowards use, devised at first to keep the strong in awe. Our strong arms be our conscience, swords our law. Now that is Shakespeare!' he said.

His sudden verbal outburst had a very noticeable reaction since our formerly close-packed fellow boozers started to surreptitiously back away, and an almost tangible element of fear and uncertainty invaded the space between us.

Ted drank the final dregs from his glass and ordered another two pints from a barmaid, who appeared to be a little curious at the sudden verbal outburst, and the unusual space that had developed between us and the others.

'Hopefully, Dickie's troubles will soon be over,' Ted continued. 'Frobisher will walk, and Basil will receive a considerable amount of public-sponsored legal aid funding for his company, of which I hasten to add, he is a major shareholder. Apart from a very nice salary, he receives an annual premium bonus from his company shares. The way I see it, mate, it is a win-win situation for all concerned.'

'I can't help my feelings, Ted,' I replied.

Blowing out a long, clearly exasperated puff of air from his puckered lips, he replied, 'It is clear to me that you are one of those people who take more than the recommended daily dose of vitamin I. Too much is simply not good for you.'

'I appreciate what you are saying, Ted, but whatever you may say, I still believe that the whole issue is morally questionable. I believe that I am right, and I really can't help the way that I feel about the situation.'

Smiling, he replied, 'How many references to that naughty little personal pronoun did you make in that relatively short statement?'

I had to smile. 'OK Ted, you have made your point, I won't mention the issue again.'

As I left, I asked him where Tina was hiding.

'Dunno mate,' he replied. 'I haven't seen her for a couple of days.'

Since Happy Hour at the Glass House is a purely masculine affair, I was not over enamoured at the thought that not only had my person been violated, but the masculine *anal-orifice* responsible had been some low-life inebriated cretin who had probably not washed his face for weeks, let alone his hands!

Later, I had a message from Lenka stating that Zora-Aleena had invited us all to dinner at the pub, which I thought was a very nice gesture. A table would be available from 18:30 onwards.

Having an hour and twenty minutes to spare, I sauntered down to the Bread Bin. Apart from Rosheen and a couple of blokes that I hadn't seen before, the places was as empty as a hermit's address book.

Having bought a drink, I quite unconsciously made my way to a seat that I like to occupy while on the premises. It's easy to understand how certain actions in life become habitual. For example, before I finally go to sleep at night, I quite robotically flip the pillow over to the cold side, which seemingly must activate my subconscious light switch, since I am asleep almost immediately thereafter.

Rosheen gave me her usual warm greeting and then introduced me to the two strangers. One was Fergal, her brother, and the other was a friend of his called Shamus. I was to find out later that they were both lifelong companions, albeit coming from very differently political and religious backgrounds. Fergal was born in the Republic and Shamus was brought up in Belfast. They greeted me warmly, and I felt at ease with them in no time at all.

Sadly, making friends of complete strangers in a lonely unforgiving place like London isn't easy. But it is considerably trouble-free when being introduced by a loved and respective friend or relative. Seemingly, if I was a well-thought of friend of Rosheen, clearly no further test or investigative character-identifying small talk would be necessary.

The stereotypical Londoner has been described as an arrogant, unfriendly, miserable and stingy eccentric. Which isn't too bad I suppose, particularly since they missed out on the inbred self-indulgent toffs in monocles, the light-fingered cockney pickpockets, the anti-Highway Code suicidal cyclists, the unfriendly workaholics, and last but not least, the Stella-swilling wife-beaters.

Sadly there is no mention of the undeniable fact that London is also an enormous worldwide racial melting pot, and home to some of the most talented and interesting specimens of humanity who have chosen to live here among us – warts and all. Frankly, it would be a very miserable place without them.

In no time at all, our level of conversation was both interesting and outrageously funny, with both of them displaying very profound verbal narratives, and I really enjoyed their witty repartee. I cannot remember a time when I have laughed so much. I was quite sad to have to leave them.

I arrived at The Magpie at 18:20 and made my way through the posh bar into the restaurant area. This is a part of the pub that I had never visited before, mainly due to the fact that The Magpie is simply my watering hole, a place where I go for a little liquid refreshment, periodically enhanced by the unforgettable camaraderie of like-minded individuals who as a collective, enhance my very existence – and then of course there are also my friends.

My three girls, resplendent in their best party frocks, were seated at a very elaborately decorated table. On a sumptuous golden silk taffeta tablecloth, a four-cover place setting arrangement had been made, and clearly a lot of thought and detail had been put into the exercise.

As I arrived at my chair, Zora-Aleena suddenly appeared from out of the darkness and greeted me very warmly. It may be my imagination, but I have never seen this woman in a distant well-lit area. As mentioned before, she simply seems to materialise, like Bela Lugosi in his 1931 film *Dracula*. Suffice it to say, that on more than one occasion, her sudden appearance has completely altered my normal daily bowel movement, necessitating my own very hasty *evaporation* from the immediate area somewhat faster than a toupee in a hurricane! Another reason why I always carry a handy supply of diarrhoea relief tablets and a packet of aloe-vera infused wet-wipes.

'Good evening, Mr Paul,' she said, shaking my hand warmly and looking at Lenka for some kind of visual response.

Lenka smiled and quietly made a hand-clapping motion, which brought an embarrassed but clearly appreciative smile from Zora-Aleena.

I was graciously invited to sit down and our hostess obligingly pulled the chair back for me, smiling sweetly.

We all had a marvellous time, and frankly we were treated like visiting royalty by both Zora-Aleena and Vlado, who in between refilling the almost bottomless glasses of a few of the lads in the Gay Bar, periodically made a very nervous appearance.

Just before we left, my diminutive bum-pincher-ninja arrived.

'Just thought that you'd like to know, Paul,' she said, smiling radiantly, 'I have submitted DNA samples from both yourself and Stephen Mullins and can confirm that you are not the biological father of Stephen.' She handed me a copy of an official-looking document.

I thanked her for her kind support and effort, and she stopped long enough for me to buy her a drink. Being a very resourceful lady, I didn't enquire how she had managed to obtain our respective DNA samples. As they say, 'least said – soonest mended!'

'I think that this issue is now completely resolved,' she said on leaving.

We were all home at 21:45, filled to the brim with good food and drink, and the warm appreciative glow of an evening that will be remembered for a long time.

Gabriel was waiting for us on our arrival, and Maria collected an overnight bag for her and Elisha. Apparently, they were staying overnight at Gabriel's home, since tomorrow he is taking them out for the day again (bless him).

Apart from Jimena, I had the flat to myself for the rest of the evening since Lenka was meeting up with Tina a little later in the evening.

Goodnight, Ginny.
P xx

31st March 2012

Good morning, Ginny

Thank you so much for your birthday wishes, but as you know I am basically a very shy and retiring person when it comes to people making a fuss of me, and birthdays have always been at the bottom of the barrel when it comes to the kind of overt extravagance and ego-boosting goodwill that I have to usually contend with on this, the annual celebration of my birth.

Jimena and I had a very peaceful night, and we were up at 07:50. The flat was like a morgue, and apart from Jimena's vocal requests for food, my flat was ominously still, uncomfortably so. But then I am never satisfied, it seems. I was almost driven to distraction during the time that *Gob Almighty* and her infantile demolition experts were residing in the flat above mine, and now I can't stand the almost unbearable silence.

Following a shower and a couple of pieces of toast washed down with coffee, I was ready to start another day.

Being in mooch-mode, a little later I was on a bus into town. I had just missed one by a gnat's eyelash, but a few minutes later, several more arrived, so I could quite literally have taken my pick. That is one of the good things in relation to living in such a vibrant, bustling Met-trollops like London; buses are relatively frequent, with minutes between them. Having hailed one at a request stop, if one doesn't like the look of the driver, one can refuse to board in the certain knowledge that like the proverbial bad penny, another miserable looking *fatherless-person* driving a potential alternative, would be bringing his bus to a tyre-screeching and passenger-reshuffling stop a few minutes later. For the uninitiated London first aiders, this is the main reason why defibrillators are installed close to betting offices, National Health dental surgeries and request bus stops. Sadly however, most Londoners wouldn't be able to identify a defibrillator, even if they were *urinating* on one, let alone know how to use one!

Thirty minutes or so later, I was meandering along the spiritual centre of London, Trafalgar Square, and thereafter along Whitehall towards Westminster Bridge. I never tire of revisiting London landmarks; it's like meeting up with old friends. Sadly, on a personal level, I feel that I have precious few of them at the moment.

Crossing Westminster Bridge I sauntered east along the Southbank, which at 11:50 was very busy with locals and visiting tourists alike, checking out the various interesting sights. First of which, along this particular thoroughfare, is the impressive London Eye, which is apparently the tallest cantilevered observation wheel in the world. But then I've never really liked heights, although it's not so much the height that disturbs me, but the dreadful widths make me very giddy.

I mean, not wishing to put a too finer point on the issue, the last time I managed to pull *Alfie the Dip* out from under his collapsed shed, I paid for his taxi to the local A&E, and following the stitches, I collected him again in another one. I painstakingly replaced the concrete lintel over the door of his shed, so that when his injuries were better, he could continue in the breeze block structure. I have never met a person who is more accident prone. In fact, he seems to run into accidents that were originally intended for someone else. The fact that I strained my back and spent a considerable amount in cab fares is neither here nor there. But did he hear me complaining? Or did I ask for financial reparation? Not on your life!

The Tate Modern, a little further along the South Bank (as the name would suggest) is home to a collection of modern and contemporary art, which is housed in a great big ugly lump of a building, which was formerly the Bankside Power Station. Frankly, I have never been too keen on modern art since most of the exhibits that have been raved about are comparable with what one might find adorning the walls of nursery or infant schools. Besides, I have never seen the need to visit a building that offends my inherent love of architectural beauty, just to see infantile art works, particularly since I would also have to pay for the pleasure.

My gifts of financial aid to *Lenny the Ponce* have been an ongoing issue throughout our association. There have been times when in wild carefree abandonment I have run the gauntlet at Sainsbury's (and still have the scars to prove it) simply to stock up his ever-empty larder. Has he ever returned one shekel of the vast sums of money that I have donated to his cause over the years? Not on your life!

There is always a crowd of awe-struck spectators looking at the replica of Shakespeare's Globe Theatre. The original was built in 1599, but sadly it was destroyed by fire in 1613. Another was built in 1614 on the same site. The present reconstruction of the Globe opened in 1997.

Even Ted has never been backward in coming forward during times of trouble. I have helped him out on many occasions when, that fickle phantom *lady luck*, has deserted him. Apart from nicotine and alcohol, gambling is another one of his abiding addictions, and on more than one occasion he has realised the truth behind the saying that *gambling away the rent money is a moving experience,* and 'muggings' here, has always been around to provide the: requisite solace, when he has been troubled with suicidal thoughts. I have also provided the temporary accommodation necessary to keep him dry and warm at night, together with sufficient food to aid in the restoration of his bodily tissues, and to temporarily postpone his mental and physical deterioration, following yet another horse's *hesitation* at coming out of its stall with the rest of the runners. And thus sadly, yet another *certainty* is destined for a milk round or the glue factory!

I called into the Swan pub again and enjoyed a pint of their best bitter. As mentioned before, the view from their outside seating area is truly awe-inspiring. Looking across the river, I was suddenly struck with the thought that in the grand design of things, we are all pretty insignificant. A miniscule part of something far greater – an atom in the cog of the wheel of existence. And yet as inconsequential as we may be, we are all important in our own ways.

Of all of my so-called close friends, the incidences where I have provided care, solace and assistance, often to my own detriment, is legendary. Each and every one of them has at some point received help in one form or another, whether it is physical, financial or spiritual, and I have never desired to receive any recompense, thanks or acknowledgement. After all, that's what friends are for. Sadly, as far as mine are concerned, not one of the *fatherless-people* has remembered my birthday! No cards, no texts, not even a measly phone call from a collective which could be justifiably referred to as a bunch of ungrateful, two-faced *pud-wappers!*

At around 17:15 I arrived in The Cut, Southwark, famous for the Old Vic theatre.

Established in 1919, it was originally called the Royal Coburg Theatre. Over the years, notable thespians such as Dame Sybil Thorndike and Sir Lawrence Olivier have captivated thousands of hungry culture lovers in this beautiful theatre. In the good old days, for those in the know, following a performance both could be found sampling the joys and pitfalls of *grape and grain* in a few of the local hostelries, and as Maurice Micklewhite, aka Sir Michael Caine (who was brought up locally), would have said, 'Not a lot of people know that!'

At around 19:00 I found myself at Marble Arch, feeling inexplicably miserable. I caught a bus towards Kilburn and a little later arrived home. I spent half an hour or so writing up your email.

** INTERLUDE**

1st April 2012

Good morning, Ginny.

I am sorry that I didn't finish or send you yesterday's email, which I will submit with today's entry. Although on second thoughts, I might not send that one at all.

Having walked into the Gay Bar last night, the place was as empty as a mourning heart. Vlado asked me if I could assist him in the posh bar, and of course I readily agreed to do so. The place was in complete darkness, and pointing to the light switch behind the bar, he asked me to put the lights on.

What greeted me, once the lighting was re-established, was positively marvellous. With the exception of *Whispering Jim,* the place was packed out with all of my friends, old and new. My three girls rushed towards me, and nearly smothered me to death. A band on the stage played a very loud, heavy metal rendition of *Happy Birthday* and frankly, I was overcome with *emulsion*, as Alfie would have said, and tears streamed down my face. I felt such a fool! But that was the last thing that I was to remember with any degree of certainty!

Needless to say that my actions and just what went on thereafter is a complete mystery. I am told that I had a real good time, and apparently, on leaving during the early hours of this morning with the girls, Dave and Lenny had to carry me home. Apparently, they also put me to bed. And thankfully I can't remember if they gave me a kiss goodnight.

I awoke this morning at 10:25. I was suffering from one hell of a hangover; my mouth felt like a gorilla's armpit and I had a severe headache. Once up, I was very unsteady on my feet and crawling on all fours towards the kitchen, I needed the support of Jimena who thankfully led me in the right direction. I was very disorientated indeed and felt quite nauseous, but I forced myself to the bathroom, and fighting back the urge to vomit, I cautiously showered.

Both Maria and Elisha were out when I got up, and Lenka's door was closed, so I assumed that like me she had slept late, but in her case she was still down to it at 11:10, which for her is most unusual. But then recently she has been busier than a centipede at a toe counting contest.

I prepared Jimena's morning repast which consisted of minced mackerel and tuna, the smell of which had me gagging. I was grateful that apart from the cat, no other living entity had witnessed my disgraceful condition, compliments of what could be described as a considerable amount of alcohol poisoning. But as delicate as I was feeling, I managed to force down a couple of slices of dry toast, remembering my revered mother's words that 'Breakfast is the most important meal of the morning!'

I met *Whispering Jim* outside Brenda's Breakfast Emporium as arranged at midday, and he was very smartly dressed in a Jimmy Savile lookalike tracksuit and trainers, although the well-rounded paunch of belly fat that refused to defy gravity, hung down dejectedly over his very tight-fitting waistband, and looked both painful and somewhat ridiculous. As for the suggestion that he was an athletic type, during a former discussion on the importance of exercise, he once reasoned:

'If God had intended me to touch me toes, he would have put them on me kneecaps!'

He appeared to be a little nervous and asked if we could visit Rosheen at the Bread Bin before we went into the Gay Bar. Initially, I was a little reluctant, since I had arranged with Ted to have him inside the Gay Bar at around 12:15, but I relented and sent Ted a quick text to say that we had been delayed and I that I would text him again a little later.

Rosheen was absolutely delighted to see him, and having grappled with him into one of her customary welcoming hugs, he had to be helped to a vacant seat by the pool table. Having regained his composure, he opened up a small ruck sack that he had been carrying and took out what looked like a female purse. He tipped a considerable amount of pound coins onto the table and within minutes the jukebox was blasting out Jim Reeves numbers.

An hour or so later, fortified with a little tension-dissipating alcohol, we made our way to The Magpie and as promised, I sent Ted a quick text to say that we were on our way.

On our arrival, Jim and I were met at the Gay Bar threshold by both Zora-Aleena and Vlado. Jim became quite emotional when Zora-Aleena took his hand and, welcoming him back to the pub, gave him a much unexpected hug. Vlado just smiled, shook his hand and led him into the bar. It really was so nice of them to go to such trouble, and I was convinced that their welcoming sentiments were sincerely meant.

There were around fifteen or so regular pub faces in attendance who, having clearly rehearsed it all before our arrival, sang a very commendable rendition of that beautiful Celtic ballad 'Danny Boy' and it frankly brought tears to my eyes. Jim was almost inconsolable as he was led to his usual table by the jukebox, on which stood two perfectly pre-poured pints of Guinness, and a small pile of one-pound coins. On the front of the jukebox, a very elaborate card had been placed bearing beautiful italic script which read *Welcome Home Jim* within an artistic border of small green shamrocks, shillelaghs and harps.

At around 14:45, Lenka arrived and Zora-Aleena was clearly very pleased to see her. They embraced warmly, followed by what looked like a stage-managed verbal greeting:

'Good afternoon, Miss Lenka,' Zora-Aleena said, shaking her hand.

'Good afternoon, Miss Zora-Aleena,' replied Lenka,

'It is really good to see you again, and you are welcome to take a seat anywhere in the bar.'

'That's very kind of you, Zora-Aleena.'

Lenka then gave Jim a very enthusiastic hug and joined us at our table.

I congratulated her on the most amazing improvement in Zora-Aleena's proficiency in the English language. Her diction was almost perfect, and her confidence was quite remarkable, given the short time that Lenka has been giving her tuition.

Apart from becoming very close friends, Lenka confided that she had found Zora-Aleena to be a very interesting, albeit enigmatic person, with a quite profound sense of respectability in everything that she became involved in. Her apparent aloofness was simply a mask behind which she sheltered to disguise her modest and self-effacing nature.

Lenny, Alfie and Dave joined us, and the banter improved as each new round of drinks arrived. Jim was on good form. Needless to say, his choice in music was a little predictable, although when his attention had been averted sufficiently, Dave slipped in a crafty pound or two, selecting music from the sixties and notably his personal favourite, Billy Fury.

Whispering Jim's only real comment was, 'Who the feck put this load of shite on?'

'What's your favourite drink, Jim?' asked Alfie, who trying to change the subject was clearly in a little mischievous mood, and was bent on a little *Jim-baiting.* However, the wind was taken out of his *urine-soaked* sails when Jim replied, 'The next one! And I can't feckin wait to get it. Whose round is it anyway?'

As is usually the case, happiness multiplies when you share it with others, and as the afternoon and evening slipped by, the Gay Bar quite literally reverberated with unbridled laughter and merriment. Even Zora-Aleena made herself available, smiling at everyone and mingling amiably with the very surprised Gay Bar regulars. She really is a changed woman, and clearly her time spent with

Lenka has been very beneficial indeed. Let's hope that it lasts.

At 19:30, my little bum-pincher-ninja arrived. She had a playful look on her face and was smiling like a Cheshire cat. She walked back to the bar door and beckoned to someone outside. I almost fell through the floor when Stephen Mullins entered the pub.

As he approached me, his extended right hand invited a similar response, and smiling at me good-naturedly, he had clearly hoped on a reconciliation of our earlier differences.

All was forgiven and forgotten within minutes of his arrival, and after a very sincere apology in relation to the theft of Spike, and the erroneous belief that I was his biological father, within thirty minutes or so we were happily chewing the fat together like two old friends who had lost contact with one another.

You remember the court case where for the first time I was able to take a good look at him facially, and I commented that he reminded me of someone? Well that someone was his mother Anna. In close proximity to him, I could see just how much he resembled her. I was very saddened to hear about her untimely death.

Later, having come back from the loo, as I sat down at Jim's table I suddenly felt very ill at ease. *Whispering Jim* was giving Stephen the fish-eye treatment and I noticed that on the table both his fists were clenched and the whites of his knuckles were very evident.

I quietly asked Lenka what was going on, and it seems that when Jim went to the bar, he casually asked Tina who Stephen was. She had quite innocently told him that he was the man responsible for stealing Spike.

I held Stephen's arm and, inviting him to stand, I cautiously led him to the bar door. Tina followed us. I explained to him on the way that Jim was very fond of Spike and that he had been told the truth behind his disappearance. He nodded understandingly.

Outside, I apologised, but explained that Jim likes to take things apart to see why they don't go, and that under the circumstances it would perhaps be prudent for him to therefore go! He got my general drift, and shaking my hand once again, he apologised profusely for all the trouble that he had caused.

Tina gave him a hug and they were last seen walking hand in hand north along the High Road towards Kilburn Park tube station. And a perfect couple they looked.

Jim was in fighting mode when I returned to the bar, and I pacified him as best as I could. Vlado had earlier noticed Jim's facial discomfort and had lifted the bar counter in preparation for his reluctant hasty leap into the crowded room should it become necessary. I gave him a reassuring thumbs-up, which he acknowledged by smiling, and shaking his head he lowered the bar counter again and breathed out an audible sigh of relief.

There were no further problems, and later having thanked his hosts, Jim tottered out to his homeward bound taxi, contentedly wide-eyed, and legless.

On our return home, Maria's door was closed, so my three other girls were safely ensconced within, and due to the lack of any sound, were clearly fast asleep.

Lenka joined me for a little night cap before we retired.

Goodnight, Ginny.

P xx

2nd April 2012

Good morning, Ginny.

Elisha and Maria had monopolised the bathroom at 07:15 this morning, and in an effort to take my mind off a rather urgent need in relation to my bladder, I prepared Jimena's breakfast.

The steamed-up bathroom became vacant at 07:42 precisely, and as my two newly scrubbed girls made their way to their bedroom, I shot past them like a greyhound out of a box.

It's my big day with regard to my *Ernie* reversal procedure today. From midnight last night I have had to fast, although I was encouraged to drink plenty of water, which I did before bed. I had to shower this morning using a special medicated gel which presumably is used pre-op to prevent infection, although having dressed, the antiseptic smell was quite overpowering.

Maria made breakfast for herself and Elisha this morning, and I have to say that her enthusiasm for domestic duties is commendable and for the spectator highly entertaining. She is relatively thorough in a disorganised sort of way, and this morning Elisha had scrambled eggs on toast, albeit that she was expecting a peanut butter sandwich. Well near enough, I suppose?

Maria left with Elisha at 08:50 to take her to playschool, and as she was leaving she asked if I would still be home on her return at around 09:10. It seems she wanted to have a chat about something.

On her arrival back home, she stated that Gabriel had asked her to move in with him. I was initially against the idea, but purely for selfish reasons. The thought of not having my beautiful girl around was quite heartbreaking. She has been part of my life for such a long time now that frankly I would be quite lost without her.

Gabriel lives in a rather nice flat overlooking the Regents Canal at Little Venice as it is called locally. Actually, it is a mere stone's throw from Warwick Avenue tube station, which is less than a ten-minute walk away from Susan Atkins Court, so at least my darling little monster-muncher would only be a stone's throw away.

I left her at around 10:30 en route for St Mary's hospital Paddington.

** INTERLUDE **

Hello again Ginny. It's now 21:35 and I have just got back home. My two big girls were waiting expectantly for my arrival, and with their interrogative questioning, I couldn't get a word in edgeways. Elisha was sound asleep, and I blew her a kiss before I closed Maria's bedroom door.

My hernia reversal procedure was a complete success, and although I am feeling a little sore at the site of the wound, I feel so relieved that it is now all over and hopefully in the not-too-distant future I shall be able to visit my gym again, which I have missed terribly.

Maria appeared to be very excited at the prospect of moving in with Gabriel, and an unmistakeable glow of intense happiness and expectation shone from her beautiful blue eyes. My own feelings are a mixture of sadness at my impending loss, and trepidation at the giant step that my little girl would be taking. However, I am very fond of Gabriel, he is a thorough gentleman and is clearly besotted with her, as she is with him. So what could possibly go wrong? Besides, this is not likely to happen for about a month or so, since Gabriel will be out of the country on an assignment, which is all pretty hush-hush and Secret Squirrel.

As far as Elisha is concerned, Maria stated that she'd like to continue in her present role and wanted to carry on in what she referred to as *The School Run,* and will drop and collect Elisha daily. I was very pleased about this since it would mean that I would continue to see her regularly. However, I insisted that should she continue in this function, that I would pay her a weekly fee, which I think is only fair.

I mentioned that in the near future (no official dates had been forthcoming) I would need to attend a one day a week training course to learn fostering skills, and she stated that on the day in question, having collected Elisha from her playschool, that she would take her back to my place, and would remain with her until my arrival home. She clearly had given all of this a lot of thought.

However, it then suddenly dawned on me that with Maria away, who would carry out Elisha's morning and evening ablutions? Lenka would not always be available due to her work commitments, and while I had assisted with this duty when my own kids were children, I didn't feel that it would be appropriate for me, an unrelated male foster parent, to have this kind of responsibility.

I am sure that the main reason why I was selected as a potential foster-parent in the first place was because Stockton & Brand were aware that I had two women living at home, one of whom has effectively carried out the role of *Substitutus Matrem Suam* (stand-in mother) from the day that Elisha arrived. Later, I mentioned these issues to Lenka and her jaw dropped.

Clearly concerned, she said, 'I hadn't thought about that. What she obviously needs is a long-term stable relationship with a couple who would in effect bring her up as their own. Either that or she must officially be put up for adoption.'

I really didn't like the idea of us discussing our dear little girl as though she had become a simple commodity, like some raw material that needed refining.

A little later, Lenka was in the mood for a couple of social libations and a little intellectual intercourse, but we settled on a couple of drinks at the Bread Bin and an initial meaningless chat with *Alfie the Dip* instead.

'Have you heard about Lenny?' he enquired, as Lenka and I entered the pub.

'No, I haven't Alfie.'

'He's just got divorced!'

'That would be a little difficult Alfie, since he hasn't got married yet,' I replied, giving Rosheen a little wave as she came into the bar from her office.

Giving me one of those vacant looks which have been known to confuse traffic wardens long enough to enable the escape of appreciative penalty-dodging motorists, and had on one occasion been responsible for an over-zealous first aider attempting to resuscitate him, he replied, 'Yeah well they couldn't get married could they? Ted told me they've been banned from the church!'

'I think that you are getting your wires crossed, Alfie,' I said. 'Probably what Ted told you was that they have been reading the Banns at the church.'

'Wass 'at then?' he replied.

Lenka thankfully joined in on the conversation. 'When a couple want to get married in the Church of England, it has to be announced in the church in which they intend to marry. This gives a chance for anyone to announce a reason why they should not lawfully marry. Their intention to marry is read out on three consecutive Sundays. It's an ancient tradition dating back over many centuries,' she said.

'So If I didn't want them to marry, I could say so!' said Alfie.

'Well not quite,' said Lenka. 'You have to present a justifiable reason why they can't be legally married. One of them could already be married for example, which would make the intended marriage illegal.'

'Bigotry, you mean! That's when a bloke has more than one wife,' Alfie said, smiling triumphantly.

'The word is bigamy, Alfie!' I said.

Taking a long guttural swig of his cider and lemonade, he belched resoundingly, and wiping an area of froth from his mouth with his jacket sleeve, which had earlier picked up an unidentifiable black mess of detritus, he liberally spread a large evil-smelling swathe of whatever it was across his chin, mouth and nose, the smell of which momentarily brought him to his senses. Looking around accusingly at those nearest to him he said, 'So what's the penalty for having two wives then?'

'Well apart from a considerable prison sentence, which the bloke in question might have desperate need of anyway,' I said.

'Have you ever thought about the dreadful suffering involved in having two bleedin mother-in-laws? That has to be punishment enough!' said Dave, who physically shuddered at the suggestion.

Ted arrived a little later and asked me to join him outside. I followed him out of the bar. He informed me that Dickie O'Toole, aka *The Tesco Kid*, had been remanded in custody on a charge of conspiracy to pervert the course of justice and sundry other offences. Like Albery's case, it would be heard at the Crown Court at some future date, and in the meantime he would once again be happily incarcerated at *Her Majesty's Pleasure.*

Ted was in court to witness the proceedings and from what he told me, Dickie appeared to be as happy as a mosquito in a nudist colony, and as he was led down, he smiled at Ted and gave him double thumbs-up. This didn't go unnoticed by an observant reporter from *The Kilburn Times,* who was covering the case, and on leaving the court, had foolishly questioned Ted about his relationship to the accused. Clearly the reply that Ted gave him could not be adequately expressed in terms of a simple or suitable euphemism and is definitely not for the ears of those with delicate or easily offended dispositions.

The charges against Frobisher have been dropped and it appears that he will be reinstated in his job. Basil is very happy with his client's innocence and release, although apparently he appeared to be a little confused as to why an elderly man like Dickie would want to frame Frobisher in the first place. He was convinced that there was more to this issue than was apparent, and how right he is!

As for me, it was all so bittersweet. On the one hand, I felt considerably relieved that an innocent man's life and reputation had not been ruined, and yet conversely I felt tremendous sadness that an unfortunate soul, who is frankly unable to cope with life on the outside, was once again back within the confines and deprivations of the only real home that he'd ever known. If ever there was a clear example of society's failure, it has to be personified in the very unfortunate life of Richard O'Toole. I sincerely hope that he will spend whatever time he has left in peace, contentment and happiness.

As Lenka and I made our way home, once again she held my hand. She seems to sense when I am feeling low, just like my dear old Spike, although I'm pleased to say that thankfully, my Lenka wouldn't be tempted to chew one of my table legs, or feel inclined to have a dump on the kitchen floor.

Goodnight, Ginny.
P xx

3rd April 2012

Good morning, Ginny

My day started off with the usual hilarious morning antics of Maria and Elisha, which had me laughing uncontrollably. I cannot think of a better way of starting a new day, and I am clinging on to a kaleidoscope of mental pictures of them, which I hope will be downloaded onto my subconscious *hard drive* for future recall and enjoyment.

I believe that true mental happiness can be achieved by erasing all saved distressing or unhappy images from the past and replacing them with happy recollections instead. In some instances, having a retentive memory is a useful thing, but perhaps not so for those unfortunate guilt-ridden individuals who have to continually suffer the torment of their former mistakes or regrets in life. They say that we often take for granted those things that we should cherish the most, which is perhaps the main reason why I unconsciously tend to count my blessings daily. As far as the impending loss of Maria from my life and daily routine, with all that goes with it, I am quite literally treasuring what could be our last memorable moments together.

As she left to take Elisha to school, I asked her if she'd like to join me for a little trip down to the South Bank for a couple of hours, and on the way back we could collect Elisha together and take her to McDonald's for an evening meal. She was all for the idea.

A little later, we were on the first of our southbound buses en route to Victoria, where a little later we changed for another that took us over Vauxhall Bridge. We arrived at London Bridge at around 10:35.

It was a beautiful day weather wise, and although it was a little chilly, particularly near the river, the sky was blue, there was not a cloud in the sky, and the sun shone down on us benevolently.

We called into the Swan and as a fitting memory, I suggested a visit to St Paul's Cathedral and a little later, we crossed over the Millennium Footbridge to Sir Christopher Wren's masterpiece. It was a perfect day to fulfil the last of my outstanding lifelong ambitions in life: to climb to the very pinnacle of this magnificent structure. Maria was all for joining in on this once in a lifetime experience.

Having walked through the beautiful nave, we started the initial climb up to the Whispering, Gallery which was the first of the three viewing platforms. Then the going got a little more strenuous up a steep winding staircase to the Stone Gallery, and finally up a steep almost vertical ladder to the Golden Gallery which is 85.4 metres or around 280 feet above the Cathedral floor.

As fit as he was, I am sure that even Sherpa Tenzing would have needed a bit of a sit down had he climbed up with us. As that old saying has it:

'Life is not measured by the breaths we take, but by the moments that take our breath away.'

Our 528-step, twelve-minute climb (with a couple of rest periods in between) certainly proved the truth behind this saying. At the top, we were both quite literally gasping for breath like two old forge bellows, but the beautiful view of London that was presented far below us quite literally took our breath away. It is an experience that will remain with me for the rest of my life.

At that truly memorable point in time, I felt a quite overwhelming compulsion to hold my beloved Maria close, and I surprised her momentarily with my affectionate cuddle, as I whispered:

'Do you know, just how much I love you, my darling?' to which she replied:

'Nearly as much as I love you, my Paul!'

The tension was broken when she said, 'I'll race you to the bottom,' and with a display of amazing agility, she bounded down the first group of steps, and her laughter echoed resoundingly as she made her way down.

At the bottom, we were greeted by a couple of very miserable looking officials. One had a dead-pan expression and the other looked like he had sucked a dozen lemons for breakfast.

'Have you forgotten that this is the house of God?' he asked.

'Indeed not sir!' I replied. 'I am sorry if we have been a bit noisy, but I'm sure that even the Almighty wouldn't mind us rejoicing in this his magnificent temple!'

Thereafter we were reunited with secular society, and on our way back to the homestead. At the bus stop, Maria held my hand briefly and kissed me three times on the cheek which was accompanied by her usual verbal MWAH! MWAH! MWAH!

We collected Elisha from her playschool at 13:00 and a slight structural adjustment ensued with Elisha walking in between Maria and I. She was soon swinging in between us like a young gymnast on a trapeze. She giggled delightfully just about all of the way along the High Road, and once at our destination, my left arm was as limp and lifeless as *Wino Lucy's* legs following a lunchtime session on the Bulgarian *Pisse-Druppa Beaujolais.*

We had a relatively early dinner at McDonald's and Elisha took over, ordering various dishes which on previous visits she had sampled. I have to say that her choices were very good indeed, and not being too keen on what they refer to as *fast food,* I was pleasantly surprised at the quality and quantity of the fare.

On our way home later, I received a phone call from Muhulin who appeared to be in a very distressed condition. She stated that she needed to see me urgently. We therefore arranged to meet up again at the *Coffee & Cream* restaurant in the High Road at around 18:30.

I dropped the girls off at home at around 16:45 and then sauntered off to the pub. The Gay Bar was relatively quiet, with Dave and Ted in attendance. They were engaged in conversation as I entered.

'He has the personality of a mop in a bucket of *urine!'* said Ted authoritatively.

'That's a bit unfair, mate,' said Dave, 'I think he's alright. Least wise he's never done me any harm.'

Needless to say, I never did find out who they were talking about, since as per usual, the subject matter changed with boring predictability, and neither of them paid me any attention as I entered. I am beginning to fully appreciate the truth in the saying that 'the older that a person gets, the more invisible they become!'

'And a very good evening to you both too!' I said sarcastically, ordering a pint from the ever-attentive Vlado, who shook my hand as I arrived at the bar.

Nudging Dave, Ted said, 'I thought that alcoholics were supposed to be anonymous?'

Smiling contemptuously, I took a seat at the bar, winked at Vlado and replied, 'Save your breath Ted, you'll need it to blow up your girlfriend later!'

An elderly chap sitting by the cigarette machine, whom I'd not seen before, started to laugh, and eventually regaining his composure he said, 'I'll have to remember that one, it was very funny!'

To laugh at a friend is a normal and an acceptable part of male camaraderie, but to have a complete stranger laugh at a shy and sensitive person like Eduardo Filepe Cordona, aka *Ted the Pleb,* and to get away with it unchallenged, was pushing his luck to the extreme.

Ted glared at him menacingly, and to prevent any suggestion of a potential nasty altercation, I walked across to the stranger and introduced myself to him. Sitting down at his table, I engaged him in conversation and found out later that he was a retired schoolteacher by the name of Jack Siddall, who had recently moved into the area from Scunthorpe.

It didn't take him long to ingratiate himself with Ted and Dave, which he carried out with humour and considerable dignity, although buying them both a pint with a large whiskey chaser, slightly tipped the uncertain balance in his favour. He came across as a very nice bloke, and within an hour or so he was chatting and laughing with us as though he had known us all for years. I had a feeling that he was destined to become an additional cherished member of our team.

I bade them all farewell at 18:10 and hastened along the High Road to the *Coffee & Cream* restaurant, where I met up with a very tearful Muhulin.

As I entered, she rushed into my arms sobbing pitifully. Fortunately, the restaurant was very quiet, and apart from the waitress, the two other customers adopted a typical Kilburn response and stirring their coffees with evident nonchalance, appeared to be completely disinterested and simply looked away. This kind of behaviour accounts for the fact that Kilburn has the lowest incidence of broken noses or black eyes in the northern hemisphere, although a typical Kilburnian can be readily distinguished from other Londoners, in that apart from retaining their natural good looks and innate charm, most of them have rather large ears.

Sitting her down at a table at the rear of the restaurant, I ordered us two coffees and a couple of *Goblin Buns* (which are bigger than fairy cakes). Having regained her composure sufficiently, she apologised profusely and then went on to say that overnight Jasmine had unexpectedly suffered a heart attack, and despite the best efforts of the in-house medical team, she had sadly passed away.

Naturally, I was very sorrowful at hearing this unexpected news and I tried my very best to comfort her. A little later she mentioned Jasmine's former husband, a bloke called Nabil. I was very surprised to learn that Muhulin had been in regular contact with him from the time that he had left the family home. From what she told me, I had clearly got his story all wrong. I was under the impression that he had abandoned Jasmine after she had been diagnosed with multiple sclerosis.

Muhulin told me that the reason why Nabil had left, and had then subsequently divorced her, was due to her very open proclivity for clandestine affairs, and her almost insatiable attraction for other men. Nabil naturally couldn't cope with the anxiety and distress that this caused him, and all of this happened some two years before she had been diagnosed with MS.

Apparently it broke his heart to leave the children, although he has continued to provide for them financially ever since the divorce. Where all of this money had gone is a mystery, since Jasmine never appeared to have a pot to *urinate* in, or a window to chuck it out of. When he was told that his son had been put into care, he subsequently filed for custody, and given Jasmine's condition, this was granted. Muhmud is now living with him and attends a special needs school, where he is apparently doing well.

The conversation then turned to Elisha. Muhulin told me that being her next of kin, Nabil will be likewise filing for custody, and it seems highly likely that this too will be granted. Sadly, we will miss her a great deal, but then I am so very happy for this beautiful little girl who has brought such happiness and joy into our lives. She will always hold a very special place in our affection.

Frankly, I really didn't like the uncertainty that was forever looming over her, and hopefully she will now have a normal life in the bosom of a loving family. Nabil hasn't married again, although Muhulin told me that his partner (Katie) loves children, so it all looks very promising indeed.

As we were leaving, the waitress smiled at us and said, 'Don't worry folks, I'm sure it will all work out for the best. Jasmine's dad sounds like a very nice bloke, and remember, young children are so very adaptable. You'll be laughing about all of this in a couple of weeks!'

The other couple gave us a supportive smile and a little wave as we left.

When I got back home, my four girls were in Maria's room watching a cartoon DVD called *The Little Fairy Princess* Well three of them were, Jimena was curled up in a tight little ball, fast asleep on the windowsill.

Not wishing to disturb them, I quietly slipped into my room, and putting my audio headphones on, I listened to Mozart's *Requiem*, which didn't exactly lift my wretched mental condition, in fact it simply heightened my sadness and sense of impending loss. I really am not looking forward to telling Maria this distressing news, and wondered if this might be an opportune time to take a short break away on holiday. A six-month safari in Kenya would probably fit the bill rather nicely.

Goodnight, Ginny.
P xx

4th April 2012

Good morning, Ginny.

My initial attempts at sleep last night were a little futile, but that was to be expected I suppose, given the considerable amount of mental anguish that I had suffered earlier. My mind searched for a way of dealing with our impending loss of Elisha, and more particularly how this would affect my dear Maria. Even my usual cognac-laced cocoa had little or no effect.

Jimena had decided that rather than sleep in the girl's room, she would occupy the lower half of my bed, but as mentioned before, she has a bit of previous for attacking toes under the duvet, and every time that I changed position, the slightest movement of my feet resulted in a swiftly executed attack, which frightened the life out of me each time. Fortunately, the thickness of my duvet's fibres provides adequate protection from her little claws and teeth.

At 02:20, having been roused from my slumber by yet another aerial attack on my feet, I decided to get up. As I got out of bed, Jimena crept stealthily under my duvet, presumably looking for the phantom that was hiding someone at the bottom. It was quite amusing watching her shape warily making its way towards her anticipated prey, and she clearly didn't know what to expect.

As she neared the end of the bed, I ran my hand cautiously under the duvet and tickled her bum. This clearly startled her since she screamed in alarm and shot out from under the duvet like an ejaculation of toothpaste from an over-squeezed tube. She dashed up to the top of my bedroom curtains in record time, panting heavily. The pupils of her eyes were wide and black with annoyance, and she looked about as pissed off as a mosquito in a mannequin factory.

While I did not intend to alarm or hurt her in any way, it was just what I needed to release my pent-up feelings of frustration, and it temporarily lifted my spirits immeasurably. However, it took me quite a time thereafter to extricate her from the curtains, and to stop myself giggling like an adolescent schoolboy.

Having eventually managed to prise her from my curtains, I gently lifted her down. She rushed to my bedroom door and looked back at me appealingly. I let her out into the hall, and quietly opening Maria's bedroom door, she vanished into the darkness, where her natural curiosity would no longer be aroused and her safety therefore assured.

Since it is clear that 'an action will inevitably cause a reaction', I realised later that due to my puerile behaviour, my former beautiful feline sleeping companion would not be too keen on spending another night on my duvet, and therefore any further opportunity for me to cement the bond between us has been irrevocably lost. From here on, I shall have to be especially nice to her. Which might be a bit of a problem, since I am always nice to her anyway.

I was back into bed at 03:25 and despite my feelings of guilt and remorse, I went out like a light and slept heavily, until the delightful sounds of Elisha's unfettered laughter awoke me again at 07:10.

As I lay there in the semi darkness, it suddenly struck me that the way to alleviate the dreadful sadness that Maria would inevitably suffer would be to pre-empt this eventuality, by implanting in her mind the very real observation that what Elisha needed most in her life was the love, guidance and protection of a normal family environment.

As with most tragedies in life, it is the initial shock of it all that causes the most distress, and I felt sure that Maria would be inconsolable at having to deal with the loss of our sweet little child, which for her, would be as distressing as the bereavement of her own beloved daughter. Likewise, I am sure that Elisha would also be dreadfully upset at losing the only real mother-figure that she has ever known. However, I consoled myself slightly when I remembered the reassuring words of that eavesdropping nosey waitress at the café, '*Young children are so very adaptable*,' she asserted, and frankly looking at a woman who appeared to have been through life's mangle a few times, I believed that she knew what she was talking about.

Apart from perhaps a like-minded group of randy swingers, nobody likes change, but I was resolute in my determination to find an answer. We have a very appropriate aphorism in English which states *Little strokes fell great oaks* and by adopting this truism, I will likewise use a little systematic brainwashing to periodically introduce negative statements with regard to the uncertainty of Elisha's future, should she remain in our care.

It is clear that Nabil will have to go through the Family Law Courts to get legal custody of our little girl, although frankly I see this as a mere formality. Thankfully this process will take a little time which will be very useful, since it will give me the space to put my plans into operation.

Time is of the essence, and I shall put my first suggestive seed into the compost of hope over breakfast. However, before I could put my plan into action, I received a rather disturbing phone call from that maestro of the anti-climax and accomplished orator in the art of spontaneous diatribe, Alfred John Tillington, aka *Alfie the Dip*. Initially he questioned the parentage and integrity of his former employer, whom it would appear had dispensed with his services following an in-house investigation into the systematic disappearance of entire packets of ginger nuts from his desk drawer, and a box of toilet roles from his office bathroom.

Without seemingly taking another breath, he then went into another sizeable rant about Ted, who had apparently been taking 'electrocution lessons' and now speaks 'all posh and plummy like a butler with a silver spoon up his bum!' He ended the call on a positive note however, asking for a short-term loan of £500, repayable over a twelve-month period, with a two per cent *'confounded interest rate'*.

I finished the call by assuring him of my future support, but as for the present, could he kindly *'GO AWAY AND PREFERABLY NOT MULTIPLY!'* (or words to that effect).

Lenka was working last night, and her bedroom door was closed when I got up, so she was clearly sleeping.

After their fun-filled time together in the shower, both Elisha and Maria presented themselves in the kitchen at 08:00, looking expectantly hungry as did Jimena, although in her case, I felt that the look she gave me was bordering on one of contemptuous disdain. However, it softened when I placed an extra-loaded bowl of food down for her.

As usual, my breakfast experience was both entertaining and joyful. Elisha's almost endless ticker-tape reminiscences of her recent experiences were both interesting and amusing. Out of the earshot of Elisha, as they were about to leave for her playschool, I simply mentioned to Maria how well that Elisha had settled in with us, and pointed out that as a short-term measure, this had been very useful. However, I suggested that it would be far better for Elisha to be living with a proper family of her own!

She smiled at me complacently and whispered, 'That would be a bit of a problem. Her mummy is not well and cannot be to look after her properly. Her daddy is done a runner and gone, and her brother is like a rabbit running all around the place in March! That's why she has *us* instead!' They both left a little later.

Well, my first tentative step into the art of brainwashing went down with a bang like a fat kid on a seesaw, and didn't exactly go as expected. Still, there's a long way to go yet and I will keep presenting those little strokes that hopefully will eventually wear her down enough to get her out of her comfort zone, and to finally topple her resistance and reluctance to change.

While my *Ernie* wound is still a little tender, I thought that I'd pay a very overdue visit to my gym for a poach in the steam room, followed by a shave and a refreshing shower.

Danielle, our beautiful receptionist, appeared to be genuinely pleased at seeing me, and she gave me a very warm and affectionate cuddle on my arrival.

It has been some time since I saw Lenny, and I was very pleased to find him on the rowing machine. He was looking very fit indeed, and he confessed that daily exercise has made him a new man. Perhaps it was just my imagination, but he seemed to be more intelligent since the last time that we had met, which I think, was our meal together when I was introduced to his beautiful fiancée Eugenia.

He seemed vibrant and very self-assured, and totally unlike the blathering idiot of a few months ago. He made the comment that, 'Exercise and boozing were similar in many ways, they both produced feel-good sensations.' He confessed that he had become a bit of an *endorphin junkie,* and that out of the two, he would prefer a good old workout, instead of a pint of unnecessary alcohol!

Clearly Eugenia was straightening him out splendidly. Since being with her, he had curtailed a considerable number of his filthy habits (which I won't go into) and he has even suggested the possibility of avoiding alcohol altogether.

I was absolutely astounded when, having clearly committed it to memory, he quoted an entry that Samuel Pepys, the seventeenth century diarist had apparently made, following a dry January:

'Thanks be to God, since leaving drinking of wine, I do find myself much better, and do mind my business better, and do spend less money, and less time in idle company.'

After my ablutions, we met up in the reception area and on leaving he stated that the wedding will take place at 14:00 on Saturday 21st April, and it was to be a formal affair. He advised me to hire a black tuxedo, white shirt and black bow tie from Moss Bros, and he would reimburse me the costs. He reminded me that as his best man, I should read up on my duties, and to prepare an appropriate speech for the evening reception (which apparently will be held in our estate hall).

At 11:50, as I walked across the road to the Gay Bar, I really could not believe the miraculous change that has taken place in one of life's congenital unfortunates, and clearly this has been due to the love and guidance of a very special woman, and I couldn't be more genuinely happy for him.

The Gay Bar was completely empty when I arrived until the arrival of another very special woman appeared in the shape of Zora-Aleena, who welcomed me enthusiastically. She shook my hand warmly and greeted me in what I would suggest was very passable English. She informed me that she was meeting up with Lenka for a 'working lunch', and it seems that this is now a regular occurrence in her social calendar. This not only provides her with consistent lessons in English, but also provides her with much needed confidence-building exercises.

I gather that Vlado is pretty impressed with her progress thus far, as evidenced by allowing her to take a more active hands-on share in the day to day running of the pub. A few short weeks ago, he wouldn't have dreamt of leaving her alone in the place while he nipped off to the cash & carry, but clearly that is what he had done this morning due to his absence from the place.

This amazing bit of simple deduction had me thinking about Basil (not erotically you understand) and as if by some strange telepathic coincidence, he phoned me a little later. He asked me if I'd be free to have a meet-up later in the day, and checking my diary and finding that I had nothing pressing, I agreed to meet him at the Glass House pub after *Happy Hour* at around 17:30.

I wasn't really in the mood for alcohol this morning, so I had an orange juice and a bag of wild duck and cucumber flavoured crisps instead. Vlado arrived a little later. He gave me a perfunctory smile as he struggled into the bar carrying two heavily laden shopping bags. His face was bright red and he was panting like a lizard on a hot rock.

'You need a few sessions at my gym, Vlado,' I called, as he vanished behind the bar.

Dropping the bags noisily, he looked back at me and sighed. 'No Paul,' he said, trying to catch his breath.' I need a body of the dog, to do all of my hard pub's work!'

My thoughts immediately turned to Alfie, who having recently joined the ranks of the *vocationally idle,* may have need of a little gainful employment in the near future. As a secondary consideration, getting him back into work might alleviate his immediate need to deplete my limited financial resources, which I am wholeheartedly in favour of, particularly since David 'Borough' would have more chance of shoving cooked spaghetti up a shag's bum, than I would have in getting it back.

'I may have the dog's... I mean, man, that you need Vlado! (Crossing my fingers) A local man with impeccable credentials,' I said, taking another sip of my orange juice.

'I am not bothering if he is a star in the films, but he must be happy to break his back with the energy and eagerly hear me when I call him names!' he replied.

I kind of understood what he was trying to say, although, perhaps my Lenka could give him a few pointers with regard to elementary English diction and advanced employment law, particularly as it affects employers in cases brought against them for unlawful employment practices (which I feel that he may have need of anon). I also thought that a course in SBESFL (Stress-Busting Exercises for Speakers of Foreign Languages) might also prove useful.

I met Basil at 17:30 as arranged, and he seemed genuinely pleased to see me, as I was him.

The main bar was in a disgusting mess and looked like a group of marauding elephants had passed through it. The indescribably rank smell was positively disgusting. Frankly, I felt a little nauseous.

Sensing my discomfort, he pointed to the door. We were back out into the relatively clean carbon-monoxide-infused air of Cricklewood Broadway a little later.

Being a relatively warm evening, we decided to make for the Gay Bar, and it was a pleasant walk. Our conversation revolved around matters of an inconsequential nature, and saturation point was reached within ten minutes or so. Thereafter, it took on a more serious direction.

He started to question me about Ted, and in no time at all I was feeling very apprehensive indeed. Given his legal experience, his interrogation was tactfully indirect and I found myself giving him guarded answers. When asked how I would describe Ted's typical characteristics, I replied honestly in that from my own personal experience he had always been of an entrepreneurial disposition, ever on the lookout for money-making opportunities. He was the personification of *a rough diamond*, in that while he was lacking in manners, style or grace, he was of a kindly disposition. His general character was that of a typical Kilburnian (apart from having relative small ears) and he was known for his generosity and caring demeanour for those whom he deemed less fortunate or unable to fend for themselves. In essence, he was a shining example of an altruistic, tender-hearted individual. From the time of his breech birth, where he sadly lost his mother, and following a very tumultuous childhood, he learned to fend for himself, and developed considerable strengths and abilities when it came to dealing with life's challenges, and fearlessly confronted any problems that came his way. Suffice it to say, he was not a man to suffer fools gladly, particularly those who had no consideration for their own safety, or that had a particular fondness for hospital cuisine.

As we neared the Gay Bar, he seemed satisfied with my candour since he changed the subject. But on peering into the bar, he saw Alfie and 'suddenly remembered' an urgent appointment. Just before he left, he whispered, 'I'll cut to the chase Paul. Is Ted capable of fitting a person up?'

'We are all capable of doing that, Basil,' I replied, trying to be as direct and yet as non-committal as I could.

He smiled at me wryly, and putting an index finger up to the side of his nose, he tapped it a couple of times and said, 'Thanks for your help, Paul. It was good to see you again.' He hailed a passing cab and left.

As I walked into the bar, I breathed a sigh of relief. And without wishing to sound unkind, I took one look at Alfie and, like Basil, I also 'suddenly remembered' an urgent appointment, and before he could utter a word, I hastily left the premises.

Later, I actually read Elisha a bedtime story, which I enjoyed a great deal. Elisha was a little non-committal either way, although she did mention that Lenka was the best at storytelling and she didn't even need a book. Lenka heard her comments as she passed through the hall and laughed. She came into the bedroom and thankfully took over from me.

Maria was sitting out on the balcony, so I thought that I'd have another attempt at a little *oak-felling,* and this time she wasn't so confidently assertive, and initially appeared to be open to a little positive suggestion. I simply mentioned the fact that while I was relatively young at heart, other parts of my anatomy were considerably older and some were well past their use by date.

She looked at me sympathetically and tried to make light of this obvious truth. But clearly it had touched a raw nerve, since for a time she was lost in thought.

A little later, I went on to the attack again and casually mentioned that, 'I'd had a good life, with few regrets, and that if I passed away tomorrow, I'd be the fittest looking bloke in the mortuary and the happiest new arrival in the nest.' She clearly didn't understand what I was talking about until I reminded her of my lifelong love of the gym, and then went on to clarify the matter in relation to my belief in reincarnation and my hope that I would be reborn as a bird. And since I was halfway there as it were, I suggested that a likely or possible candidate could be *The Bald Eagle*.

Her eyes started to well up with tears and I rushed across to comfort her, however I realised that this was not an expression of intense sadness, but on the contrary, it was due to her attempting to restrain her laughter. Suddenly the noise she made was comparable with a drunken alpine yodeller who had inadvertently trapped his dick in the zip of his new lederhosen, and from such a slight frame she emitted an unbelievably loud tsunami of discordant and raucous screams, which echoed through the courtyard of the estate, much to the consternation of the residents. Within minutes, many of them were hanging out of their windows, frantically searching for the cause of this unwelcome disturbance.

Lenka and Elisha rushed out to the balcony in alarm, and grabbing Maria's hand, I pulled her up from her seat and pushed her and my two other girls back into the relative safety of the flat.

Thereafter, we all dispersed into our own private rooms, and as I could still hear Maria's laughter, I plugged my earphones into my Walkman CD player and listened to The Brighouse and Rastrick Brass Band, which negated all other sounds.

Later as I went to bed, my ears were buzzing like an old fridge on its way out, and the pulsating throbbing noise in my head felt like a bomb was about to go off. But the distinctively rousing mellow sounds of a British brass band are quite beautiful. It certainly clears away any mental cobwebs, and when listened to using headphones, it is pre-eminently useful in loosening stubborn ear wax as well.

Goodnight, Ginny.
P xx

5th April 2012

Good morning, Ginny.

I was wide awake at 01:10 this morning thinking about Alfie, and more particularly how I could cunningly divert the potential loss of five hundred very dear friends of mine. However, I was in a bit of a quandary. I realised that my actions yesterday were based on panic rather than rational considerations, since when it became clear that Vlado was looking for help in the bar, without thinking, my own selfish thoughts turned to Alfie. Clearly, in the short term, getting him back into gainful employment would alleviate the immediate threat to my limited financial resources. But there are far greater issues at stake here, notably my self-respect and reputation.

At 01:20 I decided to have a chat with him about it, since as they say, 'There's no time like the present!' Besides, he has made it very evident that he likes a little stimulating conversation (earlier than most) so I thought that I'd give him a call.

His mobile phone rang twice, and then I heard him say, 'You have reached the voicemail of Alfred Tillington. Kindly leave your message after the beep.' There wasn't one!

'Good morning, Alfie,' I said cheerfully. 'I am feeding the Fringillas earlier this morning, so I thought that I'd give you a call.'

'Cor blimey! You are a martyr to them hamsters,' he said, sounding very light-hearted and alert.

'I know that you are a busy boy, Alfie,' I said, 'but I wondered if you'd like to join me for a spot of breakfast this morning at the café?'

'That'll be nice, mate,' he replied. 'But they are not open yet, are they?'

'No Alfie, Brenda is probably still happily ensconced in her staple.' I said.

'Actually, that's quite lucky cos I'd run out of milk, and eating dry Weetabix is *effin* horrible,' he said. 'And take it from me, mate, porridge made with water isn't much better!'

We arranged to meet at Brenda's café at 10:00. Thereafter, I slept on until the dawn chorus (which turned out to be a single asthmatic wood pigeon coughing) awoke me at 06:30.

Our own usual break-fest followed, although I simply had a cup of coffee. Sitting opposite me at the kitchen table, with her first mouthful of various culinary delights, Maria cautiously looked up at me, and finding me looking back at her enquiringly, she suddenly coughed out her semi-masticated food in my general direction. I tried to duck, but to no avail. She rushed out of the room, laughing hysterically, and Elisha just sat there in stunned silence.

Having cleaned myself and the table top as best I could, Maria cautiously re-emerged from the hall, looking very embarrassed indeed. 'I'm so sorry, Paul,' she said, with no real conviction in her voice. 'I can't get Bald Eagle out of my head!'

As arranged, I met Alfie at the café, and we had an enjoyable full-English breakfast each. Thereafter, I engaged him in probably the first real *fatherly chat* that he's ever had. I'll give you a short account of what transpired between us. I simply mentioned that Vlado was looking for an honest, dependable and hard-working man to assist him in his daily duties at the pub.

'And you thought of me!' he said, excitedly.

Being as straightforward as I could, I said, 'Well you are the only bloke I know who is currently a *Pro-Bono TV Remote Control Tester,*' I replied.

'That's so kind of you, mate,' he said. 'I was seriously beginning to wonder where me next bottle of milk would be coming from.'

'They don't sell milk at the pub, Alfie,' I said, 'which, given your penchant for purloining anything that isn't screwed down, is just as well. And, I hasten to add, Vlado does not have any secret caches of ginger nuts either!'

'Oh you heard about that,' he said. 'I dunno what all the fuss was about, I mean it was only a few packets of biscuits!'

'What about the toilet rolls then?' I asked.

'Well I bought meself a toilet roll holder for Christmas, and I thought it'd be nice to put some *real* toilet paper on it.'

'Christmas, Alfie?' I said in amazement. 'If you haven't used toilet paper since Christmas, what have you been using to wipe your...?'

Newspaper!' he replied. 'A quality newspaper though, not one of them tits 'n' bums jobbies, I have always preferred the broodshits.'

'The word is *broadsheets,* Alfie,' I said.

'*The Times* offers its readership an unbiased, objective and balanced view on world events, and having cut it up into bite-sized pieces so to speak, one single edition with give me over three weeks of very useful *spankerchief bumba-klarts,* as me old Jamaica friend Winston would say. It also is keeping me tits up on current local and international affairs.'

'I think the word that you're looking for Alfie is *abreast,*' I said. 'But that aside, I have to say, that your use of the English language is generally improving Alfie, and I am more than simply impressed at your imaginative rhetorical eloquence. It is not what I have come to expect from you at all.'

'Well it might start to go downhill now that I have proper toilet paper,' he said. 'I mean, there's nothing to read on it!'

Losing interest in any further discussion on this particular subject, I stated that I would be willing to put his name forward to Vlado, but if he was to let me down, that I would immediately pass the issue over to a very good friend of mine called *Big-Juri,* who would undoubtedly introduce him to his pigs.

'I love pigs!' he said excitedly.

'Believe me Alfie, you wouldn't like these ones very much!' I replied.

Before we parted, he asked me for a two-pound loan to buy a bottle of milk, and then as a secondary thought (there wouldn't be a third) he asked if he could have an additional two pounds for a box of Weetabix. I gave him a tenner together with a Sainsbury's voucher which I found in my wallet. It gave the fortunate owner a two-pound reduction when spending eleven pounds on milk and cereals.

Back at home a little later, I had a phone call from Simon Stockton from social services, asking me to pop in and see him. He said that it was 'rather urgent'.

I arrived at the social services offices again at midday. I was invited into his office a little later, and after the usual pleasantries had been dispensed with, he got down to business.

He told me that Elisha's father (Nabil Al Tajir) had filed for custody of his daughter, which didn't come as any real shock. I explained to him that Muhulin, Jasmine's niece, had kept me informed with regard to his custody of Mahmud and the probable impending custody of Elisha.

Simon stated that Nabil would like to meet me and Elisha whom he hadn't seen since she was three years old, before the custody issue was settled. I commented that it would be nice for Maria to accompany us, since she had been so actively involved in Elisha's life, and I couldn't help myself, I was suddenly overcome with *emulsion,* and had to wipe a couple of tears away. Simon's frumpy-dumpling assistant Emily kindly gave me a couple of tissues, and I felt so very embarrassed. But then I am sure that Stockton and Brand are no strangers to the lamentations of others. Their chosen profession has to be one of the most heart-rending and emotional of occupations known to man, and I am sure that there have been many occasions when they too have had to reach for the tissues. Thankfully there wasn't a toilet roll to be seen anywhere, although I did notice a current copy of *The Times* resting on the top of a briefcase.

For security reasons, Simon suggested that the meeting should take place in his office, which I was more than happy about. He will contact both me and Nabil to arrange a mutually convenient date and time in the 'very near' future.

On leaving, Simon shook my hand and thanked me for my cooperation, and Emily held my other hand tenderly as she escorted me to the door. Women seem to be doing that quite a lot recently. Is it because like one of them sniffer dogs, they can sense that something is medically wrong? Or is it that they simply feel safe in the presence of a stereotypical pipe and slippers pensioner, with his (assumed) loss of sexual libido – age-related low testosterone level, and shrivelled up nob with more wrinkles than a Californian raisin? The fact that he carries a *London Transport Freedom Pass* doesn't exactly help in dispelling these erroneous beliefs, since the general consensus among discerning women is that even if he were nice looking, oozing with charisma, and well off... being over sixty, he probably wouldn't be able to raise a gallop anyway!

I called into The Magpie on my way home and had a long chat to Vlado about Alfie. Without telling any *porkies,* I gave it to him straight, stating that like us all, he had his faults, but he wasn't a lazy man and I felt that provided he was made to feel like *part of the team* he would prove himself a very useful person to have around.

Fortunately, Vlado has always liked Alfie, and in common with the rest of his customers, he knows little or nothing about his previous life or calling, and that's just as well!

Before I'd taken a sip of my beer, Ted arrived. He was dressed very smartly indeed, wearing a grey shirt with a contrasting grey and white striped tie, a pair of black trousers with razor-sharp creases, a pair of shiny black patent-leather shoes, and a black blazer, with an unknown heraldic crest emblazoned on its left breast pocket.

In a very plummy voice he said, 'Good afternoon, Mr Shaughnessy, I hope that you are as well as you look!'

'Alright Ted, what's going on?' I said.

'I have enrolled as a trainee toastmaster and I have my first assignment this afternoon.'

'Oh, I see, that's what Alfie meant about you talking all plummy and posh!'

Dave suddenly appeared out of the loo area, doing up his flies. 'Oh Gawd not another money-making project. What happened to the doughnuts on wheels venture?' he said.

'On my first day of business, my one and only employee had a rather nasty accident with a drunken cyclist! I gave up the idea afterwards because the skates were ruined and my one operative had a broken ankle. I landed up having to give away a veritable fortune in doughnuts,' he said bitterly.

'Well, we didn't get any of them!' said Dave, clearly disappointed.

'So where are you going for your first and probably your last assignment, in the exciting world of the itinerant toastmaster?' I said sarcastically.

'It's a society wedding in Stratford,' he replied.

'You're having a laugh!' said Dave in disbelief. 'The East End is the *anal-orifice* of London, and Stratford is halfway up it! The only nobs that you are likely to encounter in Stratford mate are those naughty little things that you might be secretly looking at in the urinal next to yours!' said Dave, chuckling to himself.

At around 14:45, Lenka arrived with Zora-Aleena. Having bid a very fond farewell to Lenka, she gave me a little wave and disappeared behind the bar. I gave my Lenka a hug and brought her up to date with regard to Elisha. She took the news better than I had expected, and was genuinely happy particularly since our little girl would be finally reunited with her own family once again.

Being the coward that I am, I asked her to stay with me when I broke the news to Maria, and felt that like an irritating bronchial infection, the quicker I got it off my chest the better. I phoned Maria to make sure that she'd be home this evening. Elisha has her bedtime story at around 19:00 so I asked her to make herself available for a meeting with Lenka and me at around 20:00. She was more than a little inquisitive, but I simply told her that it was nothing to worry about.

At 19:45, Lenka and I returned home to find Maria patiently waiting for us in the lounge. Elisha had fallen asleep some twenty minutes before. As perceptive as ever, as we sat down she said, 'It's about Elisha, isn't it!' I nodded, and then gave her a comprehensive rundown of the issue.

She sat there patiently listening, and at the end of my ten-minute explanation, she gave me an embarrassed smile and then burst into tears. Lenka gave her an affectionate cuddle and whispered, 'It's all for the best, Maria,' to which she tearfully replied, 'I know it is. But I shall miss her so much!'

'We all shall, love,' I said. 'Now, all that has to be done is to tell Elisha.'

'I'll do that,' Maria said confidently. 'I'll make her so excited to see her daddy again!'

I really was so very moved at her response and the maturity that she has shown, in what for her must be a particularly difficult emotional time (bless her little wooden maracas).

Just before we all said goodnight, Maria tearfully said, 'If I do move in with Gabriel, do you think that I could take Jimena with me?'

I looked at Lenka who nodded her approval, and smiling at her I said, 'Of course you can, my darling.' She gave us both a wonderful hug and quietly made for her bedroom.

Before getting into bed, I realised that like my erroneous belief that *Whispering Jim's* life would fall apart following his departure from The Magpie, my estimation of Maria's response to the news of Elisha's impending departure was likewise hopelessly wrong. She has displayed a level of strength and resilience that one would expect to find in a more seasoned adult, and I couldn't be more proud of her. I just hope that I will be able to match the same level of maturity when I have to bid farewell to her and Jimena.

Goodnight, Ginny.
P xx

6th April 2012

Good morning, sugarplum.

I switched my mobile phone on this morning at 06:25 and found that I had a missed call from Alfie, which was timed at 02:39 (the *pud-wapper*). Having clearly not received a reply, he then sent me the following text, which I thought I should send to you for posterity.

> 02:44. I tryed to fone you, but u did nt speek so I fort to sed a txt.
> I fink at I hav got a job at tha pub wiv LADO. I start at ate
> So must go aslip an see yoo arfter.

At times like these, one really has to appreciate just how wonderfully fulfilling life can be. With people like Alfred J. Tillington in one's immediate circle of friends... Sorry love, I am just being a little facetious. In all honesty, my life would be considerably duller without his involvement in my daily activities, and like *Whispering Jim,* he would be sadly missed if he were no longer around. As stated before, most of my favourite friends are lovable quirky eccentrics and I wouldn't have them any other way.

But seriously, life can be so interesting given the way that nothing ever seems to remain constant or certain, well apart from death and taxation that is. Change is inevitable (well never from a condom machine in a pub toilet that is). And clearly in a crowded hostelry, nobody would be thick-skinned enough to complain about it. Well apart from one possible candidate (who I'm sure thinks that they are party balloons anyway). Bless his little restocked toilet roll holder!

Yesterday at around this time, I was contemplating a breakfast and a modicum of stimulating conversation with the aforementioned lost soul, who is an absolute bundle of effluent humour and non-rhetorical wit. This morning, apart from Elisha's excited reminiscences of her playschool adventures, our breakfast was a pretty sombre affair. Maria was very quiet indeed, and I guessed that she was working on her master plan to gently ease Elisha into accepting the prospect of living with a real family once again.

Being Good Friday, Elisha is off now for her Easter break, and Maria and Lenka are going to take her for a visit to Madame Tussauds to see the waxworks, followed by a visit to Regents Park. I gave Lenka twenty pounds to help out with the costs.

I too felt in need of another mooch, and an hour or so later, I was aimlessly strolling around Borough Market.

Apparently, it is one of the oldest food markets in London dating back to the twelfth century. At this time of the day, it is usually busy with sight-seeing tourists with not a local in sight. But then it was a little after 11:30 and the lunchtime office rabble, colloquially called the *half of bitter and watercress roll brigade,* had not yet left their offices, bent on inflicting their oxygen diverting and annoying space-invading bodies on the innocent and unsuspecting visitors.

The Market is a vibrant and exciting place, and an ideal venue to sample the vast array of al- fresco food from an almost overwhelming supply of street-food vendors. There is even an area charmingly called *The Farmer's Market,* where outrageously priced but good-quality fruit and vegetables are to be found in abundance. But without wishing to sound hopelessly sceptical, I had noticed that most, if not all of the traders had unmistakable cockney accents, and I simply couldn't think of any active banana plantations in or around Bow, Whitechapel or Limehouse.

On my travels abroad, like any discerning British tourist, I have always gravitated to the restaurants and bars frequented by the locals. One can generally be assured of the best well-stocked *nosebags* with scrumptious ingredients, together with a suitable liquid accompaniment, which (unlike the cost of a half a dozen Columbian bananas at the Borough Market) doesn't cost the equivalent of Latvia's GDP. Not surprisingly, these desirable venues are always to be found well away from the rip-off tourist areas, and in many cases their geographical locations are a closely guarded secret.

The main difference between the typical Londoner and his European counterpart is that irrespective of the ridiculously high prices, the Londoner seeks out fashionable or trendy locations simply *to be seen!* Borough Market is as fashionable now as Carnaby Street was back in the sixties, and both have been used as credible places for the indigenous *poseurs* to been observed.

Being *one of the faces* is just as important now as it was then, but for many of the impecunious native youngsters back in the sixties, to seriously consider spending money at one of the fashionable shops or nearer to home, in one of Borough Market's banking organisations masquerading as public houses, was simply out of the question. One stratagem that we used back then, was to dress up in a variety of miscellaneous clothing of the trendy variety (the more outrageous the better) and to carry an acquired bag from one of the more expensive shops. These were highly prized and sought after accessories and fetched a good price on the local black market. They would be filled with any old jumpers purchased from a local charity shop. Actually, this practice can still be observed today, with the occasional shopper at PRIMARK, who always leaves with their purchases carried out in a HARRODS' bag.

The term *promenading* suggests a leisurely stroll around, simply to meet, or to be seen by others. The other modern-day term of *cottaging* (which has nothing to do with estate agents) has a similar import, since it is also means that the person thus engaged also wants to *be seen*. However, the main problem with this type of social gathering is that potential meeting places are few and far between, and despite a largely liberal-minded population, for some (notably the local constabulary) such harmless pursuits could be construed as importuning in a public place, which like *urinating* in a public fountain is still against the law.

We did a lot of that back in the sixties (promenading that is), and carrying our exclusive bags we could readily identify with the Kinks' *Butterfly* and would be able to *flit from shop to shop*, doing nothing more outrageous than simply browsing at the ludicrously expensive clothing, but more importantly, 'BEING SEEN!'

During the week, the pubs and eating venues in and around Borough Market are frequented by the aforementioned *half of bitter and watercress roll brigade,* who like hungry wildebeest trek across London Bridge at lunchtime and arrive again after their release from their office captivity a little later in the day. At the weekends it becomes the domain of the tourist.

A former old friend of mine, who worked in the city, related this tale a few years ago, on the understanding that his identity would be withheld, and that he would remain completely anonymous.

Following his hard day's malingering,

Barrington S. Coddlinton-Bysshe, dob 01/08/48, of 14, Dibdin Mansions, Balham, SW12 would escape the tedium of his confined space within an air-conditioned office complex, and like a considerable number of other daily commuters awaiting their ever late/cancelled/de-railed trains back to their suburban nirvanas, he would be tempted to join the office elite of trendy lads at one of the local pubs, being ever cognisant of his need to be regarded as *one of the faces*.

On a Friday evening, he would reluctantly join a few of his more reckless colleagues for a few libations at one of Borough Market's hostelries. On a summer evening they would stand outside one pub in particular, that used a large upturned oak barrel as a table. With a round of drinks costing the same as the weekend groceries for a family of three, he would refuse to get involved in *the syndicate* (which is a collective, where all the participants throw in money to pay for the drinks). Initially he bought his own drinks, but he cunningly decided that in future, he would bring his own liquid refreshments.

On the first Friday night that he joined in as it were, he craftily retrieved one of his small cans of Sainsbury's Budweiser from his rucksack. The main problem now was that unfortunately the pub did not serve beer in cans, so he had to get a glass from somewhere before his deception was rumbled by one of the eagle-eyed bar attendants, and his status as *one of the faces* was irrevocably compromised. He got around this by volunteering to collect the next round from the bar, and while doing so, he asked the bar person for a glass of ice. On his return, he simply replenished the top of the oak barrel with fresh pints. He then surreptitiously emptied the ice away, and (like a latter-day Tommy Grasscon) he stealthily filled the now empty glass with his own considerably cheaper beer, and not wishing to leave any trace of his chicanery visible, he would put his empty can back into a rucksack, the inside of which was inevitably to smell like a barmaid's apron.

Thereafter, on every Friday morning, having read the back of his conditioner bottle (for the umpteenth time) he would then load his rucksack with a pint glass and four cans of Budweiser, in preparation for his evening sojourn with the lads. During the following fifteen years with the same company, and joining in as his did with the lads every Friday evening, his deception was never rumbled by the ever-vigilant bar team.

Apparently he retired in 2010, and having patented the idea, he had a short spell involved in the manufacture and sale of rucksacks with internal pouches around their inside rim, which could easily accommodate six cans of beer/lager/cider etc. He was last heard of in Balham, but following numerous enquiries regarding his whereabouts, he seems to have simply disappeared, which is very disappointing, since the unprincipled *fatherless-person* still owes me a considerable sum of money.

(Should his whereabouts become known, kindly forward the details to Basil Lang c/o Burt Lang & Forthright (Solicitors) 15, The Chambers, Kensal Rise, London, NW10. Information leading to his conviction and subsequent imprisonment and/or deportation will be favourably rewarded with a small financial gratuity.)

London is full of interesting places, and Borough Market is just one of them. When I think about my home town, I always tend to feel rather emotional about this ever-sprawling madhouse of a city. However, I cannot help feeling immensely proud and not a little humbled at being born in such a wonderful place. But London is for the young, and my tenure is just about up. Hopefully, I shall be relocating to a place out in the country soon, and frankly I can't wait.

Borough Market survives purely on the ever-present twice-daily tidal wave of the *office-wallas,* and the innate friendliness and patronage of our very welcome visitors and foreign tourists. Long may they grace our shores!

I was back in Kilburn at 15:30 and I called into the flat. Elisha came rushing down the hall and jumped up into my arms. 'I'm going to see my daddy!' she said excitedly.

Maria walked into the hall and, holding my hand, she led me into the lounge where we all made ourselves comfortable. Lenka had left earlier to meet up with Tina.

'He's my daddy, and he wants me to live with him and Mahmud,' she said happily, a beaming smile on her face. 'We are going to see him...?' She looked at Maria.

'Soon!' said Maria.

'Soon!' she repeated. 'Can we go to McDonald's?'

Needless to say, a little later, we were once again sitting in a restaurant that is becoming an essential part of my weekly social calendar.

Elisha is a very popular customer and is always so enthusiastically welcomed by the charming counter staff. They all make such a big fuss of her and I have come to realise that her love for the place is not only because of the food, but she seriously enjoys the warmth and hilarious banter that she has with them. The looks of amazement that they give her following one of her honest meal appraisals has them rolling about in the aisles. For one so young, she is a very astute and critical reviewer of their dishes and drinks.

As we ate our meals, I looked at my beautiful Maria and gave her an appreciative smile and a wink of gratitude.

She smiled coyly and blew me a kiss, which I caught in my right hand and put in my inside jacket pocket for later. Elisha looked a little confused at my actions, but giggled happily when I told her what I'd done.

While my two girls were getting stuck into a dessert of banana waffles liberally doused in maple syrup and cream, I bade them farewell and made for The Magpie.

Vlado greeted me warmly and was positively gushing with praise for Alfie, who had completed his first four hours' work in the pub at midday. I didn't stay long, and I dare say that I will be hearing from my newly employed friend in the not-too-distant future. But for my peace of mind, I shall be ensuring that my mobile phone is switched off early tonight.

We all had a quiet evening and both Maria and Elisha were sound asleep at 21:30.

Goodnight, Ginny.

P xx

7th April 2012

Good morning, Ginny.

I was awake at 06:35 this morning, and all was quiet. I checked my phone and was a little disappointed to find that from the time that I had switched it off last night (18:45) I hadn't received one call or text. Some people are never satisfied! I mean, I moan when I get a call, and then moan when I don't? I was hoping that at least I would have had a text from Alfie, detailing his first morning's work at the pub. I really do enjoy starting a new day with a good old-fashioned belly laugh, and let's be honest, Alfie does have a quite unique style when it comes to expressing his thoughts in writing.

As soon as I opened my bedroom door, Jimena dashed passed me and shot up my curtains like a rat up a drainpipe. However, she has now mastered the return trip and can safely get back down again using her little claws like grappling irons. She cautiously takes little backward movements, although I think that she might be a little scared of heights, since she looks straight ahead all of the way down.

They say that a cat has 'nine lives' and that no matter how high up, 'a cat will always land on its feet!' I wonder if they mean that figuratively or quite literally. I mean, Lenny 'landed on his feet' recently, what with his new financial windfall, which is more than can be said for Alfie, who having celebrated a two-pound win on a scratch card last week, on his way out of the shop, he tripped over the newsagents free-standing paper display, knocking the neatly presented newspapers all over the place. During what could be described at man's first attempt at non-mechanical flight and not wearing a crash helmet, he dived headlong into the magazine display, bashed his head and landed up lying in an untidy heap by the front door. Ranbir Sarka gave him a mop and a bucket of water and asked him to clean up the blood, but to add insult to injury, he had to pay four pounds fifty pence for the ruined newspapers as well (which he asked to be put on his slate). When he finally passes through this mortal coil, God forbid that he should ever come back as a cat. He wouldn't last five minutes!

Over breakfast this morning, we had a conversation about animals, and I explained to Elisha that most animals, like us, live in families. 'There are many different families of cats,' I explained, and naming a few I said, 'There's the tiger, the lion, the leopard as well as lots of others.'

Jokingly, I asked her if she could name three other members of a cat family.

She sat and thought for a moment and then replied, 'The daddy cat, the mummy cat and the baby cat!'

Maria almost choked on her egg and sausage sandwich, and I couldn't catch my breath for laughing. What's not to love about this beautiful little girl?

At around 10:20 I ventured over to the gym. It was very quiet indeed, and for the first time even the two scary looking cleaners were sitting on chairs in the weights room looking thoroughly depressed. Still, to lighten up their day I took a couple of turns on each of the cross-trainers (all eight of them), picked up a couple of dumbbells, got under the bench press bar, and ran my hands along it, and finished off with blowing my nose on a tissue, which I 'inadvertently' dropped.

As I walked towards the steam room, they leapt into action spraying and wiping every item that I had touched. One of them finished her two minutes of enthusiastic activity with a quite beautiful ballerina-type flourish as she swept up my dropped tissue and disposed of it in a waste bin.

Watching their dejected figures making their way back to their chairs actually made me feel rather depressed. However, it was short lived since having had a refreshing shower and a shave, as I passed the pub on my way home, I had a chat with Alfie who was busily sweeping the outside seating area.

'Good morning, Alfred,' I said, putting my gym bag on one of the tables.

His smile brightened up my day. 'I couldn't have said it better meself! Vlado is learning me to speak Albania,' he said. 'It's only me second day and he has already let me sweep the front! I've cleaned the toilets, filled up the Brylcreem machine, and that... *other* machine,' he said bashfully. 'I have two breaks in the morning, and for me brekkies this morning, I had porridge with banana and honey. Zorro-Alooney is a great cook!'

'It's Zora-Aleena,' I said.

'Pardon?' he replied.

'It doesn't matter, Alfie,' I said, picking up my gym bag. 'You can tell me all about it later.'

'It's much better than Weetabix, even with milk on!' he shouted as I made my way home.

As I stepped into the flat, my phone rang. It was Alfie. Answering it I said, 'I'm sorry but the person that you are trying to reach is unavailable. Kindly leave your message after the beep...

'**BEEP!**' I screamed. A short pause followed.

'Hello Paul, sorry I missed you. Ted asked me to tell you that if I saw you, I should tell you to give him a ring. I saw you just now! So will you give him a ring?'

'Yes I will, Alfie,' I said, and hung up.

I joined Maria and Lenka in the lounge. They were in quiet conversation as I entered.

'I miss him so much,' said Maria, stroking Jimena who was purring happily on her lap.

'He'll be back soon, and I'm sure that he is sending you daily texts,' replied Lenka.

'Yes he is, but it's not the same,' Maria replied.

Having my two girls together seems to be a bit of a rare treat these days, and not having had a lot of time with Maria, out of Elisha's hearing, I congratulated her on the way that she had dealt with the issue relating to our beloved little girl's impending move and change of household. Lenka was also very supportive with regard to the way that she handled what was essentially a very delicate situation. Just as we had finished speaking, Elisha poked her head around the door and said 'BOO!' and theatrically we all jumped. This had her laughing hysterically.

Lenka will be out having a working lunch with Zora-Aleena at midday, and Maria and Elisha are going down to Gabriel's flat to give the place 'a little tlc with a vacuum cleaner and a feather duster'. There wasn't much point in asking Jimena what her plans for the day were, since after Maria had got up, she dashed into my bedroom and was asleep on my pillow in no time.

I phoned Ted thereafter and since his first few sentences were not about his experiences in Stratford on Thursday, and being ever perceptive to the feelings of others (particularly those with pugilistic tendencies), I decided to keep my mouth shut, and thereby later in the day felt relatively confident that I would be able to retain what teeth I have left! Besides, I am sure that his latest *unfortunate* experience will be the talk of Kilburn anon.

I met him at his favoured *equine actuary* in the Cricklewood Broadway at midday. I really do not feel comfortable in betting establishments, although when the day comes where I see a bookmaker putting on his bicycle clips in readiness for his homeward journey, I can say in all honesty, that I might take a more active interest in the bookie-enriching *Sport of Kings.*

As I entered the betting shop, Ted was sitting on a high stool, screwing up a small piece of paper, which I assumed was yet (another) losing bet. He was visually glued to an aerial television screen watching a horse race, and the look on his face, which remained constant throughout our less than exuberantly joyful verbal exchanges, suggested a modicum of bitterness, dejection, unhappiness and despair. 'Out of fifteen runners it was a two-horse race!' he said to nobody in particular.

Having suddenly come back down to earth, he looked at me in surprise. 'My money was on the favourite, *Margo with a Tee*. She got beaten from the word go. She didn't leave her bleedin stall!' he said despondently.

'So who won?' I asked disinterestedly.

'It was a very close thing, but looking at the photo finish, my money would have been on *Gornorf Again*,' he said confidently. As he finished speaking, the result was announced. 'In first place by a short head the winner is *Hoof Hearted* at 4–1 with *Gornorf Again* a close second at 2–1. The 11–4 favourite, *Margo with a Tee*, failed to come out of her stall.'

Smiling, I said, 'Well that's alright Ted, at least you'll get your stake money back.'

'Dream on sunshine!' he replied. 'If a horse is withdrawn before the start, you'll get your money back, but if it's in its stall and comes under starter's orders and fails to respond to a whip or an enthusiastic verbal *giddy-up!* by the jockey, all bets are settled as losers.'

Despite the fact that smoking has been banned in public places for years, this over-crowded hovel was like a Chinese opium den, and was filled in a warm, stuffy fug of tobacco smoke (try saying that with a mouthful of chocolate maltesers). It was an absolutely disgusting environment to be confined in, no matter what the reason, or what you were sucking, and frankly an oxygen cylinder would have been far preferable.

Holding my hand (which I'm beginning to get a little worried about), Ted led me out into the equally dreadful carbon-monoxide-infused air and vehicular uproar of a very busy thoroughfare. He guided me along the Broadway like a carer leading a leper, and due to the speed of our progress, I figured that he had some very urgent business to discuss with me. However, once inside the *Hippo Public House* (which was busier than a centipede's chiropodist) he dashed off to the loo, shouting over the discordant pandemonium, 'Get the drinks in, mate!'

You will remember the last time that I was in this pub, and I was interrogated by that bar girl who thought that I was a DHSS snooper? Well she was working again, and she gave me a little wave of recognition. I mouthed out what drinks I wanted, and nodding in acknowledgement, she poured up our two pints and left them on the counter. She raised her arm up high above the crowd, with her index finger pointing down to their location (bless her little beer-sodden pinafore). When I had eventually fought my way to the bar to collect and pay for them, she just smiled at me and waved me away.

Carefully carrying my two pints of lager, I made for the door area, which was the only square footage in the place that appeared to be clear. It had a small rectangle of space that seemingly had been missed by my fellow imbibers (which aroused my suspicions enough to check out the area thoroughly). Happily, I didn't find any grenades, used condoms, animal faeces or other unsavoury detritus, so I simply stood there, awaiting the return of my itinerant *urine-head* compatriot. A little later, I saw him tracing his steps back through the *miscellaneous rabble* (who were packed together tighter than a clam's bum at high tide) and I was beginning to feel far from well.

Ted downed his pint in what must be world-record time and having taken one sizeable gulp, I left the rest, and placing the glass on a nearby window ledge, I thankfully legged it out of the place.

Ted (like most of his horses) came in a close second. He went to hold my hand again, but this time I pulled it away sharply and asked him why he was being so tactile?

As we walked towards Kilburn, he started to behave like a spoilt brat that couldn't have his own way. 'Oh don't be such a stroppy *fatherless-person*,' he said, making a very overly exaggerated show of putting both of his hands in his pockets. 'It's just that sometimes you appear to be a little lost.'

'What lost as in I dunno where I am, kinda thing, or lost as in a tad mentally confused?'

'It's a bit hard to explain,' he said, appearing to be a little uncomfortable.

'Frankly mate, I am getting very concerned at the amount of people doing the same thing. It's one thing for women to do it, but totally out of the question when it comes to the blokes!'

Stopping suddenly, and looking at me intently, he theatrically put his hands on his hips and said, 'That's an audaciously sexist remark Paul, and frankly I am very disappointed in you. So I would be obliged if you would kindly change the subject.'

'Certainly,' I said. 'How about the money that you owe me? That would be a very stimulating conversation indeed!'

Needless to say that from that moment on, any further physical contact was avoided, and our normal exuberant verbal interaction became as silent as a nun's confessional. However, as The Magpie's public house appeared like a desert mirage through the distant fog of carbon monoxide fumes, Ted started to arouse from his meditative stupor, and a little later as we reached the pub's hallowed portal, he became animated once again.

'Well aren't you going to ask me how my toastmaster event went?' he said.

'How did your toastmaster event go, Ted?' I asked obediently.

Hustling me forcefully through the door of the Gay Bar he said, 'Don't *effin* ask!'

As we entered the bar, Alfie was taking off a plastic apron.

'Thanks very much, Vlado,' he said. 'That was the best pumpkin crumblie that I've ever had. You are so lucky, having a lady what can cook!'

Alfie didn't stay long and as we walked up to the bar, he waved us a farewell and was gone.

To cut a very long story short, Ted was a little concerned at the way Basil was acting. He couldn't quite put his finger on the problem, other than to say that he was acting very distant and not his usual friendly self. My own recent meeting with Basil was no less strange, and I was a little concerned at the third-degree type questioning he put me through in relation to Ted's character. As I have mentioned before, Basil is far from stupid and he seems to have a bit of a sixth sense when it comes to sniffing out a little underhanded or unscrupulous monkey-business.

I am clearly the piggy in the middle here. I am very fond of both of them and I really couldn't place one above the other. Hopefully, I will never be in the unenviable position of having to choose between them. For the time being, I will not dwell on the issue, and hope that my concerns are unfounded.

Back at home, Elisha brought me up to date with regard to Gabriel's home, and I was most impressed at the quality of our evening meal that Maria had prepared. She is certainly becoming more confident in her culinary adventures, and as if the main course of cottage pie, carrots and peas wasn't enough, the apple pie and custard to follow was absolutely scrumptious.

Having finally washed up and had systematically cleared away all of the plates and cutlery, like a dutiful mum she took Elisha for her evening ablutions. Later having tucked her and *Jose* (her Spanish teddy bear) up in bed, she patiently read them both a story, until Elisha's tired little eye's closed again for another day.

Frankly listening to Maria's beautifully gentle soothing voice, she would have had me snoring like an old organ flue in minutes.

Goodnight, Ginny.
P xx

8th April 2012

Good morning, Ginny.

Following a very good sleep and a lukewarm cup of coffee, I hastened out of the flat at 07:30. Both of my girls' bedroom doors were closed and there was no sound coming from either.

Apart from it being the Easter weekend, today is traditionally observed by many Buddhists as the birthday of Gautama Siddhartha, the founder of Buddhism. He was apparently the son of a tribal leader in an area that is now Nepal. He is believed to have been born around 563 BC, in the village of Bodh Gaya in the northeast Indian state of Bihar.

One thing that we both have in common is that we share the same birth sign (Aries), so like me he was brave, self-assured, honest, optimistic and skint. But unlike him, my own lifelong inability to retain financial wealth was not caused by enlightenment and the subsequent rejection of worldly concerns, but rather a spiritual exercise in being able to bravely go without from time to time. Being self-assured enough to recognise that my present state is due to my errors or mistakes of the past. Being completely honest in my acceptance of any karmic sanction, and as a simple sentient being, to optimistically believe that 'something will eventually turn up, albeit perhaps a few thousand years too late!'

A rather pleasant young bus driver welcomed me aboard my Oxford Street bound bus this morning. Actually, he was as miserable as a frost-bitten apple in July, but it's nice to start a new day's mooch with an optimistic thought, albeit perhaps a little fanciful.

I didn't manage to order the requisite clothing that I will be expected to wear at Lenny's forthcoming wedding (which falls a week on Saturday) simply because the shop in question was deemed to be of the larger kind. By law, in England and Wales any store that is over 280 square metres in size must close on Easter Sunday and Christmas Day. Even on a normal Sunday, the larger stores can only open for six consecutive hours between 10:00–16:00. In this particular issue, size really does matter, and it clearly puts the Christian religion above all other secular concerns.

The trading laws in Scotland are devolved to their own parliament and are considerably more relaxed however, and it seems that the only rule of note is that employers cannot force anyone to work on a Sunday. This is a very sensible exception since without wishing to stereotype, a goodly proportion of the populace would have been out the night before (sampling the grain) and as a result could be visually and/or manually compromised. Measuring a bloke up for a suit for example, requires a modicum of clear unblurred vision to be able to read the measurements, and a steady hand is imperative in obtaining reliably accurate measurements in general, and a semi-reliably inside leg measurement (free from any later civil action) in particular. It's bad enough for a lifelong teetotaller with a rock-steady hand to take this kind of space-invading measurement, let alone a *half-pished* jock with all of the manual refinements of a visually impaired three-toed Malaysian Sloth!

On my bus back to Kilburn later, I seriously wondered why Lenny had insisted on his wedding being a formal occasion. He has never been to a formal gathering in his life, well apart from perhaps his christening, and even then, excluding the officiating religious practitioner and a representative from the orphanage, I am sure that the poor little soul would have been on his own. Clearly, the story that he was told in relation to his father's continual absence, was nothing more than a smokescreen. Besides, the bulbs in lighthouses do not need to be constantly changed.

But getting bank to Lenny's wedding, I am sure that this upmarket decision was made by Eugenia, who like a heat-seeking missile is the guiding influence in their relationship, and I do believe that she has been on target from the word go. But power to her elbow, I have to admire her determination and ingenuity in finally getting a lifelong social claimant off benefits. Although perhaps marrying him to do so, could be considered a little extreme! I jest of course and I couldn't be happier for them both.

I arrived at The Magpie at 12:35 and stepped into the Gay Bar just as Vlado was handing Alfie a pint of lager. 'You are much welcome, Alfred,' he said. 'I must make you strong, for the pubs work. Your soldier man, he said, that his troops march on his belly!'

'Ahhh that'll be Alan Tischmarch,' said Alfie. He's one of them gardener blokes, but he got fed up with marching 'em up and down that hill, so he threw in the trowel! He now writes phonographic novels, which he says; keeps him in clover!' Looking at me imploringly he said, 'Wass 'at then?'

Before I had time to correct Alfie's grammatical faux pas, and to enlighten him on the meaning of the aforementioned idiomatic expression, my day was brightened considerably with the arrival of *Whispering Jim,* who was welcomed wholeheartedly by us all. Vlado was pouring his drink as soon as he saw him.

On entering a pub, Jim does not say anything to anyone until he is seated with a pint of Guinness in front of him. He takes the carriage of his pints of *the blonde in the black dress,* from the bar very seriously indeed, and is completely non-communicative until his *latest affair* had safely taken her seat on his beer mat at his table.

In the time that I have known him he has never spilled a drop, whether drunk or sober, and he positively refuses to allow anyone to deliver them to him. His reasoning is quite interesting in that as mentioned before, he drinks on average twelve pints of Guinness daily. This is split between his twice daily sessions, during the hours of 11:00–15:00 and 17:00–23:00 respectively. In the past he has estimated that his daily twelve visits to the bar, as well as the inevitable bladder evacuations, at the Water-Loo, accounts for all of his regular exercise.

In the past he has estimated that at The Magpie he had walked on average 1.2 miles daily, and has pointed out quite convincingly, that were he a non-drinker, he would have denied himself a potential 8.4 miles of life-enhancing aerobic exercise every week! As daft as it sounds, there is an element of truth in this statement, although I am sure that the medical profession would not entirely endorse his somewhat confused logic.

Having successfully lowered his newly poured pint on its virgin beer mat, he rummaged in his jacket pocket and placed a large handful of pound coins on the table. Within minutes of his arrival, the bar was echoing to the subtle velvet orchestration and dulcet baritone voice of Jim Reeves, and frankly it was as though he had never been away.

The two of us joined him at his table, ostensibly to have more of a chance of hearing what he was saying. He brought us up to date with all of his adventures since our last meeting. Much of it was apparently quite funny, since occasionally following a couple of inaudible sentences he would chuckle away merrily.

However, as he tried to make sense of what Jim was saying, the pained expression on Alfie's face kept both Vlado and I very amused indeed.

When Jim's lips stopped moving, I assumed that his present discourse was at an end, and jokingly I asked him how his love life was going. I was more than a little surprised to learn that he had struck up a bit of a friendship with one of the female tenants at his home. I got to understand that her name was *Brigit O'Riley* (a sprightly sixty-year-old spinster from Bantry Bay). Sensing his evident embarrassment however, I changed the subject.

Ted suddenly made an appearance, looking a little worse for wear. But nevertheless, he gave us all a perfunctory smile before he ordered his gin and grapefruit.

Seemingly not wishing to be left out, Alfie mentioned that he'd also struck up a bit of a promising friendship with a young 'frisky-prumpling' that he had met at our local launderette. Apparently, *Amanda* had told him that, 'She'd like a man like him to be the father of her children!'

'Well that's absolutely marvellous, Alfie,' I said. 'I thought that you were in line to become a lifelong bachelor!'

'So what did you say to her?' said Ted.

'I just said, well I dunno, being a dad, it's a big responsibility.' But then I had a bit of a think, and I thought, well I do like kids, I'm in full-time job, I'd make a good daddy! But I didn't wanna look too keen like, so...'

'Get on with it, Alfie for gawd's sake. What did you say to her?' said Ted, beginning to lose his patience.

'Well the only thing I could say, I asked her how many children she had.'

There followed a bit of an uncomfortable silence. Ted and I just stared at him in disbelief, and *Whispering Jim* went to the toilet. The look that Vlado gave him was a mixture of concern, sympathy and disbelief, and I came to the obvious conclusion that being in close confinement with him over these last couple of days he had rightly deduced that while his latest employee was a very gentle larger-than-life character, he is also a fruit bun short of a picnic.

Since Ted and I made no further comment, for a very short time Alfie looked at us enquiringly. But since our silence often follows many of his verbal utterances, he is now mentally programmed, as it were, to either keep quiet thereafter or to change the subject completely. On this occasion, he went for the second option.

Looking at Ted, he said, 'Did Basil ever thank you for helping him out with that Frobisher bloke?'

Ted appeared to be completely oblivious to Alfie's question, and walked up to Vlado at the bar and ordered four more pints.

Suddenly, the horrific enormity of what Alfie had said hit me forcibly, and I went into panic mode. Grabbing him by the arm, I pulled him up from his seat. Ted was otherwise engaged on getting the next round in, so I said to nobody in particular, 'We will be back in a minute folks. Alfie needs a few groceries from next door.'

I guided him out of the bar, and still holding his arm, I took him a little distance away from the pub. He looked at me nervously. 'What's wrong, Paul?' he said.

'What do you know about the Frobisher issue, Alfie?' I said, as we sat down on a low wall outside of the newsagents.

'Well, only that Ted got him off,' he said, looking at me accusingly. 'What's this all about, Paul? I've got half a pint in there and Ted's just buying me another one!'

'You are not supposed to know anything about Malcolm Frobisher, Alfie, and speaking to Ted about it isn't very wise. It is all supposed to be confidential.'

'Wass 'at then?'

'It's supposed to be secret Alfie! It mustn't be spoken about – nobody must know about it – mum's the word!'

'I haven't got a mum, mate, well that's not quite true. No, I mean I must have had one once 'cos I'm here and...'

'Alfie, please listen!' I said, as I started to have difficulty in breathing and felt that I was in the early stages of an imminent panic attack. 'This is a private matter between Ted and...'

'Dickie O' Toole, yeah I know,' he said. 'Ted told me about it a few weeks ago. I like Dickie, he's a nice bloke. Basil would have got a lot of money for getting that other bloke off, so I thought it only right that Ted should get some of it.'

'You told Basil about it?' I said in exasperation.

'When I was leaving he said that I owed him for the biscuits and toilet rolls, and I just said and you owe Ted for getting Frobisher off!'

'Did you say anything else to him?' I asked.

'No, I just left.'

'So how do you know Dickie O'Toole?' I asked.

'I met him and Ted in the Bread Bin one night. He's gone back to Ireland now.'

'So how did Ted get Frobisher off then, Alfie?' I said, trying to sound innocently interested.

'I dunno, he didn't say did he. I suppose it was with his usual animal cunning and gurl.'

'The word is guile, Alfie,' I said, starting to relax again.

As we walked back towards the Gay Bar he said, 'That school teacher bloke, Jack I think his name is, he was asking me about Ted and Dickie too!'

I held his arm before we entered the bar. 'Keep that to yourself for the time being, Alfie,' I said, which initially he seemed to think was rather funny, until he realised that there was nothing playful in the very severe eyeball treatment that I was giving him. He nodded understandingly.

Sitting down again with the boys, he necked the remaining lager from his first glass, and looking at me timidly, he slowly pulled his other full pint towards him like a naughty schoolboy who had just been admonished for not doing his homework.

Later in the Water-Loo I quietly said to him that I needed to speak to him urgently.

'I'll give you a ring later,' he said, tapping the side of his nose with his right index finger.

'No you won't, Alfie,' I said. 'I shall be home at around six, so give me a call then.'

Needless to say, I didn't receive the call from Alfie at 18:00 as requested and throughout the evening I tried to phone him several times. It seems that the annoying little *person* had switched his phone off.

Goodnight love.

P xx

9th April 2012

Good morning, Ginny.

Alfie phoned me at 06:00 this morning, and since I had suffered a very uncomfortable night having been tossed and turned like a locust in a hurricane, I was feeling somewhat delicate, and having heard his voice, my usual morning bonhomie was lost in a confused verbal tirade of abuse. Once I was satisfied that he had fully understood my need to offload certain disagreeable sentiments, I patiently listened to what he had to say.

The first issue related to my phone call request. He thought that I had meant 06:00 this morning and hence his call. Although in fairness, I felt obliged to compliment him on his punctuality, since as my phone rang, my ornate reproduction Georgian clock was chiming six.

Thereafter we discussed the Jack Siddall issue and it became clear that the bloke is either an undercover police officer or a private investigator. I told him in no uncertain terms that in future he was not to discuss the Frobisher, Ted or Dickie issue with him, or *anyone else* for that matter, and that should he be approached about the subject again, he was to notify me immediately. I do believe that this time he understood the seriousness of my request since on closing our conversation he said, 'Don't worry Paul, I won't let you down, I promise!'

Listening to the morning news at 07:00 I heard a newsflash which stated:

During the early hours of this morning two unidentified fly tippers had completely blocked the front doors and the garage entrance to Kilburn Police Station. Early reports suggest that this is the work of animal protesters since the offensive material used in this audacious act was raw horse manure. No police representative has as yet been available for comment.'

While I am ever amazed at Ted's somewhat innovative ways of seeking satisfying revenge on others whom he considers worthy of a little karmic redress, I shall seriously have to temper my own disappointed or disillusioned opinions on the actions or omissions of others, and keep such opinions completely confidential. This particular righter of wrongs is becoming a positive liability, and while he is full of the bull variety, I really cannot comprehend where on earth he is getting all of this horse shit from.

Elisha, Maria and Jimena arrived in the kitchen at 08:15 and I fed Jimena, while Maria prepared cheese on toast for Elisha and herself.

A little later, Maria asked if she could take Elisha away for a couple of days to a cousin of hers who lives in Surbiton. Elisha was very excited at the prospect and stated that *Isabella* has a little dog called *Luna* and could she go please? How on earth could anyone refuse such a request?

I asked Maria how they would get there, and she stated that they would be collected by Isabella's husband *Mateo*. Before I had given her my consent, Maria was on her mobile phone to Isabella to arrange a pickup time. While they were happily packing a few clothing items, Maria informed me that Isabella was a primary school teacher and Mateo was a doctor. I insisted that she gave me their full names and current address, together with their home and mobile phone numbers. This she did immediately. I understood their excitement, because I too enjoy a change of scenery from time to time. Maria stated that she would ring me daily and that they would be home on Thursday morning.

I trust her implicitly and know that Elisha will be well cared for, so I didn't feel in the least dubious about allowing them out on this little adventure. From my understanding, they will be leaving one loving team and simply spending a little time with another one. I am sure that it will do them both the world of good.

A little later, I visited the gym and did a little cardiovascular-type exercise, and to awaken my limpness of musculature I completed a little weight training. I really enjoyed the later visit to the steam room followed by a shave and a shower.

Back at the flat at around 11:30, Mateo arrived. And what a charming bloke he is. The girls gave me a lovely hug before they left, and a little later Jimena was wandering around the flat, visiting each room in turn looking for them (bless her little inquisitive whiskers).

I felt a mooch coming on, and I really was in a bit of a quandary with regard to the recent revelations that had come about over the last couple of days. I needed to talk to someone about, it, someone completely unbiased and neutral. Clearly, the last thing that I want to do is to involve anyone else in the Frobisher mess. But what else can I do? I decided that I would have a chat to my Lenka about it. I sent her a text, asking her to give me a ring when she was free.

In the meantime, I felt that a good stretch of the legs would do me the world of good, and hopefully it might clear away the considerable amount of mental uncertainty that I am going through at the moment.

At around 13:10 I was wandering around a nearby ancient area known as Hampstead Heath. It comprises of some 790 acres of rambling heath, together with modern and ancient woodland, which is ideal terrain for the jogger or more sedate moocher bent on a little physical or mental exercise. The name Hampstead is apparent derived from the Anglo-Saxon word for 'homestead'.

One of the greatest pleasures associated with walking is that it allows one the opportunity to engage in wonderfully irrelevant thoughts and memories of the wool-gathering variety. These fleeting observations race through one's mind like small summer clouds, although initially mine were confined to the Frobisher issue. The more I thought about it, the more I realised that Basil had smelled a rat, and his first line of investigation would naturally concern those nearest to the issue, notably Ted. His own suspicions would have naturally been reinforced with Alfie's innocent remark to him about Ted 'getting Frobisher off!' Quite apart from this, Basil had grilled me recently about Ted's character generally which concluded with his question of whether he was capable of 'fitting someone up?' It all became pretty clear as my aimless stroll ensued.

On my way home later, the sight of a young girl with her mum reminded me of Deirdre Jane Ramsbottom, our junior school's beautiful blonde boy-eater. She was the first to shun my fumbling, romantic advances, although perhaps the back of the bike sheds wasn't exactly the best place to initiate an amorous affair. But then, space for any outside extra-curricular activities at junior school was never at a premium.

At a mere twelve years of age, Deirdre was a mischievous temptress who quite literally was (single-handedly) responsible for the sexual awakening of a considerable number of eleven-year-old boys. She was the first real love of my life who taught me many things. She instructed me in the dexterity required in tying up shoelaces, and how to blow my nose effectively and hygienically. These days, I don't have any problem when it comes to blowing my nose, although I still have a little bit of an issue in relation to doing up my shoelaces. Now I simply can't reach the buggers!

Apart from her instructions in relation to my bodily needs, she was also very keen on teaching me the rudiments associated with 'getting my leg over'. A term she used for riding a bike. A little later, she was to use this expression when it came to some of our other more energetic outdoor activities. Through her guidance, I was to realise that in the affairs of men, the females were destined to play a very active and important part. They were considerably more than just a supporting act, as it were. Indeed, I was convinced that those beautiful semi-docile beings were simply waiting for the right opportunity to launch their domestic *coups d'etat,* which, from personal experience, I can confirm normally occurs within the first five years of their marital lives. It results in the awakening of a considerable amount of formerly complacent men, who erroneously believed that like Maria's misguided dad that they too were the boss.

337

Deirdre was a guiding light in my early life, and I have a lot to be thankful to her for, since apart from acquiring a pretty comprehensive knowledge in relation to *matters of the heart,* I was a competent cyclist at a very early age and was to become pretty conversant with the concept and usage of the euphemism, which I was to use later in many of my junior school's literary compositions.

In her early twenties, she went into the legal profession and was subsequently called to the bar (the judicial variety, that is), and later still, she went on to become one of the youngest stipendiary magistrates in the land, bless her little white bicycle pump!

But with regard to exercise, out of all of my friends, I am the only one that uses a gym on a more or less regular basis, apart from Lenny, who would only ever use it for personal hygiene issues anyway. The nearest that he ever came to meaningful exercise related to his reluctant morning sit-up to hit his snooze button on his alarm clock. Why he had one that was timed to wake him up in the first place was always a bit of a mystery to me. He certainly had nothing to get up for. And now, he could quite literally lounge about in bed for the rest of his life (should the mood or inclination take him). Ironically, the gym is now a serious competitor to the Gay Bar, or any other pub for that matter.

As I was leaving the Heath, I had a call from Lenka and we arranged to meet somewhere incognito and I suggested the Hippo pub at 17:30.

I met her as arranged and over a couple of drinks I brought her up to date with regard to *some* of the issues that were worrying me. I didn't feel it prudent to go into the full details however, other than to express my concern relating to Basil's need to question me about Ted.

As supportive as ever, she felt sure that there was nothing to worry about. However, she stated that she would have a general chat with Tina to see if she could throw any light on the matter.

I concluded our little *tete-a-tete* with emphasising the point that discretion was very important, and that Tina must not suspect that her interest in Basil generally was nothing more than simple girl-talk. She nodded understandingly.

Maria phoned as we were making our way back to the Gay Bar, and Elisha was clearly enjoying her visit. She was having great fun it seems with Luna, who was 'very clever and could do lots of tricks!' Maria, as considerate as ever, stated that, 'They were both having a wonderful time, and that I mustn't worry.' She will phone me again tomorrow.

When we arrived at the Gay Bar pub, Lenny and his betrothed were in conversation with Ted.

'Well I thought a few sarnies cut up into them petite little shapes, and a few vol-au-vents and assorted cakes would be enough. I mean, there's not going to be that many guests at the evening reception, are there? Besides, I know that you've got a few bob now son, but that doesn't mean that you've gotta chuck it around like a bloke with no arms! Besides, no peers of the realm will be attending, so we can probably dispense with the carpaccio of veal fillet dressed in pink peppercorn cream cheese and wild duck crispy onion canapés, together with the 49 claret, and stick to good old-fashioned anti-posh nosh. How many people are you expecting anyway?'

'About fifteen in all, I think,' Lenny said, looking at Eugenia for confirmation.

'Yes, and most of them will be your friends!' she said, with a suggestion of disappointed resignation in her voice. 'I shall be bringing two people – my mum and a niece.'

'Well one doesn't get married every day, love,' he said. 'It's a once-in-a-lifetime experience, or at least it should be! I feel that it would be only proper, that those dear friends of mine, who have stood by my side in those days of misery and adversity, should all witness the momentous event.'

Ted took a long audible guzzle of his lager and looking at Eugenia he said, 'I have to hand it to you love, your influence upon a former wastrel has borne fruit. His vocabulary has improved a great deal, and he's not even married yet!'

Eugenia took his comment good-naturedly and smiled at him wryly. 'All it takes is a little kindness, a teeny-weeny bit of guidance and a considerable amount of luck!' she replied, holding her hand out towards Lenny, who put his arm around her affectionately and kissed the top of her head.

'Getting a little emotional,' he said. 'I owe this little lady my life.'

'I wish you were quite so enthusiastically sentimental when it came to the considerable sum that you owe me!' Ted replied unkindly.

Eugenia looked up at Lenny enquiringly, and I was rather annoyed that Ted could be so self-centred at a time like this. I pointed my right index finger at him accusingly.

Clearly embarrassed, he tried to make light of the situation and said, 'Lenny knows that I'm only teasing him. He's as dear to me as my own flesh and blood, ain't that right son?'

With tears in his eyes, Lenny said, 'I don't know where I'd be without you, Ted.' He walked across towards him and hugged him warmly.

Ted was clearly taken aback and his body language registered panic, embarrassment, anxiety and despair, and gently prizing Lenny's arms from around him, he led him back to Eugenia and gently placing Lenny's right arm around her shoulder, and looking at me for support, he said, 'Truth be told, son, it's time for another to pick up the reins,' and smiling sweetly he regained his seat, which coincidentally was as far away from Lenny as it could be.

Having ordered a drink for Lenka and me, Vlado was full of complimentary comments about Alfie's general capabilities and his pleasing personality. 'He has hard-working is, with eagerness and happy face,' he said enthusiastically.

Being on our own this evening I suggested to Lenka that we visit the Chinese buffet for our evening meal and she was very enthusiastic at the suggestion.

As we were leaving the pub, Jack Siddall arrived and I was very surprised when he smiled at Lenka and said, 'We meet again Lenka, how are you?'

'I am very well, thank you Jack. What brings you to these parts?'

339

'Oh I've been here before; it's a very nice bar, and the locals are friendly enough. I just thought that I'd pop in for a couple of pints and a bit of a chinwag.' He shook my hand as we passed each other.

As we made our way to the Chinese buffet, I casually asked her about Jack. She stated that he was working with Ted and Tina. She had met him one evening at a pub near Basil's office and was introduced to him by Tina. She then went on to say that he was a retired teacher, and was related to Basil in some way.

Over our meal a little later, I told her not to worry about the Basil issue, and that I would have a little chat with him myself, and in the meantime to not mention anything to Tina.

Things are going from bad to worse, and frankly I really don't know which way to turn.

Goodnight love.
P xx

10th April 2012

Good morning, Ginny.

I am sure that at some point in my life I must have spent a worse night, but for the life of me I couldn't remember when it was. I had little or no sleep and at 06:10 I kicked my legs out of bed, dressed quickly and a little later I was assaulting the punchbag at the gym with all the finesse of a raging bull suffering from a toothache. In the steam room, having got over my puerile tantrum, I tried to make sense of this very convoluted issue. Clearly the two main characters in this drama, Malcolm Frobisher and Richard O'Toole, are both presumably more than happy at the final curtain, as it were, since Frobisher had regained his former good character and job, and Dickie is back where he feels he belongs. So for all intents and purposes everything should be hunky dory.

The only real problem now is Basil. Knowing him as I do, he will not rest until he finds out the full story, and this could result in the two main protagonists, Dickie and Ted, being subjected to another police investigation which would probably result in Dickie's original conviction being added to by being Ted's accomplice on another charge of conspiracy to pervert the course of justice, and other side issues of the perjury, fraudulent misrepresentation, contempt of court type of thing, which wouldn't really be too much of a problem for Dickie. However, Ted's involvement and guilt wouldn't be under any doubt since he was the mastermind behind it all, but in his case, a term of imprisonment would be about as welcome as a wet fart in a mankini.

I feel quite confident that both of them would be banged up for a considerable time. As a side issue, I too could be seriously at risk since while I was not actively involved in the finer details, I was aware of what was going on. Although I don't think that there is any legal obligation for a person to report a crime or to get involved in the matter should they not wish to do so. However, I could be wrong. I'm sure all will become clear as time passes.

Under the present circumstances, I have to arrange a meeting with Basil to discuss the whole issue. I naturally feel loyalty to all of the people involved here, but he has forced my hand. The fact that he has Jack Siddall snooping around is far from satisfactory and frankly, it's only a matter of time before he finds out about the whole sorry business. I feel that I should put us both out of our respective misery before this happens.

Back at home, I had breakfast with Lenka, who will again be meeting up with Zora-Aleena for a working lunch. As perceptive as ever, she asked me if there was anything wrong, and I smiled at her, grateful for her concern and simply stated that I was fine, just a little tired. I think she saw through that however, since she smiled at me ruefully and said, 'If I can help in anyway, just give me a call.' What's not to love about this beautiful young lady? She extends her love so unconditionally.

Norman Frederick Chisholm, aka *Norn the Post,* arrived at 11:30 bringing with him glad tidings of great joy. Not from him personally you understand, but through a letter that he had confidently shoved through my letterbox. It was a request from those people bent on getting me and the other *old farts* out of London, asking me to phone them. There being no better time than the present, I phoned them before Norman had left our block.

I was told by a very nice lady operative that a two-bedroomed bungalow was available in the village of West Togram in Hampshire which I was informed is around nine miles west of Southampton. I thought it must be a good omen, because Spike and his new partner (Beryl Young live in Hampshire). The Bungalow at 4, Birdcage Way was empty and I could view it at my leisure. Access could be gained by the electronic key box inside the front porch. Once I had keyed in the code 1949 the box would open and the front door key would then be available. I was to ensure that when I left, that I had replaced the key back into its key box. On closing the door, it would automatically lock itself. This was very welcome news indeed, and it was just what I needed to lift my spirits albeit perhaps briefly.

However, firstly I am determined to rid myself of any further anxiety or self-recrimination and grief over my part in relation to the Frobisher affair. I therefore phoned Basil and asked him if he would be available for a meeting. Fortunately he could fit me in on Thursday at midday, and I suggested the Bread Bin.

A little later, I took a walk to Rosheen's pub to be greeted in her usual enthusiastic way, although prior to my arrival she had apparently cleaned out the function room in readiness for a retirement party later this evening, and therefore her normal Herculean strength had thankfully been considerably reduced.

I asked her if her *private room* would be available on Thursday, it was and she was more than happy to let me use it. I explained that I would need it for around two hours maximum. While I was there, Maria phoned again to say that Mateo would be dropping her and Elisha home at around 10:00 tomorrow morning.

Later as I walked back to the Gay Bar, I started to mentally formulate my plan of action, and to chronologically elucidate the series of events that resulted in Frobisher's fall from grace together with those that led to him being exonerated of any legal wrongdoing. I fully accept responsibility for my own actions and will face whatever sanctions, whether legal or otherwise, that Basil deems appropriate. However, this is a very delicate issue, and I would hate to think that later I would be accused of disloyalty or duplicity, and therefore felt that it would be wise for me to take along a trusted friend to act as an independent witness.

As has been seen again recently, my self-appointed karmic assessor does take his retaliatory responsibilities seriously, and from what I understand, his latest show of reprisal towards our boys in blue in general, and the Kilburn nick in particular, has received world-wide coverage by the media. Apparently, during the two days that the station personnel were *confined* to their desks at the nick, supplies had to be lobbed into the station yard by a bloke on a cherry-picker, whose only comment of note recorded in *The Evening Standard* was 'It's a living!'

The Gay Bar was empty on my arrival, apart from *Tony the Tube*, who in every respect of being a discreet and trusted friend, would be an ideal candidate and companion to join me on my meeting with Basil. Fortunately, he is off work for a couple of days and will be happy to join me, more from curiosity than anything else, since I was somewhat evasive in giving him a reason for this hastily arranged meeting. We agreed to meet at the Bread Bin at 11:45 on Thursday.

I have to be honest and state that the prospect of this encounter frightens the life out of me. In the past, I have dealt with many difficult situations, but they have never involved having to explain the unsavoury machinations of myself and friends to another. The fact that, this particular *other* happens to be a member of the legal establishment, does add to my general sense of foreboding and trepidation. But then I comforted myself with the truth that in the unlikely event of Siddhartha Gautama finding himself in a similar situation, that he would have faced the issue fearlessly, and would have manfully accepted whatever punishment was due. And if he can do it, so can I!

Simon Stockton phoned me at around 17:15 to say that Nabil (Elisha's dad) would be free on Friday at around 10:00 and if that was convenient with me, he would phone him back. I replied in the affirmative. Simon phoned again a little later, to reaffirm that the meeting was now scheduled.

I had a quiet night of reflection at home.

Goodnight, Ginny.
P xx

11th April 2012

Good morning, Ginny.

I slept surprisingly well last night and was determined to spend the day with Elisha and Maria. The trouble is, not being an expert on the type of entertainment that would be suitable for a six-year-old child, I would have to obtain Maria's advice on the matter.

As promised, Mateo dropped the two girls off at 10:00 and I was pleased to have them both home again. I suggested to Maria that we should all go out for the day, which was very enthusiastically received by Elisha.

Without asking her, Maria suggested the children's zoo at Battersea Park, and Elisha screamed with delight. You see, it's all very simple when you put other minds to it!

The biggest problem with this was that getting there would be a bit of a trek, and realistically most of the journey would have to be made by tube. Driving would be out of the question since I would have more chance of being mugged by a daffodil than finding a parking space in Battersea. I really didn't feel that I could cope with the tube journey however, so I checked various maps and realised that we could take a bus to Victoria, another to Vauxhall and then yet another from there to Battersea Park. We could keep Elisha amused showing her the various London sights *en route,* so after a quick bite to eat, we caught the first bus on our London adventure at 11:15.

We got to Battersea Park at 12:45 and from the time that she arrived until the time we left Elisha was an absolute bundle of energy, rushing from one pen to the next, and squealing with delight at the various animals on show. Much of the emphasis was on baby animals, and there was an amazing variety of them to see. The children were encouraged to stroke the baby rabbits, and some of them could be fed with little bits of lettuce, but Elisha's favourite was a small enclosure that housed a number of tiny piglets.

A photographer with a small monkey wandered around touting for business and of course, Elisha wanted a picture holding the monkey. Having paid the chap, I gave him one of my cards and he said that the photograph and its negative would be sent through the post.

Maria insisted on buying us all scrummy ice creams, and as usual when we are together, we shared a lot of fun and laughter, and my previous melancholic mood was thankfully consigned to history, at least for the time being.

On leaving at 15:25, Elisha stated that she hoped that 'Her new daddy would bring her again', and Maria, smiled at her lovingly and said, 'Well if he doesn't, I'll smack his bum!' which set Elisha off giggling again. I thought that the zoo was a beautiful experience for the children as it was for the adults, and I won't forget our wonderful adventure to the Battersea Park children's zoo.

On the various buses home, Elisha relived the sight of just about every new animal that she had seen, and as we neared home, inevitably she asked if we could go to McDonald's for dinner.

When we arrived at Kilburn, I gave Maria enough money to adequately cover the cost of their evening meals, and I gave them both a hug and a kiss and then made for the Gay Bar.

Ted was in very animated conversation with Dave and Jack Siddall as I arrived, in fact so engrossed were they that I didn't even get a nod of recognition as I walked past them to the bar.

'Jim is a one-off, Jack,' Dave said. 'He has had us in fits of laughter over the years.'

Being the superb raconteur that he is, Ted said, 'One of his best, related to that story about his uncle Conor,' Dave nodded encouragingly having remembered the anecdote and chuckled away to himself.

'Apparently being in his eighties at the time,' Ted continued, 'on one occasion in an attempt to liven up their non-existent sex life, his wife *Erin* dressed up in a *Wonder Woman* costume that she had earlier hired from a local fancy dress shop, and just before pub closing time she hid in their bedroom wardrobe. As Uncle Conor tottered into the bedroom slightly worse for wear, she leapt out of the wardrobe and shouted *Super Vagina!* Which clearly took him by surprise.

'Apparently, looking up at her timidly, he slowly got up from the floor panting like a pair of blacksmith's bellows, and having finally got over the initial shock, he sat down wearily on the bed and replied, *I'll take the feckin soup!*'

A great deal of laughter followed, and for the first time I thought that Vlado had actually understood the joke, since he laughed along with the rest of us, which is more than can be said for Alfie who had listened to Ted's tale patiently, and following the punchline and the laughter that followed, initially looked at us all enquiringly. Clearly he had no idea what it was all about, but rather than offend anyone, he decided to laugh anyway. Such is the gentle innocent naivety of the man. He might not be the sharpest crayon in the box, but he is a very endearing member of the team.

I wanted to have a chat with Ted in relation to his latest encounter with the local constabulary but felt it could wait until Mr Siddall was no longer around. But later, as Jack made for the Water-Loo, Ted said to me that he needed to talk to me 'urgently' and before I could reply he said, 'Bread Bin at seven!' Due to the considerable amount of urgency in his voice, this was a command that clearly could not be ignored.

With a little over thirty minutes to spare, I dashed home just to make sure that the girls were alright, and to have a quick freshen up. I arrived back at Rosheen's hostelry just before the appointed hour.

Ted was sitting away from the bar at a table by the dartboard when I arrived, and there was a pint of lager waiting for me. To cut our very long and quite disturbing conversation into manageable bites, in his usual inimitable style, he explained that he knew all about my intended meeting with Basil, and then went on to state that I was being 'cunningly tested'.

He informed me that with regard to the Frobisher issue that he had come clean with Basil and told him the whole story a few weeks ago. However, the 'complete truth' had been slightly altered. Basil believed Ted's story that Frobisher had indeed been set up with regard to the jewellery that had been found in his garage. Ted convinced him that this was due to a long-standing grievance between Frobisher and a *certain party* that was bent on his destruction both socially and domestically. He made it clear to Basil, however, that he was not prepared to divulge the culprit's name, but for *a modest sum* he could provide a very obliging scapegoat who would be willing to exonerate Frobisher fully. Apparently, Ted then went on to describe Mr O'Toole's very sad tale.

Initially, Basil wasn't happy about Dickie becoming *the fall guy* (as you Americans would say) but he had a chance to discuss the issue with him personally, and like me, he realised that it was the best option for both of the parties involved. The evidence against Frobisher was pretty conclusive, and from what Ted told me, Basil wasn't very hopeful that his man would walk free.

All of this subterfuge was going on without my knowledge, and as if that wasn't bad enough, I wasn't very impressed with what followed. Apparently, some time later Basil and Ted had a bit of an argument with regard to the question of loyalty. Ted was of the opinion that I would never betray him to another, whether under duress or through bribery, and while Basil was likewise in agreement that I perhaps couldn't be bought, he believed that he could get me to, as he put it, 'spill the beans' following a systematic plan of action bent on targeting my main weakness (which is my conscience). Basil is all too aware that like my heart, I always carried it on my sleeve.

Cleverly, Basil knew that his questioning me about Ted's integrity, and the planting of Jack Siddall as a potential snoop, would have alerted me to the suggestion that he was closing the net, as it were, and that he would inevitably find out the truth. He believed that I would come clean about the situation before this happened, and he had estimated my reaction correctly. But that aside, I was very annoyed to learn that I was being systematically set up just as surely as Frobisher had been.

I was likewise horrified to learn that they had a hundred-pound wager between them – Basil believing that at the meeting tomorrow I would tell him the complete unabridged story, which would ultimately incriminate Ted, which was in complete opposition to Ted's belief that I would never *grass* on a friend in general and him in particular.

'There is more chance of Basil phoning Alfie and offering him his job back than of you grassing me up to Mr Lang tomorrow,' he said confidently. 'I can almost see those one hundred pounds, in used ten pound notes, resting comfortably in my chaise lounge piggy-bank,' he said.

This set my ever-rampant imagination on a little cunning plan of my own. 'You are that sure that I won't drop you in the proverbial tomorrow?' I said.

'Absolutely mate!' he replied.

'Well be that as it may, I thank you whole-heartedly for your faith in me, although I think that you could be wrong in your assumption that Basil wouldn't give Alfie a second chance, and give him a little tinkle and offer him his job back,' I said. 'Stranger things have been known to happen, Ted.'

'No chance!' he said. 'If Alfie was the last person on this earth, take it from me son, Basil would not employ him again. Having proved himself untrustworthy, he is quite simply *persona non grata,* as far as Basil is concerned.'

'You're a bit of a gambling man, how's about a little wager on it?' I said.

'Go on then,' he said. 'How much would you like to donate to my retirement fund?'

Oh I dunno... how's about fifty?'

'Make it a round hundred and you've got a bet!'

We shook hands on it, and I bade him a fond farewell. Thereafter I made my way home.

On going to bed, I was feeling very downcast indeed and not a little disappointed that two people whom I have held in such high regard could behave so despicably. However, as it has turned out, I am very pleased that Ted had given his tale to Basil, and more importantly that he had told me about it since had he not done so, I would have been left in the unenviable position of either concocting a similar story, or ultimately telling Basil the truth. I am therefore very thankful indeed that I no longer have to make a choice between the two.

However, as I was drifting off to sleep, the rudiments of a plan started to develop. I realised that being privy to the intentions and expectations of both conspirators gave me a slight advantage, and that therefore I could play them at their own little game. Frankly, they both need to be taught a lesson. The first step would be to have a word with Alfie tomorrow morning at the pub, prior to my meeting with Basil.

However, Alfie's memory might just prove to be the fly in the ointment.

Goodnight, Ginny.

P xx

12th April 2012

Good morning, Ginny.

I slept surprisingly well last night and was awake and ready to 'get out there amongst it' at 06:30 this morning.

I dashed over to the gym first thing, and had a very enlivening weight-training workout followed by a little cardiovascular exercise on the cross-trainer. Thereafter, I enjoyed a poach in the steam room for a while, where I finally decided on my plan of action. This was followed by a shave and an invigorating shower, and in all honesty I cannot think of a more satisfying way of starting a new day. I felt on top of the world on my way home.

I was back at the homestead at 07:55 and all was very quiet indeed as I tiptoed into the kitchen. Both of my girls' bedroom doors were still closed, and I crept quietly around the flat like a caterpillar checking out a rose bush.

Within minutes of my arrival however, I heard a rustling sound coming from Maria's room, a noise which slowly built up in volume. It peaked as Maria's door was suddenly flung open, and Maria and Elisha came charging down the hall like two March hares, in search of a little out of character behaviour. Jimena followed up the rear, stopping halfway along the hall, and with one back leg pointing skywards, she started to clean her undercarriage in that inimitable feline way. It's a shame that Ted wasn't here to witness the spectacle, since I'm sure that it would have set him up for the day.

Breakfast was completed at 08:30 and as is now the case, Maria cleared the table, washed up, and systematically replaced all of the breakfast crockery and cutlery into their designated places.

Following their morning ablutions, Maria stated that she was taking Elisha to the park. It was a pretty cold morning so I advised her to make sure that they were both well wrapped up. As they were leaving, I told Maria that they would both be needed tomorrow at around ten to see Mr Stockton. Initially, she didn't understand. I cautiously pointed towards Elisha who was busily checking out her day bag and gave her a wink. She suddenly nodded as the penny dropped, and she intimated to me that I should give her a call on her mobile anon.

Once they had left, I gave it around ten minutes or so and then I phoned her to confirm that Elisha would be meeting her father at the social services office at 10:00 tomorrow morning.

A little later, I visited The Magpie and met up with Alfie who was busy sweeping outside the Gay Bar entrance. I have never seen him looking more radiantly happy.

After the usual pleasantries were concluded, I informed him that in the near future he may receive a phone call from Basil asking him if he'd be interested in returning to work for him. He looked at me as though I was mad, but I allayed his concerns and then gave him the whole story. I went over it all again to ensure that he fully understood what I had told him, and I reminded him that like the Frobisher issue, he was not to discuss it with *anyone.*

As arranged, I met Tony outside the Bread Bin at 11:45. He was still very inquisitive about the whole issue, but I stated that he will be put out of his misery very shortly.

I wasn't in the mood for a drink and led Tony into Rosheen's private room which was at the back of the premises. Basil was already in attendance and was sat at a small circular table on our arrival. As we entered the room he stood up. We shook hands and I then introduced Tony, stating that due to the delicacy of the meeting that I thought it best to have an independent observer present. Basil nodded understandingly, and then obligingly shook Tony's hand as well. He was smiling good-naturedly and before anything else took place he asked if we would like a drink. We both politely declined. Thereafter we made ourselves comfortable on the two other vacant chairs.

Once all was quiet, Basil opened his briefcase and collected an A4 pad and a pen, which he placed in front of him. I was rather impressed when Tony took a small reporter's notebook and pen from his pocket, which he likewise placed down on the table in front of him.

It was all so very dramatic and with writing pens at the ready, like lances at a mediaeval jousting session, Basil invited me to make my opening statement.

Firstly, I thanked them both for attending and then for Tony's benefit, I gave what could be considered as an outline of the issues, explaining that a few weeks ago, a very unfortunate miscarriage of justice had taken place which ultimately led to a man being deprived of his livelihood.

Basil nodded in agreement and wrote a few things down, as did Tony.

Looking up from his notepad, Basil stated that I had forgotten to mention that the person in question was in fact completely innocent of the crime and had in fact been 'fitted up!'

I pointed out however that this was not correct, in that Alfie had made no bones about the fact that he had stolen the ginger nuts and the toilet rolls, and there was no suggestion of him having been fitted up! He had freely admitted his guilt and accepted his subsequent loss of employment stoically.

Basil looked at me in surprise and then asked me what on earth I was talking about.

To cut a very long-winded saga down to the salient points, I stated that the purpose of my requesting the meeting was to plead the case of Alfred John Tillington, who had been sacked from a job that he loved, for stealing a few ginger nut biscuits and an undisclosed quantity of toilet rolls.

Before Basil had time to interrupt, I went on to provide what I considered to be a perfectly feasible reason behind the theft of the items of property that belonged to Basil. It was a lengthy discourse and to add to its considerable disturbing quality, I introduced a little pathos, with my voice faltering periodically and intermittently falling silent as though trying to control my apparent distressed condition. My theatrical performance had clearly been convincing because at one point, dear old Tony gave my hand a supportive squeeze under the table.

My story revolved around Alfie's (fictitious) elderly aunt who had been living in almost indescribable poverty in an undisclosed charitable foundation. Being the last of his relatives, she had sadly been diagnosed with terminal pancreatic cancer and had since passed away. Alfie had been giving her almost all of his meagre salary which he had received while working for Basil, and sadly just before she died, she developed chronic dysentery. In the hope of making her final days comfortable, instead of her using the dreadful shiny non-absorbent toilet paper (familiar to school children in the fifties) which was supplied by the home, reluctantly Alfie decided to *borrow* a few rolls of Basil's superior grade toilet tissue. He fully intended replacing them when his finances improved.

Needless to say, *Aunt Maudie's* favourite biscuits were ginger nuts, and again going against his innately honest character, he took a few of Basil's abundant supply of biscuits to give her as a little treat. Sadly over the years she could not afford to replace her ill-fitting dentures, and in her last few weeks of life she could only ingest vitamin- and mineral-fortified milk drinks, but could also manage to suck the odd biscuit or two which she enjoyed immensely. Throughout my discourse, Tony had been scribbling away busily.

Throughout all of this lengthy discourse, Basil just sat there with his mouth agape, but slowly his shoulders started to slump forward in a posture of utter wretchedness and despair. He hadn't written anything down on his notepad, and just periodically nodded as my sad tale unfolded.

When I had finished, Basil looked up and judging by his facial expression he had been clearly moved by my story. I left it at that, making out that I was too distressed to continue. On standing I shook his hand and thanked him for allowing me the opportunity to offload the terrible feelings of guilt and unhappiness that I had suffered, and I wished him well. He was very quiet indeed as Tony and I left.

Once out into the fresh air I quite literally breathed an audible sigh of relief. I thanked Tony for his very kind assistance, and believing that he deserved an explanation, I told him the full story. He found it all rather amusing and complimented me on my acting capabilities.

I thanked him for his help and complimented him on his very attentive behaviour during the meeting, but was curious to know what he had written down on his notepad. He gave me his notes to examine, and I had to laugh when I realised it was nothing more than a pretty comprehensive weekend shopping list.

Thereafter we hastened to the Gay Bar where Vlado was in conversation with Alfie.

'Yeah it was all very upsetting Vlado, and I did what I could,' said Alfie, biting into a sandwich. 'Auntie Maudie was my last living realative,' he said.

'The word is relative, Alfie,' I said helpfully.

He looked at me and smiled. 'She died with a broken pancake and a sore bum.'

'I am very sad for the loss you have Alfred, and have kind wishings for your easy mind,' said Vlado, clearly trying to be as supportive as he could.

When Vlado had vanished from the bar, I asked Alfie what he was doing, and why had he mentioned the story about his Aunt Maudie?

'I just didn't want to forget, in case someone asked me,' he said.

Bless his heart, I understood what he was saying, but reminded him, that from here on in the subject was closed. However, I reminded him that he may have a phone call from Basil, and just to make it clear again, I went over the reason why he had taken the biscuits and the toilets rolls. I also suggested to him that it would be a nice gesture on his part to tell Basil that now that he is working again, that he would be willing to pay for the items that he took. He nodded at me enthusiastically.

On leaving later, I asked him to contact me immediately if Basil should give him a call and let me know what was said.

'Do you think he will call?' he asked.

'Well I have a hundred good reasons why I sincerely hope that he will, Alfie!' I said, and tapping the side of my nose with my right index finger, I left for home.

I wasn't in the mood for socialising thereafter and had a quiet afternoon and evening at home. I met up with Lenka briefly, as she left for work and thereafter as I lay in a relaxing bath with Sebastian surfing in the suds, I considered the day's events. I have not been very happy at my less than honest behaviour, but at least I need no longer be troubled about the Frobisher issue, which like my conscience can now be finally put to rest.

Goodnight, Ginny.

P xx

13th April 2012

Good morning, Ginny.

There was a lot of noise coming from the bathroom at 06:10 this morning, and getting up to investigate, I heard what sounded like Maria and Elisha splashing about in the bath. This was very unusual since they normally take a morning shower.

Jimena was her normal predictable self however, and as I made for the kitchen to enliven my coffee percolator, she jumped up onto the kitchen table and having graciously allowed me to stroke her head, made it quite evident that despite the noise, her breakfast preparations should continue as normal. I duly complied a little later, and having finished her breakfast, she washed her paws and face and then trotted out into the hall. A little later, drowning out the sounds of the girls' merriment in the bathroom, she proceeded to *barf* violently on the hall carpet.

I rushed out of the kitchen and found her looking up at me apologetically, although it was short lived, since she felt the urgent need to let off a little frustrated steam and shot off down the hall as though her bum was on fire. She bashed into the wall on the way down and, like a bullet ricocheting off a rock, she bounced headlong into Maria's bedroom.

I cleaned up the very unwelcome mess and then thoroughly washed the carpet with hot water and disinfectant. I was on my hands and knees as the girls vacated the bathroom wrapped in towels. They looked at me enquiringly.

'I am so sorry my ladies,' I said, getting up and dusting myself down. 'The dowager duchess had a little accident this morning. Soames is cleaning out the stables and the scullery maid is on holiday. May I prepare breakfast, Lady Elisha?'

She looked at me in bewilderment. Maria squeezed her hand and said, 'He's just being silly!'

Elisha rushed down to me and hugged my leg, and in a rather concerned voice she said, 'Are you just being silly?'

'Of course I am my darling,' I said, picking her up and giving her an affectionate hug.

Thereafter, I made us all breakfast which was full of the inevitable fun and laughter, although Maria was unusually quiet and was clearly fighting back tears. Elisha simply couldn't stop talking about her adventures at the zoo yesterday, and I have no doubt that the experience will remain with her for the rest of her life (as it will me).

Later, Maria carefully dressed Elisha in her best little outfit. We left home at 09:35 and walked along to the social services office, where on our arrival we were met by Simon Stockton who was seated in the reception area. We all went up in the lift to the third floor, and he invited us into an office which looked very plush and was clearly meant to be used for meetings of this kind.

As we entered, Emily Brand and Nabil stood up, and Simon invited us to sit in the three chairs opposite them. Emily sat down, but Nabil remained standing as though he was riveted to the spot.

Elisha clearly had no idea as to the purpose of this visit, but like most children of her age, she would have unquestioningly followed us through the gates of hell, provided I was holding her hand (bless her little white mittens).

Once we were seated, Simon welcomed us all and then introduced us to Nabil, who smiled at us good-naturedly. But from the time that we had entered the room, his full attention was on Elisha, and he had remained standing as though he was suddenly in the presence of royalty. His adoring eyes were transfixed on his little girl from the moment that we had entered the room. Simon had to gently awaken him from his trance-like state, inviting him to regain his seat.

'Oh I do beg your pardon,' Nabil said apologetically, and clearly embarrassed, he quietly sat down, absentmindedly checking that his tie was still around his neck.

Emily Brand was the first to open the proceedings.

'Thank you all for coming,' she said, enthusiastically. 'This is one part of our job that both Simon and I enjoy immensely. But before we go any further, I would like to officially introduce Nabil Al Tajir who has come forward to claim legal custody of his daughter Elisha. I have made diligent enquiries into his claim and from my investigation can confirm that the man that you see before you is the said Nabil Al Tajir, and likewise that he is the biological father of Elisha.'

She produced a passport and another official-looking document. 'These are Nabil's credentials, which consist of his Iraqi certificate of birth and his British passport, which are clear proof of his identity.' She passed them to me for my scrutiny.

Opening a file, she produced three other documents. She placed them down on the desk and said, 'This is the birth certificate of Elisha Amira, who was born in London on the 25th May 2006. The parents are named as Nabil Al Tajir and his wife Jasmine Al Tajir (*nee* Asghar) who sadly passed away on the morning of the 3rd April this year.' Holding up a small certificate she said, 'I have her death certificate, should you wish to see it. These documents are available for your inspection today, and certified copies of them will be held in Elisha's file for any later inspection.'

Throughout Emily's discourse, Nabil did not take his eyes off Elisha. It suddenly went quiet, and I heard Elisha say to Maria, 'Is that my daddy?'

Maria was clearly overcome with emotion and had to leave the room. I held Elisha's hand and walked her around the table to where Nabil was sitting. He turned his chair around to face her as we approached. I released her hand a few feet away from him, and she timidly walked towards him.

'Are you my daddy?' she asked quietly.

Holding out his hands to her he said, '*Naeam ana amirti, wana ahibuk.*' Which for us non-Arabic speakers he kindly translated, 'Yes I am my princess and I love you!'

She rushed into his arms, and they were locked in a quite wonderful embrace, until Maria returned doing her utmost to raise a smile and attempting to fight against those dreadfully disconcerting emotions that had clearly moved us all.

So far, I had put a brave face on the proceedings, but seeing how distressed Maria was, Elisha hastened around to her and jumped into her arms. I heard her whisper, 'Don't worry, I think he will take me back to the zoo!' which had Maria howling in delight, and frankly it was just what we needed to clear the awkward intensity of the moment.

A little later, coffee, lemonade and cakes were brought in, and Elisha didn't waste any time sampling the various tempting treats. She didn't leave Nabil's side thereafter, and frankly the poor bloke couldn't get a word in edgeways as she gave him a much-remembered narrative detailing her numerous adventures with us. She effortlessly glided through her chronicles with the expertise of a seasoned newsreader, and Nabil sat attentively listening to her discourse clearly enchanted. There was no mistaking the very strong feelings that he had for her.

Periodically, he smiled happily at me and Maria, who following the rather swift ingestion of two jam doughnuts, two chocolate hobnobs and a cup of coffee, had regained her normal composure and sat patiently listening to Elisha's tales. Her eyes shone with unbridled affection for a little girl who had captivated our hearts so completely, and I could not have been more appreciative of the gentle guidance and care that she had given our little one so unconditionally. Frankly, I could not remember another who could equal the profound effect that she has inspired in us, and there is no doubt that when she finally leaves, our mutual feelings of loss will be quite unprecedented.

I would have liked to have had the opportunity of getting to know Nabil a little better but reasoned that this was not the time or place. However, I felt confident that like his daughter, he too would inevitably become part of our extended family. Frankly, I liked the man a great deal and looked forward to our next meeting.

On that subject, Simon stated that Nabil had mentioned before our arrival that he would like Elisha to spend a couple of days with him and Mahmud at his home in Ruislip. In our presence he added that he'd be very happy for Maria to come along too, if she wished.

Elisha, was very excited at the prospect and said, 'Please come too Maria... please... please!'

Maria smiled and nodded her approval. Looking at Nabil and smiling, she said, 'That would be very nice, and yes, thank you, I'd love to come.'

Before we left, Nabil suggested collecting the girls on Monday morning and he would bring them home on Wednesday evening.

I shook his hand and gave him my card. I just reminded him that I would need his full home address and his home and mobile phone numbers before he collected them. He wrote these details down and gave me his business card. Thereafter, we bade him a fond farewell.

'Goodbye daddy,' Elisha said sweetly, giving him a kiss and a cuddle which almost tipped Maria over the emotional edge again, but she managed to control herself.

I thanked both Emily and Simon for their kind attention, and on leaving Simon said, 'I'll be in touch, Paul, and if there is anything that I can help you with, please feel free to give me a call.'

A little later, with Elisha swinging in between us again like that little trapeze artist, we made our way back home, all of us in very high spirits and like those mad March hares, were full of the joys of spring.

Back at home, Lenka greeted us all excitedly, having eagerly awaited our return following Elisha's meeting with her father.

Elisha took her hand (which I thought was absolutely delightful) and guided her into the lounge, where for a child of such tender years, she gave her a quite amazingly accurate account of the meeting. We all listened intently to her charmingly sweet narration of the events that had excited her so completely, and like her usual bedtime story, we had become very real participants in what was effectively her first real-life fairy story. A tale which we all hoped would have an ecstatically happy ending.

The rest of the day was spent in the company and cherished familiarity of my loved ones, and just for a change, for our evening meals, I ordered a takeaway from our local Chinese restaurant, which excited Elisha a great deal. She has never eaten oriental food before.

I was in no mood to venture out this evening and was more than simply content to have a relaxing lounge in the bath before retiring to my bed.

As I was soaking in the suds, my mind produced a kaleidoscope of beautiful images of today's events, and I came to the conclusion that the experience of watching such happy occasions must be very beneficial and pre-eminently therapeutic for one's mental well-being. I reasoned that for those unfortunate souls who were suffering from depression for example, that part of their treatment should consist of hourly bouts of therapy sitting in the arrivals lounge of any of our airports to watch the indescribable happiness and joy of people being reunited with their loved ones. I believe that it would beat any number of hours of psychiatric treatment or counselling, and indeed it could put a number of pharmaceutical companies out of business, particularly those involved in the manufacture of anti-depressant drugs, which I have always firmly believed do more harm than good.

Goodnight, Ginny.
P xx

14th April 2012

Good morning, Ginny.

Another Saturday morning took Kilburn High Road completely by surprise, and people were deliriously dashing around as though the end of the world was nigh. For some it was a very real possibility, particularly those who were bent on grabbing a 'little something' for their own *stinky ties* back at the reservation who in their diligent search, were totally oblivious to the homicidal tendencies of the Saturday morning drivers, all bent on finding that non-existent parking space.

Tying up one's steed in Kilburn is never exactly trouble free at the best of times, and at weekends it is almost impossible. But following their journey's abroad and having been subjected to the infuriating habits of people creeping out of their hotels before sunrise and putting their *Bayern Munich* towels on loungers before breakfast, many canny Kilburnians had adopted a similar stance by parking their cars in the abundant spaces late on a Friday evening. A practice that is considered 'highly irregular and beastly unfair' by visiting shoppers from the more upmarket areas like Maida Vale and St John's Wood, who on principle would not behave in such a despicable manner. Although to be fair, many of those that complain can generally afford to take their own sunloungers with them on holiday anyway.

Lenka, Maria and Elisha were out on another girls' shopping day, and I was on a quest to hire my formal attire for Lenny's wedding which takes place in a week's time. Due to the relatively unpretentious circles in which I am normally to be found, I have never needed to wear formal clothing, but not wishing to upset the boy on his big day, I will comply with his wishes.

On my bus into town I had a thought. (I seem to be doing that quite a lot lately.) Given my ancestral heritage, I suppose I am what could be described as a multicultural Englishman when it comes to my Celtic descent. Although I could also be considered as Anglo-Irish and Anglo-Scots since my original ancestors (like most of the world's western population) came from Ireland. Mine then moved to Scotland and later still, branches of my immediate family travelled south into England.

Where is all of this leading, I hear you ask? Well, given my general reluctance in ever wishing to clothe myself in the trappings of the socially elite, and being at heart an innate socialist, by way of compromise I had seriously considered wearing Scottish formal attire for Lenny's wedding. Apart from any other consideration, this would probably be the last chance I shall ever have of legitimately wearing the kilt. However, before I could actually make a decision, I felt that it would be better to speak to him about it first.

When I got off the bus at Marble Arch, I phoned Lenny to discuss the matter, and he was positively gushing with enthusiasm at the prospect, adding that he thought that it would constitute 'a certain other-worldly classy element to the proceedings' which at best went completely against my reasons for wearing Scottish formal attire in the first place. Thereafter a modicum of uncertainty and indecision prevailed against a formerly untroubled mind, and my optimistic carefree spirit evaporated quicker than a squirt of fly killer in a desert. I think that had he appeared a little less pretentious, that I would have gone along with the idea, but I had no intention of wearing proof of my cultural ancestry in anything less than a respectful and honourable manner; totally free from any hint of high-blown pomposity.

In agreement with Ted's observations recently, Lenny's happy-go-lucky personality is slowly being eroded in favour of Eugenia's staid expectations in relation to what she demands in her future husband. His use of the Queen's English and his independent thought processes have improved considerably, and her influence has been quite remarkable. His life and aspirations have gone from the former stumbling blocks of chaos and uncertainty to the stepping stones of order, balance and symmetry. But such is the love of a good woman, who like her feminine counterparts, are by nature congenitally adept at the modification of the masculine psyche.

I firmly believe in the old saying that 'boys will be boys' but that only applies until the females arrive on the scene, and then suddenly they metamorphose into men, just as surely as an awkward uncouth looking caterpillar with dreadful table manners, changes into a beautiful, sophisticated butterfly. The wedding ceremony could quite literally be used as an analogy in relation to what is to be expected of a 'boy's life' following his marriage. The blushing bride enters the church and coincidentally, in the correct chronological order, the first three things that she sees are:

AISLE...ALTAR... YOU...

I managed to hire the necessary (penguin suit) as they are called, and was back on the bus at midday. All that I have to work on now is a suitable best man's speech for the evening reception. The flat was empty on my arrival home, and Jimena did her usual party piece, hurtling along the hall and skilfully clambering up my outer clothing and parking herself on my shoulder, purring contentedly.

Alfie rang ten minutes or so after my arrival home, inviting me to join him at the Goose, and being very interested in what he had to say, I ventured off to spend a little time with him.

As I entered the pub, he came rushing over to me, spilling a fair quantity of his beer on the way. Fortunately, the less than appreciative glares that Thomas Patrick O'Mahoney was giving him went completely unnoticed as he shook my hand excitedly.

He told me that Basil had phoned, requesting him to visit the office at three on Monday. Well that's the first part of my bet secured, I thought, now all that is needed is for Basil to offer him his job back and I'll be one hundred pounds better off.

'That's marvellous Alfie,' I said.

'What do you think he wants to see me about?' he asked.

I sat him down at an empty table and tried to calm him. I reminded him about the story of his Aunt Maudie and said, 'Well with a bit of good luck, he will offer you your job back.'

'But I don't want to work there anymore,' he said defiantly. 'I like to work with Vlado at the pub instead... he is a good boss... I get a lovely breakfast and yesterday, he showed me how to change a barrel of beer, and he might let me do it again tomorrow,' he said excitedly.

'What are your hours of work?' I asked.

'I work four hours from eight till twelve, with my break in the morning for breakfast.'

'Well if Basil wants you to work with him again, why not say that you'd only be available part time. It's a good idea to not to burn your bridge, Alfie,' I said.

He clearly didn't understand what I meant, so to clarify the matter I said, 'It would be good to work with Ted and Tina again, but only sometimes. You could still be part of the Kilburn Unreliables, but only when Basil needed you, and when you were not working at the pub. It would give you extra money too; you could be

Basil's undercover agent!'

He sat thinking for a minute or two. 'I'd be like a secret agent, like one of them spies on the telly!' he said, taking a long swig of his beer, and smiling happily.

'That's right, Alfie,' I said. 'Just think, in a few months you could be working for MI5.'

'No I don't think so, I really shouldn't be driving, 'cos I'm banned!' he replied.

As I was leaving I reminded him (yet again) about the Aunt Maudie story, and the reasons why he had stolen the toilet rolls and biscuits from Basil. He nodded enthusiastically like one of them stupid looking annoying nodding dogs that you see in some of the old bangers owned by a sub-section of the miscellaneous rabble, many of whom it seems, need reminding where they should sit since they have their names emblazoned on the inside top part top of the windscreen for all the world to see.

I walked into the Gay Bar at around 13:50 and nodded at two strangers who were sat at *Whispering Jim's* old table. They were playing cribbage, which is a favourite card game of mine.

Vlado was in a very good mood and he seemed to be considerably more relaxed that I have ever seen him. He poured me a pint of lager and taking it from the bar, I walked over to my usual seat by the window, where my beloved Spike would normally have sat watching the passers-by while munching his way through a split bag of crisps, and growling at them contentedly.

Suddenly the door flew open and the diminutive figure of *Scotch Andy* walked into the centre of the room and glared at the two strangers. He then looked at me and in a very agitated broad Glaswegian accent he said,

'Who are you looking at, and what are you doin sittin in ma fecking chair?'

I stood up quickly and replied, 'Oh I'm dreadfully sorry, mate,' as I nervously walked back towards the bar. 'I forgot, I'll just finish my drink and…''Just sling ya hook afor a lose ma temper!' he said menacingly.

Looking at the two strangers who were clearly very apprehensive indeed, I put the glass down on the bar and slowly walked to the door. Smiling at them awkwardly, I left. I took a seat outside and checked my watch.

At the moment, the record for people hastening out of the bar following our little ruse is around one minute and five seconds, and this was achieved by what turned out to be a Welsh Baptist minister and his wife from Pontypridd, who were on a weekend sabbatical and were hoping to catch one of the current West End shows. They didn't make it however, since they spent the rest of the afternoon and evening enjoying the banter and genuine fellowship of the boys in the Gay Bar. They stumbled back to their hotel at 23:45 apparently (*Brahms and Liszt*) singing that beautifully patriotic Welsh song 'Men of Harlech', having clearly enjoyed their first visit to London, compliments of The Magpie pub in general and the Gay Bar regulars in particular.

Our latest victims left the pub, two minutes and eleven seconds after I had left, and once they were out, I shook their hands warmly, introduced myself to them and then told them that this was a bit of a routine 'wind-up' that we follow whenever we welcome new people to the bar. Once back inside, Andy likewise greeted them enthusiastically, and dropping his Glaswegian accent in favour of his normal pleasantly gentle Dr Finlay-type lilt, he bought them two more drinks. In truth, Andy is to physical violence what Fanny Craddock was to Gas Tungsten Arc Welding. But then, our prospective audiences are clearly not aware of that. All that they see is a very confident, somewhat diminutive man, intimidating a bloke just about twice his size.

Fortunately, this dramatic routine can only occur when all of the elements of the subterfuge are present. Firstly, apart from the targets (strangers to the pub), the bar must be otherwise empty on my arrival. Secondly, *Scotch Andy* must by sheer coincidence enter the pub to set the drama into operation. We have managed to do it a couple of times before, and Vlado (fortunately) finds it all just as amusing as we do. It has never resulted in any trouble, and the people duped have always taken it all in good part. On their return visit, those that have been through the process often relive their first memorable experience at The Magpie, and they are always greeted warmly by the Gay Bar regulars. Lots of fun and merriment usual ensues thereafter.

We spent an hour or so chatting with our newly initiated friends, who introduced themselves as Peter Webb and Danny Gillespie. They were very talkative individuals, particularly Danny, who wanted to know all about the pub and the local area generally. He stated that they were both from Brixham in Devon and had promised themselves a weekend in London. Strangely, neither of them had the type of accents to be expected from people who originate from that part of the world. Added to which, Danny seemed annoyingly familiar, but for the life of me, I couldn't remember where I had seen him before.

I haven't seen or heard from Ted since Wednesday evening, which is quite unusual, although I was told by Andy that he'd seen him on Thursday morning. It is also quite unusual for Andy to be seen at the weekends since his wife (Elaine) had him very well under control, and the chances of him to behave like that aforementioned caterpillar are normally few and far between. However, he was allowed to revert back to his much-lamented boyish self again this weekend, since his wife is away visiting relatives, and clearly he fully intended making the most of it.

Back at home, following their hedonistic bout of what has been called 'retail-therapy', a term which describes the distinctly feminine experience associated with aimlessly wandering around among the traders and costermongers in places like Oxford Street, the girls were all in slow come-down recovery and were in urgent need of a comfortable chair, a little caffeine and a pair of verbal-diarrhoea-resistant ears, down which a veritable diatribe of utterly boring blathering could be stuffed. And while I had attempted to make a casual strategic withdrawal from the immediate area, stuffed down it was!

In Maria's case, she was initially more interested in replenishing her bodily tissues with the ingestion of a substantial quantity of bread pudding and a sizeable slab of chocolate gateau. Elisha was happy with a glass of passion fruit and a biscuit, with Lenka being happier still with a large glass of 'corporation wine' (which my beloved grandma used to call water) and a fairy cake.

However, having been *captured* by them in the kitchen with no real chance of escape apart from possibly leaping out over the balcony railings into the curate's hydrangea plant below, which was not a very appealing thought, particularly since I didn't have my Spider Man outfit handy, and not wishing to put a dampener on the closing stages of their morning adventure, I sat patiently listening and perfunctorily oohed and aahed as the more 'exciting' aspects of their boringly dull ho-hum story unfolded. Finally, having exhausted themselves on the more mundane aspects of the trip, they finished on their *piece de resistance,* which related to the dreadfully insipid tea and tasteless currant buns that was served to them in the John Lewis customer cafeteria.

Later, when all of the morning's reminiscences had been consigned to their mental hard drives, Lenka prepared and cooked an absolutely scrummy pork goulash, with rice and assorted vegetables for out evening meals, and thereafter we all retired to our private domains.

Following an evening soak in the bath, I was happy to have a little read and an early night.

Goodnight, Ginny.
P xx

15th April 2012

Good morning, sugarplum.

Well frankly my day didn't start off too well, since at 01:25 this morning I was awoken by an urgent banging on my front door. I wearily made my way along the hall passageway and opening the door slowly, I peered out into the darkness and could just about make out the silhouette of a man slumped across the stairwell railings. On opening the door wider to give more light to the area, I found that it was my old pal Andy. He looked up at me and gave me one of those truly ridiculous smiles normally associated with a drunkard that doesn't have full control of his senses, let alone his facial expressions.

I helped him into the flat and guided him into the lounge. I sat him down on the sofa and he was clearly in a very inebriated state. Following his initial indecipherable utterances, I got to understand that he'd lost his door keys. I collected a spare duvet from my bedroom cupboard and when I returned to the lounge he was flat out on my sofa fast asleep. I gently took off his shoes and covered him with the duvet, and tiptoeing out of the room and turning off the light, I silently closed the door behind me.

Back in bed as I was drifting off to sleep again, I thought about the very few occasions when I had allowed myself to become wide-eyed and legless, and on those very rare occasions, I realised that despite my mental and physical incapacity the night before, that I had always managed to wake up in my own bed the morning after. Well there was that one very unfortunate incident when I landed up in a girl-guide's sleeping bag instead of my own... but as she said, 'I won't go into that!'

At 07:30 this morning, Compton and his itinerant band of aural-assaulting campanologists were rudely awakening all slumbering entities (whether sober or otherwise) within a two-mile radius of St Benedict's Church.

On entering the kitchen to enliven my coffee percolator, I went out onto the balcony and saw Father Marcus walking into the courtyard. He waved up at me enthusiastically, and then with a very creative mime-dance routine, he intimated that he would be phoning me. But since he was quite literally a matter of feet away from me, he could have just as easily told me verbally. Still, I nodded at him enthusiastically, intimating that I had deciphered his message and gave him a smile with double-thumbs up.

A little later as I was sipping my first cup of coffee, a very distraught and dishevelled Andrew Cunningham-Stewart, aka *Scotch Andy,* shuffled into the kitchen. He was looking absolutely dreadful. I didn't say anything initially but poured him a long glass of cool water from my fridge bottle, which he seemingly needed desperately. Following a long and evidently grateful draught, he apologised profusely for being such a nuisance, and hoped that he hadn't caused too much of a disturbance last night. He then went on to relate a rather disjointed tale of his alcoholic debauchery, which he narrated with considerable uncertainty in relation to the venues in question. He believes that he had ended up at the Goose, although it was all a little confused.

He vaguely remembers arriving home, only to find that he had lost his door keys. With Elaine being away, he had no alternative but to seek shelter at my humble abode. Apparently, she will be arriving back home at around 16:00 today and in the meantime, I suggested to him that having a shower and a shave might make him feel a little better, and that once the girls were up, that I'd make him a bit of breakfast. I gave him a fresh towel and he sauntered off to the bathroom.

He came back into the kitchen around twenty-five minutes later, looking considerably better, and was clearly refreshed. His arrival coincided with that quiet unidentifiable rustle that will inevitably increase in volume, and ultimately result in an exuberantly joyful rush of eight legs of various shapes and sizes along the hall, all of them being bound for culinary sanctuary in the kitchen.

As predicted a little later, Maria, Elisha and Jimena arrived, all bent on a little brekkie-nosebag. Andy decided that he wouldn't stay for breakfast but thanked me for my hospitality. On leaving, I asked him if he would be free for 'a quick livener later' in the day, and he smiled at me ruefully and stated that he would 'possibly' be available until around 15:30. The cat's arrival home at around 16:00, presumably putting paid to any further rodent activity for the day and indeed the foreseeable future.

Lenka was beaming happily and seemingly couldn't wait to 'get out there amongst it' this morning and suggested taking the girls to Camden Lock. This was met with an enthusiastic howl of delight from Elisha who clearly didn't need any persuading, and Maria smiled and nodded happily, which also registered her similar approval at the suggestion.

I made us all an assortment of breakfasts: Lenka just wanted toast, Elisha had a bowl of cereal with chopped banana and yogurt and my Maria had pancakes and chopped bananas liberally coated in maple syrup, followed by a peach and a couple of chocolate hobnobs. I was happy with a yogurt followed by a toasted ham and cheese sandwich. Naturally, copious quantities of coffee and mango juice were drunk, although following her morning meal of tuna in gravy, Jimena preferred a nice cool saucer of semi-skimmed milk, which she lapped up in her usual delicate manner.

At around 10:30 they all left, and on the way out Lenka stated that I shouldn't worry about their evening meals since they would all eat out. I had the distinct feeling that another evening trip to McDonald's would be on the cards.

Given the circumstances, were I to find myself presently enslaved in that unnatural union with a woman that they call marriage, today in particular, being temporarily free from the censorial eyes and dictates of my women folk, I could have acted like an unattended coal fire and simply have gone out. However I am spoiled, since unlike the matrimonially shackled, I do not have to cram a number of weeks of boyish behaviour into a twenty-four hour bout of hedonistic debauchery, with all of the over-indulgent excess that this clearly entails.

All seasoned drinkers have learnt that alcohol in moderation can be a very obliging servant, but taken in excess, it changes into an unforgiving tyrannical master. However, we have all been there. It's just that boys in general are considerably slower to forget painful experiences, albeit that many are happy to avail themselves in 'action replays' just as soon as their womenfolk's backs are turned, and the irresistible opportunity of enjoying an additional period of hedonistic pleasure had presented itself once again. Women on the other hand appear to be far more forgetful when it comes to physical pain than their male counterparts. In quantifying this assertion, I believe that I can state quite categorically that the worst possible pain known to the human species has to be the agony experienced by women during childbirth. For men (lacking in imagination) it has been compared with the type of discomfort felt by a man trying to pass a rugby ball out of their anal-orifice, or perhaps more realistically, the dreadful debilitating pain of being kicked in the groin.

A few months after going through the awful pain of childbirth, many women having seemingly forgotten all about it, are happy to consider having another baby and going through it all again. However, I have yet to hear a man state that he's looking forward to his next kick in the bollocks!

I am singularly blessed with having a mind of my own, which is completely uninfluenced by the dictatorial demands of a member of the so called 'fairer sex'– a term used to describe women as a collective, and of course this includes wives. By inference therefore one could argue that the males must be considered as the 'unfair sex' and given the rise in cases of assaults on women and domestic violence generally, this designation could be justifiably appropriate. However, in recent years, cases of 'husband bashing' have been reported in ever-increasing numbers, so it's clearly not a one-sided issue. It certainly suggests limitations to the term 'weaker sex,' and perhaps this could explain why those men, who have been present at childbirth, never mention the possibility of having additional children, at least until a couple of years later, when both he and his wife had completely forgotten about the pain and dreadful trauma entirely.

I believe that if it were the men who were responsible for giving birth, adoptions would rise dramatically, maternity wards would become obsolete, apart from providing a limited service for the occasional kick in the groin enthusiast, and this planet's dreadfully overcrowded population would halve in less than a generation.

'Men are from Mars and women are from Venus' seems to conveniently sum up the differences between the sexes, but I feel that this simple definition is totally inadequate and completely misses what I believe to be a fundamental truism. Despite what the learned geneticists and anthropological scientists tell us, I am convinced that girls are genetically programmed to reach maturity by the age of six, whereas boys are simply destined to mentally remain infants for the rest of their lives, and hence my own adaption to the very well-known saying 'boys will *always* be boys'.

With the afternoon to myself, I checked out the internet for the exact location of West Togram. I found that from Southampton City centre I could get an X21 bus to the village, which apparently is around a twenty-minute ride away. With Maria and Elisha being with Nabil on the forthcoming Monday and Tuesday, I would be totally free to go down and visit what could be my future home. I then checked out British Rail and found that around three trains an hour leave from Waterloo to Southampton daily. I decided therefore that on Tuesday morning I would leave bright and early and check out the bungalow that awaits my inspection at 4, Birdcage Way, in the village of West Togram, Hampshire. How on earth did we ever manage without the internet?

Thereafter I then spent an hour or so making notes for my forthcoming best man's speech at Lenny's wedding, and I remembered some very funny anecdotes that I thought I could use.

At around 18:30 I decided to take a stroll down to the Bread Bin, and was very surprised to find Andy sitting at the bar. Apparently, at around 16:10 he had met

362

Elaine on her arrival outside of Kilburn Park station, and she was quite touched that he had taken the trouble to meet her. Hand in hand he had accompanied her home – and they say that romance is dead?

He naturally didn't tell her about the loss of his flat keys, or his alcoholic adventures during her absence, and allowed her to use her fob and key to gain entry to the estate and their flat.

Fortunately, once inside their home, he found his own keys on the toilet cistern, and reasoned that before he had left yesterday afternoon, he had clearly visited the bathroom to brush his hair, splash a little aftershave around and have a slash, before he set about the serious business of getting as much booze down his neck as was humanly possible. With his mind on such hedonistic thoughts, it is quite understandable why he had left his keys behind.

Elaine was very happy to be home, and by way of showing a little gratitude for his selfless act in meeting her from the station, she suggested that as a reward, he should go out and have a few beers. He was very grateful for her unexpected and very kind gesture, since he was still suffering from his former booze-fest and was in desperate need of *the hair of the dog*, which is a belief that drinking more booze will relieve the very unpleasant symptoms associated with alcohol over-indulgence. It stems from a very ancient old wives tale type of thing, which suggests that the cause of an ailment can also be used in its cure. However, medical research suggests that drinking more booze during a hangover is doing nothing more miraculous than simply relieving the main symptoms of alcohol withdrawal, which are the usual very unpleasant feelings associated with the common hangover.

Following a phone call from Elaine, Andy left for home at 18:45 and for a very short time I was friendless until my dear Lenka phoned asking for my whereabouts. She arrived at the pub a little later, and for the next thirty minutes or so she entertained me with a very funny account of her earlier experiences with Maria and Elisha.

We were on our second drink when Bunny Longhurst walked past the pub, and noticing us sitting in the saloon bar, his former homeward trajectory was spontaneously changed and he called in and joined us. He looked like he had just returned from a Kenyan safari, and I was not far wrong, but his quarry had not been the lion, the elephant or the rhino, nor had he just returned from Africa. Apparently he had spent the entire weekend camping in the highlands of Scotland hoping to catch sight of one of the rarest birds to be found in the UK. His excitement was almost overwhelming when he showed us a number of beautiful digital photographs on his very professional-looking camera of the capercaillie, which apparently prefers the Scottish pinewood, which according to learned ornithologists is 'a rare and vulnerable habitat', and as a result, its population had declined so seriously that there was a very real risk of it becoming extinct altogether. Sadly it is on the RSPB 'Red List' of endangered species.

Jokingly, I said that I wondered if I should put *Ted the Pleb* on the endangered list since I hadn't seen or heard from him since last Wednesday. After all, The Magpie pub was not 'a rare and vulnerable habitat' for one that uses it more frequently than a vagrant visits a soup kitchen.

And then suddenly like an unexpected bolt of lightning, I remembered where I had seen Danny Gillespie before. Some weeks previously (perhaps you will remember) when on a similar Sunday, I had visited the Bread Bin, and Bunny and I had disturbed the two other well-dressed blokes in the bar? Well, I asked Bunny about whether he could remember the incident. He initially didn't recall it, but when I mentioned the part about them being possible Jehovah Witnesses, he smiled and then repeated what he'd said on the day in question that 'they were out-of-work burglars looking for unattended houses'. This apparently was said in jest, and he had simply repeated what was believed to be nothing more than malicious gossip. But then from my experience of the stereotypical nosey *fatherless-people* that are known to frequent this particular pub, and being the unashamed serial people-watchers that they were, that on occasion those same questionable snippets of malicious gossip had proved to be correct.

A few years ago, an apparent unsubstantiated rumour was being spread around that the pub would be closing. Nobody took much notice but following its 15:00 closure on one fateful Sunday afternoon, before the locals had even sat down to enjoy their normal roast dinners, a team of covert demolition experts came in and bulldozed the entire building, lock, stock and barrel.

After a last-ditch attempt by the landowners to 'legally' clear the site in readiness for the proposed building of a luxury housing complex, the pub was demolished illegally. But being a 'listed' building, the avaricious *fatherless-people* responsible were served with an official court order, to rebuild the pub, brick by brick to its original specifications. Thank goodness for good old British common sense and the luck of the Irish. Apparently, the presiding judge at the court case was from County Cork.

Before our subject of conversation had changed, Bunny went on to say that our 'two suspected burglars' had been seen in the Bread Bin on numerous occasions, which certainly contradicted Mr Gillespie's story that they were visitors from South Devon. But then perhaps I was simply being a little overly suspicious because they both appeared to be pretty genuine blokes.

Bunny left at around 20:50 looking absolutely exhausted, but he had clearly enjoyed his weekend away following his interesting and much cherished pastime.

Once he had left, Lenka ordered another couple of drinks and placed a very large cognac in front of me. She then went on to explain that she had been offered a teaching post back in Slovakia, working with mentally retarded children, and she asked me what I thought. As I spoke, I started to feel a little emotional but I answered her as honestly as I could, stating that her selfless concern and support for the dispossessed or disadvantaged was beyond question. Her humble self-effacing personality and the quiet way that she went about caring for others was one of her more endearing qualities, and clearly her teaching capabilities as evidenced by the miraculous change in Zora-Aleena's confidence, quite apart from her proficiency in spoken English, was quite remarkable. Reluctantly I had to admit that if she did not accept the position, a lot of very unfortunate children would miss out on her very special caring qualities and her undeniably talented teaching abilities.

She smiled at me bashfully, and as a tell-tale tear made its way down her cheek, she said,

'I shall miss you a great deal, my dear Paul.'

With a very uncomfortable lump in my throat, I replied, 'As I shall you my beloved girl, and be assured that my love for you will remain unconditional and eternal.'

Needless to say, our quiet and gentle walk home together will remain a cherished memory with me until the end of my life.

Goodnight, Ginny.

P xx

16th April 2012

Good morning, Ginny.

Father Marcus called this morning at around 09:15, just as our breakfast wreckage was being cleared from the kitchen table. Initially he was very apologetic for not phoning me yesterday as promised, but he had apparently become involved in what he called a *pastoral matter,* which could have been anything from a serious and pressing issue relating to one of his parishioners, to a legal method of preventing a number of nomadic goats, owned by a recently arrived traveller group from eating his newly planted spring vegetables, which had been growing in unused burial plots around the church grounds.

Following two pieces of toast, liberally coated with peanut butter, three custard cream biscuits and a cup of coffee, the reason for his visit became clear. Not having Nobby Caxton's new address which he believed was 'somewhere up north' he thought that I might have it. He wanted to send him the proceeds of his collection. I checked my notepad and wrote down Nobby's new Huddersfield address which I handed it to him.

On leaving, I asked him how much he had collected and he replied proudly, 'Twenty-nine pounds and thirty-eight pence.' I was appalled! Nobby Caxton was always such an industrious man, ever helpful and considerate to the residents, and out of the 220 flats on the estate, less than thirty measly pounds had been collected – ten pounds of which I had donated!

'Frankly, Father Marcus, I am absolutely disgusted,' I said. 'He has worked at Susan Atkins Court for over twenty years, and I am quite ashamed that I live among such ungrateful skinflints!'

'Indeed Paul,' he said. 'Take it from me, it doesn't take too long to count up the meagre offerings from my Sunday collection plate. But then we shouldn't judge; many are pre-eminently generous of spirit, and most of them wish him all the very best for the future.'

Walking him to the front door, and searching for my wallet I said, 'Well at least let me bring it up to a round figure.'

'No Paul,' he said, theatrically holding his hands out in front of him. 'You have given quite enough already.' Opening my front door, he put his right index finger to the side of his nose, he tapped it twice and said, 'Leave that to me – I'm sure that I will be able to rustle up the requisite twelve pence!'

My mouth was still agape as I walked into the lounge, where Maria and Elisha were sat, waiting expectantly for the arrival of Nabil, a small overnight bag in front of them.

Lenka was carrying out her morning ablutions as Nabil arrived. He shook my hand enthusiastically, smiled at Maria and lifted Elisha up into his outstretched arms as she came rushing down the hall to greet him. Once all of the excitement had died down, Nabil stated that he'd have the girls back at around 19:00 hours on Wednesday evening, and during the interim, he could be contacted on his mobile phone should the need arise. I confirmed that likewise, I could also be reached on my phone.

Once they had left, I phoned Poppy at Elisha's playschool to tell her that our little girl will no longer be attending the playschool. I told her the happy news that she was being reunited with her father and would be moving away from the area. Poppy stated that she will be missed a great deal by the other children and the teachers alike, which came as no surprise to me whatsoever.

Thereafter, I phoned Basil to ask if he knew where Ted was hiding since he hadn't been seen for a few days, which for a man of such annoying predictability was very strange indeed.

Basil said that he had left the office at around 15:00 on Wednesday afternoon, but was generally only around when he was needed, as was Tina. Recently, he hadn't any real reason to call upon his services, although he confessed that he had been using Tina's invaluable talents quite a lot recently.

Thereafter, I tried to phone Ted again but got no reply. The infuriating bugger hasn't got voice mail, but then he has always been a bit of a traditionalist and swears by his uncomplicated, easy to operate, *First Edition* Nokia 1011 mobile phone of a circa. 1992 vintage, which he believes will *one day* become a very desirable and ultimately expensive collector's item.

But frankly I am beginning to get a little worried, since normally Ted is never too far away and is about as predictable as the hourly chimes of Big Ben. Besides, I have been more than content with the way things have been going recently, and apart from a few small issues, I am extremely happy with the current *status quo* and would seriously like it to remain as it is.

Back in the kitchen as I was drinking my second cup of coffee, Lenka arrived and over a bowl of crunchy nut cornflakes and chopped banana, she stated that following our chat last night, she had been very encouraged by my comments and had decided to take the teaching post after all. I was very happy for her, since I am sure that she has made the right decision and will subsequently prove herself to be a very important asset in any new teaching environment. However, like a couple of other ladies in my life, she too will be missed dreadfully.

I told her about my visit down to West Togram tomorrow, and being on her days off, she asked if she could tag along, and of course I was very happy for her to join me. Moving home is a serious business, and perhaps like her, I need the right kind of objective encouragement to finally take what is for me a momentous step into the unknown. For many years I have lived the life of a would-be dazzling urbanite with a simple dream of one day settling into a rural area, to gently wile away whatever years I had left. But in search of that classical rustic idyll, simple dreams can sometimes become a little distorted and clouded with unrealistic expectations.

Tomorrow the scales will hopefully fall from my eyes, and instead of fanciful dreams, I will be able to get some positive idea about the reality of rural living, together with becoming aware of some of the pros and cons that adopting such a completely different lifestyle will entail. Having a woman like Lenka at my side will be very helpful, since even with my eyes fully open, I could miss the very obvious issues that could mean the difference between everlasting contentment and happiness, and the abject misery of making a terrible mistake, and suffering thereafter for the rest of my life.

Lenka will be meeting up with Zora-Aleena again at around midday, and I decided that a good hour of exercise was needed, so grabbing my gym bag I hastened across to my sweatshop. I had an enjoyable time completing twenty minutes on the rowing machine followed by fifteen minutes on the cross-trainer. After my brief visit to the steam room, and a shave and shower, on leaving for home I felt that I could have completed a full round in the ring with Muhammad Ali – him chasing me around it that is!

Just as I put my door key into the lock, *Scotch Andy* rang, asking me to call up to his flat as a matter of urgency. I threw my bag into the hall and hastened across the courtyard. Andy lives on the third floor of a block opposite. Following my knock, he cautiously opened the door. He was looking like he had spent the night out poaching in some forest and was in a very dishevelled state. I knew that something catastrophic must have taken place, and it appeared that he had earlier experienced a quantity of that indefinable character-building process associated with a woman's scorn, and was suffering from a small bruise on his forehead, a slight nosebleed and what looked like defensive scratches to his right forearm. I instinctively felt that it would be better for him to do the talking.

He wearily led me into his lounge, and as we sat down he related a very disturbing story. Apparently, following Elaine's phone call to him while we were together at the Bread Bin last night, on his arrival home, she had asked him if he had moved her jewellery box. To cut a rather long story short, they both searched the flat from top to bottom but it couldn't be found. It apparently contained some of Elaine's most cherished items of jewellery, which included some prized rings and gold chains that had belonged to her mother. Thereafter they realised that other items of their property were also missing, which included some five hundred pounds in cash, an old Rolex watch that had belonged to Andy's grandfather, an antique silver half-hunter watch and chain, together with other personal items of property, including their passports. They had been burgled!

The police were called, who completed a detailed crime report. Apparently, there were no obvious signs of a break-in, and the officer in charge of the investigation was of the opinion that access had been gained to the flat with the use of a key. The new caretaker was invited to attend the scene, where he was interviewed and asked to see if any of his master keys could open Andy's front door. He duly obliged and all of them were laboriously checked, but none of them fitted the lock. However, Andy did explain that the original door lock had been changed many years ago. Thereafter as a follow-up, the caretaker's movements on the day in question would be verified later.

At around 08:15 this morning, Andy had been *invited* to attend Kilburn Police Station (which is far preferably than being unceremoniously lobbed into the back of a police van instead). Fortunately, the earlier rather offensive example of *Ted the Pleb's* wrathful karmic vengeance had been cleared, although apparently the former drab Victorian edifice had undergone a remarkable facelift. Apparently, the inner yard and walls were now festooned with numerous pots of beautiful roses, and a large concrete plot which was formerly used for stray dogs had been cordoned off, and having been filled with fresh top soil mixed with a considerable amount of well-rotted horse manure, a large area of dormant crowns of rhubarb had been planted. Isn't it just delightful how earlier misfortune can be used to such wonderful effect.

DS Blackstock (whom you will recall is an old acquaintance of mine) is dealing with the case, and he asked Andy to officially identify items of jewellery and other miscellaneous items of property that had come into police possession. There was no mistaking that the articles were those that had been taken from his flat. He was asked to make a written statement and happily against signature, all of his stolen property was restored to him, although the missing cash had not been recovered. However, he was told that enquiries were still ongoing.

Later, DS Blackstock stated that the man suspected of the burglary was a well-known local villain who had been arrested during the early hours of Sunday morning. Apparently he was found walking along the Cricklewood Broadway dressed in the stereotypical clothing of a burglar, and was wearing a black domino mask, a blue-striped shirt, and a woollen flat cap. Across his shoulder he was carrying a large sack on which the word **SWAG** was emblazoned. He was slightly inebriated and apparently had told the arresting officers, whom I was later to learn were nicknamed 'Spastic and Crutch' by their police colleagues, that he was on his way home 'following a reunion party'.

On checking out his sack (which isn't a euphemism), apart from a few innocuous items, they had found the stolen items of jewellery and the passports. According to the very smug detective sergeant, 'It was a very clear example of splendid police work and an open and shut case of burglary, together with the added bonus that the property stolen had been recovered and the person responsible had been caught – bang to rights!'

Due to an unprecedented rise in local burglaries, the despicable *pud-wapper* was being held in police custody pending his appearance at Westminster Magistrates Court tomorrow morning.

Having made us both a cup of coffee, I looked at Andy and he smiled ruefully and said, 'I suppose that I can forget about the money. That will mysteriously have gone missing prior to the other stuff reaching the nick!'

'No I am not convinced that the police officers would have helped themselves to that. I still have a modicum of belief in the honesty of our boys in blue,' I said. However, I had to mention that I was not so enthusiastically confident in the less than transparent integrity of our plain clothes undercover (pigs in blankets).

Laughing loudly for the first time, Andy said, 'But then what kind of absolute numbskull-cretin would parade along a High Street in the middle of the night, wearing burglar's gear and carrying a sack full of stolen property?' We both regarded one another thoughtfully, and suddenly, as if we had mysteriously conjured up some ancient medieval oracle, the obvious candidate simultaneously came to our minds and together we uttered, 'Eduardo Filepe Cordona!'

Laughing hysterically, the more we thought about it the more it made sense. Ted is an inveterate prankster, who unashamedly had modelled his erratic and unconventional behaviour and antics on his all-time favourite man of action:

369

Oliver Reed (a complete off-the-rails head case) who seemingly possessed a considerable amount of congenital fearlessness and an almost suicidal disregard for his own safety and well-being. I am confident that had he ever been in a combat situation, like his American counterpart, he too would have been 'highly decorated' since without doubt he was a walking Victoria Cross recipient in waiting.

Without needing any confirmation, we were both in agreement that it was *Ted the Pleb* who was presently safely ensconced in a police cell at the Kilburn nick, savouring the aromatic fragrance of well-rotted horse manure wafting in through the small window at the top of his cell. However, we were just as convinced that he would not have been responsible for the burglary at Andy's flat. He would never lower himself and steal from one of his friends, no matter how desperate his personal circumstances. There had to be some other logical reason why he was carrying the stolen property and knowing his often very shady affairs with the local underworld, a considerable number of very compelling possibilities presented themselves.

A little later I had a call from Tina, who suggested that we meet up for lunch at around 14:00 at a pub in Queens Park called *The Volunteer*. I am not very familiar with the area, but she gave me very detailed instructions on how to get to the place, which was apparently close to the tube station.

I arrived a little early and having got parked on a vacant stool at the bar, I bought myself a pint. Once Tina had arrived, I bought her a drink and we sat at an empty table in the relatively quiet saloon bar. She had changed her appearance quite dramatically. Her hair was longer, there was a hint of make-up on her face, and frankly she was looking quite beautiful. Her usual page-boy type clothing of tight leotard leggings and tighter vest had been replaced by a very feminine pair of beige slacks, and a matching cardigan, over which she wore an elegant raincoat. Actually, I could have walked past her in the street without recognising her.

She seemed to be in a bit of a rush and ordered a sandwich from the menu and then went into her reason for wanting to have a chat with me. Primarily it was about Ted. She had been informed by a close lady friend who worked in the Admin Department at the Kilburn Police Station that he was currently being held, although she didn't know on what charge. 'Did I know about it?' she asked.

I told her about as much as I knew which had all been nothing more than second-hand information. But her main concern was that Basil was not to be informed about Ted's arrest. I was quite surprised at this apparent disloyal and deceitful suggestion. But once she had explained her motives, I understood her reason behind what I initially thought was very uncharacteristic behaviour.

In a nutshell, she explained that both she and Basil had become very fond of a man who had more than proved his unquestionable allegiance to the firm. Being a rather shy man when it came to expressing emotion, she believed that he had displayed, in a rather awkward and embarrassed way, considerable loyalty and had watched over them both like a protective mother-hen, which she perceived was his way of showing the unconditional love and respect that he had for them as individuals. He was a rough diamond indeed, but he was looked upon as a family member rather than a business associate. He had made it very evident to Tina that he enjoyed working for Basil, whom he looked up to as a bit of a surrogate father figure, and were Basil to know that he had been arrested, it could compromise their intimate friendship and business relationship irrevocably. His loss to Basil personally and to the business in general would be dire, and indeed it would break Ted's heart to no longer be a welcome part of the team. She made it plain that she would consider anything rather than allow that to happen.

Just before she left, I mentioned the appointment that Alfie had with Basil later, and nodding enthusiastically she stated that her and Ted had a wager on the outcome of his decision. I was a little surprised to learn that she was aware of what the meeting was all about, but clearly Basil had discussed the issue with them both, if for no other reason than to get their valued input to presumably help him arrive at a just and equitable decision.

On leaving, I gave her a hug and asked her what the bet was about. She replied that it was a two-hundred-pound wager whether or not Basil would re-employ Alfie. She was of the opinion that given Alfie's evident dishonesty, that Basil wouldn't use him again, whereas Ted was confident that being the kind and forgiving person that he was, he would give Alfie a second chance.

On the bus home, I had to smile to myself when I thought about the outright conniving cunning that I had so effortlessly been subject to. Normally being a non-gambling man, Ted must have realised that I was backing a certain winner, and by hedging his bets as he has done, he would still be a hundred pounds better off, provided that is, that Basil was willing to give Alfie a second chance. However, were he to decide against re-employment then *as usual* Ted would have come in second place and would be a hundred pounds out of pocket. But I instinctively felt sure that 'Mr Tillington', being the odds-on favourite that he was, would come romping home a clear winner with no photo finish necessary. All that I had to do now was to wait for the official result.

I had a very quiet evening at home and following a nice soak in the bath with Sebastian doing his usual theatricals in the suds, I left a note for Lenka to state that I anticipated leaving home at around 08:00 in the morning, and that if she still wished to join me for my visit to West Togram, that I would be making a light breakfast for around 07:15.

Before lights out, I phoned *Paul the Cab* to ask him if he'd be free to convey Lenka and I to Waterloo Station tomorrow morning and if so, would I need to take out a bank loan to cover the cost of the fare. He stated that he could accommodate us, and since he had been booked to take a parcel to the Elephant and Castle already, he could drop us on the way at the reduced non-meter running fee of a tenner.

Goodnight, Ginny.

P xx

17th April 2012

Good morning my dear.

I was aware of movement and the unmistakeable sound of cascading water in my shower as my new day started at 06:10. Clearly my Lenka was eager to 'get out there amongst it' this morning. Once she had completed her morning ablutions, I followed likewise, but thereafter having nothing interesting to read on the loo, I was cooking our breakfasts of scrambled eggs with smoked salmon trimmings a little later. Once our reviving cups of coffee had been drunk, I too was ready for our day's adventure.

On leaving the estate promptly at 08:00, Paul and his cab were waiting for us outside. He held us spellbound with his stories about the famous people who had been sitting where we were now sat, together with an assortment of amusing anecdotes of a kind particular to the repertoire of a seasoned London black cab driver. Actually, he didn't stop talking from the time that he had collected us until he had dropped us off at Waterloo railway station (an hour and ten minutes later) and even then having paid him, as we walked away, I am sure that he was still talking.

Having collected a couple of return tickets to Southampton Central, we were safely aboard the 09:40 train and thirty minutes or so later we were heading south through some quite beautiful countryside.

Lenka and I chatted about her time in London and she commented that given the innumerable happy memories, it would always be remembered with fondness. In relation to the inevitable sadness that she would feel when it was time for her departure back to Slovakia, she felt it would be like saying farewell to a cherished but unrequited love affair, which I didn't quite understand until she explained that to say goodbye to a lover while being dreadfully sad, could with time be accepted and inevitably forgotten. But in a metaphorical sense, an unrequited love could never be truly forgotten, since there would always be the possibility of revisiting it in the hope of that love becoming mutual. She can be very profound sometimes, and having discussed the issue further, she elaborated by explaining that while ever she remembered London as an unrequited love, she was assured that it would never be forgotten, and that therefore she would always return.

As the train left Farnborough station, she asked me why I thought that some people preferred to sit in seats with their backs in the direction of travel, while others preferred to face the opposite way. It was another quite profound but interesting question. Looking along our particular carriage, which had seats facing in both directions, most of the passengers were facing the direction of travel, but others had clearly chosen other seats facing backwards. Personally, I have always preferred to face the direction of travel, which I suppose could suggest that in life I like to plan my steps forward, which frankly would be true. Generally, I don't ever like looking back. Lenka thought the same. But what of those that choose to look backwards? Does it mean that those people are not forward-thinking people, or was that just a ridiculous unfounded assumption, prompted by our *craic-type* waffling on about inconsequential *sphericals*?

A lively young guard came wobbling along the aisle towards us checking tickets, and having given him our return tickets for inspection, I questioned him about the train's seating arrangements. He stated that most trains had an equal quantity of forward and backward-looking seats, for the simple reason that unlike a plane, a train doesn't always go in one direction. There is a driver unit at both ends, so having taken the forward trip out, in effect on the return journey it would be going back in reverse. Basically, were all of the seats facing a forward direction on the return journey, all of the passengers would be sitting in a backwards position. He then went on to enlighten us further by stating that research had indicated that some people feel unwell when sitting against the direction of movement, so whatever the direction of travel, passengers would always be assured of a choice. Smiling good-naturedly, he then went on to remind us of British Rail's excellent record when it came to public safety and customer comfort, and bidding us farewell, he wobbled off along the aisle to diligently clip the remaining virgin tickets of the other passengers, and to continue in his ever-vigilant search for suspicious-looking unattended articles, or people behaving in a less than acceptable manner as defined by section two of the 1927 British Rail rule book (as amended) which related to customer etiquette and deportment (not a lot of people know about that!)

Our train arrived at Southampton Central station at 11:17 and once out of the station, I questioned a few locals in relation to where I could catch an X21 bus, and the first somewhat inebriated *pud-wapper* replied, 'At an X21 bus stop probably!' and then shuffled away. Lenka found it quite amusing, although I would have been quite happy to punch his lights out, since drunk or sober, I hate sarcasm!

A little later, we were on that illusive bus, which apparently runs from the

Civic Centre Building to Furrow End Station at two minutes and thirty-two minutes past the hour. Clearly my first major adjustment to rural living would entail having to accept a considerably slower more disciplined pace of life, particularly if I had to rely on the local public transport. But one thing that struck me immediately was the very courteous way that the driver behaved in relation to the safety and comfort of his passengers. As Lenka and I boarded, he waited until we were seated before he drove away, which is not what happens in London. The term 'Hold Very Tight Please', while a command no longer used on public transport due to the loss of conductors in favour of one-man buses, visitors to London would be well advised to look upon boarding a London Transport bus with the same trepidation that one would feel when attempting to negotiate an army assault course. Failure to do so could result in serious injury.

The route to West Togram village was very pleasant indeed and on the way the bus meandered along small country roads with an abundance of arable land and pasture on either side. We also passed through a number of very pleasant sleepy looking villages, where the absence of vehicular traffic conjured up wonderfully satisfying mental visions of their agricultural past. We arrived in the village high street at around midday.

Following the very detailed instructions given to us by a very pleasant 'sober' local, we arrived in Birdcage Way, where I simply stood gazing along at a series of semi-detached bungalows and marvelled at the quite beautiful surroundings. Opposite the bungalows, a small meandering babbling brook ran along close to a footpath, and a quaint wooden bridge spanned it, across which verdant pastures with a near view perspective of invitingly mysterious woods could be seen. The vista was quite stunning, and holding my hand, Lenka guided me to the second bungalow along where having obtained the key from its porch master box, we entered inside.

The hall had an aroma of newly applied paint, and checking each room, I realised that it had been very tastefully decorated throughout. It consisted of two bedrooms, a very spacious lounge, a tiled bathroom and kitchen, with what appeared to be brand new cupboards. The garden, which was south facing, measured about 100 x 80 feet, and clearly the former resident had been a very keen gardener because it was well cared for and consisted of lawns and flowerbeds.

Lenka was clearly impressed and mentioned that it was nothing like what she had imagined, and I was very impressed indeed. A little later, we crossed over the little wooden bridge and checked out the beautiful common land and an area which was called Alice Woods on the other side. It backed on to an area of forestry which included a large amount of sycamore and oak trees. In between what looked like a former cultivated area, wild plum trees were in abundance, and to add to this delightful pastoral scene, on our way back to the bungalow, a young woman riding a chestnut mare passed us. Frankly, I was utterly smitten, as was Lenka.

Possibly an hour had passed during our inspection and being in the mood for a little exploratory mooch, having locked up the back door which led to the garden and having made sure that the front door was closed, I returned the key to its box. We sauntered back into the general direction of the high street. It consisted of an assortment of shops which included a post office, chemist and a small bakers shop, but then slightly hidden from the road, as though waiting to surprise us, we found a delightful ancient looking pub called The Queen's Arms. Its position just off the main road and its appearance reminded me of the stereotypical coaching inns of the past. It had a very low front door, small windows and white stuccoed walls, on top of which was a beautiful, thatched roof. I asked Lenka to pinch me just in case I was dreaming.

Needless to say that when I thought about our breakfast which was a long time ago this morning, I felt in great need of a little sustenance, as did Lenka, so we excitedly made our way inside,

We made a couple of old locals jump at our swift and purposeful arrival, although in minutes we were both made very welcome indeed. Being a rural village pub with its usual regular trade, it didn't take long for the locals to identify us as visiting foreigners, and thankfully we were treated very cordially by the five regulars who were in various stages of intoxication. One of the lads explained that it was nice to have people from what he called 'the real world' in the pub, and raising his voice so that the others could hear he said, 'The level of intellectual discussion in here is about as interesting as listening to *Match of the Day* in Bengali!'

Loud laughter and a modicum of unrepeatable derision from the attendant customers followed, and I was really beginning to feel at home. On top of which I was very happy indeed to find that one of my favourite real ales was on tap, and completely gobsmacked to be told by the diminutive licensee (a robust, seen-it-all-type, Liverpudlian woman of some sixty-five summers) that it was 'One pound ninety-seven pence a pint.' In London, you couldn't buy a tomato juice for less than two pounds fifty, and that was at Happy-Hour prices.

Clearly other visitors had queried the price of her drinks in the past, but before I could put the question to her, she said, 'I know what you are going to say and… before you ask, we don't take cheques, or cards, and no, we don't have any of them fangled Happy Hour palavers in this pub neither.'

Lenka wasn't in the mood for an alcoholic drink, and was happy with a coffee, and I was more than a little *delightfully blithesome* to stop *Hilda's* latest keg of real ale from going sour, and managed to squeeze down five pints before, during and after our lunch of salt beef sandwiches, chips with curry sauce and a slice of lardy cake, which I was assured by the lads in the bar was 'a cherished local delicacy'.

Having briefly discussed the matter with Lenka, and having weighed up all of the considerable advantages and the almost non-existent arguments against my proposed escape from London to West Togram, at 14:45 I bade a fond farewell to Hilda and a group of like-minded *Jolly Boys* who, for better or worse, were destined to become my new drinking companions.

Apart from falling helplessly asleep on the train back to London, and to use

Lenka's exact words was apparently snoring like 'a bull elephant seal' for most of the journey, we were sitting in the Bread Bin at 18:40.

Alfie greeted us excitedly like a puppy that had been left at home alone and was very proud to announce his return to the Kilburn Unreliables as a part-time associate. As expected, Basil had reinstated him and I was very pleased at the outcome, albeit feeling a little guilty at the dugskullery that I had used in the process. But Alfie's additional news was a complete blow to my system, and any semblance of my former complacent happiness simply evaporated like the steam from a dog's turd.

Apparently, at 11:00 this morning Ted had pleaded guilty to a charge of burglary and had been remanded in custody for later committal to the Crown Court for sentencing. I was absolutely devastated. I couldn't come to terms with the fact that he would admit to a crime that he had simply not committed. Clearly there was far more to this issue than was apparent.

I phoned Tina immediately who was aware of Ted's unfortunate downfall, although Basil was at this time blissfully unaware of the news. Being more or less Basil's secretary, I asked her to check his diary so that I could come in and see him. If anyone should be responsible for giving him the dreadful news, then I figured that it should be me.

A little later, Tina rang me back and stated that Basil could see me around 14:00 tomorrow, and I confirmed that I'd be there,

On our way to the flat, I felt the almost overwhelming desire to visit the Gay Bar. Lenka was tired and needed sleep, so she didn't join me, but before we parted, I gave her an appreciative cuddle and offered her my sincere thanks for joining me today. Breakfast, as mentioned earlier, appeared to be a long time ago this morning, but leaving The Queen's Arms seemed to be infinitely longer.

I arrived at the Gay Bar at around 19:30, and as I stepped through the door to the bar, Vlado pointed to the posh bar. I therefore left and walked around to the saloon bar entrance which, apart from a single punter, was deserted.

Vlado explained that he had heard about Andy's unfortunate issue, and that he had something that I should see. He seemed a little evasive and refused to answer my questions but stated that I should visit him before opening time tomorrow, when he would explain. I confirmed that I would call back at around 10:30 in the morning.

All was quiet when I arrived home a little later, and following a much-needed shower, I hastened to bed quite exhausted.

Goodnight, Ginny.
P xx

18ᵗʰ April 2012

Good morning, Ginny.

I am sorry that I didn't send you my usual epistle last night, but frankly I was quite exhausted by the time that Lenka and I had arrived back at Waterloo yesterday. I completed it this morning first thing, so while it is a little late (for which I apologise), at least I know that you have got it.

Following my very welcome shave and shower this morning, my first enjoyable task was to contact my new landlords regarding my decision to accept the vacant tenancy at West Togram. They will send me a tenancy agreement that I have to examine, and once they had received a signed copy of it, they would set the wheels in motion. I really am very excited at the prospect of finally moving out of London. But like Lenka, I shall always look upon my home town as an unrequited love, and shall visit it often, if for no other reason than to meet up with my old beloved friends again, a few of whom I shall miss a great deal.

On Vlado's suggestion last night, I visited the pub at 10:30 this morning. He took me upstairs to his private flat above the bar. Zora-Aleena greeted me very warmly indeed and invited me to make myself comfortable in their lounge. Vlado brought us in coffee and biscuits, and a little later he switched on his television set and, putting in a VHS tape, without saying a word he simply pointed to the screen.

I was very surprised to be watching a recording of last Saturday afternoon's action in the Gay Bar, that had been clearly recorded using a covert camera situated somewhere above the optics. The recording's date was 14ᵗʰ April 2012 and it initially showed the antics that Andy and I had got involved in with the strangers who later identified themselves as Messrs Webb and Gillespie.

I was seen leaving the premises at 15:10. Thereafter, Andy was in animated conversation with our newly made acquaintances, and he was drinking vodka tonics with amazing rapidity. As time passed, his actions portrayed what seemed like the typical hedonistic devil-may-care-attitude of an irresponsible man that had temporarily regained his boyish freedom. He tottered out of the bar, clearly worse for wear at 16:48 precisely. His front door keys, which he had obviously forgotten to collect, were clearly visible on the top of the bar counter. On leaving, the door had not fully closed behind him as Gillespie is seen to grab them with amazing dexterity, and just as swiftly he is then seen putting them into his jacket pocket. At 17:14, both men are seen leaving, bidding Vlado farewell. They turned right out of the Gay Bar in the general direction of the old homestead.

It quickly became evident that it was our erstwhile friends who were responsible for the burglary at Andy's flat and presumably to provide a little confusion in relation to how entry had been obtained, the cunning *fatherless-people* had placed the keys on the top of Andy's toilet cistern to suggest that he had left the flat without them. This was very clear evidence that Ted was not responsible for the burglary and that now all that had to be determined was how exactly Andy's property had landed up in his swag sack on that fateful early morning. And that could be a very different proposition altogether.

Not wishing to confuse the issue unnecessarily, I told Vlado that Ted had been arrested on suspicion of being responsible for the burglary at Andy's home and that his tape was vital evidence to prove otherwise. He gave it to me without hesitation which I thought was not only very noble of him, but it proved the unquestionable loyalty that he had for his customers in general, and one undeniable mad-arsed but lovable cretin in particular. On leaving, I embraced him fondly and shook his hand, although on the way down to the bar he intimated that he didn't want the covert bar camera to become common knowledge, and I assured him of my complete discretion.

I met Alfie outside who was busy sweeping the front steps, and was clearly in a joyful mood, whistling a very off-key version of that beautiful aria from Madame Butterfly *Un bel di, vedremo*. I was at a loss to determine just where, or under what circumstances he would have heard this piece of music. It certainly wasn't from the jukebox in the Gay Bar. However, I decided not to question him about it since I really wasn't in the mood to be on the receiving end of an earth-shattering revelation, particularly since I was wearing clean underwear. Diverting my thoughts quickly away, I congratulated him again on his reinstatement with Basil, and then asked him what he knew about Ted's Saturday evening caper. He invited me to sit down on one of the outside chairs and then went into a comprehensive account of the events which ultimately culminated in the abrupt incarceration of *Ted the Pleb*, to await *Her Majesty's Pleasure*. Alfie's story was very entertaining indeed.

Apparently, once a year a local scoundrel's reunion takes place. Ted dresses up as his villainous alter-ego hero known to the local underworld as *The Bandit*, and hence why he was wearing a burglar's outfit when he was stopped by the police. I really had to fight back an almost overwhelming desire to laugh, when I thought of Ted likening himself to another one of his favourite actors, a certain 'Mr Reynolds', who starred in one of his all-time favourite films, *Smokey and the Bandit*. It was all the funnier however when I considered that out of the two famous thespians named Reynolds, my egotistical friend acted more like Debbie than Burt – but it would have been a very brave person to have told him so!

Having regained my composure sufficiently, Alfie then went on to say that he was told that the party had been raided by the police, and he suggested that this was probably why Ted had decided to leave and was subsequently found walking home. He added bitterly, 'Ted has never liked people what wears them uniforms. He says it makes 'em look like the Justapo.'

'But dressed like a burglar, he was almost inviting the police to give him a tug. So why didn't the silly bugger drive home instead?' I asked.

He regarded me thoughtfully for a moment and then with a level of innocent candour that quite simply couldn't be challenged he replied, 'Ted has never ever drunk and droven!'

I arrived punctually at the offices of Burt Lang and Forthright at 13:45, where I was initially met by Tina who took me into Basil's office, where, emulating a butler, she announced my arrival.

Basil greeted me cordially, and as Tina was about to leave I asked her to remain. I'm sure that on later reflection she would have preferred to have been elsewhere, but she obligingly sat down wearily. I sat down next to her, and Basil looked at us expectantly.

I ran through the whole sorry tale of Ted's party, his later stroll along Cricklewood Broadway in the early hours of Sunday morning dressed as a burglar, his arrest, his appearance at court together with his guilty plea, and finally his subsequent retention in custody awaiting committal proceedings for sentencing at the Crown Court.

Basil's facial expressions amply mirrored his innermost feelings. But before he could make any comment, I told him about the encounter with Messrs Webb and Gillespie, and my own suspicions that they were responsible for the burglary which Ted had pleaded guilty to. I handed him Vlado's VHS tape, which would prove beyond any doubt that Gillespie was in possession of Andy's door keys on the day of the burglary.

This issue had clearly taken Basil by surprise, and initially he seemed lost for words. Tina left to make coffee and Basil walked to his office window and appeared to stare out blankly, completely lost in thought. A little later he seemed more like his old self and, sitting down at his desk again, he thanked me for my visit and stated that he would take a trip down to Kilburn Police Station later in the day.

As I left, he shook my hand and said, 'Leave it to me, Paul, I'll see what can be done.'

At around 15:10, as I was on the bus home, Simon Stockton phoned to say that following the official Family Court application and the subsequent decision, Nabil was now at liberty to take over full legal custody of Elisha.

This was followed by another phone call from a very distraught Lenny who had apparently just heard the news about Ted's 'judiciary allotted confinement' and then suddenly dropping his Eugenia inspired supercilious verbal utterances, he blurted out,

'Paul!... What the fuck am I goin to do about me weddin reception nosh?'

I sensed a modicum of anxiety in this very expressive enunciation, and initially I tried to calm him down. The first question that I needed to know was how many people were expected. To which he replied, 'Around fifteen including myself and Eugenia.'

And then quite out of the blue, I started to panic as well, indeed becoming quite breathless. However, help was at hand. Hastily I dashed off the bus in Kilburn High Road and sprinted into the Goose like a hare being chased by a greyhound, and breathing in a good lungful of its restorative putrid aroma, reminiscent of a large quantity of well-ripened Gorgonzola cheese that had been matured for months in a sealed cask of urine, I was back to my old self again in no time.

Actually, it had occurred to me in the past that provided this quite unique malodorous stench could be replicated and its vapour distilled, the landlord should seriously think of marketing it as a medicinal essence designed at reviving people following panic attacks, fainting spells or near-death experiences. It could seriously become a cheaper rival to the usual restorative smelling salts being currently sold at ridiculously high prices. As an alternative, it could be put into aerosol cans and used by women as a self-defence spray. One squirt in the face would be guaranteed to deter the most ardent assailant, or indeed it could change the directional trajectory of any overly enthusiastic uniformed equivalent, bent on issuing another poor motorist with a Penalty Parking Notification. Actually, I didn't see one single yellow line in West Togram – but then I didn't see very many cars there either.

Having regained my composure, I smiled and waved at a very annoyed looking Thomas Patrick O'Mahoney, who was busily squeezing out his ever-present mop, the head of which had seen better days and was blacker than a coal miner's lunchbox. But then thinking about it later, I suppose I too would have been a little upset if under similar circumstances I had witnessed what appeared to be a very distressed man rushing into my pub, who then without so much as a by your leave, sits down and puts his head between his knees (an action quite unique in drinking establishments). But then adding a certain attention-distracting element to his bizarre performance, the bloke then suddenly jumps to his feet and takes large gulps of air which he noisily breathes out again through fluttering puckered lips that look like a chicken's bum. Clearly, it has been known for people to enter a public house less dramatically, but strangely as I made my way out, there wasn't a murmur of complaint from any of the locals, and the only sound to be heard was the familiar chortling from poor old Buster Crimmond, who was seated in his usual place by the door, critically examining the menu. Some things never change it seems!

On the way home, I phoned Rosheen to find out if her function room was free on Saturday. However, being at the eleventh hour as it were, I wasn't overly optimistic. However, she stated that it had been booked for a retirement party but due to the sudden illness of the retiree, it was cancelled a couple of days ago. I immediately phoned Lenny and asked him to join me at The Bread Bin.

His reply, while being initially tinged with a perceptible amount of understandable trepidation, quickly reverted back to its usual uninspiring drivel when I told him that I might be able to provide an alternative. 'I'll be with you in an hour,' he said excitedly.

Once back inside the wonderfully refreshing pine and furniture-polish smelling Bread Bin, together with Rosheen I discussed hiring the function room for Lenny's Saturday evening reception. I then went on to discuss various options when it came to his catering needs. She was very helpful indeed, and she gave me plans of the possible seating arrangements, the names and phone numbers of two very good outside teams involved in corporate and social catering events, and a first-class band that specialised in wedding receptions in particular.

Before Lenny had even stepped through the door, we were well on our way to providing him with a completely different set of arrangements for his wedding reception evening. He had initially booked our estate hall, but frankly in my opinion it would be far too big, whereas Rosheen's function room would be perfect given the amount of people attending.

On his arrival, he was looking a little flustered, and it's a shame I didn't have a small bottle of that imaginary restorative distillate, 'Essence of Goose' or its French equivalent labelled as 'Essence d' Oie'. However, he slung a pint down his *Gregory Peck* quicker than one of them star-nosed moles can snatch and eat a worm, and thereafter his eye's glazed over, a stupid smile developed on his face and a low audible sigh confirmed that his former period of uncertainty and anxiety had been temporarily supressed, compliments of Rosheen's newly arrived 5.6% real ale called *Badger's Nob*.

While I sat there sipping orange juice, Lenny was just about sold on the idea of changing his wedding reception venue to Rosheen's function room. Thereafter, he contacted one of her suggested catering teams, who would visit him at home tomorrow, and on Rosheen's advice he booked the band over the telephone.

Had he ingested a further pint of the aforementioned ale, I felt pretty confident that I could have convinced him to book his forthcoming stag night in Lanzarote. Fortunately, I would never engage in such utterly childish behaviour, particularly since I was fully aware of the quite outlandish tales associated with the antics of 'so-called mates' at stag parties, which are numerous and legendary. But a place like Lanzarote would be completely out of the question, particularly since there are a plethora of alternative locations considerably nearer to home like Malaga or Torremolinos.

Before he left for home to impart the pending revised arrangements for the approval and official sanction of his new lifetime managing director, we ventured forth *a trois* into the function room, where he seemed very pleased with what it had to offer. The décor was bright and tasteful. A line of very comfortable looking chairs ran along two walls and a raised stage dominated one end. The flooring was polished mahogany and the chairs and tables, which had evidently been left in position following the last function, were scattered around the room. Clearly being a small number of attendees, his seating and table arrangements could be placed at one end of the room in a comfortable and intimate fashion, leaving sufficient space for a little dancing later in the evening. Rosheen would supply the well-stocked bar, and had I been left with the decision, I would have had no hesitation in hiring it. It would provide a very comfortable venue for Lenny's wedding reception, and as he left, his smile and enthusiastic cuddle gave me every hope that this last-minute adjustment to the original plans would allay his fears, and that he could finally look forward to a smooth and happy transition from a relatively carefree irresponsible child-like bachelorhood, into that man-making state of semi-cooperative captivity known as marriage.

I was back home at 18:50 and was greeted by Lenka and my ever-fun-loving bundle of feline fluff, who did her usual dash up my outside clothing, a feat in which she has now become very proficient indeed.

Nabil and my two other girls arrived at 19:20. They had clearly had a great time although they were looking absolutely exhausted. Elisha was almost unstoppable in her excitement and Nabil quietly asked me if he could have a word. Lenka took them into the lounge, and Elisha's joviality and laughter inspired Maria to join in.

Nabil wanted to confirm that I had been contacted by Simon Stockton and advised of his now formal status as Elisha's legal guardian. I shook his hand and congratulated him and stated that his little treasure would be missed dreadfully. Kindly, he suggested picking her up on Monday morning, which would effectively give Maria, Lenka and I time to really get used to the idea of Elisha's final departure from our home. It would also allow space to collect her meagre belongings together and for us to work on some kind of strategy to help alleviate the dreadful sense of loss that we are all going to feel in a few days' time.

Once Nabil had left, I had a relaxing bath, and I left the girls alone to spend and enjoy what little time they had left together. I was feeling very tired indeed on going to bed and I certainly didn't need any rocking.

Goodnight, Ginny.
P xx

19th April 2012

Good morning, Ginny.

Alfie was at it again at 04:10 this morning and I was far from amused. 'Sorry!' he said. 'Did I wake you?'

'No not at all, Alfie,'I said. 'I was reading the final chapter of my latest bed book entitled *How to get away with the perfect murder.*'

My phone suddenly went dead, and there followed a long silent pause.

'Hello?' he suddenly said. 'Can you hear me?'

'Sadly, yes I can hear you Alfie,' I reluctantly replied.

'Sorry, I accidentally put my phone on mute, and when you do that the people listening at the other end can't…'

'What do you want Alfie?' I said, my voice quavering with a seething mass of pent-up frustration and anger.

'Ted asked me to give you a message.'

'How long ago, Alfie?' I asked.

'About twenty minutes!' he replied.

'Alfie!' I screamed. 'Ted is being held at Her Majesty's Pleasure and I'm relatively confident that at this time of the morning, he would not be allowed to make an outside phone call!'

'He called from a phone box and wants you to meet him there outside the gates of Paddington Park by the Bowling Green. He didn't want to phone your mobile, like I am, in case your phone had been... been... tampooned with by the Justapo!'

Suddenly I was wide awake, and sitting up in bed and switching on my bedside lamp, I said,

'When should I meet him, Alfie?'

Another pause followed. '...About twenty minutes ago!' he replied.

I finished our little chat with a stern warning that under no circumstances was this matter to be discussed with anyone, least of all Basil or Tina.

'Don't worry,' he said cheerfully, 'I'll keep it close to me breast!'

'It's chest Alfie!'

'Yeah, there as well!' he replied.

I dressed in record-breaking time, which was well worthy of an award of a cherished Blue Peter badge and grabbing my heavy-duty torch, I silently left the flat. It was a bitterly cold morning and it was very foggy. I made my way to the park following a well-used familiar route, but even then I had to stop occasionally to ensure that I was going in the right direction. Having eventually found the telephone box, I thought it best to not look too suspicious by standing outside it with a torch in my hand, so I got inside and waited.

A couple of minutes passed and then suddenly the phone box door opened and Ted appeared. Happily, his burglar get-up had been changed for what looked like prison attire. Looking around him cautiously, he intimated that we should leave the area. As we made our way back to the flat, I took off my duffle coat and wrapped it around his shoulders because he was clearly very cold indeed.

Back in the flat, I made him a hot toddy to warm him up, and then he related his latest adventure. Apparently at around 02:40 this morning a prison van had collected him and another remand prisoner from Kilburn Police Station. As luck would have it, en route to Brixton prison the van was in collision with an articulated lorry that, due to the heavy fog and a sizeable quantity of black ice on the road, had apparently jack-knifed. The prison van was forced to swerve heavily, causing it to tip over on its side. In the ensuing moments of confusion that followed, those that could walk were off loaded, but two who were apparently unconscious, were left inside waiting for the arrival of the emergency services.

The two prison van officers being distracted with the injured prisoners and trying to warn other motorists of the accident, gave Ted the opportunity to slip away and make his escape. He kept to the back streets keeping low on the approach of any vehicle and slowly made his way back to Kilburn.

As far as the events of last Saturday night, he stated that the reunion was going very well indeed. At the venue he was sitting in the garden enjoying a glass of Chablis when suddenly an uninvited marauding 'abomination of filth' smashed their way through the front doors. As Ted made his less than dignified exit attempting to clamber over the back fence, one of his criminal associates frantically stuffed what was later identified as the valuables stolen from Andy's flat, into his swag sack. Ted had no idea of what was effectively being planted on him, and frankly he couldn't have cared less, since at the time he was far more interested in an action that *Dave the Voice* would have colourfully described as 'making like a hockey game and getting the puck outa there!'

Feeling much revived after my toddy he asked if he could have another one, and I duly obliged. Thereafter, he stated that he was utterly gobsmacked when he had been stopped by *Spastic* and *Crutch* since he was a mere two streets away from home. He was fully aware that stolen property had been planted on him, but where it had come from was a mystery. At the station he denied any knowledge of it, albeit that it had been found in his sack.

At the court hearing on Tuesday morning he had pleaded guilty to the charge of burglary, as a simple matter of course. As he explained this was the normal procedure since being an honest and loyal member of the local fraternity of villains whose motto was *'ut eam claudat'* (which as any grammar schoolboy knows means 'keep it shut!') he was well aware of his fraternal obligation to never 'grass up' a fellow associate, no matter what the provocation or enticement. The ancient proverb of 'Honour among thieves' was to be observed at all times, and severe punishment would follow any transgression, no matter how innocent or unintentional. Frankly, I was very impressed indeed.

Given the unfortunate circumstances of his case, however, he was confident that before his person was brought before the Crown Court, a suitable scapegoat would be provided, probably chosen from one of the fraternity's younger members, who having a relatively clean police record, and being eager to please, would sacrifice himself in favour of a respected seasoned felon like Ted. The likelihood of the younger member receiving a severe sentence was remote but given Ted's long and infinitely varied history of criminal activity, any additional conviction could prove very costly indeed and could seriously compromise his future bookings at Butlin's Skegness for the foreseeable future. But before this could be initiated, Ted would have to respectfully present his case to the fraternity's governing body, which would then be put before the membership for consideration.

Having told him about my encounter with Messrs Webb and Gillespie, he confided that these two individuals were active paid-up members of the fraternity, although the names that they were using were fictitious. He was understandably reluctant to divulge their true identities, other than to say that their underworld *noms de plumes* were *Butch* and *Sundown* – with no prizes for guessing which 1969 film these came from.

He would phone one of the senior members later this morning to plead his case for what he called 'captivity exchange' and thereafter, following a couple more toddies, he would 'bash his forehead around a bit, and perhaps make a slight incision on his left ear' to suggest that he was suffering from a head injury. Thereafter, he would creep back to the park, and after the gates had been opened, he would lay along one of the paths as though in an unconscious state. I would notify the park authorities and phone for an ambulance. Later he would claim that he couldn't remember what had happened or how he had arrived at the park. Naturally, the police would put two and two together, only now, suffering from an apparent head injury and possible amnesia, he would be confined in the warmth, comfort and care of St Mary's hospital Paddington instead of a draughty uncomfortable cell in Brixton Prison.

With some hour or so before the park gates would be opened, I suggested to him that he should try and grab a little sleep. He didn't need asking twice and, having leapt on my bed with all the finesse of a warthog, he was snoring like a chainsaw having a punch-up with a rampant grizzly bear in no time. I took my latest bed book, *Aliens like Pork Scratchings*, with me to the kitchen and made myself a cup of coffee.

Lenka came home from work a little later and we had a quick chat before she went to bed.

At 07:30, while the sun had arisen about an hour earlier, visibility was still very limited due to the fog, but it was time to 'get out there amongst it'. I awoke Ted, who appeared to be much disorientated. I gave him my duffle coat and, carrying a rucksack, we quietly left the flat. On the way using my phone, he made a call to one of his senior members wishing to invoke the aforementioned 'captivity-exchange' application, and he seemed to be pretty confident of the outcome.

When he gave me my phone back, I saved the number he had called, putting it into my contacts list under the name of 'Micky Mouse'.

When we got to the park gates, I suggested that it might be better to be found on the pavement outside rather than inside the park, since giving the ambulance people directions to his exact location might prove a little difficult. I therefore phoned for an ambulance, giving the operator full details of what I'd found and stating that, 'The unconscious man was breathing and that being a qualified first aider, I had placed the patient in the recovery position and covered him with my coat.'

We stood around for about ten minutes or so, when in the distance I could see flashing blue lights. Ted quickly slipped off my duffle coat and then laid face down. Once on the ground he hit his forehead a couple of times on the pavement and his nose started to bleed. I covered him up again with the duffle coat.

As the ambulance neared our position, I flashed my torch and waved it down. Within minutes of its arrival, having recovered my duffle coat, Ted was wrapped in a warm woollen blanket and was on his way to St Mary's hospital where a nice warm bed was awaiting him and then later on, feeling it was time to regain consciousness, he would then engage the medical staff in a considerable amount of *urine-taking* of the 'lead-slinging' variety.

Following my unexpected early morning adventure, on my arrival home I found Elisha and Maria eating their breakfasts. Jimena wasn't in the mood for her usual athletic greeting and looked at me with eyes that portrayed a modicum of bored indifference. However, she became considerably more animated and friendly as I opened her new tin of mackerel and pilchard cat food – the hussy!

Maria and Elisha will be visiting Gabriel's flat again to give the place another little clean-up of the flicking a duster around type of thing, which would be followed by a cursory vacuuming of the more noticeable areas like the carpets and stairs. Actually, Maria's domestic activities have improved considerably over the last few weeks and surprisingly she seems to be enjoying the experience immensely. I wanted to have a word with her about Elisha's departure date, but I simply couldn't get a word in, such was their incessant chatter. However, I did manage to state that I would be giving her a call later in the day and clearly she understood what I meant.

In the meantime, following a light breakfast of fruit and honey yogurt, I hastened across to the gym to give my limpness of musculature another rude awakening, which despite the glares from the two cleaners sitting in the wings, I carried out with considerable aplomb. On my way home later, as I passed the Gay Bar, Alfie came rushing out to meet me. But slowing down as he approached, he suddenly stopped. Looking at the newsagent's shop, he acted like a ventriloquist without the dummy, or in his case a dummy without the ventriloquist. Without his lips moving to any noticeable degree, he asked if this morning's operation had been successful. I smiled at him and nodded in affirmation.

He then went on to enquire why he had to remember some things like the Aunt Maudie issue, and then had to forget other things like Ted's phone call. He seemed more than simply pleased with my reply when I told him that, 'Undercover agents are very clever people, who have to remember and forget a lot of very important things!'

As I made my way home, he smiled at me happily and said, 'Don't worry, Paul, your secrets and the stuff that you want me to forget are safe with me!'

I really didn't want to ponder on this, and having dropped my gym bag at home, I decided that a brisk mind-clearing walk would do me good, and I therefore made for *Whispering Jim's* watering hole in Notting Hill, and I was in an adventurous mood. But as that well-known line taken from Robert Burns' delightful poem, which describes the amusing antics of a mouse states:

'The best-laid schemes *o'Mice an' Men Gang aft agley.'* It is not known whether Mr Burns had been sampling the delights and creative qualities of that other *wee Scottish Beastie* during the composition of this enchanting poem, but in translation this line would suggest that, irrespective of how well we plan our actions, there is always the risk of having to endure unforeseen problems and that as a consequence, one's expectations have been known to go *tits up* and… *tits up* mine went!

I was later informed, by a very excited Alfie that apparently, 'as I had commenced my epic walk to the Pig and Whistle at my end, Jim was boarding his cab bound for the Gay Bar at the other,' and like those proverbial ships in the night, we had passed one another en route, although happily unlike the metaphor, we were destined to meet up again later.

Just as I walked into Jim's new watering hole, I had a phone call from Vlado. 'Jim wanted to know where I was?' he said. 'Tell him, Paul said that I'm in the pub.' It then got a little complicated, what with Vlado's basic command of the English language and Jim's barely audible utterances. It became all the more convoluted however, after Vlado had passed the phone to Alfie, whose opening gambit was, 'I am in the pub, but I can't see you in here.' In sheer frustration I put on my very best supercilious operator voice and said, **'Beep!**… You have dialled an incorrect number… please hang up and try again… **Beep!'** He hung up, and I switched my phone to silent mode.

Danie made me very welcome, and we chewed the fat for a while. Viljoen was apparently at the local groomers, having whatever type of completely unnecessary pampering that an Indian mynah bird in captivity has to endure. But then apart from *Whispering Jim,* he too was a star attraction. People would travel miles to see him and listen to the very amusing things that he had to say, and they enjoyed Viljoen's comical outbursts as well! Although this delightful bird had the slight edge on Jim since he at least could be understood.

On leaving, I switched my phone back on to find that I'd had sixteen missed calls from Alfie and a voicemail from Lenny asking me to phone him. I had forgotten all about my anticipated call to Maria, and accordingly I phoned her straight away to give her the news that Elisha would be finally leaving us during the morning of Monday 23rd April. She took it all very well indeed and stated that both she and Elisha would be dining out this evening. Lenny wanted another meet-up at the Bread Bin and, checking the time, I stated that I would see him at around 16:30.

I decided to give my London Transport chauffeur a little more time off and had another invigorating walk back to Kilburn. As I passed St Mary's hospital I was tempted to call in and see how my former fugitive had settled in, but decided against it. I was sure that by now his story and identity would be known and that in all likelihood, he would be under police guard. My visit would do nothing more than simply draw very unwanted attention to myself.

At the Bread Bin later, Lenny was like a little boy who had just bought a new engine for his electric train set. He was positively beside himself with pent-up excitement, and couldn't wait to offload his news which during the following fifteen minutes without respite, consisted of Eugenia's approval in relation to the change of wedding reception venue, the choice of food as discussed with the newly appointed caterers, and confirmation that the band for the evening would be the one recommended by Rosheen, which she described as 'a very versatile group, specialising in music from the seventies and eighties with particular emphasis on the 'oldie-goldies' who went by the name of *Plonker and Sons'*.

Before I left for home, Lenny gave me an invitation card to attend his forthcoming stag night celebrations which will be held in the *Gay Bar* of The *Magpie public house* tomorrow night, where ticket holders would be invited to avail themselves of the buffet and free bar. The festivities would commence at around 19:00. However, despite all of the clandestine efforts to keep the forthcoming event secret, the news of an imminent free bar at The Magpie would have been passed around every pub this side of the Watford Gap, quicker than a box of *Rennies* at the local Indian restaurant.

With this very obvious fact in mind, Lenny emphasised that entrance would only be allowed on the production of an official invitation, and for the chancers, the doorman for the night, a Chelsea Pensioner called Staff Sergeant Amos John Gripple BEM, was a non-smoking lifelong teetotaller with no interest in women, football or gilt-edged securities, and since his army discharge following 'that little misunderstanding with the colonel's valet', he was completely incorruptible.

Back at home, I felt quite exhausted. I spent a little time with Elisha and Maria before my bed in general and my pillow in particular had convinced me that I should give it some head. I complied almost immediately thereafter.

Goodnight, sugarplum.

P xx

20ᵗʰ April 2012

Good morning, Ginny.

My four girls were all up bright and early this morning and more than simply eager to 'get out there amongst it!' Following their respective breakfasts, which ranged from yogurt and choco-pops cereals to bacon sandwiches and pilchard pate cat meat, Lenka suggested a visit to the Battersea Park children's zoo, if for no other reason than to finally get to see the place that Elisha had raved about so enthusiastically. To say that our little girl was excited at the prospect is a bit of an understatement. She dashed into Maria's bedroom to get herself dressed in 'suitable attire' and to load her little day bag with a few essentials like a box of wet wipes, a small hand towel, a hairbrush and an unopened box of chocolate hobnobs for the journey.

Apparently, Lenka is aware of Elisha's impending departure, and I am sure that her sudden decision to take two days' holiday was prompted by her genuine desire to make our little girl's final days with us enjoyable and as memorable as possible.

Before they left, I told Lenka that I would be 'otherwise engaged this evening' and didn't expect to be back home until the early hours of Saturday morning. I also asked her to arrange their evening meal. I gave her £50 to hopefully cover the costs of the day's expenses.

Being in the mood for a bit of a purposeful mooch, I initially dropped off a formal letter at the Estate Office giving them notice of my intention to end my tenancy in Susan Atkins Court. I will be vacating my flat by the very latest on Monday 7ᵗʰ May 2012, and this will effectively give them a month's notice (give or take a few days) – which is a condition of my signed tenancy agreement. Having spent many happy years in residence here, I would not wish to leave in anything less than a respectful and dignified manner.

Later, I visited a small local removal company to get a quote in relation to my impending move. I spoke to the proprietor, whom I guessed was in or around his mid-thirties. He was relatively small in stature, but what he lacked in height he certainly made up for in bodily size. He was very stocky indeed and had a very swarthy complexion, which suggested that his lineage was of a Latino/Hispanic provenance. I couldn't have been more wrong however, since in the unmistakeable accent of a born and bred Geordie, he introduced himself as Dimitri Fedorov. Shaking my hand with a vice-like grip, he smiled and in an evidently much used response to my surprised facial expressions he said, 'Ahh! Away bonny lad? I'm used to bein mistaken for a Spaniard or a Greek, but actually I'm neither. Me parents were from the Ukraine. They emigrated here when I was a bairn, and in fact I were brought up in Gateshead, yah nah.'

Giving him one of my cards, he stated that he would ring me early next week to make an appointment to call. During his visit, he would make a complete inventory of the property to be moved. A day or so later, he would then supply me with what he described as 'a very competitive written quotation which would not be bettered locally'. I was suitably impressed.

I called into the café for a cup of cappuccino and as I sat there sipping its milky goodness, I became lost in thought. It suddenly occurred to me that there is now a mere twenty-seven hours before my friend Leonard M Ficks, aka *Lenny the Ponce,* would finally bid farewell to his childhood. For many, marriage is naturally a very unsettling time; a period in a boy's life, which has been compared to the bodily confusion and bewilderment of puberty. One minute he has complete control of his life and actions and then following the wedding ceremony, a few glasses of champagne and a celebratory 'knees-up Mother Brown', it quickly becomes apparent that his days of unfettered hedonism are numbered and his former individualism in general and his complete unrestricted autonomous control of the TV remote in particular are now at an end. I suddenly felt overwhelmingly down in the dumps!

But a modicum of despondency deflecting help was at hand. As I poked my head into the Gay Bar, Vlado and Alfie were busy putting up stag-night themed party decorations, with lines of triangular bunting depicting a very amused looking smiling stag with enormous antlers, over which was written in bold capital letters: **STAG NIGHT.**

Alfie was clearly in party mood and was enjoying himself immensely. I naturally offered my help but Vlado smiled and having thanked me, intimated that together with his newly employed *general factotum*, that they had it all under control.

Getting his crumpled-up party invitation from his back pocket, he waved it about proudly and stated, 'Don't forget to bring your thingie tonight, cos if you ain't got one, then that army bouncer bloke what is trained in unarmed origami, won't let you in!'

Rushing down the stepladder, he pointed to the RSVP lettering on the invitation and said, 'Wass'at then?'

'It's short for the French expression, Alfie,' I said. 'It means *respondez s'il vous plait.'*

'Wass 'at then?'

'It simply means, reply please. When you get an invitation with those letters on it, you should tell whoever sent you the card, that you will be attending.'

Vlado was stood at the top of another stepladder pinning balloons to the ceiling, and as Alfie suddenly dashed passed, it wobbled uncontrollably. Fortunately it didn't fall over, but it produced a bright scarlet blush on the usual pallid complexioned cheeks of our revered landlord, and his momentarily widened eyes (resembling chapel hat pegs) stared back at me in alarm.

Having grabbed his mobile phone from the optics shelf, Alfie punched in a number quickly and a little later I heard him shout, 'I'm coming Lenny!... N-N-N-No!... N-N-Not that!... I mean I'm coming to your party tonight!... Oh?... Well that's alright then!… Yeah… I'll see you later crocodile!'

Rushing back into the bar he said, 'Lenny knew I was coming!'

Alfie, whom I have estimated to be around thirty-five years of age, albeit with the mental age of a boy of around eleven, has never married, and in fact, I am not too sure if he has ever had a girlfriend. Facially, I suppose he could be considered as nice looking, with auburn hair which is always neatly trimmed, and a rather patchy facial growth which he likes to keep at what closely resembles *designer stubble*. His eyes are emerald green, and his boyish smile is quite charming…I am having a little difficulty writing this, Ginny, since it is making me feel quite emotional. I am already beginning to think of people in the past tense, which I find very disconcerting.

Back at home, I had a nice long soak in the bath, and then thought I'd get myself dressed in a little finery of the smart-casual kind, and having avoided alcohol all day in readiness for what could become a veritable booze-fest this evening, I sauntered down to the Chinese buffet. I figured quite rightly that I should put a considerable amount of heavy stodgy food into my stomach prior to getting involved in the possible liquid over-indulgence to come. Actually, I took my time, and while my gastronomic intake was nowhere near the quantity that Maria had ingested on our last visit, I managed to tuck away a sizable offering of various culinary delights, many of which I was at a complete loss to identify. But suddenly remembering that famous idiom-proverb about the fate of that 'nosey cat', I didn't pursue the matter. I left at around 19:20 and made for the Bread Bin.

I have never liked to arrive early at any social gathering where the consumption of alcohol has taken place, preferring to put in an appearance later. From my experience, I have found that it is far better to arrive once the attendees have settled into their new social environment, and the relaxing qualities of alcohol in its various guises had taken effect. To arrive early where the soberly bored or indifferent looking individuals are wandering around aimlessly, is about as exciting as watching a damp plank warp. But thankfully, there is no such thing as *punctuality* when it comes to social gatherings of this kind, as any person who has *a bit of previous* for always arriving on time will tell you.

That metaphorical well-fed early bird will soon realise that there's more to life than eating. By arriving a little later in the day, apart from having a better night's kip, his mid-morning breakfasts will no longer be solitary affairs. As an added bonus, he will now be able to make additional like-minded friends from among his new dining companions, so it then becomes a win-win scenario.

Additionally, if it is the *early bird* that catches the worm, is it right to assume that there is more to the common earthworm – *Lumbricus terrestris* – than meets the eye? Generally speaking, they live in the soil and are hidden from the sight of potential predators (which includes birds suffering from insomnia). However, it is not uncommon to find earthworms above ground and there is a number of compelling reasons why. For example, should they decide to do a *moonlight-flit* and move to a better neighbourhood, they would be able to cover far greater distances up above than through the soil below. In addition, the common mole – *Talpa europaea* – feeds almost exclusively on earthworms, and unfortunately the vibrations of raindrops on the soil above, replicates the sounds made by a mole searching for din-dins. It is understandable therefore why body-swerving worms break cover and 'make like a hockey game and get the puck outa there!'

But I have a more romantic notion believing that under cover of darkness, worms like to socialise and party. Being out of the ground they are no longer at risk from hungry moles, and apart from the nocturnal birds like the beady-eyed owls, are generally safe from their (diurnal) cousins (who like to get their heads down at night). Presumably those worms that are still above ground at daybreak, are clearly reluctant to leave the festivities, and like their drunken human counterparts are willing to 'get a mouthful from an angry wife' or in the worm's case, 'become a couple of mouthfuls for a solitary avian diner', rather than become 'a party-pooper' and leave for home early.

It is a well-documented fact that following a night's party, some revellers (like the fun-loving earthworm) have found themselves in some very unlikely places, which nicely brings me back to the duties and responsibilities of a best man, primary of which is the safe, timely and unhindered arrival of the groom at the wedding ceremony. In this regard, this evening I shall be ever vigilant to the puerile actions and drunken suggestions of the Gay Bar regulars and more particularly Lenny's closefriends, notably Dave, Tony, Jim, Lenny and Paul.

I am familiar with just about all of the Gay Bar regulars, albeit that many are simple acquaintances who for one reason or another have not become members of my close inner-circle of friends. I would estimate that there are some fifteen to twenty regulars and they appear to be made up of three separate groups, or cliques. But don't get me wrong Ginny, they are all friendly enough, it's just that they simply choose to mix socially with some people more than others, as indeed do I.

Some people complain about the whole concept of being neatly compartmentalised into groups of any kind, which I find somewhat strange, particularly since we are by nature gregarious animals who like to mix in social collectives. But the truth is that from our earliest experiences in life, we all spend most of our time in little social groups of one kind or another. From those halcyon carefree days spent in nursery and secondary schools (imprisoned in scholarly groups), we then progress into adulthood and the work environment, where again we become members of other collectives that are known as 'work colleagues'. For many, this has the potential for becoming a very enlightening and rewarding experience (there are great quantities of very interesting people out there) but for others, it is a veritable nightmare, particularly when one's 'opposite number' is an enthusiastic member of the Jimmy Savile appreciation society, or a serial killer aficionado with a penchant for reading crime novels together with an abiding interest in Bangkok in general, and Asian lady-boys in particular.

Unlike our relatives, we are at liberty to select our own personal friends from the numerous potential candidates that life or personal circumstance may throw our way. But sadly, occasionally mistakes can occur. For those unfortunate enough to realise that they had made a very serious error of judgement in relation to this exacting selection process, it is worth remembering that 'to air is human' and 'mistaeks like sheet happens!'

My own little preferred group comprises of *Ted the Pleb, Lenny the Ponce, Dave the Voice, Tony the Tube, Whispering Jim, Alfie the Dip* and *Paul the Cab* – bless em all!

On my arrival at the Bread Bin, I was absolutely delighted to find Nobby Caxton. He was in very animated conversation with Rosheen and Bunny Longhurst, and was looking very good indeed. Apparently Nobby is an old friend of Lenny's, who had invited him and his wife to his wedding, paying for his rail fares together with his local hotel costs. I thought that this was not only a kind and very generous gesture, but it went some considerable way in augmenting the utterly disgraceful amount of money that had been collected on Nobby's behalf by that indefatigable and much underrated eccentric cleric, Father Marcus Byron Tanner (bless his little white surplus).

At around 22:10, Nobby, Gretchen and I wandered down to the Gay Bar which was in full swing. We could hear the music from some considerable distance away.

** INTERLUDE **

21ˢᵗ April 2012

Good morning, Ginny.

I am very pleased to report that Lenny's stag do was a resounding success, with no incidents of a puerile and/or disputatious nature taking place. I had been particularly careful to watch my own alcohol intake and apart from the occasional visit to the Water-Loo, I had my eyes on Lenny almost continuously, and under no circumstances would I have tolerated any reckless or stupid behaviour, particularly if it was aimed in the direction of my vulnerable charge. I took my responsibilities as best man very seriously indeed, and I was adamant that no mishaps, accidents or unwanted incidents would occur on my watch. Although I did breathe an audible sigh of relief as I loaded Lenny into his pre-booked cab at 01:30 this morning. Before he left, we had agreed to meet up at the gym at 08:00 this morning to simply purge and pamper our bodies with a cleansing and relaxing session in the steam room, followed by a shave and an invigorating shower.

I was sitting in the steam room at 08:10 this morning. Lenny arrived a little later. We chatted about last night's festivities and he thanked me for my help. We then had a bit of a heart to heart and for the first time, despite his former confident manner, he seemed to be a little ill at ease.

It was clear that last night's fun and laughter had made him realise that the party was nothing more than the closing act on his freedom, as it were. In a few hours, he would have a wife to consider and last night was a reminder of the passage of time and of things past. He freely admitted that what really mattered now was the future.

However, he lightened up considerably when I reminded him of the fact that 'most of the Gay Bar regulars were still in their salad days, where the colour green had nothing to do with their decision-making capabilities, but related to the general hue of their skin following their ever-indulgent and patient battle with alcohol. He, however, was a seasoned artisan who had passed through that boyish apprenticeship, and now being on the cusp of maturity as it were, had to move on to more responsible manly pursuits and considerations. Booze and all that went with it, would now be simply recognised as being a part of his growing-up process. But he was a big boy now, and those days were well and truly over!'

As he was leaving the steam room, I reminded him of those very wise words of St Paul, who said, 'When I was a child, I thought like a child, I reasoned like a child. When I became a man, I put the ways of childhood behind me.'

Standing at the door he said, 'You make it all sound so very simple, mate.'

'Just remember, Lenny,' I said, 'life is what you make it; just take one step at a time!'

He confidently pushed the door open, stepped out, tripped and with a resounding sickening thud, fell headlong on to the floor.

I rushed out after him, and found him lying face down, groaning loudly. His right foot was at a very strange angle and I realised immediately that it was broken.

I called for assistance and one of the cleaning girls rushed up to the reception. An ambulance was called and two paramedics arrived shortly afterwards. He was clearly in pain but he asked me to get his phone from his locker. While the ambulance boys were doing their bit, Lenny phoned Eugenia, giving her my number. Shortly after, he was stretchered out of the place and was conveyed to the A&E Department at St Mary's hospital, Paddington.

As he left, he offered out his hand to me which I held momentarily. 'I'll have to put those impending manly pursuits and considerations on hold for a while,' he said, smiling at me ruefully.

Back at home a little later, I had a call from Eugenia who was understandably very concerned indeed. Clearly the wedding arrangements would have to be put on hold, and she asked me if I could contact the various people concerned. She gave me the phone numbers of the caterers and the band, and I would personally contact Father Marcus and Rosheen.

All of my girls were up when I arrived back from the gym, and Lenka had very kindly organised their various meals. I wasn't really in the mood for eating and, given all of the unexpected events at the gym earlier, I had forgotten to have a shave and shower. I remedied that almost immediately thereafter.

A little later, I phoned Rosheen and she was very understanding and hoped that Lenny would make a swift and full recovery. Father Marcus was just as supportive and stated that he would place a note on the door of the church notifying people that the wedding planned for 14:00 had been temporarily postponed. He added that the free time would allow him to engage in what he called 'a lickle-shuggles diggy-diggings'. I must ask him to get me a box of whatever pills he's on!

Thereafter I left a message on the band leader's mobile phone, cancelling the booking, and I spoke to a very charmingly young lady at the caterers notifying her about Lenny's accident and stating that the event would be on 'the back burner' pending his recovery.

At around 10:15, Alfie called to ask if I could give Basil a ring and I duly obliged. Although why on earth people feel it necessary to contact the monkey rather than the organ-grinder is another one of life's enigmatic unanswerable questions like, why doesn't Tarzan have a beard when he lives in the jungle without a razor? Or why is it that people say 'they slept like a baby' when babies wake up every two hours?

Basil stated that he would be visiting Ted at the hospital for around 11:00 and would I like to join him. I thought that by accompanying Ted's solicitor, the police would naturally conclude that I was part of his legal team and that I could therefore slip in unnoticed. I therefore agreed to meet him outside the main entrance to the hospital at eleven bells.

Being Saturday again, the girls were bent on another little 'retail therapy' expedition, and I left home at 10:20 en route for St Mary's hospital.

Once on the bus, I thought about this impending visit and was determined to stop any further cloak and dagger *sphericals* of the skulduggery kind, and to come clean with Basil about the reasons why Ted had pleaded guilty to the burglary charge and then to explain Ted's impending 'captivity- exchange' issue. Although I felt that this would be better coming from him. I reasoned that the more that Basil knew about this unfortunate affair the better. Hiding behind any more smokescreens or giving him any further false information would inevitably become counter-productive, and therefore I decided against that particular course of action. Besides, I want to go to bed at night with a clear untroubled conscience (for a change).

I met Basil as arranged, and having identified ourselves to a police constable who was sitting outside of Ted's private room, we were given permission to enter.

This little break from Ted's normal daily routine has been clearly beneficial. Frankly he was looking a picture of health and as we entered he was eating an apple. He appeared to be very pleased to see us and invited us to sit down on the two chairs available.

Thereafter, for Basil's benefit I asked him to provide a full unexpurgated version of the events that brought him to his present comfy position. I insisted that he was not to withhold any of the salient facts from the evening of his villain's reunion to his arrival at the hospital.

Listening to his very interesting account of the events, I realised that he would make an excellent bed-time storyteller. Basil listened attentively. Once he'd finished, I reminded him of the 'captivity-exchange' scenario which he had conveniently forgotten about.

Before leaving, I suggested that in relation to this issue, it might be helpful for me to have the name and telephone number of his current *Mr Big* to enable me to follow up on his application. I would suggest to the man in question that I was a visiting villain from up north who was a distant relative of Ted's, who simply wanted to know when I could expect to pick him up from prison.

Reluctantly, he gave me the mobile phone number of the present head of his hoodlum group, who predictably is simply called *The Don* and when and if I deemed it necessary, I would put on my very best (English version) of a James Cagney voice and give the *anal-orifice* a call.

Before we left, Ted quietly explained that he'd be in the hospital for a little while longer (because of the dizzy spells) and on parting, I shook his hand and mentioned that he was greatly missed by all at The Magpie, and I do believe that this hit a raw nerve because he appeared to become a little emotional. His eyes started to blink rapidly and he turned his head away.

Basil and I visited the A&E on the way out, and I was told that Lenny was undergoing surgery. It was pointless exercise therefore to hang around unnecessarily.

Basil gave me a lift back to Kilburn, and on the way he expressed serious concern in relation to Ted's future liberty. He was absolutely astounded following his revelatory tale about his membership of the local villainous fraternity and their intriguing rules and regulations. This was a very disturbing disclosure for him, and apart from being found in works of detective fiction, he had no idea that such clandestine criminal organisations really existed.

He kindly dropped me off outside the Gay Bar, and for the first time I sensed that my diminutive former super-sleuth was going through a distinct period of uncertainty. His usual confident panache was gone and in its place he exuded a very disagreeable aura of righteous indignation, which if not exactly passive was bordering on a non-participating level of restrained anger and frustration. Frankly, he was acting like a rubber tyre that had been over inflated and was just about ready to blow. I wasn't going to be around when it happened however, and after wishing him a fond farewell, I calmly got out of the car and then burst through the doors of the Gay Bar as though a demented taxman was after my non-existent assets.

I frightened the life out of Alfie who was engaged in polishing the bar counter.

'Sorry, Alfie,' I said, panting like a forge bellows.

'Downt madder,' he said, thoughtfully examining what looked like small initials that had been carved into the woodwork and then had been covered over with a bar mat.

'AJT,' he said. 'I wonder who?' He suddenly put his hand over the mark, gave me what appeared to be a rather embarrassed smile, and then slowly covered up the evidence of his ancient graffiti with its innocuous beer mat.

Dave and Tony arrived a little later having apparently read the note left by Father Marcus on the church door. Wearing what could be described as their best 'going out suit ensembles', they both looked and smelled pretty dangerous. They were both shocked when I gave them the unhappy news about Lenny's unfortunate accident, but a little later with that all forgotten, they enthusiastically recounted their own memorable little anecdotes from last night's festivities.

Both Vlado and Zora-Aleena were genuinely sorry to hear about Lenny's unfortunate accident and asked me to convey their best wishes to him and to wish him a full and speedy recovery.

My little bum-pincher ninja phoned me a little later. Apparently, she had some very important information for me and asked if we could meet up tomorrow just after opening time at the Volunteer pub in Queens Park. I agreed to meet her there just after midday.

Thereafter, my afternoon was thrown into confusion. Apart from my morning meeting with Lenny at the gym, my intended early afternoon's itinerary had to be shelved. But I had it all meticulously planned and had it gone ahead it would have consisted of the following: 13:00 – get into my penguin suit. 13:30 – make my way (on foot) to St Benedict's Church. 13:40 – meet Lenny at the church and welcome guests and assist in getting them to their respective seats. 14:00 – Standing next to Lenny in the church, and holding him firmly (to prevent his escape), give him Eugenia's wedding ring, and watch the wedding ceremony. 14:30 – Following the newly-weds exit from the church, assist the photographer with the photoshoot. 15:30 – Following the newly-weds departure in their limousine, collect the guests and in 'an orderly fashion' escort them (on foot) to the Bread Bin Public House to commence the evening celebrations. 'And a Partridge in a Pear Tree!'

Both Tony and Dave were in the mood for a little 'cultural exchange', which for them generally implies getting out of Kilburn for a while. However, instead of going out on what would simply degenerate into a pub crawl (albeit in an unfamiliar area), I suggested a trip to our local cinema instead. I was more than a little surprised when they both became very excited at the prospect. The latest James Bond film *Skyfall* was currently showing in a local cinema at Marble Arch and having checked on the web, I found that the next performance was scheduled to start at 18:40.

We had a couple of hours to kill, so we could all have our evening meals and whatever else was necessary before we caught up with our town-bound chauffeur a little later. Having heard our conversation, Alfie timidly asked me if he could come too. He was over the moon when I smiled at him and said, 'Of course you can Alfie, on condition that you buy the first round of ice creams.' This produced a very evident rush of excitement which resulted in a facial floridity comparable to that of a newly smacked buttock, and trying to catch his breath he said, 'I love the pictures... the last film that I saw at the pictures was that one with that 'orrible shark what was eating all them poor swimmers.'

Being clearly in *urine-extraction* mode, Dave said, 'Oh yeah! I saw the trailer for that; I thought it was just an advert for toothpaste!'

'No it was definitely a film, cos I saw it, and it went on for a long time... Adverts only go on for a little while and...' He was still talking as we left. 'See you later, Alfie,' I said. 'Don't be late!'

Our agreed meeting time would be 17:30 at the bus stop. Thereafter, I went back to the flat and met up with my girls. They all looked pleasantly exhausted following their earlier shopping expedition.

As I entered the kitchen, Jimena looked up at me enquiringly, her left offside leg pointing skyward, like a freeze-framed photograph of a feline ballerina, and then following a rather disinterested yawn she continued in her afternoon grooming session. Lenka was in the process of creating another one of her exotic Slavic-inspired meals, and Maria was watching her with an intensity that was quite distracting (bless her little wooden maracas). My beautiful little Elisha was busy using her crayons to enliven the basic outline drawing of a butterfly in her colouring-in book. For one so young, her imaginative use of the various colour combinations was very intuitive and quite charming.

Our visit to the cinema was both enjoyable and thankfully uneventful. We decided to walk back to Kilburn, and there were no slips, trips or mishaps of any kind as we sauntered along visiting a number of unfamiliar pubs on the way, which was not only very educational but culturally rewarding.

In pubs south of the Marylebone Road flyover, the cost of alcohol is far more expensive than those on our side of the divide. The needs and aspirations of the locals also appear to be considerably different to those who, having won the jackpot on the scratch card of life, were born and raised in Kilburn and its environs. Many of the younger types we met were yuppy-wannabes, a goodly proportion of whom having escaped from the former tedium and gut-wrenching boredom of their home towns or villages (which are scattered from 'the mess' of the Watford Gap to the bonny lochs and glens of Inverpinples) had bravely left their homes, kindred and pubs (where their favourite tipple was less than two pounds a pint) to journey forth to London in search of fame, fortune, affordable accommodation and pubs selling halves of lager for less than five pounds a glass.

We were all back on home turf at 01:10, culturally enlightened and very tired indeed.

Goodnight, Ginny.

P xx

22nd April 2012

Dear Ginny.

I slept very well indeed last night and at 07:15 I visited the gym for the usual routine of aerobic exercise followed by a poach, a shower and a shave. There was only one cleaning lady around this morning, and while formerly I have not had the time or (sadly) the inclination to chat to the floor staff, this morning she smiled at me as I passed her en route for the apparatus room, and I stopped to have a little social tete-a-tete with her.

Following a lengthy introduction, I learned from *Becky* that she had travelled down to London from Bristol in May 1989. She had never married and currently shared a flat with a lady friend from Yarmouth. I would estimate that she was in her late forties. She had the figure of a former gymnast, although she confided that her only real form of exercise had been manual work of one form or another. While she was rather plain looking (without a trace of make-up) she had a pleasant face, with green eyes, black shoulder-length hair and a very endearing smile. She currently worked forty hours per week at the gym, split over a seven-day week covering the 06:00–14:00 shift. This allowed her to work an additional four hours per day from 16:00–20:00 as and when needed at our local McDonald's.

Having told her about Elisha, she suddenly became very excited indeed, and I was very pleased to learn that my little girl was a fond favourite of hers (as she was with all of the other staff). I briefly explained Elisha's story and my hope that as a final party treat, in company with my two big girls, we would bring her along for one last visit this evening.

Becky will be working tonight and I asked her if it would be possible to reserve a table. I knew that they did so for diners celebrating a child's birthday for example. She stated that she would ring me a little later in the morning to confirm, and in the meantime I would make sure that these arrangements were convenient with my Maria and Lenka.

After my anticipated aerobic exercise split between the cross-trainer and the rowing machine, I paid a quick visit to the steam room followed by a refreshing shower and shave. On my way out, I gave Becky one of my cards and stated that following her phone call that I too would also confirm with her one way or another.

Back home, the girls were all together eating their various breakfasts, and without giving the game away, I asked Lenka and Maria if they would be available tonight. Happily both are free.

Winking at them, I casually asked Elisha where she would like to go for dinner this evening and without hesitation she said, 'The Coffee and Cream

Restaurant – they have scrummy goblin buns!'

I was completely dumbstruck! Suddenly, I realised that I needed to visit the toilet, and excusing myself, I dashed along the hall and just about managed to get parked on the loo. To take my mind off of my present unfortunate condition, I got stuck into a very interesting list on the back of a bottle of anti-wrinkle regenerating cream, reading about its constituent ingredients. As one would expect, it contained mineral oil, isopropyl and sodium hyaluronate, but I was very surprised to learn that it also contained triethanolamine and tetrapeptide-7 as well. Interrupting my enlightening concentration-diverting browse, I could hear the sound of raucous and unfettered laughter echoing along the hall.

A little later, as I popped my head around the kitchen door, my three girls were suddenly struck dumb, as though they had been caught in the middle of some dreadful clandestine conspiracy. Although this unexpected silence was quite alarming, I confidently walked into the room and made myself a cup of coffee. Having sat down at the table, I made enquiring eye contact with both Lenka and Maria, who both seemed rather embarrassed. 'OK,' I said, 'what's going on?'

Elisha slowly sauntered over to me and appeared to be rather nervous. Timidly she put her little hand on my arm, which she started to stroke tenderly. 'No sorry, Paul,' she said. 'I was just kidding. I really want to go to McDonald's! Can we go please, Paul?'

I was completely lost for words and a brief silence followed. I picked her up and holding her close, I said, 'Of course we can, my darling,' and then started to giggle like a loon, which was suddenly lost in a loud supportive eruption of mirth from Maria and Lenka.

It's been a long time since I have been fooled so convincingly, but what made it all the funnier was the realisation that I had actually been 'done up like a kipper' by a six-year-old child! And while I shall always cherish this beautiful memorable incident, it will remain a closely guarded secret for the rest of my life.

Becky phoned me at around 10:45, stating that a table for four had been booked and would be available from around 18:20 this evening. Actually, I too was quite excited at the prospect.

In the meantime, I had a meeting planned with my little bum-pincher-ninja at the Volunteer pub in Queens Park to attend, so at 11:20 I got out there amongst it, and travelled the one stop from Kilburn Park tube station. My carriage was all but empty apart from two young ladies in party frocks, and an elderly bloke who was reading a newspaper. I am pleased to say that I didn't suffer any feelings of nausea or claustrophobia on the way, and I arrived as fresh as a November chrysanthemum, albeit suffering from a little annoying train-lag.

Tina, who was sitting at a table well away from the bar as I arrived, waved at me as I entered. She stood up as I joined her and gave me a very warm hug, planting a gentle kiss on my cheek.

After the usual pleasantries had taken place, she got down to business. She informed me that Basil had cleared all of his unnecessary tasks both corporate and private, to be able to devote all of his time to the Ted issue. Apparently, he had been quite inconsolable following the news of Ted's fate.

He made it clear to Tina that while he was positively against the idea of an innocent man suffering for a crime that he did not commit; he was mature enough to accept that even in criminal fraternities a binding *espirit de corps* existed, and that the members were obligated to act and abide by the common rules and regulations which govern its existence. In the same way that guilty criminals are legally punished, transgression of a fraternity's guidelines or ordinances would result in some kind of unbiased judge-like sanction, which apparently ranged from simple attention-seeking punishments like a kick in the testicles, to the more physically debilitating scourgings that the imaginative sadistic mind is capable of.

Apparently, having given Ted's predicament some considerable thought, he had come to the conclusion that under the circumstances the 'captivity-exchange' scenario was the only feasible option open to him. However, I had a very bad feeling in relation to Basil's conspicuous involvement is this issue. I suggested to Tina that (under Basil's directions) I should be the frontman, as it were, and that all of this could be discussed with him anon.

In the British legal system, the worst kinds of offences like murder are dealt with severely. As late as 1969 before capital punishment was finally abolished in the UK, those convicted of murder were sentenced to death by hanging, or on reprieve, were given whole life sentences behind bars.

In the criminal world, the British slang term 'to grass' means to inform the police or the authorities of a person's wrongdoing or activities. It comes from the rhyming slang 'grasshopper' which means 'copper' (a slang term for a police officer). So a 'grass' or 'grasser' tells the 'copper' – policeman. Among the criminal classes it is considered to be the most heinous of negative actions that a person can engage in. I think that it is fair to say that in the UK anyway, that keeping one's own counsel, minding one's own business or turning the odd blind eye to naughty issues, is instilled in children from a very young age. One would never dream of 'snitching' on a classmate for example.

Tina was her usual bubbly self, but changing the subject she asked me if the name 'Compton' was familiar to me.

I replied that the only Compton I knew was the head campanologist at St Benedict's Church.

'That's the one,' she said. 'From my investigations, I have found out that he is the head of Ted's particular criminal group. He is known as *The Don*,' she said, smiling. 'You really couldn't make it up!'

I nearly choked on my sausage roll! 'So you're telling me that Wilfred (never late) Compton, a bloody bell-ringer, is the Mister Big in charge of our local villainous fraternity?'

'Well believe it or not, stranger things have happened,' she said. 'Ted Bundy the serial killer, who eventually admitted to committing thirty-six murders, was at one-time a director at the Seattle Crime Prevention Advisory Commission.'

I felt that I should arrange another very urgent meeting with Basil, and asked Tina if I could call in to see him at around 11:00 tomorrow morning. She said that she would confirm by text later on in the day. She gave me a big cuddle and another delicately placed kiss on the cheek as we parted.

I wasn't in the mood for another tube ride, so I walked back to Kilburn, calling in at the Bread Bin on the way. At 15:45, Tina texted me to say that a meeting with Basil was arranged for tomorrow at 11:00 as discussed.

Later in the evening, our time spent at McDonald's was quite wonderful. On our arrival, Becky welcomed us, making a big fuss of Elisha, who ran into her outstretched arms and planted a kiss on her cheek together with its obligatory 'MWAH!' which had everyone laughing deliriously.

Holding Elisha's hand, Becky escorted us to our little spot for the evening which had been beautifully decorated with small helium-filled balloons on strings that floated motionless above the centre of our table. A little printed card was placed on one of the place settings which simply read **'Elisha's Seat'**. A Ronald McDonald jigsaw and a small, wrapped present were on her chair.

Once we were all seated, three young girls behind the counter waved at Elisha, and laughing she raised bother her arms and waved back at them enthusiastically. 'That's Adela, Jolanta and Kinga,' she said excitedly. 'They live in Poland!' she stated confidently.

Stratford in East London will be hosting the summer Olympics this year, with the official opening ceremony taking place on the evening of Friday 27th July. The inside of the restaurant was festooned with Olympic paraphernalia and photographs of many of our competing athletes were hanging from every square inch of available wall space. It certainly gave the place a very special festive ambience. All of the staff was wearing 'Team GB' clothing, with replica gold medals hanging around their necks, and clearly many liked the idea of being associated with Olympic medallists, and their enthusiasm was almost palpable.

Our meals were very nice indeed, and the staff made a great fuss of our little girl, but the evening finished on a quite spectacular note. While we were eating our dessert ice cream, that well-known McDonald's TV theme tune suddenly started to play and Ronald McDonald himself made an appearance. With the usual clown's make-up face, he wore a bright red afro-style wig, a red and white stripe undershirt, over a bright yellow jumpsuit, and he was carrying what appeared to be a birthday cake on which were six lighted candles.

Elisha was positively riveted to the spot, her eyes wide with disbelief and her mouth gaped open in wonderment. The other children in the place were all just as surprised and started to clap excitedly. The expectant hum of enthusiasm quickly turned into a chaotic roar of jubilant mirth.

Ronald placed the bright yellow cake down in front of Elisha and blew her a kiss (which she caught and put into her little bag) and then obligingly she blew out the candles. It was clear that the management and staff had gone to a lot of trouble to make the evening a very memorable and special one for a little girl who was clearly one of their most enthusiastic and beloved patrons. Frankly, we were all tickled pink, and it was all such a beautiful way for our little girl to spend her last night in Kilburn.

On top of Ronald's cake written in red piped icing was the quite beautiful message:

FOR ELISHA – COME BACK SOON xxx

On leaving, I met the manager, a young trendy-looking man of around thirty-five summers, and thanked him profusely for all of the kind effort that he and his staff had made to ensure that Elisha's visit was so special. I gave Becky twenty pounds by way of appreciation, and thanking her for her help, I gave her a little cuddle of gratitude. She appeared to be somewhat embarrassed (bless her little white pinafore). But I am so pleased that I took the time to have that little chat with her this morning, since apart from it resulting in a lovely final evening for Elisha, I had made a new friend.

Just before we left, Elisha rushed behind the counter and gave Becky, Adela, Jolanta and Kinga a cuddle each, which completely compromised Maria's very tenuous grip on her emotions, and she hastened out of the restaurant gently sobbing.

Back at home, we all had a very quiet evening, with each of us backing up our own mental hard drives as it were, to ensure that our evening experiences would be forever saved.

Goodnight, Ginny.

P xx

23rd April 2012

Good morning, Ginny.

We all slept well, and for our Elisha's last breakfast I made us all banana pancakes with maple syrup. Needless to say, the main topic of conversation were the events of last night.

Nabil arrived at 09:30 and Elisha was ecstatically happy to see him. She ran down the hall and leapt into his arms. I was so very happy for her. Judging by her opening words on his arrival, the poor man was certainly in for a veritable earbashing, particularly in relation to her meeting with Ronald McDonald. He gave my two big girls beautiful bouquets of flowers, which I thought was very generous of him, and he hugged them both appreciatively.

Before they left, Elisha hugged me and planted a slobbery kiss on my cheek. She then gave Lenka a cuddle and a kiss, and, searching in her little day bag, she gave her Ronald McDonald's jigsaw.

Finally, opening her little day bag again she put her hand inside and making a grabbing motion, she brought her clenched fist out and slowly opening it. She gently tapped Maria's cheek while simultaneously making a loud verbal 'MWAH!' Smiling at Maria tenderly, she said, 'I was saving Ronald's kiss especially for you!' Maria's eyes started to fill up again, and she smiled sweetly.

As I walked them to the front door, Nabil shook my hand and gave me a sealed envelope.

'This is just a small token of my sincere thanks for looking after my precious little girl so well, and be assured that we shall be meeting up again in the very near future, my dear friend.'

'I hope so Nabil!' I said. And then suddenly they were gone and a cherished chapter of our lives was at an end.

Thereafter, it was business as usual. I phoned Eugenia who stated that Lenny was doing well following his surgery. His right foot and ankle are now in plaster, and he is expected to be at home later on this afternoon. Apparently, he will need crutches for a week or two until the plaster is taken off; and then he will need physiotherapy to assist in quite literally getting him 'back on his feet'.

Father Marcus arrived a little later and kindly assisted me in clearing out the biscuit tin of my remaining custard creams, and then went on to enquire about the present health status of Lenny. I gave him a quick summary of his condition, made all the quicker when I noticed that he was surreptitiously 'giving the eyeball' to an unopened packet of what Alfie would call 'chocolate suggestives'. However, I was feeling decidedly mean as he was leaving, so I gave him a chocolate hobnob for the walk home, which as the crow walks is a distant of around fifty-two feet.

Lenka will be working an afternoon shift today (14:00–23:00) and was all in favour of spending a quiet and uneventful morning resting in her room, and Maria will be meeting one of her college friends for lunch.

Opening Nabil's envelope in my room, I found a handwritten note thanking me and the girls for the love and care that we had given to Elisha. I felt inclined to send him a written reply, describing just how much unconditional love and affection that Elisha had given to each of us in return. I was then quite flabbergasted to find five hundred pounds in fifty-pound notes. I called the girls into the kitchen and gave them the money, which I felt was only fair. Lenka went one better, however, by stating that Maria should have the lot, and frankly I had to agree with her.

Of all the emotional quirks currently available on my Maria's beautiful physiognomy, it is very rare indeed to see her in a state of abject embarrassment. Initially, her cheeks became quite rosy coloured, her mouth suddenly gaped open like a dying codfish, and she was lost for words (which is another very unusual personal departure from the norm). However, following a sizeable lump of bread pudding and a couple of chocolate hobnobs, she regained her composure sufficiently to give us one of her endearing smiles. Blowing us both a kiss, she gently picked up Jimena and, casually scooping up the cash from the table, she sauntered off to her bedroom.

I then received two phone calls in quick succession. The first one was from Tina who stated that due to an urgent matter, Basil would be unavailable to have a meeting with me today. She thought that 14:00 tomorrow would be better. I checked my social calendar, and with no pressing engagements pending, I was pleased to accept her invitation.

The second call was from Alfie, asking if I'd be free to say farewell to Nobby Caxton and his wife, who would be returning home from the Bread Bin at around midday. I stated that once I had fed 'the hamsters' that I'd be on the first bus! Before he could make any further comment, I hung up and switched my mobile to silent mode.

Having secured the padlock on the fridge door and slapped a liberal squirt of *Hai Karate* aftershave 'on me boat' (boat race = face), I left for the Bread Bin at 11:50.

Rosheen gave me one of her usual friendly greetings and, like Father Marcus, wanted to know how our injured prospective bride groom was faring. I gave a summary of his condition to the assembled group which consisted of Bunny Longhurst, who had dashed into the pub for 'a quick lunchtime livener', Nobby and his wife Gretchen, together with Jack Sidall who was in the company of a rather corpulently disposed frumpy dumpling of some forty-five summers.

The general level of conversation was energetically charged and bounced around from one subject to another with considerable rapidity. But unlike the general level of meaningful discourse in the Gay Bar, it was both entertaining and mentally stimulating. But perhaps more importantly, each area of discussion reached a logical conclusion before another subject was introduced.

Before he left, Nobby indicated that he wanted to have a quiet word with me. I asked Rosheen if her private room was available for a short time, and a little later Nobby and I were in discussion.

Sadly, his first topic was Albery Groupenhourst. Nobby had been instructed through a court summons (issued to his legal team) to appear at Southwark Crown Court at 10:00 on Monday 21st May for a preliminary hearing. As expected, Albery will be pleading 'not guilty' to what his own legal team referred to as 'the ridiculous trumped-up charges'.

On a personal level, Nobby's legal team were optimistic that his involvement in the illegal machinations of Albery were influenced as a direct result of coercion viz. (the threats made against him and his immediate family) which would provide considerable mitigation in relation to his own reluctant involvement in the case. His main fear, however, was that if he was given a custodial sentence, inevitably he would be identified as an informer (grass) and as such, would be treated like a despicable pariah whose life would not be worth living. He explained that in prison there were two main socially unacceptable inmates, 'the nonce' (a paedophile) and 'the grass,' (an informer) and out of the two, 'the grass is worse than the worst nonce!'

We then got on to the more pressing subject of Ted. Nobby was surprisingly well informed about the whole issue. And he was clearly very well versed in the structure and the rules and regulations of our local villainous fraternity. Apparently, each London group has a name, which is an anagram of the area which it represents. Our local Kilburn group goes under the collective name of the 'BLIK-NUR'. Likewise, the Bermondsey fraternity south of the river went under the anagram of the 'SEREB-NOMDY'. Both of which, any reasonably intelligent schoolboy could have deciphered.

Trying to bring a little light relief into the discussion, I made the comment that, 'Wilf and his team had been watching too many episodes of Doxon of Dick Green!' And suddenly, he appeared to be very ill at ease and not a little nervous. He was very surprised and rather concerned that I knew the name of 'The Don' and cautioned me to be very careful when it came to this particular man. He emphasised that even Albery was very wary of him; and frankly that was all the justification that I needed to take Nobby's warning seriously.

A little later, we all bade Nobby and his wife Gretchen a fond farewell. Alfie arrived just as they were leaving. Looking at me anxiously he said, 'I tried calling you on your phone, but it kept ringing.'

'Sorry Alfie, but I was otherwise engaged,' I said.

'No, you weren't engaged cos when it's engaged it goes beep-beep-beep...' Looking around him, he walked to the end of the room and then using his head to motion me (at least it's good for something), he engaged in his ventriloquist's dummy routine again. He passed me a small slip of paper, and without any noticeable movement of his lips he said, 'Ted wants you to ring that number.'

I checked the number that was written down and then went through the motions of dialling the number. Alfie stopped me. 'No not now!' he said, evidently in panic mode. 'Ted was very Pacific.'

'The word is specific, Alfie,' I said.

'Well, Ted said that you can only ring that number at eight o'clock at night!'

'Does he want me to ring it tonight then, Alfie?' I asked.

'Oh... I dunno,' he said, looking decidedly flustered. An ominous silence followed. Suddenly he started to laugh. 'How stupid of me,' he said. And then getting his phone out from his jacket pocket, he said, 'All I've gotta do is give him a quick ring – what's the number?'

I simply stared at him in disbelief. No euphemistic sentiment could fully describe the verbal onslaught that followed. A close approximation of the words used would be, 'Alfie – you are a silly billy!' (or words to that effect). Suffice it to say, that he was left in no doubt about my general feelings on the issue.

Having 'suddenly' remembered another pressing engagement, he smiled at me pleasantly (which following my earlier admonishment was very considerate of him) and, taking a few tentative steps backwards, he said, 'See you later, crocodile!'

As he walked away, I felt so terribly mean and I called him back. I gave him a hug. 'Do you know how many bags of sugar that I love you, Alfie?' I said.

'Five?' he said, appealing. 'Not even close – nine and a half!' I replied.

He smiled radiantly. 'As many as that,' he said. 'I was going to say eight, but then I thought that that might be too much.'

'Alfie, you remember when I told you how clever those undercover agents are, who can remember and forget all of those secret things?'

He nodded and smiled, but before he could make a reply I said, 'Well this is something that I want you to remember – it's very important indeed!'

I can't recall a time when I had seen him looking so eagerly attentive. It reminded me of the time when, having a bit of a disagreement with Spike, he realised that there was a slice of bread pudding on the cards, provided he let me have my slipper back.

'In future, Alfie,' I said, 'before you say anything, mill it over in your mind and if you think that it might be a silly thing to say, then just don't say it. That would be a very clever thing to do!'

'But what if I don't think that it's a silly thing to say?' he asked.

'Well then just don't say it anyway!'

He had a somewhat bemused look on his face as he walked back towards the bar.

The rest of my afternoon was spent at home, doing what comes so naturally to me these days (nothing of any importance). Jimena was my only companion, although she was more than happy to get on with her own mental wool-gathering, and the occasional perfunctory lick or two of her paws.

At 20:00 precisely, I rang the number that Alfie had given me. The person who answered clearly didn't want to discuss matters of a social nature, and simply stated that 'The Bandit' had asked him to give me the simple message that, 'his 'captivity-exchange' application had been unsuccessful, and that he wanted to send his best wishes to me and all at The Magpie. On remand, he is allowed three one hour visits a week, and looks forward to seeing some of the boys again soon.

He closed this brief conversation with a somewhat veiled threat. 'Your number is now blocked on this mobile, and I would strongly advise you to delete my number, or any other that you might have from your phone's memory.'

A little later, I did as instructed, clearing the number, and just to be on the safe side, I also cleared the other number that Ted had given me. Discretion is indeed a better part of valour!

Goodnight, Ginny.

P xx

24th April 2012

Good morning, Ginny.

I had a dreadful night's sleep, and having got up for a pit stop at 02:20, I simply couldn't go back to sleep again. Due to my constant tossing and turning, at 03:50 Jimena had clearly had enough of the constant disturbances and was scratching noisily at my bedroom door. As I let her out into the hall, she emitted a very strange sound which could only be described as a very annoyed 'MEEEOOOOWWWWTHHHHUUUUPPT'. But not being an expert on the vocal utterances of animals in general, or pissed-off moggies in particular, I was convinced that this very clear paroxysm was nothing more than a show of utter frustration of the 'Oh for fuck's sake!' kind of thing. I apologise for using the vernacular form, Ginny, but following today's adventures I am feeling far from amused, and need to let off a bit of steam, a bit like Jimena's tantrum this morning. I wonder if cats can suffer from Tourette's syndrome?

When I finally kicked my very frustrated legs out of bed at 06:15, I was in a foul mood and decided that following my cup of reviving coffee, I'd wander across to the gym for nothing more strenuous than a ponder in the steam room, followed by a shave and a shower.

I didn't see Becky during my visit, and perhaps it was just as well, since I really wasn't in the mood for socialising, although had I met her, I would have naturally pushed myself out of my mental lethargy and would have become as polite as an encouraged Jehovah's Witness who had been asked to call again.

The girls were both out this morning, and I was missing them and really could have done with a little amusing rapport of the kind that only they could provide. Jimena seemed a little better on my return from the gym. As I walked into the kitchen she jumped up onto the table and allowed me to stroke her. Following her morning repast of the bits of salmon and pilchard that are not fit for human consumption, she gave me a kind of look that suggested uncertainty and then vanished along the hall in the direction of Maria's room.

Following my own breakfast of boiled eggs and toast soldiers, I left home at 10:10 en route for the offices of Burt Lang and Forthright in Kensal Rise. I arrived at 10:55 just in time for a cup of tea and a slice of tiffin.

It didn't take long to complete the usual pleasantries and to eat the confection, and thereafter we got down to the important issues relating to our mutual friend, Eduardo Filepe Cordona, aka *Ted the Pleb.*

Basil was flabbergasted when I told him about Ted's unsuccessful 'captivity-exchange' application, and he was clearly very angry indeed. His initial response was to 'arrange a meeting with Mr Compton', which I didn't like the sound of whatsoever. However, as he had pointed out earlier, it would be a wise move to keep one's enemies close, so at some stage, getting a little nearer to the *pud-wapper* would be a very positive step. However, I felt it unwise for Basil to get involved in this personally, and suggested that I should lead the attack, as it were.

As of today's date, Ted will have been under 'judicial custody' for ten days. I am aware that he had spoken to Wilf, or at least a senior member of his fraternity last Thursday morning. Ted had given me Wilf's mobile number, but following the less than friendly warning that I received last night, I had cleared the number from my phone. Besides, how on earth could I initiate a conversation with a man that I had never met, on a subject that was so dreadfully complicated? No, I would have to take the bull by the horns at it were, and arrange a face-to-face meeting with Mr Compton.

Using my video record facility on my mobile phone, I asked Basil if I could record the section of the VHS tape where Messrs Webb and Gillespie are seen in Andy's company on the afternoon of the burglary. This undoubtedly puts them both in the area on the day of the crime. Additionally, it clearly provides very incriminating evidence against Gillespie, who is seen to pocket Andy's door keys. That was his first mistake. The second mistake was to leave the keys inside Andy's flat (as could be verified by his wife). The fact that he had spent the night at my place would also give a certain amount of credibility to the belief that his door keys were missing. While this evidence was all circumstantial, I believe that on the 'balance of probability' it would be enough to convict the two *anal-orifum* of burglary, which just for the record, is contrary to section 9.1(a) of The Theft Act of 1968 as amended. Basil was very impressed with my legal knowledge, although I really don't know how on earth we ever managed before the arrival of the internet and its various search engines.

Given the clear evidence that *Butch* and *Sundance* were responsible for the burglary at Andy's flat (compliments of Vlado's video), I felt that I have a slight advantage. Additionally, since happily I am not a paid-up member of any criminal fraternity or ancillary organisation, this affords me a certain freedom of action of a type which is not available to the general membership. For example, I am under no obligation to abide by any rules applicable to any such fraternity, and can therefore confidently *grass-up* whomever I should choose. Therefore, being an upstanding and respectable citizen, I feel that I would be doing the general public a great service in assisting the police to rid society of two unscrupulous thieving *fatherless-people*. Unless of course, the powers that be (Compton and Co) are willing to arrange for the timeous release from police custody of one Eduardo Filepe Cordona, aka *The Bandit* – who is more familiarly known as *Ted the Pleb.*

I left Basil's office with a new sense of purpose and a confident bounce in my step, until I skidded along on an enormous unseen pile of dog shit that is, and nearly ruptured myself in the process. Fortunately, nothing was broken apart from my short-lived feelings of complacency. It certain brought me back to earth with a bump. And not wishing to be in any confined space with the travelling public, since smelling like a bloke whose jeans were covered in dog shit I wouldn't have been enthusiastically welcomed on any bus or tube. I therefore walked home instead, using the less frequented back streets.

As I entered my block, on the way up the stairs I took off my jeans, and as I walked into the flat, I found Father Marcus, Maria and Lenka standing in the hall. It was, to say the very least, a bit of an embarrassing encounter. I dashed into the bathroom, depositing my jeans together with a handful of washing powder into the bath. I ran a goodly quantity of hot water over them and putting on a pair of rubber gloves, I gave them a thorough scrub. Thereafter, I left them to soak for a while and checking that the hall was now clear, I sprinted across it like a geriatric poofter in boxer shorts, breathing an audible sigh of relief once I was in the safety of my bedroom.

A little later, I rejoined the good Father and my girls who were all in busy conversation in the kitchen. I made my profuse apologies and explained the reason for my rather unusual method of entry into the flat, and having allowed them to get over their loud expressions of unfettered mirth, I made myself a cup of reviving coffee.

Before Father Marcus left to go and complete his normal rounds of spiritually uplifting verbal advice to those who were reckless enough to answer their doors to him, I asked him If he would be available to have a quick meeting with me at some time later in the day, suggesting the Bread Bin as a possible venue.

He stated that he would be free at around 16:30, for about thirty minutes. We agreed on the time and place and I bade him farewell a little later.

As inquisitive as ever, Lenka asked if she could tag along, and I thought that not wishing to deceive her in any way, I could simply have a general chat with Father Marcus along the lines of my possible interest in joining his current team of bell-ringers. Inevitably this would quite innocently lead the conversation from the history of their formation on to the names and personal particulars of its members. Thereafter I would cunningly steer the conversation towards 'old crusty-bollocks' himself, Wilfred (never late) Compton, Campanologist-Extraordinaire and supreme *anal-orifice* of this fair parish.

I do not dislike very many people and can't think of anyone that I can truly say that I hate. So for me to loathe this individual, having never personally met him, is a quite new and unique experience. Frankly, I am quite looking forward to meeting him, if for no other reason than to confirm that my unreasonable feelings for the bloke are completely justified.

With time on my hands, I told Lenka that I would call in at the Gay Bar for a while. I asked her if she'd like to join me, but she declined, stating that she would see me at the Bread Bin later.

At the pub, Dave, Tony and Alfie were in lively conversation. 'They are stealing the food from out of our mouths!' said Dave, who was clearly very agitated.

'In the medieval days, people caught clipping the realm's coinage would be severely dealt with, often ending up on the block!' said Tony.

'What block? Like as in an estate block?' said Alfie, as inquisitive as ever.

'No, the chopping block,' Tony replied, with an unmistakable amount of exasperation surfacing in his voice.

Wass 'at then?' asked Alfie.

'It was a place where people what clipped the realm's coinage lost their heads,' said Dave helpfully.

'How can you lose your head – it is part of your body, and it don't just come off and get lost, like a packet of fags, or a...'

'In those days, Alfie,' I said, trying to be as patient as I could. 'The coins were mainly all made of silver and gold. So a sixpence for example was made up of six pennyworth of silver. But what people used to do, was to cut a little bit off and save it until they had enough to take it to a pawn shop or money dealer and sell it. They could even give it to a silversmith to make a snuff box or a small candlestick out of it, if they had enough of it. Trouble was that by clipping a little bit off of the coin meant that it wasn't worth sixpence anymore, and this caused all kinds of problems. Anyone caught clipping the coins or who were found with clippings, could have their heads chopped off.'

'Well you wouldn't have caught me doing it, I can't stand the sight of blood and looking...'

'Alfie, you remember what I said about them very clever people, who think before they say something?' I said.

He seemed very embarrassed and nodded.' Sorry!' he said. 'I won't say nuffin else.'

'No Alfie, you must join in on our conversations, it's a very educational experience, and everyone should engage in social intercourse whenever they can!' I said.'I never talk about dirty things!' he said indignantly, and grabbing his coat from behind one of the chairs, he walked to the door resolutely and said, 'Arivvedoochee crocodilio,' and vanished out into the non-critical anonymity of the Kilburn High Road.

And suddenly, I was feeling pretty guilty and somewhat miserable again. He is the only person I know who can instil in me such conflicting emotions.

You may have gathered that the earlier conversation had its origin in the fact that many of our consumer products from soap and toiletries, to cleaning fluids and consumables, are being cunningly reduced in size by unscrupulous manufacturers. This devious and insidious form of deception appears to be all pervasive, and as far as I am concerned, it is just as despicable as the less than respectable actions of people like Compton and his associates.

Actually, the earlier conversation was initiated by Dave who had mentioned that his favourite chocolate confection had got to such a small size, that glasses were now needed to see it. The cost of it, however, had not shrunk in a similar manner. Dave has always been a very liberal-minded, gentle sort of individual, but he is totally uncompromising when it comes to people, or manufacturing organisations, that have the audacity to mess about with his food, his beer or his women (in that order).

Our meeting with Father Marcus was a relatively quiet affair, as a direct consequence of a pair of eagle eyes that had spotted him on his way to the pub. The eight or more other bar attendees shot out of the back door faster than a group of centipedes who had been dropped onto hot sand, and in an effort to conceal the evidence of their swift departure, Rosheen quietly placed the various glasses under the counter.

I bought Father Marcus a sherry on his arrival and after the usual pleasantries were concluded, I introduced my reasons for wanting to see him. He appeared to be quite relieved when he realised that I was not in need of spiritual guidance or any form of pastoral care, and was very surprised to learn about my latent interest in campanology as was Lenka.

I learned that there were five bell-ringers including Compton and when we got round to him, Father Marcus had nothing but praise for the man. Apparently, he was in his late sixties, was quite small in stature, and he described him as 'a Wilfred Brambell look-a-like', who was an actor famous for his portrayal of a grimy and grasping old man in a father-and-son rag-and-bone team, called Steptoe and Son. It was a very popular British sitcom back in the sixties.

Apparently, Compton was a moderate once-a-week drinker, who would usually 'join the boys' on their Sunday lunchtime sessions at a pub in St John's Wood called *The Raven's Bill*. I had never heard of the pub before, but then when it comes to satiating my desire for alcoholic beverages or convivial company, I do not wander too far away from my beloved Kilburn and its environs.

Father Marcus left at around 17:20 and I was in an adventurous mood. I asked Lenka if she'd like to join me on a little 'fact-finding mission' into the wilds of St John's Wood to see if I could locate the watering hole of Wilfred (*the bells made me deaf you know*) Compton, 'The fiend of St Benedict's Church'.

'What about Maria?' she said.

'I don't think that she drinks in a pub in St John's Wood,' I said.

My attempts at the innocent replica of a classic Alfred Tillington reply, resulted in what my revered old mum would have described as a 'fourpenny one', as Lenka's right fist pounded into my arm. Holding her clenched fist under my nose, she said, 'Now!... What about Maria?'

I phoned Maria immediately and told her that Lenka and I were on a fact-finding mission and did she wish to join us. Her reply was pretty succinct.

'No, gracias,' she said and hung up.

We eventually located the Raven's Bill pub, along a small affluent backstreet. It was a very small place of the 'nothing to write home about kind' with a pool table, a dartboard and a well-used shove-ha'penny board which had seen better days. The 'bar person' who was the spitting image of Margaret Thatcher (in drag) was busily wiping the bar top down as we arrived.

There certainly weren't any diminutive Albert Steptoe look-a-likes present, and it didn't take us long to finish our drinks and to 'make for the hills' once again.

On the way home, we called into our local Turkish restaurant and had a very nice meal, and then on our way back to the flat, I had an action replay of this morning's shit-skidding incident. However, this time Lenka prevented me from falling, which was very fortuitous indeed in that it saved me the trouble of handwashing another pair of jeans. But then having to dig out dog poo from the tractor-tyre like soles of my Reebok trainers wasn't exactly the first word in pleasant activities either!

Goodnight, Ginny.
P xx

25th April 2012

Good morning, Ginny.

I shall be doing a little more snooping around today and thought that on opening time I'd pay a visit to the 'Raven's Bill' and have a friendly chat with the locals. I would have to be careful however, since like the former *Beast of Susan Atkins Court,* I was sure that Mr Compton would have a fair amount of his underworld spies knocking around the place, and that clearly none of the pub's patrons could be trusted as far as I could throw them.

Lenka was up and out early this morning, but following her morning shower, Maria made an appearance in the kitchen at 07:45 with Jimena trotting in behind her. Now that her caring duties are at an end, she will be resuming her MBA studies. She is clearly feeling a little superfluous to requirements however, particularly now that Elisha is not around, although she confessed that she wouldn't have missed the experience for the world. We had an enjoyable breakfast together.

My visit to the Raven's Bill pub later in the morning proved to be a very enlightening experience indeed. As I write these lines, I am still feeling very apprehensive about my own well-being and safety. Given the considerable amount of information that I have received today, I truly have to question whether my intended course of action is wise or simply bordering on the imbecilic.

I arrived at the pub at around 12:30. There were two other punters in the bar, and the Margaret Thatcher look-a-like bar person was in attendance again.

I ordered a pint of Guinness and waited patiently for its frothy goodness to settle. In places like Ireland, fifteen minutes before opening time, numerous half-filled glasses of Guinness just about cover the length of the bar tops, awaiting the arrival of the thirsty customers. Once they are through the doors, the glasses are then filled with infinite care, ensuring that they are graced with an obligatory ten millimetres of creamy white head. Pouring the perfect pint of Guinness is a true art form, and inexperienced or shoddy bar persons who have the temerity to serve up a bad pint, have more chance of actually wearing it than being paid for it.

Having collected my 'blonde in the black dress' as *Whispering Jim* would have said, I sauntered over to a vacant window seat by the door. Having taken a swig, I nearly choked on spotting Alexander Barrington Scott (my court hero) who walked into bar from a back room. He was clearly just as surprised at seeing me.

Walking out from behind the bar, he rushed across to me, and shaking my hand said, 'Well this is a very fortuitous meeting, Paul.' And sitting down at my table, he said, 'I had fully intended having a word with you, and I know why you are here.' He then went on to explain that Wilfred Compton was his mother's brother, making him his nephew. The bar person was his wife Gloria, and they were the pub managers. Smiling at me almost apologetically, he then went on to state that the pub was owned by his uncle Wilf. I was absolutely flabbergasted.

Lowering his voice, he then went on to say that he was aware of his uncle's underworld activities, the details of which he had no desire of knowing about. Likewise, he was not involved in any of his uncle's affairs whether legal or otherwise. As he stated apologetically, 'That one can choose one's friends, but when it came to family, you simply had to take what you were given.' But then he went on to confirm that he had assisted his uncle in a rather serious territorial issue with Albery Groupenhourst. In a show of strength, Albery had challenged Wilf stating that if he could arrange for an innocent person convicted of an offence to be released before conviction, then he would relinquish his former hold on a disputed two square mile area between the Brondesbury Road and the Harrow Road flyover.

On the orders of Albery, the 'innocent person' chosen to be subjected to this despicable iniquity was none other than 'yours truly'. This resulted in the shed issue and what I thought was Alexander's heroic defence, where he told the truth and admitted his share of the blame. It appears that the bloke who was renting shed number 23 was bought off, allowing Alex, with the help of Nobby Caxton, to achieve his *coup de grace*. However, what Wilf didn't know was that Albery had another trick up his sleeve. Should the initial plan fail, he had a secondary back-up option. He had the illegal fiddling device installed in my electric meter at the same time as the shed break-in issue. And should I get off the first charge, he was confident that I would be convicted on the second one.

The plan didn't go exactly to plan since when DS Blackstock had searched the flat, he hadn't spotted the fiddling device in the electric meter cupboard. The fact that I got off of the theft charge meant that Albery had lost the bet, and accordingly he had to relinquish a two-mile square area of his former territory.

Out of spite, he anonymously notified the Electric Company about the presence of the fiddling device in my electric cupboard, which resulted in my being arrested again on another charge, this time of the Fraudulent Abstraction of Electricity, which is contrary to section 13 of the Theft Act 1968.

It was only Nobby's timely intervention on the day of the trial that turned the tables. Without his selfless and noble assistance, I would have undoubtedly been found guilty. He did this of his own volition, effectively going against the directions of Albery, which potentially put him in a very serious position indeed and as they say, 'the rest is history.'

Alex made it very clear, that Nobby Caxton's actions were due entirely to Albery's very real threats and demands. Likewise, his own involvement in the shed saga, while being instigated by his uncle, he was happy to get involved in, since he honestly believed that by doing so, an innocent man would be saved and that therefore his actions were honourable and not influenced by any sinister motives.

We then discussed the Ted issue, and he fully understood my desire to assist. But emphasised that the 'BLIK-NUR' fraternity was a serious democratically run organisation, and that it was the membership who held the power, particularly on contentious issues, or votes like the one held recently on the fate of Eduardo Filepe Cordona alias *The Bandit*.

I asked him if he could arrange a meeting between me and his uncle to 'discuss this matter' to see if an alternative course of action would be possible, but with blood being thicker than water, I decided to keep my plans close to me chest. What I have to say to Mr Compton will be between him and me, and since he was instrumental in all of the needless discomfort and worry that I have suffered recently, I feel that it was time for me to likewise give him a little 'something' to think about. However, I shall tread very carefully indeed.

Having drunk my delicious well-presented pint of Guinness, I thanked Alex for his candour and giving him one of my cards, I reiterated that I would like to have a chat with his uncle, and while it might be a bit of a futile exercise, I felt that 'someone outside of the fraternity should speak up on Ted's behalf'. He nodded understandingly.

On leaving the pub, I phoned Basil, giving him a very basic outline of my meeting with Alex, and he asked me to call in and see him first thing in the morning.

On my way back to Kilburn, I had a call from Maria who was very excited indeed, so much so that she couldn't quite catch her breath as she was trying to speak. Finally, having calmed herself down sufficiently, she told me that Gabriel will be returning to the UK on Saturday morning. His flight is expected to land at Heathrow at around 05:45.

Needless to say, I have a feeling that my darling girl will be on the missing list for the foreseeable future. But then like Lenny, I am so happy that she has finally met the love of her life.

Being around a thirty-minute walk from *Whispering Jim's* pub, I thought that I'd pay him a visit. Following a much need brisk walk, I arrived at the pub feeling almost euphoric, with those naughty little 'feel-good' endorphins having brightened up my mood considerably.

Danie gave me a wave from the bar as I entered, and Jim was engaged in conversation with a little lady. Having spotted me, he joined me at the bar, and ordered two pints. Viljoen did his little party piece which as ever, brought a wave of laughter throughout the bar.

Following the obligatory wait allowing for the stout to settle, Jim mentioned that he was in the company of 'his friend' Brigit, and seemed to be a little embarrassed (bless his little soggy beer mat).

Brigit was a sprightly lady of some sixty-five summers. She was of small stature, with blue eyes and almost white medium-length hair, which she wore in what I believe is called the pixie cut. She must have been quite stunning in the lovely April of her prime, since now approaching her late autumnal years as it were, she was still a fine-looking woman. On being introduced to her, she made it very plain that Jim was 'simply a friend', which I assumed meant that they were not involved in any of the 'under the duvet wubby-couching'. Why on earth she felt it necessary to clear up any misunderstanding that I may have had in relation to this issue, was beyond me. Frankly, it wouldn't have mattered to me if she was a geriatric nymphomaniac in endurance training. But then, she'd probably had a very strict Catholic upbringing, which would have been similar to Jim's but unlike him, she had not forsaken her faith or had turned her back on the *bells and smells* at the first taste of the communion wine, or in Jim's case, the start of his lifelong relationship with *the blonde in the black dress.*

I could see why anyone would enjoy the company of this very appealing lady, since her level of intellect was surprisingly good, and her razor-sharp wit cut through any semblance of pretension or twaddle. Smiling at Jim tenderly, she put her hand on his arm and said, 'He has been my rock!'

I was to learn a little later that she had been diagnosed with inoperable pancreatic cancer and that if she were to accept treatment, she would have between eight months to a year of life. Without treatment, she would have at best around six months. She bravely chose the latter.

Her dominant level of belief and faith in the Almighty was all consuming, and when she spoke about the happiness and the joy that she had experienced in her life, I felt so very humbled at meeting someone with such unshakable conviction and belief that her saviour had died for her sins and had risen on the third day. A little later I bade them both a fond farewell.

On the walk back to Kilburn, I was genuinely feeling spiritually uplifted and felt so very grateful that I had met a true and faithful ambassador of the Christian faith and frankly I felt blessed by association.

Dimitri Federov phoned at 15:10 to ask if it was convenient to call at around 16:20 to carry out an inventory of my belongings in relation to my forthcoming move. I was back home at 16:00 and Dimitri arrived a little later. He was very thorough and stated that he would drop in his quote tomorrow afternoon at the latest.

Both of my girls were out when I had arrived home and Jimena appeared to be genuinely excited to see me. I played with her for a while, but feeling a little restless, and needing a little friendly company, I visited the Gay Bar, but apart from Vlado and Zora-Aleena the place was as empty as a cobbler's curse, so I returned home, grabbed my bag and hastened over to the gym, where I simply had a long meditative poach in the steam room followed by a shave and a shower.

I had a very quiet uneventful evening.

Goodnight, Ginny.

P xx

26th April 2012

Good morning, Ginny.

I had a very long and infinitely refreshing sleep, getting up at 06:50. All was very quiet, apart from Jimena, who having heard her morning breakfast provider rousing, joined me in the kitchen, purring noisily and looking up at me appealingly. Needless to say, I duly obliged and a little later she was getting stuck into minced salmon eyebrows and pilchard belly buttons, and evidently enjoying the feast, periodically looked up at me adoringly. It is clear to me that apart from a man, the way to a cat's heart is also through its stomach.

I was feeling somewhat rebellious this morning, and as a primary exercise at 08:00 I phoned Tina and asked her to give Basil the message that 'something had come up and that I can't get to his office this morning, but if convenient, I'd meet him at the Glass House pub at midday'.

She said that she'd give him the message when she got to the office and that if I hadn't heard back from her by 10:00, then Basil would meet me as requested at the time and place stated.

I phoned Eugenia to enquire after the health and general mental condition of Lenny, and was given a very favourable assessment of his present state, and was afforded an enthusiastic invitation to pay them both a visit. A little later, I took a stroll along the Cricklewood Broadway and was welcomed by Eugenia at her flat, which was situated just behind the Horse and Plough pub.

Lenny appeared in fine spirits. His injured leg was encased in plaster, from his kneecap to his foot, and Elisha would have had great fun drawing pictures on it, had she been around (bless her little day bag).

As I walked into Eugenia's lounge, Lenny was seated in a very comfortable looking chair, with his plastered foot propped up on a small poof (no offence intended to the LBGT brigade).

'Don't get up!' I said as I entered.

'You have more chance of seeing a double amputee sitting in a chiropodist's chair!' he replied smiling affably, which cheered me up considerably.

It now appears that they have made renewed plans for the wedding, which will now take place at 2 pm on Saturday the 5th of May. All the necessary bookings have been made again, and all have confirmed their attendance. Rosheen has put off an earlier enquiry to hold a birthday party on the same date, the band is free on the evening of the 5th and the caterers are also available, so it seems that it's all systems go for the 5th May provided that his plans do not *gang aft a-gley* (again). And not wishing to tempt fate, he will be avoiding the gym for the foreseeable future.

I was a ten-minute walk away from the Glass House pub, and not wishing to be late, I bade Eugenia and Lenny a fond farewell at 11:40. Just before I arrived,

Dimitri phoned to ask if he could call at around 16:00. Apart from my meeting with Basil, I was free for the rest of the afternoon, so I stated that I'd see him at the flat at the appointed time.

When I arrived at the pub, Basil was sitting at a table away from the bar. A rather nice pint of Guinness awaited my arrival.

'So what urgent matter had altered your plans this morning?' he asked, taking a sip from a glass of Coke.

'It was a simple determination on my part – to change the very one-sided nature of our future meeting arrangements, which hitherto have been undemocratically directed by you. Normally it entails your request, nay command, to visit you at your office. I am no longer a client of yours, Basil, and with the greatest of respect, I should no longer be treated like one.'

He smiled at me ruefully and said, 'Oh dear, how remiss of me! My sincere apologies, should I now call you Mr Shaughnessy or would a simple…'

'OK… OK, enough of the sarcasm,' I said. 'I simply believe that from here on in, Basil, a little more give and take – and in your case a little more give – is needed in our relationship.'

Smiling, he said, 'You are right of course, I'll try and do better next time!'

Thereafter, I gave him a complete rundown of yesterday's meeting with Alexander Barrington Scott, the licensee of the Raven's Bill pub. He listened attentively throughout my lengthy discourse, occasionally raising an eyebrow or two as the story unfolded. Having explained that I had given my card to Alex, asking him to get his uncle to give me a call, I had to admit that I didn't really hold out too much hope that Mr Compton would oblige. I therefore suggested that if I was not to receive a call from him by Sunday, which would have given him six days to respond to my request, I would take the bull by the horns and seek him out myself. I was aware that on Sunday lunchtime, following his come-down after having given the local populace a veritable ear-hole bashing with his bells – *they made him deaf you know* – he is known to join the lads in a beer or two at his pub. (Sorry about the flippancy Ginny, but every time I think about the man, I cannot get Charles Laughton and his marvellous portrayal of the Hunchback of Notre Dame out of my mind.) Basil wasn't very enthusiastic at this suggestion however, believing that I was potentially putting myself at considerable risk. But I reiterated my belief that I still had the upper hand, but it could not be dealt without a face-to-face meeting with the man. We parted company at 13:25.

Back at home, my Maria was cleaning out her bedroom with a degree of determination that was almost breathtaking. Jimena was sat on the windowsill watching her intently. Her bedding and window nets were piled up in the hall awaiting an appointment with the washing machine, my newly purchased replacement vacuum cleaner was standing to attention ready to commence its first major expeditionary suck of her shag-pile carpet, and an array of various cleaning aerosol cans were crammed on to the top of her dressing table.

'Sorry I wasn't very much around yesterday, but I was cleaning Gabby's flat. He's coming home on Saturday!' she said excitedly. 'It's just two more sleeps!'

Dimitri arrived a little later and gave me a written estimate for my removal costs, which I thought was very reasonably priced. Unless otherwise directed, he would collect most of my belongings during the morning on Sunday 6^{h} May; the final arrangements would be made nearer the time. I gave him a two-hundred-pound deposit with the balance being paid on completion.

At the Gay Bar, I found Lenka and Zora-Aleena having a social tete-a-tete over a libation or two. As I entered, Zora-Aleena made a somewhat over exaggerated show of welcoming me, wishing me a very good afternoon, complete with a double-cheek French- type kiss, which I believe is called *Faire la bise,* in French, which was both unexpected and delightfully charming. I was likewise most impressed that she had managed to achieve this manoeuvre without poking me in the eye with her nose or giving me a *Glasgow kiss,* which is a quaint Scottish euphemism for a sudden sharp head-butt to the nose, which normally results in the recipient's hooter looking like a plate of bolognese.

Vlado was clearly impressed, and his facial expressions of pride and happiness could be compared with those seen on the facial physiognomy of the Best of Breed's owner in the winner's enclosure at Crufts. Not that you could compare Zora-Aleena with a dog. But if I had to do so, she could be likened to the beautiful long-haired Afghan hound. They are so very eye-catching, with a somewhat aloof aristocratic bearing, which compares favourably with Zora-Aleena who initially appeared to be ever at a distance, or almost untouchable. However, having spent some considerable time with my Lenka, her transformation has been quite remarkable.

'It's so nice to see you again, Paul,' she said, smiling at me radiantly and guiding me to the bar. On our arrival, she graciously released my arm, and as a courteous gesture, I took her right hand in mine and kissed it gently. 'It's also so nice to see you again, Zora-Aleena,' I said, smiling radiantly.

Behind the bar, Vlado was gently chuckling to himself, and appeared to be somewhat embarrassed. He smiled at my coyly. 'You are as they says, a smoothy bugger!'

Having previously given him instructions on the correct way to pour a pint of Guinness, when I had entered earlier, he had half-filled a pint glass, which he started to top up when his wife and I had arrived at the bar. As he placed what was undoubtedly the perfectly poured pint of Guinness in front of me, and feeling in a bit of a mischievous mood, I said,

'Good evening Vlado,' shaking his hand. 'I'll have a pint of lager please.'

Placing both hands on the bar, his shoulders suddenly slumped forward and he groaned audibly. Reaching under the counter for a clean glass, I said,

'I'm just teasing you, Vlado, I'll take that pint of Guinness if you please, and my sincere compliments on the way that it has been poured.'

Smiling good-naturedly he said, 'I think you having me over, you have, you naughty smoothy bugger.'

A considerable amount of laughter followed, which frankly is a defining feature of this particular watering hole.

Alfie was unusually quiet and didn't seem to be in a very sociable mood and was sitting on his own by the jukebox. I sauntered over to him and sat down at his table.

Some minutes passed before our eyes met, but when they did, he smiled at me timidly.

'I'm in a little bit of a fix,' he said, looking out of the window quickly, as though in fear of being seen talking to me and being overheard.

Following a brief ominous silence, he gazed around him anxiously and then adopting his ventriloquist dummy routine again, he explained that following his unexpected dismissal from Basil's workforce some weeks ago, he was a little strapped for cash. He reminded me about the request he'd made to me for that loan. An acquaintance of his had apparently given him the phone number of a friend of his, who was apparently in the 'banking business'. Following a brief meeting, he borrowed five hundred pounds. A week or so later, he was back in gainful employment with Vlado, and thereafter not needing so much money, he returned four hundred pounds of the original loan. However, as his tale unfolded, it quickly became apparent that he was dealing with unscrupulous loan sharks. Despite the fact that he now only owed one hundred pounds, the compound interest rate on the original loan had amounted to a further two hundred pounds. On the last visit to Alfie's flat, the two people involved made it abundantly clear that if the outstanding money owed (three hundred pounds) was not paid within the next four weeks, that he would then be in default and would be liable to what they described as 'punitive damages of the physical kind'.

On getting a description of the two men involved, I wasn't surprised to find that they bore a remarkable resemblance to our erstwhile Devonian visitors, Messrs Webb and Gillespie, the despicable *anal-orifum*. It is one thing to deceive a well-adjusted intelligent adult, but to dupe a bloke like Alfie, who has the mental age of an eleven-year-old boy, is almost bordering on inciting a minor to commit indecent acts.

But then Alfie is one of life's survivors who, when it comes to the very important things (like his immediate survival), he has always managed to avoid the odd out-of-control vehicle, the run-away tractor, or the rampaging bull, and even though his parents moved around a lot, he always managed to find them.

I gave him as much encouragement as I could and reminded him that his kneecaps were safe; at least for the next thirty days or so, and in the meantime I assured him that I would leave no stone unturned in my search for a solution to his problem. Trying to bring a little levity into our conversation, I jokingly advised him that I knew a very good lodging house on the Isle of Mull in the Scottish Inner Hebrides, which went down with a bang like a fat kid on a seesaw.

He looked at me sheepishly, and suddenly I was overcome with *emulsion* and felt the overwhelming desire to protect this little boy trapped in the body of a man. I hugged him reassuringly, and said, 'I'm just kidding Alfie, don't worry son, it will all work out, so you just relax.'

Thankfully Tony unwittingly came to my rescue, breaking the intensity of the moment by shouting, 'Hoi! Stop that! This is a respectable establishment!'

As he passed me on his way to the Water-Loo, Alfie gave my hand a secretive squeeze.

On walking back to the bar, Lenka seemed a little concerned. To allay her fears, I simply mentioned that Alfie was going through a little difficulty, which would be overcome in a day or two. I asked her if she had seen Maria, and smiling at me she confirmed my own belief that the only thing that she had on her mind was her beloved Gabriel.

I phoned her anyway to ask what arrangements she had made for her evening meal, and she stated that she was meeting a friend from college at a Chinese restaurant in St John's Wood.

I therefore invited my Lenka to join me for a meal at our local Turkish restaurant, and she was very enthusiastic at the suggestion. We subsequently had a superb meal, followed by a couple of nightcaps at the Bread Bin.

Goodnight, Ginny.
P xx

27th April 2012

Good morning, Ginny.

I didn't sleep particularly well last night. My overactive mind preventing my much-needed mental shutdown. Maria's room had not been slept in, and peering in at 07:20 this morning, I simply couldn't believe just how clean and tidy it was. Jimena was walking around on her bed looking decidedly ill at ease, and seemed completely oblivious to my presence, as I cautiously entered to take a closer look. Frankly, I found the extraordinary cleanliness and neatly ironed duvet cover and pillowcases quite disturbing. Her dressing table had been given a thorough dusting, and the very sweet smell of furniture polish was still evident. There wasn't a trace of dust to be found on it anywhere. As I slowly walked back into my own room, I became acutely aware of just how untidy and out of condition my own living space was by comparison. I suddenly felt quite envious. As I walked to the bathroom bent on relieving my feelings of physical grubbiness, the biblical term 'cleanliness is next to godliness' came to mind, and having had an invigorating shower and a shave and musing upon the divine nature of hygiene, I found myself absentmindedly cleaning the soap.

Having got over this silly nonsense, I fed Jimena, had scrambled eggs on toast for breakfast, cleaned the kitchen and bathroom thoroughly, vacuumed the hall and my bedroom, changed my bedding, polished the furniture, tidied my wardrobe and had a dump. Thereafter, I replaced the lovely fresh-smelling slab of blue toilet-bowl cleanser in my cistern and exchanged my current reading material with a bottle of talcum powder, the back of which I shall start reading tomorrow morning.

Given the considerable mental uncertainty that I have been going through in relation to the Compton issue, together with the less than comforting situation that Alfie had found himself in, I decided to pay another visit to my old former police pal, Jock Robinson.

I was therefore on the Euston bound train at 09:15. I managed to control my dreadful symptoms of claustrophobia for the ten minutes that I was incarcerated and breathed an audible sigh of relief once the automatic doors were opened once again, and my bum was left alone on my journey to the ticket barrier.

Jock was very pleased to see me, as I was him. He gave me a quick rundown of his adventures since our last meeting, followed by a brief state of play as it affected his wife and children, and I was so very pleased to hear about his grandchildren, and the very satisfying progress that they were making at their respective schools. It suddenly brought back so many happy memories of my beloved Elisha.

He asked me how my covert camera operation was going, and I explained to him that now that Albery Groupenhourst was no longer on the scene, it had just about become redundant. But that gave me the opportunity to bring up the Compton issue, together with Lenny's ongoing debacle with Webb and Gillespie. He listened intently, making written notes as my lengthy tale unfolded.

With regard to the possible meeting with Compton, he advised wearing discrete body camera and recording equipment. He showed me a couple of examples, and I was completely astounded at the minute size of the articles. He even showed me a pair of glasses with an inbuilt camera.

He then went on to describe his 'close protection team', which consisted of two professional operatives. One was a former South African Special Forces soldier and the other was a highly decorated officer in the French equivalent of our SAS. I was very impressed indeed.

I explained that I was anticipating a meeting with Compton at around 13:00

this Sunday, and he very kindly agreed to have Dirk and his compatriot Francois on standby. They would be available for an initial meeting early on Sunday morning, to set up the covert camera and recording equipment on my person, and would then be available to provide a little discreet, but menacing, close protection of my person at the pub. I was to confirm with Jock by no later than 18:00 on Saturday evening that the operation was 'a goer' and then the final details would be made.

I was absolutely ecstatic with praise and gratitude and left his shop with a renewed positive bounce to my step. But this time however, instead of purposefully striding out with my nose in the air, I scanned the footpath in front of me looking for any signs of faecal deposits, or the tell-tale pavement skidmarks left earlier by an unobservant pedestrian with his head in the clouds.

On my almost empty train back to Kilburn, I was feeling very optimistic indeed. Not only do I have a considerable amount of bargaining power for Mr Compton to consider, I also have a formidable team of professionals at my side, who will clearly ensure my own well-being and safety, as well as having the wherewithal to give Webb and Gillespie what could be described as 'a change in direction' in relation to their designs on Alfie. Like all cowardly bullies, the threat of having a meeting with Dirk and Francois will I am sure have them running for cover, the lily-livered *pud-wappers!* But nevertheless, I feel that they should pay for all of the worry that they have given Alfie, and it is now my turn to decide on an appropriate punitive damages award.

Back in the Gay Bar later, Tony, Dave and Alfie were in heated debate. Initially I thought that the conversation was about religion. However, it didn't take long to realise that there were racial overtones. As I walked to the bar, Dave said, 'Well it stands to reason that Adam and Eve were white!'

'How can you possibly make such a ludicrous assumption?' said Tony, taking a sip of his beer. 'Recent research has suggested that for them to have had the correct genetic make-up to be able to produce the various colours of mankind, they would have had to have been of a medium-brown or golden-brown colour.'

'Well that's not what Lenny Da Vinci and his mob thought,' said Dave. 'For centuries, that lot have drawn and painted them looking like, blonde, blue-eyed white people that had just stepped off a boat from Sweden.'

'Yeah, but that's all nonsense,' said Tony. 'It's a complete impossibility for two whites to produce a brown or black baby.'

'Well not immediately like,' replied Dave. 'But over billions of years, what with those what lived in hot climates, their skin would have naturally darkened.'

'Mine goes dark when I sit in the park sometimes,' said Alfie, helpfully.

'But you're getting away from the point, Tony. What I am saying is that historically in all of the ancient drawings produced in every part of the world, when have you ever seen a drawing or a painting that shows a brown-coloured

Adam and Eve?'

'Well sometimes it just goes red,' said Alfie.

'Yes I know what you are saying mate, but that is just romanticised bullshit! Don't forget racial prejudice is not a twentieth-century phenomenon, it has been around for a very long time,' said Tony authoritatively. 'It would have been heretical for a medieval Italian painter, for example, to have produced a religious painting depicting a dark-skinned Adam and Eve. The poor bugger would have probably been burnt at the stake!'

'Well I think that they should have been Chinese,' said Alfie, as he nonchalantly walked towards the Water-Loo.

Momentarily interrupting his train of thought and clearly getting a little out of his pram, Dave said loudly, 'What the *flip* are you *flipping* talking about!'

Putting his index finger to the right side of his nose, he tapped it twice, smiled and said, 'Chinese people eat snakes!' And then vanished into the dark anonymity of the loo passageway, whistling a very discordant version of, 'The Sempre libera aria' from Verdi's opera, *La Traviata.*

It was a very thought-provoking and profound hiatus-invoking statement, which brought that particular conversation to a very abrupt and unexpected end. Within minutes, however, the discussion had reverted back to its usual pointless, going-nowhere waffle complete with a modicum of uneducated conjecture, designed more to baffle than to convince. But then, apart from the alcohol, that is one of the main reasons why most men like to visit their local pubs. It gets them away from the similar pointless, going-nowhere waffle and uneducated conjecture of their partners back at the homestead. But as they say, 'a change is as good as a rest!'

Back at home, I peered into Maria's room again just to make sure that I wasn't hallucinating this morning, and sure enough, it still looked like a perfect bedroom setting on a stand at the Ideal Home Exhibition. I phoned her to ask if she was OK and she was in a very cheerful mood. She had been cleaning Gabriel's flat (again) and stated that she would be staying overnight to welcome him on his arrival home in the morning (bless her little wooden maracas). Such is the power of love. Lenka was working this evening, so apart from Jimena, I was alone with my thoughts (and we weren't very good company).

Goodnight, Ginny.

P xx

Good morning, Ginny.

I slept surprisingly well last night, although my large mug of cognac-laced cocoa had a wonderful sleep-inducing effect.

Having obeyed the less than fickle demands of my feline bed companion, I duly complied with her request and placed her morning bowl of cat food on her little plastic cat mat and topped up her water bowl. She took a cursory glance at them, and then dashed off to her litter tray. I know that feeling only too well.

Lenka's bedroom door was closed, so she was clearly at home and in all probability was fast asleep, having completed another night shift at her club.

Following my appointment with the 'yawning crapper-trapper' and a rather disappointing read of the back of my newly positioned talcum powder bottle, I had a shower and shave. It then suddenly occurred to me that as far as my would-be nemesis is concerned, I haven't a clue what he looks like other than Father Marcus's pretty unreliable description of 'a rather small man who resembled Wilfred Brambell'. It would be very helpful to have a photograph of the bloke, and with this in mind, having quickly thrown on a few clothes, I ventured downstairs and knocked on the curate's door.

A little later, I was enjoying a cup of coffee in the good Father's lounge. In an effort to give him a plausible reason why I wanted a photograph of the bell-ringing team, I crossed my fingers and simply stated that I'd like to see the group that I might be destined to join. He produced a large photograph album which contained numerous pictures of former memorable events, visually capturing various 'bring and buy sales, church outings, and religious festivals'.

Having reverentially thumbed his way through its pages, he finally located the pictures of his bell-ringing team and, pointing to a large head and shoulders photograph of the somewhat wizened visage of an elderly man, Father Marcus identified the Head Campanologist, Wilfred Roscoe Compton. To say that he had a bit of a 'lived-in face' would be a bit of an understatement. Indeed, my first thought on seeing him was to ask Father Marcus if anyone else was hurt in the explosion. I resisted the temptation, however. One thing is for sure, I won't ever forget his face (much as I'd like to).

Back in my own flat, unexpectedly Jimena came hurtling along the hall towards me and ran up my outer clothing, parking herself on my right shoulder. It seems highly probable that in one of her previous existences she had been a parrot, although I am pretty thankful that she cannot speak, and more importantly perhaps that she prefers to do her business in her litter tray rather than from a loftier position.

At around 10:45, I phoned Jock Robinson just to confirm that operation 'clapper' was definitely a goer. He enjoyed my choice of name for this little adventure and confirmed that 'the boys would be at my flat for around 09:30 in the morning'.

Without wishing to sound hopelessly optimistic, I have a very good feeling about the outcome of this little shenanigan. I count my blessings for the support that I am receiving from Jock and his team of close-protection professionals (bless their little mobile thumbscrews). Provided that everything goes to plan, Ted will return from his vacation spent at *Her Majesty's Pleasure* and Alfie's current financial status will improve considerably.

Changing the subject, I'd love to be a fly on the wall at Gabriel's flat this morning to witness his homecoming. I cannot think of anything more wonderful than to witness the kind of ecstatic joy and happiness that this reunion will engender. From the time that she has known of his imminent return, my Maria has been like a cat on a hot tin roof. Her outward show of excitement and longing has been almost palpable in its intensity, and frankly, I believe that meeting Gabriel has been a defining factor in this young woman's present and future happiness. They are clearly meant for one another, and I wish them all the happiness in the world.

As I was leaving the flat to take a walk down to Sainsbury's, Alfie phoned to say that he needed to see me. He was just finishing work at the pub so I joined him a little later. The poor bloke was in a terrible state. Despite the chilly conditions, he was sweating profusely and was trembling noticeably. Apparently, Messrs Webb and Gillespie had paid him an unexpected visit late last night, demanding money. He gave them what little he had, and on leaving, they made it very clear that, 'they would be back!' I tried to calm him as best as I could and, holding his hand, I took him into the *Coffee and Cream* restaurant and (throwing financial caution to the wind) I bought him a strawberry milkshake and a goblin bun. I simply ordered a glass of tap water and a serviette.

Having eventually calmed him down sufficiently, he said that he felt very disinclined to return to his lodgings. Apparently, he had been living in a small bed and breakfast place in Maida Vale, sharing the one-roomed accommodation with an old friend of his. It wasn't ideal since he had to sleep on a camp bed, but he only uses the place to get his head down and to complete his daily ablutions. Apparently, it is run by a very elderly spinster who is happy for Alfie to share the room, particularly since she doesn't have to cook him breakfast. Although, when he is working, Zora-Aleena takes care of his morning eating requirements. As a reciprocal gesture for his free accommodation, he carries out any little odd jobs that are needed, which includes a weekly cleaning of the windows.

He accompanied me around Sainsbury's a little later, and thereafter I took him home with me. On our arrival, he suddenly became quite excited and asked if he could see the hamsters. Naturally I had to think up a story pretty quick, and I told him that I had donated them to the Battersea Park children's zoo. Like a doting father, I simply couldn't resist his excited pleas of 'Can we go – can we go? Please can we go Paul?'

A little later we were on the first of the considerable number of buses on our way to Battersea, and like my former visit with Elisha and Maria, en route I pointed out all of the places of interest.

At 14:30, Alfie and I were wandering around the zoo, looking at the various pens and cages housing a considerable variety of baby animals. Like any young person, Alfie was absolutely captivated, although in all honesty, so was I. Many could be stroked, and he particularly enjoyed the rabbit enclosure, where he was allowed to feed them with little bits of vegetable matter.

If nothing else was achieved, it certainly took his mind off his present worries, and on our way back home, I suggested that he could stay at my place overnight. If one could estimate how happy he was by the amount of physical force he used in hugging my neck, one would have had to concede that he was absolutely delighted at the prospect. It quite literally took my breath away, and for a short time I could see stars! It's easy to forget, that while he may have the mentality of an eleven-year-old boy, he also has the strength of a middle-aged man.

On our way home, having told him to dash home and grab some clean socks and underwear, he got off the bus at Maida Vale. We arranged to meet up again in the Gay Bar later on in the evening

Back at home, I phoned Basil and gave him a complete update on 'operation clapper' and he sounded very enthusiastic at the news. However, he advised extreme caution.

I visited the Bread Bin at around 19:30 and on my arrival, Alfie was chatting to Bunny Longhurst. Apart from Rosheen and Bunny, the other eight bar attendees had all been given the news (whether needed or not) that Alfie would be staying at my place overnight (bless his little sleeping bag). Bunny was explaining to Alfie the difference between an eagle and a hamster. As you are aware, Alfie has a particular fondness for the latter.

'You can't really keep an eagle in a cage, Alfie,' Bunny explained. 'Quite apart from the fact that an eagle is not meant to be kept as a pet at home, even if you had an outside aviary big enough, it would cost you a fortune to feed it!'

Pondering over this, Alfie replied, 'What 'bout if I got a miniature one?'

Chuckling to himself, Bunny replied, 'There's no such thing as a minute eagle, Alfie, all eagles are big, and they're carnivorous.'

'Wass 'at then?'

'It means that they are meat eaters, Alfie.'

'Well, our school hamster; *Harry,* he was a meat eater too. I gave him one of my school dinner sausages once. I cut it up small for him, and without anyone seeing, I put it in his cage. Next morning when I went to school, it was gone. The bits of sausage were still there though!' he said thoughtfully. 'Maybe he got took by a hungry eagle?' he said bitterly.

Looking at Bunny, our eyes met briefly and a pitiful look of mutual compassion passed between us.

Trying to lighten the mood, I asked Alfie where he would like to go for dinner this evening and without hesitation he said, 'McDonald's, their little buggers are scrummy!'

'The word is burgers, Alfie,' I said.

'No, I meant the little Polish buggers what makes the burgers.'

I had the distinct feeling that I was in for a highly entertaining evening, and I wasn't disappointed.

We arrived at McDonald's at 19:30 and I was very surprised to find that Alfie was greeted very warmly by the girls behind the counter. He told me that he would often call in for a takeaway meal, but this was the first time that he had eaten one on the premises. I didn't see Becky so assumed that she was off for the evening. Before we had decided on just what to have, Alfie was smiling and waving at the girls behind the counter. 'I like Adela the best,' he said, nodding in the direction of a very petite-looking blonde-haired girl, who could just about be seen standing behind the till. 'She always blows me a kiss, when I leave. Sometimes I come back in again, so I can get another one,' he said, smiling happily. I couldn't help thinking that his long winter evenings must simply fly by!

After studying the menu for some considerable time, he stated that he'd like a double egg cheese burger with cheesy fries, an extra bun and a Coke. I wasn't really in the mood for eating, so I settled on a doughnut and a cup of coffee.

A little later, I watched with interest as Alfie prepared his burger and cheesy fries. It was an eye-opening experience in every sense of the word. Firstly, he separated the bun into two halves. Then he cut the burger patty into half-inch strips which he divided equally between the two halves of bun. He did the same with the eggs which had been poached to a firm consistency. On top of these, he layered the cheesy fries. Finally, he applied a liberal coating of ketchup and mayonnaise, and then topped each with the two halves of the extra bun. At the completion of this quite amazing transformation of a single burger into two, he patted the top of each one affectionately, and smiling at me contentedly he said, 'Bono-appa-tits-oh,' and then determinedly demolished his culinary creation with quite amazing gusto and considerable speed. When he had finished, there wasn't a single crumb left on his plate.

Later, on the way home, we had a quick couple of libations in the Gay

Bar. Vlado was very surprised to see Alfie again, since he is an early evening drinker and is never seen 'out mooching' after 20:00. Apart from any other consideration, I do believe that he might be a little frightened of the dark.

Back at home, I put up the camp bed at the bottom of mine, and having given Lenny my torch, I wished him a pleasant sleep. All was quiet a little later, although as I was dropping off to sleep, I began to realise what it must be like to sleep in a lighthouse. Clearly I was right about Alfie's fear of the dark since he was quietly humming to himself and periodically my bedroom was lit up, casting dreadfully unnerving shadows all around the room, which didn't exactly give him any real comfort. I wasn't completely over enamoured about the constant visual interruptions either. In the end, I had to take it off him. But to pacify his endless chatter, I told him a bedtime story instead, and he was soon fast asleep (bless his little fluffy teddy bear).

Goodnight, Ginny.

P xx

29th April 2012

Dear Ginny.

I slept fitfully during the night and awoke at 04:00 to the gentle snores of Alfie, which had Jimena rummaging around in my duvet, trying to locate the source of this unfamiliar sound. Having never been able to discover the identity of those 'end of duvet ruffians', she appeared adamant in her determination to capture the culprit making this 'additional' annoying nocturnal distraction. In the dim twilight of my bedroom, I was aware of her creeping along the duvet, but before I could grab her, she recklessly leapt out into the unknown, aiming into the general direction of the disturbance (which happened to be Alfie's head and more precisely his breathing apparatus). It set off a cacophony of rumpus that at 04:10 on an otherwise very quiet Sunday morning; would have made the Allied bombing of Dresden sound like a blown fuse in a cake shop.

Alfie howled in anguished fright, causing Jimena to ricochet off his head into the darkness, presumably hoping for a safe landing (which wasn't there). She crashed into the top of the television, skidded along the sideboard, knocking picture frames and various items of objet d'art all over the place, and finally bounced into the sanctuary of my armchair.

Switching on my bedside lamp, Alfie's very frightened face appeared sheepishly peering at me from over the end of my bed. He was panting like a forge bellows and was shaking uncontrollably. But if it was any consolation, Jimena had possibly had the fright of her life. Her pupils were very black and dilated, her ears were flat against the sides of her head, her back was arched with her fur standing on end and she was clearly very agitated. When she saw Alfie on the camp bed, she made an awful noise, hissing and spitting aggressively, which I believe was nothing more than her way of effacing the humiliation of it all. Having got up, I opened my bedroom door and she shot out of the room as though the devil himself were after her. I eventually pacified Alfie's very evident fears and a little later he was gently snoring again. We both slept on once more until 07:35 when an urgent visit to the Water-Loo prompted him to get up. He looked along the hall cautiously and then quietly tiptoed out of the room, gently humming to himself.

A little later, I peered into Maria's room. Jimena was curled up on her pillow, and hearing me enter she momentarily looked up at me, got up, had a luxuriant stretch and then returned to her snooze with the humiliation and annoyance of her early morning escapade clearly forgotten.

As expected, Maria's bed hadn't been slept in, and clearly Alfie would have been far more comfortable in her room. But I really did not want to disturb her yesterday, neither did I want to offer Alfie her bed, just in case the unthinkable happened and she came home unexpectedly during the night.

My Lenka's bedroom door was closed, so at some point during the early hours of the morning she had arrived home. But as considerate as ever, her entrance like the Scarlet Pimpernel is always as quiet and secretive as the selfless concern that she has for the well-being and care of others.

Following our ablutions, Alfie and I had a very nice breakfast of pancakes and chopped banana, laced with a liberal quantity of maple syrup, followed by coffee. Thereafter, I took him into the lounge and gave him a complete rundown of my forthcoming adventure and he was almost beside himself with excitement. However, I omitted any mention of Compton.

At 09:30 as arranged, Dirk and Francois arrived. I introduced them to Alfie, who putting on his best 'big boy' routine, shook their hands and then asked them if they knew James Bond. It didn't take them long to assess Alfie's condition and Dirk very kindly replied that he didn't know him personally but knew a lot of his friends. Thereafter, Alfie didn't take his eyes off him and listened attentively to his every word.

Francois was the strong-silent type who clearly wasn't in favour of small-talk or flippancy. But nevertheless he also behaved very considerately towards Alfie.

Both were pretty rugged-looking individuals. Dirk was around 6ft in height and was very stocky. Actually, he reminded me of a small wardrobe that I had recently seen in MFI. There was no visible sign of a neck and his head seemed to have been placed in the middle of his shoulders as an afterthought. His facial features were angular, with a misshapen nose that looked like it had been trapped in a mangle, and the top part of his left ear was missing, which together with the additional vertical scar that ran down the right side of his face, would safely evince to any onlooker that he was not employed as a children's entertainer. Although without the need for any make-up, he would have made a very convincing pantomime villain.

Francois, on the other hand, was taller than Dirk, but was just as stocky. He had a very swarthy complexion, and I suppose one could consider him as being rather handsome. There were no evident signs of facial injury, although he walked with a very slight limp. But then, as the small scratch on the bodywork of a Ferrari wouldn't affect its performance, I was convinced that this slight physical imperfection wouldn't have any impact on his general 'persuasive efficiency' or his boyish fun-loving 'body-altering' capabilities. Frankly, I wouldn't have wanted to meet either of them in the centre of a flood-lit football pitch, let alone a dark alley at night!

Following a little get-to-know-you-chat and a cup of coffee, Francois got down to business. He was very pleased that Alfie was available since he could be used to 'flush out' Webb and Gillespie. I had not intended using Alfie on this adventure, but I understood Francois' train of thought.

When he discovered that he was going to be used in a real-life undercover mission, Alfie became almost uncontrollable. So much so that I had to excuse ourselves from the lounge, and escort him into the kitchen where I gave him a good 'talking to'!

A little later we returned, and Alfie was full of profuse apologies, which the boys ignored.

I explained Alfie's story in relation to Webb and Gillespie and they nodded understandingly.

Having been inside the Raven's Bill pub, Francois asked me to do a quick pencil drawing of the place, detailing the entrance door, the bar and the gent's toilets. Having done so, he then went into a very thorough explanation of the course of the action that would follow at the pub. Initially, both he and Dirk would enter the bar separately. Five minutes later, Alfie was to enter, followed by me a little later. If Webb and Gillespie were in, Alfie was to briefly engage them in conversation and then walk to the toilet. I would seek out Compton and deal with him personally. Both Alfie and I were then warned that if at any time things started to get out of control or more particularly if one or either of us felt threatened, then we should – get out of the place immediately and leave the area as quickly as possible.

Alfie gave them a 'very rough' description of Webb and Gillespie, and I showed them the photo that I had of Compton on my phone. Dirk commented that he looked just like that old man in Steptoe and Son. Alfie suddenly became very vocal stating that his favourite was *Hercules* the horse! This utterance fell on very disinterested, irrelevance-deflecting ears.

Before we left, Dirk fitted the minute camera and microphone looking like a small poppy of the type worn on Remembrance Sunday, to the outside of my jacket lapel. It was very small indeed and quite innocuous looking. It is operated by a remote control, which was placed in my trouser pocket, which was operated by a simple on/off button.

At 12:30, we all piled into Dirk's Hummel, which frankly looked like something you'd expect to see coming towards you on a German battlefield. (Discrete it was not.)

We parked up at 12:43, a couple of streets away from the pub. Francois gave us a quick reminder of the plan of action. Francois would enter the pub at 13:00 precisely, followed by Dirk at 13:05. Alfie would enter at 13:15. He was reminded of his role: if Webb and Gillespie were present, to engage them in brief conversation and then walk to the gent's toilet. I would then follow up at 13:20 precisely. It all sounded straightforward enough.

We put operation 'clapper' into operation at 13:00, with Francois entering the premises. As planned, Dirk and Alfie followed.

As I walked in at 13:20, I saw Francois with his right hand behind Gillespie's left trouser leg. He had hoisted him up uncomfortably and had quickly led the off-balance moron towards the gent's toilet door. Webb then followed, with Dirk in hot pursuit. The bar was busier than my last visit, and had a number of customers, none of whom appeared to be aware of the quick disappearance of two of its former customers.

I spotted Compton sitting at a table with his nephew Alex. Both of them were very surprised at my arrival. Alex's mouth suddenly dropped open as I sat down. Compton looked at me enquiringly and then, leaning towards me aggressively, her said, 'And who might you be?'

With my heart thumping away rapidly like a headboard in a brothel, I replied, 'I might be your guardian angel, but I'm not!' I located the video extract on my phone that I had copied from Vlado's recording and for his benefit, I played it for him.

Having watched it he said, 'Is this meant to mean something to me?'

'You will no doubt recognise two compatriots of yours... Now let me see... Ah yes, I believe that you know them as, Butch and Sundance.'

Before he could speak further, I related the tale of Andy's burglary and then pointed out the fact that Gillespie is seen stealing Andy's keys on the day in question.

He shifted uncomfortably in his chair. 'So what has this got to do with me?'

'A very good friend of mine had items of stolen property, which had come from this aforementioned burglary, planted on his person. He is totally innocent of the charge of burglary, which, being a loyal member of the BLIK-NUR fraternity, he has recently pleaded guilty to!'

Compton's mouth suddenly opened and he blew out a long audible sigh. Leaning towards me again he said, 'So what is it you want?'

'I want you and your fraternity members to change their decision in relation to his recent 'captivity-exchange' application and, provided that Eduardo Filepe Cordona, aka *The Bandit*, is released by the latest Sunday 6th May, my solicitor will not release the full DVD video that he is holding to the police. It clearly provides very strong evidence against your two villainous colleagues; one of whom was responsible for fitting up Mr Cordona! It's a simple mathematical equation. By providing your own scapegoat in exchange for Ted, you will be safeguarding Messrs Webb and Gillespie's freedom.'

He took a slow purpose swig of his lager and said, 'You are either very brave or very stupid in coming in here alone, and having the audacity to threaten me!'

Timed to perfection, Francois and Dirk, together with a very frightened-looking Alfie, made their way towards us. They stopped at Compton's table.

'Oh I am not alone,' I said. 'Let me introduce you to my two compatriots. Jehovah Witnesses they are not!'

Francois leaned across the table, looking into the startled eyes of Compton, who sat back in his chair in alarm. 'Two of your compatriots are awaiting release from their cable ties in the toilet. And just to clarify the issue, should they or any of your other minions bother this kind and very unassuming soul again (nodding in Alfie's direction), we shall see to it personally that both they and you will be on disablement benefit for the rest of your lives.'

Guiding Alfie out of the door, they both left.

'Well I hope that has clarified the matter,' I said. 'Remember! I expect Ted to be released by the very latest, next Sunday. And just for the record, should you be contemplating any unnecessarily beastliness, this little meeting of ours has been visually and audibly recorded for the benefit of my solicitor. He will naturally be seeking judicial reparation should I or any of my associates be harmed in any way or any of my property damaged.' I gave them both a little patronising wave as I left.

Back outside, Alfie was very quiet indeed as we all walked back to the car. Dirk commented that the mission had been a complete success, while Francois remained broody and quiet. Having dropped us off again outside of Susan Atkins' Court, they both shook our hands and then drove away, our memorable day's adventure over.

If ever I have needed a drink, it was this afternoon. Alfie and I walked into the Gay Bar at 14:30. The usual crowd were in attendance and they all seemed very inquisitive as to where we had been. I simply stated that, 'You probably wouldn't believe us if we told you!' This had the desired effect and the subject matter changed almost immediately.

Alfie and I left at 16:50 and throughout the time that we spent in the bar, Alfie did not utter one single word. But on the way to my flat, he suddenly became very talkative as though he had suddenly awoken from a heavy sleep. 'They really gave those two a bashing,' he said, almost disinterestedly.

'Well they deserved what they got, Alfie,' I said. 'It wasn't very nice of them to frighten you like they did. They will think twice about bothering you again!'

'Yeah, but they took all of their money as well!' he said. 'It was a lot of money too!'

'Well, perhaps they had stolen the money from other people, like they were going to do to you,' I replied.

He then pulled out a large amount of twenty-pound notes from his jean's pocket, which had been folded. 'They gave me this, and said that this was what they took from me. They didn't take all of this!'

'Don't worry about it, Alfie. You just put all of that into your piggy bank,' I replied.

'Aven't got one, it broke! But I've got a post office book though,' he said, smiling happily.

Back at the flat, he collected his belongs and indicated that he would go back home. He didn't feel that he would be bothered again by 'those nasty men' and I had to agree with him.

Before he left, he gave me a cuddle, and dashing into my bedroom, he collected my torch from under the sideboard. 'Can I keep this one for a while, the battery on my torch is dead,' he said.

After he had left, I had a quiet evening watching the television. At 21:40, my Maria phoned to ask if I would mind her collecting her belongs tomorrow with Gabriel. Sad as I was at the prospect, I put on a brave face. 'I'll bring a cat box for Jimena as well,' she said. She will call at around 10:00 in the morning.

Goodnight, Ginny.

P xx

30th April 2012

Good morning, Ginny.

Jimena and I slept very well last night, but before she settled down on my duvet, she cautiously peered over the end of my bed and then carried out a very thorough inspection of the floor area. Having satisfied herself that it was free from any bodies (foreign or domestic), she curled herself into a little ball and was sound asleep a little later.

Gabriel and Maria arrived at 10:15, and I was greeted by them like a long-lost son. Gabriel had a hint of a suntan and my Maria was an absolute picture of happiness. On their arrival, Jimena did her usual acrobatics, dashing up the side of Gabriel's clothing and parking herself on his shoulder. Following a quick rundown of their adventures, Maria started to put her clothing into a suitcase that she had brought with her. They had also brought a proper cat carrying box.

Having collected all but a few items of clothing which simply wouldn't fit into the case, Maria said that she would collect the remaining items at a later date, Following a lot of hugs all round, together with a few tears, at 11:20 my two beautiful girls and Gabriel left.

I felt pretty miserable once they had gone, and grabbing my gym bag, I hastened across to the gym. I had a nice chat with Becky who took my mind off the dreadful sense of loss that I was suffering, and thereafter, I went through a very vigorous cardiovascular routine on the cross-trainer and the rowing machine, followed by a shower. On the way out, I was feeling considerably better and ready to get on with the next chapter of my life.

Apart from Lenka, Maria and now Gabriel, I have kept my impending move quiet, although now that it is a week away, I felt that I should make my intentions known to my immediate friends.

As I passed The Magpie, Alfie was washing down the front windows of the Gay Bar. Which perhaps could be more appropriately described as 'slapping a greasy water-soaked rag over them!' He had his back to me as I approached and yet again, he was whistling a Tillington adaption of a well-known classical piece of music. This time it was 'The Queen of the Night' aria from Mozart's opera *The Magic Flute.*

Being up on the fourth run of a ladder, I crept up behind him and determinedly poked him in the bum. He wobbled unsteadily and emitted what sounded like a very annoyed girlie-type scream.

Looking around at me in surprise, he said, 'Gawd, you frightened the life outa me!'

Climbing back down the ladder, he squeezed out his chamois leather, and then threw it into his bucket of black water, which had a very interesting rainbow-coloured oil slick on its top.

'I'd cover that up if I were you, Alfie,' I said. 'If the RAF were to spot it, they might bomb it!'

Clearly in panic mode, he searched the skies above and picking up the bucket, he hastened into the Gay Bar, leaving a trail of greasy water behind him. Vlado was clearly not amused at his less that quiet entrance, and folding his arms determinedly, he frowned at him in evident disapproval.

'Sorry Vlado!' Alfie said apologetically. 'Had to get in quick, in case Biggles dropped one!'

He rushed through the bar and vanished along the Water-Loo passageway, with water slopping all over the place. Looking at me appealingly, Vlado repeated, 'Biggles?'

Shrugging my shoulders and trying to control a pent-up giggle that was vying for release, I looked out of the front windows and said, 'He's been reading too many comics again!'

Casually glancing at his facial demeanour, it was clear that this did not clarify the matter, but before he could utter another word, I dropped my gym bag on one of the tables, and rushing out I said, 'Be back in a minute Vlado – just popping out to the newsagents.'

Once outside, I was giggling to myself as I entered the paper shop. Rudesh looked at me enquiringly. Dave was busy putting on his Irish lottery bet, and during such times he is totally incommunicado. He treats it all very seriously indeed and spends a considerable amount of money on this type of thing.

It has been estimated that there are around 180 lotteries held worldwide, although he concentrates on those closer to home, generally ignoring Third World countries. Although a few months ago he confessed to winning what he described as 'a substantial amount on the Indian Kerala State Lottery'. The fact that it has not changed his lifestyle one iota, and that he still carried around his bicycle clips, certainly suggested that it wasn't a life-changing amount. However, a few weeks later, following a tongue-loosening amount of alcohol (which in Dave's case would knock a brewery dray horse sideways), he admitted that he had won 'one thousand rupees', which to an Indian local lad might have provided a few luxuries, but to a seasoned dazzling urbanite like Dave, it would hardly have induced him to start packing his Speedos, suncream and Ray-Bans. In fact, at the current exchange rate, his nine pound eighty pence winnings, minus his initial five pounds stake money, would have just about allowed him to buy an off-peak, one-way tube ticket to Marble Arch!

Meanwhile back at the Gay Bar, *Tony the Tube* had arrived, having finished his day's refresher first aid course, rummaging around on an office floor performing 'cardiopulmonary resuscitation', simply known as CPR, together with performing the requisite 'rescue breaths' on a life-sized training mannequin called *Resusci Anne*. Apparently, like bus drivers, Underground personnel have to be trained in first aid, and having become a qualified 'First-Aider' they then have to go through it all again on an annual refresher course. But that aside, apparently it's a good way to keep in touch with old friends, and inevitably a few glasses of 'cream sherry' are usually had following the course conclusion.

As Dave and I entered the Gay Bar, Tony was describing the correct method of administering CPR to Alfie, who was listening intently. He was agog with enthusiasm. When Tony mentioned the 'rescue breaths', Alfie commented that his roommate 'Trevor' was very good at first aid and he had his own *Resusci Anne* which he would practise on. He then went on to explain that his one was called *Olga*. 'But before he could use it, he had to blow her up first!' The topic of conversation changed quickly thereafter.

The short-lived verbal hiatus that followed, allowed me the time to inform them of my intended departure. It was met with a variety of responses. From the heart-rending sobs of Alfie to the incredulous utterances of disbelief and dismay from Tony, to the loud, unfettered applause and boisterous antics of Dave, who was clearly in *urine-extraction* mode. Vlado didn't fully understand what I had said, but Zora-Aleena was at hand to translate, all compliments to the efforts of my Lenka. They both appeared to be very saddened at the news, although my main concern was Alfie, who was clearly very upset indeed. I told him that I was going to pay a visit to my new home on Wednesday and if Vlado was willing to release him for the day, that he could come along with me. Zora-Aleena again acted as translator. One could not mistake the look of expectation on Alfie's face.

After some thought, Vlado smiled benevolently and said, 'OK Alfie, but you owe me will of four hours for the future!'

'Like my dear old Spike on being told that he was about to 'go walkies', Alfie's excitement and the noise and rumpus that he made were almost seismic in their intensity. It took a great deal of quiet verbal encouragement and three pints of lager to pacify him.

Lenka arrived a little later, and we had a very nice meal in our local Turkish restaurant. Over dinner she too wanted to discuss her impending departure. Apparently, Tina had very kindly volunteered to drive her to Luton for her early morning flight to Kosice on Monday 7th May. Talking about it made me realise that in the space of a mere thirteen days, I will have lost four of the most influential, life-altering and beloved females that I have ever known. The only real joy in saying farewell is the hope of being reunited, and in adopting Lenka's philosophy, I shall always consider them 'as unrequited lovers' – thus ensuring that I will be mentally programmed to see them all again.

Goodnight, Ginny.

P xx

1st May 2012

Good morning, Ginny.

My normal daily routine has been completely thrown into confusion. Sadly, I no longer need to consider the bodily needs of my Spanish monster-muncher and our lesser needful loved ones, who normally at 08:00 most mornings would be sitting around my kitchen table, sampling various culinary delights. But as I sat on my lonesome around a table that had become synonymous with intense joy and laughter, this morning it had reverted back to its original cold and uninviting state, and I felt thoroughly expendable, excessively lonesome and utterly bored.

Basil was away all day yesterday visiting a relative of his in Edinburgh. He was completely unreachable telephonically throughout the day. I tried to contact him on his mobile phone a number of times, but to no avail. However, Tina informed me that he would be back in the office today, so hopefully I may be able to bring him up to date with regard to the Compton affair anon. Actually, I was more than a little surprised that he had not taken the time or trouble to contact me. Like a cliffhanger instalment of *The Magic Roundabout,* I would not have been able to rest until I had seen the next episode, or in his case, had been given the outcome of our meeting with Mr Compton and Co.

I was not in the mood for the gym today, so having murdered the brown snake, rinsed away any bodily detritus that may have occurred during the night and given my face a good old muzzlepuff with a newly installed replacement razor blade, I was ready for my breakfast of porridge and chopped banana, liberally doused in maple syrup, or at least I would have been, had I felt so inclined. But I wasn't feeling that adventurous or energetic, so I simply lobbed a couple of slices of bread into the toaster instead. This example of apathetic behaviour usually occurs following any off-balance shift in my usual daily routine, and given the considerable changes that have taken place recently, I have prepared myself for the inevitable out-of-character disruption that will follow; at least until some semblance of order, balance and symmetry had been restored,

Basil phoned at 10:15 offering profuse apologies for his uncommunicative status yesterday, but apparently, having been caught short in the departures lounge of Heathrow Airport, he had inadvertently dropped his mobile phone into the loo rendering it irrevocably damaged and beyond repair. But then its loss is tax deductible, so behind every dark cloud…

I gave him a summary of our afternoon's adventure with Compton and company, and his response was enthusiastic and eminently positive and reassuring. His clock is now ticking, and on my instructions (which makes a change) he will release all of the available evidence against Webb and Gillespie to the police. The ball is now in Compton's court, and if he chooses not to cooperate, he can almost certainly bid farewell to two of his former compatriots. But either way, Ted is in a win-win situation and like my dear old Spike, I am sure that he will also be very excited at the prospect of 'going walkies'. And that's just what I intended to do later today.

However, a potential destination, together with a justifiable reason for wanting to visit that particular place, seemed a little illusive. I settled on a purposeful visit to Waterloo rail station to purchase two cheap day return tickets to Southampton for tomorrow's visit for myself and Alfie.

As you know, I have been a lifelong moocher. Getting out and about has been a very important aspect of my life, and when I was a boy, I would plan little expeditions around my local area guided by a small local map. Following the unfamiliar and circuitous routes which I had mapped out from home to unknown geographical locations, which I found both interesting, and mentally stimulating. As my prowess at map-reading improved, my simple exploratory strolls became veritable star treks of discovery. My old mum (bless her heart) used to refer to it as 'wanderlust' and all of these years later, I am still never happier than when I am mooching around unfamiliar locations. Provided one has the time and the inclination, no distant speck on the horizon is unreachable. But before I left home this morning, I had to make a quick phone call.

In all of the excitement that I have been involved in lately, I had completely forgotten all about contacting my *penguin suit* providers to apologise to them for not returning their hire clothes. I should have returned them on Monday 23rd April. The chap that I spoke to, however, was very understanding and simply stated that there would be an additional rental charge. His voice seemed strangely familiar. I confirmed that, provided nothing untoward happened in the interim, I would return them during the morning of Sunday 6th May.

At 11:30 I left home and a little later I was sitting in a relatively empty underground carriage heading south. The early morning flow of lemming-like commuter hoards had passed away, and had been spread across the town like a urine puddle on blotting paper, seeping into every available square inch of commercial and industrial space. The sparsely inhabited carriage with its innumerable empty seats suggested a kind of intangible sadness of the type felt in an empty theatre following an entertaining and lively performance. But it will be short-lived, since in a few short hours the tide will turn again, and the vast crowds will be on their way back home once more.

It didn't take me long to purchase the train tickets, and thereafter being in town, I thought I'd have a little mooch. But then I remembered that chap that I'd spoken to about the late return of my hired clothing this morning. I was sure that his voice was familiar, but for the life of me I couldn't put a face to it. The logical thing to do therefore would be to visit the shop and seek this person out.

I arrived at around 12:50. On entering the store, standing behind the counter of the menswear department, I came face to face with my old friend and former work colleague Barrington S. Coddlington-Bysshe, dob 01/08/48, formerly of 14, Dibdin Mansions, Balham, SW12.

Faciallly and physically he had changed quite dramatically. I engaged him in general conversation for a while and then suddenly the penny dropped. His jaw fell open, his eyebrows suddenly shot up quicker than an astronaut's life insurance premium on take-off, and his eyes, that took on the appearance of a couple of chapel hat pegs, nearly shot out of their sockets. He became very breathless as he blurted out, 'Jim Shaughnessy! As I live and breathe... is that really you?'

He was creating quite a rumpus, and I was aware that a rather officious, regimental-looking individual with a curly moustache was giving us the eyeball, so I gave him my card and asked him to give me a ring. As I bade him farewell he said, 'Honest injun Jim, I was under the impression that you had emigrated. But be assured, when we meet up next, I will return the money that I owe you.'

'Well you've got a week Baz, since I will be leaving for pastures anew on the 7th May,' I said. 'But in any event, now that fate has thrown me into your general direction, I hope that our friendship can continue unhindered by fracture clinic attendances or civil court proceedings.'

Leading me to the shopfront doors, he smiled at me ruefully and said, 'I'll give you a ring Jim. You can count on it; I only work here part time, so I have plenty of time off!'

As I wandered off towards Charing Cross tube station, I was relatively convinced that while our meeting had been totally unexpected, and given the circumstances relatively good-humoured, I was sure that I wouldn't be seeing him again. And when all's said and done, that would suit me just fine. Losing a former friend is always better when it's on one's own terms. As my old mate *Detritus Norman*, a lorry driver pal of mine with a bit of previous for fly-tipping, once remarked, 'It is better to have dumped and to have lost, than never to have dumped at all!'

I was back at the Magpie at 13:50 looking for a little light relief from my depressed condition. Vlado was busily cleaning his optics on my arrival, and *Scotch Andy* was studying the racing page of *The Sun* newspaper, running a pen down the list of horses that were due to run at Kempton today.

'Feeling lucky, Andy?' I said, as I walked to the bar.

'Well whatever horse I choose today, it can't do any worse than the one that I backed yesterday.'

Alfie suddenly arrived from the Water-Loo passageway, smiling happily. 'I'm doing extra work today,' he said cheerfully. 'I won't owe Vlado any four hours then!'

Vlado shook my hand and, picking up a glass from under the counter, he nodded towards it enquiringly.

'Go on then,' I said. 'I'll have a blonde in the black dress, and if it won't put you or Zora- Aleena to any trouble, I'll have a crocodile sandwich as well and… could you make it snappy!'

Vlado looked at me in surprise and clearly didn't understand what I meant. Alfie was just as confused.

'Didn't think that you could eat a crocodile?' he remarked innocently.

Watching with keen interest as Vlado's calm and experienced hand poured out my drink, in an effort to change the subject, I asked Andy about his racetrack experience of yesterday.

'I couldn't resist putting a couple of bob on her. She had the same name as me missus, she was called…'

'Old misery guts indoors!' said Alfie helpfully.

Andy's calm facial demeanour suddenly changed into one of absolute panic. 'No Alfie, I only say that when I'm joking. And it should never be repeated,' he said, fanning his face with a beer-mat. 'The horse's name was *Jolly Elaine.*'

'So what happened to it?' I asked, taking a small sip from my perfectly poured pint of Guinness.

'She came in so late, she had to tiptoe into her stable so that she didn't wake up the other horses.'

Alfie burst into rapturous laughter, which had an amazing infectious quality, and within seconds had us all roaring in uncontrollable mirth. The enquiring disembodied head of Zora-Aleena suddenly appeared from the darkness of the Water-Loo passageway which added an addition unexpected slap-stick quality to the proceedings, and even she couldn't resist a little giggle before she vanished once again.

But this was just what I needed to shake off my depressive lethargy, and the dreadful feelings of loss and loneliness. Which are arguably two of the most mentally debilitating feelings imaginable.

Before I left for a quick shopping expedition to Sainsbury's, I had a chat with Alfie about our trip down to Southampton tomorrow, and he was clearly very excited at the prospect (bless his heart). We arranged to meet outside Maida Vale tube station at 08:00 in the morning.

Having collected a few grocery items and a couple of sandwiches and soft drinks for our train journey tomorrow, I ventured home and on the way I collected fish and chips for my evening supper.

Goodnight, Ginny.

P xx

2nd May 2012

Good morning, Ginny.

Following an hour or two of television last night, I had an early night and slept very soundly indeed. I was feeling far better this morning, so much so that at 06:05 I walked into the gym. I had a good CV workout followed by a shave and shower. I was back home at 07:15, which gave me enough time to have a little breakfast of poached eggs on toast followed by coffee.

I left home at 07:50 and joined Alfie who was eagerly waiting for my arrival outside of Maida Vale tube station. He carried a small rucksack.

We had an uneventful journey to Waterloo, and his non-stop chatter provided all of the distraction that I needed to control my feelings of claustrophobia. However, I was more than simply relieved to get off the train at Waterloo.

We were safely aboard the 09:35 train to Southampton Central, and having chosen seats with a table, as the train gently eased its way out of the station, Alfie opened his rucksack and placed a sudoku puzzle book and a small personal stereo device, together with very small set of earphones on to the table.

I likewise opened my carrier bag and placed a cheese and pickle sandwich, a box of his favourite chocolate éclairs and a strawberry milkshake in front of him. He was absolutely delighted. It didn't take too long to realise that he was very hungry indeed, since his food vanished quicker than one of those star-nosed moles. I was just starting my second sandwich triangle, as he was licking his lips following the last of his éclairs. I duly pulled out two wet wipes from my carrier bag, which he used to wipe his hands and face, an operation that he completed with the minimum of fuss. However, having decided to clear out his nasal cavities as well, he covered his nose with the tissues, breathed in deeply and let rip with an almighty earth-shattering blast, which was comparable to that of a ship's foghorn. It certainly didn't go unnoticed by a goodly number of our fellow passengers, and one bloke in the seats behind us made a big theatrical show of getting up and walking further along the carriage. Another woman a few aisles away, cast a very disapproving glance in my direction, Alfie being out of her line of vision. I gave her a very embarrassed smile, which she chose to ignore.

Having shoved his little plastic drinking straw into his strawberry milk carton, he put in his earphones, and a little later, in between the lusty slurping and sucking sounds he was making drinking his milkshake, I could just about hear a muffled version of the 'Madamina, il catalogo e questo' aria from Mozart's opera, *Don Giovanni*. Well at least, I now know from whence his earlier discordant and out of tune whistling had come from. I was to learn later that he has had an abiding interest in classical music, and more particularly opera, for many years. In fact,

I was to learn considerably more about this enigmatic young man as our day together progressed.

The speed at which he was completing the various sudoku puzzles was almost breathtaking, and initially I thought that perhaps they were all of the easier variety. But I would check that out, once an opportunity to take a crafty look presented itself. As we left Woking station, he wandered off in search of a Water-Loo, and in his absence I checked the book out and found that all of the puzzles were designated as 'challenging'.

Clearly, this amazing ability would suggest a very high level of expertise, gained from many hours spent in concentration and practice. I believe that any child can develop certain abilities or inclinations earlier than expected, if it is simply left alone for long enough. Give a child a set of colouring pens and a sheet of empty paper for example, and a beautiful colourful picture will inevitably result. Given enough well-deserved praise would be encouragement enough for the child to create another, and so it would continue *ad infinitum*. In addition, I do not believe that precociousness in a child is divinely ordained, but rather that it is as a direct result of one of the two polar extremes of parental guidance: the over-indulgent or the non-existent. In Alfie's case, sadly it was the latter.

Over the years, he had lanquished in various government-sponsored institutions of one kind or another. From his childhood days where he was diagnosed with suffering from oppositional defiant disorder (ODD), to custodial institutions for young offenders, progressing to ever-lengthening periods of detention at *Her Majesty's Pleasure* in various penal institutions. But Alfie isn't a bad person; in fact he is quite the reverse. A more kind, caring and considerate individual would be very difficult to find, particularly in a society such as ours, which with many notable exceptions is made up of egocentric individuals with very evident over-inflated notions of their own self-worth and invincibility. (Malcolm Frobisher suddenly came to mind.)

Throughout the journey he was relatively quiet, and his only observation of note came as the train left Winchester station. 'There's one thing missing on this train,' he said.

Imitating his usual enquiring reply, I said, 'Wass 'at then?'

'An ice-cream lady. I could murder a choc-chip vanilla ice cream with a large waffle cone, topped with a sprinkling of hazelnuts, as well as an extra-extra-large flake.' His eyes glazed over at the prospect and he started to salivate just like my Spike used to do whenever I offered him a jam doughnut.

Sucking in a little residual spittle, he sighed audibly, smiled at me pleasantly and then returned to his puzzle book, banging another one out pretty quickly (and that isn't a euphemism).

Our passage out of Southampton Central Station was uneventful, and arriving at the X21 bus stop at 11:05, our Southampton chaffeur arrived ten minutes later. Once aboard, I pinged my freedom pass (which I can use anywhere in England, although it doesn't include Scotland and Wales since apparently we do not have a reciprocal arrangement with these nations). Strangely, to call one's self 'English' is often associated with racist leanings or sympathies, but not so when it comes to our concessional travel document. It is one area where we can proudly declare ownership of an 'English' Freedom Pass, unhindered by the puerile remonstrations of university snowflake fraternities, or the ridiculous politically correct officinados. However, these observations didn't lessen the impact of having to part with two pounds twenty pence, to pay for Alfie's transit.On the way to the village, he informed me that Vlado had employed another young bloke to work in the pub. Apparently, Vlado was keen to train him as a bar/cellarman, and my little friend was very excited at the prospect. I congratulated him on this achievement, and he seemed very embarrassed when I did so. Clearly, he is not used to such encouragement or praise. He will start to learn the intricacies of the bar cellar work on Monday at 08:00 when the new bloke will take over his old position. I felt so very happy for him.

The village of West Togram sits on a plateau of slightly higher ground to the surrounding countryside, and as the bus chugged up the last part of the incline into the village centre, I was a little overcome with emotion, which I covered up as best I could with inconsequential chatter, pointing out the post office and the baker's shop as we passed by.

Ten minutes later, we were inside my new home and Alfie's excitement was almost overwhelming. He rushed out into the back garden, checking out every nook and cranny, like a child let loose in a chocolate factory. His antics were boisterous and a little mischievous and not having met my immediate neighbour, I had to quieten him down, since he was making one hell of a noise.

But I really could understand his immense feelings of freedom. Throughout his life he has been confined to relatively small areas. Even now his living space is shared with another, which by all accounts, is so small that they can both reach the light switch from their own beds. Spacious it is not.

Having explored the garden thoroughly, he said, 'There's one thing missing in this garden.'

'Wass 'at then?'

'A dog,' he replied. 'Dog's love to have their own private little areas to play in, and Spike would have loved this one.' Standing by the kitchen door and looking out, he smiled at me wistfully and said, 'I've never had my own garden, but if I did, I'd grow lots of flowers and maybe... even some veggies.'

It was a quite beautiful cloudless spring morning, and following a thoroughly 'beastly' winter, the sun's benevolent patronage was very welcome indeed. We were both pretty eager to 'get out there amongst it' and a little later we ventured off and took a gentle meander through Alice Woods, which was full of aural and visual surprises. The first of which was a quite dazzling display of bluebells, which like Wordsworth's 'Golden Daffodils', came as a stunning visual treat that momentarily left me speechless. Somewhere far into the forest the haunting but unmistakeable sounds of a cuckoo was heard, which was in considerable competition with an assortment of other delightful avian calls from the blackbirds, chiffchaffs, and warblers.

I was very surprised indeed when Alfie made the comment that 'Beethoven's symphony number 6 was inspired by his many walks through the countryside. He hated living in the city,' he said. Standing still suddenly he said, 'Listen! Those sounds that you can hear, or some of 'em he used in his music. If you listen very carefully to those sounds you can hear birds singing, the tinkling of little streams, pipes played by shepherds. You can even hear rain falling; and there's also a loud thunderstorm!' His thoughts and my mouth abruptly closing were interrupted by the arrival of a couple of miniature daschunds whose owner, a young lady of around twenty-three summers, informed us were called Mitzie and Teddy. They were beautiful little creatures, and Alfie played with them happily. Sitting down on the grass with his legs crossed, they both jumped into his lap and it took a little time for me and his owner to gently coax them away from their new very obliging friend.

We followed many well-used forest paths which had presumably been made by dog owners, many more of which we passed on our walk. Most of the animals encountered were off lead, and would come trotting up to us enquiringly. Naturally, Alfie made a great fuss of them all, and he didn't display any fear or trepidation, as two great lumbering Italian Spinones the size of small ponies came rushing up to greet him. I think that it is fair to say that dogs that live in rural areas are far more relaxed and friendly than their urban counterparts, as are the people. I have never seen Alfie so happy.

Back at the bungalow, I made sure that everything was secure and then we made out way up to the village. The sun had passed its meridian, and our earlier snack on the train was a long time ago this morning, and we were in need of a little additional tissue-restoring sustenance and a drink or two.

When we arrived at the Queens Arms, there were two other locals in the bar, and Hilda was standing watch behind the bar counter. She recognised me immediately and gave me what I would consider to be a very unpretentious, no-nonsense greeting, and from her opening gambit, I was convinced that we were in for an entertaining hour or so. 'Hello again our kid. Couldn't stay away again then is it?' she said, smiling sardonically.

I introduced Alfie to her who suddenly became very nervous and embarrassed.

Leaning across towards him as if to impart some secretive observation, she said, 'He's not yer daah is he chook?'

'No he's not... but how did yer know that?' Alfie asked.

Sniffing defiantly and nodding in my general direction, she replied, 'Nothing that ugly could have produced such a fine-looking young man.'

Alfie was lost for words and the sudden rosy hue to his cheeks betrayed his formerly unflappable *Mr Cool* persona.

One of the locals, who was a very 'well-nourished' individual of advancing years, peered over the top of his *Daily Echo* and smiling at me wrly said, 'Don't you go listening to her boy, she's got more gob than Jabba the Hut!'

We both enjoyed a few well-deserved pints and had a very enjoyable lunch of Hunter's chicken with chips and curry sauce, followed by apple crumble and custard.

Throughout our stay, Hilda and Alfie got on famously. She was very interested to learn that he had been working in a London pub, even though he didn't have any real experience of working behind a bar. Her answer to that was, 'Well if I can do it, anyone can do it.'

Raymond Shore, aka *Rocky,* the bloke who had given me that little bit of useful advice earlier, remarked disparagingly, 'What you do in this pub, Hilda, they could teach a chimpanzee to do,' laughing hysterically.

His mate, Bryn *The Rarebit* Bennion, a former Welsh miner from Bridge End, Glamorgan, was a younger looking man, possibly in his late fifties. Walking expectantly towards the bar with an empty pint glass in his hand, he quipped, 'You must stop sittin on the bloody fence Rocky boyo and beatin 'bout the bush. Just say what you want to say!'

Clearly, this pub was really beginning to grow on me, and I was feeling well at home.

At around 14:00 I thought that we had better be making our way back to Southampton. I asked Hilda what time the next town-bound X21 bus was due and Hilda, Rocky and Bryn in perfect unrehearsed unison replied, 'They run at fifteen minutes past and fifteen minutes to the hour!'

On bidding farewell to our new friends, Hilda made a point of saying to Alfie that if he were ever thinking about moving and was looking for a job, he should give her a call. The phone number of the Queens Arms, West Togram, could be found in the telephone directory.

We arrived at Southampton a little later, and we were safely on the 15:39 train back to Waterloo. Alfie had clearly enjoyed his day's outing out into the wilds of Hampshire, and particularly liked Hilda, who had made him feel so welcome. A little later he was banging out his sudoku puzzles again and listening to a replay of extracts from Mozart's delightful opera *Don Giovanni*. The gentle rocking of the train tempted me to close my eyes for a short period and I opened them again (five minutes later) following Alfie's determined shake of my arm, as our train was slowly pulling into Waterloo station.

We were back on home turf at 18:25 and I was happy to simply go home. Alfie wanted to visit the Gay Bar, presumably to enlighten everyone about his day's adventure. But before we parted, he gave me a very affectionate hug.

Goodnight, Ginny.

P xx

3rd May 2012

Good morning, Ginny.

I went out like a light last night and certainly didn't need any rocking. I was awake at 07:20 and was feeling much more like my old self. On getting up, I found my Lenka sitting at the kitchen table sipping coffee.

Apparently, Maria and Gabriel had called in yesterday afternoon to collect the remaining items of Maria's clothing and little bits and pieces. Apparently, Maria was looking a picture of health and from what Lenka said, appeared to be 'deliriously happy' (bless her little wooden maracas). Jimena had apparently settled in well at her new home, which was considerably larger than her former dwelling, and still liked to welcome guests in her usual inimitable manner. Thank providence that they don't live in a nudist colony!

Lenka's return flight home to Kosice has been now booked, and she will be leaving during the early morning on Monday 7th May, as will I later in the day. My destination, however, will be slightly closer to my former home. Hers will be around fifteen hundred miles further away. She has finished work now, and will be having a farewell drink with some of her favoured colleagues this coming Sunday evening. She asked me if I'd like to tag along. But with all of my packing and clearing issues, I had to decline. But then both she and Maria have been invited to Lenny's wedding, and this will allow us the opportunity to kill two birds with that proverbial single stone.

I had a call from Lenny during the morning to say that it was full steam ahead for his rescheduled wedding that will take place in St Benedict's Church at 14:00 this coming Saturday. Sadly, he still cannot walk unaided and will need to use crutches, but he doesn't think that this will be a problem. Needless to say, he will not be having another stag night. Although he stated that he'd like to have a quick meet-up before the big day for a few social libations and a chinwag, which I was all in favour of. We agreed to meet up at our favourite watering hole at 19:00

tomorrow evening.

There's still no news with regard to my poor unfortunate incarcerated pal. I spoke to Basil during the morning and he had no encouraging news to impart. But the deadline is still four days away, and as I have stated earlier, whatever decision Compton makes, Ted will 'go walkies' either way.

While my mind was engaged in backing up its mental hard drive, I had a very unexpected phone call from Mr Coddlington-Bysshe, inviting me to lunch at a very upmarket restaurant in Covent Garden called the *Casa Marino.* Following my call, he planned to book a table for midday.

I had planned to visit *Whispering Jim* today, since apart from Ted, he is the only other member of my inner circle that I believe is not aware of my impending move. I therefore gave Danie Goosen a call at the Pig & Whistle, asking him to inform Jim that I would pay him a visit at around three of the clock. Danie stated that had I called fifteen minutes later, I could have spoken to him personally. Apparently they can set their clocks around him. Usually he arrives punctually at 11:15.

As for me at 11:15, I was boarding a sparsely patronised tube carriage to Piccadilly Circus where I would need to change onto the Piccadilly Line and then travel the two further stops up to Covent Garden. I arrived at the Casa Marino restaurant with ten minutes to spare. Barrington had already arrived and was seated in a quiet corner.

This man was a very good friend of mine years ago, but due to what appeared to be his sudden disappearance, we simply lost track of one another. I hadn't seen him for ten or more years and in that time, from a rather nice looking athletically built man, he had morphed into an unattractive overweight lump of unhealthy blubber, who when I went to join him at his table, fought his way to his feet to greet me. It brought to mind those unforgettable lines from the book, *Moby Dick* – 'It riseth Cap'an Ahab!' His boyishish good looks had changed to those of a hideous villain in a pantomime, and when I first saw him, momentarily I thought that he was wearing a gas mask.

Over an aperitif, he brought me up to date with the somewhat boring circumstances of his wasted life. Frankly, I was far from interested in another story, which related to the money that he owed me. However, to his credit, he passed me an envelope containing the money that I had loaned him (which at the time was my entire life savings) which amounted to £3,700. The cash was all in crisp fifty-pound notes. He had clearly got these from a bank.

We had a nice lunch (which he insisted on paying for) and on leaving at around 14:00, I bade him farewell and gave him my new address. I was on my way to the Pig & Whistle pub a little later.

Not wishing to be walking around in central London with a considerable sum of money, I called into a local branch of Barclays Bank. I handed the cash to the teller, and she started to put the bundle of notes through one of those amazing note-counter machines. She suddenly stopped and asked me if I'd like to take a seat. She stated that due to the amount it would be counted by a colleague in their back office. I duly took a seat and checked through my phone's email messages.

A little later, two chaps came into the bank and asked me to accompany them to the bank manager's office. They identified themselves as police officers.

It appears that the bank people had identified what they believed to be a counterfeit fifty-pound note in among the other genuine notes. I was questioned about where this rather large amount of cash had come from, and I gave the officers a complete rundown regarding my meeting with Barrington, and explained that this money was payment for a long-standing debt. A little later, the bank manger joined us and stated to the police officers that another counterfeit note had been found.

I was subsequently asked by one of the police officers if I'd mind accompanying them to the local police station, where the matter could be investigated by a more senior officer. The cash would be painstakingly checked by the bank staff in the interim, and I was given a receipt for the entire £3,700 on leaving the bank.

At the police station, seemingly as a formality, I was asked to empty my pockets, and I was then physically searched. A little later I was questioned by a bloke who identified himself as Detective Inspector Stanley Hodges of the Regional Crime Squad. During the search, my own wallet was checked. I had forty-five pounds in notes of various denominations and two pounds sixty-seven pence in loose change. The notes were checked and found to be 'all correct', which I believe is a customary term used by junior police officers when meeting a senior officer.

I was later informed by him that it was believed that 'some of the notes' that I had presented to the teller at the bank were suspected of being counterfeit. However, in DI Hodges' favour, he accepted my explanation and would contact the restaurant and hopefully their CCTV would provide clear proof in relation to my explanation. Naturally, Mr Coddlington-Bysshe will be contacted first thing in the morning at his place of work, and I gave the investigating officer his mobile phone number. I was advised that while the investigation was ongoing, that I should not contact him and the cash would be held by the bank in the interim. Each note would be meticulously checked, by experts, and I can only surmise that this would be done by officials from the Bank of England. I was allowed to leave a little later and informed by DI Hodges that I would be contacted in due course, and surprisingly he gave me his private contact number.

It was 17:50 when I walked out of Bow Street Police Station and figured that Jim would now be at home. From what I understand, his first *shift* at the pub is between 11:00–16:00 followed by a two-and-a-half-hour break at home for rest and recreational activities like bathing and palate cleansing, in readiness for his evening *shift* which runs between the hours of 19:00 until close. I phoned the pub and asked Danie to send my apologies to Jim when he arrived later this evening, explaining that I had been unavoidably detained, and hopefully that I would catch up with him tomorrow morning.

On my way home I had a social call from my Maria, who hoped that both she and Gabriel could have a meet-up with me before my departure next Monday. She gave me a complete account of her life since leaving the old homestead, and she was positively gushing with enthusiastic chatter. I reminded her about Lenny's wedding which she had completely forgotten about. Clearly, her mind at this time is engaged on matters romantic, and she can therefore be forgiven for the inevitable mental hard-drive crash. She closed by saying that she had missed us both, and with us all being together again on Saturday, 'it would be just like old times!' Would that it were so simple?

Goodnight, Ginny.

P xx

4th May 2012

Good morning, Ginny.

At 05:15 this morning I had a phone call from Alfie (some things never change). He sounded very excited indeed, which contrasted superbly with my general lack of enthusiasm for humanity in general and Alfred John Tillington in particular. I was very tempted to simply terminate the call, switch off my phone and try to have another quick meeting with *Brother Morpheus*. However, Alfie has the most annoying ability of instilling a little reluctant interest in his verbal utterances, if for no other reason than to confirm that they are of a very mundane nature, and on later reflection that a fart in a spacesuit would have been considerably more stimulating.

Following a couple of minutes of utter *bullcock* (as they would say in Slovakia), he finally got around to enlightening me as to the main reason for his phone call. Apparently a friend of his (whose name was presumably omitted for brevity) had asked him to look after his three-month old Jack Russell terrier for the afternoon on Saturday. This was apparently to enable his friend to visit 'a sick auntie' who was in hospital. Having mentally registered the distinct possibility that there was an ulterior motive behind this request, before I could warn him to exercise caution, he said, 'See you later crocodile,' and rang off.

I tried to call him back several times, but it just kept going into his voicemail.

It was all so frustrating. Needless to say, any further suggestion of sleep was impossible, simply because I was worried about him. He is a very easily led bloke, and in the past certain unscrupulous *pud-wappers* have been known to take advantage of him. Still, I had anticipated catching up with him following my quick visit to the gym during the morning. However, he wasn't anywhere to be seen at 10:00 as I passed the pub on my way home from the gym.

Vlado would not be opening the doors for another hour and I had planned to be at the Pig & Whistle at that time. I had let Jim down yesterday and had no intention of it happening again today, provided of course that my plans did not *gang aft a-gley.*

After my morning workout at the gym, my next challenge of the day was to prepare my solitary breakfast. With my mind still in neutral, during my tinned fruit and yogurt breakfast I very very nearly choked to death on a prune stone that had momentarily gone down the wrong hole. On later reflection I realised that had I died at my kitchen table, no doubt my death would have been recorded as 'an accident' or 'death by misadventure' to use the correct legal description of a seasoned coroner.

Arguably all death is a misadventure, no matter what the cause. And when my time's up, I don't want it to happen by accident, I'd prefer it to take place on purpose.

I was on my way to Jim's watering hole at 10:15, and to take my mind off my temporary confinement in the tube, I thought about Ted's rather amusing joke about the snail that was crossing the road when he was run over by a tortoise. A police officer attended the scene of the accident and asked the snail how it happened. 'I don't remember,' said the snail. 'It all happened so fast.'

This particular joke always brings a smile to my face, but my giggles went completely unnoticed by my fellow travellers, who as seasoned professionals when it comes to ignoring the foibles and antics of other passengers, carried on knitting and playing with their teddy bears disinterestedly.

I arrived at the Pig & Whistle ten minutes before *Whispering Jim's* expected arrival. Viljoen was his usual entertaining self. Jim's half pint of Guinness was resting on the bar waiting for his arrival, and clearly Danie had received appropriate training in the correct procedure for pouring the perfect pint. I ordered one for myself, and both pints could then be topped up together once Jim had made an appearance.

In the interim, I had a quick discussion with Danie, whose endless stories about my dear old friend were as numerous as they were amusing. At 11:15 precisely, Jim arrived and wishing all of those in the bar (me and another bloke) a very good morning, he wandered over to his table. Having waved at Danie, he made himself comfortable, and resting his hands on the table, he looked at me expectantly. It is customary that when two friends have arranged to meet in a bar, the first to arrive takes on the responsibility of providing the liquid refreshment for the other on his later arrival. In this regard, there are those that will always cunningly arrive behind schedule, and later in the proceedings have to suddenly leave, when coincidentally it is their turn to provide the finance and the requisite balloon juice to order the next round. These unscrupulous *mummy-violators* are to be avoided like a leper's flipflop.

Not wishing to incur the wrath of my expectant friend by spilling one single drop of my precious cargo, I cautiously made my way towards him. I breathed a sigh of relief as I gently lowered the two glasses down on to his table. He stood up and shaking my hand said, 'Thanks Paul. Aren't you having a drink yourself?' Smiling at me mischievously, he gently pushed one of the glasses towards me and said, 'Go on then, you can have this one while you are waiting.'

We spent a wonderful time together, and making sure that I was as close to him as would be decent in public, I just about heard all of his stories, which related to his life and those of Brigit O'Riley, whom it seems has become foremost in his regard and affections. I am so very happy for him, although sadly, given Brigit's terminal medical condition, I fear that ironically this new-found love will be a temporary issue, and on this occasion he had sadly arrived around twenty years too late.

He appeared to be genuinely upset that I will be moving away, but wished me ever success in my future endeavours. Both he and Brigit (health permitting) will be at Lenny's wedding tomorrow, so our final goodbyes can wait until then. I left the pub at 15:45.

Being so close to Compton's pub, I actually considered calling in, but I am pleased to say that I resisted the temptation. That would have been pushing my luck a little too far, and coincidentally, while I was considering the visit, Alfie phoned. He stated that this morning he went with Vlado to the 'Cash and Curry' in Willesden, which he enjoyed very much. He was now at McDonald's and the girls behind the counter had talked him into having his meal on the premises. Before I had time to question him about his impending 'puppy-sitting' venture tomorrow afternoon, he said, 'After a while alligator' and rang off. They say that man cannot live by incompetence alone. But Alfie has managed to do so thus far (bless his little furrowed brow).

With a couple of hours to spare before I was due to meet up with Lenny, I thought that I'd take an impromptu mooch down memory lane and visit Victoria. It was here that I took my first tentative steps into the adult world of full-time employment. I left school at the age of sixteen with no formal qualifications, as did most of my contemporaries. Our teachers were all well aware of this and provided that (most) of the pupils could leave their academic days with the ability to read and write, anything else was of little importance. Accordingly, secondary modern school teachers in general were a bunch of lazy, sadistic, cane–wieding *anal-orifum*, bent on doing as little as possible from the day of their teaching deployments to the presentation of their gold-plated retirement thumbscrews.

Baffin and Leach was a small photographic printing establishment situated in a vehicular prohibited cul de sac off Eccleston Street, in Victoria SW1. It comprised of a basement photographic developing studio, a first-floor office, stationery and postal department and a top-floor printing area. My first real employment began in April 1972 and without doubt they were the happiest days of my entire working life. I was employed as a trainee photographic printer and back in those excitingly memorable halcyon days free from the pointless daily imprisonment within the educational system, I received the most important life skill lessons, which were to remain with me throughout my life.

It was within the unassuming Victorian façade of Baffin and Leach that I was to learn that the adult world wasn't entirely made up of moronic *pud-wappers*. The considerate guidance and gentle encouragement that I received from my elderly colleagues was unforgettable, and I was genuinely heartbroken when, in the latter part of 1975, the company went into liquidation.

The building was still standing, but the paint was cracked and dry. (that would make a fantastic opening line for a song). There was no hint of its present use from the outside. It wasn't exactly derelict, but the outer facade, apart from the state of the paintwork, bore evidence of considerable neglect. Actually it didn't appear to be used in any way. It didn't house any form of corporate venture, neither had it been converted into luxury apartments. It simply stood there like a sad, forgotten memorial to its once vibrant commercial past. But even in its sorrowful lonely state, it evoked such warm and comforting feelings, similar to those experienced when visiting the graveside of a departed loved one. Being aware that this would probably be the last time that I would stand in this cul de sac, and being the stupid old sentimental bugger that I am, as I left, I made a point of placing my hand on its front door briefly, as though I was consciously bidding a fond farewell to a very dear friend and a place that had been so important in my early transition from an ignorant schoolboy into an awkward but awakened wage-earning adult.

Would that my little friend, Alfred John Tillington, had been so fortunate. I am sure that he would have benefited enormously from the experience, and who knows, his life may have been irrevocably changed for the better as a result.

On my journey back to Kilburn, I received a phone call from DI Hodges confirming that a Mr Coddlington-Bysshe had been interviewed and his story that he had withdrawn the £3,700 from his bank on Thursday morning had been verified. A thorough check had been carried out by my bank and two counterfeit fifty-pound notes had been found, among the seventy-four notes examined. £3.600 had therefore been credited into my account, and the outstanding £100 would in all probability be paid into my account as soon as a full investigation had been conducted.

Back on home turf later, I met up with Lenny and a few of the boys at the Gay Bar. He still had to use crutches, and I have to say that his use of them was very impressive indeed. But then, back in the days when he had to rely on state handouts to keep his mind, body and soul together, he had an almost questionable interest in the various contraptions that were available to the disabled, and became a veritable expert when it came to using most of them. Similarly, he had an almost morbid obsessive interest in illness in general. Actually, he would have made a very good medical practitioner, since he could readily identify every known maladay that has beset mankind, from asthma and bubonic plague to syphilis and ingrown toenails.

When it came to chest complaints, one of his more notable observations was that 'out of all of the non-life-threatening illnesses, laryngitis was the only one that you couldn't tell anyone about until you were cured.'

Dave and Andy were in animated conversation when I arrived.

'The only real man-eating predator that lives in the sea is a shark. The worst one is the great white,' said Andy authoritatively.

Taking a long swig of his lager, Dave said, 'There are loads of things that can kill you that happen to live in the sea, mate, a shark is just one of them.'

'I'm talking 'bout predators,' replied Andy defiantly. Laughing loudly he said, 'I'd like to see a man-eating fish!'

Smiling mischievously, Dave said, 'I'll bet you a fiver that I can tell you where you can see a man-eating fish.'

The bar went deathly quiet waiting for Andy's reply. A few minutes past, and Dave walked over to the jukebox, shoved a pound coin into it, which made a resounding crash into the bottom of a newly emptied tin, and as he walked back to the bar, shortly afterwards the dulcet tones of Billy Fury singing 'Halfway to Paradise' echoed throughout the room.

Looking at me for support or inspiration, Andy was now a little unsure. I shrugged my shoulders, ordered a pint of Guinness and sat down on a stool at the bar. I winked at Vlado, who was seemingly captivated at the almost palpable tension that had been created.

Just as Dave's record finished on the jukebox, Alfie sauntered into the bar whistling an off-key version of 'Caro nome' from Verdi's opera *Rigoletto*. While he may not be the brightest bulb on the Christmas tree, Alfie's relatively quick assessment of the situation confirmed his belief that 'something' was not quite right. As he slowly made his way through the deathly quiet room, his body language registered concern bordering on panic. Reaching the bar, he smiled nervously at Vlado, and looking around at the faces that were regarding him critically, he said, 'So wass up then, boys?'

This innocent question seemed to break the concentration abilities of the assembled group, who as a collective were still trying to mentally identify the name of a man-eating fish.

Andy remarked, 'Nothing to worry 'bout Alfie. That plonker! (pointing at Dave) said that he could show me where I could see a man-eating fish.'

'Well I've just seen Dickie Mumford at the chip shop,' said Alfie, 'and he was a man eating fish – cos he was scoffin cod and chips – but he had a saveloy and a gherkin an all.'

The noise that followed was almost deafening. Smiling sardonically, Andy put his arm around Alfie's shoulder and said, 'Well done Alfie boy... you've just saved me five pounds. What'll you have?'

Warming to the unexpected laughter that he had unwittingly caused, he said, 'I suppose a pint of cod's wallop and a packet of scampi-flavoured crisps would be outa the question?'

This brought another somewhat restrained titter of mirth from the assemblage, although I thought that for Alfie it was a pretty fine effort. He has never been very quick-witted, although as time passes he has become aware of the wonderfully warm and happy feelings that are produced by making other people laugh.

I managed to talk to him about his dog-minding activity tomorrow afternoon, and he reiterated that the dog's owner was a friend of his and that it would only be for a few hours. I asked him what he anticipated doing with the animal during this time, and he stated that he'd 'take him for a nice long walk, and then play with him in the park'. Maybe I am simply being a little over cautious, but when it comes to Alfie, I am ever concerned about his welfare, and in situations like this one, alarm bells start to ring. He won't be attending the wedding ceremony at 14:00 tomorrow afternoon, although he will be joining us for the evening reception after the dog – which apparently is called *Bradford* – had been collected. All being well, he expected to join us at around 18:00.

My dear Lenka arrived at around 19:30 carrying two large shopping bags. She had spent the afternoon shopping, buying gifts for friends and family. Zora-Aleena was absolutely delighted to see her, and dashing out from behind the bar, she embraced her affectionately. They were soon completely oblivious to their surroundings, and engaged in that very special kind of verbal rapport, that is exclusively feminine and not for the ears of men. However, at 20:00 hours precisely, the bells of St Benedict's Church quite suddenly assailed the very surprised *external acoustic meatus* (ear holes) of the populace and visitors to Kilburn and its near environs. This is all very well during the fixed canonical hours to call worshippers to the church for a communal service, but a little annoying when the deafening sounds interrupt one's evening recreational periods in front of the television or ruining one's concentration during an important league shove ha'penny final in one's local watering hole.

It is becoming abundantly clear that Compton uses his bells (they made him deaf you know) to send some secret messages to the members of his criminal fraternity. This would explain the innumerable number of times that I have heard bells ringing outside of 'permitted hours' so to speak. I must ask Father Marcus to put his foot down firmly and ask him 'nicely' to desist in this unacceptable antisocial practice, or risk formal censure from the bishop, which may have severe ecumenical ramifications for UK campanology in general and Compton and his motley group of 'belfry head-bangers' in particular.

Having *temporarily* exhausted their current riveting topics of conversation, Lenka rejoined our less than inspiring male equivalent a little later.

This evening being probably the last chance that she and I will be able to share a quiet meal together, at least for the foreseeable future, we left the revellers in the Gay Bar at around 21:20 and called in at our favourite Turkish restaurant for our evening meal. As usual, it was absolutely delicious, as was the company. I am gearing myself up to say farewell to this wonderfully endearing woman, but am confident that in years to come our paths will cross again.

Goodnight, Ginny.
P xx

5th May 2012

Good morning, Ginny.

Leonard Maynard Finks is to relinquish his bachelor status at 14:00 today, and he will finally bid farewell to any vestiges of his boyhood. That small gold token that Lenny places on Eugenia's finger will not only signify his love for his wife, it could also be regarded as a social tourniquet, since it will certainly stop his circulation for the foreseeable future. But then he has had plenty of time to consider his lot over these last couple of months. I am confident that he has chosen wisely, since Eugenia is a very special lady in so many ways, and in the relatively short time that they have been together, great improvements have taken place in Lenny's mental processes. In fact, they have been nothing short of miraculous. Frankly, I couldn't be happier for them both, and from tomorrow he will be able to sit in their marital home, safe and thoroughly relaxed. Perhaps drinking a beer or two and nibbling a few snacks while watching Eugenia's favourite television programmes (for the rest of his natural life).

I had no intention of testing fate's fickle hand by visiting the gym this morning, and following my shower and shave at 08:00, I joined Lenka in a light breakfast of cereals and fruit. She won't be attending the wedding ceremony, since she has a few last-minute arrangements to attend to, but will be joining us at the wedding reception a little later in the evening.

In the quiet of my bedroom, I went over the notes for my best man's speech, and have tried to memorise most of it, since in my view nothing looks so insincere than having to read out a speech from written notes. It's all very well to refer to them periodically if one loses the chronological order, or forgets a line or two, and given the fact that there will be plenty of free alcohol available, things like that has been known to happen. However, not on my watch! I will be consciously limiting my alcohol consumption, at least until after my speech.

Dimitri gave me a quick call during the morning, just to confirm that he and a colleague would call tomorrow morning to make a start on loading the bulk of my goods and chattels in preparation for the move. He will collect the remaining items first thing on Monday morning and is hopeful that provided everything goes according to plan, we should be on the road for midday at the latest.

I gave Lenny a quick call to make sure that none of his plans had *gang aft a-gley* during the intervening eleven hours since I had seen him last. I am pleased to report that at the time of calling, all was in order in the lives of our potential bride and groom. Lenny reconfirmed our earlier arrangement to meet at the church at around 13:30.

Having donned my *penguin suit* at 13:15, I took a slow walk around to St Benedict's. The front door was open and I had a chance to have a quick chat with Father Marcus, who was flicking a duster around the first two lines of pews. He was wearing very simple but elegant white vestments with a large, embroidered silver cross on the front of its cream-coloured surplus.

I briefly discussed the unacceptable out-of-hours bell ringing of Compton and team, which apparently had reached the diocese hierarchy and was 'being dealt with' expeditiously.

A little later, I saw Lenny sedately cruising into the church grounds without crutches, but sitting in a wheel hair with a walking stick strapped to its back. I was more than a little surprised to see that he was wearing traditional Highland attire. Actually, in spite of the plaster on his foot and ankle, he cut a rather fine looking figure of a man. He stated that with me by his side waiting for Eugenia's arrival, on Father Marcus' nod, he would stand without the use of on any external aid and will remain standing throughout the ceremony. He mentioned that the person whom he had chosen to escort his bride down the aisle 'may come as a bit of a surprise'.

I was very intrigued. Dave, in company with my Maria and Gabriel, arrived a little later and as others started to arrive, I escorted them all to their respective seats. The groom's relatives and friends I directed to the pews on the right and the bride's relatives and guests to those on the left.

There is a lot of traditional issues with regard to procedure and the correct positioning of people at weddings. The groom for example stands on the right of his bride at the altar and there are numerous reasons or theories behind this. I like to favour the more romantic and chivalrous explanations. One of which is the belief that by standing on the bride's right, the groom is able to draw his sword in her protection to prevent her molestation or potential abduction.

A pervasive practice known 'as marriage by capture' in which a hopelessly love-sick or excessively horny man abducts the woman he wishes to marry was rife in our mirky but interesting historical past. It all sounds like something that you'd read about in one of Sir Walter Scott's novels, but apparently it happened quite a lot in the Middle Ages. It would suggest that during this period there was a distinct shortage of available women. Mind you, the Church's pervasive penchant for burning a considerable quantity of females accused of being witches, simply because of their ugly crone-like or snuggle-toothed appearances, didn't exactly help the situation. Having a hairy lip or being a cat lover at the time was definitely unhelpful in avoiding the censorial scrutiny of people like Matthew Hopkins and other toxic misogynistic and self-righteous *anal-orifum*.

Ultimately, many poor innocent women were subjected to dreadful confession-producing torture, and were subsequently condemned to death at the stake. From the mid-fifteenth century until around 1750, around 200,000 poor souls were hanged or burnt in Western Europe. But I digress!

A little after 14:00, Father Marcus, who had a clear unrestricted view along the nave, spotted Eugenia and her escort entering the church. He nodded at Edwina Fewpit who was itching to get at her organ (instrumental kind) and began to play 'The Bridal Chorus' from Wagner's opera *Lohengrin*, which we all know a 'Here comes the Bride'.

Both Lenny and I couldn't resist a crafty look behind us. Eugenia was looking absolutely beautiful in a white off-the-shoulder bridal gown, and a lace see-through veil. But my day was blessed when I realised that Eugenia was gently being led along the aisle by none other than Eduardo Filipe Cordona. He was dressed in formal attire (the smartest that I had ever seen him) and was smiling radiantly.

The wedding ceremony was conducted beautifully by Father Marcus. My only active part in it was to hand Lenny Eugenia's wedding ring, which I completed without incident.

At the end of the ceremony, Father Marcus collected Lenny's wheelchair, and

I assisted my newly wed friend into it. Thereafter, I stood behind his temporary carriage awaiting the final nod from Father Marcus, which would enliven Edwina's musical talents again. As she started to play the 'Alla Hornpipe' from Handel's *Water Music*, we slowly made our way back along the aisle and out of the church.

The photographer was waiting outside, and a very happy group of people joined in on the photographic session. A great deal of laughter and merriment ensued.

When I finally had the opportunity to have a word with Ted, I couldn't resist giving him an affectionate hug. He was clearly very embarrassed at this unexpected show of affection and hid his evident discomfort behind a lot of inconsequential chatter of the type heard at a dyslexia conference.

Due to his disabled status, Lenny had cancelled the limousine which would have conveyed both him and Eugenia to the Bread Bin for their wedding reception. He was of the opinion that apart from the indignity of watching him squeezing awkwardly into the back of a car, particularly since he'd be wearing a kilt, that since Eugenia had recently 'plighted her troth' and had accepted her husband for 'better or worse', she could push him the short distance to Rosheen's pub. In addition, he thought that it would add a rather unique and charmingly romantic element to the proceedings. However, *Paul the Cab* would be on standby nearby, just in case the morning weather forecast of 'mainly sunny with cloudy periods' suddenly changed into 'cyclonic winds and torrential rain', as it so often does.

Fortunately, our journey to the pub was both pleasant and enlightening. Ted had been released from Brixton Prison at 08:30 yesterday morning, and was collected by the ever-obliging *Paul the Cab,* who put the cost of the fare on Ted's slate.

On our way to the pub, Ted explained that his 'captivity-exchange' application votes had been erroneously miscounted, and that he had received profuse apologies from the 'head man and committee' of the fraternity. He was also advised that his annual membership fees would be wavered, and that henceforth he would become a life-member. As a good will gesture, £200 would be paid into his building society account, and a further £100 would be put behind the bar of the Raven's Bill pub to be used at his convenience (or in the pub if he preferred).

Ted and I were the last to enter the Bread Bin, and as he pushed the door open he stopped momentarily and, putting his face close to mine, said, 'You can't... ever... keep a good man down!'

I made a beeline for Gabriel and Maria who were both in party mood. Lenka would be arriving a little later in the evening. It was a shame that she wasn't at the wedding feast because it was absolutely delicious. My speech brought a few laughs, and even Lenny chuckled along when I revealed some of the more amusing anecdotes relating to his former misspent youth.

The band was brilliant and *Whispering Jim* was delighted when they agreed to play a few Jim Reeves numbers later in the evening. He even got up and had a very cuddly dance with Brigit when they played that beautiful ballad, *I Love You Because.*

As is usually the case at such gatherings, people seem to naturally gravitate to their preferred little cliques. Mine consisted of Maria and Gabriel, Lenka (who arrived later), Tina and Terry (a boyfriend of hers), *Whispering Jim* and Brigit (who was looking surprisingly well) and a very quiet *Dave the Voice,* who following a rather large second helping of each of the four courses was quite literally left panting and uncommonly speechless. Sadly, *Tony the Tube* was away in Barbados with his partner Janey. We were all having such a wonderful time until 21:50 when a very dishevelled and distressed-looking Alfie arrived carrying a small puppy.

To cut a very long-winded story into comprehendible bite-sized bits, it seems that contrary to what he'd told me earlier, the owner of the puppy was not a friend of his. He was a young man whom he had met in his local pub. Without wishing to stereotype, his description would suggest membership of that often maligned group known as travellers. Apparently, this stranger went by the name of Micky, known to his friends as *Micky the Mouse,* which confirmed my worst fears. The final nail in the coffin as it were, came when Alfie mentioned that he had loaned him thirty pounds, 'so that he could buy his sick auntie flowers and some chocolates.' Worse was to follow in that in desperation he went home to his digs, explained the situation to his landlady who was completely unsympathetic and refused point blank to allow him into the place with a dog. So effectively in a few short hours, a young puppy had been dumped on him, he has been conned out of £30, and on top of everything else, he has been rendered homeless.

I told him to return to his digs and collect all of his belongings and in the meantime I would keep an eye on the puppy.

Alfie was out of the pub faster than a buttered howitzer shell, and a lot of interest was suddenly aroused by onlookers, most of whom wanted to become acquainted with my endearing little bundle of mischief. However, having a puppy at a wedding reception evening is a little out of the ordinary and while both Lenny and Eugenia were very supportive when I mentioned Alfie's problem, I felt that once Alfie had returned I'd call it a night and head off back home.

In the interim, Lenka arrived and I had a lovely time with my two girls, who were both in party mode and had managed to get everybody on their feet dancing. Gabriel like me had given up on this outdated form of courtship ritual, since having won the heart of my Maria, he had no further need of it. However, my reason was more of a humanitarian gesture. Back in the day, I was a bit of a slick-mover and wasn't called the 'John Travolta' of the Streatham Locarno Dance Hall for nothing. Not wishing to put all of the men to shame when it came to dancing… I'm sure that I need not elaborate further.

A very out-of-breath Alfie arrived back at 22:35 carrying two heavily laden carrier bags and what appeared to be an even heavier rucksack. As soon as my little ball of fluff saw him, he displayed intense happiness, which included liberally dowsing my hired trousers in urine. However, I now had another legitimate reason for leaving the gathering early.

Having bid farewell to all present, Alfie, Bradford and I made our way home. On the way, Alfie was clearly very anxious and was offering profuse apologies, but I tried to make light of the situation by stating that 'things will look better in the morning', although frankly, this veritable mess will need a considerable amount of thought. But foremost on our list of considerations was the welfare of our little puppy, which made himself completely at home as soon as we arrived back at the old homestead.

I offered him a bowl of milk first thing, which he clearly needed since it was gone in no time. I asked Alfie if the dog had eaten anything. Apparently, earlier in the afternoon they had shared a jumbo sausage roll. Bradford had eaten the sausage, and Alfie had scoffed the pastry. Clearly both were very hungry indeed, so I heated up two of my frozen chicken stews for them to share.

I separated some of the warmed chicken, cutting it up into small bits, which I mixed with a little cooked rice, and offered the small bowl to the little one who devoured it enthusiastically, and Alfie's considerably larger meal of the remaining chicken, vegetables and rice vanished quicker than a weekend jolly boys outing to Margate. As helpful as ever, Alfie downed the last three cans of lager that I had resting in my fridge door and having given Bradford a little more milk, I was more than happy that my unexpected guests had been suitably fed and watered.

With no further possibility of Maria returning home, I let Alfie and his little dependant have her room for the night. Not having his torch with him, I suggested that he could leave the bedside lamp on overnight. He was very happy at the suggestion.

Having completed my pre-bed ablutions, before I turned in I checked on my guests. Alfie was safely tucked up in bed with the puppy fast asleep on the duvet beside him. Creeping in quietly, I sat on the bed.

'So why is his called Bradford, Alfie? I asked.

'Dunno. When I asked Micky the Mouse about it, he said it was because of his colour.'

'I don't understand?' I said.

'Neither do I… it had something to do with *brown and black with a small white area.*'

Getting up and heading for the door, I said, 'Well I'll tell you what you can do in the morning, Alfie.'

'Wass 'at then?'

Smiling I said, 'Well you can give him a much nicer name for a start!'

He was suddenly lost in thought and was still nodding enthusiastically as I quietly closed the bedroom door.

Goodnight, Ginny.

P xx

6th May 2012

Good morning, Ginny.

My penultimate day at Susan Atkin's Court began at 05:10 with a phone call from Alfie, who was in the adjoining bedroom, which was around twelve feet along the hall. He wanted to know where I kept a bucket and a cloth since he needed to 'clean up a little mess that *Charlie* had made during the night'.

'Did it not occur to you to simply knock on my door?' I asked.

'No I didn't want to do that in case I woke you up!'

Search as I might, I simply could not arrive at a feasible or logical answer to explain Alfie's train of thought, preferring to mentally ponder over the mathematical equation associated with Einstein's theory of relativity instead, which given the two, was infinitely easier to understand.

I didn't hear Lenka coming in last night, but as usual her nocturnal activity is always very quiet and considerate. Her bedroom door was closed, so clearly she was at home, but unlike me was sound asleep.

I decided to have one last morning visit to my gym, and left home at 07:30 ostensibly to bid farewell to the reception team. However Danielle was the only one on duty, but I'm pleased to say that Becky (the cleaning lady) was also on the premises. Before I left, I gave them both an affectionate cuddle, and felt quite emotional on my way back home.

I called into the newsagent on my way back and bought a tin of puppy food for Charlie, and when I arrived home, Lenka was up and was sitting in the kitchen with Alfie. She had the puppy on her lap and was clearly enjoying herself. Charlie didn't appear to be averse to the attention that he was receiving and clearly was enjoying the experience as well. He seemed very excited at my arrival, and his little stump of a tail was shaking energetically as I gently stroked him. I felt that I was being very cunningly seduced by this very endearing little fellow. But clearly some positive action has to be taken with regards to the welfare and safety of both Alfie and his dependant. In less than 24 hours I shall be leaving for West Togram, and it has fallen to me at this eleventh hour as it were, to sort out what is clearly one hell of an unwelcome mess.

I offered Charlie a small bowl of the puppy food and he obligingly finished the lot. Thereafter he lapped up a considerable quantity of water from Spike's former drinking bowl.

I made us all a substantial cooked breakfast of bacon and eggs, with buttered toast followed by coffee. Thereafter I brought Lenka up to date with regard to Alfie's rather unfortunate meeting with Micky the Mouse, and how he subsequently acquired Charlie. But the loss of his thirty pounds was nothing compared to the forfeiture of his accommodation and the indignity of having been done up like the proverbial kipper. Lenka was very sympathetic and giving Alfie a supportive hug, she did her very best to allay his fears. Teasing her, I mentioned that there were a number of things that were worrying me, but while I was thinking about them, asked if I could have a cuddle anyway. She smiled at me sardonically and then gave me a sizeable clump.

Dimitri and a great muscular lump of an associate arrived at 09:10. They carried out a quick inventory of the items that could be taken immediately. Lenka will be spending the night at Tina's place in readiness for her early morning trip to Luton airport in the morning. She had earlier cleared her room of her own belongings, and the bed and her wardrobe were the only items left. These were the first pieces of furniture to be loaded onto the furniture van.

Lenka will be available for most of the day and she kindly agreed to look after the boys while I returned my penguin suit. I was on the bus to Oxford Street a little later. On the way I phoned Ted,

Lenny, Tony and Dave, asking them if they could provide a temporary shelter for Alfie and his little dependant. But none of them could offer a reliable sanctuary; neither could they suggest a viable alternative. I was running out of time and options.

At the men's clothing establishment, Mr Coddlington-Bysshe was nowhere to be seen and apparently he was having a day off. I returned my hire-clothes and parted with an extortionate £55 due to the extended length of the hire. Still, thanks to my former friend, my finances had improved considerably. I hope that now when I make a deposit at my bank, the tellers will no longer high-five each other.

On the bus back to Kilburn, I phoned Vlado asking him for an urgent private chat. As accommodating as ever, he said that as soon as I arrived at the pub, we could vanish off into the posh bar for awhile. I was walking through the doors at midday just after he had opened the pub for business. Zora-Aleena was holding the fort as it were, while Vlado and I ventured into the posh bar.

I gave him a complete rundown of Alfie's latest adventure from start to finish. He listened attentively, albeit that a couple of times I had to repeat myself. It was clear that he was very dismayed at the news. It was also apparent that he was extremely fond of my unfortunate friend, and stated that he would be happy to assist him in any way possible. However, when I asked him if it would be possible for the boys to board at the pub until alternative accommodation had been found, he stated that he had a spare room and Alfie would be more than welcome to use it. But the dog would not be able to come with him, since Zora-Aleena suffers from a serious allergic reaction to animal fur. He was my last hope.

Before I left, I told him that in all probability Alfie would no longer be available to work at the pub, since knowing him as I do, there is no possible way that Alfie would abandon Charlie. He nodded understandingly, and asked me to convey to him his sincere best wishes. I was also to tell him that a job would always be available should his circumstances change. On leaving, I gave him and Zora-Aleena an affectionate hug, and I reminded them that this was not a final goodbye since 'unfortunately for them' they would be seeing me again from time to time.

When I returned home, much of my furniture had been loaded onto Dimitri's van and the flat was looking very bare indeed apart from two double beds, my laptop and a few neatly packed tea chests. These would be collected first thing in the morning.

Alfie and Charlie greeted me warmly on my return, as did my Lenka. Apparently, Alfie's unexpected arrival had created an additional problem. Lenka and Maria had organised a little farewell party which was to take place from 19:00 at the Bread Bin this evening. Her story about meeting up with a few work colleagues was simply a ruse to distract my attention, and to assist in hopefully keeping the intended surprise gathering secret. I was so overcome with emotion that I simply had to give her another cuddle. This failed to elicit any comment, but prompted another summary clump.

At midday, Alfie and I took Charlie out for what was effectively his first snuffle romp across the verdant pastures of Paddington Park. He clearly enjoyed the experience, as did Alfie.

During the afternoon, I started cleaning the flat from top to bottom. I had no intention of leaving the place in an untidy or dirty condition. Strangely, I felt a kind of reverence for this now almost empty unrecognisable shell of a home, where I had spent some fifteen memorable years of my life. Alfie cleaned the bathroom to an almost professional standard, and was keen to wash down the windows, but I didn't feel that this would be necessary.

Later in the evening, with Alfie and Charlie, I left home en route for the Bread Bin and my 'surprise farewell bash'. As we arrived, Elisha came rushing into my arms, and just about all of the important people in my life, including *Tony the Tube* and his endearing lady Janey, who had arrived at Heathrow a couple of hours earlier, were in attendance. They were both looking thoroughly exhausted, but did not wish to miss my farewell bash (friends indeed).

Naturally, Charlie became the centre of attention and Elisha was absolutely enthralled at this quite beautiful little puppy, which she wouldn't allow out of her sight all evening.

We all had a wonderful time, but given that tomorrow was going to be a very busy day, at around 23:15, having put off the inevitable misery associated with saying farewell, I approached each of my beloved friends individually, and bade them a fond farewell. There were a lot of tears; and my friends were a little upset too.

I left my two girls until last, and trying to act all macho and brave, we formed a little six-armed scrum, cuddling one another affectionately. I was lost for words and, grabbing Alfie's hand, we made a very swift exit.

On our walk home, Alfie said, 'I'm really going to miss you, Paul.'

'Why?' I replied. 'Are you planning on going somewhere?'

'No, but you are!' he said timidly.

Stopping to face him in the street, I replied, 'I'm not going anywhere without you and Charlie, Mr Tillington.'

I am sure that I need not tell you how joyful he was following this statement. And apart from those unavoidable little annoyances that may cause our future plans to *gang aft a-gley,* I would hope that like the best fairy tale we will all 'live happily ever after'.

Bye for now, Ginny.

P xx